DICTIONARY OF

NORTHERN MYTHOLOGY

DICTIONARY OF NORTHERN MYTHOLOGY

Rudolf Simek

TRANSLATED BY
Angela Hall

D. S. BREWER

First published 1984 as *Lexikon der germanischen Mythologie*
by Alfred Kröner Verlag Stuttgart

English translation first published 1993
by D. S. Brewer, Cambridge
Reprinted 1996, 2000, 2006, 2007

Transferred to digital printing

ISBN 978-0-85991-513-7

D. S. Brewer is an imprint of Boydell & Brewer Ltd
PO Box 9, Woodbridge, Suffolk IP12 3DF, UK
and of Boydell & Brewer Inc.
668 Mt Hope Avenue, Rochester, NY 14620, USA
website: www.boydellandbrewer.com

A CiP catalogue record for this book is available
from the British Library

This publication is printed on acid-free paper

CONTENTS

PREFACE TO THE ENGLISH EDITION

The English translation of the *Lexikon der germanischen Mythologie*, first published in 1984, has been renamed *Dictionary of Northern Mythology* as an English audience will associate most of the material presented in it with the northern mythology of the Eddas and sagas of medieval Scandinavia. The scope of the book is, however, wider than that: the mythology and religion of all Germanic tribes – Scandinavians as well as Goths or Angles and Saxons – have been dealt with insofar as they are Germanic in origin; hence, of the English mythology of heathen times, the religion imported by the Germanic tribes is included, but not that of the older Celtic population.

This English version is not only a translation of the original dictionary, but has also been updated, enlarged and indeed thoroughly revised by the author. New studies in the field have, as far as possible, been included, and the corrections and additions of some two hundred reviews of the German original have received due consideration. A number of entries are completely new and have been written especially for this English translation.

R. Simek
Gmunden, Summer 1992

INTRODUCTION

Mythology

'Myths are tales about the gods' according to J. de Vries in the preface to his volume on the history of research into mythology. Even if this definition is true, it still limits the concept of myth quite considerably. In this *Dictionary of Northern Mythology* I have looked at not only Scandinavian, but also Germanic mythology on a wider basis attempting to present the beliefs of the heathen Germanic tribes as revealed by archaeological finds, pictorial representations and written sources, in their entirety. Looking at mythology in this way means that it is no longer restricted to 'tales about the gods' but includes beings from lower levels of belief: elves, dwarfs and giants. It deals with the beginning and the end of the world, with the creation of man, fate, death and afterlife. It includes the ways in which the gods were worshipped, the cults surrounding them, burial customs and Germanic attitudes to magic. In this reference work I have endeavoured to explore the entire Germanic history of religion, reviewing Germanic mythology in its broadest sense. However, it does not include the extensive area of Germanic heroic poetry, although the distinction may not always be clear. Hence the figures of Wayland and Siegfried will not be found in this dictionary, as they do not relate to heathen Germanic religion.

Germanic heathendom and sources

The period of time in which we can speak of heathen-Germanic religion starts in the Bronze Age (1500–500 B.C.) and ends with the Christianization of the Germanic tribes which began earlier in the south than in the north: the Goths were converted to Christianity during the Migration Age in the third and fourth centuries, followed by the Anglo-Saxon and Germanic tribes. Scandinavia remained heathen for far longer and cannot be considered to be fully Christian until the mid-eleventh century. Germanic religion existed for 2500 years and was found over an area settled by Germanic tribes from Iceland to the Black Sea. It is clear that religious beliefs were by no means uniform and static during such a long period of time and over such a wide area. To make things even more complicated, the available source material is so sparse and incomplete that we know hardly anything about Germanic religion during the Iron Age (500 B.C. to 400 A.D.).

The incomplete information available can lead to a rather distorted picture of heathen religion if one looks at it uncritically. Most of our information comes from Christians and was in the main written down in Iceland, one of the last bastions of Germanic religion, where scholars wrote about Germanic beliefs two hundred years after the Christianization of Iceland in 1000 A.D. It is at this time that the younger Eddic lays were written, older ones transcribed and that Snorri Sturluson wrote his handbook for poets, the so-called *Snorra-Edda.* In this handbook Snorri attempts to present what he knows about the Germanic gods in a systematic way; but his sources are mainly poetry from Viking times (skaldic and Eddic lays) from Norway and Iceland which were hardly representative of the whole of Germania and indeed were already influenced to a considerable degree by Christian thought. Nevertheless, his works are among our main sources of information about Germanic mythology.

Even during the missionary period itself Christian historians repeatedly recorded details of the heathen religion encountered during the Christianization of the tribes, but their interest did not lie in giving a full description of Germanic beliefs and we cannot derive much information from their writings. Information about beliefs during the Migration Age comes predominantly from runic inscriptions, which are usually magical in character and only very occasionally mention the gods themselves. In addition to this we have the evidence offered by place names which reveals information about the distribution of the cults of the various gods. Roman accounts are more extensive and Tacitus' monograph *Germania* is our most important source for Germanic antiquity, even if his account idealizes the barbaric Teuton somewhat. In this work, written at the end of the first century A.D., he describes the Germanic tribes and also deals with their religion.

Undistorted evidence of Germanic beliefs is given by the monuments set up by members of Germanic tribes during Roman times and relating to the cult of matrons. These monuments were votive stones set up by Germanic people for their protective Germanic gods and were produced by Roman stone masons using Latin inscriptions. Only a few of the names of these motherly goddesses can be found in Snorri's mythography. Most of them defy any clear identification. Apart from the archaeological finds which allow us to make certain deductions about burial customs and, for example, about the worship of springs and other inanimate objects, we only have the Scandinavian rock carvings to tell us anything about the preceding 1500 years of Germanic religion. These may depict cultic scenes but they are silent about whom these cults served.

Research

Because the sources are sparse and disparate, Germanic heathen religion is on the whole less well-known than classical paganism, even in northern and western Europe; this also makes research into this religion more difficult. Snorri's scholarly reworking of his sources is basically nothing other than the first scholarly attempt at a full presentation of Germanic mythology. It was the basis for the work of mythographers during the Icelandic medieval renaissance (the Danish historian Saxo Grammaticus at the beginning of the thirteenth century also acquired his knowledge from Iceland) which continued in Scandinavia in the late Middle Ages and early modern times both in the form of late medieval popular literature (such as fairy-tales) and also as antiquarian preoccupation with pagan times (as in the case of the Swedish archbishop and historian Olaus Magnus in the sixteenth century). In the rest of Europe the knowledge of Germanic religion only slowly increased during the period of the Enlightenment through early editions of some of the sources.

At the beginning of the nineteenth century, during the Romantic period, the growing interest in Germanic religion was revealed in both art and literature, notably Wagner, as well as in the beginnings of more scholarly investigations into Germanic heathendom. This can be seen as the beginning of scholarly research proper and has continued down to the present day, fired by new impulses gained from the discovery of new sources and the development of new theories.

This present dictionary is indebted to Jan de Vries' standard handbook, last reworked and published in 1956. More recent handbooks have been either extremely short (Ström-Biezais) or else have been limited to Scandinavian religion alone (Turville-Petre). I have tried to include all the important scholarly research up to the

1990s, and an international bibliography with well over 1600 titles can be found at the back of this volume; the references given below the individual entries point to the most recent and specific secondary literature.

Reception of Germanic Mythology in Art and Literature

Against this background of continual scholarly development there are more obvious trends in the way that Germanic antiquity and religion are reflected in art and literature, its reception-history. In Denmark and also in Sweden the Nordic Renaissance led to a national reflection on their own past history. In German speaking areas Richard Wagner's music dramas, made possible by the first translations of the *Edda*, had a far-reaching effect in promoting Germanic religion and legendary matter as an important source for artistic and literary creations. Indeed, artistic interest in the material has continued into the twentieth century although it is frequently more a case of Wagner's music dramas being adopted and illustrated than the actual sources of Germanic mythology. This is clear from, for example, the numerous depictions of the valkyries.

The appearance of material reworked by Wagner from Germanic heroic poetry led, in the 1920s and 1930s, to a more intense artistic preoccupation with it in nationalistic circles. Germanic mythology proper was more or less excluded from this jingoistic interest, probably due to the church connections of the artists involved which in turn led to a taboo on the religious aspects. The awakening workers' movements in the 1920s also led to a marked interest in Germanic legends and tales about the gods but this could not develop under the shadow of the national-socialist movement which monopolized the Germanic past. Both genuinely scholarly and popular research into the Germanic peoples and their mythology increased greatly after Hitler came to power and this led to an extensive production of popular works about the 'gods of the Germanic peoples'. The fact that these publications were hardly reflected in artistic circles – with the exception of book illustrations – shows the limits of this officially supported interest in the Nordic past.

The state intervention during the Hitler period meant that after 1945 Germanic legends and mythology were ideologically suspect. For thirty years there was hardly any artistic activity in this field, whereas scholarly research continued and in the 1960s was greatly increased, especially in comparative religious and philological studies. Tentative artistic work began again at the beginning of the 1970s as a result of renewed interest in medieval times in general and a sudden upsurge in the trend for 'mythical novels'. This began in English speaking areas and as such rests more on Celtic-Arthurian mythology and legends than on Germanic. At the moment there is little more than sporadic interest from artists in specifically Germanic mythology.

This dictionary attempts for the first time not only to be a handbook of Germanic mythology and religious history but also to include information about the use of such myths in creative works. As such, it is also a motif dictionary for Germanic religion in art and literature of modern times, even if the examples given can only be a selection of works.

Choice of entries

All the names and terms which have any relevance to Germanic religion have been given entries, but also included are those names from Eddic mythology which are directly linked with mythological themes, even though they may be literary products of post-heathen times. Such names of modern invention, or others deriving from inaccurate scholarly assumptions, are given in brackets (e.g. (Cisa), (Woglinde)) whilst etymologically reconstructed names are marked by an asterisk (e.g. *Ziu). A few entries deal with the history of research and include some of the scholars whose work on Germanic religion has been of particular importance.

Structure of entries

The key word is followed by linguistic information given in brackets and as far as possible the etymological meaning of the word. Then there is a brief characterization followed by more detailed information supported by source references and finally the term is presented in connection with other areas of interest with, if necessary, a more detailed discussion of its etymology.

At the end of the entry pertinent secondary literature is listed, mostly in short titles; complete references are given in the bibliography at the back of this volume and abbreviations are given in the list that follows this introduction.

Finally, the entry closes with references to adoptions of the key word (its 'reception') in post-heathen and modern times, prefaced by R:. Wherever this information is more extensive, it is sub-divided into fine art, literature, music and others.

Thanks

My thanks must go especially to Ministerialrat Dr L. Strebl from whom the original idea for the *Lexikon der germanischen Mythologie* came but who was prevented from writing it himself. He very generously allowed me access to all his bibliographical work on the project and then continued to support me with helpful suggestions. Thanks, too, should go to a number of colleagues at the University of Vienna, as well as to Professor H. Pálsson from the University of Edinburgh and, last but not least, to my wife who supported me with her constructive criticism. Herr A. Klemm from Alfred Kröner Verlag has done more than the usual publisher's share in getting the manuscript into presentable form, and many thanks are due to him.

R. Simek
Gmunden, Summer 1984

ABBREVIATIONS

AfdA	*Anzeiger für deutsches Altertum*
ANF	*Arkiv för nordisk Filologi*
APhSc	*Acta Philologica Scandinavica*
Archiv	Herrigs Archiv für die Geschichte der deutschen Sprache und Literatur
ARW	Archiv für Religionswissenschaft
DicMA	*Dictionary of the Middle Ages*. New York 1982–1989.
DS	Danske Studier
DVjS	*Deutsche Vierteljahrsschrift für Literatur, Wissenschaft und Geistesgeschichte*
FFC	Folklore Fellows Communications
FmSt	*Frühmittelalterliche Studien*
FuF	Forschungen und Fortschritte
GR	*Germanic Review*
GRM	*Germanisch-Romanische Monatsschrift*
Hoops 2	J. Hoops, *Reallexikon der germanischen Altertumskunde*, 2nd edition. Ed. H. Beck, Berlin, New York 1968ff.
IF	*Indogermanische Forschungen*
JEGPh	*The Journal of English and Germanic Philology*
KLL	*Kindlers Literatur Lexikon*
KLNM	*Kulturhistorisk Leksikon for nordisk Medeltid*. Malmö 1956–1978.
LexMA	*Lexikon des Mittelalters*. Munich, Zurich 1980ff
MLN	*Modern Language Notes*
MLR	*Modern Language Review*
Neuphil. Mitt.	*Neuphilologische Mitteilungen*
MoM	*Maal og Minne*
NoB	Namn och Bygd
PBB	*Beiträge zur Geschichte der deutschen Sprache und Literatur*
PMLA	*Publications of the Modern Language Association*
SS	Scandinavian Studies
SSUF	Språkvetenskapliga sällskapets i Uppsla förhandlingar
TNTL	*Tijdschrift voor Nederlandse Taal en Letterkunde*
WuS	Wörter und Sachen
ZfceltPh	*Zeitschrift für celtische Philologie*
ZfdA	*Zeitschrift für deutsches Altertum*
ZfdPh	*Zeitschrift für deutsche Philologie*

GLOSSARY OF SPECIALIZED TERMS

aetiological	explaining origins
chtonic	relating to the earth
dróttkvætt	skaldic metre
Eddic	relating to the *Edda*
eponymous	name-giving
eschatological	→ eschatology
euhemeristic	→ euhemerism
fornyrðislag	Eddic metre
ljóðaháttr	Eddic metre
semantical	relating to meaning
syncretistic	mixing religions
theophoric place-names	place-names formed with the name of a god

SPELLING AND PRONUNCIATION OF ICELANDIC NAMES

ON þ equals voiceless English th, ð voiced English th and is alphabetized as th. ON ǫ is equivalent to German ö, Danish, Norwegian ø and alphabetized as oe. An accent ´ on Icelandic vowels is not a stress, but a lengthening of this vowel.

Non-English characters are alphabetized as follows:

å = aa
ä, æ = ae
ö, ø, ǫ, œ = oe
ü = ue
ð = d
þ = th

Diacritical signs such as accents and lengthening bars have been ignored for the purpose of alphabetization.

Abiamarcae. Matron name. A Roman votive stone from Floisdorf near Aachen, West Germany (CIL XIII 7898) is dedicated to the *matronis Abiamarcis*; if the reading Abiamarcae is in fact correct, then it could be interpreted to mean 'the march (or: border country) beyond (the wood)'. However, new finds giving the matron name → Ambiamarcae confirm the older supposition that the correct reading is not Abiamarcae but Ambia-.

S. Gutenbrunner, *Die germanischen Götternamen*, Halle 1936; M. Schönfeld, *Wörterbuch der altgermanischen Personen- und Völkernamen*, Heidelberg ²1965; H. Birkhan, *Germanen und Kelten*, Vienna 1970; B. u. H. Galsterer, 'Neue Inschriften aus Köln' (*Epigraphische Studien* 12) 1981.

Abirenae. Matron name? It is not certain whether the inscription found on a votive stone from Deutz, West Germany (CIL XIII 8492) should indeed be read as *matronis Abirenibus*, or whether this name is merely an addition to the previously named Hercules Magusanus. Gutenbrunner wanted to change it to Ambirenes 'The people who live on the Rhine' but this name would indicate a Celtic goddess. His theory, however, is supported by a new find from Deutz which is dedicated among others to the *Ambiorenesibus*; → Ambioreneses.

S. Gutenbrunner, *Die germanischen Götternamen*, Halle 1936; M. Schönfeld, *Wörterbuch der altgermanischen Personen- und Völkernamen*, Heidelberg ²1965; H. Reichert, *Lexikon der altgermanischen Namen*, Vienna 1987–90.

Adam of Bremen (died c.1081) wrote the *Gesta Hammaburgensis Ecclesiae Pontificum* ('History of the bishops of Hamburg') which includes a wealth of material on the Christianization of Scandinavia and hence also on the heathen religion of the North.

Adam von Bremen, 'Bischofsgeschichte der Hamburger Kirche' (*Quellen des 9. und 11. Jahrhunderts zur Geschichte der Hamburgischen Kirche und des Reiches*) Darmstadt ⁵1978; J. Martínez-Pizarro, 'Adam of Bremen' (*DicMA* 1) 1982.

Ægir (ON, 'sea'). The giant of the sea in Nordic mythology who has the characteristics of a sea-god. In *Skáldskaparmál* 23 Snorri says that Hlér and Gymir are different names for Ægir. In mythological tales in the Eddas, Ægir is frequently said to be a friend of the gods: in *Lokasenna* (and in *Grímnismál* 45) he entertains the gods and indeed this feast serves as the framework situation for the entire lay. Similarly in Snorri (*Skáldskaparmál* 1) one of the gods' visits to Ægir serves as the framework for other mythological tales: 'There was once a man called Ægir or Hlér; he lived on the island which is called Hlésey and he was extremely wise. He set out on a journey to Asgard and the gods who knew of his journey, gave him a great welcome, even if much of it was only deception.'

There are myths referring to Ægir, documented by kennings, even in the period before Christianization, e.g. the identity of Ægir and Hlér and his role as a host (Egill, *Sonatorrek* 8).

In texts about Norwegian pre-history dating from the High Middle Ages Ægir/Hlér is called the son of → Fornjótr. According to Snorri (*Skáldskaparmál* 31), the goddess of the sea, Ran, is Ægir's daughter, but in *Skáldskaparmál* 58 she is his wife, by whom he had nine daughters who were usually identified as the waves of the sea (→ Ægir's daughters). Ran owns a net with which she fishes drowned people out of the water; the drowned then go to her underwater realm and not to Hel or to Valhall.

In Old Norse, Ægir means sea-giant as well as frequently referring to the sea itself; the name Ægir is related to Gmc **ahwo*, Lat. *aqua* 'water' and thus, in the case of the sea-giant, means 'water-man' (cf. Lat. Aquarius). On the other hand it is also possible that Ægir 'sea-giant' and *ægir/ægi* 'sea' are two totally different words (Tveitane 1976).

F. R. Schröder, 'Die Göttin des Urmeeres und ihr männlicher Partner' (*PBB* West 82) 1960; J. de Vries, *Altgermanische Religionsgeschichte*, Berlin [3]1970; M. Tveitane, 'Omkring det mytologiske navnet Ægir m "vannmannen" ' (*APhSc* 31) 1976; E. F. Halvorsen, 'Ægir' (*KLNM* 20) 1976.

R: Ægir is depicted especially in fine art as the Nordic equivalent to Poseidon: N. J. O. Blommér, *Näkken och Ägirs döttrar* (painting, 1850); J. P. Molin, *Ægir* (relief on fountain); E. Doepler d. J., *Ægir* (in: E. Doepler, W. Ranisch, *Walhall*, 1901).

Ægeir is the name of a Norwegian corvette, built in 1967.

Ægir's daughters (ON, Ægisdœtra). Name given in Old Norse poetry to the waves of the sea. The nine daughters of the sea-giant → Ægir and his wife Ran are called (according to Snorri, *Skáldskaparmál* 22 and 58) Himinglæva ('the heaven-shining one' = wave), Blóðughadda ('bloody-hair'), Hefring ('the rising one'), Dúfa, Uðr, Hrǫnn, Bylgja, Bara (all synonyms for 'wave'), Kolga ('the cold one'). Apart from these nine, Snorri follows the example of the skalds in giving many other names. The names for Ægir's daughters thus appear to have been indefinite (just as is the case with, e.g. the Valkyries), and any synonym for 'wave' could be used in poetry as a name for one of Ægirs's daughters. The names are so eloquent that they were surely not coined long before the end of the heathen period. Snorri's list probably derives from his own invention and only partially from a strophe composed by Einarr Skúlason, which he also used as a source.

L. Motz, 'Giantesses and their names' (*FmSt* 15) 1981.

R: in 19th century fine art, Ægir's daughters are depicted either in the same tradition as the classical nymphs: J. P. Molin, *Nöck, Ægir o. h. döttrer* (relief on well) and N. J. O. Blommér, *Näcken och Ægirsdöttrar* (painting, 1850) or simply as the waves: H. Hendrich, *Nordische Landschaft* (*Oegir's Töchter*; painting, 1889).

Ægir's helmet (ON Ægishjálmr or actually Œgishjálmr, 'frightening helmet'). Sigurd's helmet in Nordic heroic poetry (*Reginsmál* 14 Prose, *Fafnismál* 16, 17, 44 Prose; Snorri, *Gylfaginning* 38) which he removes from the dragon Fafnir after he has killed him; previously it had belonged (according to Snorri) to Hreiðmarr, Fafnir's father.

The Ægishjálmr terrifies everyone who sees it; thus, it could be derived from Classical influences since the Greek *aigis* has the same terrifying function (in the case of Zeus, the *aigis* is a shield, in the case of Pallas Athene a cloak crowned with a Gorgon's head). The Greek word *aigis* could have become the 'helmet of terror' in folk-etymology as a result of the influence of the phonetically similarly sounding ON *œgr* 'terrible'.

Whatever the derivation of the word, the Ægishjálmr has nothing whatsoever to do with the giant of the sea Ægir.

Ælf (OE) → Elves.

Æsir. The members of the biggest family of gods in Old Norse mythology; the other family are the → Vanir.

The most important Nordic gods belong to the Æsir: Odin and his sons Thor and Baldr, also Loki. The Æsir are predominantly gods of war and government, whereas the Vanir are the gods of fertility.

In an extended sense all the gods in Eddic mythology are referred to under the general name of Æsir, the reason for which probably lies in the fusion of the two families through marriage and the exchange of hostages after the end of the wars against the Vanir. Snorri's tendency is not to make a clear distinction between the two families of gods; in his long list of the Æsir gods (*Skáldskaparmál* 1) he names Odin, Thor, Njǫrðr, Freyr, Týr, Heimdallr, Bragi, Víðarr, Váli, Ullr, Hœnir, Forseti and Loki, and as goddesses: Frigg, Freyja, Gefjon, Iðunn, Gerðr, Sigyn, Fulla, Nanna; *Gylfaginning* 34 gives in addition to these the names of more goddesses Eir, Fulla, Freyja, Sjǫfn, Lofn, Vár, Vǫr, Syn, Hlín, Snotra and Gná. Thus, the term *ásynjar* 'the female Æsir' can likewise be seen to cover all the female goddesses. All the gods live in Asgard ('court of the Æsir') to which the bridge → Bilrǫst or Asbrú ('Æsir-bridge') leads. In the myth of the creation of the world both of the families of gods share the same origins; they appear in mythological poetry together, they are all kept young by → Iðunn's apples and they are all threatened by the all-engulfing destruction at the Ragnarǫk. Thus, it is not possible to determine from the sources whether the word Æsir was originally the generic term for 'gods', which the Vanir freed themselves from, or vice versa, that it was the name of a family of gods that later became the general term.

In the mythology of the Eddas, in particular in Snorri's *Edda*, Odin is constantly the highest ranking of the Æsir and he can simply be called 'the As', just as Thor can. In *Skírnismál* it is not even quite clear which of these two is called → Asabragr 'the best of the Æsir', and in the expression of 'the almighty As' (*hinn* → *almáttki áss*) used in an oath formula it is similarly inconclusive whether the expression refers to Odin or Thor. However, the name of the a-rune (Anglo-Saxon ōs, Gmc **ansuz*) quite definitely referred to Odin.

The term ON Æsir (sg. *áss* 'god') is also recorded in Gothic as Ansis (Latinized thus by Jordanes, *Getica* XIII, 78), in Anglo-Saxon as *ēsa* (as in *ēsa gescot* 'slipped disc'; sg. ōs.) In German the name is only retained in some personal names (Ansila, Ansgeir, Anshram).

The word is Proto-Germanic and already evident during the Roman Imperial Age in the name of the goddess Vih-ansa ('battle-goddess'?) and most probably also around 200 A.D. on a runic buckle from Vimose (Denmark): *a(n)sau wīja* 'I dedicate this to the Æsir'. The basic form of the name of the gods is therefore *ans-*. However, whether it is etymologically related to Gmc **ans-* 'beam, post' so that the origin would lie in a devotion to → wooden gods or else to Old Indian *ásura-* (to *ásu* 'vitality') has not been fully ascertained as both possibilities have points in their favour.

A number of Scandinavian place-names contain the element As- (Swedish Asperg, Åslunda, Norwegian Asarâll) and these names refer to the gods in general rather than to one specific god.

The report of the origins and migration of the Æsir from Asia in the euhemeristic account given by Snorri and Saxo Grammaticus, which also transports Asgard to Asia and considers that the origin of the name Æsir is derived from Ásiámenn ('Asians'), is a product of Medieval scholarship and is by no means a reflection of Germanic mythology. The similarity of the name was simply ideal for connecting old Scandinavian genealogies with current scholarly prehistories which made the historical link between the Scandinavian peoples, and classical times and Christianity possible.

J. de Vries, *Altgermanische Religionsgeschichte*, Berlin [3]1970; H. Kuhn, 'Asen' (*Hoops* 1) [2]1973; O. Gschwantler, 'Asen' (*Lexikon des Mittelalters* 1) 1980.

R: (literature) N. F. S. Grundtvig, *Om Asalæren* (in: *Ny Minerva* 1807); P. H. Ling, *Asarne* (epic poem, 1816–33); Hans von Hammerstein, *Die Asen* (poem).
(music) W. Gerhard, *Assemblée dansante* (ballet, 1816).
(fine art) → Odin's migration.

Afliae. Name of → matrons. Two Roman votive stones from the Cologne area (CIL XIII 8211 and 8157) are dedicated to the Matronis Afliabus, or else Matronis Aflims; the Proto-Germanic dative ending of the second form of the name proves that the name is clearly Germanic and it probably belongs to ON *afl*, OHG *afla* 'power', thus 'the powerful one'; the link with the Latin name for the Eifel (Kauffmann) is unlikely.

F. Kauffmann, 'Der Matronenkultus in Germanien' (*Zeitschrift für Volkskunde* 2) 1892; S. Gutenbrunner, *Die germanischen Götternamen*, Halle 1936; M. Schönfeld, *Wörterbuch der altgermanischen Personen- und Völkernamen*, Heidelberg [2]1965; H. Birkhan, *Germanen und Kelten bis zum Ausgang der Römerzeit*, Vienna 1970; H. Reichert, *Lexikon der altgermanischen Namen*, Vienna 1987–90.

Agnarr (ON). The son of King → Geirrǫðr in *Grímnismál* 2. Agnarr helps Odin, who is there in disguise, to escape from the torture Geirrǫðr has inflicted upon him. In the younger prose framework to that lay Geirrǫð's brother is called Agnarr, and the boy is named after him.

Agni. A legendary Swedish king from the dynasty of the Ynglings who is mentioned by Þjóðólfr in his skaldic poem *Ynglingatal* 10. In this poem we hear that Agni was hanged by his wife → Skjalf, using his necklace. Snorri comments on this and extends the tale in his *Ynglinga saga*: Agni had won a battle on his military campaign to Finland and wanted to marry the daughter of the slain Finnish king. However, she (= Skjalf) knotted a rope during the night to the king's neckchain and then hanged him on a tree. Even without Snorri's exposition Þjóðólfr's stanza, which gives no reason for the woman's desire for revenge, can be compared with an Odinic sacrifice (as with Víkarr), and the role of the woman and the chain give weight to the argument. Therefore, Agni should probably be considered as one of the sacrificed Yngling kings such as Dómaldi, Jǫrundr and Sveigðir.

Snorri explains the placename Agnafit near Stockholm as being the place where Agni was burned, an explanation which is almost certainly incorrect because the more likely explanation of the name Agnafit is its etymological relationship to the innumerable Swedish placenames based on *agn-*, 'bait'.

W. Grönbech, *Kultur und Religion der Germanen*, Darmstadt [5]1954; D. A. H. Evans, 'King Agni: myth, history or legend?' (*Speculum Norroenum. Studies* G. *Turville-Petre*) Odense 1981.

R: P. H. Ling, *Agne* (play, 1912).

Ahineh(i)ae. Germanic → matrons. A votive stone (now lost) from Blankenheim near Aachen, West Germany (CIL XIII 8845) bore an inscription with a dedication to the Ahinehiae, the reading of which is not totally certain. The name of the Ahinehiae is possibly derived from a name of a river, cf. OHG *aha* 'water, river'.

S. Gutenbrunner, *Die germanischen Götternamen*, Halle 1936; M. Schönfeld, *Wörterbuch der altgermanischen Personen- und Völkernamen*, Heidelberg ²1965; H. Reichert, *Lexikon der altgermanischen Namen*, Vienna 1987–90.

Ahueccaniae. Name of → matrons. A votive altar with an inscription from Gleuel near Cologne (CIL XIII 8161), dating from 201 A.D., is dedicated to the *Ahveccani(i)s Avehae et Hellivesae*. Whether the two female figures depicted on the stone are indeed goddesses or companions to goddesses can hardly be determined. The name might indicate goddesses of springs (cf. Gmc **ahwō-*, OHG *aha* 'water'), like the Auehae, who are also named in the same inscription, or the Ahinehiae. Gutenbrunner considered that the second word element belongs to Anglo-Saxon *wiccian* 'to conjure, do magic', MHG *wicken* 'to prophesy'; Ahueccaniae could then mean something like 'prophesying female water-spirits'.

S. Gutenbrunner, *Die germanischen Götternamen*, Halle 1936; M. Schönfeld, *Wörterbuch der altgermanischen Personen- und Völkernamen*, Heidelberg ²1965; H. Reichert, *Lexikon der altgermanischen Namen*, Vienna 1987–90.

Ai (ON, 'ancestor'). A dwarf in *Vǫluspá* 11, 15 and in the *Þulur*.

Alaferhviae. Name of → matrons to whom a number of Roman inscriptions from around Jülich, West Germany are dedicated. The names appear in the form *Alaferhviabus*. On one of the inscriptions (from Patteren; CIL XIII 7862) the (damaged) word *Nymphis* appears to precede the name. The name Alaferhviae has been interpreted by Gutenbrunner and de Vries as 'the great life-giving one', from OHG *ferh* (Anglo-Saxon *feorh* 'life'). Birkhan, however, links the Alaferhviae (together with the Alaterviae, Berhuihenae and the dea Vercana) to OHG *fereheih* 'tree, oak' and interprets them as 'the goddess(es) belonging to all trees', a name which would indicate the fertility function of the matrons; this suggestion is supported by the pictures of trees on several votive stones.

W. Schulze, 'Alaferhviae' (*ZfdA* 54) 1913; S. Gutenbrunner, *Die germanischen Götternamen*, Halle 1936; H. Reichert, *Lexikon der altgermanischen Namen*, Vienna 1987–90.

Alagabiae. Name of → matrons (the exact form on the inscription is *Matronis Alagabiabus*) to whom an inscription on a votive stone dating from the 4th century A.D. from Bürgel near Solingen, West Germany (CIL XIII 8529) is dedicated; the name, which means 'the ones who give everything', presents a Germanic counterpart to the partially Celticized matron name Ollogabiae. It is possible that the same matrons were venerated under both names among the mixed Germanic-Celtic population on the Lower Rhine.

S. Gutenbrunner, *Die germanischen Götternamen*, Halle 1936; M. Schönfeld, *Wörterbuch der altgermanischen Personen- und Völkernamen*, Heidelberg ²1965; H. Reichert, *Lexikon der altgermanischen Namen*, Vienna 1987–90.

Alaisiagae. Name or epithet of two goddesses. The Alaisiagae are named on three inscriptions from Housesteads on Hadrian's Wall (Cumbria); two of them are not only dedicated to these *duabus Alaisiabis* but also to → Mars (Thingus). It might be possible to conclude from this that the Alaisiagae should be considered to be goddesses of the Thing. In both of the older inscriptions (from the second half of the second century A.D.) the individual names of the goddesses are also given, Baudihillia and Friagabis on one stone, on another Beda and Fimmilena. Following a suggestion by Heinzel, an attempt has been made to establish a link between both of the last names with Old

Frisian law terms Bodthing and Fimelthing ('summons' and 'sentence'), but an element of doubt must remain with this supposition; on the other hand the donor of the inscriptions came from a Frisian legion stationed in northern England, which would explain the Frisian link. Whilst both the goddesses' names might possibly be interpreted as being goddesses of law and justice, the interpretation of the name Alaisiagae is extremely debatable; the most likely interpretation – assuming that it is a case of an epithet for two goddesses – is 'the most venerated one' (cf. ON *eira*), although a connection with the ON goddess of healing, Eir, cannot be totally excluded.

R. Heinzel, 'Über die ostgotische Heldensage' (*Sitzungsberichte der kaiserlichen Akademie der Wissenschaften in Wien* 119) 1889; S. Gutenbrunner, *Die germanischen Götternamen*, Halle 1936; J. de Vries, *Altgermanische Religionsgeschichte*, Berlin [3]1970; H. Reichert, *Lexikon der altgermanischen Namen* I. Vienna 1987.

Alateivia. Name of a Germanic goddess. The inscription on a Roman votive stone from Xanten (CIL XIII 8606) says: *Alateiviae ex iussu [psius] Divos medicus* 'to Alateivia, on her own command, from the physician Divos'. Thus, it seems possible, but by no means certain, that Alateivia was a goddess of healing. The name Alateivia means 'the all-divine one' and is certainly Germanic as are other matron names based on *Ala-*.

S. Gutenbrunner, *Die germanischen Götternamen*, Halle 1936; J. de Vries, *Altgermanische Religionsgeschichte*, Berlin [3]1970; H. Birkhan, *Germanen und Kelten bis zum Ausgang der Römerzeit*, Vienna 1970; H. Reichert, *Lexikon der altgermanischen Namen*, Vienna 1987–90.

Alaterv(i)ae. Name of → matrons. An inscription on a Roman votive stone from the harbour at Crammond, near Edinburgh, is dedicated to the *Matrib(us) Alatervis et Matrib(us) Campestrib(us)* (CIL VII 1084). Gutenbrunner agrees with the older interpretation of the name as 'the all-loyal' (to Gmc **terwa-* 'fast, loyal, true'), whilst Birkhan explains Alaterviae, like Alaferhviae, as 'the goddess(es) belonging to the (oak-)trees' (to Gmc **terua-* 'tree, wood').

S. Gutenbrunner, *Die germanischen Götternamen*, Halle 1936; H. Birkhan, *Germanen und Kelten bis zum Ausgang der Römerzeit*, Vienna 1970; H. Reichert, *Lexikon der altgermanischen Namen*, Vienna 1987–90.

Alberich. Dwarf in the *Nibelungenlied* ('Lay of the Nibelungs') who corresponds to the Nordic dwarf → Andvari.

Alberich is adopted into Arthurian literature as early as the 14th century via the legend about Huon de Bordeaux under the name of Auberon, later as → Oberon, where he achieves literary fame as the king of the elves.

R: in Wagner's operas, Alberich is a tyrannical dwarf king of the dynasty of the Nibelungs (*Das Rheingold*, *Siegfried*, *Götterdämmerung*).

Albiahenae. Probably a matron name; it is found on four Roman votive stones, all from Ober-Elvenich near Euskirchen, West Germany (CIL XIII 7933–6). This spatial concentration suggests that the name Albiahenae could be derived from a place-name *Albiniacum, perhaps the former name for Elvenich.

S. Gutenbrunner, *Die germanischen Götternamen*, Halle 1936; M. Schönfeld, *Wörterbuch der altgermanischen Personen- und Völkernamen*, Heidelberg [2]1965; H. Reichert, *Lexikon der altgermanischen Namen*, Vienna 1987–90.

Albruna. Germanic seeress; Tacitus (*Germania* 8) mentions her in his description of the sanctity of women among the Germanic tribes: 'During the reign of the most holy Emperor Vespasian we saw that Veleda was honoured like a god in the eyes of many people; but even before this, Albruna and several others used to be revered, not by mere flattery, nor as if they were pretending that women were goddesses.'

From these comments alone, it is not clear that Albruna was a seeress, since, despite the reference to → Veleda, Albruna could also be a → matron; however, if the conjecture is correct that the name is actually documented as Aurinia, Albrinia and has been corrected to Albruna, then the name suggests the interpretation 'the one gifted with the secret knowledge of the elves' or else 'the trusted friend of the elves', and as such Albruna would indeed be a seeress.

H. Krahe, 'Altgermanische Kleinigkeiten. 4. Veleda' (*IF* 66) 1961; R. Much, *Die Germania des Tacitus*, Heidelberg [3]1967.

Alcis. Divine pair of twins whose cult is described by Tacitus (*Germania* 43). 'The Naharnavali point out an ancient sacred grove in front of which stands a priest dressed in feminine clothes; the gods worshipped there are said to correspond to Castor and Pollux among the Roman deities, for they share the same divine powers as these gods, but are called Alcis. There are no images of them and nothing suggests the influence of foreign religions, and yet they are worshipped as brothers, as youths.'

The Germanic tribe of the Naharnavali, which lived in the area now called Silesia, is only mentioned by Tacitus, who writes about sacred groves when referring to other Germanic tribes. The fact that he distinctively speaks of the *interpretatio romana* by referring to Castor and Pollux shows that he understood the Alcis as being → twin gods. The name Alcis (Gmc *Alhiz) is related, together with Gothic *alhs* 'temple', Lithuanian *elkas* 'divine grove', either to the family of OE *ealgian* 'to protect', and thus means 'protective (-ing?) deity', or else to the Germanic word *alsces* 'elks' recorded by Caesar. Since the Greek Dioskuri were partly thought of as being gods in the shape of horses, and in consideration of the etymology of Alcis as elk-, the Alcis might have been horse gods, a theory particularly substantiated in Migration Era illustrations that show a horse-shaped variant of the Germanic twin god motif (Hauck). Supporting this interpretation are the names of the Anglo-Saxon brothers Hengist and Horsa, where a clear link to horses is given.

R. Meringer, 'Indogermanische Pfahlgötzen' (*Wörter und Sachen* 9) 1926; J. Loewenthal, 'Alcis' (*PBB* 51) 1927; A. H. Krappe, 'Alces' (*PBB* 57) 1933; T. Palm, 'Der Kult der Naharvalen' (*ARW* 36) 1939; H. Rosenfeld, 'Die vandalischen Alkes "Elchreiter", der ostgermanische Hirschkult und die Dioskuren' (*GRM* 28) 1940; W. Schwarz, 'Germanische Dioskuren?' (*Bonner Jahrbücher* 167) 1967; J. de Vries, *Altgermanische Religionsgeschichte*, Berlin [3]1970; H. Kuhn, 'Alci' (*Hoops* 1) [2]1973; K. Hauck, 'Gemeinschaftsstiftende Kulte der Seegermanen' (*FmSt* 14) 1980.

Aldafaðir or Aldafǫðr (ON, 'father of mankind') is a name for Odin in *Vafþruðnismál* 5 and 53, in Bragi (*Ragnarsdrápa* 14), and in the *Þulur*. The name is formed in a similar way to Alfaðir but refers to Odin as the father of man in the meaning of Eddic → anthropogeny.

Aldagautr? (ON, 'man-Gautr'). Name for Odin in *Baldrs draumar* 2 (and 13?) which is perhaps only a scribal error; cf. Aldafaðir and Gautr.

álfablót (ON, 'sacrifice to the → elves'). *Álfablót* is recorded in Old Norse literature three times. The first reference is in the *Austrfararvísur*, written by the skald Sigvatr Þórðarson after a journey to Sweden undertaken in the autumn of 1018. He says that he was refused entry to several farms as the *álfablót* was being held there. From his ironic description it seems that he had not come across this kind of sacrifice in Norway. – This is the only definite reference to the *álfablót*; *Kormaks saga* 22 tells of a different kind of sacrifice to the elves: in this account the injured hero, Þórvarðr, is recommended to pour the blood of a bull onto one of the hills inhabited by elves and to prepare a meal for them from the meat of the bull in order to heal his injury. According to the internal chronology of the saga, this incident took place in the second half of the 10th century, although the saga itself was written only in the first half of the 13th century, so that we can assume a belief in the healing powers of the elves, if indeed it is not purely fictional anyway, only for this later period. The third account of an *álfablót* refers to King Oláfr Guðrøðarson. After a successful and fortunate reign the king died and was buried in Geirstad. His subjects called him Geirstaðaálfr and sacrifices were made to him (*Ynglinga saga* 48, 49). His great-grandfather, King Hálfdan hvítbeinn, is called *brynjálfr* in one stanza, but this seems to be a kenning for him rather than an actual name (*Ynglinga saga* 44). – Even if we do not know anything definite about the *álfablót*, it is nonetheless possible that the elves (as opposed to the dwarfs) had a cult devoted to them.

J. de Vries, 'Über Sigvats Alfablót-Strophen' (*APhSc* 7) 1932; J. de Vries, *Altgermanische Religionsgeschichte*, Berlin [3]1970; L. Motz, 'On Elves and Dwarfes' (*Arv* 29/30) 1973/74.

Alfaðir (ON). Name for Odin, → Alfǫðr.

álfar (ON) → elves.

Alfarinn (ON, 'the far-travelled' or 'the completely deserted one'?). Alfarinn is an extremely atypical name of a giant (who are normally depicted as uneducated) in the *Þulur*.

Alfheimr (1) (ON, 'world of the elves'). According to Snorri (*Gylfaginning* 16), Alfheimr is the home of the light-elves, which he obviously imagined in the heavens. In *Grímnismál* 5, Alfheimr is called the residence of Freyr, which he received from the Æsir as a teething-gift (a gift from a godparent when the first tooth appeared). Alfheimr is one of a whole series of godly residences in Asgard as listed in *Grímnismál*.

Alfheimr (2). Historically speaking, this was the name given to the area between the rivers Götaelf and Glom in the present-day border country between Norway and Sweden (*Ynglinga saga* 48). A link with the → elves can be made only insofar as the people of the Alfur lived there in legendary times. Their ruler was one of Harald Fairhair's ancestors, and they were said to be 'more beautiful than any other people' (*Sǫgubrot af Fornkonungum* 10), which could indicate a descendency from the elves.

Alfǫðr (ON, 'All-father'). Name for Odin (*Grímnismál* 48); the name also appears in the form Alfaðir in *Helgakviða Hundingsbana* I 38 and in a poem by the scald Arnórr Þórðarson (11th century); a further occurrence of the name in Þórmóðr Bersason's work (after 1000) is uncertain. Names for Odin based on *-fǫðr* (Herfǫðr, Valfǫðr) are possibly older and more likely to be heathen than those based on *-faðir* (Alfaðir, Sigfaðir), as the evidence itself seems to show. The form Alfǫðr in the *Grímnismál* could be formed in analogy to other forms based on *-fǫðr*. Snorri explains Alfǫðr in

Gylfaginning 13 as follows: '[Odin] could be called Alfǫðr because he is the father of all the gods and of all of mankind and of everything which was created by him and his power.' This explanation seems to be as much influenced by Christianity as the name Alfǫðr itself, which is possibly a translation of the Medieval Latin name for the Christian God *omnipater* (first documented in the works of Prudentius in the 4th century). The German word *Allvater* is a translation of Alfǫðr and was used to denote Odin for the first time by Gottsched in 1745.

H. Falk, *Odensheite*, Christiania 1924; H. Kuhn, 'Das nordgermanische Heidentum' (*ZfdA* 79) 1942; F. Kluge, *Etymologisches Wörterbuch*, Berlin [22]1989.

Alf or Alfr (ON, 'elf'). Dwarf named in *Vǫluspá* 16 and in the *Þulur*. Apart from this, Alfr is the name of various legendary people. For more information concerning the overlapping of the → dwarfs and the → elves see these entries.

Alfrek → elves.

Alfrigg or Alfregg (ON). Dwarf named in *Sǫrla þáttr* as being one of the four smiths who made Freyja's necklace (→ Brísingamen). Legendary figures in ON literature such as Alfrikr (*Vilkins máldagi*) and Alrekr (*Ynglingatal*) bear similar names. If Alfrigg has anything to do with these, then it means 'the mighty elf'; but 'the very experienced one' (to *al-freginn*) would also be possible.

Alhiahenae. Name of some → matrons. A Roman inscription from Neidenstein near Heidelberg (CIL XIII 6387) is dedicated to the *Matronis Alhiahenabus*. It is unlikely that the Alhiahenae are identical with other mother-goddesses called Albiahenae because of the different area in which the stone bearing Alhiahenae was found. The name Albiahenae is probably derived from *Albiniacum (nowadays Elvenich), whereas the Alhiahenae are more likely to be related either to Gothic *alhs* 'temple' or else to Gmc **alh-* 'elk', still found today in South German place-names, such as Ellwangen.

S. Gutenbrunner, *Die germanischen Götternamen*, Halle 1936; H. Reichert, *Lexikon der altgermanischen Namen*, Vienna 1987–90.

Ali (1) → Vali (1).

Ali (2). Another form of the name of Loki's son Vali (→ Vali (2)) found in Snorri (*Skáldskaparmál* 16) in a kenning for Loki, Ali's father.

Allvaldi (ON, 'the almighty'). The name given to the father of Þjazi, the giant, in *Hárbarðslóð* 19; according to Snorri he is called → Ölvaldi.

almáttki áss (ON *hinn almáttki áss* 'the almighty As'). Unnamed god in an ON oath formula which occurs both in *Oláfs saga Tryggvasonar* 201 and in the *Landnámabók* (H 268) (*hjálpi mér svá Freyr ok Njǫrðr ok hinn almáttki áss*: 'so help me Freyr and Njǫrðr and the almighty As'), where an oath is made on a temple ring and the three gods Freyr and Njǫrðr and the *almáttki áss* are called upon to witness the oath.

Repeated attempts to identify this god have led to three solutions:

(1) *hinn almáttki áss* = Ullr (Pálsson). According to the Eddic lay Atlakviða an oath was sworn to the god Ullr on a ring, and indeed it does seem that Ullr held a position

as a main god at some time or other. The main weakness in this argument is the very sparse distribution of a documented cult of Ullr (East Norway and Middle Sweden, not Iceland).

(2) *hinn almáttki áss* = Odin (F. Jónsson, Neckel, de Vries). It is inconceivable that the main Germanic god should not be called upon in an oath formula. The sparse distribution of an Odin cult in Iceland speaks against this argument, as does the fact that Odin, as an ambiguous, lawless god, would hardly be called upon to witness oaths.

(3) *hinn almáttki áss* = Thor (Olrik, Olsen, Wessén, Mogk, Turville-Petre, Tapp). It is more likely that Thor, rather than Odin, would be called upon in oaths, as he is the god who is responsible for keeping order in the world, and also because a cult of Thor is recorded in Iceland. Thor probably deserves to be called 'almighty' in regard to the daily life of men more than the other gods because of his versatility, in particular after the shift in his function from strength to other areas of life (fertility, law, family?). Thor nevertheless remains the most likely candidate to fit the identity of the *almáttki áss* for this reason (even though the sources which mention Thor being worshipped in Iceland are the Icelandic sagas and in particular the hardly reliable *Eyrbyggja saga*).

The possibility that perhaps Týr could be the unnamed god has not been seriously discussed hitherto. Despite the fact that a Týr cult is infrequently recorded in the Middle Ages (and not at all in Iceland), he should nevertheless be considered as a god of oaths since he is the ancient god of the skies and the protector of law (cf. Mars Thingsus).

The significance of the term *almáttki áss* should, however, not be over-exaggerated as the oath formula shows an obvious similarity with Christian formulae, and could have been influenced relatively early by these – indeed a medieval scholarly reinterpretation may even be present in both sources.

H. L. Tapp, 'Hinn almáttki áss – Thor or Odin?' (*JEGPh* 55) 1965; H. Pálsson, 'Ass hin almáttki' (*Skírnir* 130) 1956; J. de Vries, *Altgermanische Religionsgeschichte*, Berlin [3]1970; E. O. G. Turville-Petre, 'The cult of Oðinn in Iceland' (in: *Nine Norse Studies*) London 1972.

Almaviahenae. Matron name. A votive inscription from Thorr near Cologne (CIL XIII 12065) is dedicated to these mother goddesses. If the name is indeed Germanic, it could possibly be related to the river name Elm, OHG Elmaha, near Fulda, but this is far away from the position of the actual find; on the other hand such a river name, meaning Elm brook, is by no means an isolated case. The similarity with the Southern Gallic matron name Matrae Almahae would suggest that a Celtic origin for the name Almaviahenae is more likely.

M. Ihm, 'Der Mütter- und Matronenkultus und seine Denkmäler' (*Bonner Jahrbücher* 83) 1887; S. Gutenbrunner, *Die germanischen Götternamen*, Halle 1936; H. Reichert, *Lexikon der altgermanischen Namen*, Vienna 1987–90.

Alsvartr (ON, 'the completely black one'). Name of a giant in the *Þulur* which refers to the dirty ugliness of giants in Medieval folk beliefs (cf. Surtr, Svartr, Amr).

F. Jónsson, 'Þulur' (*APhSc* 9) 1934.

Alsviðr (1) (ON, 'the completely white one'). Name of a giant in the *Hávamál* 143. There he is said to be a giant well versed in runic knowledge.

Alsviðr (2) (ON alsviðr, 'very quick') and Arvakr are the names of the two horses which (according to *Grímnismál* 37) pull the sun over the sky. These names are also found in *Sigrdrífumál* 15 and in the *Þulur*. Snorri interprets the *Grímnismál*-stanza in the following way (*Gylfaginning* 10): 'A man called Mundilfari had two children; they were so fair and beautiful that he called his son Moon and his daughter Sun; he married his daughter to a man called Glenr. The gods, however, were angry about his arrogance and they took the brother and sister and set them in the sky and made Sol drive the horses which pulled the chariot of the sun which the gods had created from a spark which had flown from Muspellsheimr to illuminate the world. These horses were called Arvakr and Alsviðr. The gods fastened two bellows beneath the shoulders of the horses to cool them and in some sources that is called the ironblast.'

Altar. In Germanic antiquity there appear to have been two types of altar for sacrifices and for other cult activities, either a simple heap of stones (ON → *hǫrgr*), or cult frame made of wood.

Stone heaps dating from the Bronze Age to the Roman Iron Age have been found in Germanic areas and have been identified from the archeological finds of the surroundings as being places of sacrifice. Tacitus was referring to these (*Annales* I, 61), when he wrote about altars in the forests where the Germanic peoples made human sacrifices. These piles of stone are called *hǫrgr* in Old Norse (OHG *harug*, Anglo-Saxon *hearg*), a name also given to grave mounds, but predominantly to places of sacrifice (*Hyndluljóð* 10). Swedish place names such as Thorshälla (from Thórshǫrgr) and Onsjö (from the older Odenshög) point to the fact that these places served the cult of the gods even in historical times.

In addition to these stone heaps, other altars formed by wooden frames (such as those from the moor at Bangeroosterveld) are known to have been used in the Bronze Age. Four upright posts were linked on top by beams, decorated with depictions of horns and then surrounded by a stone circle. Simpler wooden frames in places of sacrifice are known from a slightly later period; the Old Norse word for this type of altar is *stallr* or *stalli* (basic meaning: frame, later altar). In 9th century scaldic poetry this word occurs several times (Þjóðólfr, Þorvaldr víðfǫrli, Egill), and in a poem by Egill Odin is even called *vinr stalla* ('friend of the altars'), which means that this kind of altar was still known at the time.

F. Jónsson, 'Hörg' (*Festschrift K. Weinhold*), Straßburg 1896; J. de Vries, *Altgermanische Religionsgeschichte*, Berlin ³1970; H. Jankuhn, H. Kuhn, 'Altar' (*Hoops* 1) ²1973.

Altar ring → Temple ring.

Alþjófr (ON, 'the perfect thief'). A dwarf in *Vǫluspá* 11 and in the *Þulur*.

***alu*.** A magical runic word which occurs over 20 times in runic inscriptions from the 3rd to the 8th centuries. Sometimes, especially on bracteates, *alu* stands alone, but otherwise it is used in connection with names, with concept runes and other magical words (*laþu, laukaR*).

Alu is also what is possibly meant by the *ǫlrúnar* ('beer-runes') in the Eddic *Sigrdrífumál* (7 and 19). The poet of the *Sigrdrífumál* first assumed the connection to *ǫl* ('beer') in order to achieve an interpretation corresponding to contemporary language usage.

Krause's interpretation that *alu* comes from an older *aluh*, which he supposed to be related to Gothic *alhs* 'temple', as 'amulet, taboo', is disputed nowadays and a connection with Hethitic *alwanzahh* 'to charm', Greek *alúein* 'to be beside one's self', Old

Norse *ǫl* 'beer' is preferred. This suggests that *alu* had a basic meaning of 'ecstasy, magic'.

W. Krause, *Beiträge zur Runenforschung*, Halle 1932; E. Polomé, 'Notes sur le vocabulaire religieux' (*Nouvelle Clio* 6) 1954; W. Krause, *Die Runeninschriften im älteren Futhark*, Göttingen 1966; E. Polomé, 'Old Norse Religious Terminology' (*The Nordic Languages and modern Linguistics* 2) Stockholm 1975; J. de Vries, *Altnordisches etymologisches Wörterbuch*, Leiden [2]1977.

Alusneihae. Matron name on two votive altars from Inden-Pier (Kreis Düren, West Germany) from the end of the 2nd century. The name is (if indeed it does not belong to the matron names based on Ala-) linked with the runic magical word → *alu* and Gmc *aluþ* 'beer, intoxicating drink'; as the second part of the name is not easy to interpret (→ Nehalennia), the interpretation of the matron name must remain undecided.

M. Clauss, 'Neue Inschriften im Rheinischen Landesmuseum Bonn' (*Epigraphische Studien* 11) 1976; H. Reichert, *Lexikon der altgermanischen Namen*, Vienna 1987–90.

Alvaldi (ON, 'the all powerful one') is the name of the father of the giant Þjazi, according to *Hárbardsljóð* 19. Alvaldi is otherwise not mentioned and possibly only serves as rhetorical embellishment to the story of Thor's killing of Þjazi.

Alvilda (= ON Alfhilda?) is the name of a Valkyrie-like king's daughter from Götaland in Saxo's *Gesta Danorum* VII, 229); Saxo obviously tried to rationalize the Valkyries of Nordic mythology and made them into warlike princesses or maiden kings. Visna and Hetha (VIII, 256–258) and perhaps also Hermuthruda (IV, 103f.) are further examples.

Alvíss (ON *allvíss*, *alvíss*, 'omniscient', 'the omniscient one'). Name of the dwarf who, according to the → *Alvíssmál*, requests the hand of Thor's daughter in marriage and, having been outwitted by Thor, turns to stone in the sunlight. As the name is otherwise not recorded and the *Alvíssmál* is a very late Eddic poem, the name would appear to be a new creation from the 12th century; the idea of → dwarfs being wise belongs to folklore.

Alvíssmál (ON, 'the lay of the omniscient one'). An Eddic lay which was probably written in the 12th century. It relates the tale of Thor's outwitting of the dwarf Alvíss. The contents are unlikely to derive from a mythical tale, but rather from poetic material, such as is found in the lists of synonyms and names in the *Þulur* (*Snorra Edda*), and is presented by the poet in an invented mythological framework: Alvíss the dwarf has been promised the hand of Thor's daughter in marriage, and he arrives to celebrate the wedding. It is then that Thor demands, as a condition for the wedding, that he must answer some questions. There then follow twice 13 stanzas, composed all in exactly the same way. In the first stanza Thor asks what the names for earth, heaven, moon, sun, clouds, wind, calm, fire, sea, wood, night, corn and beer are, and in the subsequent stanza receives the reply from the dwarf who tells him what these things are called by man, the Æsir, the Vanir, the dwarfs, giants and elves. Finally, a beam of sunlight falls into the hall and the dwarf turns to stone. The dialogue form also occurs in other Eddic lays, such as *Vafþrúðnismál* and *Skírnismál*, but the contents of the framework story (the wooing of the finally outsmarted dwarf) are not found anywhere else, although Snorri (*Skáldskaparmál*) quotes two stanzas from *Alvíssmál*; therefore, we must consider them as being the invention of the poet himself who took the → *Vafþrúðnismál* as a model. What is interesting in *Alvíssmál*, apart from the otherwise known categories of mythological beings, are the groups of synonyms which appear to put the different beings into certain language registers. On the other hand, the fact should not be ignored that the requirements of the stave rhyme partly determined the choice of expressions. *Alvíssmál* should therefore probably be seen more as a poetically reworked addition to scaldic poetry than as language registers deriving from actual mythological realities or from taboo languages.

ED: G. Neckel, H. Kuhn, *Edda*, [5]1983.
H. Güntert, *Von der Sprache der Götter und Geister*, Halle 1921; M. Thordarson, 'Alvíssmál' (*Arbók hins Islenzka Fornleifafjelags*) 1924; R. Meissner, 'Die Sprache der Götter, Riesen und Zwerge in den Alvíssmál' (*ZfdA* 61) 1924; J. de Vries, 'Om Eddaens Visdomsdigtning' (*ANF* 50) 1934; H. Klingenberg, 'Alvíssmál, das Lied vom überweisen Zwerg' (*GRM* NF 17) 1967; K. Schier, 'Alvíssmál' (*Kindlers Literatur Lexikon* 1) 1967; C. Watkins, 'Language of Gods and Language of Men' (*Myth and Law among the Indo-Europeans*) Berkely etc. 1970; L. Moberg, 'The Languages of *Alvíssmál*' (*Saga-Book* 18) 1973; J. Fleck, 'Alvíssmál' (*DicMA* 1) 1982.

Ama (or Amma, ON, 'the dark one'). A giantess in the poetry of Einarr Gilsson and in the *Þulur*. As is often the case with other giants' names it refers to the inherent ugliness of giants.

Ambiamarcae. The name of a group of → matrons. A votive stone from Deutz from 252 A.D. carries the inscription: *In (honorem) domus divinae et genio lo(ci), Ambiamarcis, Ambiorenesibus, Marti Victori, Mercurio, Neptuno, Cereri, diis deabusque omnibus* . . . ('In honour of the divine house and the protective spirits of this place, the Ambiamarcae, Ambiorenis, the victorious Mars, Mercury, Neptune, Ceres and all the gods and goddesses . . .'). Although here and on an inscription from Wardt, West Germany, from the year 218 A.D., the Ambiamarcae are not expressly called matrons, the dedication to the matrons → Abiamarcae makes this clear. These new finds confirm Gutenbrunner's theory that in this case Ambia- should be read instead of Abia-; in addition to this, there is also the recorded form Ambiomarcae. The whole group probably belongs to the place-names *Ambia (nowadays Embt); admittedly, another possibility would be the basic meaning of Ambiamarc- ('the fenced in marchlands'). The name is at any rate a Celtic-Germanic mixed formation. It is striking that both the Ambiamarcae as well as the Ambiomarcae are named together with Roman deities. Therefore, it is questionable whether Ambiamarcae are really Germanic matrons.

S. Gutenbrunner, *Die germanischen Götternamen*, Halle 1936; G. Alföldy, 'Epigraphisches aus dem Rheinland III' (*Epigraphische Studien* 5) 1968; H. Birkhan, *Germanen und Kelten*, Vienna 1970; B. und H. Galsterer, 'Neue Inschriften aus Köln' (*Epigraphische Studien* 12) 1981.

Ambiomarc(i)ae. A votive inscription from Remagen (CIL XIII 7789) dedicated by one of the soldiers from the XXX. legion begins: *I.O.M. et Genio loci, Marti, Herculi, Mercurio, Ambiomarcis* . . . The deities Ambiomarciae referred to here are possibly mother goddesses. However, the name might also simply be a place-name referring to the other previously named gods. On the other hand, new finds from the 1970s including the matron name → Ambiamarcae make it likely that Ambiomarciae is simply another form of this name.

F. Kauffmann, 'Der Matronenkultus in Germanien' (*Zeitschrift für Volkskunde* 2) 1892; S. Gutenbrunner, *Die germanischen Götternamen*, Halle 1936; M. Schönfeld, *Wörterbuch der altgermanischen Personen- und Völkernamen*, Heidelberg [2]1965; H. Reichert, *Lexikon der altgermanischen Namen*, Vienna 1987–90.

Ambioreneses. The name of a group of → matrons. Like the etymologically similar Abirenae, Ambiorenenses should probably be understood as the name for some matrons, even if this is not expressly stated as such on the recently found inscription from Deutz (252 A.D.) and the name is given together with the Ambiamarcae among a list of Roman deities. The Ambiorenenses are, then, 'the matrons who live (or are worshipped?) on either side of the Rhine'.

B. und H. Galsterer, 'Neue Inschriften aus Köln' (*Epigraphische Studien* 12) 1981.

Ambirenae → Abirenae.

Amfratninae. Name of → matrons on a dozen votive stones found only in 1980 in Eschweiler (Germany) together with inscriptions dedicated to the Alaferhviae. The name is possibly related to OHG *frad* 'capable', *fradi* 'efficiency, success', in which case these matrons would have been thought to be in charge of personal fortunes.

H. Reichert, *Lexikon der altgermanischen Namen*, Vienna 1987–90; R. Nedoma, 'Matronae Amfratninae' (*Beiträge zur Namenforschung* 24) 1989.

Amgerðr (ON, 'dark Gerðr'). A giantess in a skaldic poem by Einarr Gilsson and in the *Þulur*; Gerðr occurs frequently and is one of the best known giantesses in Nordic mythology. Many giants' names point to the dark, dirty colour of giants (Svartr, Surtr, Amr).

Ammaca. A possibly Germanic, but more likely Gallic goddess on an inscription from Maastricht. → Gamaleda.

Amnesahenae. The name of a group of → matrons. A votive inscription from Thorr near Cologne is dedicated to the *Matronis Amnesa[henis]* (CIL XIII 12066). However, the name is possibly Celtic.

S. Gutenbrunner, *Die germanischen Götternamen*, Halle 1936.

Amr (ON, 'the dark one'). A giant in the *Þulur* and also in a skaldic stanza by Ofeigr.

Amsvartnir (ON, 'the red-black one' or 'the completely black one'?). A lake, according to Snorri (*Gylfaginning* 33). The island of Lyngvi, on which the Fenriswolf is chained up until the Ragnarǫk, lies in this lake. Amsvartnir is an invention of Snorri's, as are many other names in the tale.

Amulets. Magical objects which protect the bearer from misfortune or else are supposed to endow him with some special power. The use of amulets by the Germanic tribes since the Bronze Age has been substantiated by archaeological finds. The amulets, made of animal, plant or mineral materials (pieces of shell, animal claws, roots, pearls of amber) were superseded in the Iron Age by metal pendants which found continued use in the → bracteates of the Migration Era, and plate-like amulet-pendants with magical runic inscriptions or single runic symbols of magical significance. In the last century before Christianization, set minerals or glass pearls as well as silver capsules or bags containing fragrant herbs were used in addition to these.

Other amulets, which did not give protective magic but rather established a link to a particular god, were small statuettes of gods which are archaeologically recorded for both Freyr and Thor, but ON literature only mentions them for Freyr. Small Thor's hammers (→ Mjǫllnir) as amulet-pendants were symbolic for heathendom itself in the later heathen period as were pendant crosses for Christians. The older so-called Hercules' clubs also go back to a devotion to the god Thor. It is a matter for conjecture whether the 450 so-called 'Thor's rings' found in Sweden, which are peculiar to 9th century graves, were ever worn by living people, but the suspended tiny hammers among other weapons seem to link them to Thor. Other miniature weapons may also have been used as amulets, for example small spearheads might have signified a connection to a devotion to Odin, as is also documented on the bracteates.

S. Grieg, 'Amuletter og Gudebilder' (*Viking* 18) 1954; H. Thrane, T. Capelle, H. Jankuhn, W. Krause, 'Amulett' (*Hoops* 1) ²1973; S. H. Fuglesang, 'Viking and medieval amulets in Scandinavia' (*Fornvännen* 84) 1989.

An (ON, from aða-vinr 'distinguished friend'). A dwarf in *Vǫluspá* 11. An is otherwise recorded as a male personal name.

Anarr (1) (ON, 'the other one'). A dwarf in *Vǫluspá* 11 and 15.

Anarr (2) (ON). This appears to be the name of the father of the Earth in Þjóðólfr Arnórsson's *Sexstefja* 3.

Ancestor cult → Dead, cult of the.

Andhrímnir (ON, 'the one exposed to soot'). The cook in Valhall who prepares the wild boar → Sæhrímnir in the cauldron → Eldhrímnir – that, at least, is Snorri's interpretation (*Gylfaginning* 37) of *Grímnismál* 18. In the *Þulur* Andhrímnir is found as a name for 'eagle'.

Andlangr (ON, 'the extremely long, wide one'). The name which Snorri gives to the second heaven which lies between the first visible one, and the third one called → Víðbláinn. The concept of three (or more) heavens is totally Christian. Snorri appears to have taken both the name Andlangr as well as the rest of this extract from the Medieval didactic dialogue *Elucidarius*, because the second heaven (*coelus spiritualis*) which he mentions in this work is given in the popular Icelandic translation of the *Elucidarius* as *andlegr himinn*; Snorri has changed this term for his supposedly heathen cosmology very slightly. Even his comments about the third heaven (Víðbláinn) come from the words of the Elucidarius referring to the second heaven. Therefore, Andlangr has nothing whatsoever to do with heathen mythology. – Andlangr is to be found in two later Christian poems (*Guðmundardrápa*, *Petrsdrápa*) as well as in the *Þulur*, but both examples have clearly been taken from Snorri.

Andrusteihiae. The name of a group of → matrons. The votive stones dedicated to these matrons bear the forms Andrustheihis (Bonn), Andrusteihiabus (Godesberg; CIL XIII 7995) and Andrustehiabus (Cologne; CIL XIII 8212). The Andrusteihiae belong etymologically to Old Franconian *antrustio* 'follower' and therefore are connected to a regional or people's name, as are the Celtic Cantrusteihiae (to *pagus Condrustis*).

S. Gutenbrunner, *Die germanischen Götternamen*, Halle 1936; H. Birkhan, *Germanen und Kelten*, Vienna 1970; B. und H. Galsterer, *Die römischen Steininschriften aus Köln*, Köln 1975; H. Reichert, *Lexikon der altgermanischen Namen*, Vienna 1987–90.

Andvari (ON, 'the careful one'). A dwarf in the *Vǫluspá*, the *Reginsmál* and in the *Þulur*. The prose introduction of Rm records how Loki catches Andvari in his net and how Andvari has to buy himself free with his gold. However, he puts a curse on part of the treasure, a gold ring. The gold, the ring and the curse connected to it become the motif which bring about the story of the Nibelungs. Thus, Andvari belongs more to the field of heroic poetry, where Wagner made extensive use of him, than to mythology.

Anesiaminehae. The name of a group of → matrons on a votive inscription from Zülpich (CIL XIII 7926). The name is possibly Celtic and refers to the river name Anesus, Anasus (nowadays Enns), which is however far away from the situation of the find.

S. Gutenbrunner, *Die germanischen Götternamen*, Halle 1936; M. Schönfeld, *Wörterbuch der altgermanischen Personen- und Völkernamen*, Heidelberg [2]1965; H. Reichert, *Lexikon der altgermanischen Namen*, Vienna 1987–90.

Angeyja (ON). One of the nine giant mothers of the god Heimdall, according to *Vǫluspá in skamma* (*Hyndluljóð* 37). The meaning is uncertain: 'those of the narrow island' (to *ey*: according to de Vries), 'the harasser' (Gering) or perhaps to *geyja* 'bark' (Motz)?

H. Gering, *Kommentar* 1, 1927; J. de Vries, *Altnordisches etymologisches Wörterbuch*, Leiden [2]1977; L. Motz, 'Giantesses and their Names' (*FmSt* 15) 1981.

Angrboða (ON, 'the one who brings grief'). A giantess, with whom Loki, according to the *Vǫluspá in skamma* (*Hyndluljóð* 40), begat the Fenriswolf. Snorri adds in *Gylfaginning* 19 that the Midgard serpent and Hel were also the products of this union. Whether the tradition of Loki as the father of the Fenriswolf, the Midgard serpent and Hel is ancient is difficult to judge; the telling name Angrboða is beyond doubt a late mythographical invention of the 12th century.

L. Motz, 'Giantesses and their Names' (*FmSt* 15) 1981.

Animal sacrifice. This was among the most frequent kinds of → sacrifice used by the Germanic tribes but we know little about its form apart from the ritual slaughter and the common sacrificial feast.

There appears to have been a connection between the kind of animal sacrificed and the god to whom the sacrifice was made. Goats were animals dedicated to Thor, rams to Heimdallr, boars to Freyr, bulls perhaps to Týr and horses to Odin since eating horse meat had a special religious place value. This can be seen by the fact that after Christianization it was forbidden to eat horse meat, but the custom continued for some time afterwards in Iceland as a result of the exemptions granted to the Icelanders.

Ann (ON). A dwarf, → Önn.

Annanept(i)ae. A group of Germanic → mother goddesses. The votive inscription from Wissen near Xanten (CIL XIII 8629) is from 233 A.D. and is dedicated to the *Matribus Annaneptis*. The name is possibly connected to ON Nipt 'sister; name of a Valkyrie'. The first part of the word perhaps belongs to OHG *unnan* 'grant', Gothic *ansts* 'favour', which would suggest that the Annaneptiae were the 'friendly sisters'. This interpretation is however by no means certain.

R. Much, 'Germanische Matronennamen' (*ZfdA* 35) 1891; S. Gutenbrunner, *Die germanischen Götternamen*, Halle 1936; M. Schönfeld, *Wörterbuch der altgermanischen Personen- und Völkernamen*, Heidelberg [2]1965; H. Reichert, *Lexikon der altgermanischen Namen*, Vienna 1987–90.

Annar (ON, 'the other one, the second'). According to Snorri, Annarr is Nótt's second husband; their daughter is Jǫrð. It is not clear why Snorri invented an otherwise unknown husband for Nótt, the personification of night, and also if the relationship between Jǫrð and Nótt was Snorri's invention.

Anses. A Gothic term for 'gods' used by Jordanes (a Christian historian from the 6th century) that refers to a mythical dynasty which, according to Jordanes, used to be honoured as heroes (*semideos*). Etymologically speaking, the Anses are identical with the → Æsir and the word-element Ans- is found in numerous personal names from the Migration Age, although it is not totally clear what it means. Krappe's interpretation of Anses as divine twins is somewhat shaky, and Grimm's old explanation of *ans* as 'beam' (ON *áss* 'beam') is far more likely. According to this theory, the gods were thought of as being the supporting beams of heaven; but the more likely explanation is that the word refers to the images of gods carved out of wooden beams (→ wooden gods).

J. Grimm, *Deutsche Mythologie*, Berlin [4]1875–78; A. H. Krappe, 'Anses' (*PBB* 56) 1932; E. Polomé, 'L'etymologie du terme germanique *ansuz "dieu souverain" ' (*Etudes Germaniques* 8) 1953; J. de Vries, *Altgermanische Religionsgeschichte*, Berlin [3]1970.

Anthropogeny ('the origin of man'). Tacitus is our only source for information about the religious beliefs about the origin of mankind held by the West Germanic tribes. He records that the three Germanic tribes of the Ingaevones, Istaevones and Herminones originate from a single common ancestor, Mannus, who himself was the son of Tuisto (or Tuisco), an earth-born god. Despite the apparently ancient concept of Mannus as the progenitor (cf. Manus as the progenitor in Indian mythology), this genealogy belongs more to the area of ethnogeny (→ Descendancy, myth of) which is concerned with 'the origin of the races and nations' than to the area of anthropogeny. Thus, only the two Eddas remain as sources for northern Germanic concepts regarding anthropogeny. Snorri's account of → Búri (who is licked free from the ice by the primeval cow → Auðumla and who gives birth to → Burr, whose union with the giant's daughter Bestla results in the birth of the first gods Odin, Vili and Vé), should not be understood as a myth of the creation of man since these gods subsequently create the first human couple, Ask and Embla, from two tree trunks. Although it is obvious that different and older traditions have been merged in both the *Vǫluspá* and in Snorri's *Edda*, Buri is inconceivable as the human ancestor of the gods. Therefore, the concept of the creation of man from tree trunks has to be separated from the divergent tradition of the genealogy Buri-Burr-divine triad (cf. Tuisto-Mannus-triad of tribes in Tacitus). This genealogical descendancy of man from the gods which manifests itself in the ethnographies of Germanic tribes and the genealogies of kings and thus shows itself to be the more original concept, was replaced in the late era of the heathen age by the secondary concept (perhaps contaminated by south-eastern ideas?) of the origin of the first human couple by a divine triad. According to Snorri, Odin, Vili and Vé create the first human couple, but in *Vǫluspá* 18 the divine triad is Odin, Hǫnir and Loðurr; Odin gives man the breath of life, Hǫnir the soul, Loðurr the warmth of life (if the otherwise unrecorded *lá* can be interpreted in this way). A repetition of the anthropogeny is to be found in *Vafþrúðnismál* 45 where a human couple, Lif and Lifþrasir, survive the end of the world in a tree and then become the progenitors of a new human race.

O. Höfler, 'Abstammungstraditionen' (*Hoops* 1) [2]1968; J. de Vries, *Altgermanische Religionsgeschichte*, Berlin [3]1970; G. Steinsland, 'Antropogonimyten i Vǫluspá' (*ANF* 98) 1983.

Apples. The apples of the goddess → Idun, which rejuvenate the gods when they eat them, are mentioned as early as c.900 A.D. by Þjóðólfr in his skaldic poem *Haustlǫng*. This is the source for Snorri's account of the golden apples which Idun keeps in her casket and uses to rejuvenate the gods (*Gylfaginning* 25); on one occasion the giant → Þjazi abducts Idun along with her apples, and the gods begin to age (*Skáldskaparmál* 1).

Although this myth about Idun is not very widespread, the idea of the miraculous (golden) apples can be found in other texts, namely *Skírnismál* 19f. where Skírnir offers Gerðr eleven apples as a bait.

The idea of apples as a symbol of fertility and of life appears to have been adopted by the Germanic peoples from the Romans at a relatively early period, since apples can be found depicted in Imperial Roman times as symbols of life on the altars of the → Nehalennia. The Apples of Hesperides in Classical mythology – Gaia's wedding present to Hera – could thus have served as the model for Idun's apples, but it might equally well be derived from the Christian symbolism of the tree of life. The Irish tales of the theft of the healing apples by Tuireum's sons from Hisbernia's garden, which are related to the Idun myth, could derive from similar models, but do not necessarily depend on the Nordic myth.

The question as to when the deliberate cultivation of apple trees began in Scandinavia (in the later Neolithic times? before or during the Roman Age? in the High Middle Ages?) is of little consequence regarding the magical importance of the apples, as a bucket full of wild apples has been found among the burial gifts in the Oseberg ship, and these can certainly be understood as symbols of life. The name of the fruit, which was already found in pre-Germanic times, was common to the North Germanic languages and allows one to conclude that apple trees were cultivated in Scandinavia long before Roman times.

S. Bugge, 'Iduns Æbler' (*ANF* 5) 1889; J. de Vries, *Altgermanische Religionsgeschichte*, Berlin [3]1970; E. O. G. Turville-Petre, *Myth and Religion of the North*, Westport 1975; I. Müller, D. Harmening, 'Apfel' (*LexMA* 1) 1980.

ár ok friðr (ON, approx.: 'good harvest and peace'). A formula used in Germanic cult language which summarizes what the Germanic peoples understood to be salvation (Baetke). In the description of → Fróði's peace elements, *ár ok friðr* are linked together: repeatedly good harvests, plentiful schools of fish, outward peace and inner security, a lack of any crime.

Sacrifices were made especially to the god of fertility, Freyr, so that these circumstances would be realized. The fact that this sacrifice could be the sacrifice of a king shows that the king was not only nationally in charge of and responsible for peace but that he was equally responsible for good harvests (→ Sacred kingship).

W. Baetke, 'Der Begriff der Unheiligkeit' (*PBB* 66) 1942; A. Ebenbauer, 'Fróði und sein Friede' (*Festgabe* O. *Höfler*) Vienna 1976; F. Ström, 'År och fred' (*KLNM* 20) 1976.

Arnhǫfði (ON, 'the one with the eagle's head'). A name for Odin in the *Þulur* and could possibly refer to Odin's shape-change into an eagle in the myth of the theft of the → mead of the skalds. There are, however, a number of other animal names listed among the names for Odin (Jálkr, Bjǫrn) which possibly refer to the animal disguises used in an older cult of Odin, rather than to myths recorded in literary form.

Arvagast(i)ae. Name of some → matrons. The inscription dedicated to the *Matronis Arvagastis* from Müddersheim near Aachen, West Germany (CIL XIII 7855) is from the time after 150 A.D. The name is probably derived from the Germanic personal name *Arwagasti- (cf. Franconian Arbogastes, Arvagastes, 4th/5th century).

S. Gutenbrunner, *Die germanischen Götternamen*, Halle 1936; M. Schönfeld, *Wörterbuch der altgermanischen Personen- und Völkernamen*, Heidelberg [2]1965; H. Reichert, *Lexikon der altgermanischen Namen*, Vienna 1987–90.

Arvakr (ON, 'early awake'). One of the two horses which pull the chariot of the sun (*Grímnismál* 37 and Snorri, *Gylfaginning* 10); the other is called → Alsviðr.

Arvernus → Mercurius Arvernus.

Arvolecia. Germanic (?) goddess named on a votive inscription from Brough in north England set up after 150 A.D. (*Deae Arvolecie*, if the reading should not be Arnomecte). Although the person who dedicated the inscription has a Celtic name, Maiotius, Arvolecia is nonetheless probably a Germanic name and perhaps means 'the quick healer'.

S. Gutenbrunner, *Die germanischen Götternamen*, Halle 1936; H. Reichert, *Lexikon der altgermanischen Namen*, Vienna 1987–90.

Asabragr (ON, 'Æsir-lord'). A name given to the god Thor in *Skírnismál* 33 and in the *Þulur*; the vague name serves to confirm his already well-known high rank among the Germanic gods.

Asaheimr (ON, 'world of the Æsir'). Also Asaland, a country in Asia, according to Snorri's learned pre-history, from where the Æsir originate (*Ynglinga saga* 2). The capital was Asgard which he identifies as being Troy (*Gylfaginning* 8), thus bringing about a link between classical history and the North. This is not only a mixture of classical material and deposed gods, but is also the product of Christian scholarship in medieval Iceland and as such has, naturally enough, little to do with ancient Germanic mythology.

Asaland (ON, 'land of the Æsir') → Asaheimr.

Asa-Thor (ON Asa-Þórr, 'Æsir-Thor'). A name which Snorri repeatedly gives to the god Thor. In Old Norse poetry this name is only found once (*Hárbarðsljóð* 52). Because it is an honorary name for Thor, which is found in literature especially wherever Thor's reputation is in question (*Hárbarðsljóð*; at Utgarðaloki's), it serves to increase the irony of the situation.

A. M. Sturtevant, 'Regarding the Name Asa-Þórr' (SS 25) 1953.

Asbrú (ON, 'Æsirs' bridge'). A name which Snorri (*Gylfaginning* 14) uses for the bridge leading to heaven; → Bifrǫst.

Asericinehae. The name of some → matrons which are named on three votive inscriptions in the area around Cologne: *Matronis Asericinehabus* (Odenhausen, CIL

XIII 7981), *Aserecinehis* (Odendorf, CIL XIII 7978 and 7979). It is possibly etymologically related to a Germanic personal name *Ansu-rik- (cf. Old Franconian Ansoricus, Gothic Anserigus).

S. Gutenbrunner, *Die germanischen Götternamen*, Halle 1936; M. Schönfeld, *Wörterbuch der altgermanischen Personen- und Völkernamen*, Heidelberg ²1965; H. Reichert, *Lexikon der altgermanischen Namen*, Vienna 1987–90.

Asgard (ON Asgarðr, 'home of the Æsir'). The stronghold of the gods in Nordic mythology. In mythological poetry, Asgard is found only in *Hymiskviða* 7 and *Þrymskviða* 18, and in skaldic poetry only in a poem by Þórbjǫrn dísarskáld from the 10th century. The name, which originally was probably not a name at all, is found frequently in Snorri's writings. He uses it in both *Gylfaginning* and *Skáldskaparmál* simply to denote the residence of the Æsir; → Valhall, the hall of the dead warriors, lies in Asgard, as well as → Hliðskjálf, from where Odin can see over the whole world, and → Iðavǫllr also lies within Asgard. The gods had a temple (→ Glaðsheimr) and a hall for the female Æsir (→ Vingólf) built. The other places which Grm cites as being lived in by the gods (→ residences of the gods) also lie in Asgard.

Originally, Asgard was probably understood to be part of Midgard which meant that the gods lived close to the world of men – as opposed to → Utgard, the area outside. On the other hand Snorri obviously thinks of Asgard as being in the sky, as the name → Himinbjǫrg shows. → Bifrǫst, a bridge, leads to this heavenly Asgard.

Although it is said nowhere expressly, the tale of the → Master Builder, which Snorri tells in *Gylfaginning* 41, appears to refer to the building of Asgard: the gods wanted to have a fortified castle built and a giant offered to do this within 18 months. As his reward he demanded to have Freyja as his wife and the sun and the moon as gifts. Nobody was supposed to help him in this enterprise except his horse Svaðilfari but with the help of this giant horse the work progresses so quickly that the gods had to take council three days before the time-limit expired because otherwise they would be bound to give the giant what he demanded, and they had no intention of keeping the agreement. Loki was blamed for arranging the terms with the giant and was therefore charged to find a way out of the dilemma. He changed his shape into that of a mare and diverted the stallion's attention from his work so that it was not completed on time. Thor killed the giant and Loki gave birth to an eight-legged foal, → Sleipnir, shortly afterwards. – Snorri had a completely different concept of Asgard which he included in his learned pre-history in *Gylfaginning* 2 and 8 as well as in the *Ynglinga saga* (2, 5, 9) and yet which has virtually nothing to do with Germanic mythology. Here Asgard is the capital of Asaland or Asaheimr, and in *Gylfaginning* 9 this 'old Asgard' (*Asgarð enn forna*) is even identified as Troy.

J. de Vries, *Altgermanische Religionsgeschichte*, Berlin ³1970; E. F. Halvorsen, 'Åsgard' (*KLNM* 20) 1976; J. Harris, 'The Masterbuilder Tale in Snorri's Edda and Two Sagas' (*ANF* 91) 1976.

Ash-trees. The ash was a special tree and venerated as such by the Germanic peoples. The world-tree, whose roots reach out to all parts of the earth and whose crown rises into the skies, is an ash called → Yggdrasill. However, it seems that the large evergreen tree next to the temple in Uppsala, mentioned by Adam of Bremen (*Gesta Hammaburgensis ecclesiae pontificum* IV, Scholion 138), was a yew tree.

One indication of the worship of ash-trees is given by Snorri in his mythical tale of Thor's journey to → Geirrǫðargarð (*Skáldskaparmál* 18), when he says that Thor could only save himself from the flooding river Vimur by pulling himself out on an ash; for this reason it is said that 'the ash is Thor's salvation' (*reynir er bjǫrg Þórs*), and this connexion of Thor to ash-trees is also mentioned in a skaldic stanza in the *Grettis saga* (c.1300).

It is worth noting that, according to the legend of the creation in *Vǫluspá*, the first man is called Askr ('ash-tree'), and a certain Æsc is recorded as being the mythical ancestor of the Anglo-Saxon royal family of the Æscingas (on the other hand the OE expression *æscmen* for the Danish Vikings derived from the Nordic ship's term *askr*). The ash, which was particularly wide-spread in Bronze Age Scandinavia, appears to have played a role in some of the Germanic myths of creation.

Asia. The land where the Æsir come from according to Snorri's etymology in which Germanic, classical and Christian elements are mixed together. According to Snorri, the Æsir's country there was called Asaheimr or Asaland, the capital of which was Asgard, and it was ruled by Odin (*Ynglinga saga* 2).

Askr (ON, 'ash-tree'). Askr and Embla are the first two people in the world according to the Old Norse anthropogeny of the *Edda* (*Vǫluspá* 17 and 18). Snorri tells of how Burr's sons – the gods Odin, Vili and Vé – find two tree trunks on the shore and they create man from them; Odin gives them breath and life, Vili intelligence and movement, and Vé their outward appearance, speech, hearing and sight. The *Vǫluspá*, however, says that Odin Ho*enir and Loðurr are the gods who give the progenitors breath (*ǫnd*), soul (*óðr*), life-giving warmth (should the otherwise unrecorded *lá* actually means this) and appearance (or health; *góðr litr*; *litr* actually means 'colour'). Ström has vehemently argued against the idea that *óðr* means 'soul' and interprets it as being the voice, but this hardly fits in with the list of basic life-giving functions (→ Soul). – According to Snorri, the whole of the human race comes from Askr and Embla and the gods give them Midgard as a place to live. – Askr fits in, etymologically speaking, with the myth of man's creation from a tree-trunk. A certain Æsc listed among the ancestors of the royal line of the Æscingar also lends support to the idea that this tale is not merely younger mythography. – A. C. Bang's comparison of Askr and Embla with Adam and Eve is little more than an interesting idea, even if S. Bugge's derivation of Iðavǫllr from Eden and the Urðar brunnr ('Urð's well') from Jordan are on the same lines.

A. C. Bang, *Vǫluspaa og de Sibyllinske Orakler*, Oslo 1879; J. de Vries, *Altgermanische Religionsgeschichte*, Berlin [3]1970; Å. V. Ström, *Germanische Religion*, Stuttgart 1975.

Asynja (pl. Asynjur). An Æsir goddess, → Æsir.

Atla (ON, 'the argumentative one', to *atall*). A giantess or troll-woman in the *Þulur*. In the *Vǫluspá in skamma* (*Hyndluljóð* 37) she is listed as one of Heimdall's nine giant mothers.

Atlaterviae → Alaterviae.

Atli (ON, 'the terrible'). A name for heroes and kings (Attila = Atli) in heroic poetry. In the *Þulur* Atli is also listed, however, as a name for the god Thor.

Atríðr (ON, 'attacker'). A name for Odin in *Grímnismál* 48, as well as in the *Þulur*; it refers to Odin's role as a god of war.

H. Falk, *Odensheite*, Kristiania 1924.

Atufrafinehae. Probably a name for some → matrons even if this is not expressly stated in any of the six instances of existing inscriptions from Berkum near Bonn, Germany (CIL XIII 7984–9). The name is obscure, but it certainly seems to be Germanic. Gutenbrunner's imaginative interpretation sees an etymological relationship to a place-name **at þraf(n)i-* 'at the tower, at the temple of the matrons' (from ON *þref* 'scaffold'); however, the well-documented form Atufrafinehae makes such a basic form extremely unlikely.

S. Gutenbrunner, *Die germanischen Götternamen*, Halle 1936; H. Reichert, *Lexikon der altgermanischen Namen*, Vienna 1987–90.

Atvarðr (ON, 'the defender' or 'the relative'?). A dwarf (?) in *Fjǫllsvinnsmál* 34.

Auðr (ON, 'prosperity'). According to Snorri (*Gylfaginning* 9), this is the name of the son of Nótt, the personification of night, and her first husband, Naglfari. It is unknown why Snorri here invented a first husband and a son for Nótt. In other Icelandic sources Auðr is a girl's name.

Audrinehae. Name of some → matrons; seven inscriptions on Roman votive stones from Hermühlheim near Cologne are dedicated to these *Matronis Audrinehae* (four times), *Auðrinehae, Authrinehae* or *Autriahenae* (once each). The name possibly means 'the one who gives divine support' (de Vries; to Proto-Norse *auja* 'divine protection') or else 'the friendly powers of destiny' (Gutenbrunner; to ON *auðna* 'destiny, fate'). Birkhan thinks that the Austriahenae are identical with the Audrinehae and therefore sees an etymological relationship to the name of the Austrogoti; if this is so, they could be interpreted 'the Eastern ones'. However, the geographical distribution speaks against this, since the areas where both names are found are clearly separated.

S. Gutenbrunner, *Die germanischen Götternamen*, Halle 1936; H. Birkhan, *Germanen und Kelten*, Vienna 1970; H. Reichert, *Lexikon der altgermanischen Namen*, Vienna 1987–90.

Auðumla (ON Auðumla, Auðhumla, Auðumbla). The primeval cow which is created out of the melting primeval hoar-frost. In *Gylfaginning* 5 Snorri tells how four streams of milk flowed from her udders and fed the giant → Ymir, whilst Auðumla licked the progenitor of the gods, Buri, free from the salty ice. Auðumla means 'the hornless cow with lots of (milk)' (from *auðr* 'riches, wealth' and **humala* 'hornless'). Tacitus also records that the Germanic tribes had hornless cattle (*Germania* 5).

The image of the holy cow is closely related to the figure of the Earth-mother in numerous non-Germanic religions (only the Egyptian Hathor is a cow-headed goddess of the skies); both Hera ('the cow-eyed') and especially Isis have characteristics referring back to the image of a cow. For Germanic areas, Nerthus should be mentioned, as it was he who, according to Tacitus, was placed on a chariot pulled by cattle in cult processions: here the figure of the cow is only apparent in the attributes of the goddess. – The four streams of milk from Auðumla's udders suggest a comparison with the four rivers of paradise, but it is more likely that Auðumla's four streams of milk are the result of Snorri's clerical education rather than giving proof of common origins with Near-Eastern concepts of the magna-mater.

A. Noreen, 'Urkon Auðhumla och några hennes språkliga släktningar' (*NoB* 6) 1918; F. R. Schröder, 'Germanische Schöpfungsmythen' (*GRM* 19) 1931; O. Nordland, 'Auðumla' (*KLNM* 1) 1956; J. de Vries, *Altgermanische Religionsgeschichte*, Berlin [3]1970.

R: the striking scene in which Auðumla feeds Ymir and licks Buri free from the ice was painted by the Danish artist N. A. Abilgaard (1743–1809).

Aueaniae → Aufaniae. *Matribus Aueaniabus* is a misspelling for *Aufaniabus* on an inscription from Carmona near Cordoba (Spain; CIL II 5413).

Aueha. Germanic goddess on a Roman votive inscription. The inscription comes from Gleuel (→ Ahueccaniae), and the name, as Gutenbrunner suggested, is probably etymologically related to Gmc **ahwō-* 'river' so that this Dea Aueha was perhaps a goddess of rivers or springs.

S. Gutenbrunner, *Die germanischen Götternamen*, Halle 1936; H. Reichert, *Lexikon der altgermanischen Namen*, Vienna 1987–90.

Aufanie. Matron name. Nearly 90 inscriptions are dedicated to the *Matronis Aufaniabus*, which means that this name (apart from Austrihenae) is the most frequently recorded name for matrons; the inscriptions are mostly found in Bonn and also in Nettersheim, and apart from two exceptions (from Cordoba/Spain and Lyon/France) the others are also found on the Lower Rhine. The stones have been dated to the period between 164–235 A.D., and are particularly numerous at around the turn of the century; thus, the monuments of the *Matronae Aufanie* fall into the heyday of the cult of matrons on the Lower Rhine. The inscriptions are not always expressly dedicated to the *Matronis Aufaniabus*, and the divine addressees are then called *Deae Aufanie* or *Sanctae Aufanie*, names which only confirm their high position in the cult. The name Aufanie has not yet been fully explained, but the most convincing interpretation is Much's which suggests 'generous ancestral mother' (cf. Gothic *ūfjō* 'abundance, plenty').

R. Much, 'Germanische Matronennamen' (*ZfdA* 35) 1891; S. Gutenbrunner, *Die germanischen Götternamen*, Halle 1936; B. und H. Galsterer, 'Neue Inschriften aus Köln' (*Epigraphische Studien* 12) 1981; H. Reichert, *Lexikon der altgermanischen Namen*, Vienna 1987–90.

Aumenahenae. Name of some → matrons. Two Roman inscriptions from Cologne are dedicated to the *Matronis*, or *Matribus Aumenahenis* (CIL XIII 8215 and 12054); the name probably belongs to the river name Oumena ('stream of the Aumenau') near Ems an der Lahn.

S. Gutenbrunner, *Die germanischen Götternamen*, Halle 1936; H. Birkhan, *Germanen und Kelten*, Vienna 1970; H. Reichert, *Lexikon der altgermanischen Namen*, Vienna 1987–90.

Aurboða (1) (ON). A giantess in *Hyndluljóð* 30 and *Gylfaginning* 50, Gymir's wife and Gerðr's mother. Freyr's wooing of Aurboða is told in the Eddic lay → *Skírnismál*. The meaning of the name is obscure. As it is not the name of a giantess in *Fjǫlsvinnsmál* 38 but rather of a girl, Sturtevant postulated a word *aur* (from Latin *aureum*), which would allow the name to be interpreted like a kenning: 'bidder of gold'. Nevertheless, the evidence in *Fjǫlsvinnsmál* is probably secondary. ON *aurr* could possibly also mean 'dampness' (de Vries) although it is more likely that the name, like so many other names of giants and dwarfs (Aurgelmir, Aurvangr), comes from ON aurr 'sand, gravel', a well-documented meaning. Aurboða's relationship to Gymir and Gerðr, similarily chthonic beings, would also suggest this latter interpretation.

A. M. Sturtevant, 'Etymological Comments upon Certain Old Norse Proper Names in the Eddas' (*PMLA* 67) 1952; J. de Vries, *Altgermanische Religionsgeschichte*, Berlin [3]1970; J. de Vries, *Altnordisches etymologisches Wörterbuch*, Leiden[2]1977; L. Motz, 'Giantesses and their Names' (*FmSt* 15) 1981.

Aurboða (2). One of Menglǫð's maids in *Fjǫlsvinnsmál* 38.

Aurgelmir (ON). A giant (*Vafþrúðnismál* 29f., *Þulur*), who is probably identical to Ymir since in *Vafþrúðnismál* he is called the grandfather of Bergelmir and the father of Þrúðgelmir. The derivation from *aurr* ('wet sand, gravel') is the most likely for his name, like other similar giants' names (Aurboða, Aurgrímnir). According to this, Aurgelmir would then perhaps mean 'the roarer born from sand'.

Aurgrímnir (ON). A giant (only in the *Þulur*); as with other giant names (Aurgelmir, Aurboða) it seems to be most likely that their names derive from *aurr-* 'wet sand, gravel' because of the chthonic nature of giants. Thus, the name means perhaps 'the angry one created from sand'.

Aurkonungr (ON). A name for the sparsely recorded god → Hœnir, which is only included by Snorri (*Skáldskaparmál* 15). We do not know why Hœnir is called this, but it seems extremely likely that the compounding of *aur-* with *konungr* does not mean, for example, 'sand king', but probably 'the rich king'; it might be a kenning from some lost poetry.

A. Sturtevant, 'Etymological Comments' (*PMLA* 67) 1952.

Aurnir (ON). A giant in *Grottasǫngr*; → Ömir.

Aurvandill (ON). In his *Edda* Snorri preserves the remains of a myth about Aurvandill, which Thor tells to Aurvandill's wife Gróa. He tells her that he waded through (the river) → Élivágar coming from the north. While he was doing so, he carried Aurvandill in a basket on his back. One of Aurvandill's toes peeped out of the basket, froze and then broke off. Thor picked it up and threw it into the sky and as proof made a star out of it which is called *Aurvandils tá*.

Snorri probably invented this anecdote as an explanation of the name *Aurvandils tá* (i.e. 'Aurvandill's toe') following the pattern of the tale of the creation of stars from Þjazi's eyes. Even before this, however, Aurvandill certainly had something to do with a star because the Old English equivalent of the name Aurvandill, Earendel, is a name for 'brilliance, morning star'. In a somewhat daring interpretation Much explained *Aurvandils tá* (from a **tahō* 'beam') as a star name meaning 'Aurvandill's beam' because the Greek star heroes were worshipped as horse-headed wooden gods.

The name Aurvandill has equivalents in the legends of other Germanic peoples: apart from OE Earendel, he appears as Horwendillus in Saxo (III, 85–87), as the father of Amlethus (= Hamlet), and in Middle High German as the eponymous hero of the poem *Orendel*, as well as in Langobardian (Auriwandalo) and Old High German (Orentil) personal names. The obscure remains of the myth do not enlighten this evidence.

Even the etymology of Aurvandill is unexplained: Much's interpretation as 'the bright Vandal' (from ON *aurr* 'gold'?, related to Latin *aureum* 'gold'?) is unconvincing. An equally unsatisfactory explanation is that of *aurr-* in the usual meaning of 'wet gravel' (as in Aurboða). The most plausible explanation, semantically speaking, is Much's later suggestion of 'stripe, ray of light' (from *vǫndr* 'staff, stick'), but this too is questionable even though it does suit the star-myth.

R. Much, 'Wandalische Götter' (*Mitteilungen der schlesischen Gesellschaft für Volkskunde* 27) 1926; R. Much, 'Aurvandils tá' (*Festschrift H. Seger*) 1934; S. Gutenbrunner, 'Der zweite Merseburger Zauberspruch' (*ZfdA* 80) 1944; J. de Vries, *Altgermanische Religionsgeschichte*, Berlin [3]1970; J. de Vries, *Altnordisches etymologisches Wörterbuch*, Leiden [2]1977.

Aurvandils tá → Aurvandill.

Aurvangar (ON, 'the gravelly wetlands'). A place-name found in *Vǫluspá* 14 (Aurvangasjǫt) which appears to describe a mythological place where the dwarfs live; the following place-name Jǫruvellir would appear to have the same meaning. Aurvangar is otherwise not mentioned.

Aurvangr (ON, 'the one from the Aurvangar'). A dwarf in *Vǫluspá* 13 and in the *Þulur*.

Aurvargr (ON, 'gravel-wolf'?). A dwarf in *Vǫluspá* 13 (alternative reading of → Aurvangr).

ausa (barn) vatni (ON, 'to sprinkle [a child] with water') → baptism.

Austri (ON, to *austr* 'east'). A dwarf in *Vǫluspá* 11 who, according to *Gylfaginning* 7, supports the sky made out of Ymir's skull in the east. → Vestri.

Austriahenae. Name of → matrons. In 1958 over 150 votive stones from the cult of matrons were found in Morken-Harff, all except one were dedicated to the *Matronis Austriahenis*, as far as the partially fragmentary nature of the inscriptions allows them to be read. Thus the Matronae Austriahenae are the most frequently documented names of matrons and, although none of the stones carry a date, they can be dated to the heyday of the cult of matrons on the Lower Rhine around 200 A.D., so that a significant cult centre can be postulated for Morken-Harff or the close vicinity.

Birkhan relates the name etymologically to the first word element of Austrogoti, which could be interpreted as 'the eastern ones'; he further suggests that the matrons named here correspond to the Audrinehae (from Hermühlheim) but this is rather unlikely because the areas of the finds have clear spatial separations.

H.-G. Kolbe, 'Die neuen Matroneninschriften von Morken-Harff' (*Bonner Jahrbücher* 160) 1960; H. Birkhan, *Germanen und Kelten*, Vienna 1970; H. Reichert, *Lexikon der altgermanischen Namen* I. Vienna 1987.

Authrinehae. Matron name, → Audrinehae.

Aviaitinehae. Matron name. A votive inscription from Bürgel near Solingen, West Germany (CIL XIII 8531) is dedicated to the *Matronis Rum(a)nehis item Aviaitinehis*; reading and interpretation of the name are however extremely uncertain.

S. Gutenbrunner, *Die germanischen Götternamen*, Halle 1936; M. Schönfeld, *Wörterbuch der altgermanischen Personen- und Völkernamen*, Heidelberg ^{2}1965; H. Reichert, *Lexikon der altgermanischen Namen*, Vienna 1987–90.

Axes, cult of. In northern Europe a cult of axes, in which axes unsuitable for practical use played an important role, is evident and is supported by archaeological finds dating later than the Neolithic Age. In the Bronze Age numerous rock carvings, and also the little bronze figure from Grevensvaenge, indicate a widespread cult of axes which should probably be understood as a fertility cult, as the phallic figures on the rock pictures suggest. Miniature axes as amulets are also documented since the late Iron Age and then again in the Viking Age.

As a cult of axes is not mentioned in literary sources, it has been connected with the role of the Thor's hammer → Mjǫllnir which became a symbol of heathendom in answer to the Christian symbol of the cross. The equation of axe and hammer can be explained with the function of both cult symbols in the fertility cult. The great age of the Germanic axe-cult, the relationship with the Cretan axe-cult and the parallels to the lightening weapons of the non-Germanic gods, such as Indra's and Hercules' clubs or Sucellos the Gaul's hammer, all suggest an Indo-Germanic origin of the various forms of the axe.

J. de Vries, *Altgermanische Religionsgeschichte*, Berlin ³1970; M. Puhvel, 'The Deicidal Otherworld Weapon' (*Folklore* 83) 1972; H. Jankuhn, H. Beck, 'Axtkult' (*Hoops* 1) 21973; H. Trætteberg, 'Øks' (*KLNM* 20) 1976.

Axsinginehae. Matron name on a Roman votive inscription from Cologne (CIL XIII 8216); perhaps related to Gothic *ahs* 'ear (of grain)' and thus fertility-giving goddesses?

S. Gutenbrunner, *Die germanischen Götternamen*, Halle 1936; H. Reichert, *Lexikon der altgermanischen Namen*, Vienna 1987–90.

Baduhenna. A Germanic goddess. Tacitus (*Annales* IV, 73) writes that a grove in Frisia was dedicated to Baduhenna and that 900 Roman soldiers were slaughtered near this grove in 28 A.D.

The first part of the word is probably cognate to **badwa-* 'battle'; the second part is frequently found as *-henae* in matron names. Therefore, the goddess Baduhenna would appear to be a goddess of war. Albeit the reference in Tacitus is the only mention of the name. Sacred places in woods (sacred → grove) are commonly associated with Germanic peoples.

J. de Vries, *Altgermanische Religionsgeschichte*, Berlin ³1970.

Bældæg (OE, 'the shining day'), also called Bældæg Wodning or Bældæg Wodening, is an OE mythical name which is replaced by Baldr in one chronicle (Æthelweard). In the prologue of his *Edda* even Snorri mentions 'Beldeg, whom we call Baldr', as the second son of Odin. Hence, Bældæg could be an English form of the name Baldr derived from OE *bealdor* 'Lord; Christ' and formed following the example of gods' names like Swæfdæg (de Vries; opposing this view: Philippson). The name could, however, be a mere late development of an OE tradition under the Scandinavian influence of the 10th century.

E. Hackenberg, *Die Stammtafeln der angelsächsischen Königreiche*, Berlin 1918; R. Jente, *Die mythologischen Ausdrücke im altenglischen Wortschatz*, Heidelberg 1921; E. A. Philippson, *Germanisches Heidentum bei den Angelsachsen*, Leipzig 1929; J. de Vries, *Altgermanische Religionsgeschichte*, Berlin 31970; E. O. G. Turville-Petre, *Myth and Religion of the North*, Westport 1975.

Bakrauf (ON, 'behind, backside'). Name of a giantess (only in the *Þulur*).

Baldr (ON Baldr, OE, OHG Balder). One of the most important Germanic gods and one of the Æsir. Although → Baldr's death takes a central role in Germanic mythology, our only source for it, apart from a brief reference to it in the → *Second Merseburg Charm*, is the literature of Scandinavia.

The Scandinavian version sub-divides into a Norwegian-Icelandic tradition and a Danish tradition. The Icelander Snorri gives the most detail about the Baldr myth in his *Edda*. In *Gylfaginning* 21 he describes Baldr briefly: 'Odin's second son is Baldr, of whom only good things are told: he is the best of all and everyone praises him; his appearance is so beautiful and so bright that light shines from him . . . he is the wisest of the Æsir, the most eloquent and the friendliest, but he has one problem: his decisions are not lasting. He lives in → Breiðablik which lies in heaven and where there is no impurity.' Baldr's mother is Frigg (*Gylfaginning* 21 and *Skáldskaparmál* 19), his wife Nanna, his son Forseti (*Gylfaginning* 31, *Skáldskaparmál* 5). Baldr is the owner of the ship → Hringhorni and the ring called → Draupnir (*Skáldskaparmál* 5). After the Ragnarǫk he will return from Hel together with his brother Hǫðr and will live in the new world (*Gylfaginning* 52, following *Vǫluspá* 62).

In addition to this Snorri devotes one of the longest uninterrupted parts of his *Edda* to the myth of Baldr's death and the description of → Baldr's funeral. In order to protect Baldr from harm Frigg demands that every animate and inanimate thing swears never to hurt Baldr, and receives the promise from everything except the → mistletoe. Loki hears about this and when the gods are entertaining themselves by throwing things at the invulnerable Baldr, he presses a branch of mistletoe into the hand of the blind god → Hǫðr which he then throws at Baldr, wounding him fatally. This is a terrible loss for both gods and men. At Frigg's bequest, Odin's son → Hermóðr rides to Hel in order to bring Baldr back again; Hel agrees on one condition, namely that everything in the world must weep for Baldr. Only then will she return him to them. The whole world does indeed weep for Baldr, except for a giantess called Þǫkk, and so Baldr must remain with the dead. Snorri suggests that the giantess was really Loki in disguise. In the meantime the Æsir have prepared for Baldr's funeral. Baldr is cremated together with his wife Nanna, who died of grief at her loss, on a pyre aboard his ship Hringhorni; Odin places the ring Draupnir onto the funeral pyre.

The question of lost lays arises when the search is made for Snorri's sources about Baldr's death and → Hermóð's ride to Hel. In his account of Baldr's funeral, Snorri follows the version of the poem → *Húsdrápa* (composed around 983 by the Icelandic skald Ulfr Uggason) which describes the wooden carvings in an Icelandic festive hall. In addition to this source, Baldr's death is mentioned in several Eddic lays (*Baldrs draumar*; *Vǫluspá* 31–33; *Lokasenna* 28). In *Vǫluspá*, Baldr's death is one of the events leading up to the Ragnarǫk. *Lokasenna* 28 records that it is Loki's fault that Baldr is no longer alive. This could refer both to his role in Baldr's death as well as to his prevention of Baldr's return from Hel. Loki's role in the Baldr myth certainly appears to be ancient.

The prophetic description of the events in *Baldrs draumar* offers the connection to the Danish tradition of the myth, for in the *Baldrs draumar*, as in Saxo, we hear about the revenge on → Hǫðr and Odin's fathering of an avenger with the giantess Rinda. In Saxo Grammaticus (*Gesta Danorum* III, 69f.) Nanna is the cause of the argument between Balderus and Høtherus (Saxo's Latinized name for Hǫðr). At first Baldr is defeated by Høtherus who wins Nanna. After subsequent victories which make Baldr the Danish king, Høtherus, using magic, manages to stab Baldr with the only sword that can be fatal to him. Saxo then continues with the elaborate tale of Odin's conquest of Rinda who bears for him Baldr's avenger → Bous. Although Bous kills Høtherus, he himself dies at the same time.

Saxo did not invent the idea that Baldr was a Danish king which rather derives from an older tradition which associated Baldr with the Danish royal house in → Lejre. A stanza from the Icelandic *Bjarkamál*, which mentions Baldr, suggests this, as indeed does the fact that the name of Baldr's residence Breiðablik has been found in the Danish place-name Bredebliche (near Lejre!) by the 17th-century Swedish chronicler Johannes Messenius. Thus Baldr was possibly the mythical ancestor of the Danish royal family, a suggestion further supported by the fact that in the genealogies of the Danish-influenced Anglo-Saxon chroniclers the name Bældæg is replaced by Baldr.

The etymology of the name Baldr has still not been fully explained. The various interpretations depend without exception on the respective interpretation of the Baldr myth. The oldest explanations consider the name to stem from the Indo-European root **bhel-* 'white' (Lithuanian *baltas*), thus seeing him as the god of light, probably just as Snorri describes him. Besides this idea, however, there is the suggestion that Baldr is related to OE *bealdor* and means in fact 'Lord', and therefore OHG *balder* in the *Second Merseburg Charm* may be translated in this way (this idea is vehemently opposed by Kuhn). If Baldr is considered as being related to ON *baldr*, OHG *bald* 'bold', then a warlike character might be concluded for Baldr, which, however, would be unsubstantiated in any of the sources and does not fit in at all well with our picture of Baldr. From the association with *baldr* 'bold' Schröder concluded a basic form **bal-ora-m* 'power' which would put Baldr in the role of a fertility god.

Attempts have been made to explain the obvious parallels between the Baldr myth and Christianity as a northern imitation of Christian myths. This interpretation, prevelant in the second half of the last century, was argued especially by S. Bugge who believed that the Scandinavians transferred the stories which they heard in the already Christianized England, about Christ, the son of God, onto Baldr, son of the highest god Odin, so that details such as the killing of Baldr by the blind god Hǫðr might be seen to correspond to the piercing of Christ by the blind Longinus in Christian legend.

The death of Baldr and his return to life after the Ragnarǫk (admittedly only mentioned in passing in *Vǫluspá*) have led (among the followers of Frazer) to a generally accepted interpretation of the Baldr myth as the death and re-awakening of a vegetation god (still agreeing with this, Ebenbauer 1974). Notwithstanding this, it should not be forgotten that in the actual Baldr myth Baldr does not in fact return to the living, and that the concept of the cyclic life of a vegetation god is otherwise somewhat alien to Germanic perception.

Even de Vries' explanation of the myth as an initiation rite is not totally convincing; it opens, however, the way to the clearly shamanistic context of a Germanic Odin cult to which the Baldr myth undoubtedly closely belongs. More recently, Hauck has been able to show quite plainly that on the pictorial representations of the Migration-Age bracteates, which are predominantly devoted to Odin, the basic concepts of the myth about Baldr are clearly shown 600 years before Snorri's version: Baldr's death by mistletoe, Odin's handing over of the ring Draupnir, Baldr's arrival at Hel are pictorially represented on the so-called three-god-amulets (→ bracteates).

One example of a runic abbreviation of the Baldr myth could be seen (if Gutenbrunner is to be believed) in the naming of the three gods Loki, Wodan and Thor in the runic inscription found on the 7th century → Nordendorf fibula: LOGAÞORA = Loki was the instigator of Baldr's death; WODAN = Odin was most affected by it, according to Snorri; WIGIÞONAR = Þórr vígði ('Thor consecrated') the pyre at Baldr's funeral. As ingenious as this theory may be, Odin's by no means satisfactory status in Snorri's version and the fact that → Thor should not be simply understood as a consecration god (Marold) mean that an interpretation of the inscription like this is somewhat exaggerated.

The great age of the Baldr myth, demonstrated by the gold bracteates, is confirmed by extensive non-Germanic parallels, such as the myth of Lemminkäinen's death in the Finnish *Kalevala*, or the Caucasian legends of the Ossetes, in which the identity of the roles of Loki and Syrdon, who is responsible for the death of Soslan, is especially impressive. Dumézil concludes that such common traits were the result of an Indo-European tradition of the Baldrmyth.

Although nothing definite is known about a Baldr cult, there are nonetheless several place-names in Norway, Denmark and England which are possibly related to the name Baldr, but which give no concrete evidence. Similarly unhelpful as evidence is the ON plant-name Baldersbrá (for the ox-eye daisy) which Snorri understood to refer to the splendid beauty of Baldr's eyebrows (*Gylfaginning* 21).

S. Bugge, *Studien über die Entstehung der nordischen Götter- und Heldensagen*, Munich 1889; F. Detter, 'Der Baldermythus' (*PBB* 19) 1894; F. Niedner, 'Balders Tod' (*ZfdA* 41) 1897; G. Sarrazin, 'Der Balder-Kultus in Lethra' (*Anglia* 19) 1897; F. Kauffmann, *Balder: Mythus und Sage*, Straßburg 1902. J. G. Frazer, *Balder the Beautiful*, London 1913; J. Loewenthal, 'Zur germanischen Wortkunde' (*ANF* 33) 1917; G. Neckel, *Die Überlieferungen vom Gotte Balder*, Dortmund 1920; E. Schroeder, 'Balder in Deutschland' (*NoB* 10) 1922; M. Olsen, 'Om Balderdigtning og Balderkultus' (*ANF* 40) 1924; F. R. Schröder, *Germanentum und Hellenismus*, Heidelberg 1922; E. Mogk, *Lokis Anteil an Balders Tod*, Helsinki 1925. H. Hempel, 'Hellenistisch-Orientalisches Lehngut' (*GRM* 16) 1928; K. Helm, 'Balder in Deutschland?' (*PBB* 67) 1944; H. Schneider, 'Über die ältesten Götterlieder der Nordgermanen' (*PBB* 69) 1947; H. W. J. Kroes, 'Die Balderüberlieferungen und der Zweite Merseburger Zauberspruch' (*Neophilologus* 35) 1951; H. Kuhn, 'Es gibt kein balder "Herr" ' (*Festschrift K. Helm*) Tübingen 1951; O. Höfler, 'Balders Bestattung' (*Anz. d. phil.-hist. Kl. d. öst. Akademie der Wiss.*) 1952; F. R. Schröder, 'Balder und der zweite Merseburger Spruch' (*GRM* 34) 1935; J. de Vries, 'Der Mythos von Balders Tod' (*ANF* 70) 1955; S. Gutenbrunner, 'Balders Wiederkehr' (*GRM* 37) 1956; N. Lid, 'Baldr' (*KLNM* 1) 1956; J. de Vries, [Review of] 'G. Dumézil, Les Dieux des Germains' (*PBB* West 81) 1959; G. Dumézil, 'Hotherus et Balderus' (*PBB* West 83) 1961/62; F. R. Schröder, 'Balder-Probleme' (*PBB* West 84) 1962; H. Fromm, 'Lemminkäinen und Balder' (*Festschrift F. v. d. Leyen*) Munich 1963; G. Dumézil, 'Balderiana minora' (*Indo-Iranica. Mélanges G. Morgenstierne*) Wiesbaden 1964; F. R. Schröder, 'Die eddischen "Balders Träume" ' (*GRM* N. F. 14) 1964; A. Closs, 'Irdisches Wiedererstehen' (*Kairos* 7) 1965; A. Kabell, *Balder und die Mistel*, Helsinki 1965; S. Gutenbrunner, 'Ritennamen – Kultnamen – Mythennamen' (*Namenforschung. Festschrift A. Bach*) Heidelberg 1965; W. H. Wolf-Rottkay, 'Balder and the Mistletoe' (*SS* 39) 1967; K. Schier, 'Balder-Lieder' (*KLL* 1) 1967; K. Schier, *Balder, Loki, Heimdall*, Munich 1969; E. C. Polomé, 'The Indo-European component in Germanic Religion' (*Myth and Law among the Indo-Europeans*) London 1970; J. de Vries, *Altgermanische Religionsgeschichte*, Berlin [3]1970; K. Hauck, *Goldbrakteaten aus Sievern*, Munich 1970; E. Marold, ' "Thor weihe diese Runen" ', (*FmSt* 8) 1974; A. Ebenbauer, 'Ursprungsglaube' (*Gedenkschrift f. H. Güntert*) Innsbruck 1974; J. S. Martin, 'Balder's death' (*Iceland and the Medieval World. Studies Maxwell*), Melbourne 1974; E. O. G. Turville-Petre, *Myth and Religion of the North*, Westport 1975; H. Klingenberg, 'Die Drei-Götter-Fibel von Nordendorf' (*ZfdA* 105) 1976; K. Schier, 'Balder' (*Hoops* 2) [2]1976; G. Dumézil, *Gods of the Ancient Northmen*, Berkeley 1977; J. de Vries, *Altnordisches etymologisches Wörterbuch*, Leiden [2]1977; R. Volz, 'Balder' (*Lexikon des Mittelalters* 1) 1980; A. D. Mosher, 'The Story of Balder's Death' (*SS* 55) 1983; F. Stjernfelt, *Baldr og verdensdramaet i den nordiske mytologi*, Copenhagen 1990; L. Motz, 'The Conquest of Death: the Myth of Baldr and its Middle Eastern Counterparts' (*Collegium Medievale* 4) 1991.

R: (fine art) H. E. Freund, *Balder* (statue, 1821); C. W. Eckersberg, *Balders Tod* (painting); Balder E. Fogelberg, *Balder* (marble statue, 1844, imitating Thorwaldsens sculpture of Christ); C. G. Qvarnström, *Loke och Höder* (statue, 1863); K. Ehrenberg, *Balder und Nanna, Idun und Bragi* (drawing, 1882); E. Doepler d.J., *Balders Tod* (in: E. Doepler, W. Ranisch, *Walhall*, 1901); D. Hardy, *The Death of Balder* (painting, c.1900).

(literature) J. Ewald, *Balders Død* (heroic play, 1775); A. Oehlenschläger, *Balders Död* (tragedy, 1805); A. Oehlenschläger, *Baldur hin Gode* (mythol. tragedy, 1807); L. Uhland planned a tragedy about Balder in 1812, like Fouqué and Oehlenschläger following Saxo; F. d. l. Motte Fouqué, *Baldur der Gute* (heroic play, 1818); E. T Tegner, *Frithjofssaga* (epic, 1825; invents a cult of Baldr); V. Rydberg, *Baldersbålet*, (poem, in: *Dikter*, 1882); A. Kayser-Langerhanns, *Balder und Loki* (drama, 1891);

W. Hertz, *Wie Höther Nannas Liebe gewann* (in: *Gesammelte Dichtungen*, 1900); H. F. Blunck, *Krist und Balder begegnen einander* (in: *Märchen und Sagen*, 1937).
(music) H. Vogl, *Der Fremdling* (opera, 1880, text by Felix Dahn); O. Beständig, *Balders Tod* (oratorio, 1888); C. Kistler, *Baldurs Tod* (opera, 1891, text by Freiherr v. Sohlern).

Baldr's death is described in most detail by Snorri. When Baldr is suffering from terrible dreams, the Æsir decide to protect him from harm and Frigg takes solemn oaths from all animate and inanimate things that they will not hurt him. Later the Æsir take great pleasure in shooting at or striking Baldr who is now invulnerable. Loki, however, is envious of Baldr and, having disguised himself as a woman, questions Frigg who tells him that the mistletoe has not sworn an oath because it was too young. Thereupon Loki takes a branch of mistletoe and goes to the blind god → Hǫðr who has been taking no part in the gods' game because of his blindness and his lack of a weapon. Loki points him in the right direction and Hǫðr throws the mistletoe at Baldr, who is fatally pierced and falls down dead. The Æsir are struck dumb and Odin declares that Baldr's death is the worst thing that has happened to both men and gods.

Snorri no doubt did not only use the few sparse sources we still have today for his description. Hǫðr is named as Baldr's killer in *Vǫluspá* 33 and *Baldrs draumar* 11. The kenning which Snorri quotes, *skjótandi mistilteins* ('shooter of mistletoe'), is not found elsewhere, although admittedly mistletoe is named as the cause of Baldr's death in *Vǫluspá* 31f. The fact that Loki is responsible for Baldr's death in some way can be understood from *Lokasenna* 28. The kenning mentioned by Snorri, *ráðbani Baldrs* ('adviser to Baldr's death'), is also not found in extant poetry. There is no other mention of Baldr's invulnerability.

It is obvious that although Baldr is not infrequently mentioned in skaldic poetry, allusions to the myth of Baldr's death are totally missing elsewhere, apart from in the small group of Eddic poems referred to above. Ulfr Uggason's *Húsdrápa*, which Snorri used as a source for his poetic description of → Baldr's funeral, and which itself is a description of wood-carved mythological scenes in a 10th century Icelandic festive hall, could have contained information about Baldr's death, but this is by no means certain. These scanty references to Baldr lead us to suppose that Snorri could fall back on now lost Eddic poems. Even if there were such poems, it is uncertain if it is a matter of two lays, *Baldr's Death* and *Hermóð's Ride to Hel* (Neckel, Schröder), or only one (Schneider, de Vries).

Despite the missing tradition in skaldic poetry the myth of → Baldr is very old, since the pictorial sources of the 5th and 6th century (gold bracteates) already show Baldr's death.

Lit. → Baldr.

Baldrs draumar (ON, 'Baldr's dreams'). The only Eddic lay about Baldr preserved. The title is given in the main manuscript, AM 748,4to, written around 1300. This lay of 14 stanzas, not found in the *Codex Regius* of the *Edda*, tells how the gods, worried by Baldr's terrible dreams which let him foresee his own early death, meet in council. Finally Odin rides to the Underworld (Niflhel) where he awakens a prophetess (→ Völva) from the dead. Using the assumed name Vegtamr (hence the lay in the younger manuscripts is also known as *Vegtamskviða* 'Lay of Vegtam'), he asks the seeress several questions, the answers to which reveal → Baldr's fate, his murderers and his avengers. Finally Odin shows his true identity as god of wisdom by asking an unanswerable question, and the seeress recognizes him. Although the lay has one stanza in common with the *Vǫluspá* as well as with *Þrymskviða*, it is not necessarily younger than these.

ED: G. Neckel, H. Kuhn, *Edda*, Heidelberg [5]1983.
F. Niedner, 'Balders Tod' (*ZfdA* 40) 1897; Å. Ohlmarks, 'Totenerweckungen in Eddaliedern' (*ANF* 52) 1936; H. Schneider, 'Über die ältesten Götterlieder der Nordgermanen' (*PBB* 69) 1947; F. R. Schröder, 'Die eddischen "Balders Träume"' (*GRM* N. F. 14) 1964; K. Schier, 'Baldrs draumar' (*KLL* 1) 1965; J. de Vries, *Altnordische Literaturgeschichte* 2, Berlin [2]1967; J. Fleck, 'Drei Vorschläge zu Baldrs draumar' (*ANF* 84) 1969.

R: Thomas Gray, *The Descent of Odin*, 1768; J. N. C. M. Denis, *Odins Helafahrt*, 1772; J. G. Herder, *Das Grab der Prophetin*, 1778/79.

Baldr's Funeral. Like the other parts of the myth about Baldr (→ Baldr's death and → Hermóð's ride to Hel) Baldr's funeral is described in most detail by Snorri (*Gylfaginning* 48) whose source was the poem *Húsdrápa*, written by the Icelandic skald Ulfr Uggason around 986.

Snorri tells how, after Baldr's death and Hermóð's ride to Hel, the Æsir take Baldr's body to his ship → Hringhorni in order to cremate him on a funeral pyre on board. They are, however, unable to launch the ship and so the giantess Hyrrokkin is called to help. At the first attempt she causes sparks to fly from the rollers. Thor is enraged by this and wants to strike her dead with Mjǫllnir, but the other gods prevent him from doing so. Baldr's body is then brought on board the ship. When his wife Nanna sees this, she dies of grief and is laid beside him on the pyre. As Thor is consecrating the pyre with his hammer, a dwarf called Litr runs in front of his feet. Thor kicks him into the fire where he burns to death.

Odin is present at Baldr's funeral with Frigg, his valkyries and his ravens. Freyr drives in front in a chariot pulled by a wild boar called Gullinborsti (or Sliðrugtanni). Heimdall rides on Gulltopr and Freyja drives with her cats. A number of frost giants and mountain giants are also present. Odin places the ring Draupnir on the pyre and Baldr's horse is also burned together with his master.

In many ways this description agrees with the extant stanzas of Ulf's *Húsdrápa* (handed down in Snorri's quotation only); the procession of the gods is almost identical: first Freyr (stanza 7), then Odin (8) with the valkyries and ravens (9), then Heimdall (10), a giantess launches the ship whilst Odin's warriors hold her steed, a wolf (11). The procession of gods and the launching of the ship by the giantess could have been two scenes from the wood carving in Oláfr Pá's Hall, which Ulfr describes in his poem. The fact that the other scenes – Nanna's death and the strangely unmotivated appearance of the dwarf Litr – are not found in any stanza might be coincidental, but possibly Snorri knew more verses than we do. The absurdity and the blind motifs in Snorri's version (the threatening of the giantess Hyrrokkin, the dwarf Litr) might be a result of Snorri's own first-hand knowledge of the wood carvings, whereby he interpreted the figures shown in his own way.

Höfler commented on the relationship between the wood carvings described in *Húsdrápa* and the depictions on Bronze-Age rock engravings in which quite similar pictorial elements occur and tries to interpret the threatening of Hyrrokkin and the dwarf Litr from there. Snorri interprets Thor with his raised hammer (as he can be seen on the rock carvings) once as consecrating the pyre, and then again a second time threatening the giantess (portrayed alongside). According to Höfler, the dwarf had his origins in the cult dancers who are often portrayed in strange positions over the ships on the rock engravings. – Admittedly the question remains whether it is possible to bridge the 2000 to 3000 years between the rock engravings and the wood carvings, either by postulating a basically unbroken artistic tradition, or a continuity of rituals which could lead repeatedly to similar depictions of the traditionally held rituals. Höfler found both possibilities conceivable.

Lit. → Baldr.

(**Baldruus**). Supposedly the name of a god in an inscription dating from the 3rd or 4th century in Utrecht, which allegedly corresponds to Baldr, but like *Lobbonus and *Alabuandus only rests on a rather fanciful interpretation of the text which has been deliberately ruined to make it illegibile.

C. W. Vollgraff, 'Romeinsche Inscripties uit Utrecht' (*Versl. en Medel. d. Akad. van Wetenschapen te Amsterdam, Afd. Letterk.* 70 B 5) 1930; A. W. Byvanck, 'De Inscriptionibus Traiectensibus nuper repertis' (*Mnemosyne* N. S. 60) 1933; S. Gutenbrunner, *Die germanischen Götternamen*, Halle 1936; J. de Vries, *Altgermanische Religionsgeschichte*, Berlin [3]970.

Báleygr (ON, 'the one with the flaming eyes') is a pseudonym for Odin in *Grímnismál* 47, in poems by Hallfreðr Vandræðaskáld (*Hákonardrápa* 6), Gisli Illugason 1 and in the *Þulur*. The two names for Odin, Baleygr and Bileygr, are probably identifiable with the brothers Bolwisus and Bilwisus in Saxo (*Gesta Danorum* VII, 234f.), where Balwisus urges for strictness, but Bilwisus pleads for mercy in dealing with the hero Hagbarðr. Falk assumed, with good reason, that in the case of Báleygr and Bileygr it is a question of two different aspects of Odin: Báleygr his godly and Bileygr his human side.

H. Falk, *Odensheite*, Christiania 1924.

Bands of warriors → Odin's warriors, → Wild Hunt.

Bara or Bára (ON, 'wave') is the name of one of the daughters of the sea giant Ägir and his wife Ran (Snorri, *Skáldskaparmál* 23; also in the work of the skald Gisli Súrsson). Nearly all the names of → Ægir's nine daughters represent a manifestation of the sea's surface.

Barrey → Barri (1).

Barri (1). The mythological place, according to → *Skírnismál* 41, where Freyr and Gerðr are supposed to meet each other for their wedding. In this source, Barri is referred to as a breezeless grove (*lundr lognfara*), whereas in the re-telling of this lay by Snorri (*Gylfaginning* 36) it is called Barrey (as in the Hebridean island Barrey, nowadays Barra) and as such would be an island. Barri can be interpreted etymologically in two ways. On the one hand it can be interpreted as 'cornfield' (from ON *barr* 'barley'), which is Olsen's explanation of it in his interpretation of *Skírnismál*, where he sees it reflect a marriage (→ *hierós gámos*) between god and mother earth as part of a fertility cult. On the other hand it could mean 'coniferous wood' (from ON *barr* 'conifer') which would fit the idea of a grove better.

M. Olsen, 'Fra gammelnorsk myte og kultus' (MoM) 1909; J. Sahlgren, 'Lunden Barre i Skírnismál' (*NoB* 50) 1962; J. de Vries, *Altnordisches etymologisches Wörterbuch*, Leiden [2]1977.

Barri (2) (ON, 'fool'. Also a personal name). A dwarf in *Fjǫlsvinnsmál* 24.

Barrow → Burial mound.

bauta(r)steinn (ON) A grave stone or memorial stone. These Iron Age grave monuments are frequent all over southern Scandinavia and normally consist of upright flat or thin monoliths. The name originally might have meant 'stone rammed into the earth', but the bigger ones certainly could not be forced into the earth, but were buried in the ground up to a third of their length. Only during the Viking Age did some *bautarsteinar* bear runic inscriptions, but their number is negligible in comparison with the total number of these monuments.

Beda. A goddess, one of the two → Alaisiagae on one of the votive altars from Housesteads on Hadrian's Wall, northern England, dating from the period after 150 A.D.. The inscription is dedicated to the *Deo Marti Thingso et duabus Alaesiagis Bede et Fimmilene*. As the god named here, → Mars Thingsus, is the god of the Thing, the meeting place and the court, the two goddesses Beda and Fimmilena have been brought into connection with legal expressions, namely Old Frisian Bodþing 'convened Thing', and Fimelþing 'court of judgement' (or 'moveable court'?). The dedicators of the inscription were Frisians in the legion stationed at Hadrian's Wall, and hence the connection with legal expressions from their home country is justifiable, even if the difference in time should not be ignored. Thus, Beda would be perhaps 'the mistress of the *Bedthing'. None of the other attempts at interpretation are more illuminating.

K. Kauffmann, 'Mythologische Zeugnisse' (*PBB* 16) 1892; S. Gutenbrunner, *Die germanischen Götternamen*, Halle 1936; J. de Vries, *Altgermanische Religionsgeschichte*, Berlin ³1970.

Bede, Beda Venerabilis (673–735). An Anglo-Saxon cleric and scholar, who wrote many important scholarly works (on grammar, rhetoric, computation, natural history, church history, hagiography) and whose *Historia ecclesiastica gentis Anglorum* ('A history of the English Church and people') is of great significance for the history and religion of the Germanic peoples, as it is not only a church history, but also a general history of the Anglo-Saxons. It repeatedly refers to the mythical prehistory of this Germanic tribe, and tells, for example, of the origin of Hengist and Horsa, and relates the myth of Scyld Scefing.

Beinviðr (ON). A giant in the *Þulur*. Beinviðr is also the name of a plant (holly), although it is uncertain exactly why the giant should be named after it.

F. Jónsson, 'Þulur' (*APhSc* 9) 1934.

Beldeg (ON) → Bældæg.

Beli (1) (ON, 'bellower'). A giant who fights with → Freyr at Ragnarǫk. In *Gylfaginning* 36 Snorri tells of how Freyr had to fight Beli without a weapon and therefore killed him using an antler (the significance of which is obscure in the myth). This is why Freyr is known in kennings as 'Beli's killer' (*bani Belja*, e.g. *Vǫluspá* 53). It is possible that Freyr's killing of Beli without a weapon is linked with the tale that Freyr had lent his horse and sword to his servant Skírnir, details which are known from the lay of Freyr's wooing (*Skírnismál*). Gerðr, the giantess who Skírnir woos on Freyr's behalf, is grieving in *Skírnismál* 16 about the death at Freyr's hand of her brother (name not given). We may conclude from this that Beli was the brother of Gerðr and as such the son of Gymir and Aurboða, but this is by no means certain.

K. Weinhold, *Die Riesen*, Berlin 1858; J. de Vries, *Altgermanische Religionsgeschichte*, Berlin ³1970.

Beli (2). A (mythological?) horse in the Eddic *Kálfsvísa*.

Beow, also Beav and similar (Anglo-Saxon, 'barley'). One of the mythical ancestors of Vôden (= Odin) in the genealogies of the Anglo-Saxon royal dynasties, mostly as the son of Sceldwas/Scyld. It is uncertain whether Beow is identical with the hero Beowulf of the same-named epos, as the names are not etymologically related. – Because of the meaning of the name Beow and the connection to → Sceaf, older scholarship thought of him mostly as a corn demon and linked him with ON → Byggvir. As neither Sceaf nor Byggvir can be thought of as corn gods, this interpretation for Beow is equally unconvincing. The phonetic similarity with Beowulf and the semantic similarity with Sceaf is probably the reason that Beow is found as a mythical ancestor in the genealogies.

E. A. Philippson, *Germanisches Heidentum bei den Angelsachsen*, Leipzig 1929.

Bergdis (ON, 'mountain-*dís*' = 'mountain-goddess'). A giantess in *Hversu Nóregr byggðisk* and in the *Þulur*. As giantesses' names based on *-dís* are otherwise only frequent in the sagas of the 13th and 14th centuries (Eydís, Glámdís, Skjalddís, Þordís), it may be concluded that the real characteristics of the female goddesses known as *Dísir* were no longer known and had been mixed up with the concept of giantesses.

Bergelmir (ON, 'the mountain-bellower'?). A giant in the *Vafþrúðnismál* (29 and 35). He is the grandson of the first giant Ymir (= Aurgelmir) and Þrúðgelmir's son. In Snorri (*Gylfaginning* 6) stanza 35 of *Vafþrúðnismál* is interpreted in such a way that when Ymir died, all the frost giants drowned in his blood except Bergelmir and his wife who were able to save themselves and became ancestors of the frost giants.

A. Kock, 'Ordforskning i den äldre Eddan' (*ANF* 27) 1011.

Berguiahenae. Name of matrons. Only part of the name, namely *-rguiahenis*, survives on a Roman votive inscription from Gereonsweiler near Jülich, Germany (CIL XIII 12014), but another inscription found on the same site and dedicated to the *Matronis Berhuiahenis* (CIL XIII 12013), means that the reading as Berguiahenae is fairly certain. A deviating form of the same name may be given in an inscription from Tetz which was dedicated to the B[er?]guinehis. Despite the resulting problems, Birkhan relates the name Berguiahenae etymologically to matron names based on tree names (such as Alaferhviae, Alaterviae, Vercana; cf. OHG *fereheih* 'oak').

S. Gutenbrunner, *Die germanischen Götternamen*, Halle 1936; M. Schönfeld, *Wörterbuch der altgermanischen Personen- und Völkernamen*, Heidelberg [2]1965; H. Birkhan, *Germanen und Kelten*, Vienna 1970; H. Reichert, *Lexikon der altgermanischen Namen*, Vienna 1987–90.

Berguinehae. Matron name on a lost inscription from Tetz near Aachen, Germany (CIL XIII 7878). Probably a variant form to → Berguiahenae, but the reading is uncertain.

Berhuiahenae. Matron name on a votive inscription from Gereonsweiler near Aachen, Germany (CIL XIII 12013); → Berguiahenae.

Berlingr (ON, 'short beam'). A dwarf who is named as being one of the four smiths of Freyja's necklace in *Sǫrla þáttr*. → Brísingamen.

J. de Vries, *Altnordisches etymologisches Wörterbuch*, Leiden [2]1977.

Berserks (ON *berserkr*, pl. *berserkir*) are the warriors in Old Norse literature who distinguish themselves in battle by their 'berserk-fury', during which they roar madly, bite their shields and become invulnerable.

The oldest reference to berserks is in *Haraldskvæði*, a eulogy composed by the skald Þórbjǫrn Hornklofi about the Norwegian king Harald Fairhair, after his victory in the decisive battle at Hafrsfjord (c.872), in which berserks and → Ulfheðnar had taken part. Berserks are only alluded to seven times in poetry, notably in younger Eddic lays and skaldic stanzas from the 12th to 14th centuries. Only one stanza composed by Víga-Styrr and quoted in *Eyrbyggja saga* might still be traceable back to heathen times, and even this is extremely uncertain.

Writing in the 13th century, Snorri gives a detailed account of berserks at the beginning of the *Ynglinga saga* 6: 'Odin's men went (into battle) without armour and were as wild as dogs or wolves. They bit their shields and were stronger than bears or bulls. They killed many men but they themselves were unharmed either by fire or by iron; this is what is called berserk-fury (*berserksgangr*).'

In Icelandic saga literature, berserks are stereotyped in two different literary ways. On the one hand they are élite troops who – mostly in groups of 12 – serve famous kings (*Egils saga*, *Vatnsdœla saga*, *Hrólfs saga kraka*) and on the other they are wandering trouble-makers (alone, in twos, or in groups of twelve) who challenge farmers to single combat and/or demand their daughters or wives, and can only be beaten by the respective saga hero who has to undergo a stereotype display of his masculinity (*Grettis saga*, *Heiðreks saga*).

The literary cliché figure of berserks in the Icelandic High and late Middle Ages has its ancient roots in the cult-ecstatic masked warrior of Germanic antiquity, as both the etymology of the name and remainders of old concepts in the descriptions of berserks (particularly in Snorri) show.

The etymology of berserks (from *ber-* 'bear' and *serkr* 'shirt; skin') reveals that both berserks and the *ulfheðnar* ('wolf-skins'), who are frequently referred to alongside the berserks, were warriors clad in skins as depicted on Vendel-Age Swedish helmets (Torslunda: 6th/7th centuries). The element *ber-* was misunderstood by Snorri and Scholars up to the 19th century as *berr*, 'naked' ('went into battle without armour'), and the reference to naked Germanic warriors by Tacitus (*Hist*. II,22) has supported this interpretation.

Snorri mentions the connection between Odin and berserks and *ulfheðnar*, noting that they are 'his warriors'. Odin, however, is also the god of cult ecstasy (as his name: ON *óðr* 'fury' confirms) and the berserk-fury bears all the traits of ecstatic states of consciousness: insensitivity to fire and pain (as well as not bleeding) are phenomena known from shamanic trances.

The concept of berserks and *ulfheðnar* originates, therefore, in special forms of old masked cults in Scandinavia, which manifest themselves in the existence of masked bands of warriors dedicated to Odin.

H. Güntert, *Über altisl. Berserkergeschichten*, Heidelberg 1912; O. Höfler, *Kultische Geheimbünde der Germanen*, Frankfurt 1934; N. Lid, 'Berserk' (*KLNM* 1) 1956; H. D. Fabing, 'On Going Berserk: A Neurochemical Inquiry' (*Scientific Monthly* 83) 1956; K. v. See, 'Berserker' (*Zeitschrift für deutsche Wortfoschung*, N.F. 2) 1961; G. Müller, 'Zum Namen Wolfhetan', (*FmSt* 1) 1967; H. Kuhn, 'Kämpen und Berserker' (*FmSt* 2) 1968; H. Blaney, *The Berserkr*, Colorado 1972; O. Höfler, 'Berserker' (*Hoops* 1) [2]1973; G. Kreutzer, 'Berserker' (*LexMA* 1) 1980.

Bestla (ON). A giantess, the daughter of the giant Bǫlthorn. She conceives three sons with Burr, the son of the primordial ancestor Búri, and gives birth to the first gods: Odin, Vili and Vé. These kill the primordial giant Ymir and create the world from his body (*Gylfaginning* 5 and 6). In skaldic poetry Odin is called 'son of Bestla' (Einarr skálaglamm, *Vellekla* 4), as well as in *Hávamál* 140. As the name Bestla is obscure, it appears to be very old. 'Wife' or 'bark, bast' offer themselves as interpretations, of which the latter is not unlikely, as the primordial couple of Germanic cosmology, Ask and Embla, bear the names of trees; it is nonetheless unnecessary to go as far as to try to understand Bestla as the protecting bark of the protective tree of Odin's kinship (Hunke).

W. Hunke, 'Odins Geburt' (*Edda-Skalden-Saga. Festschrift F. Genzmer*) Heidelberg 1942; J. de Vries, *Altnordisches etymologisches Wörterbuch*, Leiden [2]1977.

Beyggvir (ON). Alternative form of the name → Byggvir.

Beyla (ON). One of Freyr's servants, and the wife of → Byggvir, according to *Lokasenna* (55, 56 and prose introduction). Loki insults her by calling her 'dirty maid', but this is the only indication in the *Lokasenna* of her serving role. As is the case with Byggvir, Beyla seems to be a protective spirit. Nowadays, Beyla is mostly considered to be related to *baula* 'cow', and thus could be seen as the protectoress of dairy work. Sievers related Beyla as 'bean-woman' to *baun* 'bean' (from **baunilō*) as a counterpart to the spirit of the corn Byggvir. Dumézil, on the other hand, interprets Beyla as 'little bee' (from **bíuilō*).

E. Sievers, 'Grammatische Miszellen' (*PBB* 18) 1894; G. Dumézil, 'Deux petits dieux scandinaves: Byggvir et Beyla' (*La nouvelle Clio* 3) 1952; F. Jónsson, *Lexicon Poeticum*, Copenhagen 21966; J. de Vries, *Altgermanische Religionsgeschichte*, Berlin [3]1970; J. deVries, *Altnordisches etymologisches Wörterbuch*, Leiden [2]1977.

Biáf (ON for OE → Beow). In the prologue to his *Edda*, Snorri mentions Biáf as the son of Skjǫld, 'whom we call Bjár'. → Bjár is only found, however, as the owner of the house called Kerti in the *Alvíssmál*.

Biflindi (ON, 'the one with the painted shield'). A name for Odin in *Grímnismál* 49 and in the *Þulur*. Even Snorri includes the name (together with the variant form Bifliði) in *Gylfaginning* 2. Odin is depicted on Vendel-Age helmet ornaments and on pictorial stones as a spear-bearing rider and also with a shield. It is uncertain whether there is any connection with the name Biflindi. Perhaps Bifliði 'the one who makes the armies quake'? would be the correct form.

H. Falk, *Odensheite*, Christiania 1924.

Bifrǫst (ON). The bridge between Midgard and Asgard, identified with the concept of the rainbow (*Grímnismál* 44, *Fáfnismál* 15; *Gylfaginning* 40), was thought to have been erected by the gods between the heavens and earth (*Gylfaginning* 12). Bifrǫst ends in the sky at Himinbjǫrg where Heimdallr, who guards the bridge from the giants (*Gylfaginning* 16 and 26), lives. Every day the Æsir ride over to their court at the Urðarbrunnr (*Gylfaginning* 14), hence the other name for it, Asbrú. At the Ragnarǫk the hostile sons of Muspell will ride over Bifrǫst, and then it will collapse.

Bifrǫst either means the 'swaying road to heaven' (from ON *bifa* 'shake, sway') or else, if → Bilrǫst is indeed the more original form, 'the fleetingly glimpsed rainbow'. The interpretation as 'the multi-coloured way' is less likely. Snorri's description of Bifrǫst as a rainbow is, however, more convincing than de Vries' assumption that Bifrǫst means the milky way. Gjallarbrú, the bridge which leads to the realms of the dead and which corresponds to numerous parallels in non-Germanic concepts of the bridge leading to the Other World, should not be confused with Bifrǫst.

J. deVries, *Altgermanische Religionsgeschichte*, Berlin ^{3}1970; P. Dinzelbacher, *Die Jenseitsbrücke im Mittelalter*, Vienna 1973; A. Ebenbauer, 'Bifröst' (*Hoops* 2) ^{2}1982.

R: Hendrich, *Die Regenbogenbrücke* (painting); E. Tegner, *Bifrost* (poem, 1812).

Bifurr, also Bívorr, Bivörr (ON, 'the quaking one', to bifa?). A dwarf in *Vǫluspá* 11 and in the *Þulur*. Another interpretation would be 'beaver', i.e. 'the one who is as eager as a beaver'. This being the case, the word would be a borrowing from Low German.

C. N. Gould, 'Dwarf-Names' (*PMLA* 44) 1929; J. de Vries, *Altnordisches etymologisches Wörterbuch*, Leiden ^{2}1977.

R: Bifurr is one of the 13 dwarfs in J. R. R. Tolkien's novel, *The Hobbit* (1937).

Bil (ON, 'moment'?). A goddess who, according to Snorri, is one of the Asyniur (*Gylfaginning* 34).

However, in *Gylfaginning* 10, Bil is reduced to a mere fairy-tale figure in Snorri's tale of the picture in the moon (→ Máni) where she is one of the figures in the moon. Bil frequently occurs in kennings in poetry as a not closely defined mythological female figure, and it is clear that Bil was certainly not considered to be a goddess in the actual sense of the word in heathen times.

A. Holtsmark, 'Bil og Hjuke' (MoM) 1945.

Bíldr (ON, 'knife for blood-letting'). A dwarf in one version of *Vǫluspá* 13.

Bileygr (ON, 'the one with poor sight'). A name for Odin in the *Grímnismál* 47 and in the *Þulur* which refers to Odin's blindness in one eye. The name should be considered, however, in connection with another name for Odin → Báleygr.

Billingr (1) (ON, 'twin, hermaphrodite'). A dwarf in one version of *Vǫluspá* 13.

Billingr (2). The father of a girl (*Billings mey*) whom Odin wants to seduce in the so-called first → Odin's example of the *Hávamál* (96–102). However, he is deceived by her, finding a female dog in his bed instead of her. It is unlikely that Billingr (2) and Billingr (1) are identical as Odin otherwise sleeps exclusively with the daughters of giants (Gunnlǫð, Rinda); thus, Billingr (2) is possibly also a giant.

Billing's daughter (ON *Billings mey*) in the *Hávamál* 97, → Billingr 2, → Odin.

Bilrǫst (ON). The name given (only in *Grímnismál* 44 and *Fáfnismál* 15) to the bridge to → Asgard, namely the rainbow. The name is probably related to ON *bil* ('moment, weak point') and is possibly the original name of the bridge to heaven, although it is always called → Bifrǫst in the *Snorra Edda*.

Bilskírnir (ON, 'the one striking lightning with rays of light'). A room which, like Valhall, has 540 doors (*Grímnismál* 24). According to Snorri, Bilskírnir lies in → Þrúðvangr and in *Skáldskaparmál* 4 he says that Bilskímir belongs to Thor. A kenning for Thor used by the 10th century skald Gamli confirms Snorri's association of Thor with Bilskímir.

A. M. Sturtevant, 'Etymological Comments Upon Certain Old Norse Proper Names in the Eddas' (*PMLA* 67) 1952.

Bjár (ON). A hero from the *Alvíssmál* who is the owner of a horse called Kerti. Bjár is identified by Snorri in the prologue to his *Edda* as being the equivalent of Bíaf, i.e. OE → Beow.

Bjǫrgólfr (ON, 'mountain-wolf'). A giant in the *Þulur*; however, it would seem more likely to be a kenning for a giant than a name for one.

Bjǫrn (ON, 'bear'). The name Odin gives himself in *Harðar saga* 15, although Bjǫrn is a common personal name anyway. As a name for Odin it is closely connected with the animal disguises used by Odin's warriors (*Ynglinga saga* 6; → berserks).

H. Falk, *Odensheite*, Christiana 1924.

Bjǫrt (ON, 'the beautiful one, bright one'). One of Menglǫð's maids in the *Fjǫlsvinnsmál* 38.

Black elves → *svartálfar*.

Bláinn (1) (ON). A dwarf in the *Þulur*. For an interpretation → Bláinn 2.

Bláinn (2). Name for the first giant → Ymir in *Vǫluspá* 9, perhaps because the blue sky was created from his skull; whatever the reason for the name, it is related to ON *blár* 'blue, black'.

Blapþvari (ON, 'chatter-pole'?). A giant in the *Þulur*.

Blávorr or Blǫvurr (ON, 'the shining one' to Norwegian *blava* 'shine'?). A dwarf in the *Þulur*.

Bleik (ON, 'the blond one'). One of Menglǫð's maids in *Fjǫlsvinnsmál* 38.

Blíð (ON, 'the friendly one'). One of Menglǫð's maids in *Fjǫlsvinnsmál* 38.

Blikjanda-bǫl (ON, 'pale misfortune'). The bed curtains in the residence of the goddess of the underworld → Hel, according to Snorri's allegorizing description (*Gylfaginning* 33).

Blindi (ON, 'the blind one'). A name for Odin in the Eddic lay *Helgakviða Hundingsbana* II which probably refers to his blindness in one eye.

H. Falk, *Odensheite*, Christiana 1924.

Blindviðr (ON, roughly: 'hidden tree'). A dwarf in the *Þulur*.

blóðǫrn (ON) → bloodeagle.

Blóðughadda (ON, 'the one with the bloody hair' = 'wave'). One of the nine daughters of the sea-giant → Ægir and his wife Ran (*Skáldskaparmál* 22 and 28; Einarr Skúlason; *Þulur*), who were identical in Old Norse poetry to the waves of the sea. The name does not appear to be too appropriate for a wave, but perhaps it was supposed to convey the wispy, thread-like appearance of the water streaming from the crest of the wave. Despite the bloody name here, it is nonetheless less likely that these → Ægir's daughters should be considered as a kind of Valkyrie for the warriors killed at sea.

blót (ON) → sacrifice.

bloodeagle. The carving of the bloodeagle (ON *rísta blóðǫrn*) was a particularly cruel kind of killing during which the ribs were separated from the back-bone, folded out like eagle's wings and the lungs were pulled out, all done whilst the victim was still alive.

This kind of revenge on an enemy is recorded both in skaldic poetry (Sigvat) and in Eddic lays (*Reginsmál* 26) as well as in the sagas and could originally come from a form of human sacrifice, as performed in the *Orkneyinga saga* 8, where Jarl Einarr had his opponent killed in such a manner and thus 'sacrificed him to Odin for the victory' (*gaf hann Oðni til sigrs sér*). A similar account can be found in Saxo, *Gesta Danorum* IX, 315. Other evidence for this kind of killing suggests, however, that it could originally have been a special kind of revenge directed at the killer of one's father.

A. Ebenbauer, 'Blutaar' (*Hoops* 2) [2]1982.

boar. → Gullinborsti, → Sonargǫltr.

boat burial is a burial custom for which we have ample archaeological evidence for the Germanic tribes of North and Western Europe during the Iron Age and up to the end of the Viking Age. It is frequently referred to in Medieval literary sources where three types of boat burial are described:

(1) a burning ship was sent sailing out to sea with the dead person on board. The Byzantian chronicler Procopius records this type of burial in the 6th century in his description of the inhabitants of the North Sea coast and it is also recorded in the Old English epic, *Beowulf*. The Old Norse sources of the High Middle Ages (Snorri: *Ynglinga saga* 13, *Gylfaginning* 48) also make particular mention of the burning ship with its funeral pyre sailing out to sea.

(2) the ship was burned on land with the dead person on board; the ashes were then interred in a burial mound. Reference to this form of boat burial is found repeatedly in Saxo (*Gesta Danorum* III, 74; V, 156; VIII, 264). In addition to this there is the detailed and fascinating eye-witness account from the year 922 made by the Arabian Ibn Fadlan who described the funeral of a Varangian chieftain. He described how the corpse was not only given weapons, food and domestic animals for his journey, but a young girl was also put onto the ship with him and burned on the funeral pyre together with everything else on board; a burial mound was then erected over the ashes.

(3) literary evidence in the Kings' sagas and the Icelandic sagas, which frequently refer to inhumation in a ship over which a burial mound is then erected.

Whereas cremation on a burning boat afloat on the sea naturally enough remains archaeologically unsubstantiated, the other forms of boat burial are confirmed by numerous finds, showing that inhumation in unburned ships is somewhat more common than cremation, although there are also occurrences of cremation in unburnt ships. Archaeological finds have shown that the custom of boat burial in Scandinavia is not limited either by time or place; it is most frequent in Norway and Sweden and reaches the height of its popularity in the Vendel period and Viking Age (6th to 10th century). A form of boat burial in which the burnt remains of both corpse and boat are interred within → ship settings is found in particular in Sweden and Denmark.

The underlying beliefs would appear to differ according to the kind of boat burial chosen – the idea of a journey made by the dead person to the unknown Other World by ship can hardly hold true for the burial ships which lie at anchor, symbolically motionless, in their burial mounds. As, at least in the Viking period, the various burial customs existed side by side, a combination of several originally differing concepts must be assumed: on the one hand, the journey to the Other World by ship, on the other hand the grave as the house of the dead, in turn connected with the idea of the ship as the home of the seafarer. – As far as our late literary sources allow such a deduction, the concept of the ship of the dead → Naglfar must be dissociated from the custom of boat burial since Naglfar only occurs in connection with and as a signal for the end of the world (Ragnarǫk). The mythological counterpart to boat burial can be seen more convincingly in Baldr's death-ship → Hringhorni, which according to Snorri (*Gylfaginning* 48) was pushed out to sea ablaze.

Å. Ohlmarks, *Gravskeppet*, Stockholm 1946; M. Müller-Wille, 'Bestattung im Boot' (*Offa* 25–26) 1970.

R: a burning ship with a dead Viking on board is the stereotypical concept of Old Norse burial customs in modern times, as can be seen clearly in Sir Frank Dicksee's *The Funeral of a Viking* (1893) and all the films about Vikings. In J. R. R. Tolkien's trilogy, *The Lord of the Rings* (1954/55), Denethor's dead son Boromir is similarly laid in a boat in true Scandinavian tradition.

Boðn (ON, 'vessel'). In the myth of the theft of the skaldic mead, the dwarfs Fjalarr and Galarr catch the blood flowing from the wise giant → Kvasir and then keep it safe (according to Snorri, *Skáldskaparmál* 1) in two vessels, Boðn and Són, and in a cauldron, Oðrœrir. The three vessels pass into the possession of the giant Suttungr and it is from him that Odin finally steals the mead.

Snorri took the name Boðn from older kennings in which it is quite clearly identifiable as a vessel.

H. Lindroth, 'Boðn, Són och Oðrœrir' (MoM) 1915; J. de Vries, *Altgermanische Religionsgeschichte*, Berlin ^{3}1970.

Bǫlþorn (ON, 'thorn of misfortune'). The father of the giantess Bestla, who is the mother of the first gods Odin, Vili and Vé. Bǫlthorn is only mentioned in *Hávamál* 140 and it is from here that Snorri (*Gylfaginning* 5) took his information. Bǫlthorn's position in mythology is not completely clear as he is not mentioned otherwise as being one of the primeval giants, and yet appears to have existed at the same stage of time as the first man Buri. His name does not fit into an old mythological concept, either.

Bǫlverkr (ON, 'the evil-doer, malefactor'). The name Odin gives himself in *Grímnismál* 47. It is also Snorri's name for him in the tale relating the theft of the skaldic mead (*Skáldskaparmál* 1). Odin meets nine mowers working for Baugi the giant and involves them in an argument about his whetstone, subsequently killing them all. After this he works for Baugi for a whole summer under the name of Bǫlverkr and does the work of nine. As a reward for his work Baugi promises him a sip of the → mead of the skalds, which his brother Suttungr protects, but eventually he denies him this reward so that Odin has to use some more deception in order to steal the mead successfully.

Bǫmburr (ON, 'fatty'). A dwarf in *Vǫluspá* 11.

R: Bömburr is one of the 13 dwarfs in J. R. R. Tolkien's novel, *The Hobbit* (1937).

bog corpses (bog people; peat bog bodies; German *Moorleichen*, Danish *mosslikar*). The term is given to the well-preserved corpses found in the marshes of Denmark and North Germany (but also Britain, southern Sweden and Norway) most of which date from the end of the Bronze Age to the first century A.D.. These extraordinarily mummy-like bodies have been kept from decay by the acid qualities of the marshes and grant us an insight into different facets of the period in question. Apart from revealing much about every day life of the period (health, clothing, fashion), the most remarkable fact about these bog people is that few of them seem to have died a natural death. Many of them had been hanged or strangled before they were deposited in the marshes; some were covered or at least secured by sticks and pikes. Despite the obvious links with Tacitus, *Germania* 12, who states that the Germanic punishment for unmanly or cowardly behaviour was submerging the offender in bogs, hardly any bog people seem to have been drowned, but maybe one should not read too much detail into Tacitus' information.

It is still unknown whether bog corpses are to be interpreted as evidence for → death penalty, human → sacrifice, or as an attempt to prevent the walking of the dead (→ *draugr*), but combinations of these solutions should not be excluded as the ancient death penalty had, to some extent, a sacrificial character.

D. Strömbäck, 'Hade de germanska dödsstraffen sakralt ursprung?' (*Saga och Sed*) 1942, 51–69; A. Dieck, *Die europäischen Moorleichenfunde (Hominidenmoorfunde)* 1, Neumünster 1965; V. P. Glob, *Mosefolket*, Copenhagen 1965; H. Jankuhn, *Archäologische Bemerkungen zu Tier- und Menschenopfern bei den Germanen in der Römischen Kaiserzeit*, Göttingen 1967; H. Jankuhn, *Archäologische Bemerkungen zur Glaubwürdigkeit des Tacitus in der Germania*, Göttingen 1966; F. Ström, 'Straff. Sakrala element i straff' (*KLNM* 17) Malmö 1972; A. A. Lund, *Moselig*, Copenhagen 1976; F. Ström, 'Bog Corpses and *Germania*, Ch. 12' (G. Steinsland: *Words and Objects; towards a Dialogue between Archaeology and History of Religion*) Oslo 1986.

Borr stands in Snorri's *Edda* for → Burr.

Borvoboendoa. Name of a goddess or a matron on two Roman inscriptions from Utrecht. Possibly Celtic however.

S. Gutenbrunner, *Die germanischen Götternamen*, Leipzig 1936.

Boudunnehae. Name of a goddess or → matron on two inscriptions from the 2nd century in Cologne; possibly Celtic however.

S. Gutenbrunner, *Die germanischen Götternamen*, Leipzig 1936; B. and H. Galsterer, *Die römischen Steininschriften aus Köln*, Cologne 1975.

Bous. The avenger of Baldr, according to Saxo (*Gesta Danorum* III, 82). He is the son of Rinda who conceived him from Odin after the Finnish seer Rostiof had told Odin the prophesy that only she would bear Baldr's avenger for him. Bous proves himself to be extremely warlike at a very early age, and finally kills Hötherus, but dies of his wounds soon afterwards.

Bous corresponds to Odin's son → Vali of Eddic mythology and like him has the sole function of avenging Baldr. Bous is the Latinized form of the Old Danish name Bo (ON Búi) 'farmer'. It is questionable however whether the Old Danish vegetation demon Boui is identical with Bous and whether Bous should therefore be considered as a fertility god (de Vries).

P. Herrmann, *Die Heldensagen des Saxo Grammaticus*, Leipzig 1922; J. de Vries, *Altgermanische Religionsgeschichte*, Berlin [3]1970.

bovines → bull cult.

bragafull or *bragarfull* (ON, roughly 'chieftain's cup'). The name given, according to Snorri, to the toast used at sacrificial feasts or festive meals and banquets, which was drunk after the toasts to the gods, before the → *minni* (the cup for the dead) was drunk (*Ynglinga saga* 37; *Hákonar saga góða* 14). The diverse versions of the name leave open the question as to whether it was indeed a 'chieftain's cup' or a 'cup for the most distinguished (ancestors?)'. In the *Edda* (*Helgakviða Hjǫrvarðssonar* 30 Prose) the *bragafull* is connected with the vow at the inheritance banquet. However, as Snorri hardly bases his comments in the above-named sources on old traditions, and also as the prose addition to the Eddic lay is probably quite young, the question remains whether the drinking of the *bragafull* really was a heathen-Germanic custom or not.

K. Düwel, *Das Opferfest von Lade*, Göttingen 1971.

Bragi (1) (also: Bragi enn gamli Boddason, 'Bragi Boddason the Old'). The oldest skald whose works we know of. He composed his poetry in the 9th century (in Norway?) although the sources do not allow any closer dating. In the list of the skalds (*Skáldatal*) from the 12th and 13th centuries, Bragi is called the poet of the legendary Swedish king Beli, but also the skald of the Swedish king Björn at Haugi who has been identified as being King Bern of Birka and who was visited in about 830 A.D. by St. Anskar. According to these pieces of information, Bragi would already have been a grown man in 830, but Icelandic sources (*Landnámabók*, *Egils saga*) which include him in their genealogies, suggest that he lived between 835–900.

Apart from a few individual stanzas found elsewhere, Snorri in his *Edda* has handed down to us 20 stanzas and half-stanzas of Bragi's *Ragnarsdrápa*, a so-called shield poem which tells of the legendary and mythological scenes depicted on a shield.

In the Middle Ages, Bragi was already celebrated as being the first of the skalds and it is extremely likely that the poet Bragi is identical with the god → Bragi (2); as such, he became a mythical figure a mere 100 years after his death.

Jón Jóhannesson, 'Bjǫrn at Haugi' (*Saga-Book* 17) 1966/69; F. Jónsson, 'Brage skald' (*APhSc* 5) 1930/31; R. Frank, 'Bragi Boddason the Old' (*DicMA* 2) 1983.

Bragi (2) (ON). God of poetry. Snorri includes him in *Skáldskaparmál* 1 in a list of the gods, and in *Gylfaginning* 25 he tells of him: 'One (of the Æsir) is called Bragi; he is famous for his wisdom, but especially for his eloquence and his skill with words; he is very knowledgeable about poetry and the art of poetry is named after him (*bragr*) and a person is said to be a poet or poetess if he is more skilful with words than others are. His wife is Iðunn.' In Eddic poetry, only *Grímnismál* 44 names him in a mythological context, but nonetheless actually seems to refer to the skald Bragi (Bragi (1)); in *Lokasenna* (8–14) he argues as one of the Æsir with Loki, and here too Iðunn is said to be his wife. Otherwise, he is only mentioned in *Sigrdrífumál* 16 in a somewhat unclear connection with runes. Bragi is seldom mentioned in skaldic poetry: once as the husband of Iðunn in a stanza in *Grettis saga*, and otherwise only in the *Hákonarmál* 14

(961 A.D.) and the *Eireksmál* 3 (954 A.D.), both times as the one welcoming the lords in Valhall. There is nothing in the two skaldic poems which makes us assume that the poet Bragi is thought to be a god here; he is simply another hero who has been found worthy of admission to Valhall.

Because Bragi appears as a god in 12th and 13th century writings, notably in Snorri's *Edda* and in the *Lokasenna*, it is extremely likely that the figure of a god was created from the much venerated 9th century poet (Mogk, Turville-Petre). The systematizing treatment of Germanic mythology in the scholarly Icelandic Renaissance of the High Middle Ages means that such a deification need not necessarily have taken place in heathen times.

Snorri says that *bragr*, 'poetry', has taken its name from the god Bragi; but, as a *bragr* could also mean 'chieftain, lord' and the name Bragi was otherwise used for historical and fictitious persons, the association Bragi/*bragr* 'poetry' is not necessarily original, and possibly only encouraged the deification process of the poet.

E. Mogk, 'Bragi als Gott und Dichter' (*PBB* 12) 1887; S. Bugge, 'Der Gott Bragi in den norrönen Gedichten' (*PBB* 13) 1888; E. Mogk, 'Bragi' (*PBB* 14) 1889; W. H. Vogt, 'Thors Fischzug', (*Studier till. A. Kock*) Lund 1929; W. H. Vogt, 'Bragis Schild', (*APhSc* 5) 1930; H. b. d. Wieden, 'Bragi' (*ZfdPh* 80) 1961; J. de Vries, *Altgermanische Religionsgeschichte*, Berlin [3]1970, E. O. G. Turville-Petre, *Myth and Religion of the North*, Westport 1975.

R: (literature) F. G. Klopstock, *Wingolf* (ode, 1747); F. G. Klopstock, *Braga* (ode, 1771); F. G. Klopstock, *Die Kunst Tialfs* (ode, 1771); A. Oehlenschläger, *Bragis sang om Gefjon*, (poem in: *Nordens guder*, 1819); *Bragur* (lit. periodical, 1791–1812). (fine art) Karl von Münchhausen, *Braga* (etching, 1799); K. Ehrenberg, *Balder und Nanna, Iduna und Braga* (drawing, 1883); E. Doepler d. J., *Bragi* (in: E. Doepler, W. Ranisch, *Walhall*, 1901).

Brage is also the name of a Norwegian minesweeper, built in 1944.

Bragi (3). Also a name for Odin in the poem *Hǫfuðlausn* 31 by Egill Skalagrímsson.

bracteates. Circular decoration coins, stamped on one side only, dating from the 5th and 6th centuries A.D., which originate from an imitation of late classical medallions of the Roman emperors. Of the bracteates found up to the present time, approximately 300 come from Denmark, 190 from Sweden, 160 from Norway, 30 from England and approximately 20 from the European mainland further south than Denmark. Four main types of bracteates were distinguished by their motifs as early as the 19th century:

A-bracteates: male head in profile,

B-bracteates: one to three human figures, sometimes accompanied by animals,

C-bracteates: male head in profile above a four-legged animal,

D-bracteates: single animals or else animal decoration.

Nearly half of all the bracteates belong to group C, a quarter to group D.

An early and secondary form of bracteates are medallion imitations which bear an additional picture on the reverse side, in contrast to the actual bracteates.

Nearly a third of all bracteates bear runic inscriptions which are only partly legible or make any sense. In these inscriptions sometimes the rune master is named or else he speaks himself, but the majority are magical runic inscriptions in which the otherwise magical words *alu* and *laukaR* (→ leek) are found.

Bracteates are important for mythology not so much because of the runes, but rather because in their pictorial representations they moved on quickly from imitating the Roman imperial portrait to depicting Nordic concepts, and as such offer a wealth of religious pictorial material for a basically illiterate time.

Apart from depicting people, there are also pictures of animals, among them pigs (A-bracteates), birds (on A, B and C-bracteates), horses (C-bracteates) and fantastic creatures (on D-bracteates); the horse pictures of C-bracteates are frequently striking because of their obviously handicapped forelegs which allows a presumable diagnosis of 'shoulder lameness' (Hauck), which in turn suggests a link to the god of healing, Odin. The portrayal of the male head and of other pictorial elements on the A-bracteates and C-bracteates suggests the nowadays generally accepted theory that the place of the emperor of the late classical Roman medallions was predominantly taken over in the north by Odin, and his roles as magical doctor and lord of the gods were clearly expressed iconographically. The most frequent motif – of the C-bracteates – is that of Odin's healing of the horse, as has been preserved in writing through the Second Merseburg Charm.

On the three-god bracteates (B-bracteates) Baldr is quite clearly depicted as well as Odin; the third god is perhaps Loki, but more likely Hel, thus allowing the whole to be interpreted as a pictorial representation of the myth of Baldr (Hauck).

Extensive research has yet to be done on the interpretations of details in bracteate iconography, and a decisive explanation will in all probability not be possible in many cases, for example the three-god bracteates and the possible depiction of twin gods (→ dioskuri).

K. Hauck, *Goldbrakteaten aus Sievern*, Munich 1970; O. Höfler, 'Brakteaten als Geschichtsquelle' (*ZfdA* 101) 1972; K. Hauck, 'Zur Ikonologie der Goldbrakteaten' I–XXV (1972–1983; see bibliography); K. Hauck, 'Brakteatenikonologie' (*Hoops* 3) ²1978.

Brandingi (ON, 'the burning one'). A giant in the *Þulur*. Like the giants Eldr, Eimnir and Logi, he appears to be a personification of fire, a personification which suggests itself since it is a giant, Surtr, who kindles the world conflagration at the Ragnarǫk.

Breiðablik (ON, 'the far-shining one'). The heavenly residence of the god → Baldr, according to *Grímnismál* 12. In *Gylfaginning* 16 and 21 Snorri mentions Breiðablik as a beautiful place which will never be impure. As a name, Breiðablik is certainly a relatively young formation, hardly older than the poem *Grímnismál* itself.

Brimir (1) (ON). Name for a giant in *Vǫluspá* (9 and 37), which is used as an alternative name for Ymir. Since the sea (according to *Grímnismál* 40) was formed from Ymir's blood, Brimir is probably derived from *brim* 'Meer'.

Brimir (2). The name Snorri (*Gylfaginning* 51) gives to the room where the gods hold their drinking feasts. However, the name is obviously a misinterpretation of *Vǫluspá* 37: *bjórsalr jǫtuns, en sá Brimir heitir* ('the ale-room of the giant called Brimir') where Brimir is the name of the giant and not the room itself; → Brimir (1).

Brísingamen (ON). A piece of jewelry belonging to Freyja, according to late Old Norse sources (*Þrymskviða* 13, 19; *Gylfaginning* 34, *Skáldskaparmál* 20). Despite the form found in the manuscripts, which means 'necklace of the Brisings', it would seem to be etymologically related to Norwegian *brisa* 'to shine'. The extant name could possibly be influenced by the *Brōsinga mene* in the Old English poem Beowulf.

The myth of the theft of the necklace is difficult to comment upon because of the fragmentary and sparse source material. The Old Norse sources say the following about it (cf. de Vries):

(1) Loki is called 'the thief of Brising's belt' (*Brísings girði*) (Þjóðólfr ór Hvíni, *Haustlǫng*, 9th century);

(2) Loki is called 'the thief of Brísingamen' (*Skáldskaparmál* 16);

(3) Freyja's necklace is called Brísingamen (*Þrymskviða* 13, 19; *Gylfaginning* 34, *Skáldskaparmál* 20);

(4) In the *Sǫrla þáttr* ('Tale of Sörli'), written in the late 14th century, Loki steals Freyja's precious (here nameless) necklace at Odin's behest;

(5) Heimdall and Loki fight for an object which is possibly called → Singasteinn in *Húsdrápa* (10th century);

(6) Snorri records in *Skáldskaparmál* 8 that Heimdall and Loki, in the shape of seals, have fought for Brísingamen, a passage that presumably derives from a now lost part of the *Húsdrápa*;

(7) Snorri calls Heimdall 'the bringer of Freyja's necklace' (*Skáldskaparmál* 8).

In addition to the above, there is another reference in the Old English poem *Beowulf* (1197–1201) to the fact that Hama has stolen the *Brōsinga mene* from Eormenric's hall.

It is hardly possible to reconstruct a myth from these different references which could throw light on the meaning of Brísingamen, as well as Loki's and Heimdall's role in its theft. The most detailed version of the theft of Freyja's necklace in *Sǫrla þáttr* is by far the youngest, and it was possibly extensively reworked to fit it for its literary function in this tale, which explains the → Hjaðningavíg. The *Sǫrla þáttr* records that the golden necklace was forged by four dwarfs (Alfrigg, Dvalinn, Berlingr, Grerr). Freyja must spend a night with each of them in order to obtain it. When Loki tells Odin this, Odin forces him to get the necklace for him. Loki can only enter Freyja's bedroom in the shape of a fly; as she is resting on the necklace, he has to sting her so that she moves and he can steal the jewelry from her. When Freyja demands it back from Odin, he makes it conditional on her creating an eternal war between two kings; she finally manages this and the Hjaðningavíg is accomplished.

Even if this tale can be traced back to an ancient myth, it does not clarify the significance of the fight between Heimdall and Loki, as nothing is recorded about the regaining of the necklace by Heimdall. – The Brísingamen and its theft have been interpreted in quite different ways. Much saw it as reflecting a myth of the theft of fire, whereby he interprets Loki's appearance in the shape of both seal and salmon as referring to the aquatic nature of the god. The attempts at natural-mythological interpretations have found two explanations for Brísingamen, both in connection with Old Norse *brísingr*, Norwegian *brising* 'fire'. According to Pipping, the Brísingar are the rays of the *aurora borealis* (Northern lights) which symbolize the warriors dedicated to Odin who have fallen in battle. An older explanation sees Brísingamen as being the symbol for the rising sun, thus linking the form of a necklace with the cult of a fertility goddess (Freyja) (Müllenhoff); Scandinavian bronze figures of the Migration era, representing naked female figures with necklaces, are also considered as documentary evidence (F. Ström, Jungner). On the other hand, Pering has associated Brísingamen with the kenning *hafnýra* ('sea kidney') in the already-mentioned stanza from *Húsdrápa*, a word that he understands as the name for the kidney-shaped fruit of a West Indian plant which the Gulf Stream carries to Scandinavia (Norwegian *vettenyrer, søbønner*). This fruit would be used as birth stones, that is to say amulets for pregnant women and worn in the belt, later as necklaces.

It is by no means certain that Heimdall and Loki really fight for Brísingamen in the stanza in *Húsdrápa*, and *hafnýra* would be a sound kenning for 'island' as well as for 'ship'. – The total absence of the characters Hama and Eormenrīc, connected with the *Brōsinga mene* in *Beowulf*, in the Norse myth of Brísingamen (although Heimir and Eormanric are well known in Norse heroic poetry) has led H. Damico to the attractive, though not totally convincing, theory that the names of these figures should not be understood as personal names but as terms: OE *hāma* 'cricket' = fly = Loki, *eormenrīc* 'world-power' = Odin. Despite these various attempts at explanation it should be admitted that the true role of Brísingamen in Norse mythology as well as the function of the battle between Heimdall and Loki is totally obscure.

K. Müllenhoff, 'Frija und der Halsbandmythus' (*ZfdA* 30) 1886; R. Much, 'Der germanische Himmelsgott' (*Festgabe R. Heinzel*, Vol. 1) Halle 1898; H. Jungner, *Gudinan Frigg och Als Härad*, Uppsala 1922; H. Pipping, 'Eddastudier' (*Studier i Nordisk Filologi* 17) 1926; J. de Vries, *The Problem of Loki*, Helsinki 1933; B. Pering, *Heimdall*, Lund 1941; F. Ström, *Loki*, Göteborg 1956; A. B. Rooth, *Loki in Scandinavian Mythology*, Lund 1961; F. Jónsson, *Lexicon Poeticum*, Copenhagen [2]1966; J. de Vries, *Altgermanische Religionsgeschichte*, Berlin [3]1970; K. Schier, 'Húsdrápa 2, Heimdall, Loki und die Meerniere' (*Festgabe O. Höfler*) Vienna 1976; H. Damico, 'Sǫrlaþáttr and the Hama Episode in Beowulf' (*SS* 55) 1983.

R: a modern literary version is given in Alan Garner's *The Weirdstone of Brisingamen* (London, 1960). J. Doyle-Penrose, *Freyja and the Necklace* (oil painting, c.1890).

Brísingr (ON, 'flame'). Possibly the name of a dwarf in the poem *Haustlǫng* (9) by Þjóðólfr ór Hvíni from the 9th century; → Brísingamen.

Brokkr (ON, 'the one who works with metal fragments; blacksmith'; unlikely: 'the runner' to *brokka*). According to Snorri (*Skáldskaparmál* 33) the brother and helpmate of the dwarf → Sindri who makes the gods' treasures Gullinborsti, Draupnir and Mjǫllnir.

L. Motz, 'New Thoughts on Dwarf-Names' (*FmSt* 7) 1973.

Brünhilde (ON, Brynhildr). Heroine of the tale of the Nibelungs, referred to in Nordic sources (*Skáldskaparmál* 39; *Oddrúnargrátr* 14) as being a → valkyrie, which is connected in some way with her warlike actions.

R: Brünnhilde (soprano) is also a valkyrie in R. Wagner's *Der Ring des Nibelungen*, the daughter of Erda and Wotan whom they expel from Valhall. K. Gjellerup wrote a tragedy, *Brynhild* (1884); as in K. Moser's oil painting *Wotan und Brünhilde* (1914), Brünhilde is frequently depicted together with → Odin in the wake of Wagner's operas.

Brúni (1) (ON). A name for Odin, admittedly only found in the *Þulur*. It can be interpreted as 'the brown one' (as in the dwarf's name), but the meaning of the name is more likely 'the one with bushy eyebrows'.

H. Falk, *Odensheite*, Christiania 1924.

Brúni (2) ('the brown one'). A dwarf named in *Vǫluspá* 13.

Brýja (ON, 'Troll-woman (wife)'). A giantess in the *Þulur*; the word is probably a new formation of *brý* 'troll'.

Brynhildr → Brünhilde.

Bugge, Sophus (1833–1907), Norwegian scholar of antiquities. In his *Studier over der nordiske Gude – og Heltesagns Oprindelse* (1880ff.) (Engl.: *Studies about the origin of Nordic mythological and heroic tales*) he held the provocative theory that practically all myths in Old Norse literature derive from late classical and Christian concepts. Although Bugge may be considered a representative of the older school of comparative mythology, he broke away from all his predecessors who agreed that the Eddic lays contained predominantly heathen material. Bugge started out from the clearly Christian insertions in Eddic poetry and, by using somewhat daring etymologies (Loki from Luzifer, Urðarbrunnr from Jordan, Iðavellir from Eden, Garmr from Ceberus), managed to show that Germanic mythology was totally dependent on Near Eastern religions. Bugge believed that Viking Age Ireland and Britain were the places where the adoption from one culture to the other took place.

Bugge's theories, despite being subsequently defended by W. Golther, were in general vehemently rejected, but the possibility of south-eastern influences on Germanic religion had been pointed out and is kept in mind even today.

Buínn (ON, 'the one who is always ready'). A dwarf in the *Þulur*.

bull cult. From the Bronze Age cattle, and in particular the bull, played a role in the religious life of the Germanic tribes in which the symbolic significance was not limited to one area alone.

The main centre of the bull cult among the Germanic peoples was in Denmark and is evident in numerous archaeological finds. In particular, bull symbolism on Iron Age cauldrons and drinking horns occurs frequently and this could indicate a link between the bull cult practised by the Cimbri and a drinking sacrifice. It is difficult to distinguish whether this sacrifice and the bull cult played a role in fertility cults or should be seen as an element of the worship of Týr (Esterle). Both a bull sacrifice and the bull as a symbol of power are documented for the Anglo-Saxons, but nothing more specific can be said about this bull cult.

The origin of the Germanic bull cult has repeatedly been said to be in East Mediterranean cultures, but this is hard to prove and the assumption is also unnecessary, as the significance of cattle in all early agrarian cultures could have easily led to an independent development of the bull cult.

H Rosén, 'Freykult och djurkult' (*Fornvännen* 8) 1913); K. Schneider, 'Runische Inschriftzeugnisse zum Stieropferkult der Angelsachsen' (*Festschrift E. Mertner*) Munich 1969; G. Esterle, *Die Boviden in der Germania*, Vienna 1974.

Bumburr (ON). A dwarf, → Bǫmburr.

Búri (1) (ON, 'producer, father'). The ancestor of the gods. However, Búri is not mentioned in the cosmogonic passages of the poetic *Edda*. Snorri tells of how Búri was freed from the ice by being licked out by the primordial cow Auðumla. Búri has one son called Burr, who begat the first gods, Odin, Vili and Vé with the giant's daughter Bestla. Snorri does not explain how Burr himself was begotten, whether he was born from a giantess (like the three gods) or by autogeny (as in the case of Ymir's children).

Buri (2) or Búri (ON, perhaps to *búa*, therefore 'inhabitant'?). A dwarf in *Vǫluspá* 13.

Burial customs. In order to understand the varying forms of interment, several aspects need to be taken into consideration: the concept of life after death, the reverence for the dead by the living, the protection of the living from those already dead, the social structure of the community and not least the social position of the dead.

Although it cannot be said conclusively from which point in time the northern and western European population may be considered as being Germanic, the forms of burial customs show a continuity which possibly outlasted ethnic regrouping and therefore necessitates a common study of pre-historical and early historical customs.

The West European megalithic culture, which preceded the Bronze Age (1800–500 B.C.), was characterized by its monumental dolmen graves, which at least in one of their forms (the passage graves) were erected as family and dynasty graves. Passage graves are great stone burial chambers covered by earth mounds and accessible by a passage. In such passage graves in Denmark and Ireland the remains of up to 100 uncremated corpses have been found. These mighty stone constructions can be understood as witnesses to a marked ancestral cult as well as to the necessity of some form of protection of the living from the dead. The enormous work involved in the erection of such monumental structures as burial places for the future tribe or family could point to a rigid social structure. The orientation of the graves with their entrances to the south and the burial chamber to the north (→ Hel) allows an insight into the religious concepts of this early epoche. Traces of fire in the graves and the unique construction of the passage grave at Newgrange, Ireland, where a huge block of quartz placed over the passage entrance in the south only allows the sun's rays to penetrate into the burial chamber at midwinter, seem to presuppose a pronounced cult of the dead.

With the end of the Neolithic period and the transition to the Bronze age the burial customs changed to favour stone-cist graves and thus a tendency towards individual graves. This suggests a slackening of the social structure, as well as a lessening in the significance of the cult of the dead. Whether an increased fear of the dead can be inferred from this – the family grave had to be opened anew for each burial – is questionable. Alongside the stone-cist graves in the earliest Bronze Age there are also simple burials in barrows. The barrow, which frequently includes later burials in the side of the mound and repeated re-buildings, remains the grave form characteristic of the Bronze Age in northern Europe.

The barrow also continued as the predominate grave form, at least for the higher social classes, when cremation of the corpses and burial of the ashes began to prevail in around 1300 B.C. Neither burial mounds nor cremation are undeniable proof of an immigration of new peoples, and cremation especially should not be merely understood as a simple change of burial customs among the Indo-Germanic people. The transition to cremation in the 2nd millenium B.C. seems to occur in the whole of the Euroasian area. – The new custom need not even mean the change to a belief in a soul, as the grave-goods still suggest the concept of the 'living dead'; equally, the interpretation that the cremation of the corpses serves as a protection of the living from the dead does not give sufficient explanation for the wide distribution of the cult.

The beginning of the Iron Age in Europe shows no remarkable change in the burial customs. Gradually, however, the custom of simple inhumation began to spread from the south, from the Mediterranean, probably as a result of Roman and later Christian influence. The expansion was very erratic; Tacitus, writing in the 1st century, still only recorded the Germanic tradition of cremation in burial mounds. On the other hand, in the case of the Goths, who were Christianized earlier, inhumation had soon become the norm. From the post-Roman Iron Age to the end of the pagan era both cremation and inhumation burial can be found side by side among the western and northern Germanic peoples. Whilst in the south Christianization accelerated the transition to inhumation, which was only accepted slowly in Scandinavia, cremation continued to be the preferred form of burial by the Saxons and the Friesians until the 8th century when the Church had to take a definite stand against it.

Particularly in Scandinavia, the grave form of the barrow continued after late heathen times, and, although it was on the decrease in the British Isles in the Roman Iron Age, it asserted itself again (along with other grave forms) during the Scandinavian settlement as a sign of the social standing of the deceased. As such it was mainly used for warriors and chieftains. In this form of burial, → boat burial was extremely common from the beginning of the Migration era onwards, and all variations of cremation and inhumation have been found. Even in grave-fields without boats there are reminders of this burial form in the → ship settings, where stones in the shape of a boat surround the grave.

In ON literature burial in barrows and boat burial (with or without cremation) is the most frequent form of burial customs, but inhumation in coffins is also mentioned.

During the whole period referred to, grave goods are never missing, although they decreased greatly in the early Iron Age. The grave goods found in graves of chieftains from the Viking period, on the other hand, surpass in richness even the gifts found in Bronze Age graves and confirm the custom, mentioned in literary sources, that animals and even people (perhaps the wife or a serving girl) were put into the grave alongside the dead man; this was, however, dependent on the social standing of the deceased.

In Scandinavia during the Viking period 'bauta'-stones (memorial stones) marking the graves were common; these are distinct from other gravestones (rune stones, pictorial stones) by their size and lack of inscriptions.

O. Almgren, 'Vikingatidens grafskick i verkligheten och i den fornnordiska litteraturen' (*Nordiska Studier till. A. Noreen*) Uppsala 1904; H. Rosén, *Om dödsrike och dödsbruk i fornnordisk religion*, Lund 1918; S. Lindqvist, 'Snorres uppgifter om hednatidens gravskick och gravar' (*Fornvännen* 15) 1920; S. Lindqvist, 'Ynglingaättens gravskick' (*Fornvännen* 16) 1921; K. Helm, 'Die Entwicklung der germanischen Religion' (H. Nollau, *Germanische Wiedererstehung*) Heidelberg 1926; S. Piggot, *Ancient Europe*, Edinburgh 1965; H. Uecker, *Die altnordischen Bestattungssitten*, Munich 1966; Å. Hyenstrand, 'Gravformer och symboltecken under yngre bronsalder' (*Fornvännen* 63) 1968; J. de Vries, *Altgermanische Religionsgeschichte*, Berlin [3]1970; H. Döbler, *Die Germanen*, Munich 1975; Å. V. Ström, 'Änkebegravning', (*KLNM* 20) 1976; J. M. Coles, A. F. Harding, *The Bronze Age in Europe*, London 1979.

burial mound. The custom of burying the dead in burial mounds is wide-spread in Europe from the Neolithic period onwards and is not only limited to Germanic tribes. The form of burial within the burial mound varies (cremation, inhumation, individual grave, family grave), but it is supported by archaeological evidence from the earliest Bronze Age to the Viking period in western and especially in northern Europe among the Germanic population. Whilst other forms of burial can be found alongside this throughout (→ burial customs), it seems that the burial mound (originally probably a family grave) was mainly a chieftain's or king's grave in late pagan times.

The belief that life after death could take on the form of the living dead (→ draugr) who inhabited the burial mound was frequently and vividly depicted in literature, although belief in them was not restricted merely to those buried in burial mounds.

The concept of the dead in burial mounds is closely related to the idea of the dead living inside mountains. This is referred to in Icelandic saga literature (*Eyrbyggja saga* 11; *Njáls saga* 14) as well as repeatedly in the Icelandic *Landnámabók* (S 69, M 25, S

97 etc.). Added to these North Germanic sources are the South and West Germanic tales of kings in mountains. According to legend, Friedrich Barbarossa (also Charlemagne) is waiting in the Untersberg (Salzburg, Austria), Friedrich II in the Kyffhäuser (Thuringia, Germany), Duke Widukind in a hill on the Weser, King Arthur in Cadbury Hill (Somerset, England) – for the day when he will ride forth to save mankind. The entrancement of these kings cannot be separated from the Germanic belief in the living dead, and is rather further evidence of how concretely life after death was thought of.

J. Grimm, *Deutsche Mythologie*, Berlin [4]1875–78, Reprint 1981; E. Hartmann, 'Der Ahnenberg' (*ARW* 34) 1937; H. R. Ellis, *The Road to Hel*, Cambridge 1934; S. Piggot, *Ancient Europe*, Edinburgh 1973; H. Döbler, *Die Germanen*, Munich 1975; Å. V. Ström, H. Biezais, *Germanische und baltische Religion*, Stuttgart 1975.

Burinn (ON, to burr 'son'?). A dwarf in the *Þulur*.

Burorina. A goddess named on a votive stone from the island of Walcheren (CIL XIII 8775). The name is possibly Celtic. If it is indeed Germanic, then perhaps to Anglo-Saxon *byrele* 'giver'?

S. Gutenbrunner, *Die germanischen Götternamen*, Halle 1936; M. Schönfeld, *Wörterbuch der altgermanischen Personen- und Völkernamen*, Heidelberg [2]1965; J. de Vries, *Altgermanische Religionsgeschichte*, Berlin [3]1970; H. Reichert, *Lexikon der altgermanischen Namen*, Vienna 1987–90.

Burr, also Borr. (ON, 'son').The father of Odin, Vili and Vé (*Vǫluspá* 4, *Gylfaginning* 5,6). According to Snorri he is the son of Búri, who was licked out of the ice by the primordial cow → Auðumla; it is not clear how Burr came into being. Burr's wife is → Bestla, the daughter of the giant Bǫlthorn, and thus in Snorri's cosmogony the giants are the ancestors of the gods.

Búseyra (ON, either 'the one with big ears' or else 'the one who starves the household'). A giantess in a stanza by the skald Þórbjǫrn dísarskáld where she is named among some other giantesses who were killed by Thor. We have no further information concerning the killing of the giants and giantesses listed in this stanza, except for Hyrrokkin about whom Snorri tells that Thor nearly killed her at Baldr's funeral.

Byggvir (ON). According to *Lokasenna* 43, 46, 56 and the introductory prose of the *Lokasenna*, Byggvir is Freyr's servant. Both he and his wife Beyla are only mentioned in *Lokasenna*, and indeed without the information in the prose introduction they would hardly be thought of as servants because they take part in the argument with Loki, just as the gods do. Admittedly, Beyla is called a 'dirty maid' by Loki, but considering his other insults this need not be taken too seriously. Although no great conclusions should be drawn from this single reference to Byggvir, Byggvir and Beyla should nonetheless be considered as lesser gods or at least as protective demons, which the etymology of their names confirms. Byggvir is usually related to *bygg* 'corn', and thus would be a corn demon, a field spirit. The identification in older scholarship that Byggvir was identical to the Finnish corn spirit Pellon-Pekko (→ Fjǫlnir (2)) is nowadays generally rejected. It is more likely that there is a link with the OE Beav (Beow) who is included in genealogies as Sceldva's son. Beav and Sceldva, however, stand in the same relationship to each other as Beowulf and Scyld Scefing, of whom it is said that he was left lying on a sheaf in a ship which drifted to land (*Beowulf* 7f.), and a connexion between Scyld Scefing and a field cult is therefore obvious.

E. Sievers, 'Grammatische Miszellen' (*PBB* 18) 1894; G. Dumézil, 'Deux petits dieux scandinaves: Byggvir et Beyla' (*La nouvelle Clio* 3) 1952; J. de Vries, *Altgermanische Religionsgeschichte*, Berlin [3]1970.

Byleiptr → Byleistr.

Byleistr (or Byleiptr, Byleiftr, ON). One of Loki's two brothers (*Vǫluspá* 51, *Hyndluljóð* 40; *Gylfaginning* 32, *Skáldskaparmál* 16). The names in Loki's genealogy, most of which are only interpretable with difficulty (→ Helblindi, → Farbauti, → Nal, → Laufey), suggest that it is an ancient genealogy. The etymology of Byleistr has not been satisfactorily settled: the second element is probably related to *-leiptr* 'lightning', and the first perhaps to *bylr* 'wind'. An interpretation as 'the one who makes lightning in the storm' or else (along with Weinhold) 'the one releasing the storm' is unsatisfying, however; even less convincing is Bugge's suggestion of 'bee-lightning' which refers to the fly-like shape which the devil (and Loki) can put on.

K. Weinhold, 'Die Sagen von Loki' (*ZfdA* 7) 1849; E. Wadstein, 'Bidrag till tolkning ock belysning av skalde- ock Edda-dikter' (*ANF* 11) 1895; S. Bugge, *Studien*, Munich 1889; J. de Vries, 'Loki . . . und kein Ende' (*Festschrift Schröder*) Heidelberg 1959; J. de Vries, *Altnordisches etymologisches Wörterbuch*, Leiden [2]1977.

Bylgja (ON, 'wave'). One of the nine daughters of the sea-giant Ægir and his wife Rán (*Skáldskaparmál* 22 and 58; Ottar Svarti; *Guðmundardrápa; Njáls saga*) who in Old Norse poetry were identified as being the waves of the sea.

Byrgir (ON, 'hider') occurs in a tale told by Snorri in *Gylfaginning* 10 about the picture in the moon and is the name of the well from which Bil and Hjúki came when the moon fetched them from earth; → Máni.

Caimineae. A group of → matrons on a lost inscription from Euskirchen, Germany (CIL XIII 7969). It is not certain if the name is Germanic or Celtic.

S. Gutenbrunner, *Die germanischen Götternamen*, Halle 1936; M. Schönfeld, *Wörterbuch der altgermanischen Personen- und Völkernamen*, Heidelberg [2]1965; H. Reichert, *Lexikon der altgermanischen Namen*, Vienna 1987–90.

Cannanefates → Kannanefates.

Canninefates → Kannanefates.

Cantrusteihiae. A group of → matrons on four votive stones from the 2nd/3rd centuries. The name is possibly Celtic and derives from the tribal name Condrusi (cf. *pagus Condrustis*).

S. Gutenbrunner, *Die germanischen Götternamen*, Halle 1936; M. Schönfeld, *Wörterbuch der altgermanischen Personen- und Völkernamen*, Heidelberg [2]1965; H. Reichert, *Lexikon der altgermanischen Namen*, Vienna 1987–90.

Chandrumanehae. Name of some → matrons, to whom a votive stone from Billig near Euskirchen, Germany (CIL XIII 7968) has been dedicated (*Chandrumanehis*). As yet the name has not been convincingly interpreted.

S. Gutenbrunner, *Die germanischen Götternamen*, Halle 1936; M. Schönfeld, *Wörterbuch der altgermanischen Personen- und Völkernamen*, Heidelberg [2]1965; H. Reichert, *Lexikon der altgermanischen Namen*, Vienna 1987–90.

Channo → Mercurius Channin(i)us.

Christmas → Yule.

Chuchen(eh)ae. Matron name found on four votive stones from the area around Zülpich, Germany, probably dating from the 3rd and 4th centuries (CIL XIII 7923–4, 12008–9); the origin and interpretation of the name are obscure, unless it is related in some way to the place name Kuchenheim.

S. Gutenbrunner, *Die germanischen Götternamen*, Halle 1936; M. Schönfeld, *Wörterbuch der altgermanischen Personen- und Völkernamen*, Heidelberg [2]1965; H. Reichert, *Lexikon der altgermanischen Namen*, Vienna 1987–90.

Cimbrianus, Cimbrius → Mercurius Cimbrianus.

(**Cisa, Zisa**) is supposedly the name of a Germanic goddess who, according to a Latin historical text from the 11th century, was worshipped in Augsburg in heathen times. Whilst Grimm made extensive speculations about the identity of this goddess, today the supposition of a goddess Cisa is rejected because the source text does not stand up to critical examination.

J. Grimm, *Deutsche Mythologie*, Berlin [4]1875–78; R. Kohl, 'Die Augsburger Cisa – eine germanische Göttin?' (*ARW* 33) 1936.

Cobba. An inscription from Utrecht says: *deabus Borvoboendoae Cobbae* ('dedicated to the Borvoboendoa and the Cobba'). It is as yet unclear whether Cobba really is a goddess or even if the named deities are Germanic or Celtic.

S. Gutenbrunner, *Die germanischen Götternamen*, Halle 1936; M. Schönfeld, *Wörterbuch der altgermanischen Personen- und Völkernamen*, Heidelberg [2]1965.

Codex Regius of the poetic *Edda* (Icelandic: *Konungsbók eddukvæði*) is the name given to the main manuscript of the → poetic *Edda*. It came into the possession of the bishop of Skálholt Brynjólfur Sveinsson in 1643 who presented it to the Danish king, Frederick III in 1662 (hence the name of the manuscript, 'King's book'), whereupon it was put into the Royal Library in Copenhagen under the catalogue number Gl. kgl. sml. 2365, 4to. In 1971 it was the first of a great number of Old Icelandic manuscripts to be given back to Iceland.

The Codex was compiled in the second half of the 13th century and contains the most important collection of Old Norse mythological and heroic poetry; in the 16th or 17th centuries an eight leaf quire of the manuscript was lost, including the lays about Sigurd. Today the Codex is comprised of only 45 leaves.

K. Schier, 'Edda, Ältere' (*Hoops* 6) [2]1986.

cosmogony. We know little about how the West Germanic peoples envisaged the origin of the world. Tacitus merely records that the Teutons worship a god called Tuisto, who is descended from earth itself, and whose son Mannus is the forefather of the three Germanic tribes, Ingaevones, Herminones and Istaevones (→ Anthropogeny). Tuisto is etymologically connected to the number 'two', and was possibly a hermaphrodite being like the Nordic proto-giant Ymir who engenders children out of himself. The third stanza of *Vǫluspá* says of Ymir that he was alive before the dawn of time, 'when neither the heavens nor earth existed' (*iǫrð fannz æva né upphiminn*), when there was only the chasm → Ginnungagap. This alliterative formula of the

North-Germanic source is not only found in the OHG *Wessobrunn Prayer* (9th century; *ero ni uuas noh ûfhimil*), but also in a variant form in the Old Saxon Heliand, in OE texts, on a Swedish rune stone and also on the late Medieval Danish rune stick from Ribe (Schier, Lönnroth). Despite the frequent usage in Christian contexts the formula appears to go back to an ancient Common Germanic cosmological formula. According to the *Codex Regius* and *Hauksbók*, the first line of the already mentioned *Vǫluspá* stanza reads 'In olden days when Ymir lived' (*Ar var alda, þat er Ymir bygði*); the version in the *Snorra Edda* reads, however, 'when nothing was' (*þat er ecci var*). Snorri's version has been generally considered as the more original, even though it is reminiscent of Genesis 1,2 (*terra . . . erat . . . vacua*); *Vafþrúðnismál* 29, 30 refers to another proto-giant, Aurgelmir, whom Snorri (*Gylfaginning* 4) identifies as being the frost giants' name for Ymir, previously mentioned in *Vafþrúðnismál* 28. – According to Snorri, there were two antipoles even before the creation of the world: the icy Niflheim and the fiery Muspell. The rivers Élivágar (*Gylfaginning* 3 names them as Svǫl, Gunnþrá, Fjǫrm, Fimbulþul, Slíðr, Hríð, Sylgr, Ylgr, Víð, Leiptr, Gjǫll) subsequently fill Ginnungagap with poisonous frozen mist. The heat from Muspell, which meets the rime, causes it to melt and leads to the genesis of Ymir, an idea which Snorri appears to have taken from *Vafþrúðnismál* 31. Ymir is fed by the cow, Auðumla, which itself feeds on the rime, thus licking Buri, the forefather of the gods, free from the ice. Buri is the father of Burr who, together with the giant-daughter Bestla, begets the gods Odin, Vili and Vé, who then kill Ymir and create the earth from his flesh (*Vafþrúðnismál* 21, *Grímnismál* 40; *Gylfaginning* 7): from his bones they make the mountains, the sky from his skull, the seas from his blood. The entire giant tribe, whose existence is obviously presupposed seeing that the gods are descended from the giants through Bestla, drown in Ymir's blood, all that is except for Bergelmir (*Vafþrúðnismál* 35; *Gylfaginning* 6). When the three gods created the world from Ymir's body (*Grímnismál* 40, 41 adds that the trees are made from his hair, Midgard from his brows, and the clouds from his brain; → cosmology), they took two tree trunks from which they created the first human couple, Ask and Embla (→ anthropogony). Alongside these North Germanic (or more cautiously: Eddic) concepts of the creation, Schier has tried to interpret an aquatic cosmogony from the lifting of the earth in *Vǫluspá* 4,1 (*Aðr Burs synir bíǫðom um ypþo*); however, this inconclusive passage would be the only Germanic source and it can therefore have played no significant role. – Whereas primary sources are sparse, Germanic cosmogony has numerous equivalents in other cultures: the parallelism between the hermaphrodite figures Tuisto/Ymir and the Indian forefather (Sanskrit Yama, Avestic Yima) has repeatedly been shown, but correlation to the three generation succession of the protoplasts (Buri-Burr-Odin) with the killing of the forefathers can also be found in Greek, Phonecian, Iranian and Babylonian mythologies (Littleton). Even the creation of the world from the body of a proto-being finds equivalents world-wide.

F. R. Schröder, 'Germanische Schöpfungsmythen' (GRM 19) 1931; K. Schier, 'Die Erdschöpfung aus dem Urmeer' (*Festschrift Leyen*) Munich 1963; J. de Vries, *Altgermanische Religionsgeschichte*, Berlin [3]1970; G. S. Littleton, 'The "Kingship in Heaven" Theme' (*Myth and Law among the Indo-Europeans*) Berkeley etc. 1970; J. S. Martin, 'Ar vas alda' (*Speculum Norroenum. Studies Turville-Petre*) Odense 1981; L. Lönnroth, 'Iorð fannz æva né upphiminn' (*Speculum Norroenum. Studies Turville-Petre*) Odense 1981.

cosmology. Only the Nordic sources give us a complete view of the world, and even if Snorri does decorate this picture in his *Edda* with numerous details of non-Germanic origin, confirmation of the most important evidence in the *Edda* is nonetheless found in other sources. – The part of the world inhabited by men is called → Midgard; the gods have their fortress a short distance away in → Asgard. Outside the regions inhabited by men lies → Utgard, where the demons live, in the east, separated from Midgard by rivers, lies → Jǫtunheim, in the north and under Midgard is the realm of the dead → Hel. The fact that the south, where the fiery → Muspell lay before the creation of the world, also presents a danger, is most likely a later concept which derives from the influence of Manichaeic religions. Originally the south was associated with life and salvation as is clear from the Bronze Age burial mounds which open towards the south (→ burial customs). – The centre of the cosmic system is the world tree → Yggdrasill whose roots reach out to the ends of the inhabited world. According to archaic ideas the world tree is the support of the sky; similarly, the idea of a pillar propping up the heavens in → Irminsûl was prevalent among Continental Germanic peoples. Only in later sources, which had been influenced by Christianity, did the heavens, connected to earth by the bridge → Bifrǫst, become the dwelling place of the gods. The locations of Asgard as well as → Valhǫll, which had originally been thought of as being in Hel, were transferred into the heavens. The known world is surrounded by a sea in which the Midgard-serpent coils itself around the world. Not only Snorri but also the authors of later saga literature have tried time and again to reconcile this native Germanic cosmology with the mythological elements heard about on journeys, as well as with the ideas conveyed by scholarly Christian representation. This led to numerous varying interpretations of mythological geography; → Other world.

W. Grönbech, *Kultur und Religion der Germanen*, Darmstadt [5]1954; J. de Vries, *Altgermanische Religionsgeschichte*, Berlin [3]1970; R. L. M. Derolez, *Götter und Mythen der Germanen*, Wiesbaden 1974.

creation myth → cosmogony.

cremation of the dead can be seen as typical for the pagan Germanic peoples. It began to prevail from the beginning of the older Bronze Age (c.1300 B.C.) onwards although inhumation may be found throughout the period as well. There is evidence of various forms of cremation in the Viking Age (→ inhumation burial, → boat burial). The oldest literary evidence for cremation in Germanic times is found around 100 A.D. in Tacitus (*Germania* 27, 1) who records how the dead person is buried together with weapons and a horse in a burial mound. In late heathen times there are numerous literary examples of cremation, especially in the works of Saxo (*Gesta Danorum* I, 27; III, 74; V, 156; VI, 214; VIII, 264) and Snorri (*Heimskringla* Prologue; *Ynglinga saga* 8, 9, 13, 16, 19), more seldom in the saga literature (*Örvar-Odds saga* 31, 32, 41; *Vǫlsunga saga* 31; *Norna-Gests Þáttr* 9) and in skaldic poetry. The detailed description of the Arab Ibn Fadhlan, who was present at a cremation ceremony of the Varangians on the Volga at the beginning of the 10th century, is most interesting.

In mythology, cremation is encountered at → Baldr's funeral (Snorri, *Gylfaginning* 33) when the dead god is cremated on board his ship.

The influence of the church on the South and West Germanic peoples meant that cremation here decreased dramatically after Christianization whereas in Scandinavia – obviously as a result of the example from the south – inhumation was more usual than cremation even before the conversion.

cult objects are objects which were used in religious cults and which we know from archaeological finds as well as from pictorial representations. They are among the most important sources of religious history, although they only rarely reveal which god they favour or in whose cult they were used.

Among the oldest cult objects known are stone circles and ship-settings. From pictorial representations supported by archaeological evidence, lures and cult axes are known as cult objects from the Bronze Age. Ships, found on rock carvings, were also probably cult objects. The function of little bronze figures, which may represent worshippers but perhaps portray gods, is unknown. In contrast to this, carts with a purely religious function such as the Trundholm sun-chariot may have played a role in processions as Tacitus records concerning the cult of → Nerthus. The origins of the Iron Age → wooden gods found in Denmark, England and Germany are found on a lower plane of religious life. Drinking horns and cauldrons may also be counted as cult objects even if the religious link of the individual objects has not always been identified with absolute certainty. Bracteates are not as important as cult objects since they have more significance as amulets than as cult objects, even though in most cases a link can be made to a particular god (Odin); the case is similar to the amulet-like miniature Thor's hammers (→ Mjǫllnir). Small statues of gods (of Freyr, Thor) can be found in late pagan times, but real cult objects from this time have not come down to us. → Temple rings.

Dagfinnr (ON, 'day-finder' or 'day-sorcerer'?). Name of a dwarf in the *Þulur*. The name possibly refers to the belief that dwarfs (and similar beings) turn to stone when they are touched by sunlight. → dwarfs, → Alvíss.

Dagr (ON, 'day'). The personified day. Snorri understands Dagr to be this (*Gylfaginning* 16 following *Vafþrúðnismál* 25) when he calls him the son of → Nótt 'night' and of → Dellingr. Apart from the sources given, Dagr seldom appears in the *Eddas*. *Hyndluljóð* mentions him as being the husband of Thora, and in the fragment of the *Alsvinnsmál* he rides the horse called Drasill. Snorri also mentions (*Skáldskaparmál* 62) that Dagr is the ancestor of the line of the Dǫglingar, to which the hero Helgi Hundingsbani, who is in turn killed by a certain Dagr in a possibly cult context, also belongs (*Helgakviða Hundingsbana* II). Höfler deduced from the existence of Dagr and the Dǫglingar a mythological figure *Daguz, whom he considered to have been a personification of day and of light and was venerated by the Suebi. According to Höfler, after the migration of the Angles to Britain, this Dagr of the Suebi tribe was called Suebi-Dagr, Anglo-Saxon Swæfdæg, from which the ON name → Svipdagr developed.

O. Höfler, 'Das Opfer im Semnonenhain' (*Edda, Skalden, Saga. Festschrift F. Genzmer*) Heidelberg 1952; F. R. Schröder, 'Svipdagsmal' (GRM 47) 1966.

R: Dagr appears as a youth on a white horse in P. N. Arbos' *Dag* (painting, 1874).

Dáinn (1) (ON, 'died'). A dwarf in *Vǫluspá* 13 and in a poem by Sigvatr Þorðarson (11th c.). In *Hyndluljóð* 7 he is named, together with another dwarf, Nabbi, as having made the boar Hildisvini. This is certainly in imitation of the dwarf Brokkr, who made the god Freyr's boar, Gullinborsti. In *Hávamál* 143 Dáinn appears as the representative of the elves, but an equation of dwarf = elf is not justifiable here because immediately afterwards the dwarfs are listed as separate entities. Dwarfnames are somewhat randomly used in poetry, understandably so, as all dwarf names are relatively young. Dáinn is, however, one of the very few dwarf names which appears other than in the *Þulur* and the catalogue of dwarfs given in the *Vǫluspá*, and hence may be older.

H. de Boor, 'Der Zwerg in Skandinavien' (*Festschrift Eugen Mogk*) Halle 1924.

Dáinn (2). One of the four stags which graze on the branches of the World-ash, Yggdrasill.

dark elves (ON dǫkkálfar). A group of → elves. Snorri divides the elves into two groups (*Gylfaginning* 16), dark elves and light elves. He calls the dark elves 'blacker than pitch' and says they are very different from the light elves. – Presumably, the awareness that traditionally various mythological beings were grouped together under the term elves led Snorri to attempt to systematize them according to categories of Christian folklore. Grimm therefore may have been wrong when he thought that Snorri had identified the dark elves with devils and the light elves with angels. In fact, the dark elves and the light elves are two aspects of the same concept of demons of death which were closely related, in a similar way to that in which death and fertility cults were closely related.

J. Grimm, *Deutsche Mythologie*, Berlin [4]1875–78; E. O. G. Turville-Petre, *Myth and Religion of the North*, Westport 1964.

Darraðarljóð (ON, 'Dǫrruð's lay'). Despite frequently being called the 'lay of the Valkyries', Darraðarljóð does not belong to → mythological poetry. It refers to a historical event, namely the famous Battle of Clontarf (near Dublin) on Good Friday 1014 when an Irish and a Viking army met each other, a battle in which both the victorious Irish king Brian (hence the other name for it, Brian's battle)' and the Orcadian earl Sigurd were killed. The lay, which was composed in the Eddic metre *fornyrðislag*, appears to date from shortly after the battle as it was obviously composed still under the direct impressions left by the battle. It is possible that the skald was one associated with the Orcadian earls, a supposition supported by the place given to the frame-story. According to the accompanying prose text of the *Njáls saga* in which the lay is found, a man in Caithness/North Scotland saw 12 riders riding towards a house. Through a chink in the door he sees how these 12 → norns, of whom six are named (Hildr, Hjǫrþrimul, Sanngriðr, Svipul, Guðr and Gǫndul), weave the fates of the warriors in the battle on a loom made of human intestines, skulls, swords and spears. Finally they ride away again, six to the north and six to the south. – Although it would appear that the lay is named after the observer, Dǫrruð, this is deceptive and most unlikely as the name is repeatedly used in the lay in the kenning *vef darraðar* 'battle' (*vindum, vindum, vef darraðar* 'we are weaving, we are weaving the web of Dǫrruð'). The kenning, which also occurs already in Egil's *Hǫfuðlausn* 5, is usually interpreted as 'spear-web = battle' (hardly: 'fate'); *darraðr* is related in the meaning 'spear' to ON *darr*, OE *daroþ* 'spear'. *Darraðr* is however recorded in only a few similar doubtful kennings, such as *dafar Darraðar* 'army?' and *skúrum Darraðar* 'hail of spears'? As the word in these kennings is given in addition to this in the singular, interpretations such as 'web of spears' are most unlikely. Falk's suggestion, on the other hand, seems to be more convincing: he postulates a name for Odin Dǫrruðr instead of a **darraðr* 'spear', which would give more sense in all the cases given above. According to this theory, the lay itself would be named after Odin which would suit his function as the god of battles admirably. – It is mentioned elsewhere in ON heroic poetry that → norns or → valkyries determine the fate of the heroes. Nonetheless, the couching of the *Darraðarljóð* in the prose of the *Njáls saga* would appear to be secondary and derive from a misunderstanding; namely, the lay itself allows the supposition more of the weaving movement of the valkyries through the fighting warriors in the battle itself, rather than a weaving on a far-away loom (v. See).

ED: F. Jónsson, *Den Norsk-islandske Skjaldedigtningen*, B 1, Copenhagen 1912.

Eiríkr Magnússon, *Darraðarljóð*, Coventry 1910; A. Åkerblom, *Darraðarljóð* (Ord och Bild 25) 1916; H. Falk, *Odensheite*, Christiania 1924; A. J. Godheer, *Irish and Norse Traditions about the battle of Clontarf*, Haarlem 1938; A. Holtsmark, 'Vefr Darraðar' (MoM) 1939; F. Genzmer, 'Das Walkürenlied' (*ANF* 71) 1956; A. Holtsmark, 'Darraðarljóð' (*KLNM* 2) 1957; K. v. See, 'Das Walkürenlied' (*PBB* West 81) 1959; K. Schier, 'Darraðarljóð' (*KLL* 2) 1966; J. de Vries, *Altnordische Literaturgeschichte*, Berlin 21964; H. Uecker, 'Darraðarljóð' (*Hoops* 5) [2]1983; C. J. Clover, 'Darraðarljóð' (*DicMA* 4) 1984; R. Poole, 'Darraðarljóð 2' (MoM) 1985; G. Kreutzer, 'Darraðarljóð' (*LexMA* 3), 1986.

R: Thomas Gray, *Fatal Sisters* (in: *Poems*, 1775); J. G. Herder, *Die Todesgöttinnen* (in: *Volkslieder*, 1778/79); G. Mackay Brown, *An Orkney Tapestry*, 1969; the lay may also have influenced Shakespeare's *Macbeth*.

Darri (ON). A dwarf in the *Fjǫlsvinnsmál* 34; → Dǫrri.

death and life after death. Death did not mean the absolute end for the Germanic peoples but rather the transition into a different kind of existence. This is obvious from the grave forms from earliest times to the end of heathendom. However, the → burial customs give no information about the exact kind of life after death the Germanic peoples believed in, nor do they answer the question of what form the continued existence took, whether the form of a → soul or else as a physical entity.

It is not possible to generalize about Germanic concepts of life after death. The belief in the realm of the dead → Hel as given in Medieval sources (in particular Snorri) was already influenced by Christian and classical concepts, so that the interpretation of Hel as a realm of the dead populated by shadowy souls is hardly applicable for the heathen Germanic peoples. Apart from this belief, Medieval literature also speaks of a belief in → Valhall which appears to be rooted in ancient Germanic concepts. Another equally old concept is the journey of the dead into another world by ship, a concept well-documented by the numerous ships' graves (→ boat burial) in Scandinavia.

Detailed investigations since the beginning of the 20th century (Schreuer, Neckel, Klare) have led to the insight that it is extremely unlikely, at least for the late heathen period, that the North Germanic peoples had a dualistic belief, i.e. a distinct division between the decomposing body of the dead person and the further existence of his soul. The extant sources suggest that the concept was rather of the living corpse. Although saga literature (written 200–500 years after Christianization) is otherwise extremely unreliable for heathen beliefs, these sources do show unanimity, particularly with regard to these concepts, so widely divergent from Christian thought. Admittedly, they may be strongly influenced by the folklore of Medieval Iceland. Nevertheless we may assume that the concept does indeed reflect heathen beliefs.

Christian influence and literary expression of the heathen belief results in the following picture of the living dead in the grave: the dead person is alive and lives in the grave with full physical qualities. He is directly in touch with the world of the living; he prophesies what will happen in the future, defends his burial mound against grave robbers and terrorises his surroundings as a → *draugr*. He can be forced by the living using magic to give prophesies (*Hávamál* 157; *Baldrs draumar* 4; *Grógaldr* 1). The fact that the needs of the dead correspond to those of the living speaks in favour of the concept of a physical life after death, namely that he suffers from cold and wet (*Helgakviða Hundingsbana* II, 54) and is hungry and thirsty. The living dead looks exactly like his corpse, so that a drowned man appears to be totally wet through (*Eyrbyggja saga, Laxdœla saga*), those who have been slain appear bloody and complete with their wounds (*Gunnlaugs saga; Helgakviða Hundingsbana* II 44, 46). – Although in these cases the exact form of this appearance serves literary purposes, they nonetheless have their justification as remnants of the heathen belief in the dead.

In spite of the monistic concept of the dead in Germanic beliefs, it would be wrong to speak of the total lack of a belief in a soul. It is simply limited to that of the living person (→ *fylgja*). On the other hand, the dead live on in physical form as described above, as well as in their deeds, their fame and their descendants, apparent in the frequent occurrence of the tradition of transferring a dead man's name to a grandson.

H. Schreuer, 'Das Recht der Toten' (*Zeitschrift für vergleichende Rechtswissenschaft* 33 & 34) 1916 & 1917; H.-J. Klare, 'Die Toten in der altnordischen Literatur' (*APhSc* 8) 1933/34; R. T. Christiansen, *The Dead and the Living*, Oslo 1946; W. Grönbech, *Kultur und Religion der Germanen*, Darmstadt [5]1954; F. Ström, 'Döden och de döda' (*KLNM* 3) 1958; E. O. G. Turville-Petre, *Myth and Religion of the North*, Westport 1975; Å. V. Ström, H. Biezais, *Germanische und baltische Religion*, Stuttgart 1975.

death penalty. The question whether the death penalty had a sacred origin is still much disputed. The problem is whether the execution of a criminal can be understood to be → human sacrifice to the insulted gods (as the guarantors of cosmic order) or not. The forms of the death penalty in heathen Germanic tribes are the same as the forms of sacrifice, which leads to the surmise that the origin of the death penalty was indeed probably sacral despite all objections (Ström, Sandklef).

Hanging, which Tacitus (*Germania* 12) refers to as the death penalty for traitors and which was the punishment for theft in Medieval times, is recorded as being the sacrifice to Odin (→ Odin's self-sacrifice, → Víkarr), and is also recorded as being the main form of sacrifice at the great sacrificial festival at → Uppsala so that there can be hardly any doubt about the original cult relevance of this form of death.

Tacitus calls drowning in a bog the death penalty for cowards and for some sexual offences. The German and Danish bog men confirm the existence of this form of death, although it is not always possible to conclude from the form of killing exactly what the motive was, whether punishment or sacrificial depositions, which are also recorded in the sources. Drowning as a purely sacrificial death is recorded by Tacitus in his discussion of the → Nerthus cult (*Germania* 42) and it is also mentioned by Adam of Bremen (*Gesta Hammaburgensis Ecclesiae Pontificum* IV, 27; Scholion 138) in connection with the sacrifice at Uppsala where people were drowned in a well close to the temple.

It is similarly unclear in the case of other modes of execution whether they are a result of the death penalty or else human sacrifice. These include the carving of the → blood eagle and the breaking of a man's back on a stone, which is, however, only recorded in one saga.

L. Weiser-Aall, 'Zur Geschichte der altgermanischen Todesstrafe und Friedlosigkeit' (*ARW* 30) 1933; F. Ström, *On the sacral origin of the Germanic dath penalties*, Stockholm 1942; D. Strömbäck, 'Hade de germanska dödsstraffen sakralt ursprung' (*Saga och Sed*) 1942; A. Sandklef, 'De Germanska dödsstraffen, Tacitus och Mossliken' (*Fornvännen* 39) 1944; H. Jankuhn, *Archäologische Bemerkungen zur Glaubwürdigkeit des Tacitus in der Germania*, Göttingen 1966; J. de Vries, *Altgermanische Religionsgeschichte*, Berlin [3]1970; D. J. Ward, 'The threefold death' (*Myth and Law among the Indo-Europeans*) Berkeley 1970; H. Beck, 'Germanische Menschenopfer in der literarischen Überlieferung' (H. Jankuhn, *Vorgeschichtliche Heiligtümer*) Göttingen 1970; F. Ström, 'Sakrala element i straff' (*KLNM* 17) 1972.

dedication to Odin can be defined as the personal commitment of someone to Odin. Such dedications are quite frequently referred to in Old Norse literature and almost form a stereotypical feature in heroic poetry. Höfler dealt in great detail with the most important examples of Odinic heroes, including Víkarr, Oðinkár, Starkaðr and Helgi. The ambiguous relationship of these heroes to Odin is characteristic. He protects them in battle and gives them victory, but they are then finally dedicated to him in death. The warriors did not cut their hair as an outward sign of their dedication to the god, a feature which occurs in names such as Haddingus, Víkarr, Oðinkár.

One form of dedication to Odin might be at the bottom of Snorri's euhemeristically marked report of Odin's warriors (*Ynglinga saga* 6) → berserks.

O. Höfler, *Germanisches Sakralkönigtum*, Tübingen etc. 1952.

Dellingr (ON, 'the shining one' or 'the famous one'?). A dwarf in the *Þulur*.

C. N. Gould, 'Dwarf-Names' (*PMLA* 44) 1929; J. de Vries, *Altnordisches etymologisches Wörterbuch*, Leiden [2]1970.

Deusonianus → Hercules Deusonianus.

Díar (ON, 'gods'). Snorri (*Ynglinga saga* 2 and 6) gives this name to a group of 12 priests who, according to his euhemerisitic depiction, ruled with Odin in Asgard and then in Scandinavia. The name Díar is only found in Snorri's version of the migration of the → Æsir, but the word was already used in the 10th century by the skald Kormákr in a kenning for the mead of the skalds *día fjǫrðr* 'fjord of the gods'. The expression Díar is probably borrowed from Old Irish (Old Irish *día* 'god') and is related etymologically to the ON god Týr. Since Kormákr was of Irish descent on his mother's side, we may suppose that he first introduced Díar as a foreign loanword which was then used by Snorri who knew and quoted Kormák's stanza.

R. Lid, 'Díar' (*KLNM* 3) 1958.

dioscuri. The twin brothers fathered by Zeus with Leda in classical mythology and called Kastor and Polydeukes in Greek or Castor and Pollux in Latin. However, the term dioscuri is used in a more general sense for all divine twin brothers who occur in the mythologies of most Indo-European peoples. Lack of source material made it uncertain for a long time whether the Germanic tribes also had a tradition of dioscuri. However, there are various indications of the existence of such divine twin brothers especially in Germanic antiquity. The oldest allusion is found in the writings of the Greek historian Timaios (3rd century B.C.) who reported that the 'Celts' (i.e. Germanic tribes) on the North Sea coast were particularly devoted to the dioscuri. A short passage in Tacitus (Germania 43, 12ff.) where he mentions the veneration of a divine pair of brothers who were called → Alcis, and whom he identified expressly with Castor and Pollux, is even better evidence for the worship of the dioscuri.

Apart from the single direct reference to a veneration of the Alcis other sources point to the existence of dioscuri among the Germanic peoples. Even if the uncertain evidence of possible twin gods on Bronze Age rock carvings is disregarded (Schwarz), the little statuettes showing the figures of two gods from the Bronze Age (such as one from Zealand) should still be borne in mind.

A mythical set of brothers repeatedly appears in the tribal legends of various

Germanic peoples, and a pair such as this led the migration of the Langobards from Scandinavia (Ibur and Aio according to Paulus Diaconus, Aggi and Ebbi according to Saxo Grammaticus VIII, 284f.) and the Anglo-Saxons conquered England under the leadership of two brothers, Hengist and Horsa (Bede, *Historia ecclesiastica* I, 15; Geoffrey of Monmouth VI, 9f.). In the tribal legend of the Vandals, too, the brothers Raos and Raptos are the leaders of the Astings (Dio Cassius 71, 12).

Not every couple of brothers in myths and heroic tales should be interpreted, however, as being dioscuri. Olsen and de Vries wanted to interpret the Haddingjar as deities, who were originally dioscuri, but this seems to be as wrong as the attempt to consider the Germanic gods Freyr and Njǫrðr to be twins.

In Greek mythology the dioscuri were considered to be deities in the shape of horses. This could also be applicable to the corresponding Germanic gods as both the etymology of Tacitus' Alcis as well as the names of the Anglo-Saxon leaders Hengist and Horsa suggest a horse-shape. Confirmation for this can be found in Migration Age pictorial documents (metal helmets, bracteates, pictorial stones) where the depiction of human figured dioscuri pairs alternate with those shaped like horses (Hauck).

Even though we know little about the function and position of the Germanic dioscuri – since Hauck's interpretation of their aiding the god of battle, Odin, in helping warriors to victory is not an overly convincing hypothesis – the existence of dioscuri gods among Germanic peoples can nevertheless be assumed with great certainty.

F. Niedner, 'Die Dioskuren im Beowulf' (*ZfdA* 42) 1898; K. F. Johansson, 'Germ. Alcis (Germ. Dioskurer)' (*ANF* 35) 1919; J. Loewenthal, 'Cultgeschichtliche Fragen' (*PBB* 49) 1925; R. Meringer, 'Indogermanische Pfahlgötzen' (*Wörter und Sachen* 9) 1926; M. Olsen, *Stedsnavne og Gudeminner i Land*, Oslo 1929; A. H. Krappe, 'Les dieux jumeaux' (*APhSc* 6) 1931; E. Krüger, 'Die gallischen und die germanischen Dioskuren' (*Trierer Zeitschrift* 16 & 17/18) 1940 & 1941/42; R. Much, 'Aurvandils tá' (*Festschrift H. Seger*) Breslau 1934; H. Rosenfeld, 'Die vandalischen Alkes' (*GRM* 28) 1940; H. Neumann, 'Neue Beiträge zum altgermanischen Dioskurenglauben' (*Bonner Jahrbücher* 150) 1950; J. Sahlgren, 'Hednisk gudalära' (*NoB* 38) 1950; N. Wagner, 'Dioskuren, Jungmannschaften und Doppelkönigtum' (*ZfdPh* 79) 1960; H. Rosenfeld, 'Germanischer Zwillingsgottkult' (*Märchen. Festschrift für F. v. d. Leyen*) Munich 1963; W. Schwarz, 'Germanische "Dioskuren"?' (*Bonner Jahrbücher* 167) 1967; D. Ward, 'The Divine Twins' (*Folklore Studies* 19) 1968; H. Biezais, 'Die vermeintlichen germanischen Zwillingsgötter' (*Temenos* 5) 1969; J. de Vries, *Altgermanische Religionsgeschichte*, Berlin [3]1970; D. J. Ward, 'An Indo-European mythological theme' (*Indo-European and the Indo-Europeans*) Philadelphia 1970; K. Hauck, 'Bildforschung als historische Sachforschung' (*Festschrift H. Löwe*) Cologne, Vienna 1978; K. Hauck, 'Gemeinschaftsstiftende Kulte der Seegermanen' (*FmSt* 14) 1980; K. Hauck, 'Zur Ikonologie der Goldbrakteaten XXVIII' (*Jahrbuch des Römisch-Germanischen Zentralmuseums* 32) 1983; K. Hauck, 'Dioskuren' (*Hoops* 4) [2]1984.

dísablót (ON, 'sacrifice to the *dísir*'). This sacrifice to the → *dísir* is only recorded twice for the West Nordic region, in two rather unreliable Icelandic sagas from the middle of the 13th century. In *Víga-Glúms saga* 6 the *dísablót* is celebrated at a Norwegian farm at the beginning of winter (*af vetrnóttum*, i.e. mid-October). *Egilssaga* 44 also mentions an autumnal festival in Norway which is called a *dísablót*. The only account that both sagas give of the form of such a *dísablót* is that it was linked with a banquet. Even if these sources can only be seen as literary motifs, they nonetheless show that the Icelanders distanced themselves from this cult in their own history and localised the practice of the *dísablót* in Norway. Snorri Sturluson, writing at the beginning of the 13th century, also knew of the *dísablót* and in *Ynglinga saga* 33 he identifies it as similar to the cult at Uppsala in Sweden. Whatever Snorri says about the *dísablót* is only a supplement to the naming of the *dísablót* in the poem Ynglingatal (written by the skald Þjóðólfr ór Hvíni in the 9th century), in which the *dísablót* is obviously associated with the big cult celebrations held in → Uppsala, as Adam of Bremen describes them.

The expression → Dísarsalr in this context might indicate a more complex form of the cult and the existence of a temple. The literary sources allow the presumption that a cult of the *dísir* was more common in Sweden than in West Nordic regions, although place-names which show that the *dísir* cult was indeed ancient are not only to be found in Sweden (Diseberg, Disevi), but also in Norway (Disin).

F. Ström, *Diser, Nornor, Valkyrjor*, Stockholm 1954; J. de Vries, *Altgermanische Religionsgeschichte*, Berlin [3]1970; E. O. G. Turville-Petre, *Myth and Religion of the North*, Westport 1975.

Dísarsalr (ON, 'hall of the *dísir*') was a temple in Uppsala which served the cult of the *dísir*, according to Snorri (*Ynglinga saga* 33). The name is also found in younger sagas such as *Hervarar saga* (7). Whether this temple was identical with the great temple at Uppsala cannot be determined because of the few brief comments in the sources.

Disathing (Old Swedish disaþing) → Disting. Also recorded as a place name in Swedish Uppland.

dísir (ON dís, pl. *dísir*; Old Swedish dis). A kind of female (fertility?) deity, perhaps related to the Old Saxon → Idisi mentioned in the First Merseburg Charm. Both Swedish and Norwegian place-names suggest a belief in *dísir* in heathen Scandinavia and a sacrifice associated with it (→ *dísablót*): Norwegian Disin from older Dísavin '*dísir*-meadow' (→ Idisiaviso in Tacitus), Swedish Diseberg, Disevid, Disasen and Disaþing (from the place at which the Thing was held at the time of the *dísablót* ('sacrifice to the *dísir*'); → Disting. Two sagas from the 13th century onwards tell of a *dísablót* which was celebrated on the farms at the beginning of winter, although the accounts of a close connection between the Swedish royal house of the Ynglingar and the *dísir* (*Ynglingatal* 12 and Snorri's *Ynglinga saga* 19 and 29) seem to be more reliable sources. They tell the following. Agni is killed by his wife, Logadís. Aðils falls to his death at the *dísablót*, just as he is riding around the *Dísarsalr*. – The *dísir* seem to have still been worshipped in Norway at the end of the heathen era, as the epithet of the skald Þorbjǫrn dísarskáld seems to prove; there is only one fragment of a lay about Thor composed by this skald, used and thus kept for posterity by Snorri, but his name probably goes back to a piece of poetry he composed dedicated to the *dísir*. The *dísir* are frequently mentioned in Old Norse prose literature, mostly in the meaning of fetch-like women who appear in dreams (→ spá*dísir*). – Several of the Eddic sources might lead us to conclude that the *dísir* were valkyrie-like guardians of the dead, and indeed in *Guðrúnarkviða* I 19 the valkyries are even called *Herjans dísir* 'Odin's *dísir*'. The *dísir* are explicitly called dead women in *Atlamál* 28 and a secondary belief that the *dísir* were the souls of dead women (→ *fylgjur*) also underlies the → *landdísir* of Icelandic folklore.

In addition to this, ON *dís* also appears simply as a term for 'woman', just as the possibly related OHG *itis*, Old Saxon *idis*, Anglo-Saxon *ides* for 'woman' was perhaps used also to denote a kind of goddess. Therefore, it is problematic to draw conclusions from names such as Vanadís = Freyja (*Gylfaginning* 34) and ǫndurdís 'ski-*dís*' for Skaði, since *dís* could easily simply mean 'woman'.

The actual role of the *dísir* can only be defined with difficulty, and even the times of sacrifice are not particularly helpful in our quest, as they give no conclusive information since the *dísablót* (recorded in late sources) in Norway was held at the beginning of winter, but the Disting was apparently held in Sweden at the beginning of February. The Anglo-Saxon festival *mōdraniht* ('mothers' night') is recorded as having taken place at the beginning of the new year, and this could be best brought into connection with the West Germanic → matron cult. As the function of the matrons was also extremely varied – fertility goddesses, personal guardians, but also warrior-goddesses – the belief in the *dísir*, like the belief in valkyries, norns and matrons, may be considered to be different manifestations of a belief in a number of female (half-?) goddesses.

E. Brate, 'Disen' (*Zeitschrift für deutsche Wortforschung* 13) 1911/12; F. Ström, *Diser, nornor, valkyrjor*, Stockholm 1954; F. Ström, 'Diser' (KLNM 3) 1958; J. de Vries, *Altgermanische Religionsgeschichte*, Berlin ³1970; H. Birkhan, *Germanen und Kelten*, Vienna 1970.

R: in D. Hardy's painting *The Dises*, the *dísir* are depicted like valkyries.

***dísir* sacrifice** → *dísablót*.

Disting, also Disaþing (Old Swedish, 'thing at the time of the sacrifice to the *dísir*'). A Thing which took place at the beginning of February at → Uppsala, originally getting its name from a heathen sacrifice to the → *dísir* and retaining it after Christianisation. The Disting at Uppsala and the → *dísablót* ('sacrifice to the *dísir*') recorded as having taken place in West Nordic regions confirm, as do Norwegian and Swedish place names, the cult worship of the *dísir* in Scandinavia. The place name Disaþing in Swedish Uppland proves that there was also a Disting at other places apart from at Uppsala at some point.

K. F. Söderwall, *Ordbok öfver Svenska Medeltids-Spraket*, Lund 1900–1918; J. de Vries, *Altgermanische Religionsgeschichte*, Berlin ³1970.

dog. Dogs played virtually no role in Germanic religious observance. They were hardly ever used as sacrificial animals, even if, according to Adam von Bremen's description of the → Uppsala sacrifice, dogs were supposedly sacrificially hung up there. In mythology only the dog of hell → Garmr is known: he is the guard over the entrance to Hel.

dǫkkálfar (ON) → dark elves.

Doepler, Karl Emil (1824–1905). Painter, illustrator and costume designer, created the disputed costumes for R. Wagner's *Ring* in the Bayreuth Nibelungenfestspiel 1878. He tried to design historically and archaeologically documented imitations of Viking Age clothes. Wagner was not satisfied with the result and later productions of the *Ring* have only occasionally attempted to achieve historical accuracy.

Doepler's son Emil (the Younger, born 1855) was also interested in Nordic mythology and created the illustrations to W. Ranisch's Art Nouveau picture volume about Germanic mythology (E. Doepler, W. Ranisch, *Walhall*, Berlin 1901).

Dǫrri (ON, perhaps 'spear-fighter'?). A dwarf in *Fjǫlsvinsmál* 32.

Dǫrruðr (ON, 'the spear-fighter', from *darr-Hǫðr). Probably a name for Odin found in the kennings *vefr Darraðar* 'Dǫrrud's web, battle', *dafar Darraðar* 'army', *skúrir Darraðar* 'spear-rain'. However, in all the given cases the possibility that the kenning is based on a **darraðr* 'spear' has been considered. This, however, is not found anywhere in prose. Particularly in the first kenning given above, the most likely solution in association with the → *Darraðarljóð* is that it is Odin in his function as god of the battle and fallen warriors. Even from the etymology this name fits as the spear is Odin's attribute elsewhere, too.

H. Falk, *Odensheite*, Christiania 1924; A. Holtsmark, 'Vefr Darraðar' (MoM) 1939; F. Jónsson, *Lexicon poeticum*, Copenhagen ²1966 (s.v. *darraðr*); J. de Vries, *Altnordisches etymologisches Wörterbuch*, Leiden ²1977.

Dofri (ON). A giant in the *Þulur*. In the *Flateyjarbók* (*Haralds þáttr hárfagra*) he is the inhabitant of the mountain Dofrafjall from where the name of the giant would appear to derive. A translation as 'the lazy one' would also be possible.

Dolgr (ON, 'enemy; troll'). A dwarf in the *Þulur*.

Dólgþrasir (ON, 'the hostile fighting one'). A dwarf in the *Vǫluspá* 15. In the version of the *Snorra Edda* he is called Dólgþvari 'enemy drill'. Dólg- is found in the personal names Dólgfinnr. Þrasurr is a name for Odin.

Dólgþvari → Dólgþrasir.

dolmen. Chambered tombs from the pre-Germanic Western European megalithic culture were erected from huge boulders or stone slabs and were often mistakenly considered as late as the 19th century to be Old Germanic sacrificial tables or else 'Druid altars'.

Dómaldi. The skald Þjóðólfr mentions the Swedish king Dómaldi Vísbursson from the house line of the Ynglings in his poem *Ynglingatal* 5, where he merely records that the Swedes killed their own king Dómaldi in the hope of receiving subsequent good harvests. In his *Ynglinga saga* 15 Snorri comments as follows: 'In Dómaldi's days there was a lot of hunger in Sweden. The Swedes sacrificed oxen, next year people, but neither helped. The chieftains conferred and agreed that their king Dómaldi was to blame for the bad harvests and that they should sacrifice him in order to regain good harvests. They should attack and kill him and redden the altars with his blood, and they did this.'

The Latin *Historia Norvegiae* reports somewhat deviantly that Dómaldi was hanged as a sacrifice to the goddess Ceres (probably Freyja is meant here). This hanging would indicate, however, a sacrifice to Odin more than anything else.

The concept that the king was personally responsible for good harvests and peace is the basis of the institution of → sacred kingship. There are several examples of the sacrifice of a king for bad harvests in the *Ynglinga saga*, and such a sacrifice is also documented for the Burgundians as early as the 4th century.

W. Grönbech, *Kultur und Religion der Germanen*, Darmstadt ⁵1954; F. Ström, 'Kong Domalde i Svitjod och "kungalyckan"' (*Saga och Sed*) 1967; J. de Vries, *Altgermanische Religionsgeschichte*, Berlin ³1970; L. Lönnroth, 'Dómaldi's death and the myth of sacral kingship' (*Structure and Meaning in Old Norse Literature*) Odense 1986.

R: the fresco in the Swedish National Museum in Stockholm by Carl Larsson, *Midvinterblot* ('Midwinter sacrifice', 1911–15), shows the sacrifice of Dómaldi.

Donar. The southern Germanic equivalent of the Germanic god of thunder who is called → Thor in the north, and Þunor in Old English. The southern Germanic sources are much sparser than those referring to Thor. Veneration of Donar is only indirectly documented for Roman times on the votive inscriptions to → Hercules. It is however not always absolutely certain that these do indeed address the Germanic god. The translation of the Roman names for the days of the week, which renders *Dies Jovi* as OHG *Donarestag*, Middle Low German *Dunredach*, Frisian *Thunresdey*, Anglo-Saxon *Thunresdæg*, suggests a veneration of Donar. The alternating identification of a Germanic god with two different Roman gods as in the case of Donar = Hercules is a result of the *interpretatio romana*, in which the external attributes of the gods were apparently the criteria of major importance in identifying the gods of one culture with another: Donar's hammer was considered to correspond to Hercules' club, and their respective strength in their fights against monsters supported this identification conclusively. In Tacitus (*Germania* 9, *Annales* II, 12) the name Hercules is used to stand for Donar. On the other hand, the fact that Jupiter could be used in place of Donar is the result of the *interpretatio germanica*. A determining factor here appears to have been the fact that they are chief gods, both of whom hurl lightning. The so-called Donar's oak which stood near Geismar (Hessen, Germany) and was felled at Boniface's instigation in 725 is actually called Jupiter's oak in the text.

Veneration of Donar is evident, although not well documented, for the post-Roman period by the Nordendorf clasp, on which alongside the gods Wodan and Logaþore Wigiþonar is also named. Further proof comes from a Saxon abjuration formula which names Thunaer, Wodan and Saxnôt.

There are numerous German place-names Donnersberge, clearly based on Donar, but they are not all necessarily places of cultic significance.

J. Grimm, *Deutsche Mythologie*, Berlin [4]1875–78; E. Mogk, 'Donar' (*Hoops* 1) 1911–13; J. de Vries, *Altgermanische Religionsgeschichte*, Berlin [3]1970.

(**Donner**). Richard Wagner's version of the Germanic god Donar/Thor in the opera *Das Rheingold*. The part is for a baritone voice.

Dóri (ON). A dwarf in the *Vǫluspá* 15. The name either means 'the damager' (to Old Saxon, Anglo-Saxon *derian*), or else to Faeroese *dori* 'peg'. Motz' explanation of Dóri as 'fool' to ON *dari*, MHG *tōre* 'fool' is not uninteresting.

L. Motz, 'New Thoughts on Dwarf-Names' (*FmSt* 7) 1973.

R: Dóri is one of the 13 dwarfs in J. R. R. Tolkien's novel, *The Hobbit* (1937).

dragon (OE *draca*, ON *dreki*, OHG. *traccho*). The concept of dragons is not at all limited to the Indo-Europeans, let alone the Germanic tribes. Dragons are mentioned in sources from the 8th century A.D., and there are frequent references to dragons in OE and ON, but also OHG literature, especially in heroic poetry (in *Beowulf*, *Nibelungenlied*, *Vǫlsunga saga*, *Fáfnismál*, and a few times in skaldic poetry). The notion of the dragon as a strong, warlike, fabulous creature was possibly derived from the dragon banners of the Roman army, whence it also made its way into the Welsh coat of arms. The word itself also stems from the same source and is derived from Latin *draco*, whilst the Germanic word for dragon (cf. ON *linnr*) has only survived in German *Lindwurm*. Even the dragonships, a class of big warship with dragonheads adorning the stems, were called *dreki* in ON. The fact that beam ends on stave churches are still decorated with dragon heads may be indicative of an ancient Germanic belief in the ability of dragons to avert or create evil.

In Germanic mythology as represented in Medieval Scandinavian sources, the dragon Níðhǫggr in *Vǫluspá* is probably derived from Medieval Christian visionary poetry, but Thor's fights with dragons, even the sea dragon Miðgarðsormr (→ Midgard serpent), have traits in common with similar fights in heroic poetry, and both may go back to more ancient Germanic beliefs.

Dragons are described as crawling creatures both in *Beowulf* and *Fáfnismál*, but flying dragons (*flugdreki*) are frequently mentioned in ON sagas.

O. Höfler, *Siegfried, Arminius und die Symbolik*, Vienna 1961; F. Wild, 'Drachen im Beowulf und andere Drachen' (*Sitzungsberichte der Österreichischen Akademie der Wissenschaften* 238/5) 1962; C. Lofmark, 'Der rote Drache der Waliser' (*Festgabe* O. *Höfler*), Vienna 1976; J. A. Tally, *The Dragons Progress*, Denver 1983; R. Simek, 'Drache. Germanische Mytholgie, Kultur und Sagenüberlieferung' (*LexMA* 3) 1986.

draugr (ON). The living dead who in folk-belief led a very real life after dying and being buried in a burial mound and who consequently represented a threat to the living. In the Middle Ages the idea of there being living dead in burial mounds became a popular literary topos, and the sagas are full of descriptions of these wraiths who might involve grave robbers in fights and who became a threat to both men and animals especially at midwinter. The ultimate death of the *draugr* was usually achieved by cutting off his head, placing it on the *draugr*'s buttocks and then burning him. The ash was then buried away from human habitation (*Grettis saga* 35, *Eyrbyggja saga* 63).

This ghost-like figure in Medieval literature is the result of the many ancient beliefs in a life of the dead continuing in full vitality and physical presence (→ death and life after death), which merged with the knowledge of what a corpse looked like when it began to decompose. The belief in the final banishment of a *draugr* by fire proves that it was certainly an ancient belief. – The word *draugr* belongs to the Indo-Germanic root **dreugh*, and originally meant 'harmful spirit'.

H.-J. Klare, 'Die Toten in der altnordischen Literatur' (*APhSc* 8) 1933/34; E. O. G. Turville-Petre, *Myth and Religion of the North*, Westport 1975, Å. V. Ström, H. Biezais, *Germanische und baltische Religion*, Stuttgart 1975.

Draupnir (1) (ON, 'the dripper'). Odin's golden arm ring, from which another eight equally heavy rings drip every ninth night (Snorri, *Gylfaginning* 48, *Skáldskaparmál* 33). According to Snorri, it was forged by the dwarfs Brokkr and Sindri like the other jewels belonging to gods. Odin laid Draupnir on the pyre at Baldr's funeral, and on one occasion Baldr is named as the owner of the ring, too (*Skáldskaparmál* 5). Saxo mentions a magic ring in his version of Baldr's myth as well; this ring increases the owners' riches and could come from the same tradition. In skaldic poetry Draupnir is mentioned many times – mostly as a kenning for gold – but it is never said to which god it belongs. In the *Edda* the name Draupnir admittedly never occurs, but the ring and its properties are described (*Skírnismál* 21).

The role of the ring Draupnir has been seen to be a mythical counterpart to the → temple ring, and therefore Odin would be the appropriate owner of the mythical oath-ring. Höfler suggested that the ring was a symbol of sovereignty. Hauck was able to prove that the god's ring was depicted on a number of Norwegian bracteates from the 5th to 7th centuries, and that it was a symbol of power for Odin, who laid it on the pyre of the dead Baldr as a legitimation of power towards the goddess of the Underworld Hel. Odin is already to be seen on early Viking Age Gothland pictorial stones riding his horse Sleipner and bearing the ring. These depictions include – according to Hauck's interpretation – Odin with the ring as a symbol of power, Baldr's arrival and acceptance by Hel by producing the ring. Even if this detailed interpretation will not remain undisputed, the by no means seldom occurrence of the ring (sometimes as a knotted ring) in pictures of gods on bracteates and amulets is proof of the mythical relevance of this symbol in Migration age Germania, even if the name Draupnir is relatively young and a product of Viking Age literary embellishment.

O. Höfler, 'Das germanische Kontinuitätsproblem' (*Historische Zeitschrift* 157) 1938; J. de Vries, *Altgermanische Religionsgeschichte*. Berlin [3]1970; K. Hauck, 'Gemeinschaftsstiftende Kulte der Seegermanen' (*FmSt* 14) 1980.

R: J. R. R. Tolkien, *The Lord of the Rings* (novel, 1954/55).

Draupnir (2) ('dripper' of rings, hence 'goldsmith'?). A dwarf in *Vǫluspá* 15 and in the *Þulur*.

Drífa (ON, 'flurry of snow'). A giantess (?) in the mythical genealogy of the progenitor Fornjótr mentioned in the version of *Hversu Nóregr byggðisk* where Þorri, Fǫnn, Mjǫll and Drífa are the children of King Snær. As all of these names personify aspects of winter, it is possible that originally the genealogy was of frost giants.

Drǫfn (ON, 'wave'). A giantess, who is repeatedly said to be one of the daughters of the sea-giant Ægir and his wife Ran (*Skáldskaparmál* 58; Ormr, Einarr Gilsson, Kormákr). However, she is not mentioned by Snorri (*Skáldskaparmál* 22) among the nine → daughters of Ægir.

Drómi (ON, 'fetter'). According to Snorri (*Gylfaginning* 33), Drómi is the name of the second of the fetters with which the Æsir want to chain the wolf → Fenrir, but this rips just as the first one (Lœðing) does. Snorri cites the proverbial phrase 'to throw off the Drómi' which refers to the overcoming of severe difficulties. He probably did not invent the name himself.

Dúfa (ON, 'diveress' = 'wave'). One of the nine daughters of the sea-giant → Ægir and his wife Ran (*Skáldskaparmál* 22 and 58; Einarr Skúlason; *Þulur*); → daughters of Ægir.

Dúfr (ON). A dwarf in the *Vǫluspá* 15; probably 'the sleepy one' (to Norwegian *duva*).

Dulinn (ON, 'the hidden one'). A dwarf in the *Þulur*.

Dumbr (ON, 'the stupid one' or 'the dumb one'). A giant in the *Þulur*. Many of the Medieval Nordic giant names characterize the giants as slow, stupid or else ugly.

Dumézil, Georges (born 1900). French historian of religions who began (from 1939 onwards) to apply his theories, concerning the religions of Indo-Germanic peoples, onto the Germanic religion and as a result introduced a new direction of comparative mythology into scholarship which had already been prepared by F. R. Schröder independently from him. Dumézil's ideas, which became increasingly structuralist (or rather helped lead to structuralism) led subsequently to the development of the → Three Function Theory (1958) which he also based on Germanic mythology and which, in its outlines, is generally accepted nowadays. Dumézil repeatedly took a stance against the exaggerated criticism of Snorri's reliability as put forward by Mogk and Baetke.

Duneyrr (ON, 'the one with the downy (or brown) ears'). One of the four stags which graze in the branches of the world-ash Yggdrasill according to *Grímnismál* 13 (and Snorri, *Gylfaginning* 15).

Duraþrór (ON, 'slumber-boar'). One of the four stags who graze in the branches of the world-ash Yggdrasill, according to *Grímnismál* 13 (and Snorri, *Gylfaginning* 15 and the *Þulur*).

Durinn (ON). A dwarf in the *Vǫluspá* 10 and *Gylfaginning* 13. Etymologically the name possibly belongs to *dúra*, and as such would mean 'the sleepy one'. Should the short vowel be original, 'door-keeper' (to *dyrr*) would also be possible, or else a connection with Old Indian *dhvaras* 'demonic being'.

B. Ejder, 'Eine Vǫluspá-Stelle' (*Die Sprache* 22) 1976; J. de Vries, *Altnordisches Etymologisches Wörterbuch*, Leiden [2]1977.

Dúrnir (1) (ON, 'the sleeper'). A dwarf in the *Þulur*.

Dúrnir (2). A giant, only named in the *Þulur*.

Dvalarr (ON). A mythical stag named in the *Þulur* and probably identical with the deer → Dvalinn (2) mentioned in the *Grímnismál*.

Dvalinn (1) (ON, 'the slow one' or 'the sleeping one'). A dwarf (*Vǫluspá, Hávamál, Alvíssmál, Fáfnismál*; *Gylfaginning*), who is, according to *Fáfnismál*, the father of several norns. In the *Sǫrla þáttr* he is named as being one of the four smiths who made Freyja's necklace.

R: Dvalinn is one of the 13 dwarfs in J. R. R. Tolkien's novel, *The Hobbit* (1937).

Dvalinn (2). One of the four stags who, according to *Grímnismál* 33 (and Snorri, *Gylfaginning* 15) graze in the branches of the world-ash Yggdrasill. In the *Þulur* he is also to be found in the form Dvalarr.

dvergr (ON, 'dwarf') → dwarfs.

dwarfs (OE *dweorg*, ON *dvergr*, OHG *zwerc, gitwerc*). In folklore there is a belief in beings such as dwarfs, elves, trolls and giants which is on the whole independent from the higher forms of religion and actual mythological concepts. As these areas of folk-belief have even survived the Christianization of the Germanic peoples to all intents and purposes intact, the sources of the Christian era still give us an extremely usable impression of the concepts which the Germanic people had of these various beings. With regard to mythology the ON legendary sagas of the 14th and 15th centuries tell us more about dwarfs than the Eddas, as they belong to the standard inventory of such sagas, half believed in and half smiled at as stereotype fairy-tale elements belonging to such sagas. The names of dwarfs in the lists given in *Vǫluspá* and in the *Þulur* (which presumably go back to common sources) are a further source which enable us to find out more about the ideas concerning dwarfs. In these lists we find more than 100 names of dwarfs, nearly all of which are admittedly young and most are descriptive in some way.

Snorri equates the dwarfs with a sub-group of → elves, namely the *svartálfar*. In the *Hávamál* (143 and 160) we find dwarfs in the hierarchy of Æsir, elves and dwarfs. This would seem to correspond to their position in folk-belief. Whereas the elves seem to have played a certain role in the religious cult, the dwarfs are merely beings (mostly helpful) with whom people can associate as with their own kind. There is no suggestion in the source-texts that dwarfs were originally thought of as being particularly small. This is a concept which first appears in the sagas where they are described as being small and usually ugly. Their wisdom is much more characteristic and this is manifested in names such as → Alvíss, → Fjǫlsviðr, → Ráðsviðr. The dwarfs were thought of as being very skilful, particularly as smiths, as again numerous dwarf names suggest (Hanarr, Nýráðr, Næfr; Skirvir, Draupnir, Fjalarr, Bifurr etc.). The dwarfs made most of the treasures belonging to the gods, i.e. Thor's hammar Mjǫllnir, Sif's golden hair, Heimdall's ring Draupnir, Freyja's necklace Brísingamen and her boar Hildisvíni (*Hyndluljóð* 7). Freyr's wonderful ship Skíðblaðnir was also built by the dwarfs, namely by 'Ivaldi's sons', and the fetters (Gleipnir) put onto the Fenriswolf are also dwarfs' work. – The dwarfs live under mountains and in rocks, as both skaldic kennings from the 11th and 12th centuries and also the sagas from the 13th and 14th centuries repeatedly confirm. The ON expression *dvergmáli* for 'echo' also records the idea that the dwarfs are mountain dwellers. The younger legendary sagas mention that in order to catch dwarfs one has to watch for them in front of their rocks, and the Eddic lay → *Alvíssmál* tells of how the wise dwarf Alvíss turned to stone when the first ray of sunlight touched him outside the protection of his home. In addition to the concept of dwarfs as clever craftsmen and mountain dwellers comes the idea of their being miners and custodians of various treasures, a concept which has been retained in folk-belief in South Germanic areas until modern times. – Even magical powers have occasionally been attributed to the dwarfs (*Hávamál* 160; *Alvíssmál*), probably originally as the result of their reputation of having technical skills. – Snorri reports that four dwarfs, Austri, Vestri, Norðri and Suðri, carry the sky formed from Ymir's skull (*Gylfaginning* 7) and the kenning *níðbyrðra Norðri* 'sky' from the 10th century (→ Vestri) proves that this is not merely yet another result of Snorri's scholarly education. Similarly, we hear through Snorri (*Skáldskaparmál* 1) and the evidence of several kennings that the dwarfs (Fjalarr and Galarr) are the brewers and briefly the custodians of the → mead of the skalds which they brewed from the blood of Kvasir.

There are various traditions referring to the origin of the dwarfs in the Eddas. *Vǫluspá* 9 describes the creation of the dwarfs from the blood of the giant Brimir and the bones of the giant Bláinn as part of the cosmogeny. On the other hand Snorri describes the origin of the dwarfs as being maggot-like beings in the flesh of the progenitor giant Ymir which were then endowed with reason by the gods (*Gylfaginning* 13). Both explanations would appear to originate rather from mythographical imagination than from folk-belief.

The origin of the concept of dwarfs is either to be found in nature spirits or else in demons of death. Dwarfs' names such as Nár, Náinn, Dáinn, Bláinn and their underground homes would speak in favour of the second interpretation, Nature spirits are probably more likely to be elves. However, it is possible that there was a mixture of concepts, and a superimposition of forgotten pantheistic concepts could also be considered. The etymology of 'dwarf' is obscure. On the one hand scholars have referred to Norwegian *dvergskot* 'animal disease' and Old Indian *drva-* 'weakness, sickness' which would lead back to an Indo-Germanic root **dhuer-* 'damage', but on the other hand considerations have centred on Old Indian *dhvaras* 'demonic being'. Also the Indo-Germanic root **dhreugh* (leading to German *Traum* 'dream', *Trug* 'deception') has been considered, in which case 'deceptive picture' would be the more original meaning.

A Lütjens, *Der Zwerg in der deutschen Heldendichtung*, Breslau 1911; H. de Boor, 'Der Zwerg in Skandinavien' (*Festschrift E. Mogk*) Halle 1924; C. N. Gould, 'Dwarf-Names' (*PMLA* 44) 1929; I. Reichborn-Kjennerud, 'Den gamle dvergetro' (*Festschrift E. A. Kock*) Lund 1934; I. Reichborn-Kjennerud, 'Den norske Dvergetradition' (*Norsk Folkekultur* 20) 1934; S. Gutenbrunner, 'Eddastudien I: Über die Zwerge in der Vsp Str. 9–13' (*ANF* 70) 1955; E. F. Halvorsen, 'Dverger' (*KLNM* 3) 1958; J. de Vries, *Altgermanische Religionsgeschichte*, Berlin [3]1970; L. Motz, 'On Elves and Dwarfs' (*Arv* 29/30) 1973/74; F. Kluge, *Etymologisches Wörterbuch*, Berlin [22]1989; J. de Vries, *Altnordisches etymologisches Wörterbuch*, Leiden [2]1977; C. Lecouteux, 'Zwerge und Verwandte' (*Euphorion* 75) 1981.

R: The concept of the existence of a race of dwarfs is not only common among Germanic peoples, and has found such great interest in particular in popular literature that it is impossible to separate the reception of Germanic belief in dwarfs from that of other peoples. Cf. H. Hässler, *Zwerge und Riesen in Märchen und Sage*. Diss., Tübingen 1957.

Earendel (OE, 'sunrise, morning star') → Aurvandill.

Earthquake → Loki's punishment.

Ēastre → Ēostra.

Edda. Originally the name for the → *Snorra Edda* (also known as the *Prose Edda* or the younger *Edda*), but now the usual name for the collection of Old Norse heroic and mythological lays called the *Poetic Edda* (or wrongly the *Sæmundar Edda*). The ON word *edda* actually means 'great grandmother' which hardly suffices as an explanation of the word as a book title. A derivation from words such as *eddumál* or *eddasaga* 'grandmother's tales' is conceivable. The most frequent explanation is to relate *Edda* to *óðr* 'poetry, poem', i.e. in the meaning 'poetics'. A totally plausible explanation is that *Edda* means 'book from Oddi' as Oddi is the farm where Sæmundar, the supposed author of the Poetic *Edda*, lived and where → Snorri Sturluson spent his youth. The interpretation 'honoured book' to a supposed word **eddr* 'honoured' is, however, incorrect, whilst a derivation from Latin *edo* 'I declare' is quite possible.

G. Neckel, 'Aisl. Edda "Urgroßmutter" ' (*ZfdA* 49) 1908; W. Krogmann, 'Die Edda' (*ANF* 52) 1936; S. Gutenbrunner, 'Der Büchertitel Edda' (*PBB* 66) 1942; A. Faulkes, 'Edda' (*Gripla* 2) Reykjavík 1977 (= Rit 16); K. Schier, 'Edda, Ältere' (*Hoops* 6) [2]1986; H. Beck, 'Eddische Dichtung' (*Hoops* 6) [2]1986.

R: K. Rheintaler, *Edda* (opera, 1875).

Eggmóinn (ON, 'killed by the sword'). A dwarf in the *Þulur*. As is the case with a number of other dwarf-names, his name suggests a concept of the → dwarfs as spirits of the dead.

Eggþér (ON). A giant in the *Vǫluspá* 42. He is described in this passage as the guardian of the giantesses in the Iron Forest and is described as being jolly and able to play the harp. The name Eggþér has a counterpart in OE Ecgthéow, Beowulf's father, and probably actually means 'the one who has servants armed with knives'. Eggþér is also found as a personal name in ON as Egðir, in OHG as Eggideo, Eckideo.

P. H. Salus, P. Beekman Taylor, 'Eikinskjaldi, Fjallarr, and Eggþér' (*Neophilologus* 53) 1969; J. de Vries, *Altnordisches etymologisches Wörterbuch*, Leiden [2]1977.

Egill (ON). The giant in *Hymiskviða* 7 who allows Thor to leave his goats at his farm on his journey to Hymir. Later, in *Hymiskviða* 38, we hear that a giant had to atone for the laming of one of Thor's goats by giving Thor both his children. We can assume that this has some connection to the mythical tale of the laming of Thor's goat as told by Snorri in *Gylfaginning* 43. In this tale an (unnamed) farmer, in whose house Thor and Loki spend the night, atones for the laming of a goat, which his son has caused, by giving Thor his son Þjálfi and his daughter Rǫskva as servants. According to this, Egill is the father of Þjálfi and Rǫskva in the myth of → Thor's he-goats.

Eikin (ON, 'the furious one'). A mythical river in the river catalogue of *Grímnismál* 27 and in the *Þulur*.

Eikinskjaldi (ON, 'the one with the oak-shield'). A dwarf in *Vǫluspá* 13 and 16. It is, however, not certain whether Eikinskjaldi really is a name or if it is merely an attribute which refers to the other dwarfs in the list in the *dvergatal* of *Vǫluspá*. For a personal name the form Eikinskjǫldr would rather be expected.

P. H. Salus, P. Beekman Taylor, 'Eikinskjaldi, Fjallarr, and Eggþér' (*Neophilologus* 53) 1969.

R: Eikinskjaldi is understood as a surname for a dwarf in J. R. R. Tolkien's novel *The Hobbit* where Thorin bears the surname Oakenshields.

Eikþyrnir (ON, 'the one with the oak-like antlers'). The stag which stands on Valhall's roof and grazes from the leaves of the tree called Læraðr (= Yggdrasill?). Drips of water coming from the tips of his antlers fall into the spring Hvergelmir, which feeds all the rivers of the world. This information from *Grímnismál* 26 is repeated by Snorri in *Gylfaginning* 38. – It is not completely clear what role the stag really played in Germanic religion. The → stag cult probably stood in some sort of connexion to Odin's endowment of the dignity of kings. The dripping antlers are reminiscent of mythical food-giving proto-beings such as the proto-cow Auðumla or else the goat Heiðrun.

J. de Vries, *Altgermanische Religionsgeschichte*, Berlin [3]1970.

Eilífr Goðrúnarson. An Icelandic skald who lived at the end of the 10th century at the court of Earl Hakon in Norway. The only example of his poetry still extant is a fragment of a eulogy about Hakon, but the information of greater parts of his → *Þórsdrápa* has been preserved through Snorri's integration of them in his own works.

Eimgeitir (ON). A giant in the *Þulur*. The name is an extension of the giant's name Geitir and means 'the steaming (or burning) Geitir'.

Eimnir (ON, 'burner'). A giant in the *Þulur*. His name, like Brandingi's, means that he probably belonged to those giants (→ Surtr) who kindle the world conflagration at the Ragnarǫk. Logi (and Eldr) on the other hand are simply personifications of fire.

Einheri (ON, 'the one who fights alone'). A name for the god Thor in *Lokasenna* 60 and, as a poetic epithet, probably refers to the fact that Thor frequently fights alone against giants and demonic powers. A connexion with the *Einherjar*, who are of course Odin's warriors, is extremely unlikely.

einherjar (ON, 'those who fight alone'). The term used in Old Norse mythology for the warriors slain in battle, who are brought to → Valhall by the → valkyries after their deaths. In this warrior's paradise they spend their days in battle, but in the evenings they are all alive again (*Vafþrúðnismál* 41) and drink the mead which flows from the udders of the goat Heiðrun and is offered to them by the Valkyries (*Grímnismál* 25 and 36). Each day, the *einherjar* eat the meat from the constantly renewed boar Sæhrímnir. There is sufficient for everyone and it is prepared for them in the cauldron called Eldhrímnir by the cook Andhrímnir (*Grímnismál* 18). At the → Ragnarǫk the *einherjar* will go into battle on the side of the gods against the Fenriswolf and the other enemies of gods and mankind (*Grímnismál* 23).

In the *Edda*, *einherjar* are only mentioned in *Grímnismál*, *Vafþrúðnismál* and *Helgakviða Hundingsbana* I 38, from where Snorri took the idea (*Gylfaginning* 37–40). The skaldic poems *Eiríksmál* and *Hakonarmál* from the middle of the 10th century prove that the concept of the *einherjar* was indeed wide spread at least by the late heathen period.

M. Olsen considered that the myth about the *einherjar* originated in Rome from the constant battles of the gladiators there, who began to fight each day anew. But even if we do not want to refute totally the influence of the Roman Coliseum on the picture of Valhall (with its 540 gates) as given in the late poetic sources, the roots for the band of warriors in the Germanic paradise do not lie in Rome. The concept of the eternal battle and the daily resurrection of the slain warriors can also be found in Saxo (I, 31) as well as in the reports of → Hjaðningavíg. The Harii, mentioned in Tacitus' *Germania* (43), who are described there as an 'army of the dead' (*feralis exercitus*) are comparable with the *einherjar* and etymologically closely connected. Since Höfler, one tends to interpret these obviously living armies of the dead as religiously motivated → bands of warriors, who led to the formation of the concept of the *einherjar* as well as of the Wild Hunt. Another obvious etymological derivation of the word *einherjar* falls into place here, namely that it could mean 'those who belong to an army'.

E. Mogk, 'Einherjar' (Hoops 1) 1911–13; O. Höfler, *Kultische Geheimbünde der Germanen*, Frankfurt 1934; F. Strömm, 'Einherjar' (*KLNM* 3) 1958; J. de Vries, *Altgermanische Religionsgeschichte*, Berlin ³1970.

R: the *einherjar* are also seen as part of the picture of Valhall, for example in K. Ehrenberg's charcoal drawing *Gastmahl in Walhalla (mit einziehenden Einheriern)* (1880), or A. Oehlenschlägers poem *Einheriarne* (in *Nordens Guder*, 1819); in Klopstocks ode *Braga* (1771) they are mentioned as Einherion.

Einriði or Eindriði (ON, 'the one who rides alone', originally perhaps 'the one who rules alone'). A name for the god Thor (*Haustlǫng* 19, *Vellekla* 15, *Þulur*). In Snorri Einriði only occurs in the prologue to his *Edda* in the learned pre-history of the Æsir where Einriði is the son of Lóriði and father of Vingþor although all three names are actually simply epithets for Thor. Because the name Einriði (just like Thor's name Hlóriði) only occurs very sporadically in Medieval literary sources, but on the other hand occurs as a personal name in runic Swedish ainriþi (Grinda in Södermannland, 11th century) and runic Danish ainraþi (Rimsø, North Jutland, 10th century), it could be that these indicate an extra-literary knowledge of the name for Thor.

Eir (1) (ON). The name of an Asynia (= an Æsir goddess) who is said here to be the best female doctor. In *Fjǫlsvinnsmál* 38 Eir is one of Menglǫð's serving girls, but in the *Þulur* merely the name of a → valkyrie. The name means 'the helper' (ON *eir* 'help, mercy') and is appropriate for a healing goddess, yet the name is missing in the list of Asyniur in the *Þulur*, and therefore the valkyrie's powers to awaken the dead and their healing powers will have to be taken into account so that Eir as a valkyrie is probably the more original version.

J. Grimm, *Deutsche Mythologie*, Berlin [4]1875–78; J. Steffensen, 'Lækningagyðan Eir' (*Skírnir* 134) 1960; J. de Vries, *Altgermanische Religionsgeschichte*, Berlin [3]1970; G. Müller, 'Die Heilkraft der Walküre' (*FmSt* 10) 1976.

Eir (2) (ON). One of Menglǫð's maids in *Fjǫlsvinnsmál* 38.

Eiríksmál. Fragmentary anonymous skaldic poem (composed after 954) on the death of king Eirík Bloodaxe. The poem intensively uses heathen mythological concepts in describing the king's arrival in Valhall.

K. von See, 'Zwei eddische Preislieder: Eiríksmál und Hákonarmál' (*Festgabe U. Pretzel*) Berlin 1963; E. Marold, 'Das Walhallbild in den Eiríksmál und Hákonarmál' (*Medieval Scandinavia* 5) 1972; T. Ulset, *Merknader til en del skaldedikt*, Oslo 1975; J. Harris, 'Eiríksmál and Hákonarmál' (*DicMA* 4) 1984.

Eistla (ON). One of Heimdall's nine giant mothers in the catalogue of giantesses in *Vǫluspá in skamma* (*Hyndluljóð* 37). The meaning of the name is obscure. Gering interprets Eistla (from *eisa* 'hurry') as 'the stormy one', whereas Sturtevant derives its from *eista* 'testicles', i.e. 'the swollen, swelling, ones' which would fit his interpretation of Eistla as a sea-god. Motz relates Eistla to *eisa* 'glowing ash, fire', i.e. 'the glowing one'.

H. Gering, *Kommentar*, 1, Halle 1927; A. M. Sturtevant, 'Etymological Comments upon Certain Old Norse Proper Names in the Eddas' (*PMLA* 67) 1952; L. Motz, 'Giantesses and their Names' (*FmSt* 15) 1981.

Eisurfála (ON, 'ash-troll-woman'). A giantess in the *Þulur*.

Eitri (ON, 'the poisonous one'). A dwarf in the *Þulur*. Cf. the German expression for an unpleasant person *Giftzwerg* 'poisonous dwarf'.

Eldhrímnir (ON, 'the one covered in soot from the fire'). The cauldron in which Andhrímnir the cook prepares the boar → Sæhrímnir, time and again for the gods and the *einherjar* in Valhall; this, at least, is Snorri's interpretation (*Gylfaginning* 37) of *Grímnismál* 18.

Eldir (ON, roughly 'the fire-lighter'). Ægir's servant in the → *Lokasenna*. Following *Lokasenna*, Snorri also uses the name in *Gylfaginning* 31. Both the prose introduction of *Lokasenna* and Snorri mention another servant as well, called → Fimafengr.

Eldr (ON, 'fire'). A giant in the *Þulur*. In Snorri (*Skáldskaparmál* 26) Eldr is a brother of Ægir and Vindr and as such the son of Fornjótr. Since Fornjótr's son, who is otherwise identified with fire, is called Logi, it would appear that Eldr is not an actual name, but rather a 'personified' synonym for → Logi created by Snorri.

M. Clunies-Ross, 'Snorri Sturluson's use of the Norse origin-legend' (*ANF* 98) 1983.

elf mills → rock carvings.

Élivágar (ON pl.). The rivers which flow from the spring Hvergelmir into the primeval chasm Ginnungagap, according to Snorri (*Gylfaginning* 3 and 4). When their poisonous drops of hoar frost meet with the heat from Muspellheim, the first life began in the melting ice, namely the giant → Ymir. The interpretation of Élivágar as eleven rivers is obviously an invention of Snorri's and probably results from the plural form of the name. Snorri also names all these river names which come from the river catalogue in *Grímnismál* 27 and 28: Svǫl, Gunnþrá, Fjǫrm, Fimbulþul, Slíðr, Hríð, Sylgr, Ylgr, Víð, Leiptr, Gjǫll. However, in *Skáldskaparmál* 17, no doubt following *Hymiskviða* 5, Snorri himself says that Élivágar is only one river which forms the border to Jǫtunheim. *Hymiskviða* states that Hymir lives at the edge of the skies to the east of the Élivágar. Halvorsen has pointed out that in *Hymiskviða* the name Élivágar probably relates to *él* 'bad weather, storm', *vágr* 'sea', and can be understood to be a name for the proto-sea surrounding the world. This is a more appropriate interpretation of the name.

E. F. Halvorsen, 'Élivágar' (*KLNM* 3) 1958.

Éljúðnir (ON, 'the one dampened by rain'). The hall of the goddess of the underworld → Hel according to Snorri's allegorizing description of her abode (*Gylfaginning* 33).

Elli (ON, 'age'). Personification of old age. In Snorri's tale of Thor's journey to → Utgarðaloki (*Gylfaginning* 45f.; → Skrýmir) she is introduced as Utgarðaloki's wet-nurse, with whom Thor has to wrestle, a contest which he is bound to lose because nobody can ever conquer old age, as Snorri says in his explanation of the contest.

Elves. Beings from the lower mythology. The West Germanic concepts concerning these beings begin to differ from the Scandinavian ones even in the early Middle Ages, and in Anglo-Saxon areas an independent tradition in folklore about elves soon developed, perhaps as a result of Celtic influence.

Even in the 9th and 10th centuries there are already a number of different terms for elves in OE texts which might have been caused by the variety of elf-like beings in classical mythology, whose names were subsequently translated. However, this manifoldness might allow conclusions about an already well-developed systematization of these beings in Germanic mythology. Apart from the masculine *ælf/ylf* and the feminine *ælfen/elfen* there are also the compounds *bergælfen*, *dunælf(en)*, *muntælfen* 'mountain elf', *landælf*, *feldælf* 'field elf', *wæterælfen* and *sæælfen* 'water nymphs' and *wuduælfen* 'wood spirits'.

The Anglo-Saxon adjective *ælfsciene* 'as pretty as an elf' indicates the bright side of this being, as does its usage in personal names (Ælfbeorht, Ælfred). On the other hand, numerous names of illnesses (e.g. OE *ylfa gesceot* 'lumbago') surely document a belief in the damaging character of the elves.

In the late Middle Ages and in modern times the Scandinavian *alfar* and the dwarfs merged into the more general concept of the *huldufólk*. Likewise, the elves have never played a great role in German folk-belief. However, a strong tradition was preserved in England and it is from here that these beings were re-borrowed into German speaking areas only in the 18th century (through Bodmer, Wieland, Herder). This is the reason why the borrowed form *Elfen* is more common in German today than the original *Elben* or *Alben*.

R. Jente, *Die mythologischen Ausdrücke im altenglischen Wortschatz*, Heidelberg 1921; E. A. Philippson, *Germanisches Heidentum bei den Angelsachsen*, Leipzig 1929; R. A. Peters, 'OE. Ælf,

-Ælf, Ælfen, -Ælfen' (*Philological Quarterly* 42) 1963; N. Thun, 'The Malignant Elves' (*Studia Neophilologica* 41) 1969; E. O. G. Turville-Petre, *Myth and Religion of the North*, Westport 1975.

R: (literature) In the Anglo-Saxon world the widespread knowledge of elves has found an obvious echo in literature. Elves play a vital role in English literature from Shakespeare to Tolkien (cf. Oberon). The lighter aspect of the elves has predominated in literature and art and they are shown throughout as being delicate, sometimes winged, protective spirits who are mostly helpful to mankind. The German name Erlkönig (as in Goethe's like-named ballad) used instead of *Elfenkönig* originates from an incorrect translation of Herder's who misunderstood the Danish *elverkonge* ('elf-king') to be Erlenkönig, but attributed it to it some of the darker aspects of elves.

(fine art) Moritz v. Schwind, *Elfentanz* (painting); B. E. Ward, *Huldra's Nymphs* (painting); C. P. Sainton, *The White Elves* (painting); N. J. O. Blommér, *The Elf-Dance* (painting); in Blommér's wake a flood of kitsch elf-dance paintings were manufactured in the late 19th and early 20th century.

Embla (ON). According to Eddic anthropogeny, Embla was the first woman. → Askr and Embla were created from tree-trunks and given various functions of mental and physical life by a divine triad (*Vǫluspá* 17 and 18; *Gylfaginning* 8). Whilst Askr 'ash' is etymologically unproblematic, Embla creates more problems. A derivation from *Elm-la from *Almilōn and thus to *almr* 'elm' (Bugge) is a possibility. The more exact correspondence would, however, be *Ambilō and consequently there have been attempts to connect Askr and Embla with the Vandal kings Assi and Ambri who are mentioned in the History of the Langobards (written by Paulus Diaconus) as Ambri probably comes from *Ambrilō (Much). Sperber's suggestion that Embla might be related to Greek *ámpelos* 'vine, liana' is more interesting than this uncertain correspondence. It should be noted that in Indo-European areas an analogy would be obvious between the drilling of fire and sexual intercourse. Vines were used as inflammable wood and placed beneath the drill made of harder wood in order to ignite. The ritual making of fire seems proven for Scandinavia because of a depiction of it on one of the stone plates on the Bronze age grave from Kivik on Scania.

H. Sperber, 'Embla' (*PBB* 36) 1910; R. Much, 'Wandalische Götter' (*Mitteilungen der schlesischen Gesellschaft für Volkskunde* 27) 1926; F. R. Schröder, 'Germanische Schöpfungsmythen' (*GRM* 19) 1931; J. de Vries, *Altgermanische Religionsgeschichte*, Berlin ³1970; Å. V. Ström, H. Biezais, *Germanische und baltische Religion*, Stuttgart 1975.

Ennilangr (ON, 'the one with the wide forehead'). A name listed in the *Þulur* for the god Thor. The reason for this is unknown.

Ēostra (or perhaps *Ēastre; Anglo-Saxon). A goddess mentioned by → Bede, from whom the *Ēostur-monath* (= April) takes its name according to Bede (*De temporibus ratione* 15). Grimm concluded from this reference and also from the name of the OHG Easter festival Ôstarûn (pl. of *Ôstara) a West Germanic goddess of sunrise and of spring-time, Proto-Germanic *Austrō, OHG *Ôstara (cf. Latin Aurora). Despite repeatedly expressed doubt one should not disregard Bede's information totally. However, a spring-like fertility goddess will have to be assumed instead of a goddess of sunrise, despite the name, seeing that otherwise the Germanic goddesses (and matrons) are mostly connected with prosperity and growth. Cf. Hreda.

J. Grimm, *Deutsche Mythologie*, Berlin ⁴1875–78; E. A. Philippson, *Germanisches Heidentum bei den Angelsachsen*, Leipzig 1929; H. Wesche, 'Beiträge zu einer Geschichte des deutschen

Heidentums' (*PBB* 61) 1973; J. de Vries, *Altgermanische Religionsgeschichte*, Berlin [3]1970; H. b. d. Wieden, 'Die Runenbildtafel vom Süntel' (Schaumburg-Lippische Mitteilungen 22) 1933; Å. V. Ström, H. Biezais, *Germanische und baltische Religion*, Stuttgart 1975.

Eoton (Anglo-Saxon, 'giant'). A particular group of giants in heathen Anglo-Saxon mythology. The ON equivalent is *jǫtunn*. Grendel in the Beowulf legend is called Eoton, although he is actually a water monster.

E. A. Philippson, *Germanisches Heidentum bei den Angelsachsen*, Leipzig 1929.

Erce (OE). A mythological (?) person named in an OE benediction of the fields, where the earth is invoked with the formula: *erce, erce, erce, eorþan modor*. It is not certain whether this word is really the name of a goddess, an earth-mother, nor is the meaning of the name clear. A link with the fearsome spectre of Frau Herke (or Harke) who occurs in folklore in Saxony has been suggested but it is by no means certain and therefore does not help interpret the word any further.

E. A. Philippson, *Germanisches Heidentum bei den Angelsachsen*, Leipzig 1929; J. de Vries, *Altgermanische Religionsgeschichte*, Berlin [3]1970.

(**Erda**) is R. Wagner's version of the Germanic goddess Jǫrð. Whereas Jǫrð is called Thor's mother in the medieval sources, Wagner makes Erda the mother of the norns and Brünhilde, the valkyrie, in his operas *Das Rheingold* and *Siegfried*.

Ermis → Irmin.

Eschatology. The concepts of last things and the end of the world. The Germanic peoples' concept of eschatology is seen in Eddic mythology in the visions of the → Ragnarǫk and in the not totally explained West Germanic concept of → Muspell. These concepts are by no means applicable to all Germanic peoples and can only be established for the late heathen period.

Ethnogeny → Descendency myth.

Et(h)rahenae. Name of a matron. In both of the more complete references to Et(h)rahenae on votive stones, the Et(h)rahenae appear together with the Gesahenae: as *Etrahenis et Cesahenis* in Rödingen (CIL XIII 7890, Germany), as *Matronis Etttrrahenis et Gesahenis* in Bettenhoven (CIL XIII 7895, Germany); Ettt- is certainly a misspelling for Eth-. The Et(h)rahenae could possibly belong to OHG *ettar* 'fence, border', perhaps however to the place name Eitrach. The fragmentary inscription from Wollersheim (CIL CIII 7821, Germany) possibly points to a link between the Et(h)rahenae and the Veteranehae/Veterahenae.

M. Ihm, 'Der Mütter- und Matronenkultus und seine Denkmäler' (*Bonner Jahrbücher* 83) 1887; S. Gutenbrunner, *Die germanischen Götternamen*, Halle 1936; M. Schönfeld, *Wörterbuch der altgermanischen Personen- und Völkernamen*, Heidelberg [2]1965; H. Reichert, *Lexikon der altgermanischen Namen*, Vienna 1987–90.

Euhemerism. The system that explains mythology as growing out of real history, its deities as merely magnified men of stature from long past times. Euhemerism has taken its name from Euhemeros of Messene (circa 300 B.C.), the creator of this theory whose work was translated into Latin by Nennius.

Christian Scandinavian historians and mythographers, notably the Icelander

Snorri Sturluson and the Dane Saxo Grammaticus, are especially prone to euhemerism in Germanic mythology and it is found in most of the Icelandic historical works of the high Middle Ages, even in Ari fróði's Book of Icelanders (*Íslendingabók*, pre-1133) where he includes Yngvi and Njǫrðr as historical kings.

In Snorri's writings, euhemeristic ideas occur particularly in the prologue to his *Edda* and in the *Ynglinga saga* where he gives an account of the migration of the Æsir to Scandinavia (→ Odin's migration), whilst the actual mythography of the *Gylfaginning* is passed off as a deliberate deception of these Æsir, but then bears few traces of euhemerism. In the *Ynglinga saga* (5–7) Snorri gives a detailed account of the euhemeristic origin of the Nordic gods and religion. Odin was lord over Asgard in Asia, a great place of sacrifice which had 12 priests looking after it. When Odin settled in Sigtuna after migrating from the east, sacrifices were made to him and his college of 12 high priests (among them are Njǫrðr, Freyr, Heimdall, Thor, Baldr) and they were worshipped like gods.

Saxo's euhemerism is of a different kind. The material which he uses is admittedly Icelandic but the way of dealing with it differs from Snorrri's. For example, we hear nothing of the migration of the Æsir, but on the other hand Saxo develops a theory about the gods (*Gesta Danorum*, I, 19f.) which only has a slight influence on the rest of his work. Saxo explains that there are three kinds of sorcerers: the eldest group of giants are subordinate to the smaller but more intelligent giants, the group of prophets; the third group developed from the association between the two other groups and was not equal to its ancestors as regards greatness or power of magic, but nonetheless they were worshipped by mankind as gods.

This system remains, however, functionless and unexplained. With the first group, Saxo surely means the (proto-)giants of Nordic mythology, by the third group perhaps the Æsir and the Vanir. However, he does not put the gods, whom he always treats like men, into any order within his system, although Odin has a prominent position in his work as well, and if Ollerus or Mithotyn usurp his divine position (→ Odin's exile), this leads to their rapid downfall. In connexion with Odin's second exile (*Gesta Danorum* III, 80ff.), Saxo mentions a divine college of Æsir which possibly corresponds to Snorri's 12 priests.

There are several reasons for the euhemerism in the works of Scandinavian authors. Firstly the authors of the scholarly Icelandic Renaissance were seeking a way which would make the heathen Germanic mythology handed down to them in skaldic poetry and the Eddic lays comprehensible to their Christian audience. Secondly, euhemerism offered the possibility of dealing with heathen mythology without any contradiction of Christian beliefs, and thirdly it created an opportunity for the scholars to establish continuous links with Continental European historical traditions.

A. Heusler, *Die gelehrte Urgeschichte*, Berlin 1908; P. Herrmann, *Die Heldensagen des Saxo Grammaticus*, Leipzig 1922; R. Schomerus, *Die Religion der Nordgermanen im Spiegel christlicher Darstellung*, Göttingen 1936; F. Wild, *Odin und Euemeros*, Vienna 1941; W. Baetke, *Die Götterlehre der Snorra-Edda*, Berlin 1950; A. Holtsmark, *Studier i Snorres Mytologi*, Oslo 1964; K. W. Bolle, 'In Defense of Euhemeros' (*Myth and Law among the Indo-Europeans*) Berkeley 1970; K. v. See, 'Euhemerismus' (*LexMA* 4) 1987; G. W. Weber, 'Euhemerismus' (*Hoops* 8) ²1992.

Euthungae. Germanic matrons on an inscription from Cologne (Germany; CIL XIII 8225) dedicated to the *[Mat]ribus Suebis [.] Euthungabus* 'the Suebian mothers Euthungae'. As, however, a letter in front of the name is missing, the form is not totally certain. The name of the Euthungae probably belongs to the name of a

Germanic tribe, the Iuthungi, known from classical authors, and not as [R]euthungae to the Reudigni.

S. Gutenbrunner, *Die germanischen Götternamen*, Halle 1936; E. Schwarz, 'Die Herkunft der Juthungen' (*Jahrbuch für fränkische Landesforschung* 14) 1954; M. Schönfeld, *Wörterbuch der altgermanischen Personen- und Völkernamen*, Heidelberg ²1965; H. Reichert, *Lexikon der altgermanischen Namen*, Vienna 1987–90.

Exposure of children. An old Scandinavian legal custom which meant that the father was allowed to have a new born child exposed so long as it had not taken any nourishment or been given the (possibly unhistorical, however) heathen → sprinkling with water. Exposure was supposedly one of the exceptions to Christian law made when Iceland was Christianized in 1000 A.D. so that it was still legal for a while afterwards (*Kristni saga* 12).

Exposure of children and the later fostering of children by other people is not only known from Medieval Icelandic literature but was also an important literary motif in European fairy-tales such as *Hansel and Gretel*. This raises the question whether the significance of the motif in literature in fact led to an exaggeration of the importance of child exposure in legal sources.

(**Eyluðr**) (ON, 'island-cradle'). In the *Þulur* incorrectly listed as being a name for Odin. Otherwise, Eyluðr only occurs in a poem by Snæbjǫrn from the 11th century, where it is a kenning for 'sea'.

H. Christiansen, 'Eyluðr' (*Norsk Tidsskrift for Sprogvidenskap* 19) 1960.

Eyrgjafa (ON, 'sand donor'? or Ørgjafa 'scar donor'?). One of Heimdall's nine giant mothers according to *Vǫluspá in skamma* (*Hyndluljóð* 37). As with the other names of these mothers, Eyrgjafa is probably no older than the lay itself.

L. Motz, 'Giantesses and their Names' (*FmSt* 15) 1981.

Eysteinn Valdason. An Icelander who wrote a poem about Thor towards the end of the 10th century, of which we know nothing more. There are only three stanzas of his → *Þórsdrápa* (2) remaining and these describe Thor's fishing trip (→ Thor and the Midgard serpent). They are quoted in Snorri's *Edda*.

Fachine(i)his. Matron name. A number of votive inscriptions from the Lower Rhine dating from the 3rd/4th centuries (at least three from Zingsheim, one from Euskirchen) are dedicated to these *matronis Fa(c)hine(i)his*. The name possibly belongs to Gmc **fahana-* 'glad'.

S. Gutenbrunner, *Die germanischen Götternamen*, Halle 1936; M. Schönfeld, *Wörterbuch der altgermanischen Personen- und Völkernamen*, Heidelberg ²1965; H. Reichert, *Lexikon der altgermanischen Namen*, Vienna 1987–90; R. Nedoma, 'Matronae Amfratninae' (*Beiträge zur Namenforschung* 34) 1989.

(**Fafner**). Name of a giant, invented by R. Wagner for his opera *Das Rheingold* and not otherwise recorded in Nordic mythological and heroic poetry as the name of a giant. It does occur, however, as the name of a dragon (→ Fáfnir, → Fasolt).

Fáfnir (ON, 'the embracer'). The dragon whom Sigurð kills in Nordic heroic poetry.

Fáinn (ON, 'the coloured one'). A dwarf in the *Þulur*.

Fála (ON, 'female fool, troll-woman'). A giantess in the *Þulur*, but also in the poetry of the skald Gisli Súrsson and in two late Medieval sagas. Fála is an obvious name for a giantess if one thinks of High Medieval ideas about the stupidity and ugliness of giantesses. These figures have very little to do with the giant-daughters of Germanic mythology who even the gods find desirable (Gerðr, Skaði).

Falhófnir (ON, 'the one with the fallow hooves'). A mythical horse in the catalogue of horse names in *Grímnismál* 30 and in the *Þulur*. According to Snorri (*Gylfaginning* 14), Falhófnir is one of the horses belonging to the Æsir.

Fallanda-forað (ON, 'danger of falling', 'hindrance'). Name of the threshhold to the abode of the goddess → Hel in Snorri's allegorizing description (*Gylfaginning* 33).

Falr (ON, 'hider' to *fela*). A dwarf in a poem by the skald Hofgarðarefr in a version of *Vǫluspá* 16 (instead of Fjallar). The name probably refers to the hiding of the skaldic mead. Falr means, however, also 'tube on the blade of the spear'.

L. Motz, 'New Thoughts on Dwarf-Names' (*FmSt* 7) 1973.

Fano. Germanic god? A fragment of an altar found in Cologne in 1964 and dating from the 2nd or 3rd century A.D. is dedicated to *deo Fanoni*, as most likely is a fragment from Xanten (CIL XIII 8660). If the name is indeed Germanic – a Celtic origin is also possible – it could be related to the name of the commander of the Heruli, Fanitheus (to OHG *fana*, *fano* 'cloth, flag').

M. Schönfeld, *Wörterbuch der altgermanischen Personen- und Völkernamen*, Heidelberg [2]1965; G. Alföldy, 'Epigraphisches aus dem Rheinland' (*Epigraphische Studien* 5) 1968; H. Reichert, *Lexikon der altgermanischen Namen*, Vienna 1987–90.

Fár or Fárr (ON, either like Fáinn: 'the coloured one' or else 'danger'). Name of a dwarf in the *Þulur*.

Farbauti (ON). Loki's father, according to the information given in the *Snorra Edda* (*Gylfaginning* 32, *Skáldskaparmál* 16) and in older skaldic poetry (Þjóðólfr ór Hvíni, *Haustlǫng* 5; Ulfr Uggason, *Húsdrápa* 2). Farbauti is said to be a giant. The name means 'the dangerous hitter', which allows a natural-mythological interpretation in the sense of 'lightning' (Kock) or 'storm' (Bugge).

S. Bugge, *Studien*, Munich 1889; A. Kock, 'Etymologisch-mythologische Untersuchungen' (*IF* 10) 1899; J. de Vries, *Altnordisches Etymologisches Wörterbuch*, Leiden [2]1970.

Farli (ON, 'the travelling one'?). A dwarf named in the *Þulur*.

Farmaguð (ON, 'god of burdens'). A name for Odin in Snorri's *Gylfaginning* 10 and probably identical with → Farmatýr.

H. Falk, *Odensheite*, Christiania 1924.

Farmatýr (ON, 'god of burdens'). A name for Odin (*Grímnismál* 48, *Þulur*, and in Eyvindr Finnsson: *Háleygjatal* 11). It possibly refers to Odin as the god of trade. Wotan/Odin is identified as Mercury in the *interpretatio romana* (Falk). With regard to this, Höfler pointed out that Odin was the god of the bands of young men since it is in the connexion with trade associations and guilds that he can be more readily understood in the role of the god of trade. The assumption that the name refers to the mythological tale of the theft of the skaldic mead (de Vries) is less likely, despite the documented kenning *Odins farmr* 'Odin's burden = poetic mead', as it is hardly appropriate. For more information about the names based on -týr, cf. → Sigtýr.

H. Falk, *Odensheite*, Christiania 1924; H. de Boor, 'Die religiöse Sprache der *Vǫluspá*' (*Deutsche Islandforschung* 1) Breslau 1930; O. Höfler, *Kultische Geheimbünde der Germanen* 1, Frankfurt 1934; J. de Vries, *Altgermanische Religionsgeschichte*, Berlin [3]1970.

Fasolt (MHG). A giant in German heroic poetry. In the legend of Ecke he is Ecke's brother, and in a late charm against lightning, he is called upon for help as the master of the thunderstorm. It is questionable if, as Grimm assumed, he is identical with Kári, the giant of the winds who is similarly infrequently recorded in Nordic mythology.

Fasolt's place in Scandinavian mythology only comes, however, via R. Wagner's opera *Das Rheingold* in which the curse of the ring is immediately revealed when Fasolt is killed by his brother Fafnir as soon as both have taken possession of the treasure.

J. Grimm, *Deutsche Mythologie*, Berlin [4]1875–8.

Fatalism → Fate.

Fate. Earlier scholars were of the opinion, still frequently held nowadays, that heathen Germanic beliefs considered that everything, even the gods, was subject to fate. The influence of fate in Germanic religion is, however, extremely difficult to assess because the literary source texts, on which we are dependent, reflect Germanic thought largely from a Christian point of view. For a long time, for example, the OE *Wyrd* was considered to be the central concept of Germanic fate, but more recent research has suggested that it is as much a predominantly Christian creation as the supposedly fatalistic belief of the Germanic peoples in nothing but their own power and strength (→ *máttr ok megin*).

It is hardly assessable how far the concept of the norns, who direct the fate of men and gods in Scandinavian mythological poetry of the late heathen era, was already influenced by classical thought. It is even more risky to assume an impersonal but influential fate for the Germanic peoples, a kind of fate which can hardly be proven, even if the saga literature appears to confirm it.

F. Kauffmann, 'Über den Schicksalsglauben der Germanen' (*ZfdPh* 50) 1926; A. G. v. Hamel, 'The Conception of Fate' (*Saga-Book* 11) 1928–36; H. Naumann, *Germanischer Schicksalsglaube*, Jena 1934; W. Baetke, 'Germanischer Schicksalsglaube' (*Neue Jahrbücher für Wissenschaft und Jugendbildung* 10) 1934; W. Wirth, *Der Schicksalsglaube in der Isländersaga*, Stuttgart 1940; E. Neumann, *Das Schicksal in der Edda* 1, Gießen 1955; H. Krahe, 'Altgermanische Kleinigkeiten' 4 (*IF* 66) 1961; Å. V. Ström, 'Scandinavian Belief in Fate' (*Fatalistic Beliefs*) Stockholm 1967; G. W. Weber, *Wyrd*, Bad Homburg 1969; J. de Vries, *Altgermanische Religionsgeschichte*, Berlin [3]1970; Å. V. Ström, H. Biezais, *Germanische und baltische Religion*, Stuttgart 1975.

Fengr (ON). A name for Odin in *Reginsmál* 18 and in the *Þulur*. The word usually means 'booty, supply' but it is going too far to call Odin the god of trade solely because of this (cf. Farmaguð). Fengr is more likely related to *fá* 'catch' and as such means 'catch; catcher; the one who leads the fallen heroes to Valhall'.

H. Falk, *Odensheite*, Christiania 1924; J. de Vries, *Altnordisches etymologisches Wörterbuch*, Leiden [2]1970.

Fenja (ON). A giantess in the *Grottasǫngr*, in the poetry of the skald Þórmóðr Bersason and in Snorri (*Skáldskaparmál* 40). The interpretation of the name is most likely 'the fen-dweller, heath-dweller' (to *fen*) but this is hardly appropriate for a giantess who works in a mill. Therefore, suggestions have been made that the name means 'the remover of chaff' or 'the hard worker' but this is hardly convincing from an etymological point of view.

J. Loewenthal, 'Wirtschaftsgeschichtliche Parerga' (*Wörter und Sachen* 9) 1926; J. de Vries, *Altgermanische Religionsgeschichte*, Berlin [3]1970.

Fenrir or Fenrisúlfr (ON). The wolf which Loki begat with the giantess, Angrboða, and whom the Æsir bound in fetters. At the → Ragnarǫk, however, it will free itself and will devour Odin before Viðarr is able to kill it.

The myth of Fenrir is divided by Snorri into several independent tales: (i) the fettering of the wolf in which the god Týr loses his right hand, (ii) Odin's and Viðarr's battle with him at the Ragnarǫk, (iii) probably the passage about the way in which Garmr, the hound of hell breaks free, and (iv) the devouring of the sun by a wolf.

In Eyvind's *Hákonarmál* 20 there is an allusion to Fenrir roaming unfettered around the world at the Ragnarǫk. It seems that Snorri used this scant allusion to a myth linking it with the fairy-tale motif of invisible fetters and a legend which explains the loss of Týr's right hand and combined them into a mythical tale. In *Gylfaginning* 33 he tells of how Loki had three children from Angrboða, a giantess: Fenrir, the Midgard serpent and Hel. The gods brought up the wolf but when he grew too strong for them, they decided to tie him up. At first they tried to do so using the fetter called Lœðing, then with Drómi, but he broke free from both of these. Finally the dwarfs made the fetter known as → Gleipnir which is light and soft, and the Æsir used this to chain him up on the isle of Lyngvi in Lake Amsvartnir. The wolf, however, became suspicious and, as a pledge, one of the gods had to put his hand into his jaws so that he would allow the chain to be put on. When the wolf noticed that he could not break it, he bit the god and this is how Týr lost his right hand. Then the gods fastened the fetter using a chain called Gelgja to the rock known as Gjǫll which they hit into the earth using the stone, Thviti. Finally, they propped open Fenrir's jaws by putting a sword between them; not unexpectedly, he howled terribly and the foam from his jaws formed the river Ván. By this time, however, he was so well bound that he could only regain his freedom at Ragnarǫk.

Only *Lokasenna* 38f. alludes to the loss of Týr's hand during the chaining of Fenrir, but this poem is extremely late and it is not sure whether these tales were in fact already linked in heathen times.

The hound of hell (or wolf) Garmr, mentioned in the Poetic *Edda*, appears to be identical with Fenrir as he is said to rip free from his chains at Ragnarǫk (*Vǫluspá* 58). In *Vǫluspá* 56 an unnamed wolf fights with Odin and it too can be assumed to be Fenrir. The idea that Týr steps into battle against Garmr is probably only Snorri's as he differentiates between Fenrir and Garmr. Two more wolves are mentioned as being involved in the events at the Ragnarǫk, one of which devours the sun, the other the moon. *Vǫluspá* does not mention them, but Snorri names them at the beginning of his description of the Ragnarǫk (*Gylfaginning* 50). In *Gylfaginning* 11 he refers to a wolf called Mánagarmr ('moon-eater') from the Iron-wood and says that this wolf is identical to the wolf which in *Vǫluspá* 40 is called Fenrir. Immediately prior to this Snorri has given the wolves who pursue the sun and the moon the names Skǫll and Hati respectively. Despite the different names given to these wolves, it is likely that they are all one and the same, namely Fenrir, and the various names go back to Snorri's over-zealous attempts to systematize.

The detail of the gods propping a sword in Fenrir's jaws is recorded as early as the

10th century in a kenning by Eyvindr, and the Viking Age Gosforth cross from North England also shows a wolf with a sword between its jaws, whereas the Thorvald cross on the Isle of Man (10th century) shows Fenrir devouring Odin.

The meaning of the name Fenrir has not been fully explained, but the most likely explanation is the link with ON *fen* 'fen, marsh', and the parallel formation in the tribal name Fanesii in Pliny's writings shows the great age of this formation (Gutenbrunner). Thus, Fenrir was originally a 'fen-dweller', an appropriate name for such a monster.

The myth of Fenrir is associated with the eschatological complex of concepts surrounding Ragnarǫk which developed in the 10th century. However, the myth might have been influenced even earlier than this by south-eastern thought, such as the Caucasian legends of the fettered giant. The literary composition of the various tales and the rich variety of names for all the details is Snorri's embellishment of the myth.

E. Wilken, 'Der Fenriswolf' (*ZfdPh* 28) 1896; F. v. d. Leyen, 'Der gefesselte Unhold' (*Festschrift J. v. Kelle*) Prag 1908; S. N. Hagen, 'Om navnet Fenrisulfr' (*MoM*) 1910; A. Olrik, *Ragnarǫk*, Berlin 1923; S. Gutenbrunner, 'Fanesii und Fenrir' (*ZfdA* 77) 1940; O. Briem, 'Fenrisúlfr' (*KLNM* 4) 1959; A. Sommerfeldt, 'Har syden og vesten vaert uten betydning for nordisk hedenskap?' (*MoM*) 1976; J. de Vries, *Altgermanische Religionsgeschichte*, Berlin [3]1970; K. Elstad, 'Om tremenn og solulvar i Edda' (*ANF* 102) 1987; O. Gschwantler, 'Die Überwindung des Fenriswolfs und ihr christliches Gegenstück bei Frau Ava' (*Proceedings of the VIIth International Saga Conference*) Spoleto 1990.

R: (fine art) D. Hardy, *Odin and Fenris*, and: *The Binding of Fenris* (two paintings, c.1900); E. Doepler d. J., *Odin und Fenriswolf*, and: *Fesselung des Fenriswolfes* (both in: E. Doepler, W. Ranisch, *Walhall*, 1901); A. V. Gunnerud's metal sculpture *Fenrir* on Asköy near Bergen dates to the 1960s.
(literature) A. Oehlenschläger, *Om Fenrisulven og Tyr* (poem in: *Nordens Guder*, 1819); K. H. Strobl, *Der Fenriswolf* (novel); E. K. Reich and E. Larsen: *Til kamp mod dødbideriet* (farce, 1974).

Fenrisúlfr (ON, 'Fenris wolf') → Fenrir.

Fenris wolf → Fenrir.

Fensalir (ON, 'marsh halls'). Frigg's abode according to *Vǫluspá* 33 (mentioned also in Snorri's *Gylfaginning* 34 and 48 and *Skáldskaparmál* 90). The question whether the name indicates that a cult of springs was associated with the goddess Frigg (Edzardi) must remain unanswered.

A. Edzardi, 'Fensalir und Vegtamskviða 12,5ff' (*Germania* 27) 1882.

feralis exercitus → Harii, → Wild Hunt.

Fernovineae and Fernovinehae. Matron names. One inscription from Meckenheim is dedicated to the *matronis Fernovineis* and one from Cologne to *Fernovinehis*. Both inscriptions date from the 2nd or 3rd centuries A.D. The name could be related to a **fern-awī* 'old stream'.

S. Gutenbrunner, *Die germanischen Götternamen*, Halle 1936; M. Schönfeld, *Wörterbuch der altgermanischen Personen- und Völkernamen*, Heidelberg [2]1965; H. Reichert, *Lexikon der altgermanischen Namen*, Vienna 1987–90.

Fertility cults are cults which are supposed to stimulate nature or the gods governing it to renew the yearly cycle of growth and to maintain the rich harvests. In Germanic antiquity such fertility gods are not too frequently documented, but nonetheless ample evidence of such cults is to be found in modern folk traditions which derive from older cult forms.

One of the most archaic concepts about the re-awakening of fertility is the → *hierós gámos* (or Sacred Marriage) of the sky-god with the earth-goddess which is symbolically imitated by mankind in the fields, a custom which has continued up to early modern times. Even the rock carvings from the first milleniuim B.C. show pictures of ritual marriage scenes, and the cult of Nerthus can also be convincingly interpreted as a Sacred Marriage.

Devotion to the Vanir gods Njǫrðr, Freyr and Freyja and the sacrifices to them should also be considered as a vegetation cult. The status of these → Vanir in the beliefs of the farming population is confirmed by the great number of place-names deriving from the names of the gods. The place-names point to a considerable number of cult-places of the Vanir. → Freyr, in historical times, can be considered the main representative of these gods of the third function (nourishing or fertility function; → three-function-theory); the great sacrifice at → Uppsala, which is conceived as an integral part of a fertility cult with its lascivious songs and dances in Adam's and Saxo's descriptions, should probably be understood as a sacrifice to the god Freyr (thus → Frøsblot).

W. Mannhardt, *Wald- und Feldkulte*, Berlin ²1904; A. W. Persson, Åkerbruksriter och hällristningar (*Fornvännen* 25) 1930; E. Elgqvist, *Studier rörande Njordkultens spridning*, Lund 1925; B. Sternquist, 'New Light on Spring-Cults in Scandinavian Prehistory' (*Archaeology* 17) 1964; G. Turville-Petre, 'Fertility of Beast and Soil' (*Old Norse Literature and Mythology*) Austin 1969; J. de Vries, *Altgermanische Religionsgeschichte*, Berlin ³1970.

fetches → *fylgjur*.

Fiðr (ON, also Finnr 'Finn; magician; troll'). A dwarf (*Vǫluspá* 16 and in the *Þulur*). Fiðr is also recorded as a personal name in the 11th century. The Finns had a reputation in Medieval Scandinavia for being magicians, and the dwarf's name Fiðr appears to refer to this function.

H. Koht, 'Var "Finnane" alltid Finnar?' (MoM) 1923.

Fíli, also Víli (ON). A dwarf in *Vǫluspá* 13. In the version given in the *Snorra Edda*, the two names Hepti and Fíli have been merged to give → Heptifíli. Fíli could mean 'the filer' although this would be the only *fíli* in ON meaning 'file, rasp' and would have to have been borrowed from Low German or Frisian. Another etymological possibility is to interpret Fíli as coming from **filhja* and therefore 'the dwarf who hides the skaldic mead'.

H. Gering, *Kommentar*, 1, Halle 1927; L. Motz, 'New Thoughts on Dwarf Names' (*FmSt* 7) 1973; J. de Vries, *Altnordisches etymologisches Wörterbuch*, Leiden ²1977.

R: Fíli is one of the 13 dwarfs in J. R. R. Tolkien's novel *The Hobbit* (1938).

Fimafengr (ON, 'the one who arrives in a hurry' from *fimi* 'hurry' and *fengr* 'supply'). Ægir's servant in the prose introduction to the → *Lokasenna* where Fimafengr is killed by Loki whilst the Æsir are praising him. Snorri tells a similar tale in *Gylfaginning* 31. As Fimafengr is not mentioned in the *Lokasenna* itself nor anywhere else, it would appear to be a very late analogous invention to Ægir's other servant with the similarly descriptive name → Eldir.

J. de Vries, *Altnordisches etymologisches Wörterbuch*, Leiden [2]1977.

Fimbulþul (ON, Fimbulþul 'mighty wind'? or 'mighty speaker'?). A river in the catalogue of mythical rivers in the *Grímnismál* 27. According to Snorri (*Gylfaginning* 3 and 38), it is one of the Élivágar rivers which flow from the spring called Hvergelmir.

Fimbulþulr (ON, Fimbulþulr 'mighty speaker, mighty wise one'). A name for Odin in the *Hávamál* 80 and 142.

Fimbultýr (ON, 'mighty god'), A name for Odin (*Vǫluspá* 60) that refers to Odin's function as main Germanic god. Nerman concludes that the line in *Vǫluspá* which tells of 'Fimbultýr's old runes' the frequently occurring rune → (Týr-rune) refers to Fimbultýr. It is, however, too risky to base such conclusions about inscriptions from the Migration Age only on *Vǫluspá* without there being any links in between whatsoever.

H. Falk, *Odensheite*, Christiania 1924; J. de Vries, *Altgermanische Religionsgeschichte*, Berlin [3]1970.

Fimbulwinter (ON, *fimbulvetr* 'the enormous winter, the terrible winter'). According to Snorri, this is the harsh winter which heralds the beginning of the downfall of the world at the → Ragnarǫk whereas in *Vafþrúðnismál* 44 it seems to stand for Ragnarǫk itself. Snorri says that the Fimbulwinter was a succession of three winters, without any summers in between, with snow from all directions and frost and cold stormy winds.

Such similar mythological concepts are seldom found in other peoples but there are parallels to Iranian-Manichaeic myths; a borrowing from there is however unlikely as coldness as a cosmic danger is particular to northern Europe. The attempt to understand the Fimbulwinter as the climatic change at the turn of the Scandinavian Bronze Age to the Iron Age in around 500 B.C. (Sernander) is probably incorrect. It suffices that any succession of harsh winters would give enough reason for this concept to arise.

T. Bergeron, M. Fries, C. A. Moberg, F. Ström, 'Fimbulvinter' (*Fornvännen* 51) 1956.

Fimmilena. A goddess named in an inscription on a votive altar at Housesteads on Hadrian's wall, Cumbria, England from the time after 150 A.D. The altar was set up by members of a Frisian legion stationed in northern England and is dedicated to → Mars Thingsus and to both of the *Alaisiagis* Beda and Fimmilena. As in the case of → Beda (2), Fimmilena seems to be related most convincingly to an Old Frisian legal term, the *Fimelþing*. Although the meaning of this word itself is not totally clear ('movable thing', 'final judgement'?), Fimmilena can be thought of as being the 'mistress of the *Fimelþing*'. Schütte's interpretation of Fimmilena as the 'goddess of the Fivelland' is most unlikely.

S. Gutenbrunner, *Die germanischen Götternamen*, Halle 1936; M. Schönfeld, *Wörterbuch der altgermanischen Personen- und Völkernamen*, Heidelberg [2]1965; H. Reichert, *Lexikon der altgermanischen Namen*, Vienna 1987–90.

Finnr (ON), dwarf, → Fiðr.

Fire. The cult of fire which was widespread among Indo-Germanic tribes would appear to have no more relevance for the Germanic tribes in historical times. Caesar, admittedly, mentions Germanic peoples having a cult of a certain Vulcanus, but otherwise there is no evidence for a god of fire, despite attempts to interpret Loki as such. These rest on the unreliable association of Loki with the poetic personification of fire, → Logi. The role of fire in various religious traditions (Yule fires, midsummer fires) and legal acts (going round a piece of land with fire in order to take possession of it), does not justify assuming a Germanic cult of fire, as Huth attempted.

O. Huth, 'Der Feuerkult der Germanen' (*ARW* 36) 1939; O. Huth, *Vesta*, Leipzig, Berlin 1943; J. de Vries, *Altgermanische Religionsgeschichte*, Berlin ³1970.

First Merseburg Charm. In contrast to the → Second Merseburg Charm this charm is not a healing charm, but rather a 'releasing charm' which is supposed to release the prisoner from his chains. The first part of the charm which comprises of four long lines tells how a number of (valkyrie-like?) women ('Idisi', → *dísir*), release imprisoned warriors from their chains, and the last line contains the actual magical command: *insprinc haptbandun, invar vigandun* ('jump out of your chains, flee the enemies').

Fjalarr (1) (ON). A dwarf in the *Vǫluspá* 16. Snorri (*Skáldskaparmál* 1) calls him the brother of → Galarr. These two murdered Kvasir the wise and brewed the → mead of the skalds fom his blood. Snorri also uses the dwarf brothers to explain the kenning *dvergar farskostr* (or *dvergar skip*) 'mead' by telling how the giant Suttungr leaves the two dwarfs who have killed his father Gillingr and his mother to die on a skerry and how they buy their passage back to land by handing over the mead of the skalds. – The meaning of the name Fjalarr is uncertain: 'the hider' (to *fela*) would fit a dwarf and also Fjalarr (3) but not Fjalarr (2); because of this Fjalarr has also been related to New Norwegian *fjela* 'to spy', which, however, is not found in this meaning in Old Norse. The most recent explanation (Salus and Taylor) agrees with the link to *fela* and explains Fjalarr as being 'hider, deceiver' and comments that Fjalarr is only found as a name in its own right in Fjalarr (1) and otherwise only occurs as an epithet in which cunning and cleverness might have been emphasized.

C. N. Gould, 'Dwarf-Names' (*PMLA* 44) 1929; P. H. Salus and P. Beekman Taylor, 'Eikinskjaldi, Fjalarr and Eggþér' (*Neophilologus* 53) 1969; J. de Vries, *Altnordisches etymologisches Wörterbuch*, Leiden ²1977.

Fjalarr (2) (ON). A bright red cock in *Vǫluspá* which sits near to the giant Eggþér and crows.

Fjalarr (3) (ON). The names of several different giants in the Eddas. In *Hávamál* 14 the name is used as a synonym for Suttungr, and in *Hárbarðsljóð* 26 it appears to stand in some connexion with the myth of Skrýmir although it is not totally certain if the name denotes a giant here or a dwarf. In the *Þulur*, Fjalarr is clearly listed among the names of giants.

Fjǫlkaldr (ON, 'very cold'). Svipdagr's grandfather in *Fjǫlsvinnsmál* 6. In this lay Svipdagr calls himself Vindkaldr and says that he is Várkaldr's father. These names are merely poetic embellishments.

Fjǫlnir (1). A name for Odin (*Grímnismál* 47, *Reginsmál* 18; *Gylfaginning* 2 and 19, and frequently in skaldic poetry) which was possibly understood to be 'the one who knows much'. With regards to the etymology of F. → Fjǫlnir 2. As a name for Odin, Fjǫlnir is certainly secondary.

W. v. Unwerth, 'Fiolnir' (*ANF* 33) 1917.

Fjǫlnir (2). A legendary Swedish king (*Skáldskaparmál* 40), son of Yngvi-Freyr and → Gerðr who falls to his death into a vat of mead whilst in a drunken state at a feast (*Ynglinga saga* 11). It is clear that this tale is extremely old from a stanza, quoted by Snorri, which was composed by the skald Þjóðólfr ór Hvíni in the 9th century.

The etymology of the name is disputed and the various attempts at interpretation depend on the diverse mythological interpretations. Older scholars (Schück, Kjær, Krohn; taken up again by Sturtevant) relate Fjǫlnir (from *Felun-eR) to the ON verb *fela* 'hide' and consequently interpreted Fjǫlnir as a name for Odin: 'the one who hides the mead of the skalds'. Unwerth considered Fjǫlnir to be primarily the name of a fertility god which would mean it was related (from *FelduniR) to Gmc **felþa*, German *Feld*, Engl. field, as such 'field god'. He linked this interpretation with Olsen's theory of the identity of → Byggvir (from ON *bygg* 'corn', thus 'corn-spirit') with the Finnish corn spirit Pellon Pekko (from **beggwu bygg*). He also brought the tale of Fjǫlnir's death in the mead vat into association with this so that, according to his interpretation, the field or corn god loses his life in the beer which is brewed from grain. Ever since Dumézil's thoughts on this matter, this interpretation has been rejected since Dumézil pointed out that Pekko is actually the diminutive Pietari ('Peter'). Semantically speaking, an entirely different interpretation is more convincing, namely to relate Fjǫlnir to ON *fjǫl-* 'many' (Lexicon Poeticum, Naumann, Dumézil), hence 'the rich, mighty one', which would be well appropriate as an epithet for Freyr. On the other hand formations of this kind based on an adverb do not occur elsewhere (de Vries). Falk also suggested that Fjǫlnir could be an abbreviation of Fjǫlsviðr 'the very wise one', but this would only be appropriate for a name for Odin (→ Fjǫlnir 1).

H. Schück, *Studier i Nordisk Litteratur och Religionshistoria*, Stockholm 1904; H. Naumann, 'Altnordische Namensstudien' (*Acta Germanica* N. R. 1) 1912; A. Kjær, 'Nogle Stedsnavne' (MoM) 1914; W. v. Unwerth, 'Fiolnir' (*ANF* 33) 1917; F. Jónsson, 'Maskuline substantiver på -nir' (*ANF* 35) 1919; K. Krohn, *Skandinavisk mytologi*, Helsingfors 1922; H. Falk, *Odensheite*, Christiania 1924; F. R. Schröder, 'Neuere Forschungen zur germanischen Altertumskunde und Religionsgeschichte III' (*GRM* 17) 1929; F. Jónsson, *Lexicon Poeticum*, Copenhagen [2]1931; A. M. Sturtevant, 'Etymological Comments' (*PMLA* 67) 1952; J. de Vries, *Altgermanische Religionsgeschichte*, Berlin [3]1970; G. Dumézil, *From Myth to Fiction*, Chicago 1973; J. de Vries, *Altnordisches etymologisches Wörterbuch*, Leiden [2]1977.

Fjǫlsviðr (1) (ON, 'the very wise one'). A dwarf in the *Þulur*.

Fjǫlsviðr (2) (ON). A name for Odin in *Grímnismál* 47 which alludes to Odin's position as the wisest of the gods.

Fjǫlsviðr (3) (ON, 'much-knower'). The (giant?) guard of the virgin → Menglǫð in the late Eddic poem → *Svipdagsmál*. Fjǫlsviðr answers Svipdagr's questions about herself as well as various mythological matters. This part of the *Svipdagsmál* is therefore also known as *Fjǫlsvinsmál*. Fjǫlsviðr (3) is certainly not identical with Fjǫlsviðr (2), and hardly with Fjǫlsviðr (1).

Fjǫlsvinnsmál (ON, 'Lay of Fjǫlsviðr'). A very late Eddic lay which together with the Grógaldr is called → *Svipdagsmál*. In the 50 stanzas composed in the poetic metre of the *ljóðahattr* the *Fjǫlsvinnsmál* tells about the wooing of Menglǫð, who lives on a mountain surrounded by a wall of flames, by the hero → Svipdagr. Svipdagr asks the giant (?) guardian → Fjǫlsviðr ('much-knower') numerous questions, hiding under the pseudonym of Vindkaldr. At first these questions concern Menglǫð's following and abode, then go on to mythological topics and finally Fjǫlsviðr himself announces that Menglǫð can have no other husband but Svipdagr, whereupon the hero reveals his true identity and Menglǫð and he greet each other with mutual declarations of love.

Lit. → *Svipdagsmál.*

Fjǫlvarr (ON, 'the very careful one'). A mythical person in *Hárbarðsljóð* 16 at whose home Odin stayed for five years. As the closely related name Fjǫlvǫr is the name of a giantess, one might assume Fjǫlvarr to be a giant, but the literary sources do not allude to any myth of Odin and Fjǫlvarr. However, as Odin's comments in *Hárbarðsljóð* are intended to confuse Thor, it is quite possible that such a myth never existed in the first place.

Fjǫlverkr (ON, 'the one who works a lot'). A giant in the *Þulur*. The giants are by nature the hard workers of the mythical beings and there are various tales and legends about the giant master-builder to show this.

Fjǫlvǫr (ON). A giantess in the *Þulur*. The name could perhaps mean 'the very careful one'. For other possible interpretations → Svívǫr.

Fjǫrgyn (ON, 'earth'). A name given on several occasions to Thor's mother (*Harbarðsljóð* 56, *Vǫluspá*) 56. It could simply be another name for Thor's mother → Jǫrð (like → Hlóðyn) as even Snorri did not consider Fjǫrgyn to be a goddess in her own right. On the other hand, the fact that Fjǫrgyn does not occur anywhere in skaldic poetry, as would be expected for a purely literary alternative to Jǫrð, is somewhat conspicuous and as such perhaps warrants more critical attention.

J. de Vries, 'Fjǫrgyn en Fjǫrgynn' (*TNTL* 50) 1951; F. R. Schröder, 'Erce und Fjörgyn' (*Festschrift f. K. Helm*) Tübingen 1951.

Fjǫrgynn (ON). The father of the goddess → Frigg. He is only mentioned by Snorri (*Skáldskaparmál* 19) and in the very late *Lokasenna* 26, but not in skaldic poetry or in older mythological Eddic lays. Hence it seems more likely that Fjǫrgynn is a late analogous formation to Fjǫrgyn, but there have also been attempts to link Fjǫrgynn with the Lithuanian god Perkunas. To try and see Fjǫrgynn as the ancient god of thunder and as such Thor's predecessor is surely reading too much into the 12th and 13th century recordings of the name.

R. Much, 'Der germanische Himmelsgott' (*Festgabe f. R. Heinzel*) Halle 1898; J. Loewenthal, 'Zur germanischen Wortkunde' (*ANF* 33) 1917; J. de Vries, 'Fjǫrgyn en Fjǫrgynn' (*TNTL* 50) 1951; F. R. Schröder, 'Erce und Fjörgyn' (*Festschrift f. K. Helm*) Tübingen 1951; J. de Vries, *Altgermanische Religionsgeschichte*, Berlin ^{3}1970.

Fjǫrm (ON, 'the one in a hurry'). A river in the catalogue of rivers in *Grímnismál* 27. In Snorri (*Gylfaginning* 3 and 40) Fjǫrm is one of the Élivágar rivers which flow from the spring, Hvergelmir.

Fjǫturlundr (ON, 'Grove of bondage') → grove of the Semnones.

Fleggr (ON). A giant in the *Þulur*. The name either belongs to *flag* 'mountain wall, cliff' because the giants dwell in the mountains, or else to *flagð* 'monster, troll'.

F. Jónsson, 'Þulur' (APhSc 9) 1934; J. de Vries, *Altnordisches etymologisches Wörterbuch*, Leiden [2]1977.

(**Floßhilde**) is one of the Rhine daughters in Richard Wagner's operas *Das Rheingold* and *Die Götterdämmerung*; the name was invented by Wagner.

Fǫnn (ON, 'snowdrift'). A giantess (?) in the mythical genealogy of the mythical ancestor Fornjótr in the version of *Hversu Nóregr byggðisk* where Þorri, Mjǫll, Drífa and Fǫnn are named as the children of King Snær. As all these names personify aspects of winter, it is possible that this was originally a genealogy of frost giants.

Fǫr Skírnis ('Skírnir's journey'). The title of the Eddic lay → *Skírnismál*, given in the *Codex Regius*.

Fol → Phol.

Fólkvangr (ON, 'field of the people'; 'field of the army'?). The abode of the goddess Freyja (*Grímnismál* 14). The meaning of the name Fólkvangr, which is surely not much older than the *Grímnismál* itself, is clear from the explanation immediately following it, namely that Freyja chooses half of the fallen heroes (for Valhall), and Odin chooses the other half. In *Gylfaginning* 23 Snorri keeps close to these specifications given in the *Grímnismál* and adds that Freyja's hall in Fólkvangr is called Sessrumnir.

Folla → Volla, → Fulla.

Forað (ON, 'danger'). A giantess in the *Þulur*. Her name indicates the danger inherent in giantesses, which is clear from Thor's various adventures with them.

Fornaldarsǫgur (ON, 'mythical-heroic sagas') is the name given to a genre of → sagas, the material of which deals with the legendary pre-history of Scandinavia, i.e. with the time before the settlement of Iceland. These sagas, composed in the late 13th and 14th centuries, are by no means homogenous and some of them even bear extremely fairy-tale-like traits, whereas others deal with the old heroic tales (*Hrólfs saga kraka*) or else with pseudo-historical royal histories (*Skjǫldunga saga*). Several of the *fornaldarsǫgur* are based on older lays which are either reworked into prose (*Vǫlsunga saga*) or else used as a framework for the sagas (*Hervarar saga*). It appears that many of the *fornaldarsǫgur* have been lost but many are retained to some extent as they were used by Saxo Grammaticus in his Latin *Gesta Danorum*. Thus we at least know the contents of them even if the actual form has been lost because of the liberties taken by Saxo in his use of his sources.

Several of the *fornaldarsǫgur* retain remains of myths as well as of heroic sagas and also old genealogies and as such they are interesting as a source for Germanic mythology (*Hervarar saga*). However, as with the other sagas, care should be taken in using the *fornaldarsǫgur* as source material for dealing with Germanic mythology as their authors (like those of the sagas of the Icelanders) used heathen customs and gods in part merely in order to lend historical colour to their tales.

P. Herrmann, *Erläuterungen zu den ersten neun Büchern der Dänischen* Geschichte des Saxo Gram-

maticus, Bd. 2, Leipzig 1922; J. de Vries, 'Die Wikingersaga' (*GRM* 15) 1927; H. Reuschel, Saga und Wikinglied (*PBB* 56) 1932; H. Reuschel, *Untersuchungen über Stoff und Stil der Fornaldarsaga*, Bühl 1933; M. Schlauch, *Romance in Iceland*, London 1934; F. Genzmer, 'Vorzeitsaga und Heldenlied' (*Festschrift P. Kluckhohn & H. Schneider*) 1948; E. O. Sveinsson, 'Fornaldarsǫgur' (*KLNM* 4) 1959; M. C. v. d. Toorn, 'Über die Ethik in den Fornaldarsagas' (*APhSc* 26) 1963/64; K. Schier, 'Fornaldarsögur' (*KLL* 3) 1967; H. Pálsson, P. Edwards, *Legendary Fiction in Medieval Iceland*, Reykjavík 1971; H. Kuhn, 'Abenteuersagen' (*Hoops* 1) ²1973; P. Buchholz, 'Fornaldarsaga und mündliches Erzählen zur Wikingerzeit' (*Les vikings et leur civilisation*) Paris 1976; P. Buchholz, *Vorzeitkunde*, Neumünster 1980; Also the following papers given at the *Fourth International Saga Conference* Munich 1979: A. Bucher-van Nahl, 'Originale Riddarasögur und ihre Beziehung zu Fornaldarsögur'; P. Buchholz, 'Lügengeschichten?'; P. Hallberg, 'Some Aspects of the Fornaldarsögur as a Corpus'; P. A. Jorgensen, 'Literarisch verwandte Stellen in verschiedenen Fornaldarsagas'; H. Pálsson, 'Towards a Definition of Fornaldarsǫgur'; H. Seelow, 'Zur Rolle der Strophen in den Fornaldarsögur'.

Fornbogi (ON, 'the old bow'). A dwarf in *Vǫluspá* 13.

Fornjótr (ON). The ancestor of a family (of giants?) in a legendary Norwegian pre-history set at the beginning of the *Orkneyinga saga* (*Fundinn Nóregr*) and, somewhat differently, in the *Flateyjarbók* (*Hversu Nóregr byggðisk*). Fornjótr is said to be a king and yet from the names of his descendants it is clear that the genealogy must be mythological: Fornjótr has three sons, Hlér ('sea'), Logi ('fire') and Kari ('wind'). Either Jǫkull ('glacier') or Frosti are said to be Kari's sons. According to both traditions, Kari is the grandfather of Snær ('snow') who again is the father of Þorri (name of a winter month). According to the variant in *Hversu Nóregr byggðisk*, Snær's children are called Þorri, Fǫnn ('snow drift'), Drífa ('snow flurry') and Mjǫll ('powder snow'). This wintery genealogy could indicate that there was originally a whole genealogy of frost giants which was included in the pre-history of Norway for the first time in the literature of the High Middle Ages. On the other hand, the telling names suggest a late invention.

Only the etymology of the name Fornjótr itself is problematic and there have been many attempts to interpret it: if it is read as *forn-jótr*, then the possible meaning could be 'old Jutlander' (Grimm) or else 'proto-giant' (Hellquist); *for-njótr* would give 'previous owner' (Uhland) or else 'destroyer' (Jónsson). The most unlikely explanation is *forn-njǫtr* 'delighter in sacrifices' (Noreen), whereas *forn-þjótr* 'old bellower' (Kock) would at least fit in with the names for other giants. The spelling *fior-* in some manuscripts of the 13th and 14th centuries suggests that Fornjótr was understood at this time as being 'life-giant' (to *fjǫr* 'life'), which would possibly mean an identification with Ymir.

Although it is uncertain whether the Old English plant name *fornetesfolm* (to Fornjótr and *folm* 'hand') really goes back to Nordic influence, if it did it would show how well this giant was in fact known.

L. Uhland, *Schriften*, Vol. 6, Stuttgart 1868; J. Grimm, *Deutsche Mythologie*, Berlin ⁴1875–78; A. Noreen, 'Mytiska Beståndsdelar i Ynglingatal' (*Uppsalastudier til. S. Bugge*) Uppsala 1892; E. Hellquist, 'Om Fornjótr' (*ANF* 19), 1903; E. A. Philippson, *Germanisches Heidentum bei den Angelsachsen*, Leipzig 1929; F. Jónsson, 'Þulur' (*APhSc* 9) 1934; J. de Vries, *Altnordisches etymologisches Wörterbuch*, Leiden ²1977; M. Clunies Ross, 'Snorri Sturluson's use of the Norse origin-legend' (*ANF* 98) 1983.

Fornǫlvir (ON, 'heathen Ölvir'). A pseudonym for Odin in the *Þulur*.

Forseti (ON, 'chairman'). The name of one of the Æsir gods according to Snorri (*Gylfaginning* 31, *Skáldskaparmál* 5). He is Baldr's and Nanna's son and lives in the godly residence of Glitnir (*Gylfaginning* 31 following *Grímnismál* 15). He is only mentioned in *Grímnismál* in the whole of Old Norse poetry and here he is said to be a god who settles arguments, and hence his name 'chairman (at the Thing)'; the rest of the tale of his relationship to other gods and his residence is no doubt the result of Snorri's creative powers.

Despite the extremely sparse Scandinavian sources and the telling name, Forseti need not be a late poetic invention. In the *Vita Sancti Willebrordi*, composed by Alcuin between 785 and 797, we hear that at the beginning of the 8th century St Willebrord came to an island which lies between Frisia and Denmark called Fositesland in honour of the god worshipped there. Adam of Bremen (*Gesta Hammaburgensis ecclesiae pontificum* IV, 3) identified this island as Helgoland, but this can hardly be correct.

Because of the similarity of names between this Frisian Fosite and the West Nordic Forseti, attempts have been made to find a common base-form which might have been *Forsete or else *Forsite which then in the north, as a result of folk etymology, was re-formed to create the more comprehensible form Forseti. In the Oslo fjord there is a place-name, Forsetlund, which could also refer to this god.

The hypothesis that Forseti is, as Snorri suggests, a god of law and legal disputes (de Vries), is found wanting because the derivation of Forseti from Frisian does not give the meaning of the Nordic name any more proof and as such cannot be considered in order to support this theory, however suggestive it might appear at first sight.

F. B. Hettema, 'Fosete, Fosite, Foste' (*TNTL* 12) 1893; T. Siebs, 'Der Gott Fos(e)te und sein Land' (*PBB* 35) 1909; J. de Vries, *Altgermanische Religionsgeschichte*, [3]1979.

R: E. Doepler d. J., *Forseti* (W. Ranisch, H. Doepler, *Walhall*) 1901.

Forve (ON). A dwarf in the *Þulur*. The meaning is uncertain even if one assumes a term *Forvé*: 'unholy place' or else 'forecourt to a shrine'? Neither are really appropriate for a dwarf's name.

C. N. Gould, 'Dwarf-Names' (*PMLA* 44) 1929.

Frægr (ON, 'the famous one'). A dwarf in *Vǫluspá* 13.

Franangrsfors (ON, 'Franangr's waterfall'). The waterfall in the prose conclusion to the → *Lokasenna*, as well as in Snorri's tale of Loki's Punishment (*Gylfaginning*), in which Loki changes shape into a salmon in order to hide from the Æsir.

Frár (ON, 'the quick one'). A dwarf in *Vǫluspá* 13.

Fráriðr (ON, 'the one riding away'). A name for Odin in the *Þulur*. Perhaps the idea of Odin riding to Valhall with the slain warriors as the god of the dead underlies this name.

H. Falk, *Odensheite*, Christiania 1924.

Frea (Langobard.). According to the historical works of the Langobards, namely the *Origo gentis Langobardorum* and Paulus' Diaconus *Historia Langobardorum*, Frea is the wife of the god Wodan, and as such is the same as → Frigg.

***Frēa** (Anglo-Saxon). If the form of the name alone is considered, then Frēa would be the god corresponding to the Scandinavian god Freyr in Saxon Britain. However, Frēa is never recorded as a heathen god in Old English, and is only found in the meaning of 'lord', referring frequently even to Christ.

(**Freia**) is Richard Wagner's version of the goddess Freyja whom he has merged into one figure with the goddess Idun (the guardian of the golden apples). Freia is a coloratura soprano in the opera *Das Rheingold.*

Freki (ON, 'the greedy one'). One of Odin's wolves, according to *Grímnismál* 19 and *Gylfaginning* 37. The other is called Geri. In *Vǫluspá* (44, 49, 51) Freki is a name for the Fenriswolf.

Freyja (ON, 'woman, mistress'). The most important goddess of Old Scandinavian mythology and the beautiful goddess of lovers. She belongs to the divine family of the Vanir, is the daughter of → Njǫrðr and his sister, and sister (and probably originally also wife) to Freyr. Eddic mythology assigns her a husband Oðr (who is not otherwise mentioned) with whom she has two daughters, Hnoss and Gersimi (*Gylfaginning* 34). The names of both daughters are synonymous and mean only 'preciousness', and are as such merely later poetic emanations of the goddess herself.

Snorri describes her (*Gylfaginning* 23) as follows: 'Freyja is the most famous of the goddesses; she lives in heaven at a place called Folkvangr, and when she moves into battle, she gets half of the fallen warriors, Odin receiving the other half' (also in *Grímnismál* 14, which Snorri quotes here), 'her hall is called Sessrúmnir and is large and beautiful. Whenever Freyja travels, she sits in her carriage which is drawn by cats. She is fond of love songs and it is worthwhile calling upon her in matters of love.'

Apart from the cat-drawn carriage, Freyja's other attributes are a falcon garment (like Frigg's: *Þrymskviða* 5; *Skáldskaparmál* 1) and perhaps also the boar Hildisvíni (*Hyndluljóð* 7), and most important of all, the necklace → Brísingamen.

Old Norse literature speaks frequently of Freyja. In *Þrymskviða* the giant → Þrymr only wants to return Mjǫllnir if he gets Freyja as his wife. In *Lokasenna* 30 she is accused of whoring, whilst in *Hyndluljóð* she competes with a giantess in a contest of knowledge and in *Oddrúnargrátr* 9 she is invoked together with the goddess Frigg.

Snorri emphasises her position as the most beautiful and most important of the goddesses, and in the adventures of the giants she is the representative of the goddesses who is time and again desired by the giants, not only in *Þrymskviða* but also in the tales of the → Giant Master Builder and of the giant → Hrungnir.

The skalds of the 10th century also frequently name Freyja. An anecdote about the skald Hjalti Skeggjason throws light on Freyja's important position in heathen religion. The skald composed the following verse mocking Freyja at the All-thing in 999 A.D. during the confrontation between heathendom and Christianity: 'I don't like barking gods; I consider Freyja to be a bitch'. This verse led to him being outlawed for blasphemy (*Islenngabók* 7).

Freyja is descended from the Vanir and therefore is a goddess of fertility. She also teaches the Æsir magic, a knowledge which she brings with her from the Vanir (*Ynglinga saga* 4). With regard to this, Snorri mentions that incestuous marriage was usual among the Vanir. The gods Freyr and Freyja may thus be considered to be a brother-sister couple/married couple. It is only later, when Freyja has become one of the Æsir, that Freyja is said to have a husband → Oðr, who is once said to be away for a long time, and for whom Freyja weeps golden tears (*Vǫluspá* 25, *Hyndluljóð* 47; *Gylfaginning* 35), a tale which was also already known in the 10th century.

In skaldic poetry Freyja is known by a whole series of names, which Snorri lists (*Gylfaginning* 34): Mardǫll, Hǫrn, Gefn, Sýr, as well as Vanadís. These names characterize Freyja as a domestic guardian goddess. The name Sýr points out that Freyja like her brother Freyr is characterized with the attribute of the pig. In *Hyndluljóð* she even rides on a boar, Hildisvíni.

Also in *Hyndluljóð* 10 Freyja boasts that her protégé Ottar sets up altars to her and makes sacrifices to her, and indeed, although literary sources do not otherwise refer to a cult of Freyja, a significant number of place-names in Sweden and Norway show that there was devotion to Freyja. Norwegian place names such as Frøihov (from **Freyjuhof* 'Freyja's temple') and Swedish ones such as Frǫvi (from **Freyjuvé* 'Freyja's shrine') could point to a public cult, although a purely domestic cult would be expected of a guardian goddess or a goddess of love.

E. F. Halvorsen, 'Freyja' (*KLNM* 4) 1959; J. de Vries, *Altgermanische Religionsgeschichte*, Berlin [3]1970; E. O. G. Turville-Petre, *Myth and Religion of the North*, Westport 1975. → Freyr.

R: (fine art) H. E. Freund, *Freyja* (statue, 1821/22); N. J. O. Blommér, *Freyja sökande sin make* (painting, 1852); K. Ehrenberg, *Freyjas Aufnahme unter den Göttern* (charcoal drawing, 1881); K. Ehrenberg, *Frigg; Freyja* (drawing, 1883); E. Doepler d. J., *Freyja* (E. Doepler, W. Ranisch, *Walhall*, 1901); J. Doyle-Penrose, *Freyja and the Brisingamen* (painting).

(literature) A. Oehlenschläger, *Frejas alter* (comedy, 1818); A. Oehlenschläger, *Freias sal* (poem).

(others) As a ship's name, Freyja has been given to a Swedish supply vessel (1953) and a West German minesweeper, and since the end of the 19th century it has been a widely popular name for yachts in German and English speaking areas.

Freyr (ON, 'lord'). The most important god of the Vanir and the most powerful god of fertility of Germanic mythology.

Freyr is the son of → Njǫrðr with his sister. Freyr is Freyja's brother and after the custom of the Vanir probably originally her husband, until with the Æsir he woos the giant's daughter Gerðr (*Skírnismál*; *Gylfaginning* 36) and marries her.

Freyr owns the ship → Skíðblaðnir (*Gylfaginning* 44; *Skáldskaparmál* 7 and 33) and the boar → Gullinborsti, who (according to Snorri, *Gylfaginning* 48) pulls Freyr's chariot. Apart from the fabulous embellishments these attributes appear to be old, since the boar as a sign of fertility is connected with the Vanir and the Swedish royal house elsewhere, and an association with seafaring can similarly be traced far back with the Vanir gods Njǫrðr and Freyr.

Freyr's residence is → Alfheimr (*Grímnismál* 5) which he was given as a teething-present. Snorri describes it in *Gylfaginning* 23f. as follows: 'Freyr is the noblest of the gods; he rules over rain and sunshine and thus over the produce of the earth; it is good to call upon him for good harvests and for peace; he watches over the prosperity of mankind.' Freyr falls at Ragnarǫk in battle against the fire giant Sutr (*Vǫluspá* 53; *Gylfaginning* 50) in which, according to Snorri, he has no sword as he lent it to his servant Skírnir in order to woo Gerðr. It is at this point that Freyr is called 'killer of Beli' and Snorri (alone of all sources) tells us (*Gylfaginning* 36) that Freyr killed the otherwise unknown giant without his sword using the antlers of a stag.

In his euhemeristic rendering of the *Ynglinga saga* 10 Snorri tells of Freyr's life in quite different terms: Freyr was a Swedish king who settled down in Uppsala and was married to Gerðr who had a son called Fjǫllnir. The Peace of → Fróði began under his reign and the name of the Yngling dynasty came from his other name, Yngvi. When Freyr died, it was kept secret throughout Sweden for three years and he was not cremated so that the Peace of Fróði would not be broken; instead he became the subject of devotion and sacrifice.

It has been realized for a long time that Fróði and Freyr are identical and even Freyr's affinity to Sweden mentioned by Snorri is beyond doubt, as the cult place names (as much as anything) prove. Adam of Bremen talks of a temple at Uppsala and mentions statues there of Thor, Wodan and Fricco (= Freyr). Fricco's statue was adorned by a 'mighty phallus' (Adam: *cum ingenti priapo*). Adam also writes about the lascivious songs during the sacrifice at Uppsala which were totally appropriate within the scope of a fertility cult.

A strange tale about the devotion to Freyr can be found in part of the Icelandic *Flateyjarbók* which tells how a fugitive Icelander, Gunnar Helmingr, finds protection with a priestess of Freyr who is travelling through the land in a chariot bearing the statue of the god Freyr; Gunnar soon takes the place of the statue and travels around like this; when the priestess becomes pregnant, the people take this as being a good sign. Even if this story is late, it nonetheless fits in nicely with the procession of Nerthus as told by Tacitus and the belief in the power of the Vanir to bring good harvests and fertility so that it does not seem necessary to assume the influence of burlesque yarns from abroad.

Saxo reports a → Frøsblot which Haddingus (who has characteristics in common with the god Njǫrðr) is supposed to have instituted. Such sacrifices to Freyr, particularly in Sweden, are recorded in literature. Cult place-names based on Freyr are especially common in East Sweden, and even the sacrifice mentioned in Uppsala could have been a sacrifice to Freyr.

As to the attributes of the god Freyr, the Swedish kings appear to have had a particular affection for the boar, as the Swedish crown-jewel Svíagríss (a ring, 'boar of the Swedes') confirms; → Gullinborsti. Uppsala and East Sweden were the centre of the cult or the god Freyr and this cult was especially propagated by the Swedish Yngling-kings who counted Freyr as their ancestor.

The fact that Freyr enjoyed special devotion even outside Sweden can be seen by his position in the formula of the oath 'so help me Freyr and Njǫrðr and *hinn almáttki áss*' (the almighty god); at sacrifices held by the Norwegian jarls of Hlaðir the first draught was dedicated to Odin, but the following ones to Njǫrðr and Freyr; admittedly this report in the *Hákonar saga góða* 14 is probably not historical. Men with the by-name Freysgoði 'priest of Freyr' are repeatedly found in the Icelandic historical sources, and even a comment in a late Icelandic saga that a devotee of Freyr carried with him a Freyr amulet in his bag (*Vatnsdœla saga* 10) has been substantiated by the find of a small Viking-Age statuette (from Rällinge, Sweden) which is distinctly phallic in character.

Freyr is not only the main god of Sweden, but also he is the mythical ancestor of the Swedish royal family of the Ynglings with the cognomen → Yngvi or Yngvi-Freyr, which corresponds to the name → Ingunarfreyr mentioned in *Lokasenna* 43 and the *Oláfs saga*; it is therefore possible that Yngvi-Freyr is identifiable with the mythical progenitor *Ingwaz of the Germanic tribe of the Ingaevones, but the problem with the relation Freyr/Yngvi/*Ingwaz has by no means been solved.

S. Bugge, *Fricco, Frigg und Priapos*, Christiania 1904; G. Turville-Petre, 'The Cult of Freyr' (*Proceedings of the Leeds Phil. and Lit. Soc.* 3) 1935; H. Schück, 'Ingunar-Freyr' (*Fornvännen* 35) 1940; W. Baetke, *Yngvi und die Ynglinger*, Berlin 1964; N. Å. Nielsen, 'Freyr, Ullr, and the Sparlösa Stone' (*Medieval Scandinavia* 2) 1969; J. de Vries, *Altgermanische Religionsgeschichte*, Berlin [3]1970; E. O. G. Turville-Petre, *Myth and Religion of the North*, Westport 1975; P. Bibire, 'Freyr and Gerðr: The story and its Myths' (*Sagnaskemmtun. Studies H. Pálsson*), Vienna 1986.

R: (fine art) B. E. Fogelberg, *Freyr* (plaster, 1818); K. Ehrenberg, *Freyr und Gerda, Skade und Niurd* (drawing, 1883); E. Burne-Jones, *Freyr* (sketch); J. Reich, *Frey*

(water colour, c.1900); E. Doepler d. J., *Freyr*; and: *Freyr und Gerd* (E. Doepler, W. Ranisch, *Walhall*, 1901).
(literature) P. O. Sundman: *Berättelsen om Søm* (novel, 1977).
Freyr is also the name of a Dutch Navy vessel (1954).

Friagabis. An ancient Germanic goddess. One of the inscriptions of the votive altars in Housesteads on Hadrian's Wall, Cumbria, England (after A.D. 150) calls the goddesses Friagabis and Baudihillia together → Alaisiagae. Friagabis probably means 'generous' (lit. 'friendly giving').

R. Much, 'Baudihillia und Friagabis' (*Festschrift Jellinek*) Vienna, Leipzig 1928; S. Gutenbrunner, *Die germanischen Götternamen*, Halle 1936; H. Reichert, *Lexikon der altgermanischen Namen*, Vienna 1987–90.

Fricco. The name Adam of Bremen (*Gesta Ecclessiae Hammaburgensis Pontificum* IV, 26) gives to the god worshipped in the temple at Uppsala along with Thor and Wodan, and who was portrayed there *cum ingenti priapo* ('with a huge phallus'). Undoubtedly the fertility god → Freyr is meant with Fricco, even if the etymology of Fricco is somewhat problematic. Fricco is not identical with the name Freyr/Frø unless Adam confused him with Frigg. A derivation from **friðkan* 'lover' is more likely, whereas the popular explanation by older scholars from Thracian Priapos is not particularly convincing.

J. Loewenthal, 'Fricco' (*PBB* 50) 1927; J. de Vries, *Altgermanische Religionsgeschichte*, Berlin [3]1970.

(**Fricka**). Richard Wagner's version of the goddess Frigg in the operas *Das Rheingold* and *Die Walküre*; like Frigg, Fricka is Wotan's wife, too.

Friday. The → week-day name Friday goes back to the Common Germanic translation of the Roman *dies Veneris* ('day of Venus') by 'day of Frîja' and occured already in or before the 4th century A.D.: OHG *fríatag*, OE *frīgedeag*, ON *friádagr*. It is uncertain whether Frîja/Frigg was really considered to be the goddess of love, and was understood as being the counterpart to Venus, hence the translation, since Frigg's sexual promiscuity otherwise appears to be a characteristic rather of the younger sources than the older.

E. O. G. Turville-Petre, *Myth and Religion of the North*, Westport 1975; F. Kluge, *Etymologisches Wörterbuch*, Berlin [22]1989.

Fríð (ON, 'pretty') is one of Menglọð's maids in *Fjǫlsvinsmál* 38.

Frigg (ON) is the main goddess of the Æsir in Scandinavian mythology; of all goddesses she is second to no-one apart from the Vanir goddess, Freya.

Frigg is Odin's wife, the mother of Baldr and the daughter of an otherwise unknown → Fjǫrgynn (*Lokasenna* 26; *Skáldskaparmál* 19); her residence is in Asgard (→ Fensalir) and her servants are called Fulla and Gná (*Gylfaginning* 34; *Skáldskaparmál* 19). Her attribute is the falcon dress (*Skáldskaparmál* 18, 19). In the *Snorra Edda*, Frigg's role is particularly stressed in the myth of Baldr as it is she who demands an oath from everything in the world not to harm her son → Baldr, and it is at her request that Hermoðr rides to Hel to ransom Baldr from the underworld.

As a divine married couple who interfere in the conflicts of men, albeit on different sides, Frigg and Odin appear in both the prose introduction of the Eddic *Grímnismál* and in the history of the Langobards (Paulus Diaconus, *Historia Langobardorum*); whereas Wodan supports the Vandals, his wife Frea (= Frigg) helps the Langobards who are finally victorious by using cunning means.

Another myth about Frigg is told by Snorri in the *Ynglinga saga* 3: during → Odin's exile his brothers Vili and Vé do not only own all his property jointly but also share his wife Frigg, until Odin's return, when he claims his wife again. This myth is referred to in *Lokasenna* 26 where Loki blames Frigg for having slept with Vili and Vé. Frigg plays a completely different role in Saxo's versions of Odin's exile (*Gesta Danorum* I, 25f.) where she has a statue of Odin destroyed because of her jealousy about his renown and commits adultery with a slave; the shame as a result of this makes Odin go into exile.

In Germanic times Frigg seems to have been known outside Scandinavia: in the Second Merseburg Charm Frîja (the OHG form of the name Frigg) appears in an active role and was worshipped to such an extent as early as the 3rd and 4th centuries that when the Roman week-day names were translated, Venus was so obviously identified as the Latin equivalent to Frigg that *dies Veneris* became OHG *frîatac*, OE *frīgedeag* (Engl. Friday). In Scandinavia, interestingly enough, the South German word *frīadag* was taken over (ON *fríadagr*) instead of a native name *Friggjardagr being created. In the middle of the first millenium it appears that Frigg was more widely known in the south than in the north.

The identity of the goddess Frîja/Frigg with Venus reveals something about Frigg's character, which may be confirmed by the interpretation of her name: Frigg is most reasonably cognate to OSax *frī*, OE *frēo* 'woman', OInd *priyā* 'beloved one'. Thus, Frigg may be understood to have been originally the goddess of women, of relationships, and possibly of love. Because of the long tradition surrounding Frigg there is no reason to doubt that she was considered to be Odin's wife from a very early time; in the writings of Christian authors the divine couple took on the characteristics of Zeus and Hera.

H. Jungner, *Gudinnan Frigg och Als Härad*, Uppsala 1922; H. Jungner, 'Om Friggproblemet' (*NoB* 12) 1924; E. F. Halvorsen, 'Frigg' (*KLNM* 4) 1959; J. de Vries, *Altgermanische Religionsgeschichte*, Berlin [3]1970; L. Motz, 'Sisters in the Cave' (*ANF* 95) 1980.

R: (literature) A play called Friggja was written by the Swedish king Gustav III; H. F. Blunck, *Frau Frigg und Doktor Faust* (in: *Märchen und Sagen*) 1937.
(fine art) K. Ehrenberg, *Frigg, Freyja* (drawing 1883); J. C. Dollmann, *Frigga spinning the clouds* (painting, c.1900); E. Doepler d. J., *Wodan und Frea am Himmelsfenster*, (E. Doepler, W. Ranisch, *Walhall*) 1901; H. Thoma, *Fricka* (drawing).

Frîja, Germanic goddess, Wodan's wife, best known in the ON form → Frigg. In South German sources she is known only in Langobardian sources as Frea and as Frîja in the Second Merseburg Charm. The form of the name Frîja in the 2nd to 4th centuries A.D. is confirmed by the translation of OHG *frîatac* (→ Friday) for the Latin week-day name, *dies Veneris*.

Frisavae is the name of Germanic matres on an inscription from Wissen near Xanten, Germany (CIL XIII 8633), devoted to the *Matribus Frisavis paternis*, 'the paternal Frisiavian mothers'. These Frisavae were obviously worshipped by the Frisai (also Frisiavi, Frisaevones), one of the Frisian tribes.

S. Gutenbrunner, *Die germanischen Götternamen*, Halle 1936; J. de Vries, *Altgermanische Religionsgeschichte*, Berlin [3]1970; H. Reichert, *Lexikon der altgermanischen Namen* I–II, Vienna 1987–90.

***Frô** (OHG), which is only found in OHG in the meaning 'lord' (cf. Ger. *Fronleichnam* = Corpus Christi), corresponds phonetically to ON Freyr and thus would be the OHG equivalent to the ON god Freyr. The only evidence of a god *Frô is the Dutch place-name, Vroonloo ('*Frô's wood') which is hardly sufficient to prove the existence of a South German equivalent to Freyr, especially as the Second Merseburg Charm names a god Phol, who together with another god named there, Volla, could represent the equivalence to the Nordic divine couple Freyr and Freyja.

F. R. Schröder, *Ingunar-Freyr*, Tübingen 1941; J. de Vries, *Altgermanische Religionsgeschichte*, Berlin ³1970.

Fróði (in Saxo Frotho) is a legendary Danish king from the house of the Skjöldungs during whose reign the famous Peace of Fróði (*Fróða friðr*) lasted. This peace manifested itself in a long series of good harvests which made the farmers prosperous, lasting peace (→ *ár ok friðr*) and such a sense of inner and outer security that nobody even removed a golden ring lying on the heath at Jelling.

The Peace of Fróði is mentioned already in Einar's skaldic poem *Vellekla* (about 986), and details of it are found in Snorri's *Ynglinga saga* 10f. and *Skáldskaparmál* 40, as well as in Saxo's *Gesta Danorum* V. Only in Snorri's *Ynglinga saga* 10 is Fróði equated with Freyr and the ensuing peace attributed to the fertility god.

It is a matter of a legendary time of peace, not dissimilar to the Golden Age, which is representative for the belief in the responsibility of the king for peace and for good harvests (→ sacral kingship) as well as for the cult of the fertility god (Freyr), so that the king's reign must be crowned by peace with the god, a phenomenon which is also confirmed by Tacitus (*Germania* 40) for the cult of Nerthus. When Snorri and Saxo date the reign of Fróði as coinciding with the time of Emperor Augustus and Christ's birth, then it is a question of a Christian scholarly tendency to harmonize matters.

Fróði repeatedly appears as a figure in Germanic mythology: as Froda in the Anglo-Saxon *Beowulf* and in *Widsith* and as five different kings called Frotho in Saxo whereby the quasi-historical status of these five Frothos is quite complicated. It probably comes down originally to a single mythical-legendary king who was a son of Skjǫld, the mythical ancestor of the Skjöldungs (Ebenbauer).

K. Visted, 'Frodes Fred – Julefred' (*Norsk Folkekultur* 8) 1922; K. Schier, 'Freys und Fróðis Bestattungen' (*Festschrift* O. *Höfler* 2) Vienna 1968; J. de Vries, *Altgermanische Religionsgeschichte*, Berlin ³1970; A. Ebenbauer, 'Fróði und sein Friede' (*Festgabe* O. *Höfler*) Berlin 1976; F. Ström, 'År och fred' (*KLNM* 20) 1976.

R: J. R. R. Tolkien, *The Lord of the Rings* (novel, 1954).

Frø. A god mentioned in Saxo (*Gesta Danorum* I, 30; III, 75; VI, 185) who is sacrificed to in → Uppsala. Saxo gives especial prominence to the human sacrifice occurring then → Frøsblot. Frø is without question identical with the god → Freyr.

Frøsblot ('Frø-sacrifice'). In Saxo, this is the Swedish expression for the sacrifices to the god Frø = Freyr in → Uppsala (*Gesta Danorum* I, 30). Saxo explains the origin of this sacrifice as the atonement made by → Haddingus to the god Frø which he does by offering human sacrifice. Haddingus repeated this sacrifice annually and later it was continued by his descendents. However, other sources record that the great sacrifice at Uppsala only took place every nine years, which might also be understood in Saxo (*Gesta Danorum* VI, 185).

It is uncertain what is meant by the reference to dark skinned victims (*furvis hostiis*) which Haddingus sacrificed to Frø.

(Froh). Richard Wagner's version of the god Frô (= Freyr) in the opera *Das Rheingold*.

Frór (ON, 'nimble, light-footed, alert'). A dwarf in *Vǫluspá* 13.

Frosti (ON, 'cold, frost'). A dwarf in *Vǫluspá* 16 and in *Þulur*.

Frost giants → Hrímþursar.

Fulla (ON). One of the → Asyniur, according to Snorri (*Skáldskaparmál* 1). Elsewhere, however, Snorri says that she is Frigg's hand-maiden (*Skáldskaparmál* 19, *Gylfaginning* 34) whose duties are to carry her casket, look after her shoes, and be privy to her secrets. According to Snorri, Fulla is a virgin who has flowing hair and wears a golden band around her forehead. This allusion to the golden band refers to an old kenning for gold in which Fulla's name occurs. Fulla is also used by the skalds in kennings for 'woman'. Although Snorri mentions the fact that Baldr sends Fulla a golden ring from Hel (*Gylfaginning* 48), this does not prove that she plays any role in the Baldr myth, but merely shows that Snorri associated her with gold because of the kennings (also *Gylfaginning* 34, *Skáldskaparmál* 30, 34).

The fact that Fulla occurs in skaldic poetry as early as the 10th century means that she is probably not a late allegory of plenty (to *fylli*), but most likely that she is identical with the goddess → Volla, who occurs in the Second Merseburg Charm. On the other hand, it is not clear who this goddess really is: an independent deity or identical with Freyja (which could be suggested by the use of the name in the charm), or identical with Frigg, which could be assumed from Snorri's association of Fulla with Frigg.

Fullangr (ON, 'long enough'? or Fúllangr 'lazy smell'?). A dwarf in the *Þulur*.

Fundinn (1) (ON, 'the found one'). A dwarf in *Vǫluspá* 13.

Fundinn (2) (ON). Possibly a name for Odin in a kenning by Einarr Gilsson.

Functions → Three function theory.

fylgjur (ON, sg. *fylgja*, also *fjylgjukona* 'fetches'). The souls of people but separate from their bodies. The *fylgjur* in Old Norse literature are only seen in dreams or else by people capable of seeing them with supernatural powers. They appear in the shapes of women or animals, but are a kind of *doppelgänger* of the person and can act or else appear instead of him as an ominous sign.

Although the *fylgjur* are the only indication of a belief in a kind of → soul in Nordic heathendom, they are definitely different from the Christian concept of the soul in that they leave the person at his → death and become independent beings. On the other hand, *fylgjur* can transfer to relations so that a certain relationship of the *fylgjur* to the family must be assumed.

Fylgjur have been understood as being related in some way to the protective spirits of the Roman *genii* or else with Christian guardian angels. They are more than these, as they are bound by a belief in destiny, and they stand in association to the personified luck of a person, the → *hamingja*.

The word *fylgja* is thought to be related to the ON verb *fylgja* 'follow', and as such would actually mean 'following spirit', 'wraith', but a connexion with *fulga* 'skin, cover; caul' and *fylgja* 'afterbirth' cannot be totally rejected.

M. Rieger, 'Über den nordischen Fylgjenglauben' (*ZfdA* 42) 1898; I. Blum, *Die Schutzgeister in der altnordischen Literatur*, Zabern 1912; G. Turville-Petre, 'Liggja fylgjur þínar til Íslands' (*Saga-Book* 12) 1937–45; H. R. Ellis, *The Road to Hel*, Cambridge 1943; F. Ström, 'Fylgja' (*KLNM* 5) 1960; E. Mundal, *Fylgjemotiva i norrøn litteratur*, Oslo 1974; D. Strömbäck, 'The Concept of Soul in Nordic Tradition' (*Arv* 31) 1975; Å. V. Ström, H. Biezais, *Germanische und baltische Religion*, Stuttgart 1975.

Fyrnir (ON, 'the old one'). A giant in the *Þulur*.

Gabiae. Matron name. At least 10 votive stones are recorded as being dedicated to the *matronis Gabiabus*, four of which come from Rövenich near Euskirchen/Germany which suggests there may have been a cult centre there. The name means 'the giving ones' and the goddess Gefjon is its counterpart in Old Scandinavian mythology. On two of the inscriptions naming the Gabiae, the *matronis* is replaced by *Iunonibus*. Light is shed on this variant by the association linking of *matronae* and *iunones* on North Italian inscriptions which in turn suggest that *iunones* is either a synonym for *matronae* or else a sub-group of them. It is striking that of all the Germanic matrons only the Gabiae are called *iunones*, but this might be explained as being simply a peculiarity of the stone mason. The people who dedicated the two stones are not identical.

S. Gutenbrunner, *Die germanischen Götternamen*, Halle 1936; M. Schönfeld, *Wörterbuch der altgermanischen Personen- und Völkernamen*, Heidelberg [2]1965; H. Reichert, *Lexikon der altgermanischen Namen*, Vienna 1987–90.

Gagnráðr (ON, 'the one who advises against'). A name Odin gives himself in a battle of wits with the giant called Vafþrúðnir in the Eddic lay *Vafþrúðnismál*. Therefore, freely translated, Gagnráðr could mean 'antagonist in argument'. In the *Þulur*, the name is given as being Gangráðr which is probably the more correct version considering that another of Odin's names is Gangleri. If this is so, then the name would then mean 'the one who knows the way'.

H. Falk, *Odensheite*, Christiania 1924.

Galarr (1) (ON, 'screamer'). According to Snorri (*Skáldskaparmál* 1), this is one of the two dwarfs (→ Fjalarr) who killed Kvasir the Wise, caught his blood, mixed it with honey and brewed the → mead of the skalds from it. Snorri used the dwarf brothers Galarr and Fjalarr also to explain the kenning *dvergar farskostr* (which is identical in meaning with the kenning handed down from the 10th century *dverga skip*). In his explanation he tells how the two dwarfs murdered Gillingr the giant and his wife and were then left to die on a skerry by the giant's son Suttungr. They were only able to escape from there by handing over the mead of the skalds (metaphorically speaking the ship, as it is this which leads to them being brought back to land from the skerry). Whether this explanation of the kenning really does rest on an ancient myth is doubtful and the names of the dwarfs are certainly an invention of Snorri's.

Galarr (2). A giant, but only named in the *Þulur*.

galdr (ON, literally: 'magic chant'; in the extended sense: 'magic') was an element of the Old Scandinavian magical practices (*seiðr*). *Eireks saga rauða* 4 tells in detail about the singing of such a *galdr* (called Varðlokkur) by a woman (not the seeress herself) at a prophecy meeting in Greenland. The words of the *galdr* are not given but the presumable form can be concluded from the term *galdralag*, for a stanza with particularly strict stave rhyme connexions and emphasized parallel verse form (Snorri, *Háttatal* 101). The etymological relationship of the word with the verb *galan* 'sing, twitter' favours of the idea that the *galdr* was sung and not spoken; also, several of our Medieval sources speak of *galdr* as of a murmured charm (e.g. *Grettis saga* 79).

A. F. Hälsig, *Der Zauberspruch*, Diss. Leipzig 1910; R. T. Christiansen, *Die finnischen und nordischen Varianten des 2. Merseburger Spruches*, Helsinki 1914; M. Olsen, 'Varðlokkur' (MoM) 1916; I. Lindquist, *Galdrar*, Göteborg 1923 (= Göteborg högskolas Årsskrift 29, 1); F. Ohrt, 'Om Merseburgformlerne som Galder' (*Danske Studier*) 1938; J. de Vries, *Altgermanische Religionsgeschichte*, [3]1970; R. Grambo, 'Studiet av nordiske trollformler' (*Rig*) 1973; O. Bø, 'Trollformlar' (*KLNM* 18) 1974; O. Gschwantler, 'Älteste Gattungen germanischer Dichtung' (*Neues Handbuch der Lit.-wiss.* 6) 1985.

Gallehus horns. The two golden horns were found in 1639 and 1734 near Gallehus in Schleswig/Germany, but were stolen in 1802 from the museum in Copenhagen and presumably melted down. As a result of this we have to rely on the old illustrations of the rich pictorial decorations on the horns.

The horns are from the beginning of the Migration Era (the beginning of the 5th century) and bear pictorial decorations of people, animals and symbolic signs which suggest Celtic, perhaps even southern European influence, but the Gallehus horns are quite clearly Germanic because of the runic production mark on them: 'I, Hlewagast Holtsson, made this horn' (*Ek Hlewagastir Holtijar horna tawido*). There has been no successful interpretation of the scenes depicted on the horns and their original function is likewise uncertain (→ horn). Therefore any identification with Germanic gods and cult events has to remain purely hypothetical.

W. Hartner, *Die Goldhörner von Gallehus*, Wiesbaden 1969; J. de Vries, *Altgermanische Religionsgeschichte*, Berlin [3]1970.

Gamaleda. Name of a possible Germanic goddess invoked on an inscription from a votive stone from Maastrich/Netherlands, dedicated to the *Ammacae sive Gamaledae* (CIL XIII 3615); cf. ON *gamall* 'old'?

S. Gutenbrunner, *Die germanischen Götternamen*, Halle 1936; M. Schönfeld, *Wörterbuch der altgermanischen Personen- und Völkernamen*, Heidelberg [2]1965; H. Reichert, *Lexikon der altgermanischen Namen*, Vienna 1987–90.

gambanteinn (ON, 'magical switch') is a strange magical object with which Skírnir bewitches Gerðr (in *Skírnismál*), and which Odin (*Harbardsljóð* 20) gets from Hlébarðr the giant whom he turns mad. According to the sources, it seems to have been a magic wand. The meaning of the word *gamban-* could however suggest a kind of divining-rod.

A. G. v. Hamel, 'Gambantein' (*Neophilologus* 17) 1932; A. M. Sturtevant, 'Three Old Norse Words' (*SS* 28) 1956; J. de Vries, *Altgermanische Religionsgeschichte*, Berlin [3]1970.

Gambara. The mother of the legendary Langobardian leaders Ybor and Ajo, according to the history of the Langobards (*Origo* and Paulus Diaconus I, 3 and 7). Gambara caused the Langobards to be victorious over the Vandals by praying to the goddess Freyja. In Saxo (VIII, 284) Gambara occurs in the form Gambaruc as the mother of Ebbo and Aggo in a reflection of the Langobardian tale of their migration.

Gambara is interpreted as meaning seeress because of her name (from **Gand-bera* 'wand bearer'), but the history of the Langobards does not mention Gambara having such a function.

D. Strömbäck, *Sejd*, Uppsala 1935; Å. V. Ström, H. Biezais, *Germanische und baltische Religion*, Stuttgart 1975.

Gandálfr (ON, 'the magic working elf'). A dwarf in *Vǫluspá* 12 and in the *Þulur*, although Gandálfr is actually an elf-name (→ elves, → dwarfs).

R: J. R. R. Tolkien made him famous as the Odinic guiding figure in his novels *The Hobbit* (1938) and *The Lord of the Rings* (1954).

ganga undir jarðarmen → *jarðarmen*.

Gangláti (ON, 'the slow one'). The servant belonging to Hel, the goddess of the underworld in Snorri's allegorizing description of her dwelling (*Gylfaginning* 33).

Gangleri (ON, 'the one tired from walking'?). A name for Odin in the *Grímnismál* 46 and in the *Þulur*. Snorri also says that Gylfi who comes to the gods (*Gylfaginning* 2) is called Gangleri, but he is definitely not identical with Odin. The name Gangleri is clearly connected with Odin's frequent role as a solitary wanderer.

Ganglǫt (ON, 'the slow one'). The maid in Snorri's allegorizing description of the home of the goddess Hel (*Gylfaginning* 33).

Gangr (ON, 'gait'). A giant who, according to Snorri, is the brother of Þjazi and Iði and as such was the son of Ölvaldi. The latter divided his property so that each of his sons was allowed to take a mouthful of gold as his inheritance. This is why gold is also called 'Gangr's or Iði's or Þjazi's mouthfull'. As Gangr really does occur in several kennings for gold, it would appear that neither this association nor the fragment of the myth are purely inventions of Snorri's.

Gangráðr (ON). Name for Odin, → Gagnráðr.

Ganna. A Germanic → seeress from the tribe of the Semnones who was alive and active towards the end of the first century A.D. Like her predecessor → Veleda, Ganna appears to have had notable political influence as even the Roman emperor Domitian himself showed his respect for her when she came to Rome accompanying Masyas, the king of the Semnones (Cassius Dio, *Hist. Rom.* 67, 5).

The name Ganna is usually interpreted as being connected with ON *gandr* 'magic wand' and as such is directly related to the insignia of her calling, as in the case of the seeress Waluburg.

E. Schröder, 'Walburg, die Sibylle' (*ARW* 19) 1916–19; H. Volkmann, *Germanische Seherinnen in römischen Diensten*, Krefeld 1964; J. de Vries, *Altgermanische Religionsgeschichte*, Berlin [3]1970.

Gantunae. Matron name. The name Gantunae is mentioned only once on an inscription from Cologne/Germany dedicated to the *Gantuni[s] Flossia Pat[e]rna* (CIL XIII 8218). It is probably related to Germanic **ganta* 'goose' and thus means 'goose goddesses'. However, the cult of water birds is far more widespread in Celtic than in Germanic regions. Nonetheless, there would appear to have been syncretic occurrences as the link between geese and Germanic deities is also recorded on the stone at Housesteads dedicated to Mars Thingsus.

S. Gutenbrunner, *Die germanischen Götternamen*, Halle 1936; M. Schönfeld, *Wörterbuch der altgermanischen Personen- und Völkernamen*, Heidelberg ²1965; H. Reichert, *Lexikon der altgermanischen Namen*, Vienna 1987–90.

Gapt. According to Jordanes, the ancestor of the kings of the Amales, who was worshipped as a god. The generally accepted interpretation of the name is that Gapt is a misspelling here for Gaut which is connected with the ON name for Odin → Gautr and Anglo-Saxon Geat.

H. Birkhan, 'Gapt und Gaut' (*ZfdA* 94) 1965; J. de Vries, *Altgermanische Religionsgeschichte*, Berlin ³1970.

Garmangabis. A Germanic goddess on a votive inscription from Lanchester near Durham, N. England, dating from the time between 238–244 A.D. The votive stone was set up by members of the Suebi tribe stationed there. Garmangabis either means 'the richly giving one' (cf. Friagabis) or perhaps 'the Germanic Gabis'.

S. Gutenbrunner, *Die germanischen Götternamen*, Halle 1936; M. Schönfeld, *Wörterbuch der altgermanischen Personen- und Völkernamen*, Heidelberg ²1965; H. Reichert, *Lexikon der altgermanischen Namen*, Vienna 1987–90.

Garmr (ON). A mythological dog (*Grímnismál* 44). Garmr is chained up and howls, according to the apocalyptic vision in *Vǫluspá* (44, 49, 58), where only the name is mentioned. Snorri has him fight against Týr at Ragnarǫk and both die in the process. This, however, would appear to be Snorri's addition. There are no grounds for equating Garmr with the nameless dog of hell mentioned in *Baldrs draumar*, as is frequently done by scholars, whereas on the other hand it is possible that Garmr might simply be another name for the Fenriswolf, a case further supported by the dog's fetters. Numerous kennings prove that Garmr was a well-known figure in Germanic mythology.

S. Nordal, *Vǫluspá*, Darmstadt 1980.

R: K. Ehrenberg, *Loki and Sigyn, Hel with the dog Garm* (drawing, 1883).

Gastropnir (ON). A wall of clay surrounding Menglǫð's home in *Fjǫlsvinnsmál* 12. The name has not been satisfactorily explained.

Gaut. Probably the correct reading for the manuscript form → Gapt given in the history of the Langobards by Paulus Diaconus and the *Origo* for the Gothic deity. This is most likely a form of the ON name for Odin → Gautr.

Gautatýr (ON, 'Gautland-god'). A name for Odin in Eyvindr Finnsson's *Hákonarmál* 1 (c.961) and represents an extension of the name for Odin → Gautr according to the pattern of Hroptr and Hroptatýr; → Sigtýr.

H. Kuhn, 'Rund um die Vǫluspá' (*Festschrift H. de Boor*) München 1971.

Gauti → Gautr.

Gautr and **Gauti** (ON, 'Gotlanders'). Names frequently recorded for Odin which occur elsewhere as male personal names. The name Gautr is also found in the form Gapt/Gaut as the mythical ancestor of the Langobards, as Geat in the genealogies of the Anglo-Saxon royal houses and as Gausus in the Langobardian *Edictus Rothari*. As such, he should be considered as the eponymous ancestor of the Goths who perhaps was identical to Odin in the common Scandinavian homeland of the Germanic tribes, which would explain why he was worshipped as an ancestor in so many places.

H. Falk, *Odensheite*, Christiania 1924; J. de Vries, *Altgermanische Religionsgeschichte*, Berlin [3]1970.

Gavadiae. Matron name. Inscriptions on votive stones from the period around 200 A.D. from Jülich (six) and Mönchengladbach (two) (Germany) are dedicated to these *matronis Gavadiabus*. The name is etymologically related to Gothic *wadi* 'pledge', *gawadjon* 'betroth'. These matrons are therefore either matchmakers or else goddesses who watch over vows and oaths.

S. Gutenbrunner, *Die germanischen Götternamen*, Halle 1936; M. Schönfeld, *Wörterbuch der altgermanischen Personen- und Völkernamen*, Heidelberg [2]1965; H. Reichert, *Lexikon der altgermanischen Namen*, Vienna 1987–90.

Gavasiae. Matron name. An inscription from Thorr near Cologne is dedicated to the *matronis Gavasiabus* (CIL XIII 12067). The Gavasiae may easily be identical with the Gavadiae, but if they are separate entities one could link the name with Gothic *gawasjon* 'clothe'. This would be semantically founded insofar as matrons are frequently depicted on votive altars carrying swaddling clothes which would point to their function as midwives.

S. Gutenbrunner, *Die germanischen Götternamen*, Halle 1936; M. Schönfeld, *Wörterbuch der altgermanischen Personen- und Völkernamen*, Heidelberg [2]1965; H. Reichert, *Lexikon der altgermanischen Namen*, Vienna 1987–90.

Geat (Anglo-Saxon name of a god). Geat appears to be the mythological ancestor of Vôden (= Odin) in the genealogies of the Anglo-Saxon royal houses and he is usually explicitly called a god (*quem Getam jam dudum pagani pro deo venerabantur*), but in Nennius he is said to be the son of a god. – Geat corresponds phonetically to Gothic Gapt, named by Jordanes (*Getica* 14) as being the ancestor of the Amales, as well as corresponding to Gautr, the ON name for Odin (*Grímnismál* 54) and the ancestor of the Gautlanders and the eponymous hero of the island of Gautland (i.e. Gotland) in the *Ynglinga saga* 34.

Thus, Geat is closely associated with Odin and is, at least in Scandinavian mythology, identical with Odin. This identification did not occur however among the Anglo-Saxons or the Goths, where Geat is merely the mythical ancestor of the Gautlanders who trace their various royal houses back to him.

J. Grimm, *Deutsche Mythologie*, Berlin [4]1875–78; E. Hackenberg, *Die Stammtafeln der angelsächsischen Königreiche*, Berlin 1918; E. A. Philippson, *Germanisches Heidentum bei den Angelsachsen*, Leipzig 1929.

Gefjon (also Gefjun, ON). A Scandinavian goddess of whom Snorri tells stories in *Ynglingasaga* 5 and *Gylfaginning* 1: During → Odin's migration to Scandinavia he stayed en route in Odensø (Odense) on Fyn and sent Gefjon to look for land to the north. The Swedish king Gylfi gives her land to plough and she turns her four sons, whom she has from a giant, into bulls. She puts these in front of a plough and thus ploughs Zealand free from Sweden. Snorri adds that Zealand used to lie where lake Mälar is now in Sweden and that later Odin's son Skjǫldr married Gefjon and they lived together in → Lejre.

Snorri's reference to lake Mälar is certainly secondary, and originally this was an aetiological legend of the origin of the Öresound between Scania and Zealand which

Snorri linked with the reference to Gefjon and Gylfi in Bragi's *Ragnarsdrápa* 13 (9th century), although in this work it is not necessarily the same legend that is being referred to.

Older scholarship tended to consider Gefjon as a name for Freyja (or else Frigg) because in the *Lokasenna* 20 Loki blames Gefjon for having given herself to a 'white youth' for the sake of a gift. The *Lokasenna* however is a late composition and the reproach is too much of a stereotype to carry much weight. Nevertheless, even if Gefjon should not be identified as Freyja, she could be considered as being one of the fertility and protective goddesses because of the meaning of her name ('the giving one'). Admittedly most of the Germanic goddesses have this function, but in *Stjórn* Gefjon is equated with Aphrodite.

A. Olrik, 'Gefjon' (*DS*) 1910; R. C. Boer, 'Gylfes mellemvørende med Aserne' (*Festskrift t. H. Pipping*) Helsingfors 1924; F. Genzmer, 'Die Gefjonstrophe' (*PBB* 51) 1932; A. Holtsmark, 'Gevjons plog' (*MoM*) 1944; A. M. Sturtevant, 'Regarding the Old Norse Name Gefjon' (*SS* 24) 1952; N. Lukman, 'Gefion' (*KLNM* 5) 1960; V. Kiil, 'Gevjonmyten og Ragnarsdrapa' (*MoM*) 1965; J. de Vries, *Altgermanische Religionsgeschichte*, Berlin [3]1970; M. Clunies Ross, 'The Myth of Gefjon and Gylfi' (*ANF* 93) 1978; R. Simek, *Altnordische Kosmographie*, Berlin, New York 1990.

R: there is a Gefjon-fountain in Copenhagen with a sculpture of the goddess.

Gefn (ON, 'giver'). A name for the goddess Freyja, referred to by Snorri (*Gylfaginning* 34, *Skáldskaparmál* 35), which also occurs several times in skaldic poetry. It is possible that Gefn was originally a protective goddess in her own right, but if not, the name would refer, as other names for Freyja, to her as a goddess of plenty.

Geirahǫd. A → Valkyrie which in several Eddic manuscripts of *Grímnismál* 36 is found instead of Geirǫnul. Like numerous other names of Valkyries, Geirahǫd is actually a synonym for 'battle' (cognate to ON *geirr* 'spear' and *hǫð* 'battle').

Geiravǫr. A Valkyrie in the *Þulur*. The second part of the name is either identical with the goddess → Vǫr, thus 'spear-goddess', or else with the frequently found suffix *-vǫr* in personal names such as Geirvǫr and Hervǫr.

F. Jónsson, *Lexicon Poeticum*, Copenhagen [2]1966.

Geirdriful (ON, 'spear-flinger'). A → Valkyrie named only in the *Þulur*.

Geirlǫðnir (ON, 'the one who invites to the spear-battle'). One of the pseudonyms of Oðin in the *Þulur* which refers to Odin's characteristic weapon, the spear → Gungnir.

Geirǫlnir. A pseudonym for Odin in the *Þulur* which perhaps derives from *Geirǫnlir. As such it would mean, just like the name of the Valkyrie → Geirǫnul 'the one charging forwards with the spear'. On the other hand, Ǫlnir can be found alone as a dwarf's name.

H. Falk, *Odensheite*, Christiania 1924; F. Jónsson, 'Gudenavne – dyrenavne' (*ANF* 35) 1919; F. Jónsson, *Lexicon poeticum*, Copenhagen [2]1966; J. de Vries, *Altnordisches etymologisches Wörterbuch*, Leiden [2]1977.

Geirǫndull → Geirǫnul.

Geirǫnul, Geirrǫnul, Geirǫmul, Geirǫlul. Different spellings for the name of a → Valkyrie in *Grímnismál* 36. Whether there is a connexion with Odin's name Geirǫlnir and the dwarf-name Ölnir, and what the second part of the word means, is uncertain. One possible interpretation might be 'the one charging forward with the spear' (to ON: *ana*). With regard to the form, Geirǫlul, a connexion with the magical rune-word *alu* might just be possible.

F. Jónsson, 'Gudenavne – dyrenavne' (*ANF* 35) 1919; F. Jónsson, *Lexicon poeticum*, Copenhagen [2]1966; J. de Vries, *Altnordisches etymologisches Wörterbuch*, Leiden [2]1977.

Geirroðr (ON). The protagonist in the story forming the narrative frame of the Eddic lay *Grímnismál* (2, 51), and unquestionably a literary and not a mythological figure. The even younger prose framework of → *Grímnismál* names this king as a son of Hrauðungr and gives him a brother Agnarr to boot; in the poem itself, however, reference is only made to Agnarr, who is said to be Geirroðr's son.

Geirrǫðargarð (ON, 'Geirrǫðs farm or court') is the home of the giant → Geirrǫðr in Jötunheim.

Thor's journey to Geirrǫðargarð and his fight with Geirrǫðr are described in detail in Snorri (*Skáldskaparmál* 18) who followed the poem *Þórsdrápa*, written at the end of the 13th century by the skald Eilífr Goðrunarson: Geirrǫðr had taken Loki prisoner, had locked him into a chest and only wanted to release him under the condition that he should bring Thor to Geirrǫðargarð, albeit without his hammer, girdle of power and his iron gauntlets. Thor sets out on his journey, accompanied by Þjálfi (according to *Þórsdrápa*) or Loki (in Snorri's version). He stops on the way at the home of the giantess Gríðr who lends him her girdle of might, iron gauntlets and the magic staff Gríðarvǫlr. He comes to the river Vimur which rises during his crossing. When Thor notices that the reason for this is the giant's daughter, Gjálp, who is standing up river and urinating, he picks up a stone and throws it at her in order to dam the river at its source; finally he crosses the river with the support of the magic staff and goes to Geirrǫðr. Whilst staying there, he sits down on a chair which is then lifted high into the air by the giant's daughters Gjálp and Greip, who are attempting to crush the god on the roof in this way. Thor presses against the roof with the staff and thus breaks the backs of the two giantesses. Then Geirrǫðr challenges Thor to a sporting contest of strength, whereby the giant is pierced through and dies.

The result of the contests is also described by Saxo (VIII, 290) where the legendary ruler Geruthus (Geirrǫðr) is portrayed with a pierced body, his three (instead of two, as in Snorri) daughters with broken backs. Other than this, there is little to be found of this myth in Saxo and his portrayal is heavily interspersed with elements from Medieval Christian visionary literature. Geirrǫðargarð is certainly identified in Saxo as the underworld, whilst it was part of → Utgarð in the original myth, as far as that is still recognizable.

In late Medieval romantic retelling Thor's journey to Geirrǫðargarð is also to be found in *Þorsteins saga bæjarmagns* (14th century) where Thor is replaced by a Norwegian called Thorstein.

It is possible that already in the mythological story told by Eilífr and by Snorri two older myths have been blended together: Thor's fight with Geirrǫðr on the one hand, and the more burlesque adventure with the giant's daughters on the other hand.

R: E. Doepler d. J., *Thor durchquert den Wimurfluß* (E. Doepler, W. Ranisch, *Walhall*, 1901).

Geirrǫðr (ON, 'protection from spears') is the name of a giant who is Thor's opponent in the apparently very well-known mythological tale about Thor's journey to →

Geirrǫðargarð. Geirrǫðr is also named in several kennings in skaldic poetry and in the *Þulur*.

Following the poem *Þórsdrápa* (written by the skald Eilífr), Snorri tells how Geirrǫðr challenges Thor to sporting contests and throws a red-hot piece of iron at him which Thor catches in the iron gauntlets, lent to him by the giantess Gríðr, and hurls back at Geirrǫðr, who is hiding behind a pillar, with such a force that it goes through the pillar, the giant and the wall before it sticks into the ground outside.

It seems that Geirrǫðr is identical with Geruthus in Saxo's writings (*Gesta Danorum* 8, 286ff.) who is said to be the ruler over a legendary kingdom north-east of Scandinavia, in which the hero of the saga Thorkillus undertakes a journey. When the expedition, which is helped on the way by Guðmund, Geirrǫðr's benevolent brother, arrives at Geruthus' terrifying palace, the travellers find the pierced body of Geirrǫðr (since Thor pierced him with the piece of metal), flanked by three women with broken backs; these three are clearly recognizable as Geirrǫðr's daughters, mentioned by Snorri (*Skáldskaparmál* 18), who however refers to only two daughters (Gjálp and Greip).

In *Þorsteins saga bæjarmagns* (14th century) Geirrǫðr and Guðmundr are the rulers over two neighbouring kingdoms of legendary fame: Geirrǫðr's people are dark and unpleasant, whereas Guðmund's are said to be bright and friendly. Elements of late Medieval Icelandic concepts of the topography of the Other World can be seen here, elements which rest on popular Christian ideas taken from visionary literature and which were later built into late Icelandic literature in the nordic geography of the sagas and embellished more and more, so that only slight traces of the original cosmology of Germanic mythology remained.

P. Herrmann, *Die Heldensagen des Saxo Grammaticus*, Leipzig 1922; E. Mogk, 'Die Überlieferungen von Thors Kampf mit dem Riesen Geirröð' (*Festskrift Pipping*) Helsingfors 1924; H. R. Ellis, *The Road to Hel*, Cambridge 1943.

Geirrǫlul → Geirǫnul.

Geirskǫgull (ON, 'spear-battle'). A → Valkyrie recorded repeatedly (*Vǫluspá* 30, *Þulur*), whose name is cognate either to ON *skǫgull* 'battle' or to the name of the Valkyrie called Skǫgull (*Vǫluspá* 30, *Grímnismál* 36).

Geirstaðaálfr (ON, 'the elf from Geirstad'). According to Snorri's *Heimskringla* (*Ynglinga saga* 48 and 49), this was a posthumous pseudonym of the legendary king Oláfr Guðrøðarson, who lay buried in Geirstad where the people made sacrifices to him after his death and worshipped him because of his particularly prosperous reign; → Elves, → Alfablót.

Geirtýr (ON, 'spear-god'). A pseudonym for Oðin in *Hákonarkviða* 21, written by Sturla Þórðarson in the 13th century, and as such a late imitation of Oðin-names based on -týr (→ Sigtýr). The spear is Odin's predominant attribute both in literature and in iconography.

H. Falk, *Odensheite*, Christiania 1924; H. de Boor, 'Die religiöse Sprache der Vǫluspá' (*Deutsche Islandforschung* 1) 1930.

Geirvimull (ON, 'river bubbling with spears'). One of the mythical rivers in the river catalogue in *Grímnismál* 27 and is named by Snorri as one of the Élívágar (*Gylfaginning* 3). The name brings to mind the weapon-bearing rivers of Christian visionary literature, which are reflected in the rivers of the underworld described elsewhere in the literature of the north (*Vǫluspá* 36: Slíðr, and in Saxo I, 31).

Geitir (ON, appr. 'the goatherd'). The name for a giant in the *Þulur* and in many kennings.

Geitla (ON, perhaps 'the little goat'). A giantess in the *Þulur*. A giantess called Geit can also be found in one of the sagas, namely *Jǫkuls Þáttr Búasonar* 12. The comparison with the unpretentious mountain animals is not particularly flattering, but corresponds to the image of the giants in Medieval Scandinavian folk-belief.

Gelgja (ON, 'post, fetter'). According to Snorri (*Gylfaginning* 33), this is the name of the chain with which the fetter Gleipnir (used by the Æsir to tie up the wolf → Fenrir) was fastened to the rock Gjǫll. As with most of the names occurring in this tale, the name (at least with the meaning it has here) appears to be one of Snorri's inventions.

Gerðr (ON). The daughter of Gymir the giant. She is the wife of the god Freyr. Freyr's wooing of Gerðr is told in the Eddic lay → *Skírnismál* (retold by Snorri *Gylfaginning* 36). Their son is called Fjǫlnir (according to the *Ynglinga saga* 11). *Hyndluljóð* 30 also names her as the daughter of Gymir and Aurboða and Freyr's wife. Snorri also mentions Gerðr in *Skáldskaparmál* 1 in his list of the Asyniur.

Following Olsen's theories, Gerðr is usually understood to be an earth-goddess, and her marriage with the sun-god Freyr is interpreted as a *hierós gamós*. Olsen's idea rests on the interpretation of Gerðr as the 'goddess of cultivated land', to ON *garðr* 'fenced-in field'. Sahlgren rejects this interpretation saying that Gerðr is also a personal name and that the names of goddesses in ON never appear as personal names otherwise. L. Motz has recently shown that the common trait of *garðr* and related words do not refer to the fenced-in fertile land, but rather the fencing itself. Therefore, she interprets Gerðr as being 'the one who protects by fencing in' and sees the cultic wedding in *Skírnismál* not as a fertility ceremony but as a ritual of subordination of a representative of the giants' race which in turn represents the subordination of female powers by the masculine dominated Æsir. However, it still seems most likely that Gerðr's function was as an earth-goddess, even if it probably goes too far to relate her to → Nerthus, as Olsen does, who considers that she represents the powers of fertility in her function as the partner of the fertility god Freyr.

J. Grimm, *Deutsche Mythologie*, Berlin [4]1875; M. Olsen, 'Fra gammelnorsk myte og kultus' (MoM) 1909; F. R. Schröder, *Germanentum und Hellenismus*, Heidelberg 1924; J. Sahlgren, 'Skírnismál' (in: *Eddica et scaldica*) Lund 1928; J. Sahlgren, 'Sagan om Frö och Gärd' (*NoB*) 16, 1928; J. Sahlgren, 'Lunden Barre i Skírnismál' (*NoB* 50) 1962; G. Turville-Petre, 'Fertility of Beast and Soil' (*Old Norse Literature and Mythology*, ed. E. C. Polomé) Austin 1969; J. de Vries, *Altgermanische Religionsgeschichte*, Berlin [3]1970; L. Lönnroth, 'Skírnismál och den fornisländska äktenskapsnormen' (*Festskrift* O. *Widding*) Copenhagen 1977; L. Motz, 'Gerðr' (MoM) 1981; P. Bibire, 'Freyr and Gerðr: The story and its Myths' (*Sagnaskemmtun. Studies* H. *Pálsson*) Vienna 1986.

R: (literature) A whole series of poems by A. Oehlenschläger are to do with Gerðr in *Nordens Guder* (1819) as well as E. Tegner's fragmentary poem *Gerda*.
(fine art) K. Ehrenberg, *Freyr and Gerda, Skade and Niurd* (drawing, 1883).

(Gerhilde). A Valkyrie (soprano) in R. Wagner's opera *Die Walküre*. The name is purely Wagner's invention.

Geri (ON, 'the greedy one'). One of the hounds of hell which protect Hel in *Fjǫlsvinnsmál* 14. In *Grímnismál* 19 Geri and Freki are Odin's wolves which he feeds; Snorri also cites this in *Gylfaginning* 37.

Germania → Tacitus.

Gersimi (or Gǫrsimi, ON, 'treasure, precious object'). The name of Freyja's daughter in the *Þulur*. As elsewhere Freyja's daughter is called Hnoss, and *hnoss* and *gersimi* are synonyms, the name would appear to be a poetic variant to Hnoss.

Geruthus. The Latinized name of the giant → Geirrǫðr, the ruler of the legendary kingdom in the north-east of Scandinavia, as given in Saxo's *Gesta Danorum* VIII, 286ff.

Gesahenae. Matron name. At least five votive stones from the 2nd and 3rd centuries on the Lower Rhine are dedicated to the *matronis Gesahenis*. On two of them they are named together with the Ethrahenae. The meaning of the name Gesahenae is uncertain. Gutenbrunner suggested that it is derived from a place-name.

S. Gutenbrunner, *Die germanischen Götternamen*, Halle 1936; M. Schönfeld, *Wörterbuch der altgermanischen Personen- und Völkernamen*, Heidelberg ^{2}1965; H. Reichert, *Lexikon der altgermanischen Namen*, Vienna 1987–90.

Gestilia (ON, 'guest'). Name of a giantess in the *Þulur*. It is not at all clear how the name is supposed to be appropriate for a giantess, unless *gestr* is understood in its original meaning of 'stranger'.

Gestr (ON, 'guest, stranger'). The name Odin gives himself in *Oláfs saga hins helga*. The name is characteristic of Odin's role as an unrecognized wanderer in the *fornaldarsǫgur*.

H. Falk, *Odensheite*, Christiania 1924.

Gestumblindi (ON). A name which Odin assumes in the *Hervarar saga* 9 when King Heiðrek ventures upon a battle of wits with Gestumblindi/Odin. Odin wins by asking an unanswerable question, namely what he had whispered into Baldr's ear when Baldr lay dead on the funeral pyre. Odin also wins his battle of wits against the wise giant Vafþruðnir in the Eddic lay *Vafþrúðnismál* (54f.) by asking the same question.

In Saxo's *Gesta Danorum*, Gestumblindi is found as Gestiblindus, King of Gotland (VI, 160). The saga version and Saxo's have two things in common, namely the fact that Gestumblindi is a Gotlander and an enemy of the Swedish king, and that someone challenges this Gestumblindi (Odin in the saga, Erik in Saxo) to fight.

Wessén's convincing interpretation of the name Gestumblindi as being Gest-innblindi, 'the blind guest', a name which plays upon Odin's one-eyed blindness, is generally accepted.

H. Falk, *Odensheite*, Christiania 1924; W. Wessén, 'Gestumblinde' (*Festskrift till. H. Pipping*) Helsingfors 1924.

Gevarus. A Norwegian king, who, according to Saxo (*Gesta Danorum* III, 63), is the father of Nanna and the foster father of Høtherus (Baldr's killer). In Snorri Nanna's father is Nepr. Gevar is not a Scandinavian name and could be identical with the Saxon personal name Geb(a)heri.

F. Detter, 'Der Baldermythus' (*PBB* 19) 1894; P. Herrmann, *Die Heldensagen des Saxo Grammaticus*, Leipzig 1922.

R: King Gewar is also Nanna's father in W. Hertz's ballad *Wie Höther Nannas Liebe gewann* (in: *Gesammelte Dichtungen*, 1900).

Geysa (ON, 'the forwards streaming one'). A giantess in the *Þulur*. If the form Gessa, found in some manuscripts, is more correct, the name would probably mean 'the cheeky one'.

Giants. Giants play an important role both in ON mythology, in the Germanic myth of creation and in most of the mythological stories.

Giants can have both positive or negative dealings with man and the gods. They are the inhabitants of → Utgarðr which lies outside the area settled by man and the gods and which is cold and full of dangers. The concept of giants probably originated in the observation of various natural phenomena, in particular wintery phenomena (hence: frost giants) which overwhelmed human understanding and lay outside the close area of experience of men. Thus giants are natural spirits and among the original inhabitants of the world. In Germanic cosmogeny the world is created from a giant, → Ymir, and daughters of a race of primeval giants give birth to the first Nordic gods. Odin, Vili and Vé, for instance, come from the giantess Bestla. There is no clear distinction between the gods and the giants since the gods also marry or seduce the daughters of giants (Njǫrðr – Skaði; Freyr – Gerðr; Odin – Gunnlǫð), and the giants repeatedly try unsuccessfully to win goddesses for themselves using their strength or cunning (Þjazi – Idun; Þrymr – Freyja; Hrungnir – Sif and Freyja). The Æsir were also on peaceful terms with the giants, as the drinking bouts at the home of the sea-giant Ægir show. Several primeval giants are described as extremely wise (Mímir, Vafþrúðnir) and even the gods respected their wisdom.

However, the giants, the mighty inhabitants of Utgarð, represented a constant threat to the enclosed world of gods and men. Hence, Thor, the strongest of the Æsir, spends most of his time fighting giants (Hymir, Skrýmir, Þrymr, Þjazi, Hrungnir, Þrívaldi). It appears that as time passed the negative side of the giants gained the upper hand in Germanic mythology. In our sources, all of which come from the late heathen or Christian era, the Christian demonization of heathen mythological figures certainly helped to paint a more negative picture of the giants, but a differentiation of the various types of giants was already apparent in heathen times. The original word for giants, ON *jǫtunn*, OE *eoten*, is the generic term for giants and has no specific connotation. On the other hand, ON *þurs* had already taken on a mainly threatening character by the end of heathendom. This is clear from the rune-name *þurs* which had a function in black magic (*Skírnismál* 36). Trolls is the name given to the evil, monstrous giants. In the Middle Ages trolls were thought to be another kind of evil being, distinct from the giants.

The growing influence of Christianity could also have led to a certain trend making the giants seem less harmless, as well as demonizing them, so that in the literature of the High Middle Ages we meet a concept of giants as they are thought of in folklore today: giants are destructive but stupid and consequently easy to outwit. In Old Norse literature this picture is confirmed by the various name-formations from the 10th to 13th centuries which describe the giants and giantesses as dirty, hairy, ugly, stupid and especially loud.

K. Weinhold, 'Die Riesen im germanischen Mythus' (*Sitzungsberichte der Akademie Berlin* 26) 1858; F. Jónsson, 'Mytiske forestillinger' (*ANF* 9) 1893; C. W. von Sydow, 'Jättarne i mytologi och folktro' (*Folkminnen och Folktankar* 6) 1919; E. Hartmann, *Die Trollvorstellungen*, Stuttgart, Berlin 1936; L. Motz, 'Giantesses and their Names' (*FmSt* 15) 1981; L. Motz, 'Giants in Folklore and Mythology: A New Approach' (*Folklore* 93) 1982; L. Motz, 'The Families of Giants' (*ANF* 102) 1987.

Giantland → Jǫtunheim.

Giant Master Builder. The fairy-tale motif of the giant master-builder is found in Nordic mythology in Snorri (*Gylfaginning* 41) where he tells of the building of → Asgard.

The Æsir promise a giant that he will be given Freyja as his wife if he builds the gods' castle within one winter. He nearly manages to do so with the help of his giant horse Svadilfari, but Loki changes himself into a mare and is thus able to prevent the stallion from finishing the work at the last minute. Odin's horse Sleipnir is the result of this union. Thor then kills the giant with his hammer.

The tale of the giant master-builder is also found in European folklore and even in two Icelandic sagas (*Heiðarvíga saga* 3–4, *Eyrbyggja saga* 25, 28). This is the reason why recently Snorri's tale has been considered to be a mythologizing of a *Wandermärchen* (Harris).

The fairy-tale variants, however, miss out an important detail of Snorri's mythical version, namely Loki's change of shape and the subsequent birth of Sleipnir. As Snorri used both *Vǫluspá* 25 and 26 as well as *Vǫluspá in skamma* (*Hyndluljóð* 40) for his sources, it would be conceivable that he embellished the myth-abbreviation 'Loki begat Sleipnir together with Svaðilfari' independently in order to enrich the tale of the giant master-builder. However, it is far more likely that Snorri is simply passing on a fuller version of the myth of Sleipnir's birth and the building of Asgard that he knew than any of the other versions preserved (Dumézil).

G. Dumézil, *Loki*, Darmstadt 1958; J. Harris, 'The Masterbuilder Tale in Snorris Edda and Two Sagas' (*ANF* 91) 1976; L. Motz, 'Snorri's Story of the Cheated Mason and its Folklore Parallels' (*MoM*) 1977.

R: R. Wagner gives the tale of the giant master-builder a central position in his opera *Das Rheingold*, where he doubles the number of the giants and leaves Svaðilfari out of the proceedings. The material used in the drawing by the English book illustrator D. Hardy *Loki and Svadilfari* (c.1900) is an imaginative artistic rendering which is however closer to Snorri's version.

Gífr (ON, 'the greedy one', 'fiend'). One of the two hounds of hell who, according to *Fjǫlsvinnsmál* 14, guard the gates to Hel. The other is called Geri. The names are only late embellishments of the old but probably already classically influenced concept of dogs who guard hell.

Gillingr (ON, 'the noisy one, screamer'). A giant in Snorri's tale of the theft of the → mead of the skalds where he is Suttungr's father.

According to Snorri (*Skáldskaparmál* 1), Gillingr is killed by the two dwarfs Fjalarr and Galarr, who also murdered Kvasir, by going rowing with the giant and then allowing the boat to capsize on a rock so that Gillingr drowned. They then kill Gillingr's wife with a mill-stone. Suttungr, Gillingr's son, then takes the two dwarfs and sets them on a skerry which is flooded every high tide until they beg for their lives and offer him the precious mead as atonement.

The mead of the skalds is already referred to in Eyvindr's *Haleygjatal* (c.985) as *Gillings gjǫld*, 'Gillingr's atonement', but whether the rest of Snorri's imaginative tale is just as old is questionable. It is clear from other kennings, however, that the essential features are old even if the name Gillingr is not mentioned elsewhere.

Gimlé (ON, perhaps: 'the place protected from fire'?). According to *Vǫluspá* 64, this is a hall covered with gold in which mankind will live after the Ragnarǫk. According to Snorri, Gimlé is a heavenly place in which good people will live after their deaths (*Gylfaginning* 3 and 5) and lies in the third heaven (Víðbláinn). It is unreachable for Surt's world conflagration, destined to destroy the whole world (→ Surtalogi), and is inhabited until then by light elves. This idea is, however, quite clearly heavily influenced by Christian teaching: this is not only shown by the three heavens, the highest of which is inhabited by light elves (= angels ?), but Snorri has also understood Ragnarǫk in the *Vǫluspá* as being the Day of Judgement which will decide the damnation or salvation of mankind.

Ginnar (1) (ON, 'deceiver, bewitcher'). A name for Odin in the *Þulur*. Ginnar is related to the ON verb *ginna* 'deceive, bewitch' and as such points to Odin's function as the god of magic.

H. Falk, *Odensheite*, Christiania 1924.

Ginnar (2) (ON, 'deceiver'). A dwarf in the *Vǫluspá* 16 and in the *Þulur*.

Ginnungagap (ON). In Eddic cosmogeny the cosmic void before the creation of the world. *Vǫluspá* 3 records:

Ar vas alda þar er Ymir bygði
var sandr né sær né svalar unnir;
iǫrð fannz æva né upphiminn
gap var ginnunga, enn gras hvergi.

'It is a long time ago that Ymir lived,
there was no sand, nor sea, nor cool waves,
there was no earth nor heaven,
nor any plants, only Ginnungagap.'

From this information, it is clear that the poet of *Vǫluspá* understood Ginnungagap to be the void before creation. Snorri describes (*Gylfaginning* 4) how the icy → Niflheim came into existence to the north of Ginnungagap, and fiery → Muspellsheimr in the south. The spring called Hvergelmir lay in Niflheim, which gave rise to the poisonous rivers, the Élivágar, and which froze in the northern part of Ginnungagap. Wherever the sparks from Muspellsheimr fell onto the ice in the mild and becalmed Ginnungagap, life emerged, namely the proto-giant → Ymir and then also the proto-cow Auðumla. The first gods – Odin, Vili and Vé – killed the giant and put him into the middle of Ginnungagap where they created the earth out of his body (*Gylfaginning* 7). Snorri mentions Ginnungagap again in *Gylfaginning* 14 where he describes where the world-ash Yggdrasill is situated. One of its roots is 'with the frost giants where Ginnungagap used to be'. A later gloss on Adam of Bremen's church history (IV, 39) shows that the concept of Ginnungagap was not only limited to the Eddas, but was widespread in Scandinavia. In this text *immane baratrum abyssi* is glossed with *Ghinmendegop*.

Ginnungagap is difficult to interpret etymologically. De Vries has shown in a detailed study that Ginnungagap is more likely to mean 'the void filled with magical (and creative) powers' than 'the yawning void'. Cassidy's thoughts regarding the concepts of the Medieval Icelanders about the geographical situation of Ginnungagap have led him to the conclusion that the abyss at the edge of the world (if indeed this was in fact a Medieval concept at all and not simply a product of later scholarship) was called Ginnungagap. However, later on, Ginnungagap could have been thought to be the chasm through which the ocean surrounding the world was believed to be connected to the Atlantic. In fact the north-west passage is called Ginnungagap in Bishop Guðbrandur Þorlaksson's Icelandic map of America from 1066. These conclusions cannot however be drawn from the older ON literature.

G. Storm, 'Ginnungagap i Mythologien og i Geografien' (*ANF* 6) 1890; J. de Vries, 'Ginnungagap' (*APhSc* 5) 1930/31; V. H. de P. Cassidy, 'The Location of Ginnunga-gap' (*Scandinavian Studies. Essays Leach*) Seattle 1965; J. de Vries, *Altgermanische Religionsgeschichte*, Berlin ³1970; R. Simek, *Altnordische Kosmographie*, Berlin, New York 1990.

Gipul (ON, 'the gaping one'?). One of the (mythical?) rivers in the river catalogue of *Grímnismál* 27.

Gísl (ON, 'whip'? or else from *geisl*, in which case 'the shining one'?). A mythical horse in the catalogue of horse names in *Grímnismál* 30 and in the *Þulur*. In Snorri's *Gylfaginning* 14 Gísl is one of the horses belonging to the Æsir.

Gizurr (ON). A name for Odin in skaldic poetry (*Málsháttakvæði* 22; Sturla Þórðarson) and in the *Þulur*. The name is still somewhat obscure etymologically. However, Falk suggested a relationship with *geta* 'suppose' so that the name could refer to Odin's role in battles of wit, similar to the name Sanngetall.

H. Falk, *Odensheite*, Christiania 1924; J. de Vries, *Altnordisches etymologisches Wörterbuch*, Leiden ²1977.

Gjallarbrú (ON, 'bridge over the underworld river Gjǫll'). The bridge over the underworld river of northern mythology. Its name is only recorded quite late (only by Snorri and his nephew Sturla Þórðarson), and the concept is obviously heavily influenced by Medieval visionary literature. In *Gylfaginning* 48 Snorri describes the bridge as covered with 'glittering gold'. On his way to Hel → Hermóðr rides over the bridge which lies on the Helvegr leading to the north. It is guarded by a serving maid → Móðguðr.

It is clear from references to the bridge in Saxo (*Gesta Danorum* I, 35) in connexion with the journey to the underworld made by Hadingus, as well as in the Fornaldarsagas and the legendary romances of the late Middle Ages (e.g. *Eiriks saga víðfǫrla*, *Konraðs saga Keisarasonar*) that, despite only sporadic reference, the concept of a Gjallarbrú was widespread in Medieval Scandinavia. Nonetheless, the above mentioned sources are even more heavily saturated with literary motifs from Continental European literature than Snorri is. This is true even for the most detailed description of the Gjallarbrú in the Norwegian visionary poem *Draumkvæde* from the middle of the 13th century. Here, too, the name Gjallarbrú or Gjaddarbru occurs and such names can be found repeatedly in Scandinavian folk ballads. – On the whole, however, it is rather doubtful if the bridge to the underworld really had a place in heathen-Germanic concepts.

K. Liestøl, *Draumkvæde*, Oslo 1946; A. Holtsmark, 'Gjallarbrú' (*KLNM* 5) 1960; P. Dinzelbacher, *Die Jenseitsbrücke im Mittelalter*, Diss. Vienna 1973.

Gjallarhorn (ON, 'the loud sounding horn'). The horn of the god → Heimdall

(*Vǫluspá* 46) which he blows to warn the gods at the beginning of the Ragnarǫk. Snorri describes this in *Gylfaginning* 26 and 50, too, whilst in *Gylfaginning* 14 he understands Gjallarhorn as being a drinking horn, with which → Mímir drinks wisdom from Mímir's well; although it is not specifically mentioned there, *Grímnismál* 13 also seems to have understood Gjallarhorn as being a drinking horn since the fact that Heimdall drinks good mead is referred to. Because of the practical use of horns this double function of Gjallarhorn does not seem very surprising (and is, indeed, also known from the Old French Olifant, Roland's horn).

The horn is one of the oldest Germanic musical instruments, and, as with → lures, it seems that there were also horns used purely as sacred horns which were understood as the earthly equivalents of the mythological Gjallarhorn. Archaeological finds of drinking horns reach back to the earliest Iron Age and several examples indicate a possible function as a musical instrument. Passages in Caesar and Pliny confirm the wide distribution of drinking horns among the Germanic people at this time. From the 3rd and 4th centuries A.D. glass drinking horns have been found in Denmark, otherwise they are mostly cow horns which have been adorned with fittings made out of bronze and silver (at times very artistically worked) and frequently set onto feet to enable them to stand upright. The function of the sacred horns is reflected several times in Medieval Icelandic literature in the motif of the talking drinking horns (*Þorsteins þáttr bæjarmagns*). It is interesting that such horns in literature usually occur in pairs which recalls the pairs of Bronze Age lures. However, it would appear that the paired occurrence of horns derives simply from the horns on the animal's head. There can be no doubt that the gold horns of Gallehus, dating from 5th century Denmark and decorated with mythological scenes, were of cult significance.

Å. Ohlmarks, *Heimdalls Horn und Odins Auge*, Lund u. Kopenhagen 1937; E. Emsheimr, 'Horn' (*KLNM* 6) 1961; J. Broendsted, *Nordische Vorzeit*, Neumünster 1960–63; C. Redlich, 'Zur Trinkhornsitte be den Germanen der älteren Kaiserzeit' (*Prähistorische Zeitschrift* 52) 1977.

Gjálp, also Gjǫlp (ON, 'seeress' or 'roaring one'). A frequent name for giantesses in Old Norse literature (*Þulur*; *Grettis saga* 4; *Egils saga* 60). In Snorri (*Skáldskaparmál* 18) one of → Geirrǫd's daughters who is killed by Thor, is called Gjálp. In *Vǫluspá in skamma* (*Hyndluljóð* 37) the name is included in a list of the nine giantess mothers of Heimdall.

H. Gering, *Kommentar*, Bd. 1, Halle 1927; L. Motz, 'Giantesses and their Names' (*FmSt* 15) 1981.

Gjǫll (1) (ON, 'loud noise'). A mythical river in the catalogue of rivers given in *Grímnismál* 28. It is named by Snorri as being one of the → Élivágar (*Gylfaginning* 3). According to Snorri, Gjǫll is the underworld river which is nearest to the fence around the realm of the dead (Helgrind), which the bridge to the underworld, Gjallarbrú, spans. As such, it clearly forms the border to Hel (*Gylfaginning* 48). Other rivers of the underworld are Vaðgelmir (*Reginsmál* 4), Slíðr (*Vǫluspá* 36) and Geirvimull (*Grímnismál* 27; *Gylfaginning* 38); all of these rivers are obviously already influenced by ideas from Christian visionary literature and are therefore hardly to be taken as being original heathen Germanic concepts.

Gjǫll (2) (ON). The stone slab on which, according to Snorri (*Gylfaginning* 33), the gods fettered the → Fenriswolf.

Glaðr (ON, 'glad one' or 'shining one'). A mythical horse in the catalogue of horse names in *Grímnismál* 30 and in the *Þulur*. According to Snorri (*Gylfaginning* 14) Glaðr is included among the horses of the Æsir.

Glaðsheimr (ON, 'bright home' or 'joy-home'). Odin's residence (in *Grímnismál* 8), also the place where Valhall is situated. Snorri (*Gylfaginning* 13) describes it as a temple for Odin and 12 other gods which is like gold inside and out and is the best and greatest building in the world.

Glær (ON, 'light one') is a mythical horse in *Grímnismál* 30 and in the *Þulur*. According to Snorri (*Gylfaginning* 14), Glær is one of the Æsir's horses.

Glæsisvellir (also Glasisvellir, ON, 'the shining fields'). An Elysian realm in the Other World where the mythical king → Guðmundr reigns, according to the Old Norse *fornaldarsǫgur* (*Hervarar saga* 1; *Þórsteins þáttr bæjarmagns* 5, 11, 12; *Helga þáttr Þórissonar* 1–3; *Samsons saga* 22; *Bosa saga* 7, 8, 10, 14, 16).

Glæsisvellir is usually linked with the Glasislundr ('shining grove') mentioned in the Eddic lay *Helgakviða Hjǫrvarðssonar* 1, where King Hjǫrvard lives, and thus is probably closely connected to the grove Glasir which, according to Snorri, lies in front of the gates of Valhall. There is no detailed description of Glæsisvellir, whereas Guðmundr's wealth and splendour are spoken of (also in Saxo → Guðmundr), so that it becomes clear that Glæsisvellir is a bright paradise-like region of the Other World, as the name itself implies; a similar idea seems to be implicit in the *wlite beorhte wang* in the OE epic *Beowulf*. The concept of such a paradisaical landscape hardly comes from Germanic heathendom, but is most likely influenced by Medieval Christian literature; the name however certainly does not come from Christian texts, although it could nonetheless be of scholarly origin, since Pliny (*Naturalis Historia* IV, 103) mentions amber islands called Glesiæ. The word Glasir-, Glæsir might originally have been related to Germanic *gleza* 'resin, amber'.

On the other hand Glæsisvellir could be connected with old concepts in folk-beliefs among Scandinavian, Baltic and Slavic peoples in which the dead live in or on a glass mountain, an idea still reflected in Central European fairy-tales.

Similarly, syncretic concepts, such as Glæsisvellir, are also at the root of the other Germanic Elysian fields of the Middle Ages, such as the Old Norse Odáinsakr, and probably also Iðavǫllr, and the Old English neorxnawang, where Christian and Germanic beliefs melt into each other.

R. Much, 'Balder' (*ZfdA* 61) 1924; K. Straubergs, 'Zur Jenseitstopographie' (*Arv* 13) 1957; J. Simpson, 'Otherworld adventures' (*Folklore* 77), 1966; N. Lincoln, 'On the Imagery of Paradise' (*IF* 85) 1980; R. Power, 'Journeys to the North in the Icelandic Fornaldarsǫgur' (*Arv* 40) 1984; R. Simek, 'Elusive Elysia, or: Which Way to Glæsisvellir' (*Sagnaskemmtun. Studies H. Pálsson*) Vienna 1986.

R: A re-interpretation of Glæsisvellir can be found in J. R. R. Tolkien's trilogy, *The Lord of the Rings* (1954), where it appears as Gladdenfields.

Glámr (ON, 'pale one'). A giant in the *Þulur*, as well as the troll in the famous Glámr-episode in *Grettis saga* 35.

Glapsviðr (ON, 'practised seducer'). One of the pseudonyms of Odin in *Grímnismál* 47 and the *Þulur*, and probably refers to Odin's romantic adventure with the daughters of giants like Rindr, Gunnlǫð, etc., which he boasts about in *Hárbarðsljóð*.

H. Falk, *Odensheite*, Christiania 1924.

Glasir (ON, 'shining one'). A grove with golden-leaved trees which, according to Snorri (*Skáldskaparmál* 34), stands in front of the gates to Valhall in Asgard. Glasir is mentioned in *Bjarkamál* in the 10th century although it is uncertain here if a grove is meant or not. Perhaps Snorri invented it as the name of a wood following the example of Glæsisvellir (an Elysian landscape).

Glaumarr (ON, 'noisy one'). The name of a giant in the *Þulur*. Giant names with this meaning are quite frequent, cf. Aurgelmir, Bergelmir, Þrúðgelmir, Þrymr etc.

Gleipnir (ON, 'open one'). The fetter with which the wolf → Fenrir can finally be bound by the Æsir after two other fetters have broken. Snorri tells (*Gylfaginning* 33) that Skírnir fetched it for the gods from the dwarfs who had put it together from the following components: from the sound of a cat and the beard of a woman, from the roots of the mountains, the breath of a fish, and the spittle of a bird, in short, from everything that does not exist, as Snorri makes clear in his explanation; and, although the fetter is extremely light and soft, the Fenriswolf cannot break it.

The elements of this tale probably come from an older tale or a riddle and Snorri simply built them into his story about the binding of Fenrir.

R: Gleipnir appears in a picture by E. Doepler d. J., *Fesselung des Fenriswolfes* (W. Ranisch, E. Doepler, *Walhall*, 1901) as a delicate pink coloured ribbon (!).

Glenr (ON, 'opening in the clouds'). The husband of Sól, the personified sun, according to Snorri (in *Gylfaginning* 10).

A. Kock, 'Studier i de nordiska språkens historia' (*ANF* 14) 1898.

Glitnir (ON, 'shining one'). In *Grímnismál* 15 this is the name of the silver covered residence of the god Forseti, whose walls, posts and pillars are made of gold, as Snorri records also in *Gylfaginning* 16 and 31 where he clearly follows this verse from the *Grímnismál*. Glitnir also occurs in *Ynglingatal* 7, but its role here is not quite clear.

E. O. Brim, 'Bemærkninger' (*ANF* 11) 1895.

Glói, also Glóinn (ON, 'glowing one'). A dwarf in *Vǫluspá* 15. As Glóinn he also occurs in the *Þulur*.

R: Glói is one of the 13 dwarfs in J. R. R. Tolkien's novel, *The Hobbit* (1937).

Glumra (ON, 'noisy one'). The name of a giantess in the *Þulur*. Giants' names with this meaning are quite frequent. Hence → Glaumarr.

Gná (ON). A goddess who is named only by Snorri (*Gylfaginning* 34) as the 14th of the Æsir goddesses (Asyniur). Snorri writes about her: 'Frigg sends her with her messages into the whole world; she has a horse which runs through the air and over water and is called Hófvarpnir [. . .]. From Gná's name something is called *gnæfa* ('towering up') if it rushes along high in the air'.

Snorri's etymology of the name is not necessarily correct but it is uncertain what the name might mean otherwise, even if Gná has been called a 'goddess of fullness'.

J. de Vries, *Altnordisches etymologisches Wörterbuch*, Leiden ^{2}1977.

R: E. Doepler d. J., *Gna* (E. Doepler, W. Ranisch, *Walhall*, 1901).

Gneip (ON, cognate to *gnipa* 'peak'). Name of a giantess in the *Þulur* and in a 14th century poem by Einarr Gilsson (*Selkollu-vísur* 3).

Gneypa (ON, 'the bent one?'). The name of a giantess in the *Þulur*.

Gnipahellir (ON, perhaps 'overhanging cave'). A mythological place in *Vǫluspá* (44, 49, 58), in front of which the dog Garmr who will break loose at the Ragnarök is chained up (similarly *Gylfaginning* 50). We know as little about the situation of this place within mythological cosmology as we do about the place Gnipalundr in *Helgakviða Hundingsbana* I. It is pure speculation that Gnipahellir is situated at the entrance to Hel.

Gnissa (ON, 'grating one'). The name of a giantess in the *Þulur*.

Goði. (ON) In ON *goði* (pl. *goðar*) is the term used for a → priest and chieftain. The sagas often also call heathen priests *hofgoði* ('priest of a → temple'); his function and his district of administration are called *goðorð*.

The term *goði* can be traced back at least to the 5th century as it is found in the form *gudija* on the rune stone from Northuglen (Norway), a form which corresponds to Gothic *gudja*; Danish rune stones from the Viking Age also mention *goðar*.

However, in Denmark the *goðar* do not appear to have been of as much importance as independent political leaders as they were in Norway and Iceland. We learn very little about the religious role of the *goðar* and their duties in the religious cult from Icelandic sources as the few details about the building and upkeep of a temple are scholarly reinterpretations, based on the later Icelandic system of privately owned churches. The *goðar* appear in the sagas as the chieftains of their districts and represent the actual political leaders.

K. Maurer, 'Zur Urgeschichte der Godenwürde' (*ZfdPh* 4) 1873; B. S. Phillpotts, 'Temple-Administration and Chieftainship' (*Saga-Book* 8) 1913/14; J. de Vries, 'Celtic and Germanic Religion' (*Saga-Book* 16) 1963/64; J. de Vries, *Altgermanische Religionsgeschichte*, Berlin ³1970; H.-J. Seggewiss, *Goði und hǫfðingi*, Frankfurt etc. 1978.

Goðheimr → Manheimr.

Gods. Our first literary sources regarding the gods of Germanic mythology come from the 1st century A.D., namely Tacitus, who says that the main Germanic gods are Mercury, Hercules and Mars, i.e. Odin/Wodan, Thor and Týr. In addition to this information there is a considerable number of names of female goddesses from Roman times, the → matrons.

Historians of the early Middle Ages cite the names of divine ancestors for many of the Germanic tribes (e.g. Langobardian Gaut, OE Woden). Even Tacitus mentions the fact that the three big Germanic tribes, the Herminones, Ingaevones and the Istaevones, are all descended from mythical ancestors, of whom at least Yngvi = Freyr was still considered to be the ancestor of the Swedish royal house of the Ynglings even in the Middle Ages.

In Scandinavian mythology, as we know it from ON sources, the gods are divided into two great families: the → Æsir (strength and government) and the → Vanir (fertility). In the poetry of late heathen times deified heroes (Bragi, Hermoðr) were included alongside the other gods in Snorri's and Saxo's scholarly mythographies. Apart from Odin, Thor, Baldr, Loki, Týr, Frigg, Freyr, Freyja and Ullr, however, very few other gods seem to have really played a proper role in the religion of Germanic heathendom.

Goðþjóð (ON, Goðþjóð). This term usually means 'the people of the *goði*' (cf. *Helreið Brynhildar* 8, *Guðrunarhvǫt* 8 and 16, *Hlǫðskviða* 13 and 18), but in *Vǫluspá* 30 Goðþjóð appears to be identical with *goðaþjóðin* 'gods'.

S. Nordal, *Vǫluspa*, Darmstadt 1980.

Gǫll (ON, 'noise, battle'). One of the numerous names of the → Valkyries which are actually only synonyms for 'battle' (*Grímnismál* 36, *Þulur*).

Gǫmul (ON, 'the old one'?). One of the (mythical?) rivers in the river catalogue of *Grímnismál* 27 and in the *Þulur*.

Gǫndlir (ON, 'magician, sorcerer'). A name for Odin in *Grímnismál* 49 and in the *Þulur* which refers to Odin's knowledge of magic.

Gǫndul (ON). A Valkyrie (*Darradarljóð* 5; *Vǫluspá* 30, also in the *Þulur* of the *Snorra Edda*). The name belongs etymologically to ON *gandr* 'magic, magic wand', but in a Norwegian charm from 1325 *gǫndul* also means 'magical animal; werewolf?'. In any case, the name awakens magical associations which certainly are connected with the function of the → Valkyries as the directors of human fate.

F. Ohrt, 'Gonduls ondu' (*APhSc* 10) 1935; F. Jónsson, *Lexicon Poeticum*, Copenhagen [2]1966; J. de Vries, *Altgermanische Religionsgeschichte*, Berlin [3]1970; J. de Vries, *Altnordisches etymologisches Wörterbuch*, Leiden [3]1977.

Gǫpul (ON, 'the gaping one'?). One of the (mythical?) rivers in the river catalogue of *Grímnismál* 27.

Götterdämmerung (German 'Twilight of the gods'). The name of Richard Wagner's opera. → Ragnarök.

Gói (ON). A giantess in the wintery genealogy of the frost giants given in the text of *Hversu Nóregr byggðisk*, a legendary pre-history of Norway. In Old Norse, Gói is usually the name of the winter month corresponding to mid-February to mid-March. The question as to whether here too, as has been supposed in the case of → Þorri, an ancient vegetation god should be seen in the personified name of the month, is purely speculative.

E. Halvorsen, 'Þorri' (*KLNM* 29) 1976.

Góinn (ON, perhaps 'land-animal'?). One of the snakes which lives under the roots of the world-ash → Yggdrasill (*Grímnismál* 34). According to Snorri (*Gylfaginning* 15), these snakes live in the spring called → Hvergelmir. Góinn is said to be the name of Grafvitnir's son in *Grímnismál*.

A. M. Sturtevant, 'Comments on Mythical Name-Giving in Old Norse' (*GR* 29) 1954.

Grábakr (ON, 'Greyback'). The name of one of the snakes which live under the roots of the world-ash → Yggdrasill (*Grímnismál* 34); according to Snorri (*Gylfaginning* 15) these snakes live in the spring Hvergelmir. Grábakr is found as a poetic synonym for the ship 'Ormr inn langi' already in Hallfreðr's *Olafsdrápa* at the turn of the 11th century.

Grave cult → Burial customs.

Grave ship → Boat burial.

Gráð (ON, 'the greedy one'? or else 'evil'?). The name of one of the mythical rivers in the river catalogue of *Grímnismál* 27.

Grafvitnir (ON, 'ditch-wolf'?). The name of one of the snakes which live under the roots of the world-ash → Yggdrasill (*Grímnismál* 34); according to Snorri, these snakes live in the spring called Hvergelmir. In *Grímnismál* Grafvitnir is the name given to the father of the snakes Góinn and Móinn.

Grafvǫlluðr (ON, 'the one digging under the plain'?; perhaps correctly Grafvǫluðr 'the one ruling in the ditch'?). One of the snakes which lives under the roots of the world-ash Yggdrasill (*Grímnismál* 34), and according to Snorri actually in the spring there, Hvergelmir (*Gylfaginning* 15).

Gratichae. The name of some → matrons to whom a votive stone from Euskirchen (CIL XIII 7971) is dedicated; the interpretation is uncertain.

S. Gutenbrunner, *Die germanischen Götternamen*, Halle 1936; M. Schönfeld, *Wörterbuch der altgermanischen Personen- und Völkernamen*, Heidelberg [2]1965; H. Reichert, *Lexikon der altgermanischen Namen*, Vienna 1987–90.

Greip (ON, 'grasp'). A giantess mentioned in *Haustlǫng* 13. In the *Vǫluspá in skamma* (*Hyndluljóð* 37) she is one of Heimdall's nine giant mothers. In Snorri (*Skáldskaparmál* 18) one of Geirrǫð's daughters whom Thor kills is called Greip.

Grendel (OE). An underwater monster in *Beowulf*. According to this poem, Grendel steals men out of King Hrǫðgar's hall every night until *Beowulf* undertakes to fight him, killing first Grendel's mother and then striking off Grendel's head. This tale which was possibly originally mythical was not only well-known in Britain but can also be found in only a slightly variant version in two Icelandic sagas, the *Grettis saga* (c.1300) and *Samsons saga fagra* (14th century) which were possibly not even directly influenced by *Beowulf*. The name Grendel, however, does not occur in either of these sagas.

E. A. Philippson, *Germanisches Heidentum bei den Angelsachsen*, Leipzig 1929; R. W. Chambers, *Beowulf*, Cambridge [3]1959.

R: J. Gardner, *Grendel* (novel, 1871).

Grerr (ON). A dwarf who is named in *Sǫrla þáttr* (in the *Flateyjarbók*, end of the 14th century) as being one of the four smiths who made Freyja's necklace (→ Brísingamen). The etymology is uncertain: either 'the bellower' (from OE *gerār* 'bellow'), or else 'the small one' (from Middle Irish *grerr* 'short').

J. de Vries, *Altnordisches etymologisches Wörterbuch*, Leiden [2]1977.

Gríðarvǫlr (ON, 'Gríðr's wand'). In the tale of Thor's journey to → Geirrǫðargarð, Gríðarvǫlr is the magic wand which Thor was given by the giantess Gríðr together with the powerful belt and the iron gauntlet during his overnight stay with her (Snorri, *Skáldskaparmál* 18). Thor can only overcome the problems posed by the river Vimur, flooded by Geirrǫð's giant daughter Gljálp urinating into the river, by supporting himself on Gríðarvǫlr. At → Geirrǫð's he presses Gríðarvǫlr against the ceiling, thus breaking the backs of both of Geirrǫð's giant daughters Gjálp and Greip who were lifting him up in his chair in order to crush him against the roof.

Whereas there have been tendencies to understand this tale merely as one of Snorri's many mythical comic tales, Schröder has pointed out that there could be an ancient myth here about the separation of the proto-parental couple of heaven and earth through their son, who presses against both, just as Thor does here against the chair and the ceiling.

Apart from this, the magic wand (*vǫlr*) mainly occurs in Germanic religion as an attribute of seeresses who take their name from it (*vǫlva*). It is otherwise seldom found and the reference to a Gríðarvǫlr-like wand in the *Samsons saga fagra* (14th century) comes from a borrowing from the *Snorra Edda*.

F. R. Schröder, 'Indra, Thor und Herakles' (*ZfdPh* 76) 1957.

Gríðr (ON, 'greed, vehemence, violence, impetuosity'). A giantess of whom Snorri (*Skáldskaparmál* 18) tells that she gave the god Thor lodging on his journey to → Geirrǫðargarð: 'Thor stayed with a giantess called Gríðr. She was Viðar the Silent's mother. She told Thor that the giant Geirrǫðr was as cunning as a fox and difficult to deal with. She lent him the powerful belt and iron gauntlets and the wand called → Gríðarvǫlr.' Despite the inauspicious name Gríðr is one of the exceptional cases of a friendly giantess which is especially peculiar in connexion with the giant-killer, Thor. The name Gríðr occurs several times in kennings, some of which date as early as from the 10th century (Kormákr, *Sigurðardrápa* 4).

Gríma (ON, 'mask'). A giantess in the *Þulur*, whose name is probably derogatory, relating to her ugliness.

(**Grimgerde**). A Valkyrie (alto) in R. Wagner's opera *Die Walküre*. The name is purely the invention of the composer.

Grímlingr (ON, 'the little one with the mask'?). The name of a giant in the *Þulur*, although the name seems extremely inappropriate for a giant. Cf. however Gríma.

Grimm, Jakob (1785–1863). J. Grimm is not only seen as the founder of German philology and antiquities but also of scholarly research into Germanic mythology so that a history of scholarship can be divided quite clearly into a 'pre-J. Grimm' and 'post-J. Grimm' era (R. M. Meyer).

After preliminary studies J. Grimm published his *Deutsche Mythologie* in 1835 in which he attempted to outline German mythology to the exclusion of Nordic mythology. Nonetheless, he repeatedly turned to Scandinavian material so that his work bears quite definitely the character of a survey of Germanic mythology. J. Grimm relied in the first instance on sources from folklore, and only then on literary tradition. As is to be expected from the time in which he was writing, archaeology played very little part in his considerations.

J. Grimm's work only achieved acclaim slowly, but was popular for a long time (2nd edition in 1844, 3rd 1854, 4th edition by E. H. Meyer and extended by one volume,

1875–78). It is a work of incredible wealth of material and still serves as the basis of the folklore branch of the study of religion, and of the whole of later scholarship into Germanic mythology.

Grímnir (1) (ON). A name for Odin under which Odin appears in the Eddic lay → *Grímnismál*. Like the similar name for Odin, Grímr, Grímnir means 'the masked one'. Apart from in *Grímnismál* 47 and 49, Grímnir is also found in the *Þulur*, in the work of Hallfrdðr the skald, in two kennings for 'poetry', and in Eilíf's *Þórsdrápa*, Ulf's *Húsdrápa* and in a poem by Earl Rǫgnvald. The occurrence of Grímnir in kennings for the mead of the skalds = poetry could indicate a connexion to the myth of Odin's theft of the → mead of the skalds, namely in his shape-change into the form of an eagle. However, it is more likely that Grímnir is (like Grímr) an age-old cult name for Odin.

Grímnir (2) (ON, 'the masked one'). Name of a giant in the *Þulur*; cf. Gríma.

Grímnismál (ON, 'the lay about Grímnir'). This mythological poem in the Poetic *Edda* contains almost exclusively mythological material in didactic verses and lists of poetic synonyms. In the still extant form of the poem it has an extensive prose framework and in addition to this stanzas 1–3 and 51–53 give the poem a framework for the actual didactic poetry.

The framework story tells of two brothers: Geirroðr, who is brought up by Odin, and Agnarr, who is brought up by Odin's wife Frigg. Geirrodr kills Agnarr in order to inherit the kingdom from his father, Hrauðungr. An argument breaks out between Odin and his wife about Geirroðr and Odin decides to put him to the test. Following Frigg's advice, Geirroðr welcomes Odin – who now calls himself Grímnir – in a most inhospitable way, leaving him tortured between two fires for eight days in order to make him talk, but finally Geirroðr's ten year old son Agnarr gives him something to drink. Then Grímnir utters 54 stanzas which, apart from brief references to the prose framework, contain a wealth of didactic material, including 194 different mythological names in a loosely connected sequence and in various poetic metres. At the end of all this, Grímnir/Odin recites 55 of his names and discloses his identity. After this, in the prose framework, we are told how Odin gets his revenge on Geirroðr who then falls on his own sword.

The central didactic poetry contains mythological material about the → residences of the gods, about the world-ash → Yggdrasill and → cosmology in general, as well as about the creation of the world and lists of mythical rivers, horses and so on.

Older scholarship (Müllenhoff, Boer, Genzmer's translation of the *Edda*, de Vries 1934) saw the actual core of the lay as being the prose framework and the few stanzas connected with it, and dismissed the majority of the other stanzas briefly as being later additions because of their obvious didactic character. The tale of the preference of one hero by Odin and Frigg respectively is also known to us from the history of the Langobards (the *Origo gentis Langobardorum* from 653 and Paulus Diaconus's *Historia Langobardorum* I, 7.8, from the 8th century) and is similar to the deception of Zeus in the 14th song of the *Iliad*. In addition to this, there are also two fairy-tale elements in the prose text which are otherwise known from other works of Old Norse literature: the fratricide for the sake of becoming king (as in *Hervarar saga ok Heiðreks*) and the motif of the son helping the magician tortured by his father (as in *Hálfdanar saga svarta* 8).

The consideration of the lay together with the prose framework as a unity goes back to the work of v. Hamel and Olsen, whose results have long been generally accepted by other scholars. These interpretations see the main didactic part of the poem to be the typical product of the end of the 10th century, the end of heathendom and the torturing of Odin as the rite of gaining knowledge, as is similarly encountered in shamanistic practices (v. Hamel, Schröder, de Vries 1970). Fleck interprets the *Grímnismál* as a battle of wits within the framework of the claim to sacred kingship. Only in 1972 did B. Ralph draw awareness to the likely possibility that the prose framework could be the later addition, which probably originated as a free decoration of the framework stanzas 1–3 and 51–53. The 54 stanzas of the *Grímnismál* could indeed form a logical sequence even without the framework. The framework stanzas (which surely belonged to the lay originally) then present nothing more than a fictitious mythologizing framework similar to that of the *Alvíssmál* and the *Vafþrúðnismál*. As Ralph showed clearly, the didactic verses of the *Grímnismál* were composed quite succinctly despite changing poetic metre. The idea of a cult origin of the lay seems unlikely and the *Grímnismál* should most likely be understood as being a late heathen didactic poem, an approach supported by the systematizing tendencies of the mythological material.

R. Much, 'Der Sagenstoff der Grímnismál' (*ZfdA* 46) 1902; R. C. Boer, 'Beitr. zur Eddakritik I. Über Grímnismál' (*ANF* 22) 1906; M. Olsen, 'Fra Eddaforskningen. Grímnismál og den höiere tekstkritik' (*ANF* 49) 1933; A. G. v. Hamel, 'Óðinn hanging on the tree' (*APhSc* 7) 1932–33; A. H. Krappe, 'Odin entre les feux (Grímnismál)' (*APhSc* 8) 1933–34; J. de Vries, 'Om Eddaens Visdomsdigtning' (*ANF* 50) 1934; F. R. Schröder, 'Grímnismál' (*PBB* West 80) 1958; G. W. Weber, 'Grímnismál' (*KLL* 3) 1967; J. Fleck, 'Konr – Óttarr – Geirroðr' (*SS* 42) 1970; J. Fleck, 'The "Knowledge-Criterion" in the Grímnismál: The Case against "Shamanism" ' (*ANF* 86) 1971; B. Ralph, 'The Composition of Grímnismál' (*ANF* 87) 1972; J. Fleck, 'Grímnismál' (*DicMA* 5) 1985; E. Haugen, 'The *Edda* as Ritual: Odin and his Masks' (*Edda. A Collection*) Winnipeg 1983.

Grímr (1) (ON). A name for Odin given in *Grímnismál* 46 and 47 (and in the *Þulur*). Grímr means 'the masked one', as does Odin's name Grímnir, and this probably refers to Odin's numerous disguises and shape-changes of which Snorri tells quite explicitly in the *Ynglinga saga* 6. On the other hand, one ought to take the Odin cult into consideration which includes masked processions of bands of young men (→ Wild Hunt) and Odin's warriors dressed in animal skins (such as berserks and Ulfheðnar). These cult maskings could also be the basis for the names Grímr and Grímnir. The fact that Grímr as a name for Odin is extremely widespread, even if it occurs less frequently in literature than Grímnir does, can be assumed from the English topographical names such as Grim's dyke and Grim's ditch for various (late Roman?) forts.

H. Falk, *Odensheite*, Christiania 1924; A. Meaney, 'Woden in England' (*Folklore* 77) 1966; J. de Vries, *Altgermanische Religionsgeschichte*, Leiden [3]1970.

Grímr (2) (ON, 'the masked one'). A dwarf in the *Þulur*.

Gripnir (ON, 'grasper'). A giant in the *Þulur*. Similar names with regard to the meaning are Harðgreipr and Víðgrípr.

Grisla (ON, 'piglet') is the name of a giantess in the *Þulur*. Other manuscripts give the name Gnissa.

Grjótún (ON, 'stone-town'). The home of the giant Geirrǫðr in the poem *Haustlǫng* 14 by Þjóðólfr the skald. The name is formed like a kenning, the stone town of the giants being the mountains.

Grjótúnagarðar (ON, 'stone-town-wall'). A mythical place-name. In Snorri's tale (*Skáldskaparmál* 17) of Thor's battle with a giant called → Hrungnir, Grjótúnagarðar is the place where the duel between the two takes place. Snorri made up the name himself by using the name of Geirrǫðr and the giant's home in the *Haustlǫng*, Grjótún.

Gróa (ON). A seeress in the Eddic *Grógaldr* ('Gróa's magical chant'), where she is Svipdag's mother. In Snorri (*Skáldskaparmál* 17) she is Aurvandill's wife. Snorri tells of how she is supposed to have removed the splinter from Hrungnir's whet-stone which was embedded in Thor's head after his fight with the giant → Hrungnir.

The name Gróa undoubtedly belongs etymologically to the verb *gróa* ('grow, thrive'); it is pointless to suppose that Gróa is an old fertility goddess because of the etymology of the name, as the name is most likely of extremely late origin.

Grógaldr (ON, 'Gróa's magical chant'). A very late Eddic lay which, together with the *Fjǫlsvinnsmál*, is known as → *Svipdagsmál*. In the 16 stanzas of this lay, which are composed in the *ljóðahattr* poetic metre, the hero Svipdag seeks advice from his dead mother Gróa concerning his dangerous journey to woo his bride Menglǫð, and Gróa tells him nine magical charms against various dangers. The wording of these spells is unfortunately not given in the lay.

Lit. → *Svipdagsmál*.

Grottasǫngr (ON, 'the lay of Grotti's mill'). An Eddic lay which is only extant in two manuscripts of Snorri's *Edda* from the 13th century, but not given in the *Codex Regius*. It is clear, however, from kennings used by the skalds (Egill, Eyvind), who call gold 'Froði's flour', that either the lay itself or – more likely – an older version of the material was known even in the 10th century.

Fenja and Menja are two giantesses whom King Froði has bought as slave-girls to turn his mill called Grotti, a mill which grinds everything which is desired. The two maids complain about their fate in a poetic dialogue (8–24) and tell of their origins and their deeds, but also of the imminent downfall of Froði's royal seat in Hleiðra (Lejre). Finally, they fall into their gigantic rage and destroy the mill and the house by grinding with the mill what they want: fire, weapons and a hostile army.

This short lay of only 24 stanzas does not belong to the mythological poetry proper, but rather presents a mixture of mythical with legendary and fairy-tale material; in particular the latter aspect is emphasized by Snorri (*Skáldskaparmál* 40). He then continues the tale of *Grottasǫngr* by relating that a viking called Mýsingr comes with the hostile army, kills Froði and destroys his royal home and that was the end of 'Froði's peace'. However, Mýsingr takes Fenja and Menja together with the mill along with him and makes them grind salt until his ship sinks with the weight of it. This is the reason why the sea is salty, and the movement caused by the mill sinking created a whirlpool.

The lay combines the European fairy-tale motif of the wishing mill, which Snorri has combined with other etiological motifs, with the mythical-legendary king Froði whose legendary peace is well-known to us from numerous other Nordic sources. The name of the mill and the two angry giant maids are the addition of the lay itself, or else of its direct precursor.

A. W. Johnston, 'Grotta sǫngr and the Orkney and Shetland quern' (*Saga-Book* 6) 1908–09; E. Schnippel, 'Der Grottasong und die Handmühle' (*ZfdA* 61) 1924; A. H. Krappe, 'The song of Grotte' (*MLR* 19) 1924; A. Holtsmark, 'Grotta sǫngr' (*KLNM* 5) 1960; J. de Vries, *Altnordische*

Literaturgeschichte, Berlin ²1964; H. Beck, 'Grottasǫngr' (*Kindlers Literatur Lexikon* 3) 1964; A. Ebenbauer, 'Fróði und sein Friede' (*Festgabe f.* O. *Höfler*) Vienna 1976.

Grotti (ON). A mythical-legendary mill, → *Grottasǫngr*.

Grottintanna (ON, 'the one with the gaping teeth' or else 'the one with the grinding teeth'?). Name of a giantess in the *Þulur*.

Grýla (ON, 'ghost, troll woman'). A synonym for giantess in the *Þulur*.

Guðmundr (ON), also known as Guðmundr of Glæsisvellir. The legendary king of Glæsisvellir, a mythical kingdom in the north-east of Scandinavia. In contrast to his brother (or only a neighbour?) → Geirrǫðr, he is not expressly described as being a giant, even though his huge figure is referred to by Saxo (where he is called Guthmundus).

The most detailed (and oldest) description is given by Saxo (*Gesta Danorum* VIII, 286ff.) in which Thorkillus, who is on an expedition to visit Geruthus (= Geirrǫðr) in faraway Bjarmaland, unexpectedly runs into his brother Guðmundr, who wants to bring Thorkill and Gorm's men under his power by his luxurious hospitality, a plan which does not succeed, however, due to their abstinence (cf. Odysseus's adventures with Kirke). On their way to Guðmundr's house, Thorkill and his companions see a golden bridge over a river on which they are not allowed to step as the river is the border between the world of men and the Other World. Finally Guðmundr helps the travellers to cross the river so that they can continue their journey to Geirrǫðr.

In *Þorsteins saga bæjarmagns* (14th century) Guðmundr is the king of Glæsisvellir and lord over a bright people who are friendly towards humans but who are tributaries to the evil Geirrǫðr; with the help of the hero, Þorstein, Geirrǫðr is vanquished.

Guðmundr of Glæsisvellir is portrayed in a far more negative manner as a king of a ghost-world and sorcerer in the equally young *Helgis Þáttr Þórissonar*, whereas *Hervarar saga* describes him simply as the king of → Glæsisvellir, which lies in Jǫtunheim. He lives there in a place called Grund (the land of Earl Agdis, one of Geirrǫðr's hench-men according to *Þorsteins saga*) and sacrifices were made to him after his death.

If the (admittedly unreliable) *Hervarar saga* is to be believed, and not disputing the unquestionable connexion between Glæsisvellir and Medieval concepts of paradise, it seems that Guðmundr may have been originally worshipped as the lord of a realm of the dead. This supposition is not totally unfounded as can be seen from the worshipping of a 'wooden Gudmund', a wooden idol, in Telemark (Norway) at the beginning of the 18th century (Höfler).

Nonetheless, Guðmundr and Glæsisvellir are hardly derived from old pagan-Germanic beliefs, but are more likely the product of the High and Late Middle Ages in Scandinavia and the way in which the topography of the Other World was developed under foreign influence.

O. Höfler, *Kultische Geheimbünde*, Frankfurt/M. 1934; H. R. Ellis, *The Road to Hel*, Cambridge 1943; C. Tolkien (ed.), *The Saga of King Heidrek the Wise*, Edinburgh 1960; J. Simpson, 'Otherworld Adventures' (*Folklore* 77) 1966; R. Simek, 'Elusive Elysia' (*Sagnaskemmtun. Studies H. Pálsson*) Vienna 1986.

Guðr (ON). Name of a Valkyrie. Alternative form to → Gunnr.

Guinehae. The name of → matrons on an inscription from Tetz/Germany (CIL XIII 7878); perhaps it should be completed to read Berguinehae? Otherwise unexplained.

M. Schönfeld, *Wörterbuch der altgermanischen Personen- und Völkernamen*, Heidelberg [2]1965.

Gullfaxi (ON, 'golden mane, golden horse'). The horse of the giant → Hrungnir, who challenges Odin to a contest on Sleipnir. He is slower than Odin, but in the pursuit of Odin he only comes to a halt in Asgard, where, as a consequence of his boasting, he is eventually killed by Thor in single combat. Thor gives the horse Gullfaxi to his three year old son Magni, his son by the giantess Járnsaxa, and is reprimanded by Odin for that, who thinks that Thor ought to have given the horse to him, his father, rather than to the giant-offspring Magni. Apart from the last episode, the whole tale gives the impression of being a new invention of Snorri's in *Skáldskaparmál* 17, leading up to the single combat between Hrungir. In the *Þulur* Gullfaxi is mentioned as one of the horses of the Æsir.

Gullinborsti (also Gullinbursti, Gullinbyrsti, ON, 'the one with the golden bristles'). Freyr's boar. The name is only mentioned by Snorri (*Gylfaginning* 48 and *Skáldskaparmál* 7) who probably invented it on the lines of a kenning for 'boar' in Ulf's *Húsdrápa*.

Gullinborsti, who is also called Sliðrugtanni, pulls the chariot which the god Freyr drives (*Gylfaginning* 48) and can run faster through the air and over water than any horse, whether it is day or night, as his bristles shine brightly. Gullinborsti was made by the dwarf Brokkr. These fairy-tale-like elements are most likely only Snorri's embellishments.

Even Ulfr in the year 986 was aware of the boar as the animal associated with Freyr and the *sonarblót* (sacrifice of the boar → Sonargǫltr) was held as a harvest blessing from early on. Admittedly, the generally accepted association of the boar with Freyr does not occur often in literary sources, although the boar as the symbol of Swedish kingship on the ring → Svíagríss and as a Swedish helmet decoration suggests an association with the Vanir.

H. Beck, *Das Ebersignum im Germanischen*, Berlin 1965.

R: A. Oehlenschläger, 'Loke skaffer Aser Kleinodier hos dværgene' (poem in: *Nordens Guder*, 1819).

Gullinkambi (ON, 'golden comb'). A cock in the *Vǫluspá* 43 which announces the dawning of the Ragnarǫk by its crowing. There are two other cocks in the *Edda*: Fjallar (*Vǫluspá* 42) and Salgofnir (*Helgakviða Hundingsbana* II 49). The cock does not only warn the gods for it seems that his crowing has some significance in the awakening of the dead. The idea that cocks had a place in the Nordic death cult appears to be documented in Saxo (*Gesta Danorum* I, 31) from a passage in the journey to the Other World made by → Haddingus where Haddingus' female guide kills a cock which she throws over the wall into the Other World and which immediately comes to life again.

Å. V. Ström, H. Biezais, *Germanische und baltische Religion*, Stuttgart 1975.

Gullintanni (ON, 'the one with the golden teeth'). An epithet for the god → Heimdall, which Snorri gives in *Gylfaginning* 26 and which he explains by saying that Heimdall had golden teeth. This name is one of the reasons why Heimdall (according to Snorri 'the white god') has been seen as a god of the sun, of the day, or of sunrise.

Gullmævill (ON, actually 'little golden seagull', but perhaps 'rich sea-king', as Mævill can also be found as the name of a sea-king). A dwarf in the *Þulur*.

C. N. Gould, 'Dwarf-Names' (*PMLA* 44) 1929.

Gulltoppr (ON, 'golden mane'). A mythical horse in the catalogue of horse names in *Grímnismál* 30 and in the *Þulur*. The fact that Gulltoppr is Heimdall's horse must surely be solely ascribed to Snorri's attempts at systematization (*Gylfaginning* 26, 46, *Skáldskaparmál* 8).

Gullveig (ON, 'golden-drink, golden-intoxication' or 'golden-power'; at any rate 'the personified greed for gold'). A magician or seeress in the *Vǫluspá*. The name Gullveig is found exclusively in the *Vǫluspá* 21 and 22 and even these stanzas are by no means clear:

Vǫluspá 21:

'Then she remembered the first war of the world,
when they thrust Gullveig with spears
and burnt her in the hall of the High One;
three times they burnt the three times born one,
often, not seldomly, but she lived.

Vǫluspá 22:

she was called Heiðr in every house she came into,
the true prophesying seeress,
who understood magic.
She charmed wherever she could, she charmed into trances,
ever the delight of evil women.'

This is followed by the description of the → Vanir wars.

The Gullveig-episode gives a lot of room for interpretations. Gullveig is called a seeress, but whether she is identical with the seeress whom *Vǫluspá* is called after – as J. Grimm assumed – is very doubtful. Gullveig only becomes a sorceress after her three-fold rebirth under the name of Heiðr. Heiðr is the name of a seeress both in the *Landnámabók* and in *Hrólfs saga kraka*, but it is not a synonym for seeress because of this. Gullveig/Heiðr places her seeress abilities at the service of the Vanir. This is adequately proven by the fact that the Æsir burn her (Hár 'the High One' is Odin) which brings about the war between the Æsir and the Vanir. It is too much of a simplification of Gullveig's role to consider Gullveig simply as a 'witch' who is burnt by the Æsir (de Vries).

Gehrts has interpreted the Gullveig-myth as the reflection of a sacrifical rite and Fischer (following Müllenhoff) of an alchemistic rite of purification of gold. Krause pointed to parallels with Pandora, and Dumézil to parallels with Tarpeia. In both cases it is likely that the links are only of a typological nature. The most convincing explanation up to now has been Turville-Petre's (based on Dumézil) who interpreted Gullveig as being Freyja. Freyja was the goddess most closely associated with gold (e.g. the Brísingamen belongs to her, and her daughters are called Hnoss and Gersimi, both meaning 'jewel'). She is one of the Vanir, but is found with the Æsir after the Vanir wars (as a hostage?), and she is the exponent of the form of magic known as → *seiðr*. It is possible that Gullveig/Freyja should be seen as a Vanir 'agent' who is supposed to sow greed for gold, lust and magic among the Æsir. Even the three-fold attempt of the Æsir to rid themselves of these temptations comes to nothing and Gullveig lives on. De Vries suggested that this corruption was limited to a sexual orgiastic one which the

Æsir (a 'strictly patriarchal upper class') wanted to end. On the other hand, the emphasis of the element 'gold' in the names of Gullveig and Heiðr speaks against this. However, the etymology is not indisputable. *Gull-* means 'gold', but *veig* (even in the female names Rannveig, Sǫlveig, Þórveig) is obscure, but usually means 'alcoholic drink', but also 'power, strength' and perhaps also 'gold'. The 'greed for gold' would appear to be most appropriate even if the name is young, as de Vries assumes. Heiðr is also semantically close to this in meaning: since *heiðr* means 'fame' as well as (as an adjective) 'light, clear'. Although Gullveig is called by another name after her re-birth, the meaning has not changed essentially.

J. Grimm: *Deutsche Mythologie*, Berlin [4]1875–78; G. Dumezil, *Tarpeia*, Paris 1947; T. H. Wilbur, 'The Interpretation of Vsp. 22, 4: Vitti Hon Ganda' (*Scandinavian Studies* 31) 1959; J. de Vries, 'Vǫluspá Str. 21 und 22' (*ANF* 77) 1962; R. W. Fischer, 'Gullveigs Wandlung' (*Antaios* 4) 1963; H. Gehrts, 'Die Gullveig-Mythe der *Vǫluspá*' (*ZfdPh* 88) 1969; E. O. G. Turville-Petre, *Myth and Religion of the North*, Westport 1975; J. de Vries, *Altgermanische Religionsgeschichte*, Berlin [3]1970; W. Krause, 'Gullveig und Pandora' (*Skandinavistik* 5) 1975.

Guma (ON). A giantess in the *Þulur*. The suggestion that Guma is only a feminine form of *gumi* 'man' is hardly convincing. Perhaps cognate to Gymir?

Gungnir (ON, 'the swaying one'). Odin's spear, which is one of his typical attributes. Even Bragi in the 9th century calls Odin *Gungnis váfaðr* ('Gungnir's shaker') and Egill calls him *geirs drótinn* ('lord of the spear'); Kormákr names Hroptr (= Odin) as being Gungnir's bearer. In → Odin's self-sacrifice the god is wounded by a spear, and this kind of injury is also known from the recordings of sacrifices to Odin (→ Víkarr), and in the *Ynglinga saga* 9 Snorri describes euhemeristically how both Odin and Njǫrðr graze themselves with a spear in order to dedicate themselves to Odin. Odin kills warriors in battle with the spear and then fetches them for himself. A spear thrown over the hostile army dedicates it to Odin.

According to Snorri (*Skáldskaparmál* 9 and 33) Gungnir was made, like the other godly attributes, by the blacksmith dwarfs, Ivaldi's sons, who Loki had forced to do this work. According to *Sigrdrífumál* 17 there are runes carved into the point of the spear Gungnir. Runic inscriptions on Migration Age spears are known from archaeological finds. The Bronze Age rock carvings found in southern Scandinavia give evidence of a spear-god who is surely identical to Odin. On Viking Age pictorial stones the spear rider is marked out to be Odin because he is accompanied by birds, and occasionally by the eight-legged horse Sleipnir.

However, it is not very likely that the 'rise' of the spear god Odin and a 'fall' of the older sword god Týr reflect an actual change in the form of battle from the sword to the spear (Schwietering); perhaps the spear is significant as the symbol of lordship which was as relevant for the god of justice Týr as well as for Odin in his function of lord.

J. Schwietering, 'Wodans Speer' (*ZfdA* 60) 1923; O. Höfler, *Germanisches Sakralkönigtum*, Tübingen, Münster, Köln 1952.

Gunnlǫð (ON, 'invitation to battle'). A giantess who guards the → mead of the skalds in the myth of its theft. When the mead's owner, Gunnlǫð's father Suttungr, refuses to grant Odin a sip of the mead, Odin in the shape of a snake creeps to Gunnlǫð through a hole drilled through the mountain by Baugi the giant. After he has slept with her for three nights, Gunnlǫð allows him to have three sips of the mead. Odin drains the containers Boðn, Són and Oðrœrir before fleeing in the shape of an eagle (Snorri, *Skáldskaparmál* 1, following *Hávamál* 103–110).

Gunnlǫð's name would be more typical for a Valkyrie than for a giant so that she has been compared to the figure of the Valkyrie handing out mead.

One parallel to the tale of Gunnlǫð's seduction by Odin is the Greek myth of Zeus and Persephone. Persephone is locked into a cave and Zeus comes to her in the shape of a snake. Zagreus is the result of this union. Despite several concurring details, however, the myth of Zagreus and the Nordic myth of the theft of the skaldic mead are hardly related.

R. Doht, *Der Rauschtrank im germanischen Mythus*, Vienna 1974.

R: Peter Cornelius, *Gunlöd* (opera, 1891).

Gunnr or Guðr (ON, 'battle'). A frequent name for Valkyries, both in skaldic poetry and in the *Edda* (*Darradarljóð* 5, *Vǫluspá* 30, *Helgakviða Hundingsbana* II, 7) and in the *Snorra Edda* (*Gylfaginning* 55). As with so many other names of Valkyries (Hildr, Herfjǫtur, Hjǫrþrimul, Hlǫkk, Skaga, Þrúðr), Gunnr indicates the influence of the → Valkyries in battles.

F. Jónsson, *Lexicon Poeticum*, Copenhagen ²1966; J. de Vries, *Altnordisches etymologisches Wörterbuch*, Leiden ²1977.

Gunnthorin (ON, Gunnþorin 'the one eager for battle'). One of the mythical rivers in the river catalogue of *Grímnismál* 27.

Gunnþró (ON, Gunn-þró 'battle groove'? is more likely than Snorri's version Gunnþrá 'thirst for blood'). A river in the catalogue of mythical rivers given in *Grímnismál* 27. In Snorri, where the river is called Gunnþrá or even Gunnþráin (*Gylfaginning* 3 and 40), it is one of the Élivágar, rivers which flow from the spring called Hvergelmir.

Gusir (ON). A giant mentioned in the *Þulur*. Whether he is identical with the legendary king Gusi of the Finns, who frequently appears in late Old Norse literature, is as unclear as the meaning of his name. Perhaps from *gustr* 'gust' and *gjósa* 'gush', thus perhaps 'the stormy one'?

Gustr (ON, 'gust'). The name of a dwarf in the *Reginsmál* 5 where it is probably only an alternative name for Andvari the dwarf.

Guthmundus. A legendary king in Saxo Grammaticus (*Gesta Danorum* 8, 286ff.) who is identical with ON → Guðmundr.

Gylfaginning (ON, 'the deception of Gylfi'). The first part of the → Prose *Edda*. In a framework story Snorri tells how the Swedish king → Gylfi goes to Asgard in disguise, calling himself Gangleri, in order to find out about the Æsir and their wisdom. In a hall he meets three gods, Hárr ('the High One'), Jafnhárr ('the equally high one') and Þriði ('the third') who answer his questions. In these answers Snorri offers a systematic presentation of Nordic mythology which is our most important source. Finally, Gylfi hears thunder and finds himself alone on a plain.

Snorri used the *Vǫluspá* as a source for his description of the gods, their attributes, their deeds and of the mythical *Weltbild* as the *Vǫluspá* also proceeds from the cosmogeny to the end of the world and the new creation. Snorri quotes over 60 stanzas from *Vǫluspá*. Apart from this, his other sources are *Vafþrúðnismál*, *Grímnismál*, *Skírnismál* and for the characterization of the gods mostly *Lokasenna*. The form of the *Gylfaginning* is that of a didactic dialogue, probably known to Snorri from Latin works such as Gregorius' dialogues and the *Elucidarius*. The treatment of the matter is free and despite the perspective of the scholarly Middle Ages, free from any Christian demonization of the ancient myths. However, the opinion that Snorri more or less believed in the things he wrote about (H. Kuhn) is extremely unlikely. Snorri deals with the myths with remarkable scholarly objectivity and distance.

E. Mogk, 'Untersuchungen über die Gylfaginning' (*PBB* 6 u. 7) 1879 u. 1880; W. Baetke, *Die Götterlehre der Snorra Edda*, Berlin 1950; A. Wolf, 'Sehweisen und Darstellungsfragen in der Gylfaginning' (*Skandinavistik* 7) 1977; G. Lorenz, *Snorri Sturluson, Gylfaginning*, Darmstadt 1984; J. Lindow, 'Gylfaginning' (*DicMA* 6) 1985; H. Klingenberg, 'Gylfaginning. Tres vidit unum adoravit' (*Germanic Dialects*) Amsterdam/Philadelphia 1986; R. Simek, H. Pálsson, *Lexikon der altnordischen Literatur*, Stuttgart 1987.

Gylfi. A mythical Swedish king who according to Snorri's scholarly pre-history took over the lordship of Scandinavia from the Æsir (*Snorra Edda*, Prologue; *Ynglinga saga* 5). In the → *Gylfaginning* ('the deception of Gylfi') Snorri uses Gylfi as the protagonist of the framework tale. In the *Þulur* of the *Snorra Edda* Gylfi appears as a sea-king which is appropriate for both the etymology of his name (from ON *gjálfr* 'sea, wave') and his function in the *Ynglinga saga* where he gives → Gefjon a piece of ploughland which she then ploughs free from Sweden, thus creating the island of Zealand. Possibly Gylfi was originally a sea-giant.

A. Olrik, 'Gefjon' (*Danske Studier*) 1910; F. Jónsson, 'Þulur' (*APhSc* 9) 1934; J. de Vries, *Altgermanische Religionsgeschichte*, Berlin [3]1970; J. de Vries, *Altnordisches etymologisches Wörterbuch*, Leiden [2]1977; M. Clunies Ross, 'The myth of Gefjon and Gylfi' (*ANF* 93) 1978.

R: P. H. Ling, *Gylfe* (epic poem, 1812); P. Hörberg, *König Gylfe empfängt Odin bei seiner Ankunft in Schweden* (sketch, 1814). A Germanic society called itself *Gylfilitenbund* (c.1880).

Gyllir (1) or Gyllingr (ON, 'the shouting one'). A giant in the *Þulur*, perhaps identical with Gillingr.

Gyllir (2) (ON, 'the golden coloured one'). A mythical horse in the *Grímnismál* 30 and in the *Þulur*. Snorri (*Gylfaginning* 14) lists Gyllir among the horses belonging to the Æsir.

Gymir (ON, 'sea'?). A giant. According to the prose introduction to the *Lokasenna* it is another name for the sea-giant → Ægir. This identification can only be found in *Lokasenna* in the poetic *Edda*, but Snorri also agrees with this (*Skáldskaparmál* 23) citing a stanza from the skald Refr. In both cases the identification could be limited to the functional exchangability of giant names in kennings. As a result of the different information concerning the family (Ægir's wife is the sea-goddess Rán and they have nine daughters), it is probably better to assume two different figures. Gymir is the father of → Gerðr (*Skírnismál*, *Hyndluljóð* 30) whom Freyr makes Skírnir woo for him. In addition to this in Snorri's re-telling of the tale (*Gylfaginning* 36) and in *Hyndluljóð* 30 Aurboða is said to be Gymir's wife. The *Þulur* also list Gymir as a giant. The mythical function of Gymir – whether as a chthonic deity or else as a sea-giant – is obscure as is the etymology of the name. However, as Gymir is probably a different figure to Ægir, etymologies have been suggested attempting to justify the supposed chthonic nature of the giant Gymir: as 'earthman' (from ON *gumi* 'man', *gyma* 'earth'); as 'the wintery one' (from *gemla* 'Yearling'); as 'the protector' (from *geyma* 'aufbewahren') or else as 'the bellower' (from *Ga-Ymir).

M. Olsen, 'Fra gammelnorsk Mythe og Kultus' (MoM 1) 1909; J. Sahlgren, 'Skírnismál' (in: *Eddica et Scaldica* 2) Lund 1928; A. M. Sturtevant, 'Three Old Norse Words' (SS 28) 1956; J. de Vries, *Altnordisches etymologisches Wörterbuch*, Leiden [2]1977.

Hábrók (ON, 'High-Hose'). A falcon, the mythical representative of its species in a list in *Grímnismál* 44. The name is most likely a reference to the leg feathering on falcons.

Hadda (ON, 'hairy'). A giant in the mythical genealogy in *Hversu Nóregr byggdisk*, a legendary early history of Norway. Hadda is said to be the daughter of the giant Svaði and the wife of Norr.

R: Hadda, the name of a Dutch patrol boat, built 1955.

Haddingjar. Two brothers who in the Old Norse sagas are known as the *tveir Haddingjar*, and in Saxo (*Gesta Danorum* V) as *duo Haddingi* ('the two Haddingjar'). The Scandinavian sources of Germanic heroic poetry (*Hyndluljóð* 23; *Örvar-Odds saga* 29; *Hervarar saga* 3) record that they were the youngest of 12 brothers and were so close to each other that only together did they have the strength of one man. The form Haddingjar is a plural form of the name of a Odinic hero → Haddingus, and probably corresponds to the Hasdingi (Vandal kings) and the Anglo-Saxon Heardingas.

Dumézil, in particular, considered these brothers to be a reflection of a Germanic concept of → dioscuri gods which occur among Germanic tribes in the Alcis. Admittedly, it is probably mistaken to interpret all possible brother pairs in mythological and heroic poetry as dioscuri.

O. Höfler, *Germanisches Sakralkönigtum*, Tübingen, Münster, Köln 1952; G. Dumézil, *From Myth to Fiction*, Chicago 1973.

Haddingus. A Danish king, of whom Saxo (*Gesta Danorum* I) has much to tell. He obviously had an important place in northern heroic poetry, although he is never mentioned on his own in the Icelandic sources and always appears together with his twin brother as the two → Haddingjar.

The name Haddingus was brought into connexion with the sacrificial hair of Odin's warriors from early on. Haddingus is the typical Odin hero in all ways. From his youth onwards he enjoys Odin's help in his numerous battles and dedicates himself to Odin at the end of his life in a spectacular way: the victorious king hangs himself in front of his subjects. There are extensive parallels with the biography of another Odin hero, King Harald hilditann, which have led to speculations about a relationship between the two legends, but such a relationship rests solely on similar structures in the lives of the two Odinic heroes.

Dumézil has perceived a reflection of a complex of myths surrounding the god Njǫrðr in the heroic life of Haddingus and there are undoubtedly structural similarities. However, why a myth as fundamental in a heroic epic as this should have been re-worked to the extent that not only all the names but also important elements of the plot have been lost, cannot even be answered by Dumézil.

P. Herrmann, *Die Heldensagen des Saxo Grammaticus*, Leipzig 1922; O. Höfler, *Germanisches*

Sakralkönigtum, Tübingen, Münster, Köln 1952; G. Dumézil, *From Myth to Fiction*, Chicago 1973.

Hadningar, Battle of the → Hjaðningavíg.

Hænbúi (ON). A dwarf in the *Þulur*. Possibly it is a variant of Hornbori, but it could also be related to the plant-name Hænbúa 'nard'.

Hæra (ON, 'the grey-haired one'). A giantess in the *Þulur*.

Haeva. A Germanic goddess on an inscription from Geldern (4th century?; CIL XIII 8705) which is dedicated to *Herculi Magusano et Haevae*. Haeva could be a way of writing the Greek goddess Hebe, but the possible connexion with Germanic **hīwan-* 'marry' suggests that Haeva is a Germanic goddess, the protectoress of families, who would be invoked by married couples for the protection of their children, as the further text of the inscription shows.

Schönfeld, *Wörterbuch der altgermanischen Personen- und Völkernamen*, Heidelberg [2]1965; H. Reichert, *Lexikon der altgermanischen Namen*, Vienna 1987–90.

Hafli (ON, 'the keeper' or 'the greedy one'?). A giant in the *Þulur* who does not appear elsewhere in Old Norse poetry, but does occur in Saxo as Haphlius. According to Saxo, both of Gram's sons, Guthorm and Hadding, are brought up by two giants, Vagn(h)ophtus and Haphlius (= Vagnhǫfði and Hafli) in Sweden (*Gesta Danorum* I, 19). Saxo's euhemeristic way of looking at things in Nordic mythology means that apart from the gods even the giants are reduced to a human level and as such can function as foster fathers to heroes. Saxo's account and the names are probably derived from (for us) lost *fornaldarsǫgur*.

P. Herrmann, *Die Heldensagen des Saxo Grammaticus*, Leipzig 1922.

Hagvirkr (ON, 'the usefully working one'). A name for Odin in the *Þulur*. The name is the opposite to Bǫlverkr, another name for Odin.

Haki (ON, 'hook'). A frequent name for sea kings in kennings in poetry. Otherwise it only appears in the genealogy of giants given in the *Vǫluspá in skamma* (*Hyndluljóð* 32) as a name for a giant who is said to be the son of Hveðna and the grandson of Hjǫrvarðr.

Hala (ON). A giantess in the *Þulur* and several kennings. The name belongs either to *helan* 'hide' or to *hall* 'smooth' of which the first interpretation would be semantically more convincing.

Halamarðus → Mars Halamarðus.

Hallinskiði (ON). A name for the god → Heimdall in the skaldic poem *Gráfeldardrápa*, composed by Glúmr Geirason (c.970), and in Snorri (*Gylfaginning* 27). In addition Hallinskiði is a name for ram in the *Þulur*. A whole list of interpretations have been put forward for the etymologically obscure name which range from 'the one with the lop-sided horns' and 'the inclining rod (= beam of sunlight)' or 'axis of the world' to 'rock cleft, crevice' (Schröder). Further information about the various explanations in:

A. Ohlmarks, *Heimdalls Horn*, Lund 1937; J. de Vries, *Altnordisches etymologisches Wörterbuch*, Leiden ²1977.

Hamavehae. Matron name with one definite (Altdorf/Germany CIL XIII 7864) and two doubtful records (CIL XIII 7847 and 12072). The name probably belongs (despite de Vries' reservations) to the tribal name of the Chamavi which is found not only in Tacitus (*Annales* XIII, 55) but also in other late classical writings from the 1st to 4th centuries A.D.

S. Gutenbrunner, *Die germanischen Götternamen*, Halle 1936; M. Schönfeld, *Wörterbuch der altgermanischen Personen- und Völkernamen*, Heidelberg ²1965; H. Reichert, *Lexikon der altgermanischen Namen*, Vienna 1987–90.

hamingja (ON). In Nordic heathendom, *hamingja* is the personification of the good fortune of a person. It is understood not only abstractly but also as a kind of soul-like protective spirit, and thus is closely associated with the → *fylgjur*.

There seems to be a second meaning to *hamingja* which occurs for the altered appearance of people who are able to change their shape. The word is probably derived from **ham-gengja* and originally referred to people who could let their *hamr* ('shape, shell') 'walk'. This motive of shape-changing is especially popular in Scandinavian folk-tales. – Possibly the concept of the *hamingja* as the personification of fortune gradually originated (via the idea of the protective spirit) from the notion that a soul could take on physical shape outside the body. After the death of a person his *hamingja* can be transferred to another person, even (in contrast to the *fylgja*) to someone outside the family.

I. Blum, *Die Schutzgeister in der altnordischen Literatur*, Zabern 1912; H. R. Ellis, *The Road to Hel*, Cambridge 1943; J. de Vries, *Altgermanische Religionsgeschichte*, Berlin ³1970; Å. V. Ström, H. Biezais, *Germanische und baltische Religion*, Stuttgart 1975.

hammer → Mjǫllnir, → Thor.

Hánarr (ON; possibly actually Hánnar 'the skilful one'). A dwarf in the *Vǫluspá* 13 and in the *Þulur*.

Hangaguð (ON, 'hanging-god'). A name for Odin in a poem by Hávarðr Ísfirðingr 14; → Hangatýr.

Hangatýr (ON, 'hanging-god'). A name for Odin (Víga-Glúmr: *Lausavísur* 10, and Einarr Gilsson, *Selkolluvísur* 7) and refers to the hanging in the cult of Odin, as told of in the saga of Víkarr (Saxo, *Gesta Danorum* VI, 184) as well as the well-known → Odin's self-sacrifice in the *Hávamál* 138 (→ Odin). For information about the names based on *-týr* see → Sigtýr.

H. Falk, *Odensheite*, Christiania 1924; E. O. G. Turville-Petre, *Myth and Religion of the North*, Westport 1975; J. de Vries, *Altgermanische Religionsgeschichte*, Berlin ³1970.

Hangi (ON, 'the hanging one'). A name for Odin used by Tindr Hallkelsson the skald (c.987). The name refers to → Odin's self-sacrifice and thus to his role as the god of the hanged, as do other names for Odin like Hangaguð and Hangatýr.

H. Falk, *Odensheite*, Christiania 1924.

hanging → Odin's self-sacrifice, → Human sacrifice, → death-penalty.

Hanno → Mercurius Channin(i)us.

Haphlius (Latin). A giant in Saxo who is identical with → Hafli.

Haptaguð (ON, 'fetter-god'?). A name which Snorri gives to Odin in *Gylfaginning* 19. It could be understood to mean a 'god who loosens fetters' or else a 'god who fetters', both of which would be appropriate for Odin. On the other hand, in kennings he is called *hapta beiðir* ('lord of the gods'; Glúmr Geirason, *Gráfeldardrápa* I) or *hapta snytrir* ('adviser of the gods'; Þjóðólfr, *Haustlǫng* 3), where *hǫpt* has the meaning of 'divine powers'. Therefore Haptaguð could also refer to Odin's position as the main god. Haptaguð would then be 'the god who binds man by his divine laws'.

H. Falk, *Odensheite*, Christiania 1924; J. de Vries, *Altgermanische Religionsgeschichte*, Berlin [3]1970.

Hárbarðr (ON, 'grey-beard'). A name for Odin in the *Grímnismál* 49, in the *Hárbardsljóð* and in the *Þulur*. Especially in saga literature, Odin is repeatedly described as an old bearded wanderer.

Hárbarðsljóð (ON, 'the lay of Harbard'). A mythological lay in the poetic *Edda* which differs from the other Eddic lays in its unusual form: a few complete stanzas in the metres of the *fornyrðislag* and *ljóðahattr* are juxtaposed with a few individual metrical lines or else almost colloquial prose passages, but these are nevertheless in an order which proves that it is not the result of chance but deliberate composition. In addition, the irony of the contents is highlighted by the disparate form.

The contents are somewhat unusual, too. Thor returns from the land of the giants as a ragged wanderer and Odin (assuming the name of Hárbarðr), disguised as a ferry-man, refuses to ferry him across a sound. Instead Odin mocks Thor, making him appear a strong man but otherwise a peasant with no intelligence or courage, and then tells of his own (love-)adventures. When he asks Thor: 'What have you been doing in the meantime?', Thor has only his diverse fights against giants (with Hrungnir and Þjazi) to relate.

The lay shows a tendency which culminates in the statement (24): 'The earls who fall in battle belong to Odin, the thralls belong to Thor' (*Óðinn á iarla þá er í val falla, enn Þórr á þræla kyn*). Weber comments on this as follows: 'The position of the poet is made clear in such sentences: we have here a man filled with the self-confident pride of a battle-stained Viking, poet and lord's henchman, well versed in the ways of the world, an adherent to Odin making a mockery of the protective god of the peasants, who lacks any comprehension of the spiritual and is not comparable to the ambivalent being of Odin.'

The situation of the lay – the travelling hero confronted by the reluctant ferry-man – can be found elsewhere in Old Norse literature, but the striking similarity is to Hagen's argument with the ferryman on the Danube in the MHG lay of the Nibelungs (*Nibelungenlied* 1480ff.).

The lay is assumed to have been composed towards the end of the heathen period (in Halogaland?). It is reasonably certain that no offence was taken during the heathen period when somebody made a mockery of a god (especially if it was in favour of another god). Within Eddic poetry, only the *Lokasenna* is an equivalent to the *Hárbarðsljóð* in this respect and seeing that a very much later dating cannot be excluded for *Lokasenna*, care is therefore also required with the dating of *Hárbarðsljóð*.

F. Niedner, 'Das Harbardslied' (*ZfdA* 31) 1887; M. Olsen, *Edda- og Skaldekvad*, Oslo 1960; J. de

Vries, *Altnordische Literaturgeschichte*, Berlin [2]1964–67; G. W. Weber, 'Hárbarzljóð' (*KLL* 3) Munich 1967; C. J. Clover, 'Hárbarðsljóð as generic farce' (*SS* 51) 1979; M. Bax, T. Padmos, 'Two Types of Verbal Dueling in Old Icelandic: The Interactional Structure of the *senna* and the *mannjafnaðr* in *Hárbarðsljóð*' (*SS* 55) 1983; C. J. Clover, 'Hárbarðsljóð' (*DicMA* 6) 1985.

Harðgreip (ON, 'the hard grabbing one'). A giantess in the *Þulur*. She is not mentioned elsewhere in Old Norse poetry, although Saxo (*Gesta Danorum* I, 20ff.) writes in detail about her, calling her by her latinized name, Harthgrepa. In Saxo, Harðgreip is the daughter of the giant Vagnophtus (Vagnhǫfði), one of the foster fathers of → Haddingus. Harðgreip is obviously Hadding's wet-nurse. However, her care of him changes when Hadding grows to be a man and wants nothing of her amorous attentions, pointing out that she is a giant and therefore somewhat over-proportioned for a human being. She replies: 'Don't be put off by the strangeness of my gigantic figure. I can change the shape of my body by will-power, becoming now small, now big, now fat, now thin, now shrinking, now growing. Now I reach nearly up to the sky, now I change myself into the smallest of all human beings.' Finally she wins him over to sleep with her by her proposals made in verse form. From this time on she accompanies him wearing men's clothes and is of great help because of her strength. On their journeys together she proves to be a sorceress when she pushes a rune-stick under the tongue of a dead man, causing him to make prophecies – a typical case of a northern *seiðr*. One night when an enormous hand pushes itself into the hut where the two travellers are staying, Harðgreip turns into a giantess again and because of her strong grip is able to keep the hand away from her charge. Whether her name comes from this incident, or whether Saxo was inspired by her name to write the episode is impossible to determine. Saxo tells that she died by being clawed to pieces by members of her own race, but does not give any reason why.

The stereotype of the giantess as a wet-nurse is also found in Icelandic sagas which, like Saxo, mix elements of the giantess in Medieval folklore with those of giants in Germanic mythology, without describing them in as much detail as Saxo does.

E. Hellquist, 'Ett par mytologiska bidrag' (*ANF* 21) 1905; P. Herrmann, *Die Heldensagen des Saxo Grammaticus*, Leipzig 1922; P. Fisher, H. E. Davidson, *Saxo Grammaticus, The History of the Danes*, Cambridge 1979/80.

Harðgreipr (ON, 'the hard grasping one'). A giant in the *Þulur* who is not referred to elsewhere, and is most likely listed merely as a male counterpart to → Harðgreip.

Harðverkr (ON, 'the hard working one'). A giant in the *Þulur*, cf. also → Fjǫlverkr.

Harðvéurr (ON, 'the strong archer'). A name for the god Thor in the *Þulur*. Thor is also called → Véurr in the *Hymiskviða*. Harðvéurr is only a reinforcement of this name.

Hariasa. A Germanic goddess. A now lost stone with an inscription on it was dedicated to Hariasa in Cologne, Germany in 187 A.D. (CIL XIII 8185). Etymologically speaking the name is related to the ON valkyrie name Herja and therefore is most likely the name of a goddess of war. – On the other hand, it could be possible that Hariasa means a 'goddess with lots of hair'.

S. Gutenbrunner, *Die germanischen Götternamen*, Halle 1936; J. de Vries, *Altgermanische Religionsgeschichte*, Berlin [3]1970; A. Kabell, 'Harja' (*ZfdA* 102) 1973; H. Reichert, *Lexikon der altgermanischen Namen*, Vienna 1987–90.

Harii (Latinized West Germanic 'warriors', cf. Gothic *harjis* 'army'). A Germanic tribe described by Tacitus (*Germania* 43) as follows: 'As for the Harii, not only are they superior in strength to the afore mentioned peoples, but they are wild and strengthen their born-in wildness with artificial means and the skilful choice of timing. They have black shields and black coloured bodies. They choose dark nights for their battles and strike fear into their enemies by the terrifying and shadowy appearance of the army of the dead, and no enemy can stand this strange, hellish sight, for in all battles the eyes are conquered first.'

The name of this shadowy army of warriors also reminds us of the → *einherjar*, who do not necessarily represent an old detail from the concept of the Germanic warrior's paradise. A more likely explanation is the night-time activity of the → Wild Hunt, which O. Höfler convincingly interpreted as a band of warriors, which he associated with the cult of Odin.

O. Höfler, *Kultische Geheimbünde der Germanen*, Frankfurt 1934; R. Much, *Die Germania des Tacitus*, Heidelberg [3]1965; J. de Vries, *Altgermanische Religionsgeschichte*, Berlin [3]1970.

Harigast (Proto-Germanic, 'army-guest', 'army-warrior'). Name on an inscription on helmet B from Negau/Slovenia, possibly from the 1st or 2nd centuries B.C. The complete inscription composed in a Venetian alphabet should probably be read as HARIGASTITEIVA, and as such could mean 'to the god Harigast' or 'Harigast to the god Teiva', or, less likely, 'Harigast, son of Te, . . .'. Most recent scholarship (Scardigli, Pittioni) considers the second interpretation as the more correct one since it would mean that Harigast was a Germanic warrior who gave up his helmet as a votive offering to a deity. De Vries, however, interprets Harigast as being the name of a god (cf. the name of the goddess Hariasa), namely Wodan/Odin, who was of course the god of the army, a function which several of his Old Norse names refer to (Herjann, Herjafǫðr, Heráss, Hertýr etc.).

J. de Vries, *Altgermanische Religionsgeschichte*, Berlin [3]1970; A. L. Prosdocimi, P. Scardigli, 'Negau' (*Italia linguistica nuova et antica I, Misc. in onore di O. Parlangeli*) Galantina 1976; R. Pittioni, *Urzeit*, Vienna 1980.

Harimella. Germanic goddess named in a Latin inscription from Birrens on Hadrian's Wall, North England (CIL VII 1065) which is dedicated to the *deae Harimellae*. An attempt to relate Harimella to the place name Harimalla on the Lower Rhine was violently rejected by Much who interpreted Harimella as a valkyrie-like figure. He related the name to the name of the valkyrie Herja and to ON *mjǫll* 'snow'. Birkhan explains the name far more logically as meaning the same as the valkyrie name Herfjǫtur 'army-fetter' and refers to the army-impeding function of the Idisi in the First Merseburg Charm (with *-mella* from Old Irish *mall* 'slow').

R. Much, 'Dea Harimella' (*ZfdA* 36) 1892; E. Schröder, 'Dea Harimella' (*ZfdA* 61) 1924; R. Much, 'Harimalla-Harimella' (*ZfdA* 63) 1926; S. Gutenbrunner, *Die germanischen Götternamen*, Halle 1936; J. de Vries, *Altgermanische Religionsgeschichte*, Berlin [3]1970; H. Birkhan, *Germanen und Kelten*, Vienna 1970.

Hárr (1) (from ON *hár* 'high'; 'the high one'). A name for Odin. The meaning 'the high one' is substantiated by the forms *hǫll Háva* (*Hávamál* 109, 111, 164) and the name Jafnhárr in *Gylfaginning*. Possibly Hár (*Vǫluspá* 21) would mean 'the one-eyed god' (from ON *hár* 'blind'). The meaning 'the grey haired' (cf. FMS X 171) is certainly only secondary.

F. Detter, 'Hárr' (*PBB* 18) 1894; H. Falk, *Odensheite*, Christiania 1924; J. de Vries, *Altgerman-*

ische Religionsgeschichte, Berlin [3]1970; J. de Vries, *Altnordisches etymologisches Wörterbuch*, Leiden [2]1977.

Hárr (2), also Hár (probably 'the grey one' from ON *hárr* 'grey, grey-haired'). Name of a dwarf, only given in the list of dwarf names in *Vǫluspá* 16 and *Gylfaginning* 17.

Harthgrepa (Latin). A giantess in Saxo, who is identical with → Harðgreip.

Hástigi (ON, 'the high climbing one'). A giant in the *Þulur*.

Hati (ON, 'despiser, hater'). A mythical wolf in *Grímnismál* 39. He is called the son of → Hróðvitnir and Snorri records in *Gylfaginning* 11 that he runs in front of the sun and pursues the moon which it will eventually devour. The wolf → Skǫll follows the sun.

R: J. C. Dollman, *The wolves pursuing Sol and Mani* (painting, c.1900).

Háttatal ('list of verse forms') → *Snorra Edda*.

Haugspori (ON). A dwarf in *Vǫluspá* 15. On its own, the name Haugspori would mean 'hill treader', but Gutenbrunner considers Haugspori to be only an epithet for the dwarf-name preceding it in the list, Hár(r). This is admittedly possible but not more likely than Haugspori as a dwarf's name in its own right. Gutenbrunner's suggestion that Hár Haugspori is a reference to Odin should be rejected at any rate as an over-interpretation.

S. Gutenbrunner, 'Versteckte Eddagedichte' (*Edda, Skalden Saga. Festschrift Genzmer*) Heidelberg 1952.

Haustlǫng (ON). Title which Snorri gives to a shield poem composed by the Norwegian skald Þjóðólfr ór Hvíni in the 9th century. *Haustlǫng* means 'the autumn-long one' and might refer to the fact that the poet took a whole autumn to compose the poem which consists of 20 stanzas written in the *dróttkvætt* metre. It is conceivable that the poem was originally longer than the still extant 20 stanzas.

The poem describes the mythological scenes depicted on a shield which Þjóðólfr received from a certain Þorleifr, but the poet draws from his own mythological knowledge in order to expand on the illustrations on the shield. Two motifs dominate the contents: the giant Þjazi's theft of the goddess Idun and Loki's adventure with him, and also Thor's fight with the giant Hrungnir.

The *Haustlǫng* is one of the oldest literary sources for Nordic mythology and even Snorri used it in his mythography.

Holtsmark's theory that *Haustlǫng* illustrated a Germanic cult drama is generally rejected nowadays.

A. Holtsmark, 'Myten om Idun og Tjatse i Tjodolvs Haustlǫng' (*ANF* 64) 1949; V. Kiil, 'Tjodolvs Haustlǫng' (*ANF* 74) 1959; A. Holtsmark, 'Haustlǫng' (*KLNM* 6) 1961; J. de Vries, *Altgermanische Religionsgeschichte*, Berlin [3]1970; K. Schier, 'Haustlǫng' (KLL 3) 1967; E. O. G. Turville-Petre, *Scaldic Poetry*, Oxford 1976; E. Marold, *Kenningkunst*, Berlin, New York 1983.

Havae. Matron name on a Roman inscription from Merzenich near Düren (West Germany) (CIL XIII 7847). The semantically closest interpretation of the name as 'the high ones' (cf. the ON name for Odin Hárr) is etymologically not convincing.

Hávamál (ON, 'The words of the High One'). An Eddic lay which, apart from short mythologcal passages which all deal with Odin, should be counted among Eddic didactic poetry. Its 164 stanzas are only given in the Codex Regius of the *Edda*. Stanza 164 refers to everything preceding it as being 'words of the high one', thus giving the lay its title. It also means that Odin is the one who utters the stanzas, and thus it creates a fictitious framework for the collection.

The first 79/80 stanzas (also called 'the old poem of morals' by German scholarship) give rules and advice for daily use: how a guest should behave when eating, drinking, in friendship, in generosity, at the Thing. Stanzas 81–95 also give didactic advice, especially in matters of love, which are exemplified especially in the so called → Odin's examples (96–102, 103–110) by relating Odin's love adventures. There are several epigrammatical stanzas included between 81–95 among the didactic stanzas, which tell what one should be aware of. *Hávamál* 112–137 then follows with a list of advice for a young man called Loddfáfnir, and is therefore known as *Loddfáfnismál*. The most important part of *Hávamál* as far as mythology is concerned follows this (138–141), the so-called 'Odin's runic poem' (*Rúnatals þáttr Oðins*) which contains → Odin's self-sacrifice. After a transition passage (142–145) the so-called magic lays follow in the last part of the *Hávamál* (also called *Ljóðatal*, 146–164) which contain the proclamations of 18 charms, but they themselves are not given.

The *Hávamál* has a unique position in the *Edda* which is not only due to the material contained in it, but also to the (at least at first glance) very heterogenous nature of its individual sections and their evaluation. In older scholarship (survey in v. See, 'Gestalt', 1972), *Hávamál* was seen as a conglomeration of predominantly unconnected and randomly ordered stanzas and lays in which the supposedly great age and true Germanic code of behaviour of the first part were emphasized. Innumerable attempts at dissecting, deleting and moving around of passages were undertaken on the rest of the piece in order to arrive at an 'original form'. V. See (1972) has convincingly shown, however, that the extant form of the *Hávamál* is not dictated by chance but was composed deliberately by the hand of an editor. The proof of the influence of Latin collections of proverbs (like the *Disticha Catonis*) has refuted the opinion that the *Hávamál* renders the unfalsified Germanic code of behaviour. As a result of this, *Hávamál*, in its extant form, should be seen as the product of the late 12th or early 13th century which uses a wealth of older material, but which otherwise, with a few exceptions, stands closer to the Christian Middle Ages than to Germanic antiquity.

A. Heusler, *Die zwei altnordischem Sittengedichte der Hávamál*, Berlin 1917; A. Holtsmark, 'Hávamál' (*KLNM* 6) 1961; J. de Vries, *Altgermanische Religionsgeschichte*, Berlin ³1970; H. Beck, 'Hávamál' (*KLL* 3) 1967; K. v. See, 'Sonatorrek und Hávamál' (*ZfdA* 99) 1970; H. Klingenberg, 'Hávamál' (*Festschrift S. Gutenbrunner*) Heidelberg 1972; K. v. See, *Die Gestalt der Hávamál*, Frankfurt 1972; K. v. See, 'Disticha Catonis und Hávamál' (*PBB* West 94) 1972; K. v. See, 'Probleme der altnordischen Spruchdichtung' (*ZfdA* 104) 1975; H. Pálsson, *Heimur Hávamála*, Reykjavík 1990.

R: J. G. Herder, *Die Zauberkraft der Lieder* (in: *Volkslieder*, 1778–79).

Heaven, → Asgard, → Andlangr. → Víðbláinn.

Hefring (ON, 'the lifting one' = 'the wave'). One of the nine daughters of the sea-giant → Ægir and his wife Rán (*Skáldskaparmál* 22 and 58; Einarr Skúlason) who correspond to the waves of the sea in mythological poetry.

Heiðr (1) (ON). The name given to the seeress → Gullveig in the *Vǫluspá* 22 after she had been burned three times by the Æsir and had been reborn again three times. Heiðr was also a seeress in the *Landnámabók* (Heiðr vǫlva) and in *Hrólfs saga kraka* 3. However, it is unlikely that Heiðr in the *Vǫluspá* should only be seen as a term meaning seeress and not a personal name (although this is de Vries's view), as the other interpretations of ON *heiðr* ('fame'; adj., 'light, beaming') fit the name Gullveig well semantically speaking.

J. de Vries, 'Vǫluspá Str. 21 und 22' (ANF 77) 1962; E. O. G. Turville-Petre, *Myth and Religion of the North*, Westport 1975.

Heiðr (2). A name repeatedly given to seeresses and witches in Old Norse literature, such as in *Örvar-Odds saga* 2, *Hrólfs saga kraka* 3, *Landnámabók* (S 179 = H 145), and possibly an epithet for 'good' witches. However, it might only be a literary name for women like → Þuriðr.

Heiðr (3) (ON, either 'honour' or 'heath'). A giant in the genealogy of giants in the *Vǫluspá in skamma* (*Hyndluljóð* 32). He is said to be the son of Hrímnir.

Heiðrun (ON). A goat in Nordic mythology which stands, according to *Grímnismál* 25 (also *Gylfaginning* 38), on → Valhall and eats the leaves on the tree Læraðr. Clear mead flows from her udder into the beakers of the → *einherjar*. In the *Hyndluljóð* 46 and 47, Hyndla insults Freyja with the remark that she is as sex-mad as Heiðrun. From names such as Heiðvanr and Heiðdraupnir, de Vries concludes that *heiðr* could have been a ritual word for sacrificial mead. Otherwise the meaning of the word is obscure. – The concept of the mead-giving goat would appear to be a specifically Nordic version of the concept of the feeding proto-cow (→ Auðumla). A related concept to Heiðrun can be found in the goat of Greek mythology, Amaltheia, whose horns are cornucopia.

S. Einarsson, 'Some Parallels in Norse and Indian Mythology' (*Scandinavian Studies. Essays Leach*) Seattle 1965; J. de Vries, *Altgermanische Religionsgeschichte*, Berlin [3]1970.

Heimdall (ON Heimdallr, also Heimdalr and Heimdali, perhaps 'the one who illuminates the world'; etymology obscure). A Nordic god, one of the Æsir, who is considered to be the guardian of the gods. Heimdall is mentioned several times in the Eddic lays, but only rarely in skaldic poetry (*Húsdrápa* 10 and a few late stanzas). Nonetheless, he appears to have played a significant role in heathen mythology.

In the *Vǫluspá* 1 as well as in the → *Rígsþula*, where he appears under the pseudonym Rígr, Heimdall is said to be the father of all mankind. Heimdall is Loki's deadly enemy (*Lokasenna* 48) and both kill each other at the Ragnarǫk (*Gylfaginning* 50). Snorri tells of Heimdall: 'he is called "the white As", and he is great and holy; he was born of nine sisters.' He is also known as Hallinskiði and Gullintanni as his teeth are made of gold. His horse is called Gulltopr. He lives at Himinbjǫrg near (the bridge) Bifrǫst; he is the the gods' watchman and sits at the end of the sky guarding the bridge against the mountain giants. He needs less sleep than a bird and can see things 100 miles off whether it is day or night. He can hear the grass growing on the earth and the wool on sheep and everything else which is louder than that. He owns the horn called the Gjallarhorn which can be heard throughout the whole world. Heimdall's sword is called Hǫfuð ('man-head': *Gylfaginning* 26). Apart from this mysterious comment which could show that Heimdall himself was killed by a man's head, there are many other things which are somewhat obscure about this god. The reference to

Heimdall being born from nine mothers, all of whom are sisters, could be understood to mean the nine daughters of Ægir (→ Ægir's daughters), the waves. Elsewhere (*Hyndluljóð* 35–37) it is said quite definitely that these nine mothers were giantesses, and the names of these nine and the names of Ægir's daughters do not concur.

Heimdall's epithet Hallinskiði is used in the *Þulur* also as a name for a ram, just as *heimdali* is, although this is otherwise a different form of the name Heimdall. Possibly Heimdall was associated with the ram, just as Thor with his billy-goats, Frey with his boar and Odin with his ravens or wolves. Much went further and wanted to see Heimdall as a ram-shaped god as the ram was unquestionably a common sacrificial animal among the Germanic peoples (cf. ON *sauðr* 'sheep', Gothic *sauþs* 'sacrifice') and was perhaps even thought of as a sacred animal.

As the gods' watchman (*Grímnismál* 13, *Lokasenna* 48) and guard over the heavenly bridge Bifrǫst, Heimdall gives a blast on his horn at the beginning of the Ragnarǫk to warn the gods (*Vǫluspá* 46; *Gylfaginning* 50). De Vries concluded from this that Heimdall ought to be listed among the gods of the second mythical function, that of strength, whereby Thor would represent the warrior and Heimdall the guardsman. Dumézil however thinks of Heimdall as the god of origin, like the Roman Janus and the Indian Dyauh of the *Mhābhārata*, not as the father of the gods, but as the god of the beginning of long life (symbolized by his nine births). In this case Snorri's information that Heimdall is Odin's son (*Skáldskaparmál* 8) is inaccurate. Schröder, on the other hand, understands Heimdall to be a god of fire who would correspond to the Indian god Agni.

The role which Heimdall plays in the fight for the → Brísingamen (Freya's necklace), of which Ulfr tells in his *Húsdrápa*, is even more obscure. A further puzzle is the meaning of his brilliant appearance in the myth and his golden teeth. A simplifying natural-mythological interpretation has suggested that Heimdall was a god of sunrise and the day, but this has since been rejected. Even Ohlmark's interpretation of Heimdall as the god of the sun – despite some interesting ideas, whereby Heimdall's horn represents the crescent of the moon – is not convincing. Even more mysterious is the reference to the *Heimdallar hljóð* (*Vǫluspá* 1) which lies beneath the World-ash, which perhaps refers to Heimdall's horn. *Hljóð* possibly means Heimdall's excellent hearing abilities, or else is used as a substitute for an ear, which, like Odin's eye, lies in Mímir's well at the foot of the world-ash as a pledge. Even Heimdall's epithet Vindlér is obscure in its relationship to the god Heimdall.

Despite numerous investigations, which have cast light on new aspects of the god Heimdall time and again, we are still today far from a complete interpretation of the character and function of the god Heimdall.

K. Müllenhoff, 'Frija und der Halsbandmythos' (*ZfdA* 30) 1886; V. la Cour, 'Heimdalls navne' (*DS*) 1923; R. Much, 'Der nordische Widdergott' (*Deutsche Islandforschung* 1) Breslau 1930; A. Ohlmarks, *Heimdalls Horn und Odins Auge*, Lund 1937; B. Pering, *Heimdall*, Lund 1941; J. de Vries, 'Heimdallr, dieu énigmatique' (*Études germaniques* 10) 1955; G. Dumézil, 'Remarques comparatives sur le dieu scandinave Heimdallr' (*Études celtiques* 8) 1959; F. R. Schröder, 'Die Göttin des Urmeeres' (*PBB* West 82) 1960; F. R. Schröder, 'Heimdallr' (*PBB* West 89) 1967; F. R. Schröder, 'Helgi und Heimdall?' (*GRM* 19) 1969; J. de Vries, *Altgermanische Religionsgeschichte*, Berlin [3]1970; E. O. G. Turville-Petre, *Myth and Religion of the North*, Westport 1975; G. Dumézil, *Gods of the Ancient Northmen*, Berkeley 1977.

R: (fine art) K. Ehrenberg, *Týr und Heimdall* (drawing, 1882); D. Hardy, *Heimdall* (painting, c.1900); E. Doepler d. J., *Heimdall an der Himmelsbrücke* (E. Doepler, W. Ranisch, *Walhall*, 1901).

(other) Heimdall, the name of a Norwegian fishery protection vessel, built 1962.

Heimlaug vǫlva (ON, 'Heimlaug the seeress'). A seeress who, through her ability to prophesy, helps the hero of *Gull-Þóris saga* (18 and 19). She is an example of the extremely popular figure of the heathen seeress in saga literature who became a literary topos in the High Middle Ages, but represented only a trace of the earlier importance of seeresses in Germanic antiquity.

Hel (1) (ON). The realm of the dead in Germanic mythology. It is the realm of the goddess Hel (→ Hel 2) who is a literary personification of the realm of the dead. Hel is the realm of the dead to which the people who have died on land of illness or of old age are admitted – the drowned belong to Rán, and those who have fallen in battle to Odin. Once in Hel, the dead can never leave again. 'Coming to Hel' is a synonym in the Eddic lays and in skaldic verse for 'dying'. In Germanic mythology, Hel is not a place of punishment, not a hell, it is simply the residence of the dead. Widukind documents this in a remark made about the victory of the Saxons over the Franks in 915: 'Where is there such an enormous hell which has room for so many dead?' (*Res Gestae Sax.* I, 23). Hel only takes on characteristics of a place of punishment, similar to the Christian concept of hell, in the High Middle Ages in the descriptions by Snorri and Saxo, as well as in the later Eddic lays. Elements of Medieval visionary literature (which was as well-known and popular in Iceland as elsewhere) flow into the picture of Hel here. The → Gjallarbrú, the bridge to the Other World over the underworld river Gjǫll, is one such element which admittedly reveals native elements, although it seems to be identical with the bridge of souls of Christian visions (*Gylfaginning* 48). Another one is the weapon-bearing river → Slíðr (*Vǫluspá* 36) or → Geirvimull ('Spear bubbler', *Grímnismál* 27; *Gylfaginning* 38) which also forms the (nameless) bridged border to the Other World in Saxo (*Gesta Danorum* I, 31). Odin's journey to Hel in the *Baldrs draumar* and Snorri's report of the journey to Hel made by Hermóðr on his attempt to free Baldr render late and ornate descriptions of a realm of shadows. The above mentioned Gjallarbrú is guarded by a serving maid Móðguðr (*Gylfaginning* 48). A dog of hell similar to the Greek Cerberus guards the entrance to Hel in *Baldrs draumar* 3 and 4. The fence around Hel is called Helgrindr; in other places it is called Nágrindr (*Skírnismál* 35, *Lokasenna* 63) or Valgrindr (*Grímnismál* 22) and the late *Fjǫlsvinnsmál* name the gate to Hel as Þrymgjǫll. Because Hermóðr is still alive when he rides to Hel and can therefore not cross the bridge, he has to jump over the fence (*Gylfaginning* 48). – Hel is quite clearly understood as identical with the Christian hell in Snorri's fantastic description in *Gylfaginning* 33 where he describes the residence of the goddess Hel in Niflheim = (here) Hel, Niflhel. Her hall is called Eljúðnir 'the damp place', her plate and her knife 'hunger', her servant Ganglati 'the slow one', the serving maid Ganglǫt 'the lazy one', the threshold Fallandaforad 'stumbling block', the bed Kǫr 'illness', the bed curtains Blíkjanda-bǫlr 'bleak misfortune'. The fact that these allegorizations have nothing to do with Germanic mythology need hardly be mentioned.

Hel was no doubt thought to be situated somewhere in the north where the home of the giants and demons is to be found in some texts. Snorri quotes a sentence in *Gylfaginning* 48 in which the way to the underworld leads to the north and downwards (*niðr ok norðr liggr helvegr*), and Hel, seen as a damp and cold place, could point to this (similarly the identification of → Niflheim and Niflhel in *Gylfaginning* 33 and 43), but not necessarily since these characteristics would also fit a realm situated under the earth. The burial mounds of western European megalithic culture always have their entrances to the south and the burial chamber to the north, and also the north-south orientation is predominant in Bronze Age ship settings and Vendel and Viking Age ship graves.

Hel is etymologically related to Gothic *halja* 'hell', OE *hell*, OHG *helan* 'to hide', in addition also Old Irish *cuile* 'cellar'. Therefore, the opinion that the origin of the idea of Hel originates from the family grave, as found in the megalithic graves covered with mounds of the Stone and Bronze Age, is supported etymologically.

H. R. Ellis, *The Road to Hel*, Cambridge 1943; E. F. Halvorsen, 'Hel' (*KLNM* 3) 1961; J. de Vries, *Altgermanische Religionsgeschichte*, Berlin ^{3}1970.

Hel (2) (ON). The goddess of the underworld (→ Hel 1), probably a very late poetic personification of the underworld Hel. The first kennings using the goddess Hel are found at the end of the 10th and in the 11th centuries. The underworld is the residence and realm of the goddess; typical kennings for the underworld are 'the halls of Hel' (*salar Heliar*: *Vǫluspá* 43) or 'house of Hel' (*rann Heliar*: *Baldrs draumar* 2). The most detailed description is found in Snorri's *Edda* (*Gylfaginning* 33) where Hel is called Loki's daughter and therefore the sister of the Midgard serpent and the Fenriswolf. He describes Hel as being half black, half white, morbid and fierce-looking; then he gives an allegorical description of her house (→ Hel 1) which clearly stands in the Christian tradition. On the whole nothing speaks in favour of there being a belief in a goddess Hel in pre-Christian times.

R: K. Ehrenberg, *Hermod, asking for Baldr's release from Hel* (charcoal drawing, 1881) and: *Loki and Sigyn; Hel with the dog Garm* (drawing, 1883); J. C. Dollman, *Hermod before Hela* (painting).

Helblindi (1) (ON, 'the blind one of the realm of death'). One of Loki's two brothers (→ Byleistr). Helblindi only appears in the *Snorra Edda* (*Gylfaginning* 32, *Skáldskaparmál* 16), but nevertheless he is most likely not merely the product of late mythographical elaboration, since Loki's genealogical tree (and thus the figures linked with it) seems to suggest great age.

J. de Vries, *The Problem of Loki*, Helsinki 1933.

Helblindi (2) (ON). Another name for Odin in *Grímnismál* 46 in most of the *Edda* manuscripts. The form → Herblindi is, however, more likely.

Helgrind (ON, 'Hel's fence'). The fence surrounding the underworld, Hel, according to Snorri (*Gylfaginning* 48). As nobody who has passed through the gate into Hel can ever leave Hel again, Hermóðr has to jump over Helgrind on his ride to release Baldr from the underworld. In other places this fence is called Nágrindr and Valgrind.

Hellivesa. A goddess on a votive stone in Glenel near Cologne, Germany from 201 A.D. (CIL XIII 8161). Perhaps related to the name of the river Elle?

S. Gutenbrunner, *Die germanischen Götternamen*, Halle 1936; H. Reichert, *Lexikon der altgermanischen Namen*, Vienna 1987–90.

(**Helmwige**). A valkyrie (soprano) in R. Wagner's opera *Die Walküre*. The name was invented by Wagner, probably in imitation of real valkyrie names, such as Hjalmþrimul.

Helreginn (ON, 'ruler over Hel'). A giant in the *Þulur*. The giants are rarely otherwise directly associated with the underworld, even if their domain, like Hel, lies to the north in Utgard.

Helvegr (ON, 'the way to → Hel'). The way to the underworld (*Vǫluspá* 47 and 52; *Helreið Brynhildar* Prose). Snorri speaks in *Gylfaginning* 48 about the fact that the Helvegr leads downwards and to the north (*en niðr ok norðr liggr helvegr*). The Dutch and Low German expressions *Helwegen* and *Helwege* for the way to the graveyard would seem to give further evidence of the idea that the dead take this road.

J. de Vries, *Altgermanische Religionsgeschichte*, Berlin ³1970.

Hengikjǫptr (ON, 'the one with the drooping chin'). Presumably another name for Odin (referring to his long beard), although the passage in *Skáldskaparmál* 40 does not exactly give this explanation in the introduction to the *Grottasǫngr*. However, as Hengikjǫptr is found in the *Þulur* among the names for Odin, it appears to be understood as one in *Skáldskaparmál*, too.

A. M. Sturtevant, 'Etymological Comments Upon Certain Old Norse Proper Names in the Eddas' (*PMLA* 67) 1952.

Hengist and Horsa. According to Anglo-Saxon tradition, these are the names of the two leaders of the Angle army during their settlement of England (Geoffrey of Monmouth, *Historia Regum Britanniae* 6, 10; Bede, *Historia Ecclesiastica* 1, 15), supposedly in the year 449 A.D. There are several cases of two brothers such as Hengist and Horsa in the myths of ethnogeny of other Germanic peoples (→ dioscuri). The meaning of the two names (to NHG *Hengst*, Eng. horse) suggests a connexion with the horse-shaped (Indo-)Germanic twin-deities (also found in Theban and Indian myth), and this being the case, Hengist and Horsa should also be understood as mythological figures. The mythical horse-shape of the brothers is strikingly confirmed by the horse heads on the gables of farmhouses in Holstein which were known as Hengist and Hors even as late as around 1875 and can still be seen there today.

K. Schreiner, *Die Sage von Hengist und Horsa*, Berlin 1921; E. A. Philippson, *Germanisches Heidentum bei den Angelsachsen*, Leipzig 1929; J. de Vries, *Altgermanische Religionsgeschichte*, Berlin ³1970.

Hengjankjapta (ON, 'the one with the hanging chin'). A giantess in a poem by Þórbjǫrn dísarskáld who tells in one stanza that Hengjankjapta was killed by Thor. Hengjankjapta is one of the numerous not particularly flattering names for giantesses which refer to their appearance.

Heorot (OE, approximately: 'the stag-hall'). The name given in *Beowulf* 78ff. to the great hall of the Danish kings in → Lejre which was decorated at the gable ends with antlers from which it derives its name. Despite influences from Old Testamentarian typology, in the description in *Beowulf* it seems possible that Heorot really does derive from a historical large festive hall situated in Lejre. The stag or antlers could have been a symbol of regality for the Anglo-Saxons, a possibility supported by the royal standard decorated with a stag which was found in the Sutton Hoo burial ship. The Bronze Age cult chariot from Strettweg (Styria, Austria; 7th century, of Celtic origin) and the South Scandinavian rock carvings show that antlers had religious symbolic significance already at an much earlier date. However, it is pure speculation to try to assign a stag cult to any particular Nordic god (e.g. Baldr), as Sarrazin does, and there can be no doubt that the stag cult had a far greater significance for the Celts than for the Germanic peoples.

G. Sarrazin, 'Die Hirsch-Halle' (*Anglia* 19) 1897; H. Rosenfeld, 'Die vandalischen Alkes "Elchreiter", der ostgermanische Hirschkult und die Dioskuren' (*GRM* 28) 1940; M. A. Lee, 'Heorot and the "Guest-Hall" of Eden' (*Medieval Scandinavia* 2) 1969; J. de Vries, *Altgermanische Religionsgeschichte*, Berlin 31970.

Hepti (ON, 'grasp'). A dwarf in the *Vǫluspá* 13. In the version given in the *Snorra Edda* (*Gylfaginning*). Hepti and the following name Víli are joined together to produce → Heptifíli, but this is not necessarily the more correct version.

Heptifíli (ON). A dwarf-name (*Vǫluspá* 13 in *Gylfaginning* 13), which replaces the names → Hepti and → Fíli found in the other manuscripts. According to Gering, Heptifíli could mean 'one who smooths handles by filing'; the word *fili* 'file' is not recorded, however, elsewhere in ON and would have to have been borrowed from German. Cf. however, *heptisax* 'kind of knife'.

H. Gering, *Kommentar* 1, Halle 1927; C. N. Gould, 'Dwarf-Names' (*PMLA* 44) 1929; L. Motz, 'New Thoughts on Dwarf-Names' (*FmSt* 7) 1973; J. de Vries, *Altgermanische Religionsgeschichte*, Berlin 31970.

Heráss (ON; Runic Norse *haras* 'army-god'). A name for Odin given in the runic inscription on a grave stone at Eggjum (Sogne, Norway) dating from the middle of the 7th century. The reading of this name is however not completely certain. If Høst's interpretation is correct, then Odin's function in the inscription is as the guide of the dead, an appropriate role for the leader of the army of the dead. – The stone also bears the drawing of a horse which could be interpreted as → Sleipnir.

G. Høst, 'To Runestudier' (*Norsk Tidskrift f. Sprogvidenskap* 19) 1960; E. O. G. Turville-Petre, *Myth and Religion of the North*, Westport 1975.

Herblindi (ON, 'the one who blinds the enemy army'). Another name for Odin in the *Þulur* and as a manuscript variant of Helblindi in *Grímnismál* 46. Since Odin could make his enemies blind and deaf in battle (according to *Ynglinga saga* 6), the form Herblindi seems to be the more original.

H. Falk, *Odensheite*, Christiania 1924.

Hercules. Roman god, originating from the Greek hero Hercules, the killer of monsters and the symbol of male strength. In the *interpretatio romana* it is most probably the name for the Germanic god of thunder *Þunaraz (Donar/Thor).

Tacitus already listed Hercules as one of the main Germanic gods along with Mars and Mercurius (*Germania* 9). However, it is by no means certain whether Hercules can really be considered identical to the Germanic *Þunaraz at this time, since the argument that Tacitus must have meant that Hercules was one of the three important gods Odin, Týr and Thor, weakens somewhat when we consider that this Germanic triad is not expressly documented for this older period, even though it may be assumed. Also, the *interpretatio germanica* translates Thor in place of the Roman Jupiter in the Latin week-day name. However, two things speak in favour of the equivalence of Hercules/Herakles and Donar/Thor. Both are, in their own specific areas, killers of monsters and giants and as such the powerful defenders of both gods and man against supernatural forces which threaten life. Secondly there are clear similarities in the divine attributes of both. Hercules with his club and Thor with his hammer Mjǫllnir are both linked inseparably in mythological tales and pictorial depictions. Hercules' club and Thor's hammer were both used in miniature form as amulet-like pendants, between which J. Werner was able to find typological similarities. This concurrence then supports a factual identification of Hercules with *Þunaraz/ Donar/Thor.

J. Werner, 'Herkuleskeule und Donar-Amulett' (*Jahrbuch des römisch-germanischen Zentralmuseums* 11) 1964; J. de Vries, *Altgermanische Religionsgeschichte*, Berlin [3]1970; H. Birkhan, *Germanen und Kelten*, Vienna 1970.

(**Hercules Alabuandus**). Supposedly the name of a god on a Utrecht inscription. However this description has been disregarded as a source because the inscription has obviously been deliberately obliterated by spiral ornamentation so that any reading must remain a hypothesis. Apart from the reading Hercules Alabuandus, scholars have read two recordings of the name Hercules Magusanus as well as *Baldruus and *Lobbonus from the one inscription.

S. Gutenbrunner, *Die germanischen Götternamen*, Halle 1936; M. Schönfeld, *Wörterbuch der altgermanischen Personen- und Völkernamen*, Heidelberg [2]1965; H. Reichert, *Lexikon der altgermanischen Namen*, Vienna 1987–90.

Hercules barbatus ('the bearded Hercules'). A god on a votive stone from Brohl on the Lower Rhine (CIL XIII 7694). As the name of the dedicator is not necessarily Germanic either, an interpretation as the Germanic Hercules (i.e. Donar/Thor) is impossible, and Hercules is certainly a Roman god here.

J. de Vries, *Altgermanische Religionsgeschichte*, Berlin [3]1970.

Hercules Deusonianus. A god who is only recorded on coins dating from the reign of the Roman emperor Postumus (258–269 A.D.). The name is generally considered to be etymologically related to a place-name, Deuso, on the Lower Rhine (present day Doesburg?). Despite the fact that it occurs on Roman coins, it could therefore refer to the Germanic Hercules, i.e. Donar/Thor.

S. Gutenbrunner, *Die germanischen Götternamen*, Halle 1936; M. Schönfeld, *Wörterbuch der altgermanischen Personen- und Völkernamen*, Heidelberg [2]1965; H. Reichert, *Lexikon der altgermanischen Namen*, Vienna 1987–90.

Hercules Magusanus (approximately 'the mighty Hercules'). A name for the Germanic Hercules, i.e. the god Thor.

Up to the present day, ten votive stones, four arm rings and two Roman coins dating from the reign of the Roman emperor Postumus (258–269 A.D.) have been found as definite evidence for this name of the god. The coins were minted in Cologne in 261 A.D. and the votive stones are from the 2nd and 3rd centuries A.D. The oldest evidence found on votive stones comes from Mumrills on Hadrian's Wall, northern England (CIL VII 1090). A stone from Rome (CIL VI 31162), put up by a Germanic cavalry man is dated 219 A.D. A recent find comes from Dacia and the other stones are all from the Roman province of *Germania inferior* on the lower Rhine. The arm rings have been found in Tongeren, Neuss, Cologne and Bonn.

Although three votive stones bear a picture of Hercules Magusanus which exactly corresponds to pictures of the Roman Hercules (club, lion skin, on one stone with a three-headed Cerberus), all the evidence has been found on Germanic soil, or else can clearly be defined as Germanic because of the name of the dedicator. Tacitus's new names for the Germanic main deities (Mercurius, Hercules and Mars) have led to

Hercules being identified with Donar/Thor, and therefore the extremely probable Germanic name of Hercules Magusanus likewise suggests that it can be interpreted as signifying Donar/Thor. The meaning of the name Magusanus is admittedly not undisputed. In the last century the name was mostly considered to be etymologically related to the Germanic verb **mag-* 'can' (cf. Gothic *magan*, NHG *vermögen*), but later it was considered to be a derivation from a basic word which contains the Celtic **magos-* 'field'. Grienberger interprets Hercules Magusanus as **magusanus 'campestris'*, whereas Norden relates the name to the place name Mahusenham (now Myswinkel near Duurstede), and Much and Gutenbrunner to Noviamagus (now Nijmegen, Holland), the main centre of the Batavi tribe in whose area the centre of the cult does indeed appear to have fallen. More recently, the name has again been interpreted as being Germanic and Magusanus has been derived from *Maguz/s-naz 'the one belonging to power' (Wagner).

F. Kauffmann, 'Mythologische Zeugnisse aus römischen Inschriften. 1. Hercules Magusanus' (*PBB* 15) 1891; Th. Grienberger, 'Zwischenvocalisches h in germanischen und keltischen Namen der Römerzeit' (*PBB* 19) 1894; E. Norden, *Die germanische Urgeschichte in Tacitus Germania*, Leipzig, Berlin [3]1923; S. Gutenbrunner, *Die germanischen Götternamen*, Halle 1936; R. Much, *Die Germania des Tacitus*, Heidelberg [3]1967; J. de Vries, *Altgermanische Religionsgeschichte*, Berlin [3]1970; H. G. Horn, 'Eine Weihung für Hercules Magusanus aus Bonn' (*Bonner Jahrbücher* 170) 1970; M. Clauss, 'Neue Inschriften im Rheinischen Landesmuseum Bonn' (*Epigraphische Studien* 11) 1976; N. Wagner, '(Hercules) Magusanus' (*Bonner Jahrbücher* 177) 1977; H. Reichert, *Lexikon der altgermanischen Namen*, Vienna 1987–90.

Hercules Maliator. Name of a god on a votive stone from Oberburg, Germany (CIL XIII 6619). Although earlier it was interpreted as 'hammer-swinging Hercules' = Thor, because of the likeness to Mjǫllnir, this has since been rejected as *maliator* is probably derived from *maliatores* 'stone workers' and as such he would be seen as the (Roman) protective patron of quarry workers, just like Hercules Saxanus.

E. Jung, *Germanische Götter und Helden in christlicher Zeit*, Munich, Berlin [2]1939; J. de Vries, *Altgermanische Religionsgeschichte*, Berlin [3]1970; H. Birkhan, *Germanen und Kelten*, Vienna 1970.

Hercules Saxanus. This name of a god was thought to be a name for the Germanic Hercules (= Thor) by scholars from the 19th century, since his attribute was a sword (cf. OHG *sahs*, OE *seax* 'sword'), but nowadays Hercules Saxanus is considered to be a Roman god who would have been the guardian for quarry workers on the Lower Rhine, a theory supported by the sub-form Saxsetanus (from Lat. *saxetum* 'quarry').

Nonetheless we may assume a mixed form between the Roman and the Germanic cult because despite the obviously Latin name, the monuments bearing the name of this god are predominantly found around Bonn and Cologne (CIL XIII 7697–7712, 7716–7720), and the Germanic peoples, who were confronted with the cult there, will surely have understood Thor to be this 'rock-breaking Hercules'.

E. H. Meyer, 'Hercules Saxanus' (*PBB* 18) 1894; A. v. Domaszewski, 'Die Religion des römischen Heeres' (*Westdeutsche Zeitschrift* 14) 1895; S. Gutenbrunner, *Die germanischen Götternamen*, Halle 1936; M. Schönfeld, *Wörterbuch der altgermanischen Personen- und Völkernamen*, Heidelberg [2]1965; J. de Vries, *Altgermanische Religionsgeschichte*, Berlin [3]1970.

Herfjǫtur (ON, 'fetter of the army'). A kenning-like name for a → valkyrie (*Grímnismál* 36, *Þulur*) which probably refers to the fortune determining function of the valkyries especially in battles.

Herfǫðr (ON, 'father of the army'). A name for Odin (*Vǫluspá* 29). It refers to the concept of Odin as the determiner of the fortune of battle. The similar name → Herjafǫðr is found more frequently.

Heri (ON, 'hare'). A dwarf in the *Þulur*. Less likely is the interpretation 'the warrior' (Motz).

L. Motz, 'New Thoughts on Dwarf-Names' (*FmSt* 7) 1973.

Herja (ON). A valkyrie named in the *Þulur*. The name belongs etymologically to ON *herja*, OHG *herjón* 'devastate', and goes back to the same form *Harjaza just as the West Germanic goddess's name Hariasa from the 2nd century does. It is almost impossible to say whether Herja was in fact an original name of a goddess even among North Germanic peoples. An independent development is equally likely in the case of a 'goddess of war'.

Th. v. Grienberger, 'Germanische Götternamen auf antiken Inschriften' (*ZfdA* 36) 1892; M. Schönfeld, *Wörterbuch der altgermanischen Personen- und Völkernamen*, Heidelberg [2]1965.

Herjafǫðr (ON, 'father of the army'). A frequent name for Odin in the mythological poetry of the *Edda* (*Vǫluspá* 43, *Grímnismál* 19, 25, 26, *Vafþrúðnismál* 2, *Hyndluljóð* 2, and also in the *Þulur*). Like Herfǫðr, it refers to the concept of Odin as the personal director of the fate of battle. Kuhn has supposed that the names for Odin based on *-fǫðr* (Herfǫðr, Valfǫðr) are older and more likely to be heathen than those based on *-faðir* (Alfaðir, Sigfaðir). Many of his names based on *Her-* (such as Hertýr and Herteitr) point towards Odin's function as a god of war.

H. Falk, *Odensheite*, Christiania 1924; H. Kuhn, 'Das nordgermanische Heidentum' (*ZfdA* 79) 1942.

Herjann (ON, 'lord'). A frequent name for Odin (*Vǫluspá* 30, *Grímnismál* 46, *Guðrunarkviða* I, 19; *Krakumál* 29, *Íslendinga drápa* 11, in Einarr Skálaglamm; in the *Þulur*; in Snorri, *Gylfaginning* 2). Herjann is a very old formation with the *-ana-* suffix, like *dróttin*, Oðinn and Ullinn and concurs with the Greek *koíranos* 'lord'.

Herjann as a name for Odin points to Odin's function as the leader of the → *einherjar*, the Wild Hunt (already recorded by Tacitus as the army of the dead of the Harii) and therefore it is probably a very old cult name for the god.

S. Bugge, 'Germanische Etymologien' (*PBB* 21) 1896; H. Falk, *Odensheite*, Christiania 1924; J. de Vries, *Altgermanische Religionsgeschichte*, Berlin [3]1970.

Herke, Harke → Erce.

Herkir (ON, 'noisy one' or 'bungler'?). A giant in the *Þulur*. The name is the male form of the more frequently recorded female giantess's name Herkja.

Herkja (ON, 'noisy woman' or else 'the plagued one'). A giantess in the *Þulur* and in the *Harðar saga* 7. The name is identical with that of Attila's wife, Erka, and the MHG female personal name Herche.

Hermóðr (ON). Baldr's brother. According to Snorri's version of the Baldr myth, Hermóðr was willing to ride to Hel on Sleipnir to persuade the goddess Hel to release Baldr (→ Hermóðr's Ride to Hel). Hermóðr is a god only in Snorri's version (*Gylfaginning* 48), Odin's son and Baldr's brother. In the *Edda*, a hero called Hermóðr is only mentioned in *Hyndluljóð* 2, whence Snorri's god in all probability originated. In

Eyvind's *Hákonarmál* 14 Hermóðr and Bragi (originally probably also a mere mortal) greet the fallen heroes on their arrival in Valhall, without the remotest allusion to their being gods.

In the genealogies of the Old English royal house Hēremōd is named among the descendants of Wodan as the father of Sceaf. In *Beowulf* (902f.) Hēremōd is a Danish king who was exiled and had to undertake long voyages, which might reflect in some way Hermóð's Ride to Hel.

E. Hackenberg, *Die Stammtafeln der angelsächsischen Königreiche*, Berlin 1918; E. A. Philippson, *Germanisches Heidentum bei den Angelsachsen*, Leipzig 1929; E. A. Philippson, *Die Genealogie der Götter*, Urbana, Ill. 1953; J. de Vries, *Altgermanische Religionsgeschichte*, Berlin [3]1970.

R: (fine art) K. Ehrenberg, *Hermod, von Hel die Herausgabe Baldur's erbittend* (charcoal drawing, 1881); J. C. Dollman, *Hermod before Hela* (painting, c.1900). (literature) *Idunna und Hermode* (title of a periodical published 1812–16 in 3 volumes).

Hermóð's Ride to Hel. An episode in the myth of → Baldr when, after Baldr's death and at Frigg's request, Hermóðr rides to Hel in order to ransom Baldr from her.

Hermóð's Ride to Hel is described in some detail in Snorri (*Gylfaginning* 48) both before and after Baldr's funeral: Frigg asks who would be prepared to ride to Hel to visit Baldr and to offer the goddess Hel ransom money to let him return to Asgard. Odin's son Hermóðr is willing and he rides off on Odin's horse Sleipnir. – A description of Baldr's funeral follows this, after which Snorri continues his account of the journey:

Hermóðr rides nine nights long through deep, dark dales until he arrives at the river → Gjǫll and rides to the Other World over the bridge → Gjallarbrú which is covered with gold and guarded by a maid, Móðguðr. She remarks that the bridge has creaked more under him than under five companies of dead men who had crossed it the day before, and concludes from this that he is not dead. She then asks him what he wants and he informs her of his quest whereupon she confirms that Baldr has indeed come to Hel. Hermóðr rides on up to the gates of Hel, jumps over them on Sleipnir, and arrives thus at Hel's hall where he sees Baldr sitting on a seat of honour. He stays the night there and when he tells Hel of his quest, she agrees to it on the condition that everything living and dead must weep for Baldr. Then Baldr accompanies Hermóðr outside the hall and sends Odin his ring Draupnir as a reminder of himself. Nanna sends Frigg linen and other presents, as well as a gold ring for Fulla. Hermóðr rides home to Asgard and tells his tale. On hearing about the condition for Baldr's return, the Æsir send messengers throughout the whole world so that everything might weep for Baldr. Indeed everything does weep, people and animals, earth, stones, trees and metals; only one giantess called Þǫkk refuses – and this giantess is really Loki in disguise.

Since little about Hermóð's ride to Hel has been passed down in poetic sources and yet Snorri's account is remarkably complete, it has been assumed that he used a lost lay which might have contained only the ride to Hel, but possibly also included Baldr's death. It is unlikely that *Húsdrápa* (which Snorri used as a source for Baldr's funeral) contained no longer extant stanzas about the ride to Hel and the only lay about Baldr in the Poetic *Edda*, *Baldrs draumar*, does not mention it, either.

Hermóð's ride to Hel belongs to the tales of journeys to the Other World which occur in the *Edda* in *Baldrs draumar* (Odin seeks out a dead prophetess) and in the *Helreið Brynhildar* ('Brynhilde's ride to Hel') of heroic poetry, and others which are frequently told of in Saxo and in the *fornaldarsǫgur*.

To try to interpret Hermóð's journey as the descent of a fertility god calling the vegetation to new life, as is attempted by extreme natural-mythological interpretations, is hardly correct. However, as → Hermóðr was probably a purely literary figure and originated from a human legendary hero, the mythological relevance of Hermóðr and his journey should not be over-exaggerated.

Lit. → Baldr.

Hermuthruda (probably from Ermunthrud). The name of a warlike queen in Saxo (*Gesta Danorum* IV, 103f.); → Alvilda.

Herran (ON). A name for Odin and a secondary form for → Herjan, found only in Snorri (*Gylfaginning* 2).

Herteitr (ON, 'the one liking armies'). A name for Odin in *Grímnismál* 47 and in *Þulur*; cf. Herfǫðr, Hertýr, Herjafǫðr.

(**Hertha**). A supposed Germanic 'earth-mother'. The name originated in earliest scholarship from a misreading for Nerthus and an etymology of 'earth' parallel to ON Jǫrð. Unfounded speculation has led to a connexion being seen with the cult of Nerthus at Herthasee and Herthaburg on the Baltic island of Rügen.

R: F. v. Hagedorn, *Der Wein*; and: *Hertha* (poems, 1745).

Herþǫgn (ON, 'hostess of the army'). Probably a name for a valkyrie although it is found in the *Þulur* as a synonym for 'battle'.

Hertýr (ON, 'army-Týr, army-god'). A name for Odin. It is only recorded once at the end of the 10th century (Einarr skálaglamm, *Vellekla* 3) at a time when the names for Odin based on *-týr* were relatively frequent; *týr* only means 'god' here and not Týr himself, just as the plural *tívar* only ever means 'gods'.

H. de Boor, 'Die religiöse Sprache der Vǫluspá' (*Deutsche Islandforschung* 1) Breslau 1930.

Heruli. The Heruli (or Eruli) were bands of Germanic warriors referred to in classical literary sources who were engaged in wars during the 3rd to 6th centuries A.D. in Greece, Italy, Spain, North Africa, Gaul and Scotland. During the conquest of Italy by the Odoaker in 476 A.D., the Heruli belonged to his main troops. After the downfall of the Danube state of the Heruli by the Langobards, the majority of the Heruli migrated to Scandinavia.

Earlier, the Heruli used to be called a Germanic tribe, but nowadays the opinion has prevailed that the Heruli must have been well organized, extremely mobile bands of warriors. The Heruli were early associated with the proto-Norse term for 'rune master' *erilaR*, recorded at least nine times in the 5th/6th centuries, which itself could have been related to the aristocratic title ON *jarl*, Anglo-Saxon *eorl* (English earl).

Höfler's very convincing theory connected the campaigns of the Heruli with the expansion of the runes. Helmet A from Negau would serve as a link, as it bears the name Erul, a Germanic centurion in Roman service from the 1st or 2nd century A.D. If this is the case, then members of the Heruli (like the above named centurion Erul) would have created the runic alphabet on Etruscan and Roman models at this early stage. This knowledge of runes could have spread quickly as far as Scandinavia because of the rigid organization and great mobility of the bands of Heruli. As a result, it is likely that for a long time the knowledge of the runes would have been considered as the privilege of the members of this band of warriors who were bound to Odin by cult.

R. Much, 'Heruler' (*Hoops* 2) 1915; O. Höfler, 'Herkunft und Ausbreitung der Runen' (*Die Sprache* 17) 1971.

Hervǫr. A valkyrie with the additional name *alvitr* 'omniscient' or else 'supernatural being, valkyrie' in the *Vegtamskviða*. Hervǫr and Hlaðguðr, daughters of King Hlǫðver, are described together with Ǫlrun as being swan-maidens who can fly with the aid of their swan-shifts. These explanations in the prose introduction to the Eddic lay have no foundation in the lay itself. In any case, both the valkyrie-names and also their connexion with the motif of the swan maidens belong to the area of heroic poetry and not to mythology, although admittedly → valkyries were also depicted elsewhere as riding through the air (*reið lopt ok lǫg*: *Helgakviða Hjǫrvarðssonar* 9 Prose, *Helgakviða Hundingsbana* II 4 Prose), but this concept is extremely distorted in the *Vegtamskviða*.

Hetha. A warrior queen in Saxo (*Gesta Danorum* VIII, 256f.); → Alvida.

Hiannanef-. Hiannanefae or Hiannanefatae is the actual reading of the matron name discussed under → Kannanefates.

hierós gámos (Greek, 'holy wedding'). The *hierós gámos* is the wedding between the god of heaven and the mother goddess of earth, whose union results in the revival of nature's fertility. It is documentarily well recorded for the Germanic peoples in the Bronze Age rock carvings, and is repeatedly evident in the myths which have come down to us. Odin's various love adventures, especially those with giantesses (one of whom is Jǫrð 'earth' with whom he begets the god Thor), should be seen as reflections of a *hierós gámos*, even if Odin was not originally the Germanic god of heaven.

Hierós gámos plays a significant role in religion in particular in vegetation cults. The marriage between the fertilizing heaven (or else sun) and the receptive earth occurs especially in the cult of the phallic god Freyr. Both Adam of Bremen (*Gesta Hammaburgensis ecclesiae Pontificum* IV, 27) and Saxo (*Gesta Danorum* VI, 185) show their disgust in their description of orgiastic scenes in this cult as described for the sacrifice in Uppsala. The Vanir Freyr and Njǫrðr appear to have played a significant role in the cult reenactment of the *hierós gámos*, since even Tacitus appears to have alluded to a *hierós gámos* in the cult of Nerthus (Njǫrðr), for which the subsequent ablution of the goddess speaks. With regard to this, the occurrence of the place names → Njarðarlǫg and Tysnes which are both on the Norwegian island of Tysnesǫ has led to speculation as to the possible union of the god of heaven Týr with the goddess of the earth Nerthus/Njǫrðr, which would be evident through the cult place-names extant there.

One reflection of *hierós gámos* may be seen in the spring-time traditions of folklore in which sexual intercourse taking place on the fields played a significant role and continued up to early modern times.

F. R. Schröder, *Ingunar-Freyr*, Tübingen 1941; S. Singer, 'Die Religion der Germanen' (*Schweizerisches Archiv für Volkskunde* 43) 1946; J. de Vries, *Altgermanische Religionsgeschichte*, Berlin [3]1970; F. Ström, 'Hieros-gamos-motivet i Hallfreðr Ottarsons Hakonardrápa' (*ANF* 98) 1983; G. Steinsland, *Det heilige bryllup og norrøn kongeideologi*, Oslo 1991.

R: A production of the Viennese *Serapion* theatre group called *Heilige Hochzeit* (holy wedding) was based on elements of Germanic mythology (1983).

Hiheraiae. Name of → matrons on a Roman Age inscription from Enzen near Euskirchen, Germany (CIL XIII 7900) dedicated to the *matronis Hiheraiis*. Gutenbrunner doubts the connexion with Germanic **hihera-* 'jay' for phonetic and semantic reasons.

S. Gutenbrunner, *Die germanischen Götternamen*, Halle 1936; H. Reichert, *Lexikon der altgermanischen Namen*, Vienna 1987–90.

Hildingr (ON, 'warrior'). A dwarf in the *Þulur*.

Hildisvíni. (ON, 'Hildi-boar'). The boar in *Hyndluljóð* 7 on which Freyja rides, and which is actually → Ottar who has been changed into an animal. He is described as *gullinborsti* 'the one with golden bristles', a clear indication that the poet was thinking of Frey's boar → Gullinborsti. The *Hyndluljóð* is a very late Eddic lay and there is the possibility that the poet got his information, if not out of the *Snorra Edda*, then more likely from scholarly sources rather than from contemporary mythological concepts.

Hildólfr (1) (ON, 'battle-wolf'). An otherwise unmentioned son of Odin's mentioned only in the *Þulur*.

Hildólfr (2) (ON). According to *Hárbarðsljóð* 8, Hildólfr is the owner (invented by Odin) of the ferry in which Odin refuses to carry Thor over the river. Hildólfr lived in Ráðseyjarsund, an otherwise equally unrecorded place-name. This stanza is part of the game with which Odin confuses the simple-minded Thor in *Hárbarðsljóð*.

Hildr (1) (ON, *hildr* 'battle'). A → valkyrie (Darraðarljóð 3, *Vǫluspá* 30, *Grímnismál* 36; *Þulur*). In Snorri's account of the battle → Hjaðningavíg (*Skáldskaparmál*, 47), night after night Hildr resurrects the warriors who have fallen in that day's combat so that they must go on fighting for ever (*Háttalykill*). It is possible that a folk-belief which thought that the valkyries had a magical healing function is reflected in this tale, for it is also a valkyrie → Skuld in *Hrólfs saga kraka* 51, who at night awakens the slain warriors to life again. The name given in the *Þulur* of → Eir ('grace', 'help'), who is otherwise said to be an Æsir goddess, could also point to the idea that the valkyries had a healing power. The motif of the resurrected warriors, which probably comes from Celtic culture, is relatively widespread. It possibly merely represents a literary topos of supernatural forces in the descriptions of battles.

J. Grimm, *Deutsche Mythologie*, Berlin [4]1875–78; F. Panzer, *Hilde-Gudrun*, Halle 1901; G. Müller, 'Zur Heilkraft der Walküre' (*FmSt* 10) 1976; H. E. Davidson, *Saxo Grammaticus*, Cambridge 1979–80.

Hildr (2) (ON). A legendary person mentioned in the Eddic lays (*Hyndluljóð* 19, *Helgakviða Hundingsbana* II 29). Hildr is Högni's daughter who could be identified equally well as the valkyrie Brynhildr (and the valkyrie Hildr?).

Hildr (3) (ON). A giantess in the *Þulur* and in the *Húsdrápa*.

Himinbjǫrg (ON, 'heaven's castle'). The name of Heimdall's heavenly domicile, according to *Grímnismál* 13 and Snorri. It lies at the end of the sky near the bridge → Bifrǫst, from which Heimdall's function as guardian of the gods arises (*Gylfaginning* 16 and 26).

Himinhrjóðr (ON, 'the destroyer of heaven'). The biggest bull in the herd belonging to the giant → Hymir in Snorri's version of → Thor and the Midgard serpent (*Gylfaginning* 47). Thor tears the head off the bull in order to use it as bait for the Midgard serpent. *Hymiskviða* 19 also refers to the bull's head as bait, but it does not give the animal a name. The picture of Thor and the Midgard serpent on the grave stone at Gosforth/England (10th century) shows a bull's skull quite clearly at the end of Thor's fishing line.

The name Himinhrjóðr is recorded in various manuscripts of the *Snorra Edda* as Himinbjótr, Himinhrjotr, Himinjóðr. As it only occurs in Snorri and in the *Þulur*, it appears to be an early creation of Snorri's. It is, however, unknown why the bull should be called Himinhrjótr.

Hirmin → Irmin.

History of Research. The history of research of Germanic mythology only really commences at the beginning of the 19th century. The few works of the Renaissance about the Germanic peoples and their religion (e.g. Cluver 1616, Schedius 1648) are simply collections of quotations from classical authors and Latin chroniclers of the early Middle Ages in which is no division is made between Germanic and Celtic mythology. Henri Mallet was the first author to use translations of Old Norse literature from the Poetic *Edda* and the *Snorra Edda* in his work *Monuments de la mythologie et de la poesie des Celts et particulièrement des anciens Scandinaves* (written in 1756 and translated into German in 1764 by Gottfried Schütze). Schütze himself was keenly interested in Nordic antiquity, but more for political than scholarly reasons.

J. Grimm's *Deutsche Mythologie* (1835) and L. Uhland's *Der Mythus von Thor* (1836) stand at the beginning of a circumspect scholarly research of Germanic mythology, of which Grimm's extensive work had by far the greater effect, and since then research into Germanic mythology has never ceased. Grimm wanted to write his mythology excluding Scandinavia, but nonetheless he used a wealth of Nordic material so that his *Deutsche Mythologie* is still today one of the most valuable presentations of the entire Germanic mythology based on folklore and literary, but not archaeological, sources. Grimm's work (1875–78 4th edition, ed. E. H. Meyer) was however less well-known than K. Simrock's *Handbuch der deutschen Mythologie* (1855) despite the fact that the latter was basically a backward step compared to Grimm with regard to the wealth of material and the reliablility of the presentation.

In his mythological investigation Uhland had already made repeated attempts at natural-mythological interpretations which then frequently led (in particular in the school of comparative mythology) to simplifying conclusions. The representatives of this school, to which A. Kuhn and W. Schwartz belonged, gave themselves the task of reconstructing Indo-Germanic religion, and M. Müller even wanted to reconstruct a proto-religion. This direction of research was later superseded by the so-called folklore mythology which proved to be of great help to Grimm in his studies. The study of folklore mythology took new paths as a result of W. Mannhardt's *Wald- und Feldkulte* (1875), and this usage of folklore customs in order to interpret Germanic mythology was continued until the middle of the 20th century. It has opened up a wealth of material to scholars of religion. Sir J. G. Frazer's monumental work *The Golden Bough* (1911–1935) is also based on this line of research.

Towards the end of the 19th century Germanic mythology became increasingly interesting to the philologists. Sophus Bugge questioned the originality of Germanic mythology with his revolutionary hypotheses about the origin of Germanic myths being exclusively in Christian and classical thought. Most of his theories are rejected nowadays, but have led the way to the critical appreciation of the 20th century. Bugge's theories were defended especially by E. H. Meyer who associated them with the old natural-mythological interpretations and this led consequently to these ideas being rejected.

E. Mogk's contribution to the research of Germanic mythology should not be underestimated. With his vehement criticism of the supposed reliability of the *Snorra Edda* he pointed out the whole problem of the reliability of Old Norse sources. He was correct to show that Snorri's mythology should be seen predominantly as a work of literature, but he lost himself in folklore mythology. While his considerations are basically still valid today, we should not forget that Snorri was a very careful collector of material which would otherwise be lost to us, and he was very knowledgeable himself concerning heathen mythology, even if he worked with it in a particularly free and imaginative way.

Magnus Olsen, the Norwegian scholar of place-names, tapped a new source for the research of Germanic mythology at the beginning of this century in his studies of place-names and wrote many books on this subject. Since then place-names have been considered to be an important source for the history of Germanic mythology. However, there is no extensive study as yet which could counterbalance the over-interpretation of the material so far investigated.

The Danish scholar of religion, W. Grönbech, examined the role of religion in the lives of the Germanic peoples, its influence on cult and custom in his work *Vor Folkeœt i Oldtiden* (1909–12, German 1937), but this work was only appreciated much later. Otto Höfler, the Viennese scholar, examined the links of mythology and cult and the significance of the cult in the lives of the individuals. His conclusions have found objections, but no real proof opposing them.

F. R. Schröder studied comparative mythology in quite a different way to the researchers of the 19th century by considering non-Germanic parallels and relations. He dedicated his studies to the entire view of the myths in the religions of the Indo-Germanic peoples. Several of his theories are not necessarily correct. Georges Dumézil has followed a similar path and has examined in addition to this the socio-cultural situation of the common pre-history of the Indo-Europeans. From this he arrived at his → Three-function-theory which has gained in importance since the Second World War despite some reservations. De Vries considered Dumézil's ideas in the 2nd edition of his *Altgermanische Religionsgeschichte* (1956/57) and one of the most recent handbooks is also based on them (Ström-Biezais). De Vries' important achievement has been always to have attempted a synthesis of previous research. His history of Germanic religion is the most extensive and still the valid handbook on Germanic mythology, even if he occasionally deals with the Nordic literary sources somewhat uncritically. De Vries (like Grönbech, Schröder, Höfler) can be counted as one of the supporters of the so-called sacral theory, attacked especially vehemently by H. Kuhn and v. See who on the whole denied the sacral as being the constitutive basic element of culture.

K. Hauck has added a new perspective by considering the pictorial documents left by Migration Age people (especially in bracteates) in which he sees the presentation of Germanic mythology, and points out the importance of pictorial documents which had up to then been completely ignored as sources for Germanic mythology.

W. Golther, *Handbuch der germanischen Mythologie*, Leipzig 1895; R. Batka, *Altnordische Stoffe und Studien* (Ergänzungsheft 2 zum Euphorion) 1896; R. M. Meyer. *Altgermanische Religionsgeschichte*, Leipzig 1910; F. Strich, *Die Mythologie in der deutschen Literatur*, Halle 1910; J. de Vries,

'Der heutige Stand der germanischen Religionsforschung' (GRM 33) 1951/52; K. Helm, 'Mythologie auf alten und neuen Wegen' (PBB West 77) 1955; J. de Vries, *Forschungsgeschichte der Mythologie*, Freiburg, Munich 1961; J. de Vries, *Altgermanische Religionsgeschichte*, Berlin [3]1970; M. I. Steblin-Kamenskij, *Myth*, Ann Arbor 1982.

Hjaðningavíg (ON, 'battle of Hedin's warriors'). A battle between the armies of Hedin and Högni related in the *Sörla þáttr* (in the *Flateyjarbók*) and in Snorri (*Gylfaginning* 48). In connexion with this Snorri also refers to Bragi's *Ragnarsdrápa* (9th century) where, however, the name Hjaðningavíg does not appear directly. According to *Sǫrla þáttr* the battle begins at Odin's instigation (→ Brísingamen), but Snorri's version relates that it is about Hǫgni's daughter and Hedin's beloved, → Hildr (1). If one considers the mythologizing introduction to the *Sǫrla þáttr* as an authentic part of the – undoubtedly mythical – battle, then a connexion could be seen with the battle between Loki and Heimdall (Ström), which is perhaps also a quest for Brísingamen and which finds its continuation at the Ragnarǫk. The kenning *Haddingjar land* 'land of Hedin's warriors' = 'Underworld' obviously refers to the continual slaying and resurrection of the warriors in Hjaðningavíg. – Grimm indicated a possible connexion between the Hjaðningar and the Wild Hunt, and Höfler also understood them to be a group of eternally fighting warriors, as a cult band of warriors.

J. Grimm, *Deutsche Mythologie*, Berlin [4]1875–78; M. Olsen, 'Hjadningekampen og Hallfreds Arvedraapa over Olav Tryggvason' (*Heidersskrift* M. *Hægstad*) Oslo 1925; O. Höfler, *Der Runenstein von Rök*, Münster, Köln 1952; F. Ström, *Loki*, Göteborg 1956.

Hjálmberi (ON, 'helmet-bearer'). A name for Odin in *Grímnismál* 46 and in the *Þulur*. Snorri repeatedly mentions that Odin wears a golden helmet (*Gylfaginning* 50; *Skáldskaparmál* 17), and the depictions of Odin on Vendel Age metal helmet decorations and pictorial stones (Stenkyrka Lillebjärs III, if Odin is indeed depicted here), also show him to be wearing a helmet.

H. Falk, *Odensheite*, Christiania 1924.

Hjalmþrimul (ON, 'helmet clatterer', 'female warrior'?). A valkyrie named in the *Þulur*.

Hjarrandi (ON). A name for Odin in skaldic poetry (in Bragi, *Ragnarsdrápa* 11 and Snorri, *Háttatal* 53) and in the *Þulur*. The name Hjarrandi, recorded by Saxo as Hiarnus and frequently used as a male personal name, is most likely to have derived from a change of the West Germanic personal names OHG Herrant, Hôrant, Anglo-Saxon Heorrenda. It is, however, unknown why Odin should be called Hjarrandi.

H. Falk, *Odensheite*, Christiania 1924; J. de Vries, *Altnordisches etymologisches Wörterbuch*, Leiden [2]1977.

Hjǫrþrimul (from ON *hjǫrr* 'sword' and *þrima* 'battle, noise', 'the sword-warrioress'). The name of a → valkyrie in *Darraðarljóð* 3 and in the *Þulur*. As with other names of valkyries (Guðr, Hildr) Hjǫrþrimul awakens associations of battle in whose outcome the valkyries have some influence.

Hjǫrvarðr (ON, 'keeper of the sword'). The father of Hveðna in the genealogy of giants in *Vǫluspá in skamma* (*Hyndluljóð* 32) and as such obviously the name of a giant. Otherwise, Hjǫrvarðr occurs frequently as the name of various legendary characters.

Hjuki (ON, 'the one returning to health'?). The brother of Bil in a tale told by Snorri about the picture in the moon. The name could refer to the waxing moon; → Máni.

A. Holtsmark, 'Bil og Hjuke' (MoM) 1945.

Hlaðguðr (ON). Name of a → valkyrie. Like her sister → Hervǫr, Hlaðguðr only occurs in heroic poetry. She also bears the name *svanhvít* 'swan-white' in *Vǫlundarkviða*. De Vries understood *Hlað-* to mean 'headdress', but this is rather doubtful and the association with Old Norse *hlaða* 'to weave' and *guðr* 'battle' giving a meaning of the name as 'the weaver of battles' seems far more likely for a valkyrie, despite the reverse order of the elements of the word (→ *Darraðarljóð*).

J. de Vries, *Altnordisches etymologisches Wörterbuch*, Leiden [2]1977.

hlautteinn (ON, 'sacrifice-branch'). A twig mentioned in Snorri's *Heimskringla* (*Hákonar saga góða* 14) and in the *Eyrbyggja saga* 4 (possibly influenced by the afore mentioned saga). At heathen sacrifices the priests were supposed to have sprinkled the blood of the sacrificial animal on the walls of the temple and over the assembled people. A similar scene is described in *Kjalnesinga saga* 2 but the concept would appear to have its origins more in the imagination of the Christian authors of the High Middle Ages, who created a heathen counterpart to the sprinkler (*asperges*) of the Christian liturgy. In fact, the real *hlautteinn* in heathen times seems to have been something like a piece of wood for casting lots (→ oracle; *Hymiskviða* 1; Þorvaldr Koðránsson).

Hlébarðr (ON). A giant in the *Harbarðsljóð* 20 with whom Thor had a fight. Otherwise we know nothing about him. It is uncertain whether the name is identical with the otherwise recorded *hlébarðr* 'wolf, bear' (from *léoparðr*, *léparðr* 'leopard').

Hleðiólfr (ON, 'protective wolf'?). A variant of the dwarf-name Hlévargr in the *Snorra Edda*.

Hlér (ON, 'sea'). Another name for the sea-giant → Ægir (*Skáldskaparmál* 1 and 23), also in the fictitious Norwegian pre-history in *Fundinn Nóregr* where he is the son of → Fornjótr. Kennings in skaldic poetry point to the fact that Hlér was used as a name for Ægir early on: *Hlérs dœtr* (in the skaldic poetry of Sveinn) are the waves known otherwise as → Ægir's daughters, and *Hlérs viti* (in Egill Skalagrímsson) means the same as *Ægis eldr* (both mean 'Ægir's fire', i.e. gold).

The name of the Danish island Hléysey (now Læssø) seems to be derived from the name Hlér. As Ægir has more the characteristics of a sea-god than a giant, Hlér is perhaps the eponymous ancestor of the island. It is going too far, however, to assume a cult centre for Hlér on the island only because of the name. In Saxo (*Gesta Danorum* VIII, 272) a certain Lerus is mentioned: he is probably identical with Hlér, as Saxo gives subsequently a detailed account of his son Snio (= ON Snær). The fact that the chronicle of Lejre in Denmark (*Chronicon Lethrense* 5) also makes a connexion between Læ (= Lerus = Hlér) and Snio allows the conclusion that Lejre was associated at an early time with Hlér and possibly also derives from Hlér.

G. Schütte, *Dänisches Heidentum*, Heidelberg 1923; J. de Vries, *Altgermanische Religionsgeschichte*, Berlin [3]1970; H. E. Davidson, P. Fisher, *Saxo Grammaticus*, Cambridge 1979/80.

Hlévangr or Hlévargr (ON). A dwarf in the *Vǫluspá* 15. Both forms of the name *-vangr* 'field' and *-vargr* 'wolf' would be possible. On the other hand Hlévangr, meaning 'wind protected plain', is not particularly logical as a dwarf's name, and Gould's interpretation of Hlévargr 'lee-outlaw', i.e. 'evil person buried in a sheltered spot' or Motz's 'sheltering, protective wolf' are equally unconvincing.

C. N. Gould, 'Dwarf-Names' (*PMLA* 44) 1929; L. Motz, 'New Thoughts on Dwarf-Names' (*FmSt* 7) 1973.

Hléysey (ON) Danish island, today Læssø in Kattegat, → Hlér.

Hliðskjálf (ON). Either the name of Odin's throne or else of his hall. Hliðskjálf is not mentioned in any of the Eddic lays and occurs only in the – apparently earlier – prose introduction to the *Grímnismál* and *Skírnismál*. In both cases Hliðskjálf seems to mean a seat from which the gods have a view over the whole earth. In Snorri (*Gylfaginning* 16) Hliðskjálf is described as follows: 'It is there in this hall [Valaskjálf] that Hliðskjálf is to be found, the high seat as it is called; and whenever All-father sits on this throne he can see over the entire world.' In *Gylfaginning* 8 however it is not the throne but rather the place where it stands that is called Hliðskjálf: 'There is a place called Hliðskjálf, and when All-father sits on the throne there [. . .]'. Hliðskjálf is mentioned in the same context in *Gylfaginning* 49, too, and the etymology of the word also suggests this: *hlið* is 'opening', and although *skjálf* cannot be interpreted with absolute certainty, the corresponding OE *scylf*, *scelf* point to 'tower'; Middle Dutch *schelf* means 'scaffolding', so that it would be possible that Hliðskjálf means perhaps 'the scaffolding over the (door-)opening: observation point, guard tower'.

V. Kiil has shown that Odin's throne Hliðskjálf from which he has a 'supernatural' view over the world can be seen in connexion with the magical platform *seiðhjallr* which allowed the seeresses (like shamans) to have a view into the Other World.

G. W. Weber is of the opinion that Hliðskjálf is shown on one of the depictions on the Altuna stone which also bears an illustration of the myth of Thor and the Midgard serpent. Despite the extremely common occurrence of throne seat-like amulet pendants in heathen Scandinavia it is not totally certain if they really represent Hliðskjálf (as Drescher and Hauck think). In any case, they have nothing in common with the picture on the Altuna stone.

According to M. Olsen, the connexion between Odin and Hliðskjálf, the link of his son Vali with Valaskjálf and his other son Vidar with a *Viðarskjálf (retained in the Norwegian place name Viskjøll) points to a link with the name Skilfingr, another name for Odin, which in turn can be derived from the dynasty name of the Skilfingar. These Skilfingar, mentioned in *Ynglingatal* 18 and *Hyndluljóð* 11 and 16 are identical with the Scylfingas who, according to the OE *Beowulf*, were the ruling dynasty in Sweden in legendary pre-history. According to this, Hliðskjálf and Valaskjálf as also *Viðarskjálf would be names of cult places referring to Odin and other members of his dynasty. It is clear, from the not totally lucid etymology and also the mentioning of the name by the skald Hallfreðr vandræðaskáld (*Lausavísur* 6) in the 10th century, that the name Hliðskjálf is at least not a completely new formation.

E. Brate, 'Betydelsen av ortnamnet Skälv' (*NoB* 1) 1913; M. Olsen, *The Farms and Fanes of Ancient Norway*, Oslo 1928; V. Kiil, 'Hliðskjálf og seiðhallr' (*ANF* 75) 1960; E. O. G. Turville-Petre, *Myth and Religion of the North*, Westport 1975; G. W. Weber, 'Das Odinsbild des Altunasteins' (*PBB West* 94) 1972; J. de Vries, *Altnordisches etymologisches Wörterbuch*, Leiden [2]1977; H. Drescher, K. Hauck, 'Götterthrone des heidnischen Nordens' (*FmSt* 16) 1982.

Hlíf (ON, 'dirt') and Hlífþrasir. The names of two of Menglǫð's maidens in *Fjǫlsvinn-*

smál 38. These names are possibly an imitation of Líf and Lífþrasir in the *Vafþrúðnismál* 45.

Hlífþrasa (ON) or Hlífþursa. The name of one of Menglǫð's maidens in *Fjǫlsvinnsmál* 38; → Hlíf.

Hlífþursa → Hlifþrasa.

Hlín (ON, 'protectress'). A goddess in Snorri (*Gylfaginning* 34) and in the *Þulur* whom Frigg installs with the task of protecting mankind. In *Vǫluspá* 53 Hlín merely appears to be another name for Frigg and in skaldic poetry Hlín frequently appears in kennings for 'woman'. By the 10th century Hlín was already a well-known mythological figure. However, presumably Hlín is really only another name for Frigg and Snorri misunderstood her to be a goddess in her own right in his reading of the *Vǫluspá* stanza.

Hljóðólfr (ON, 'the howling wolf'). Name of a dwarf in the *Þulur*.

Hlóðyn (or Hlǫðyn?, ON). Mother of the god Thor (*Vǫluspá* 56), elsewhere known as Jǫrð. The name Hlóðyn is etymologically obscure, but a connexion with the name of the goddess → Hludana has been supposed for a long time. As Hlóðyn is identical with Jǫrð, she has usually been understood to be an earth-goddess.

J. de Vries, *Altgermanische Religionsgeschichte*, Berlin [3]1970.

Hlói (ON, 'the roarer'). Name of a giant, recorded only in the *Þulur*.

Hlǫkk (ON, 'noise, battle'). Name of one of the thirteen → valkyries in *Grímnismál* 36.

Hlóra (ON). The name given by Snorri (*Skáldskaparmál* 4) to the foster mother of the god Thor (his foster father is called Vingnir here). She is only mentioned by Snorri in this passage and it seems that Snorri assumed and derived it from the name Hlórriði for Thor. As such it is a scholarly invention of the 13th century.

Hlóriði or Hlórriði (ON, 'the loud rider', 'the loud weather-god'?). A frequent name for Thor in the earlier Eddic lays (*Hymiskviða* 4, 16, 27, 29, 37; *Lokasenna* 54, *Þrymskviða* 7, 8, 14, 31), although it already occurs in the *Vellekla* 15 (Einarr Skálaglamm, c.986). Because of its obscure etymology and its similarity with Einriði, a name for Thor, the name gives the impression of being an old cult name, but on the other hand it only occurs quite late. Presumably Hlóra, the name given to Thor's mother, is derived from Hlóriði since Hlóra is only found in Snorri's *Skáldskaparmál*.

Snorri also knows Hlóriði as Lóriði in his scholarly pre-history in the prologue to the *Edda*, where Hlóriði (or rather Lóriði) is said to be the father of Einriði and the grandfather of Vingþorr (both are names for Thor), which means that Snorri was aware of an association between Hlóriði and Thor.

Hludana. Germanic goddess known from five Latin inscriptions: three on the Lower Rhine (CIL XIII 8611, 8723, 8661), one from Münstereifel (CIL XIII 7944) and one from Beetgum, Frisia (CIL XIII 8830). The inscription from Nijmegen comes from the year 197 A.D., the ones from Münstereifel between 222–235 A.D. Numerous attempts have been made to interpret the name (cf. Gutenbrunner and de Vries), and the most steadfast connexions are with Frau Holle, the German name for Mother Winter in Grimm's fairy-tales, and Huld on the one hand, and ON Hlóðyn on the other. If we can really put the group Hel, Nehalennia, Huld, Hlóðyn, Hludana and Frau Holle together and link it with OE, OHG *helan* 'hide', then this group of female goddesses would have the character of chthonic or earth-goddesses. Since Hlóðyn is Thor's mother, and he is also known as 'the son of the earth' (*Jarðar burr*) this explanation has found many supporters.

H. Jaekel, 'Ertha Hludana' (*ZfdPh* 23) 1891; F. Kauffmann, 'Dea Hludana' (*PBB* 18) 1894; K. Helm, 'Hluðana' (*PBB* 37) 1912; S. Gutenbrunner, *Die Germanischen Götternamen*, Halle 1936; J. de Vries, *Altgermanische Religionsgeschichte*, Berlin [3]1970; L. Motz, 'Gerðr' (MoM) 1981.

Hnikarr (ON, 'instigator'). The name given to Odin in *Grímnismál* 47, *Reginsmál* 18 and 19, and frequently in skaldic poetry. In heroic poetry Odin appears as Sigurd's guardian under the name of Hnikarr. Sigurd sails around a headland in a storm, he is hailed by an old man called Hnikarr and as soon as he has taken him on board, the storm abates. Hnikarr also gives Sigurd victory in the battle against the sons of Hunding (*Reginsmál* Pr 16 – Pr 26).

H. Falk, *Odensheite*, Christiania 1924; J. de Vries, *Altgermanische Religionsgeschichte*, Berlin [3]1970.

R: E. Doepler d. J., *Odin als Hnikar* (E. Doepler, W. Ranisch, *Walhall*, 1900).

Hnikuðr (ON). A name for Odin in *Grímnismál* 48, → Hnikarr.

Hnitbjǫrg (ON, 'beating rock'). It is in this moutain that the giant → Suttungr lives with his daughter Gunnlǫð and watches over the mead of the skalds (Snorri, *Skáldskaparmál* 1). Snorri cites the kenning *Hnitbjarga lǫgr* ('Hnitbjǫrgs's liquid') for the skaldic mead as proof of this. However, as this kenning is from a poem no longer extant and does not occur in Snorri's primary source for the myth relating the theft of the skaldic mead (*Hávamál* 104–110), we have no further information about Hnitbjǫrg.

It is reasonable to assume from the name Hnitbjǫrg a link with the mountains which open and close, thus forming a hideaway for treasure in fairy-tales. An interpretation of Hnitbjǫrg as the gateway to the underworld would also be conceivable.

R. Doht, *Der Rauschtrank im germanischen Mythus*, Vienna 1974.

Hnoss (ON, 'treasure, jewel'). The name of the daughter of Oðr and Freyja in Snorri (*Gylfaginning* 34, *Skáldskaparmál* 20 and 35) and in the *Þulur*. All valuable things are supposedly called after her. In the *Þulur* a synonym for Hnoss, 'jewel', namely Gǫrsemi or Gersimi, is listed as one of Freyja's daughters. It is unknown whether Snorri has taken the name from a skaldic kenning or whether he invented it himself.

Hoddmímir (ON, 'treasure-Mímir'?). In *Vafþrúðnismál* 45 the phrase *Hoddmímis holt* occurs, which is a term for the wood or the tree in which the survivors of the Ragnarǫk keep themselves hidden (→ Líf). Hoddmímir can most likely be identified with the trunk of the world-tree Yggdrasill as → Mímir and his spring are associated with Yggdrasill in the *Edda* as well as in Snorri (*Gylfaginning* 14). → Mímameiðr 'Mímir's tree' probably also means the world-tree.

Hǫdd (ON) → Hadda.

Hǫðr (ON, 'warrior, fighter'). One of the Æsir gods. In the myth he is accused of → Baldr's death. According to Snorri (*Gylfaginning* 48, *Skáldskaparmál* 13) Hǫðr is blind. He is one of Odin's sons (*Skáldskaparmál* 13) and therefore Baldr's brother. He kills Baldr with a branch of mistletoe (*Gylfaginning* 48, *Skáldskaparmál* 5 and 13) and he is finally killed by Baldr's avenger → Vali (*Skáldskaparmál* 5). In the *Þulur* he is also listed among Odin's sons. In the Baldr myth Hǫðr is not particularly prominent, and in both Snorri (*Gylfaginning* 48), in *Vǫluspá* 32 and *Baldrs draumar* 9f. he stands rather in the background of the events despite being the killer. Loki has a more important role as the one who advises Hǫðr where to aim in the Icelandic tradition, in particular in Snorri's version, whereas quite a different role is given to Hǫðr in Saxo's version of the Baldr myth in which he is called Hötherus and where he is shown in a very positive light. Here he (not Baldr) marries Nanna and after Baldr's death is killed by the avenging → Bous.

In connexion with *Vǫluspá* 62 Snorri mentions that Hǫðr and Baldr will march to the Ragnarǫk together (*Gylfaginning* 52). In skaldic poetry there is absolutely no link between Hǫðr and the Baldr myth and his name is merely used a few times as a not more closely defined mythological figure in kennings.

An episode from the Old English *Beowulf* is thought to be close to the Baldr myth because of the similar names of two brothers: Hæðcyn (= Hǫðr?) kills his brother Herebeald (= Baldr?) in a tragic accident (*Beowulf* 2434ff.). However, the use of the arrow and the names are the only similarities with the Baldr myth, and so a conjectured link does not seem to be particularly likely.

Dumézil has produced Indian parallels for the killing of the invulnerable Baldr by the blind Hǫðr and therefore sees an ancient Indo-European motif in the role of the blind god.

G. Dumézil, 'Hötherus et Balderus' (*PBB* West 83) 1961/62; J. de Vries, *Altgermanische Religionsgeschichte*, Berlin ^{3}1970; G. Dumézil, *Gods of the Ancient Northmen*, Berkeley 1977.

Höfler, Otto (1901–1987), Viennese scholar of Germanic languages, literature, religion and folklore. His work on heroic poetry, linguistics and especially Germanic mythology enriched these fields of study with important discoveries. Höfler, who can be included in the folkloric branch of mythological research, did much work, under the influence of W. Grönbech, on the religious life and the cult of the Germanic peoples with especial reference to their mythology, whereby he saw reflections of older rituals in the myths. He pointed out the importance of the sacred in the everyday life of the individual as well as in the archaic forms of society and showed the effects of this religiosity on the cult.

H. Birkhan, 'Otto Höfler' (*Almanach der Österreichischen Akademie der Wissenschaften* 138) Vienna 1988.

hǫfuð (ON, 'human head'). Name for the sword of the god → Heimdall, but this is not necessarily the proper name of the sword.

Hǫgstari (ON, = → Hugstari?, otherwise perhaps 'witty'). A dwarf in the *Þulur*.

Hǫlgabrúðr → Þorgerðr Hǫlgabrúðr.

Hǫll (ON, 'slippery' or 'guileful'?). One of the mythical rivers in the catalogue of rivers in *Grímnismál* 27.

Hœnir (ON). One of the less important gods in Eddic mythology, whose mythical position is fairly uncertain. In *Vǫluspá* 17f. the godly triad Odin, Hœnir and Loðurr appear in the myth of the creation of man, Hœnir being the one to give man his reason (*óðr*). In another godly triad in *Reginsmál* and *Skáldskaparmál* 37, Hœnir appears together with Odin and Loki, but here he is without a function. *Vǫluspá* 63 names him as one of the Æsir in the new world after the Ragnarǫk. In the *Haustlǫng* by Þjóðólfr ór Hvíni, Hœnir is named in the myth of Þjazi without playing any particular role.

His passive status is described in more detail by Snorri in the myth of the → Vanir wars (*Ynglinga saga* 4), where the Æsir give Hœnir, who is said to be tall and handsome, to the Vanir as a hostage, and these make him a chieftain. He lets himself be advised in all matters by the wise Mímir until the Vanir become aware of this and decapitate Mímir. – Apart from several kennings which link him to Odin, Snorri calls Hœnir in several other kennings 'the quick As', 'long legs' and → *aurkonungr* (*Skáldskaparmál* 15), all names which for want of further information remain uncertain.

The interpretations of Hœnir's mythological role differ greatly. He has been seen as a god of the heavens, of the clouds, even as a sun-god or as a water-god, mostly as a swan or stork shaped bird-god, a bird-shaped personification of Odin's intellectual abilities. All of these explanations are extremely unsatisfactory, and it is perhaps better to think of him (as de Vries does) as a god of taciturnity and of cult celebrations.

F. Detter, R. Heinzel, 'Hœnir und der Wanenkrieg' (*PBB* 18) 1894; F. R. Schröder, 'Hœnir' (*PBB* 49) 1918; J. Loewenthal, 'Zur germanischen Wortkunde' (*ANF* 33) 1917; J. Loewenthal, 'Religionswissenschaftliche Parerga' (*PBB* 45) 1921; W. Krogmann, 'Hœnir' (*APhSc* 6) 1932; F. Ström, 'Guden Hœnir och odensvalan' (*Arv* 12) 1956; E. Elgqvist, 'Guden Höner' (*ANF* 72) 1957; F. Ström, 'Hœnir' (*KLNM* 7) 1962; E. C. Polomé, 'Some Comments on *Vǫluspá*, Stanzas 17–18' (*Old Norse Literature and Mythology*) Austin 1969; J. de Vries, *Altgermanische Religionsgeschichte*, Berlin [3]1970.

hǫrgr (ON, 'holy pile of stones; altar; temple?'). The term is used for a kind of Germanic sacrificial altar which is documented archaeologically from Neolithic times onwards and represents an archaic form of the → altar. Originally *hǫrgr* appears to have meant 'holy place' exclusively, as the related Anglo-Saxon *hearg* could mean 'holy grove' as well as 'temple, idol'. Hǫrgr is also evident in Swedish place-names in connexion with Odin and Thor: Thorshälla (from Þórshǫgr) and Onsjö, Odenshög (from Oðinshǫgr). A development of *hǫrgr* as a term for a temple in the narrow meaning of the word is not ascertainable. However, a kind of tent construction could possibly be assumed from the Old English *heargtræf* (in *Beowulf*), and the use of the phrase *hǫrgr hátimbráðr*) ('high timbered *hǫrgr*': *Grímnismál* 16, *Vǫluspá* 7) suggests a wooden construction on or around the *hǫrgr*, perhaps as a shelter for the idols (if any) within.

F. Jónsson, 'Hǫrgr' (*Festschrift K. Weinhold*) Straßburg 1896; O. Olsen, *Hørg, hof, og kirke*, Copenhagen 1966; A. Rostvik, *Har och Harg*, Uppsala 1967; F. Jankuhn, H. Kuhn, 'Altar' (*Hoops* 1) [2]1973.

Hǫrn (1) (ON). A name for the goddess Freyja in skaldic poetry and in Snorri (*Gylfaginning* 34). The meaning of Hǫrn is not completely clear, but could belong to *hǫrr* 'flax'. It would be wrong to consider her as the goddess of the flax harvest for this reason alone (as de Vries believes), but rather as the protective goddess over all flax manufacture which belonged entirely to the female domain.

She is distinguished from the other female protective goddesses related to the matrons or the *dísir* (such as Hlín, Snotra, Vár etc.) by the the fact that the Swedish place-names Härnevi (also Järnevi), from *Hǫrnar-vé ('Hörn's shrine') point to a cult of Hǫrn.

J. de Vries, *Altgermanische Religionsgeschichte*, Berlin ³1970

Hǫrn (2) (ON). A giantess in the *Þulur*. Hǫrn is also a frequent name for the goddess Freyr. The origin of the name is unknown, though.

Hœrnavi, Hærnavi (Swedish place-name) → Hǫrn 1.

Hötherus (Høtherus, also Hotherus). According to Saxo (*Gesta Danorum* III) Hötherus is the son of the Swedish king Hothbrodus and Baldr's rival in seeking the hand in marriage of Nanna. He is successful in this quest, and later kills Baldr before falling himself to the avenging Bous. Hötherus is identical with → Hǫðr, the ON name for one of the protagonists in the myth of → Baldr.

hof (ON) → temple.

Hófvarpnir (ON, 'he who throws his hoofs about'). The horse of the goddess Gná. It is only mentioned in the *Þulur* and in Snorri who quotes a fragment of a stanza.

horn (drinking horn, musical horn) → Gjallarhorn.

Horn (ON, 'horn'). A mythological river (?) in Grógaldr 8.

Hornbori (ON). A dwarf in *Vǫluspá* 13 and in the *Þulur*. Hornbori possibly means 'hornblower' as in OE *hornbora*. De Vries suggests 'the one who was conceived in a corner'. However, even 'horn piercer' would be possible. The meaning 'the horn bearer' to *bera* (Motz) is linguistically speaking rather unlikely.

J. Sahlgren, 'Nordiska Ortnamn' (*NoB* 23) 1935; L. Motz, 'New Thoughts on Dwarf-Names' (*FmSt* 7) 1973.

Horsa → Hengist and Horsa.

Horse. The horse had a special significance among the animals associated with heathen Germanic religion, partly because of its great practical importance as a riding and pack animal, and partly because of Indo-European traditions.

The cultic relevance of the horse among Germanic tribes is shown to be a continuing factor from the Bronze Age onwards. Bronze Age rock carvings, drawings on sacred razor blades as well as the draft animal on the Trundholm sun chariot show the horse, as do a great number of Vendel Age bracteates (especially group C and D, more rarely B). Viking Age rune stones and also carvings depict horses, frequently in a religious context. On the pictorial stones of this latter period Odin is repeatedly shown astride his eight-legged mythological horse → Sleipnir which possibly had the function of the horse of death.

Horses were not only dedicated to Odin but also perhaps to Freyr. However, indications for this are only to be found in the earlier and less reliable texts (*Hrafnkels saga*, *Vatnsdœla saga*, *Oláfs saga Tryggvasonar*) and should be treated with care. Horse sacrifices are archaeologically documented and Adam of Bremen records in his description of the sacrificial feast in → Uppsala that horses were sacrificed alongside men and dogs and then hung up in the trees. It is difficult to decide to whom this sacrifice was made – whether to Odin, Freyr or else to some other god. The eating of horse meat at the sacrificial meal was such a deeply rooted custom that it took on a symbolic significance for heathendom in its conflict with Christianity. His heathen compatriots force the Norwegian king Hákon to eat horse meat (*Hákonar saga goða*) and the permission to eat horse meat (otherwise forbidden for Christians) was one of the conditions under which the Icelandic All-thing accepted Christianity in the year 1000. → Vǫlsi.

H. Rosén, 'Freykult och djurkult' (*Fornvännen* 8) 1913; O. Höfler, *Kultische Geheimbünde der Germanen*, Frankfurt 1934; W. Koppers, 'Pferdeopfer und Pferdekult der Indogermanen' (*Wiener Beiträge zur Kulturgeschichte und Linguistik* 4) 1936; G. Gjessing, 'Hesten i førhistorisk kunst og kultus' (*Viking*) 1943; A. Holtsmark, 'Sleipnir' (*KLNM* 16) 1971.

Horwendillus (Lat., Old Danish). The father of Amlethus (= Hamlet) according to Saxo (*Gesta Danorum* III, 85–87). It seems that Saxo, however, was the first to link the name to the Hamlet legend. The name comes from mythology → Aurvandill.

Hotherus → Hötherus.

Hræsvelgr (ON, 'corpse eater'). According to *Vafþrúðnismál* 37, a gigantic eagle who sits at the end of the world in the north and creates the winds by beating his wings. The concept that the wind is created by the beating of the wings of a giant bird is found among other cultures as well. Because the eagle feeds from carrion, the name Hræsvelgr is appropriate. His gigantic dimensions mean that he is said to be a giant (and is listed among the giants in the *Þulur*). Therefore it is absolutely wrong to conclude that Hræsvelgr is a demon of death merely because of his name.

J. Loewenthal, 'Germanische Cultaltertümer' (*PBB* 47) 1922, 1922; J. de Vries, *Altgermanische Religionsgeschichte*, Berlin [3]1970.

Hrafnaguð (ON, 'raven-god'). A name for Odin, only given by Snorri (*Gylfaginning* 37) when he mentions the Odinic ravens Huginn and Muninn, and which possibly stands for → Hrafnáss in skaldic poetry.

Hrafnáss (ON, 'raven-As'). The name given to Odin twice in skaldic poetry (*Haustlǫng* 4; Refr.), as he is accompanied by two ravens, → Huginn.

Hrauðnir (ON, 'destroyer'). A giant in the *Þulur* and in the poetry of the skald Tindr.

Hrauðungr (1) (ON, 'the destroyer' or else 'the armed one'?). A king in the early prose introduction to the Eddic lay → *Grímnismál* and the father of Geirroðr and Agnarr. A person called Hrauðungr also appears in *Hyndluljóð* 26 as Hjǫrdís' father. Hrauðungr can also be found in the *Þulur* as the name of a sea-king. Thus, Hrauðungr is a literary and not a mythological figure. The name could simply be given to any legendary king.

R. Much, 'Der Sagenstoff der Grímnismál' (*ZfdA* 46) 1902.

Hrauðungr (2) (ON). A giant in the *Þulur* and in one skaldic kenning. Like the semantically cognate Hrauðnir, Hrauðungr refers to the destructive force of the giants as enemies of man and gods alike.

Hrêðe or Hrêða (OE, 'the famous', 'the victorious'?). The eponymous goddess of the OE name of the month Hrêdemônað (= March) mentioned by Bede in his *De temporibus ratione*. An OHG female personal name Hruadâ tempted J. Grimm to connect the name with ON *hróðr* 'fame'; thus the goddess could have a similar meaning to the eponymous Roman god of the same month, Mars.

J. Grimm, *Deutsche Mythologie*, Berlin [4]1875–78.

Hríð (ON, 'stormy weather, tempest'). One of the mythological rivers in the catalogue of rivers given in *Grímnismál* 28. In Snorri (*Gylfaginning* 3) Hríð is one of the Élivágar rivers which originate in the spring Hvergelmir.

Hrímfaxi (ON, 'soot-horse'). The name of the horse which brings the night, according to *Vafþrúðnismál* 14. The horse who brings the day is called → Skinfaxi.

Hrímgarðr (ON, 'frost-gerðr'). A giantess in *Helgakviða Hjǫrvarðssonar* (and in the *Þulur*). She is said to be the daughter of the giant Hati and allows herself to be drawn into a verbal duel with the hero Atli. Therefore, Hrímgarðr is a creation of heroic poetry. The name is a link between the Hrímþursar ('frost-giants') and the name of the most well-known giantess → Gerðr.

Hrímgrimnir (ON, 'hoar-Grimnir'). A giant who, according to *Skírnismál*, lives in the realm of the dead. Skírnir threatens → Gerðr that she will send her to Hrímgrimnir. The name is an intensification of the giants' name Grimnir in combination with the Hrímþursar 'frost-giants'.

Hrímnir (ON, 'the one covered with hoar-frost' or else 'the sooty one'). A giant, referred to in both skaldic poetry and the Eddic lays, *Skírnismál* 28 and *Hyndluljóð* 32 (and in the *Þulur*), without this having any particular status in the myth. In *Hyndluljóð* his children are named Heiðr and Hrossþjólfr, but this probably has more to do with the rules of alliteration than anything else. It is also unclear whether the link in the name to the Hrímþursar is intentional.

Hrímþursar (ON, 'hoar-frost giants'). These giants are mentioned in several places in Old Norse literature (*Hávamál* 109, *Grímnismál* 31, *Skírnismál* 30 and 34; Snorri, *Gylfaginning* 4–6 passim), probably because the ancestor of the giants, Ymir, was created from ice and therefore is a frost-giant as well (*hrímþurs*: *Vafþrúðnismál* 33). Ymir was a hermaphrodite proto-being who reproduced by one of his legs begetting a son with the other. It is from this son that the giants descend. The term Hrímþursar is appropriate since it was thought that the forces which could threaten life, such as the giants, lived in the cold north and north-east of Scandinavia.

I. Christiansen, 'Rimtusser' (*KLNM* 14) 1969.

Hringhorni (ON, 'ship with a circle on the stem'). The ship in which, according to Snorri (*Gylfaginning* 48, *Skáldskaparmál* 5), Baldr was burned.

It is not very likely that Hringhorni was linked with Baldr in pagan times and it seems more plausible that Snorri invented the name. Snorri's main source for the description of → Baldr's burial was Ulf's skaldic poem *Húsdrápa* which describes the mythological scenes depicted on an Icelandic wood carving made around 980. Snorri appears to have known, either from a lost stanza or from personal knowledge of the wood carving, that the ship shown carried a ring on its stern, and therefore gave the ship the corresponding name. The depiction of ships together with sun symbols (for this is surely what the circle on the stern is) stood in a long iconographic tradition by the 10th century, supported by diverse evidence and reaching back to Bronze Age rock carvings (Simek 1977).

A ship linked with the sun is a clear reference to the ship of the fertility god (Freyr's ship Skíðblaðnir) which, because of its association with Baldr's burial, Snorri did not recognize as being associated with Freyr and therefore re-named it Hringhorni.

Two basically unconnected strands of tradition overlap in Hringhorni – or rather the depiction from which it gets its name: on the one hand Skíðblaðnir, the sun ship of the fertility god, Freyr, known from pictorial representations, and on the other hand the death-ship (→ Naglfar), which Snorri naturally knew from the widespread boat burial customs of the Viking Age. Therefore, Hringhorni should be seen as a scholarly construction of the post-heathen (at the earliest, late pagan) times. The ship was only brought into association with the god Baldr in connexion with his funeral.

O. Höfler, 'Balders Bestattung' (*Anz. d. phil.-hist. Kl. d. öst. Ak. d. Wiss.*, Jg. 1951, Nr. 23) 1952; R. Simek, 'Skíðblaðnir' (*Northern Studies* 9) 1977; R. Simek, *Die Schiffsnamen*, Vienna 1982.

Hringvǫlnir (ON, 'the one with the staff with the ring'?). A giant in the *Þulur*.

Hripstoðr (ON). A giant in the *Þulur*. The meaning of the name is unknown.

Hrist (ON, related to ON *hrista* 'shake, quake' thus, 'the quaking one'). The name of one of the 13 → valkyries in *Grímnismál* 36. It is frequently found in kennings meaning 'woman'.

Hróarr (ON; otherwise a male personal name). A giant in the *Þulur*.

Hróðvitnir (ON, 'fame-wolf'). According to *Grímnismál* 39 (and hence also in Snorri: *Gylfaginning* 11) this is the name of the father of the wolf, Hati, who pursues the moon on its course. Hróðvitnir is also said to be a wolf in the *Þulur*, and the Fenriswolf is called Hróðrsvitnir in *Lokasenna* 39. Thus, Hróðvitnir is probably identifiable with Fenrir.

Hrǫkkvir (ON, 'the bent one'). Name of a giant in the *Þulur*.

Hrǫnn (1) (ON, 'wave'). One of the (mythical?) rivers in the river catalogue in *Grímnismál* 28.

Hrǫnn (2) (ON, 'wave'). One of the nine daughters of the sea-giant → Ægir and his wife Rán (*Skáldskaparmál* 22 and 58), who were synonymous in Old Norse poetry with the waves of the sea.

Hrolfr (ON). Name of a giant, the son of → Svaði and the brother of Hadda, cited in the legendary pre-history of Norway. He married Gói of the Fornjótr dynasty.

Hroptatýr (ON). A name for Odin used by the skalds of the second half of the tenth century (Eyvindr Finnsson: *Hákonarmál* 14; Ulfr Uggason: *Húsdrápa* 8) and in the *Edda* (*Grímnismál* 54, *Hávamál* 160). As in the case of → Hroptr there has been no satisfactory interpretation of the meaning of Hroptatýr as yet, but it is most likely old and in any case definitely heathen in origin.

S. Bugge, 'Altnordische Namen' (*Zeitschrift für vergleichende Sprachforschung* 3) 1854.

Hroptr (ON). A name for Odin which is extremely frequently used in both the Eddic lays (*Vǫluspá* 62, *Grímnismál* 8, *Lokasenna* 45, *Sigrdrífumál* 13) as well as in skaldic poetry (Kormákr: *Sigurðardrápa* 7; Tindr: *Hákonardrápa* 9; Þórarin svarti: *Máhlíðingavísur* 9; Ulfr Uggason: *Húsdrápa* 8 and 11; Þord Kolbeinsson: *Eiríksdrápa* 5). The datable references all fall into the fifty years around the end of the tenth century, and there is even one reference to → Hroptatýr dating from this time. Thus, it seems to be a question of a name in vogue at a time when heathendom was already in open confrontation with Christianity.

The majority of Eddic references for Hroptr, just as the references for Hroptatýr in *Hávamál* 160 and *Grímnismál* 54, date to the height of the heathen Renaissance during the High Middle Ages. Saxo's Latinized forms of Hroptr, Rostarus/Rosterus (*Gesta Danorum* IX, 304; III, 79) also date from this period.

The meaning of the name is obscure, despite several attempts to interpret it, all of which are highly improbable. The old interpretation of Hroptr and Hroptatýr as meaning 'speaker of the gods' (cf. OHG *hruoft* 'cries, clamour') is impossible, and, should in fact Hroptr and Rostarus belong together, so are the interpretations 'implorer' (from OHG *hrópa*: according to Vogt) or 'hider' (cf. Old Frisian Cruptorix). Most unlikely of all is Bugge's derivation of Hroptr/Rosterus, Rostarus from Christus.

S. Bugge, *Studien*, Munich 1889; F. Kauffmann, 'Dea Hludana' (*PBB* 18) 1894; W. H. Vogt, 'Hroptr Rǫgna' (*ZfdA* 62) 1925; H. de Boor, 'Die religiöse Sprache der Vǫluspá' (*Deutsche Islandforschung* 1) Breslau 1930; J. de Vries, *Altgermanische Religionsgeschichte*, ^{3}1970.

Hrossharsgrani (ON, 'horse-hair-Grani'). A name for Odin in the *Þulur* and in *Gautreks saga*, where Odin disguises himself as Starkað's foster father Grani. Grani is however also a name for a horse, and so Hrossharsgrani could point to Odin having a (cultic?) connexion with horses (→ Sleipnir). Jalkr, another name for Odin, also suggests this.

H. Falk, *Odensheite*, Christiania 1924.

Hrossþjófr (ON, 'horse thief'). A giant in the *Þulur* as well as in the genealogy of giants in *Vǫluspá in skamma* (*Hyndluljóð* 32), where he is called Hrímnir's son.

Hruga or Hryga (ON, 'heap, pile'). A giantess in the *Þulur*, surely the pejorative name for a fat person.

Hrund (ON, cognate to *hrinda* 'prick, push'?). Name of a valkyrie in the *Þulur*, not recorded elsewhere.

J. de Vries, *Altnordisches etymologisches Wörterbuch*, Leiden ^{2}1977.

Hrungnir (ON, 'brawler, rioter'). A giant who challenges Odin to a horse race and who is finally killed by Thor in single combat.

The myth of Hrungnir was clearly well known in medieval Scandinavia as many kennings in skaldic poetry and the Eddic lays also mention him (*Hárbarðsljóð* 14f.;

Hymiskviða 16; *Lokasenna* 61, 63; *Grottasǫngr* 9). The myth briefly outlined in Þjóðólf's poem *Haustlǫng* is told in detail by Snorri in *Skáldskaparmál* 17.

Odin rides to Jǫtunheim on his stallion Sleipnir. He meets Hrungnir there who asks him what his horse's name is and admires the horse, whereupon Odin boasts that there is no horse in the whole of Jǫtunheim to compare with Sleipnir. Hrungnir, however, praises the merits of his own horse → Gullfaxi and gallops after Odin and although he is unable to overtake him, he is nonetheless able to ride so fast that he only comes to a standstill in Asgard. The gods invite him in for a drink and in his drunken stupor he begins to make wild boasts that he will carry Valhall back home with him to Jǫtunheim, sink Asgard and kill all the gods apart from Freyja and Sif, and these two he would abduct. Finally, the gods, weary of his insults, turn to Thor for help, and he immediately challenges the giant, but as Hrungnir is unarmed, they agree to hold the single combat later at Grjótúnargarðar. When Thor and his servant Þjálfi arrive there, they find Hrungnir with his heart of stone and Mǫkkurkalfi, an artificial giant made of clay with the heart of a mare, waiting to oppose them. Þjálfi warns Hrungnir that Thor will attack them from below whereupon Hrungnir stands on his shield. When Thor hurls Mjǫllnir at him, Hrungnir retaliates by throwing his own weapon, a whetstone which shatters in mid-air collision with Mjǫllnir. The fragments of the stone fall to the ground where they become quarries for whetstones. One piece of the whetstone, however, pierces Thor's skull and he falls to the ground. In the meantime Mjǫllnir smashes into Hrungnir's head, and Þjálfi is able to kill Mǫkkurkalfi. As Hrungnir falls, one of his legs sprawls over Thor who is unable to get up until his three-year old son, Magni, comes and frees him. The sorceress → Gróa is supposed to rid Thor of the whetstone splinter in his head, but whilst she is treating him he tells her the story of her husband → Aurvandill, and out of sheer joy she forgets her magical incantations, and this is why the whetstone is still lodged in Thor's head, which in turn is why one should not throw a whetstone, as this makes the stone in Thor's head move.

In this version we have one of Snorri's typical compilations of various myths to make a tale, which contains numerous older elements. One of the natural mythological interpretations of a battle between the god of thunder, Thor, and the rock giant of the mountains (Golther's suggestion), is not completely supported by the myth. It is also not necessary to assume (as Wais does) the migration of the myth from the Orient to northern Europe at a time when the use of metals was spreading, as the conflict between the recent intrusion of iron and the old stone weapons meant a sufficiently drastic change in every culture to be translated into myth. There is much to be said in favour of Dumézil's suggestion that the battle should be seen as a reflection of an initiation rite since fighting apparent monsters (such as the clay giant Mǫkkurkalfi here or an already dead dragon in *Hrólfs saga kraka*) play a role in such rites. The problem is then, however, the question why the actual hero, the initiate Þjálfi, does not appear in *Haustlǫng* (Snorri's source). As we do not know if Snorri had any other sources apart from *Haustlǫng*, it is somewhat incautious to read too much into individual details, such as the shield under Hrungnir's feet. Nonetheless, Bragi makes use of 'leaf of the feet of Þrúðr's thief' as the kenning for a shield, which could point to the fact that Hrungnir abducted Þrúðr, Thor's daughter. This would be without any doubt a more important motive for Thor's combat with Hrungnir than merely Hrungnir's empty boasting at Asgard, but here too the question arises as to why no mention or reference is made of Þrúðr in *Haustlǫng*.

An important motive is → Hrungnir's heart with its three points as, because of this, Thor's fight with Hrungnir may be compared with Indra's fight against the three-headed monster Trisiras in Indian mythology. From inscriptions on rune stones it is clear that both Hrungnir's heart and the whetstone in Thor's head had a fixed place in heathen folk-beliefs which confirms Snorri's comment about the unjustified throwing of whetstones. Another folk custom was to hammer nails into pictures of Thor on the high seat pillars (*reginnaglar*). The myth of the whetstone appears to have been widespread, as in the Irish legend of Cuchulain there was a growth as big as a whetstone on his forehead, even if the meaning of the myth is no longer recognizable.

W. Stokes, 'A few Parallels between the Old Norse and the Irish Literatures and Traditions' (*ANF* 2) 1885; W. Golther, *Handbuch der germanischen Mythologie*, Leipzig [2]1908; F. R. Schröder, 'Thor und der Wetzstein' (*PBB* 51) 1927; H. Schneider, 'Die Geschichte vom Riesen Hrungnir' (*Edda, Skalden, Saga. Festschrift F. Genzmer*) Heidelberg 1952; K. Wais, 'Ullikummi, Hrungnir, Armilius und Verwandte' (*Edda, Skalden, Saga. Festschrift F. Genzmer*) Heidelberg 1952; J. de Vries, *Altgermanische Religionsgeschichte*, [3]1970; G. Dumézil, *Gods of the Ancient Northmen*, Berkeley 1977.

R: (fine art) E. Doepler, *Thor den Hrungnir bekämpfend* (in: E. Doepler, W. Ranisch, *Walhall*, 1901).

Hrungnir's heart (ON, *Hrungnis hjarta*). A symbol, the name of which we only know from Snorri (*Skáldskaparmál* 17) where he describes Thor's fight with the giant, → Hrungnir. Snorri tells us that 'Hrungnir had a heart made of hard stone and pointed with three corners, just like the carved symbol which has been called Hrungnir's heart ever since.' This description points to a symbol which can be seen on rune stones and on picture stones from Gotland and consists of three interwoven triangles which are called *valknuter* in Norwegian (probably 'knots of those fallen in battle') and show certain similarities with the triskele (the three-legged swastika). The Norwegian name of this symbol and the fact that it appears exclusively on pictorial stones together with Odin, as well as being carved into funereal gifts on the Oseberg ship, point to a role for it in the cult of the dead.

The symbol is to be found on the early Viking Age pictorial stone of Lillbjärs/ Gotland together with a similar symbol showing three interwoven (drinking?) horns. This last symbol, which could also fit Snorri's description, is also found on the rune stone from Skoldelev. It is possibly only a stylistic variant of the symbol formed from three triangles. Perhaps consideration ought to be given to whether the three horns known as Hrungnir's heart are not actually totally different from the *valknuter*.

The function of both symbols in Germanic religion is nonetheless clear from the context given on the pictorial stones.

J. de Vries, *Altgermanische Religionsgeschichte*, Berlin [3]1970.

Hruodâ (OHG) → Hrêða.

Hrygða (ON, 'the sorrowfull one'). A giantess named in the *Þulur*. There are several sorrowful giantesses worth mentioning in Nordic myth. Two notable ones are Skaði, because of her unfortunate marriage to Njǫrðr and the death of her father Þjazi, and Gunnlǫð, because she was seduced by Odin and then robbed of the skaldic mead.

Hrymr (ON). Name of a giant who, according to *Gylfaginning* 50, steers the ship Naglfar at Ragnarǫk. However, in *Vǫluspá* 51 the helmsman is said to be Loki, and Hrymr is merely an armed giant in *Vǫluspá* 50, who fights against the gods. Hrymr is not otherwise mentioned and the etymology of his name is obscure.

Hugi (ON, 'thought'). The personification of thought (because of his speed) in the mythological tale of → Thor's journey to Utgarðaloki (Snorri, *Gylfaginning* 45ff.), where Thor's servant Þjálfi tries to race against Hugi, but is beaten because nothing is as fast as the flight of thought.

Huginn (ON, 'thought'). One of Odin's two ravens, the other being Muninn. Huginn is considerably more frequently referred to than Muninn, occurring in the *Edda* (*Grímnismál* 20, *Helgakviða Hundingsbana* I 54, *Reginsmál* 18 and 26, *Fáfnismál* 35, *Guðrúnarkviða* II 29) as well as in skaldic poetry where it is mostly found denoting the generic term for 'raven'. Snorri refers to the two ravens in *Gylfaginning* 37: 'Two ravens sit on his (Odin's) shoulders and whisper all the news which they see and hear into his ear; they are called Huginn and Muninn. He sends them out in the morning to fly around the whole world, and by breakfast they are back again. Thus, he finds out many new things and this is why he is called 'raven-god' (*hrafnaguð*).'

The connexion between Odin and the ravens is ancient and is well documented by numerous kennings already by the tenth century, even if the names had not then been coined. Odin is clearly the god of the ravens, and these are called Odin's birds. Ravens are very frequently called birds of the battlefield so that the fallen warriors – who come to Odin in Valhall – are also called 'food for the ravens'. Thus, they were also the birds of battle and we know from Scandinavian sources (*Orkneyinga saga*, *Njáls saga*, *Þorsteins saga Síðu-Hallssonar*) as well as from several English chronicles that it was quite common for the army banners of Viking Age Nordic armies to depict a raven. It seems that the raven banners were woven in such a way that the fluttering banner would give the impression of a raven beating its wings.

Attempts have been made to interpret Odin's ravens as a personification of the god's intellectual powers, but this can only be assumed from the names Huginn and Muninn themselves which were unlikely to have been invented much before the 9th or 10th centuries. However, Vendel Age pictures of Odin accompanied by birds (6th and 7th century) suggest that Odin was associated with the ravens much earlier. Decorations on a helmet found in a Swedish grave of the Vendel period show Odin as a rider with a spear accompanied by two birds. On golden bracteates of the groups A, B and C Odin is repeatedly identifiable iconographically by his bird companions, an identification which is further supported by other attributes (divine breath, spear, healing of horses). In the depictions on the bracteates the birds (or one of them) are often shown perched near the ear of the god (as in Snorri!) or on the ear of the horse which needs to be healed. This could lead to the supposition that the ravens were originally not only Odin's companions on the battle field, but also Odin's helpers in animal form in his veterinary function. Hauck goes a step further and suggests that Odin's companions are bird-shaped valkyries but this claim seems to be somewhat extreme.

A. M. Sturtevant, 'Comments on Mythical Name-Giving in Old Norse' (*GR* 29) 1954; J. de Vries, *Altgermanische Religionsgeschichte*, Berlin ³1970; E. O. G. Turville-Petre, *Myth and Religion of the North*, Westport 1975; K. Hauck, 'Zur Ikonologie der Goldbrakteaten XV: Die Arztfunktion des seegermanischen Götterkönigs' (*Festschrift f. H. Beumann*) Sigmaringen 1977.

R: The ravens are repeatedly depicted as → Odin's companions; R. Wagner sees them as a symbol of a new world (similar to Noah's doves) in his poem *On the 25th of August 1870*.

Hugstari (ON, 'the stubborn one'?). Name of a dwarf in *Vǫluspá* 15 (*Gylfaginning* 13).

However, according to all the main manuscripts apart from the *Snorra Edda* he is called → Haugspori.

Hulda (ON). Name of a giantess. According to *Sturlunga saga*, the Icelander Sturla Þorðarson told the Norwegian King Magnus Hákonarson a saga about Hulda, which seems to have especially pleased his queen. However, there is no saga about Hulda still in existence (if indeed it ever did exist). A text called *Huldar saga*, printed in Iceland in 1911, is an 18th century fabulation.

It is uncertain whether this giantess Hulda really has anything to do with the German fairy-tale figure Holda/Frau Holle (= Mother Winter). A connexion with the Icelandic *Huldrufolk* is just as unsure. All together all these beings seem to be 'the hidden one' as the etymology of the name suggests.

L. Motz, 'The Winter Goddesses: Percht, Holda, and Related Figures' (*Folklore* 95) 1984.

R: César Franck, *Hulda* (opera, 1894).

Human sacrifice. Both Tacitus and Procopius record that human sacrifice not only occurred among the Germanic tribes, but that it was the highest form of sacrifice that the community could accomplish. Human sacrifice was not bound to any particular use and it could occur at the regular sacrificial festival (→ grove of the Semnons, → Uppsala sacrifice) or in time of crises such as famines (Dómaldi) and wars, as sacrifices of expiation (Tacitus) or as sacrifices to Odin.

The difference between human sacrifice and the → death penalty, which could be understood as being a sacrifice of expiation to the angry gods, is difficult to define from the older sources as, although Tacitus lists crimes carrying the death penalty, he gives us little information about the link between religion and law here. Similarly, the Iron Age Danish and English peat corpses do not allow any definite conclusions to be drawn as to whether they were the bodies of criminals or the victims of human sacrifice.

Human sacrifice made at the regular sacrificial festivals of the cult communities as Tacitus describes them in the sacred grove of the Semnons, the great Viking Age → Uppsala sacrifice and the frequent examples of human sacrifice to Odin were unequivocally sacred. Even Tacitus (*Germania* 9) speaks of the fact that human sacrifice was only offered to Mercury (= Odin). The typical form of sacrifice to Odin was for the victim to be hung and pierced with a spear, as we know from → Odin's self-sacrifice and from the sacrifice to Odin of King → Víkarr. In the case of the sacrifice at Uppsala as well, the corpses of the sacrifical victims were hung up in a grove, and pictures of such people hung in groves are recorded on Viking Age tapestries. In addition to this the carving of the → blood eagle (ON *blóðǫrn*) was also understood to be a sacrifice to Odin (*Orkneyinga saga* 8).

A bloody human sacrifice by slaughtering the victim (as opposed to hanging) is shown in Migration Age pictures such as the Gotland pictorial stone Lärbro Hammars I and a Danish golden bracteate (→ sacrifice). On the other hand, one form of human sacrifice by breaking the back of the victim on a particular stone (Þórssteinn: *Eyrbyggja saga* 10; *Landnámabók* S 85 = H 73) is probably only the result of the imagination of the Christian author, probably based on a topographic name such as Þórsness. Human sacrifice to Thor is not recorded at all.

E. Mogk, *Die Menschenopfer bei den Germanen*, Leipzig 1909; E. Mogk, 'Ein Nachwort zu den Menschenopfern bei den Germanen' (*ARW* 15) 1912; E. Klein, 'Der Ritus des Tötens bei den nordischen Völkern' (*ARW* 28) 1930; F. Ström, *On the sacral origin of the Germanic death penalties*, Stockholm 1942; A. Cordes, 'Lassen sich "urgermanische Menschenopfer" mit Tacitus beweisen?' (*Heimat* 67) 1960; H. Beck, 'Germanische Menschenopfer in der literarischen Überlieferung' (H. Jankuhn, *Vorgeschichtliche Heiligtümer*) Göttingen 1970.

Hundálfr or Hundolfr (ON, 'dog-elf', the 'dog-wolf'). The extremely strange name of a giant in the *Þulur*.

Hurst(ae)rga. A Germanic goddess named on an inscription from Tiel/Holland, dating from the 2nd/3rd century A.D.

H. Reichert, *Lexikon der altgermanischen Namen*, Vienna 1987–90.

Húsdrápa (ON, 'House Lay'). *Laxdœla saga* 29 records that an Icelander, Ólafr Pá (Olaf Peacock), had a magnificent hall built in Hjarðarholt whose interior walls were decorated with wood carvings depicting scenes from Germanic mythology. A skald Ulfr Uggason recited a poem in which he described these carved panels in Olaf's hall in honour of a wedding, dated in the saga between 980 and 985. He mentions the battle between Loki and Heimdall (→ Brísingamen), Thor's fight with the world-serpent (Miðgarðsormr) and goes into some detail about → Baldr's funeral. Only 12 stanzas and half-stanzas remain extant in the *Snorra Edda*, but according to Snorri (*Skáldskaparmál* 8) it used to be much longer. In his *Edda* Snorri obviously made copious use of the mythological material contained in the *Húsdrápa*

ED: F. Jónsson, *Den Norsk-islandske Skjaldedigtning*, B 1, Copenhagen og Christiania 1912; F. Jónsson, *Carmina scaldica*, Copenhagen [2]1929 (Reprint 1960).
K. Schier, 'Die Húsdrápa von Ulfr Uggason und die bildliche Überlieferung altnordischer Mythen' (*Minjar og menntir. Afmælisrit helgað Kristjáni Eldjárn*) Reykjavík 1976.

Hvalr (ON, 'whale'). A giant in the *Þulur*. In the late adventure and legendary sagas sorcerers frequently turn themselves into whales.

Hveðna or Hvæðna (ON). A giantess in *Vǫluspá in skamma* (*Hyndluljóð* 32) as well as in Bragi's *Ragnarsdrápa*. In the genealogy of giants in *Hyndluljóð* 32 she is called Hjǫrvarðr's daughter. The name is probably only a variant of Hveðra.

Hveðra (ON, cognate to *hveðurr* 'ram' or to OE *hweoðerian* 'roar'?). A giant in the *Þulur* and in the works of Einar Skúlason 13, 14.

J. de Vries, *Altnordisches etymologisches Wörterbuch*, Leiden [2]1977; L. Motz, 'Giantesses and their names' (*FmSt* 15) 1981.

Hveðrungr (1) (ON, perhaps 'roarer'?). The name of a giant in the *Þulur*. In *Vǫluspá* 55, Viðarr takes revenge for the death of his father, Odin, by killing 'Hveðrungr's son', who, according to Snorri (*Gylfaginning* 50), must be the Fenris wolf. As the father of the Fenris wolf is Loki, Hveðrungr would therefore be a name for Loki. The term *Hveðrungs mær* for Hel, who is also a daughter of Loki's (*Ynglingatal* 32), would support this.

S. Nordal, *Vǫluspá*, Darmstadt 1980.

Hveðrungr (2) (ON). A name for Odin which only occurs in the *Þulur* and which perhaps is the result of a misunderstanding of *Vǫluspá* 55; → Hveðrungr 1.

Hvergelmir (ON, 'the bubbling cauldron'?). The name of the spring in Niflheim and the source of the Élivágar rivers, according to *Gylfaginning* 3. In *Gylfaginning* 15 and

38, however, Hvergelmir is the spring under the world-tree Yggdrasil. The Eddic lays only cite the name Hvergelmir in *Grímnismál* 26 where it refers to the spring from which the rivers of the world arise. In Eddic mythology alongside Hvergelmir, there are also other springs near Yggdrasill, namely the Urdarbrunnr and Mimisbrunnr, but de Vries is undoubtedly correct when he considers all three differently named springs as being originally one and the same mythical spring. In *Gylfaginning* 51 Snorri also adds that the dragon Níðhǫggr lives in the spring. – The name Hvergelmir is certainly quite young. It is strange but noteworthy that otherwise giants' names are based on *-gelmir*: Þrúðgelmir, Bergelmir, Aurgelmir. → Water.

J. de Vries, *Altgermanische Religionsgeschichte*, Berlin ³1970.

Hymir (ON). A giant. It is from Hymir that Thor wants to fetch a cauldron for the Æsir. Thor's adventure with Hymir, to which the myth of → Thor and the Midgard serpent also belongs, is told in the Eddic lay → *Hymiskviða* and, a slightly deviating version, in Snorri (*Gylfaginning* 17). In Snorri's version the stress is laid on the story of Thor and the Midgard serpent. In this Hymir cuts through the fishing line on which the Midgard serpent is caught, and is therefore thrown overboard by Thor in his fury at losing his catch. In *Hymiskviða* on the other hand Hymir plays an important role as the possessor of the gigantic cauldron which Thor is supposed to fetch for the gods to brew beer in. Although Hymir is named here as the father of Týr, he is one of the hostile giants, indeed a typical protagonist in all Thor's adventures, and he is finally killed by Thor. Older kennings in skaldic poetry also mention Hymir, but even they do not say much more than that he is a giant. Nonetheless, they confirm that he was known as a figure in mythical tales even in heathen times and not only for the first time in the 12th and 13th centuries when *Hymiskviða* was composed and Snorri wrote his version. In *Lokasenna* 34, Hymir's daughters, who apparently use Njǫrð's mouth as a toilet, are mentioned. They are not referred to in *Hymiskviða* though, but this by no means signifies that a comic tale about the god Njǫrðr and Hymir's daughters was unknown. Reference to Hymir as the father of Týr is to be found only in *Hymiskviða* 5, whereas Týr is the son of Odin in Snorri's writings. It is possible that an ancient godly figure existed who 'sank' down to become the giant Hymir, but the fathering of Týr does not prove this supposition any more than the uncertain etymology of the name Hymir.

F. R. Schröder, 'Das Hymirlied' (*ANF* 70) 1955.

Hymiskviða (ON, 'the lay of Hymir'). A 12th or 13th century mythological poem in the *Edda* which, like the *Þrymskviða*, relates one of Thor's adventures. Part of the material, namely → Thor and the Midgard serpent, can also be found in Snorri (*Gylfaginning* 47), otherwise only one line from the so-called *First Grammatical Treatise* and several younger kennings point to the myth of Thor and the giant Hymir as told in the 39 stanzas of *Hymiskviða*.

Hymiskviða begins with a planned feast for the gods, for which the giant → Ægir is supposed to brew the beer. However, he refuses initially because of the lack of a sufficiently large cauldron. Consequently two gods, Thor and Týr, here described as friends, make their way eastwards to visit the giant Hymir, Týr's father, in order to get a cauldron from him. Thor leaves his goats with Egill the farmer (the father of Þjálfi and Rǫskva?). The first person they meet at Hymir's is his 900-headed mother. His wife who is dressed in gold (originally a goddess?) hides them under the giant's cauldron (9) and prepares Hymir for the visit of the guests. His look, however, smashes the pillars behind which they were hiding and nine cauldrons fall to the floor, all but one breaking. During the following meal and to the horror of the giant, Thor eats two out of three bulls which Hymir has brought. Hymir then announces that because of this, they will have to go out fishing next day, and so he sends Thor out looking for bait. Thor pulls the head off the biggest of Hymir's bulls (called Himinhrjóðr) and takes it with him fishing. Thor then proceeds to row out further than Hymir actually wants to go and while the giant catches two whales, Thor catches the Midgard serpent using the bull's head as bait on the end of his fishing line. Thor's feet break through the planks on the bottom of the boat as he pulls in the line so that the giant panics and, just as Thor is getting out his hammer in order to kill the monster, Hymir cuts the line (a detail not mentioned in *Hymiskviða*, and added in Snorri's version) and the monster disappears into the sea (24). On the way home Thor carries both whales and the oars, but Hymir can still not refrain from testing Thor's strength even further. He has a goblet which no-one can break unless he is really strong. When Thor throws this against a pillar, the pillar breaks, and only when Thor, following the suggestions of Hymir's wife, hurls it against the giant's skull, does the goblet itself smash (31). Hymir regrets the loss of the goblet, but doubts whether the gods could carry the cauldron (which he now owes them after severe tests of strength?), and Týr is certainly unable to do so. It is only when Thor puts it on top of himself like a turtle that he manages to carry it away. Hymir and his giants still follow Thor, but they are all killed by Mjǫllnir (36). On the way home one of Thor's goats falls and lames himself (blamed on Loki). A giant (→ Egill?) has to give Thor both of his children (Þjálfi and Rǫskva) as retribution for this. Finally, they arrive at Asgard again along with the cauldron, and Ægir is able to brew the beer for the feast (39).

Essentially, *Hymiskviða* consists of three interlocking myths: Thor's fetching of the cauldron from Hymir's, Thor and the Midgard serpent, and finally the laming of Thor's goat. Whilst, apart from in the *Hymiskviða*, the myth of the fetching of the cauldron is only handed down to us in a line retained by chance in the *First Grammatical Treatise* 'the handle was to be heard as Thor carried the cauldron' (*heyrðr til hǫddu þá er Þorr bar hverin*), Snorri tells (*Gylfaginning* 47) in detail of Thor's fishing trip with Hymir, admittedly with a slight deviation: Thor throws the giant over-board using his fist when he has cut Thor's fishing line. Snorri has integrated the third myth about the laming of Thor's goat into another of Thor's adventures, namely Thor's journey to Utgarðarloki (*Gylfaginning* 44; → Skrýmir) where the farmer's son Þjálfi bears the blame for the laming of the goat (→ Thor's goats).

Snorri's knowledge of the episode about the Midgard serpent (and his lack of knowledge about the fetching of the cauldron) have led to various theories about the dating of *Hymiskviða*. Because of certain linguistic parallels K. Reichardt wanted to date it between 1225 and 1250. The only thing that is certain, however, is that the lay was written during the scholarly Icelandic Renaissance between 1100 and 1250. The fairytale-like elements of *Hymiskviða* (such as the 900-headed giantess) are not atypical of poetry of this time. Whereas older scholarship considered *Hymiskviða* to be a conglomerate of myths united by a single poet, Schröder has attempted to show that most elements which occur have parallels in the Indian myth of Indra, Tvastar, and the theft of the drink of the gods. Consequently, the basis of *Hymiskviða* is an ancient myth about a drink for the gods which has been replaced here by the receptacle of that drink as representing it, namely the cauldron. This old myth was relevant in Nordic mythology until Odin replaced Thor as the thief of the skaldic mead. Although the parallels to Indra in fact rather point to Thor as the god who brings the skaldic mead, the safe position among Germanic tribes of Odin as the keeper of the mead does not allow Schröder's opinion to stand.

ED: G. Neckel, H. Kuhn, *Edda*, [5]1983.

E. Hellquist, 'Om naturmytiska element i Hymiskviða' (*ANF* 18) 1902; K. Reichardt, 'Hymiskviða' (*PBB* 57) 1937; J. de Vries, 'Das Wort goðmálugr' (*GRM* 35) 1954; F. R. Schröder, 'Das Hymirlied' (*ANF* 70) 1955; G. W. Weber, 'Hymiskviða' (*KLL* 3) 1967.

Hyndla (ON, 'lapdog'). The name of the giantess in the lay named after her, *Hyndluljóð*, who was obviously extremely well versed in genealogies. Her home, a cave, is the stereotypical home of giants; her steed, a wolf, is more unusual. It is also a most original idea of the thirteenth century poet to attribute such extraordinary knowledge of genealogies to a giantess, of all people, called Hyndla.

L. Motz, 'Giantesses and their Names' (*FmSt* 15) 1981.

Hyndluljóð (ON, 'Lay of Hyndla'). An Eddic lay not found in the Codex Regius, but only in the late 14th century *Flateyjarbók*. It cannot be assigned without problems to either the mythological lays or to the heroic lays. The lay is organized as a mythologizing framework story with genealogic lists forming the middle part. This middle part is further extended by an interpolated independent lay, the → *Vǫluspá in skamma* (stanza 29–44). The genealogies of the actual *Hyndluljóð* contain over 80 personal names and family names, names which are partly from heroic epos, and partly historical and pseudo-historical Norwegian names.

The framework story begins with Ottar (in the shape of Freyja) visiting the giantess Hyndla to ride with her to Valhall so that Hyndla can give Ottar information about his ancestors. The reason for this is that Ottar has made a bet with Angantýr – no doubt about genealogical knowledge. The giantess astride her wolf reluctantly follows Freyja, riding her boar Hildisvíni. Hyndla names Ottar's ancestors. (At this point, the → *Vǫluspá in skamma* which I deal with separately is interpolated without any attempt to integrate it into the *Hyndluljóð*). When finally Freyja urges her to give Ottar the memory potion, Hyndla begins to insult Freyja very much in the style of the *Lokasenna*. Only by threatening fire magic can Freyja finally manage to get the giantess to give Ottar the potion.

According to de Vries' explanation, the *Hyndluljóð* is a didactic poem written for a person, almost certainly a Norwegian, who was close to Ottar, about whom we know nothing else. References to and borrowings from the *Hakonarmál* point to the fact that the poet knew this poem as well as the *Helgakviða Hundingsbana* I and II; the lay was probably written in the 12th or 13th centuries. Klingenberg considers *Hyndluljóð* to be the product of a collector from the 13th century who compiled two older parts (the genealogies and the *Vǫluspá in skamma*) and added a framework story to these. Fleck on the other hand interprets *Hyndluljóð*, as well as *Rígsþula* and *Grímnismál*, as a functional cult poem which reflects the handing down of knowledge (in the case of *Hyndluljóð* of genealogies) within the framework of individual dedication in Germanic sacred kingship, a theory that seems somewhat far-fetched for young poems such as these. Gurevich considers Ottar's genealogies to be merely the means of stating legal claims on an inheritance, and he interprets the *Hyndluljóð* as a result of this as a mythologization of an inheritance quarrel between Ottar and Angantýr which was conceived as a stylized representation of the battle between Midgard and Utgard.

ED: G. Neckel, H. Kuhn, *Edda*, [5]1983.

H. Gering, 'Ottar heimski' (*ANF* 36) 1920; A. Holtsmark, 'Hyndluljóð' (*KLNM* 7) 1962; J. de

Vries, *Altnordische Literaturgeschichte*, Berlin ²1964–1967; H. Beck, 'Hyndluljóð' (*KLL* 3) 1967; J. Fleck, 'Konr-Ottar-Geirroðr: A Knowledge Criterion for Succession to the Germanic Sacred Kingship' (SS 42) 1970; A. Y. Gurevich, 'Edda and Law. Commentary upon Hyndluljóð' (*ANF* 88) 1973; H. Klingenberg, *Edda – Sammlung und Dichtung*, Basel, Stuttgart 1974.

Hýr also falsely Lýr (ON, 'the shining one'). A mythological hall in *Fjǫlsvinnsmál* 32. It is probably the building in which Menglǫð lives surrounded by a wall of flames.

Hyrrokkin (ON, 'the one who has withered from fire'). A giantess of whom Snorri recounts (*Gylfaginning* 48) in the story of → Baldr's funeral that she was called upon by the gods when they were unsuccessful in launching Baldr's funereal ship. '. . . and she came riding on a wolf and had poisonous snakes as a harness. Then she jumped off her steed, and Odin called upon four berserks to keep watch over it, but they could not hold it until they knocked it down. Then Hyrrokkin went to the prow of the ship and pushed it away at the first attempt so that sparks flew up from the rollers and all the lands quaked. Then Thor became angry and took hold of his hammer, and he would have smashed in her skull, had not all the other gods begged him to have mercy on her.' Hyrrokkin does not appear to have escaped Thor's anger totally, as in Þorbjǫrn dísarskald she is named among the giantesses who were killed by Thor.

R: (fine art) Hyrrokkin is found in an illustration by E. Doepler the Younger, *Balders Bestattung* (in: E. Doepler, W. Ranisch, *Walhall*, 1901).

Icelandic sagas → Sagas of the Icelanders.

Iðavǫllr (ON). The mythical plain in *Vǫluspá* 2 and 60 which lies near to Asgard and which is part of the home of the gods. After the end of the world at Ragnarǫk Iðavǫllr is the place where the gods assemble in the new world. – Iðavǫllr has been interpreted (since Krogmann) as being related to ON **iði* 'splendour'. This interpretation is, however, not convincing despite comparable parallels (like Glæsisvellir) as the name Iðavǫllr is certainly a young formation and **iði* or related words are not recorded. Older attempts link the name to *íðja* 'activity'. The name could thus mean 'field of activity', a not inappropriate interpretation as the gods in *Vǫluspá* 2 are described doing all kinds of activities here. Iðavǫllr is most likely a creation of the poet of the *Vǫluspá*, who found a name appropriate to the circumstances and activities of the gods. Another possible interpretation of Iðavǫllr would be 'the continually renewing, rejuvenating field', from *iðuliga* 'continual' and *íðgnógr* 'more than enough', since Iðavǫllr represents the newly created world after the Ragnarǫk. Bugge, on the other hand, considers Iðavǫllr to be a corruption of the Christian Eden (just as he explains Urðr from Jordan), which arrived in the north via Anglo-Saxon intermediaries.

S. Bugge, *Studien*, Munich 1889; W. Krogmann, 'Neorxna wang und Iðavǫllr' (*Archiv* 191) 1955; A. Holtsmark, 'Iðavǫllr' (*Festschrift K. Reichardt*) Bern, Munich 1969.

Idban(?)gabia (or: Idbans?). The last surviving fragments of the name of a Germanic goddess on a Roman Age votive inscription from Pier near Düren, Germany (CIL XIII 7867): *Deae Idban[. . .]gabiae*. Gutenbrunner reads *Idian.gabiae* and relates it to ON *íðinn* 'hard-working', but the fragmentary state of the name does not allow any definite interpretation.

S. Gutenbrunner, *Die germanischen Götternamen*, Halle 1936.

Iði (ON, 'the moveable, the hard working one'). A giant who, according to Snorri

(*Skáldskaparmál* 1), was the brother of Þjazi and Gangr and thus Qlvaldi's son. Qlvaldi shared his possessions so that each son was allowed to take a mouthfull of gold as his legacy. This is why gold is also called 'mouthfull of Iði or Gang, or Þjazi'. As Iði indeed occurs in numerous kennings for gold, this genealogy and the tale of the legacy are probably the remains of an ancient myth.

Idisi (Old Saxon). Female beings in the → First Merseburg Charm:

> Eiris sazun idisi, sazun hera duoder.
> suma hapt heptidun, suma heri lezidun,
> suma clubodun umbi cuoniouuidi:
> insprinc haptbandun, invar vigandun.
>
> 'Once the Idisi sat, sat here and there,
> Some bound fetters, some hampered the army,
> some untied fetters:
> Escape from the fetters, flee from the enemies.'

These Idisi are obviously a kind of valkyrie, as these also have the power to hamper armies in Old Norse mythology: cf. the name for a valkyrie, Herfjqtur 'army-fetter'.

Apart from this, Old Saxon *idis*, OHG *itis*, Anglo-Saxon *ides* means a dignified, well respected woman (married or unmarried), possibly a term for any woman, and therefore glosses exactly Latin *matrona*. Apart from the above cited charm nothing points directly towards a religious significance of Idisi in southern Germanic regions, although admittedly as a result of the identical meaning of *itis* and *matrona*, a connexion to the widespread → Matron cult in the area of the Lower Rhine between the 1st and 5th centuries A.D. would be conceivable. A link to the North Germanic → *dísir* would be a reasonable assumption, but it is not undisputed. – The name of a battlefield on the Weser, Idistaviso, mentioned by Tacitus (*Annales* II, 16), was amended by the two 19th century scholars Müllenhoff and Grimm to → Idisiaviso 'women's meadow', which likewise does not allow any conclusions to be inferred.

O. Schade, *Altdeutsches Wörterbuch*, ²1872–82; J. Grimm, *Deutsche Mythologie*, Berlin ⁴1875–78; F. Kögel, 'Idis und die Walküre' (*PBB* 16) 1892; E. Brate, 'Disen' (*Zeitschrift für deutsche Wortforschung* 13) 1911/12; G. Eis, 'Eine neue Deutung des ersten Merseburger Zauberspruchs' (*FuF* 32) 1958; J. de Vries, *Altgermanische Religionsgeschichte*, Berlin ³1970; H. Birkhan, *Germanen und Kelten*, Vienna 1970.

Idisiaviso (corrected from the version Idistaviso given in manuscripts). The plain near the Weser where in 16 A.D. a battle took place between Arminius and Germanicus (Tacitus, *Annales* II, 16). Idisiaviso means 'plain of the Idisi', 'women's meadow'. As the → Idisi are supposed to have an influence in the outcome of a battle, similarities with the valkyries suggest themselves. Idisiaviso would thus be a place at which the Idisi had once been instrumental in a battle. – A tempting, but daring interpretation of the otherwise not fully explained Old Norse → Iðavqllr would be from a possible *Ið[is]avqllr, which would correspond exactly to Idisiaviso.

K. Müllenhoff, 'Verderbte Namen bei Tacitus' (*ZfdA* 9) 1853; J. Grimm, *Deutsche Mythologie*, Berlin ⁴1875–78.

Idun (ON, Iðunn, 'the rejuvenating one'). A goddess in Old Norse mythology who is very rarely mentioned. In pre-Christian times she only appears in Þjóðólfr's poem *Haustlqng* (c.900), which Snorri used for the description in his *Edda* (*Gylfaginning* 25): 'Bragi's wife is Idun; in her casket she guards the apples which the gods have to eat if they are aging so that they can all become young again; this is how it will go on until

Ragnarǫk'. Snorri tells the myth of → Þjazi in detail, in which Idun together with her apples is abducted by Loki and the giant Þjazi. However, the gods force Loki to fetch Idun back with the help of Freyja's falcon costume. During her escape from Þjazi Loki carries Idun in the shape of a nut (only in Snorri) and is pursued by Þjazi in the shape of an eagle, until the Æsir finally kill the giant.

Snorri might have used other sources apart from the *Haustlǫng* for the myth of Idun's abduction, but of the extant sources we know the goddess Idun is only mentioned in the very young *Lokasenna* 17 where she is blamed for having slept with the murderer of her own brother. This reproach is not found anywhere else, as is the case with similar accusations of this kind in *Lokasenna*.

In the myth of the theft of Idun the concept of the rejuvenating → apples is linked with the common tale of the theft of a goddess by a giant, and although this myth was obviously not particularly well known and might have been influenced by tales of classical mythology about Hesperides' apples, this could have happened already long before the literary age. Perhaps it was the scholarly Icelanders of the 12th and 13th centuries who first united the classical legends with the information in the *Haustlǫng* and the golden apples, which are mentioned in *Skírnismál* 19.

If Idun was indeed venerated as a goddess in pagan times, she would belong to the fertility goddesses because of her apples.

S. Bugge, 'Iduns Æbler' (*ANF* 5) 1889; E. Brate, 'Disen' (*Zeitschrift für deutsche Wortforschung* 13) 1912; A. Holtsmark, 'Myten om Idun og Tjatse i Tjodolvs Haustlǫng' (*ANF* 64) 1949; E. F. Halvorsen, 'Iðunn' (*KLNM* 7) 1962; J. de Vries, *Altgermanische Religionsgeschichte*, Berlin ³1970; E. O. G. Turville-Petre, *Myth and Religion of the North*, Westport 1975.

R: (fine art) H. E. Freund, *Idun* (statue, 1821); C. G. Quvarnström, *Idun* (statue 1843), and: *Idun som bortrövas av jätten Tjasse i örnhamn* (plaster statue, 1856); C. Hansen, *Iduns Rückkehr nach Valhalla* (painting), and a woodcut by C. Hammer of the name (1862) modelled on Hansen's painting; K. Ehrenberg, *Bragi und Idun, Balder und Nanna* (drawing, 1882); B. E. Ward, *Idun* (watercolour, 1905); E. Doepler d. J., *Idun* (E. Doepler, W. Ranisch, *Walhall*) 1901; J. Doyle-Penrose, *Idun and the apples* (painting).
(literature) F. G. Klopstock, *Wingolf* (ode, 1762); J. G. Herder, *Iduna, oder der Apfel der Verjüngung* (article on Norse mythology in: *Die Horen*, 1796): N. F. S. Grundtvig, *Idunna* (poem, 1810); A. Oehlenschläger, *Idun* (two poems in: *Nordens guder*, 1819); *Iduna* (periodical of the Gothic League, ed. by H. G. Geijer, 1811–1835); *Idunna und Hermode* (periodical in three vols, 1812–1816).

Ifing (ON, 'impetuosity, violence'). A mythical river on the border between the giants and the gods mentioned in *Vafþrúðnismál* 16. If it were ever to freeze, the giants could cross over it. This is the only time Ifing is named, but the idea that Asgard and Midgard were thought to be separated from Jǫtunheim, out in Utgard, by one or several rivers is confirmed in other sources as well. In *Hymiskviða* 5 these rivers are called Élivágar.

Ifles. Name of a matron on a votive stone from Gohr, Germany (CIL XIII 8520), as yet not satisfactorily interpreted. The name is, however, by no means related to the Afliae, as has been occasionally supposed.

Íma (ON, 'battle' or 'the dusty one'?). A giantess in the *Þulur*; → Imgerðr.

Imðr or Imð (ON). A giantess (*Þulur*; *Helgakviða Hundingsbana* I, 43) who is named as one of the nine giant mothers of the god → Heimdall (*Vǫluspá inn skamma: Hyndluljóð* 37). Etymologically, Imðr is probably related to *íma* 'wolf', because of its colour and as such could mean 'the grey, dirty one'. An interpretation as 'the thundering one' (to *yma*) would be conceivable; → Ímgerðr.

A. M. Sturtevant, 'Etymological Comments on Certain Words and Names in the Elder Edda' (*PMLA* 66) 1951; L. Motz, 'Giantesses and their Namens' (*FmSt* 15) 1981.

Ímgerðr (ON). A giantess in the *Þulur*. Like other giantess-names, Ímgerðr is a variant of Gerðr, the most well-known giantess in Nordic mythology, but the interpretation of Ím- (cf. also Íma, Ímðr, Ímr) is not totally clear: either from *íma* 'battle' or else from *ím* 'dust'.

Ímr (ON). A giant in the *Þulur*. According to Jónsson 'the dark one', but more likely the interpretation is one of the meanings like those of the giantess names → Ímgerðr, Íma, Ímðr.

F. Jónsson, 'Þulur' (*APhSc* 9) 1933.

Ineae. Name of matrons on a Roman inscription from Bonn, Germany (CIL XIII 8174) which was dedicated to the *Matronis Ineis*.

H. Reichert, *Lexikon der altgermanischen Namen*, Vienna 1987–90.

Ing (Anglo-Saxon). The ancestor of the Ingaevones. His name corresponds to Scandinavian → Yngvi. Ing only occurs in the Old English rune poem where he is ranked among the East Danes, more exactly among the Heardingas (= Hasdingi = Haddingjar). In the poem he drives a chariot which might indicate a cult-chariot, as in the cult of Yngvi or in the cult of Nerthus. The etymology of the name is as yet unexplained despite numerous attempts to do so.

J. Loewenthal, 'Zur germanischen Wortkunde' (*ANF* 33) 1917; W. Krause, 'Ing' (*Nachrichten der Gesellschaft der Wissenschaften, Phil.-hist. Kl.* 3) Göttingen 1944; J. de Vries, *Altgermanische Religionsgeschichte*, Berlin [3]1970.

Ingi (ON). A dwarf, → Yngvi 2.

Ingunar-Freyr (ON). The name given to the god Freyr in *Lokasenna* 43 and the longer version of *Oláfs saga hins helga*.

This name for → Freyr should probably be considered as another form of the East Norse → Yngvi-Freyr. The name of a Danish king in the Old English *Beowulf* (1319), who is called Frea Ingwina 'lord of the friends of Ing' (or else 'lord of the Ingaevones'?), has been compared with Ingunar-Freyr. This name is however certainly not identical with Ingunar-Freyr because Freyr never meant 'lord' in the north, and therefore one would have to interpret Ingunar-Freyr at least as 'god-Freyr of the friends of Ing'. On the other hand, the older interpretation of Ingunar-Freyr which derives the name from an *Inguna-ár-freyr 'the harvest-giving god of the friends of Ing' is usually rejected.

H. Schück, 'Ingunar-Freyr' (*Fornvännen* 35) 1940; F. R. Schröder, *Ingunar-Freyr*, Tübingen 1941; E. O. G. Turville-Petre, *Myth and Religion of the North*, Westport 1975.

Interpretatio christiana. The close contact between the Roman and the Germanic cultures in the first century A.D. led to an attempt to come to terms with the religion of the other people. This in turn meant that each culture tried to identify the gods it worshipped with the gods venerated by the other (→ *interpretatio romana*, → *interpretatio germanica*). For believers in monotheistic Christianity this was not possible. Although most of the late Classical and Medieval Christian authors were well acquainted with the usual *interpretatio romana*, their own way of viewing the problem was necessarily quite different. Whilst syncretism was a form of cultural expansion for the Imperial Romans, heathendom for the Germanic clergy after Christianization was either a level of religion which had finally been overcome or else one to be conquered, and, what is more, one to which no way should lead back. The means for this was a *interpretatio christiana* which meant a diabolization of the heathen gods and a demonization of all beings of lower mythology (i.e. dwarfs, elves, trolls, giants). Only the Medieval Icelandic authors were far less radical in their rejection of heathen religion than elsewhere, and during the conversion of Iceland there are even several cases where heathen myth and Christian thought merged into each other (→ Thor and the Midgard serpent). Snorri's presentation of Germanic mythology is frequently influenced by Christianity without causing any conflict, however.

H. Achterberg, *Interpretatio Christiana*, Leipzig 1930; O. Gschwantler, 'Christus, Thor und die Midgardschlange' (*Festschrift* O. *Höfler* 1) Vienna 1968.

Interpretatio germanica. The term used to describe the renaming (and thus identifying) of Roman gods with the names of Germanic gods by the Germanic peoples at a time when both cultures came into closer contact in the first century. The reverse process is known as → *interpretatio romana*. In both cases it is a question of the adoption of concepts from foreign religions which calls them by already known names. The only reliable insight into the *interpretatio germanica* which we have is in the Germanic translations of the Roman → week-day names. Latin *dies Martis* is rendered as the day of Zîu/Týr (→ Tuesday), the day of Mercurius as the day of Wodan/Odin (→ Wednesday). The day of Jupiter became the day of Donar/Thor (→ Thursday), although Thor actually appears in the *interpretatio romana* as Hercules. Finally, the Roman goddess Venus was identified with Fríja/Frigg (→ Friday). These examples and the perhaps surprising correspondences make the problematic nature of *interpretatio germanica* obvious. The divine attributes appear to have been decisive factors for the correspondence between the Roman gods and Odin and Thor, but nonetheless in the other cases we have to rely on speculation. We know far too little about the real role which the Germanic gods played in contemporary belief to be able to use the identification with particular Roman gods to trace their situation in the Nordic Pantheon.

Interpretatio romana. Roman interpretation. When the Romans came into contact with the Germanic peoples, both peoples tried to come to terms with elements of the foreign religion by giving the foreign concepts their own names. The naming of the Germanic gods by the Romans is called *interpretatio romana*, and the naming of Roman gods by the Germanic peoples is called → *interpretatio germanica*. There were also formal criteria for the interpretation, such as the attributes of the gods. Hermes/Mercury's hat and staff were so strikingly similar to Wodan/Odin's hat and spear, that the gods, although hardly comparable in written sources, were considered to be identical. Because Germanic religion predominantly lacked pictorial illustrations of their beliefs and gods, the Romans were undoubtedly also dependent on information gained from the Germanic people in order to understand more about the Germanic beliefs, and in this the functions of the gods might well have served as the point of comparison, even if these functions are no longer clear to us today. The *interpretatio romana* and the *interpretatio germanica* could produce different results: a Roman who was looking for a Roman god similar to Donar/Thor might have learnt from Germanic informants that he fought monsters and killed giants, and therefore Hercules sprang to mind, whilst his Germanic counterpart in search of a correspondence to the thunder and lightning hurling Jupiter would naturally think of Thor.

Examples of the *interpretatio romana* can already be found in Caesar and later especially in Tacitus who calls Mercury the main Germanic god, an interpretation confirmed by the numerous votive altars dedicated to Mercury on Germanic soil. Tacitus names Hercules and Mars (*Germania* 9, 1) as the Germanic gods in second and third in rank. Hercules is identified as Thor who, however, appears in the *interpretatio germanica* of the week-day names as Jupiter. Mars appears to denote Týr/Tíwaz, despite certain Odinic characteristics which are recognizable in Mars.

J. de Vries, *Altgermanische Religionsgeschichte*, Berlin ^{3}1970; R. L. M. Derolez, *Götter und Mythen der Germanen*, Wiesbaden 1974.

Íri (ON, 'the Irishman'). A dwarf in *Fjǫlsvinnsmál* 34.

Irmin. The only reference to a god with this name occurs in the *Res gestae Saxonicae*, written by the monk Widukind of Corvey in around 967 A.D., who, in a literary way, adorns the record of the Franconian annals for the year 772 about the destruction of the → Irminsûl by Charlemagne. He tells that the 'Hirminsul' had been erected as a sign of victory for the Saxons and that the name Hirmin is the same as Hermes and Mars, which is why older scholarship in particular thought of Irmin as a name for the Germanic god *Tīwaz (Zîu/Týr).

Moreover, attempts have also been made to derive the supposed god Irmin or Ermin from the Germanic tribal name of the Hermiones (actually Ermiones?) as given in Tacitus. Using Dumézil's theories, de Vries tried to explain Irmin as the representative of the 'third function', corresponding to the Indian Aryaman. However, as the only reliable reference to the god Irmin is the Irminsûl, and this is best of all explained as 'enormous pillar', any thoughts about the identity or function of this god must remain purely speculative.

Lit. → Irminsûl.

Irminsûl (Old Saxon/OHG, 'huge pillar'; unlikely: 'pillar of the god Irmin'). Irminsûl is referred to in the reports about the campaign of Charlemagne in Saxony in the year 772 when he conquered Eresburg and destroyed the Irminsûl at the same time. This event is recorded in numerous Franconian annals for the year 772, but in most detail in Rudolf of Fulda's *Translatio Alexandri* and Widukind of Corvey's *Res Gestae Saxonicae*. The annals call the Irminsûl a *fanum*, *lucum* or else *idolum*, and in Rudolf it is a huge tree trunk erected in the open air. In Widukind it is a sign of victory called Hirminsul, and in this source Hirmin and the god Hermes are thought to be identical. The word also occurs in some South German glossaries where it glosses Latin *colossus*, *pyramides*, *altissima columna* without any hint of cult significance. It is still found as 'gigantic pillar' in the *Kaiserchronik* in the 12th century. Although there have been attempts to conclude from the Irminsûl that there was a Germanic god Hirmin or Irmin, from whom the Germanic tribe of the Hermiones are supposed to derive, all other sources support the interpretation 'gigantic pillar'. The Old Norse words → *jǫrmungrundr*, Old English *eormengrund* 'earth', as well as in particular ON → Jǫrmungandr 'Midgard serpent', speak in favour of this, as their names did not derive from a god's name but simply meant 'gigantic serpent'.

Similarly, as Grimm pointed out, OHG *irmindeot* in the lay of Hildebrand is more appropriate as meaning 'great god' than as denoting any individual god. The evidence of the sources speaks against the existence of a god Irmin.

The Irminsûl might be incorporated into a → pole cult. Widukind's report, which was written over 200 years after the events themselves took place, admittedly refers to a 'sign of victory' but this does not say very much. De Vries collected evidence supporting a cult of world-pillars, which can be considered as for the Germanic area and which has its counterpart in the north in the world-tree Yggdrasill. Older scholarship attempted to identify the Irminsûl with the widespread Roman → Jupiter columns along the Rhine. Nowadays it is certain that these were not Germanic but Gallo-Roman cult monuments. In addition to this, the Eresburg does not fall within the area of Jupiter-column finds.

However, the Irminsûl can be seen in a larger context of the veneration of poles and beams, documented since the end of the Bronze Age. (→ pole gods, → *reginnaglar*).

J. Grimm, *Deutsche Mythologie*, Berlin [4]1875–78; K. Müllenhoff, 'Irmin und seine Brüder' (*ZfdA* 23) 1879; W. Braune, 'Irmindeot und Irmingot' (*PBB* 21) 1896; A. Olrik, 'Irminsul og gudestøtter' (*MoM*) 1910; G. Neckel, 'Irmin' (*Festschrift Siebs*) Breslau 1933; E. Schröder, 'Irminsúl' (*ZfdA* 72) 1935; S. Gutenbrunner, 'Der Kult des Weltherrschers bei den Semnonen' (*APhSc* 14) 1939/40; K. Helm, 'Erfundene Götter?' (*Festschrift Panzer*) Heidelberg 1950; J. de Vries, 'La valeur religieuse du mot germanique irmin' (*Cahiers du Sud* 36) 1952; J. de Vries, 'Sur certain glissements fonctionels de divinités dans la religion germanique' (*Hommages à G. Dumezil*) Brüssel 1960; J. de Vries, *Altgermanische Religionsgeschichte*, Berlin [3]1970.

R: in modern times Irminsûl stands in particular for the German components of Old Germanic religion. This can be seen, for example, in F. v. Hagedorn's poem *Der Wein* (1745) or in F. de la Motte Fouqué's drama *Die Irminsäule*. Irminsûl has a great pre-eminence as a symbol of twentieth century neo-Germanic movements: as the heraldic arms for the *Nordische Glaubensgemeinschaft*, which existed from 1927–45; as the title of the Irminsul-Schriftenreihe for 'New Germanic religion' in the Twenties; as the title of the magazine *Irminsul*, the 'Voice of the Armanenschaft' (since 1969); or as in the name of the New-Germanic religious movement *Treukreis Artglaube Irminsul*'.

Iron gauntlet of the god Thor, → *járngreipr*.

Iron wood → Járnviðr.

Irpa (ON). A goddess who, according to the *Njáls saga* 18 and *Jómsvíkinga saga*, was worshipped in the 10th century together with the goddess → Þorgerðr Hǫlgabrúðr in Norwegian Hálogaland. The name is probably related to *jarpr* 'dark brown', but it is doubtful whether we should conclude the existence of Irpa as a chthonic goddess (Schröder)

F. R. Schröder, *Ingunar-Freyr*, Tübingen 1941; J. de Vries, *Altgermanische Religionsgeschichte*, Berlin [3]1970.

Isis. Originally an Egyptian goddess who was subsequently venerated in the whole of the classical world. Tacitus mentions in his *Germania* 9 that part of the Germanic tribe of the Suebes makes sacrifices to a goddess called Isis. Whether it is really a question of the Suebes here or another tribe is debatable. The question of which Germanic goddess Tacitus refers to in his → *interpretatio romana* as Isis is more important. His indication that the sign of this goddess was a ship (*liburna*) suggests either the Frisian goddess → Nehalennia, on whose votive stones from the 3rd century a ship is repeatedly depicted, or else the West Germanic goddess → Nerthus (identical with the Scandinavian god → Njǫrðr), as Njǫrðr was obviously a god of seafaring before being replaced in this function by Freyr. It is by no means certain whether the → ship as a cult object, well-documented for the whole of the Bronze and Iron Age, really stood in any connexion to the cult of the Germanic Isis.

K. Helm, 'Isis Sueborum?' (*PBB* 43) 1918; R. Much, Die *Germania* de Tacitus, Heidelberg [4]1967.

Iulineihiae. The name of → matrons on a votive stone from Müntz near Jülich, Germany (CIL XIII 7882) and is undoubtedly derived from the place-name Iuliacum, the present Jülich. The Iulineihiae can only be spoken of in terms of a Germanic name of a matron insofar as the place falls within a Germanic area and the cult of this matron was surely borne by a Germanic population; the place name Iuliacum is, however, Latin (from Iulius).

S. Gutenbrunner, *Die germanischen Götternamen*, Halle 1936; M. Schönfeld, *Wörterbuch der altgermanischen Personen- und Völkernamen*, Heidelberg [2]1965; H. Reichert, *Lexikon der altgermanischen Namen*, Vienna 1987–90.

Ívaldi (ON). The father of the dwarfs who built the ship Skíðblaðnir (*Grímnismál* 43 and *Gylfaginning* 42). *Skáldskaparmál* 33 names the same dwarfs as the manufacturers of Sif's golden hair and Odin's spear Gungnir. It is not said if Ívaldi is a dwarf himself. The etymology of the name has led to speculations: it might mean 'owner of the bow' (from a basic form **iwawaldan*), that is, perhaps, Ullr, but might equally be 'the deity who rules in the yew-tree', corresponding to Skaði (according to Schröder). A derivation from *Inhu-waldan would put Ívaldi close to Yngvi. But neither the sparce information from the literary sources nor these attempts at etymological interpretation can satisfactorily explain the position of Ívaldi.

M. Olsen, *Hedenske Kultminder*, Kristiania 1915; F. R. Schröder, *Ingunar-Freyr*, Tübingen 1941; J. de Vries, *Altgermanische Religionsgeschichte*, Berlin [3]1970; J. de Vries, *Altnordisches etymologisches Wörterbuch*, Leiden [2]1977.

Íviðja (ON). A giantess in the *Þulur*. The meaning of the name is obscure. It either belongs to *víðr* 'wood', thus, 'the one who lives in the wood', or else to *ívið* 'malice', 'the malicious one'. Most unlikely is 'the swathing one' (to *viðja* 'withy').

J. de Vries, *Altnordisches etymologisches Wörterbuch*, Leiden [2]1977.

Jafnhárr ('the just as high'). A name for → Odin in *Grímnismál* 49, but in → *Gylfaginning* it denotes a god in the godly triad of Hárr, Jafnhárr and Þriði. As all three of these names (and also the name, Gangleri, assumed by Gylfi) are found elsewhere as names for Odin it is possible that, by using these names for Odin, Snorri wanted to elucidate the 'deception of Gylfi' further.

H. Falk, *Odensheite*, Christiania 1924; J. de Vries, *Altgermanische Religionsgeschichte*, Berlin [3]1970.

Jaki (ON, 'icicle'). A dwarf in the *Þulur*. The reading is uncertain, and Toki would also be a possible reading. The name might perhaps only be a variant of → Jari.

Jalkr (ON, 'gelding'). A name for Odin in *Grímnismál* 49 and 54, in the *Þulur*, and several times in skaldic poetry. Jalkr also occurs as the name of a sea-king. The original meaning in ON suggests a link with other mythological persons with horse names, such as Hengist and Horsa, who are (according to Bede) descended from Odin.

H. Falk, *Odensheite*, Christiania 1924.

jarðarmen (ON, 'strip of turf'). The Icelandic sagas repeatedly refer to a custom called *ganga undir jarðarmen* as being a rite for conferring blood brotherhood (*Gisla saga* 6; *Fostbrœðra saga*; *Þorsteins saga Víkingssonar*). In other texts (*Njáls saga* 119; *Vatnsdœla saga* 33, *Laxdœla saga* 18) this custom has been adapted to serve other purposes (humiliation, judgement of the gods), presumably from a lack of knowledge about its role in blood-brotherhood.

In the actual ceremony, a strip of turf (*jarðarmen*) was cut out of the ground so that the ends of the turf remained attached whilst the middle piece could be supported in the air by an upright spear so that two men could carry out the rite of mixing their blood beneath the turf-arch thus created. This, at any rate, is how the aforementioned sagas describe the procedure. The practical problems resulting from carrying out the rite in this way must have been tremendous, and therefore speculations regarding possibilities about an older, simpler version have been made whereby the turf was cut out of the earth in a semi-circle so that the lifting and supporting in the air would be much easier (Hellmuth).

Although the importance of the *ganga undir jarðarmen* as a symbolic re-birth of the blood-brothers from the earth is generally accepted, the question about the actual distribution of the custom as a legal procedure must remain open.

M. Pappenheim, 'Zum ganga undir jarðarmen' (*ZfdPh* 24) 1892; J. de Vries, 'Der altnordische Rasengang' (*APhSc* 3) 1928/29; L. Hellmuth, *Die germanische Blutsbrüderschaft*, Vienna 1975.

Jari (ON, 'the quarrelsome one', from *jara* 'quarrel'?). A dwarf in *Vǫluspá* 13.

Járnglumra (ON, 'iron-roarer'). A giantess in the *Þulur*.

járngreipr (or *járnglófi*, ON, 'iron gauntlet'). One of Thor's attributes, along with the hammer and the belt of strength (→ *megingjǫrð*), which is first ascribed to him by Snorri. Only with the help of the *jarngreipr* can he throw his hammer (*Gylfaginning* 20), and in his fight with the giant → Geirrǫðr it enables him to catch a piece of glowing metal which the giant hurls at him and throw it back at him.

Járnsaxa (ON, 'the one with the iron knife'). A giantess in the *Þulur*. Snorri in *Skáldskaparmál* 17 also calls the giantess with whom Thor begets Magni by this name. In the *Vǫluspá in skamma* (*Hyndluljóð* 37) Járnsaxa is named among Heimdall's nine giant mothers. However in *Skáldskaparmál* 21 Járnsaxa is used as a name for the goddess Sif.

L. Motz, 'Giantesses and their Names' (*FmSt* 15) 1981.

Járnviðja (ON, 'the one from the iron forest'). A giantess in the *Þulur*. Apart from this, the name only occurs in the plural, namely Járnviðjur 'those who live in the iron forest', referring to the giantesses who live in the mythological Járnviðr ('iron-forest') (Snorri, *Gylfaginning* 11; Eyvindr Skáldaspillir, *Haleygjatal* 3). The question remains open as to whether the name of the giantesses (from which the compiler of the *Þulur* derived Járnviðja as a synonym for giantess) or the name of the forest is the original one, since although the forest is mentioned in *Vǫluspá*, the reference to the giantesses in Eyvind occurs as early as the 10th century.

Járnviðr (ON, 'iron-forest'). The forest in the east, according to *Vǫluspá* 40, where a troll-woman gives birth to wolves. Snorri embellishes the passage as follows (*Gylfaginning* 11): 'A troll-woman lives in the east of Midgard in the forest called Járnviðr. In this forest the troll-women who are called Járnviðjur live. An old troll-woman gave birth to many giants as sons, all of them in the shape of wolves, and the wolves are descended from them.' One of them, called Mánagarmr, will devour the sun, and is identical with Fenrir. The name of the inhabitants of the forest, the Járnviðjur, is obviously also derived from Járnviðr, in the same way that the *íviðjur* (*Hyndluljóð* 48) are derived from the *íviðr* in *Vǫluspá* 2. All these names however are merely the products of late mythographical embellishment. – A wood in Holstein, Germany was also called Jarnwith (or German Isarnho).

J. Grimm, *Deutsche Mythologie*, Berlin [4]1875–78; K. Müllenhoff, *Deutsche Altertumskunde*, Berlin 1870–1908.

Jǫkull (ON, 'glacier'). A giant who is the father of King Snær in the genealogy of mythical ancestors Fornjótr (following the tradition in *Hversu Nóregr byggðisk*). Jǫkull's father is Kári ('wind'), and his brothers are Logi ('fire') and Ægir ('sea'). Because Snær's children in particular are only personifications of wintery weather, it would seem reasonable to understand the whole family as a genealogy of natural mythical beings like the frost-giants.

Jǫrð (ON, 'earth'). An Æsir goddess, even though she is also called a giantess. She is Odin's wife, and Thor is frequently said to be her son (*Haustlǫng* 14; *Þrymskviða* 1, *Lokasenna* 58; *Gylfaginning* 37; *Skáldskaparmál* 4). According to Snorri, Jǫrð is the daughter of Nótt ('night') and her second husband, Anarr (*Gylfaginning* 9). In the late heathen period, as recorded in our oldest literary sources, Jǫrð appears to have only been known as Thor's mother, and she plays no further role as an earth-goddess – as she certainly once was. It is uncertain whether the names Fjǫrgyn, Hlóðynn, Fold, and Grund (all meaning 'earth') were merely poetic synonyms for the mother of Thor created by the skalds, or whether they are various names for the old earth-goddess Jǫrð. However, the first suggestion seems to be more likely. Tacitus refers to the veneration of the earth-mother Nerthus (→ Njǫrðr) in his *Germania*. Just as Thor's counterpart in Indian mythology, Indra, is begotten by the god of the heavens Dyaus and the Earth, so Thor is also a son of the Earth, just like the proto-ancestor Tuisto, referred to in Old Germanic → myths of descendency (as mentioned by Tacitus). The Earth as the mother of the gods can no doubt also be understood from the Eddic cosmogony where the giantess Bestla is the mother of the first gods Odin, Vili and Vé, since the giants should be seen as chthonic beings.

Jǫrmungandr (ON, 'huge monster'). A name for the Midgard serpent, according to *Vǫluspá* 50 and Snorri (*Gylfaginning* 33, *Skáldskaparmál* 16). The fact that it occurs in Bragi's *Ragnarsdrápa* 16 (9th century) proves that it is old, just as related formations are. The word element *jǫrmun-* is also found in the name for Odin Jǫrmunr, in the name Jǫrmungrundr 'earth' and in the personal name Jǫrmunrek(k)r, as well as in Old Saxon Irminsûl 'world-pillar' and in OHG Irmindeot in the lay of Hildebrand (→

Irmin). Gandr, otherwise 'sorcery, magic wand', can be found in the meaning of 'monster', also in Vanargandr 'Fenris-wolf'.

J. Sverdrup, 'Bemerkungen zum Hildebrandslied' (*Festschrift E. Mogk*) Halle 1924; J. de Vries, *Altnordisches etymologisches Wörterbuch*, Leiden [2]1977.

Jǫrmungrundr (ON; OE *eormengrund*, runic Swedish *iarmunkrunt-*). An old poetic name for 'earth'. The Old Norse Jǫrmungrundr is found in *Grímnismál* 20 and in Sturla Þórðarson, the runic Swedish form in the Karlevi inscription from around 1000 A.D., the OE in *Beowulf*. The meaning of Jǫrmungrundr is 'mighty ground', although a link with a god Irmin has been postulated with regard to the names based on *jǫrmun-*.

J. de Vries, *Altnordisches etymologisches Wörterbuch*, Leiden [2]1977.

Jǫrmunr (ON, 'the mighty one'). A name for Odin in the *Þulur*. The meaning in the form given is simply 'the great one, mighty one', cf. Jǫrmungandr. The idea that there might be a connexion to the Germanic tribe of the (H)Erminones is no more than speculation; (→ Irmin).

H. Falk, *Odensheite*, Christiania 1924. E. O. G. Turville-Petre, *Myth and Religion of the North*, Westport 1975.

Jǫruvellir (ON, 'sandy plain'; unlikely to be from *hara* 'battle'). An undefined mythological place in *Vǫluspá* 14, which appears to be linked in some way with the place → Aurvangar (of similar meaning).

S. Nordal, *Vǫluspá*, Darmstadt 1980; J. de Vries, *Altnordisches etymologisches Wörterbuch*, Leiden [2]1977.

Jǫtunheim (ON, Jǫtunheimr or plural Jǫtunheimar 'world of the giants'). The name for a region in the east according to Old Norse literature, and not only mythological literature. In Eddic cosmology it stands for the demonic realm of the giants situated to the east of Midgard, and which is separated from the world of man by rivers and the iron forest (*Vǫluspá* 8, 48, *Skírnismál* 40 and Pr., *Þrymskviða* 7, 9 passim). Snorri uses it very frequently in this meaning, but it was also used by the older skalds (Þjóðólfr, Egill). In later prose literature, when Jǫtunheim has been firmly established as a literary motif and as the realm of the giants, it was no longer thought to be situated in the east and indeed it moved further and further to the north as the increasingly empirically understood geographical picture of the world demanded.

jǫtunn (ON, plural *jǫtnar*). One of the general designations for 'giant' (apart from *þurs* and *troll*). It is the least derogatory negative of all the words for giants, whilst *þurs* and *troll* usually have a perjorative connotation. As yet it has not been totally explained whether the word originally belonged to *eta* 'eat' (thus, 'the big eater') or to the tribal name of the Etiones.

J. de Vries, *Altgermanische Religionsgeschichte*, Berlin [3]1970; J. de Vries, *Altnordisches etymologisches Wörterbuch*, Leiden [2]1977.

jól (ON) → Yule

Jolareidi (Norwegian, 'Yule-ride') → Wild Hunt.

Jólnir (ON). A name for Odin (in Eilífr's *Þórsdápa* 12) which refers to Yule-tide (ON *jól*). It would be conceivable that the fertility sacrifices made at the mid-winter feast were also directed towards Odin, but it is more likely that he was associated with the mid-winter veneration of the ancestors as the god of the dead. He also had a link with the feast of Yule as the lord of the Wild Hunt. Because the etymological origin of the word Jul could point to a magical feast, a connexion with Odin as the god of magic would also be conceivable here.

The derivation of *jól* from Jólnir, as cited in the Medieval Norwegian tale in *Agrip af Nóreg's Konunga sǫgum* (c.1190) is naturally wrong.

H. Falk, *Odensheite*, Christiania 1924.

Jordanes (6th century). Gothic cleric, who was perhaps Bishop of Kroton, and who later lived in Thessaloniki or Constantinople. In 551 he wrote a history of the Goths for a friend (*De origine actibusque Getarum*, or with the abbreviated title, *Getica*), which includes information about the origin and history of the Goths as well as a few comments about their cult, and which relies heavily on the lost history of the Goths written by Cassiodor.

Journeys to the Other World. These are repeatedly found in Old Norse literature. In the Eddas the most well-known such journey is → Hermóð's ride to Hel, when Hermóð rides to Hel at Frigg's behest to ransom the dead Baldr, an unsuccessful venture (Snorri, *Gylfaginning* 48). In the Eddic lay *Baldrs draumar* it is Odin who rides to Hel on Sleipnir to hear something about Baldr's fate from a dead → Vǫlva. Despite the title and the prose frame the Eddic lay *Helreid Brynhildar* (Brünhilde's journey to Hel) is not a journey to the Other World, but rather a justification of her life.

Thor's journey to → Geirrǫðargarð can also be understood as a journey to the Other World. It is recorded as early as the late 10th century in Eilíf's *Þórsdrápa* and then described in detail by Snorri (*Skáldskaparmál* 18). This tale can also be found in Saxo among the journeys of Thorkillus to Gerruthus, as well as in the journey to the Other World told in *Þorsteins saga bæjarmagns* (in the 14th century). Following on from these there are other such journeys or else motifs taken from them in the younger → *fornaldarsǫgur*, for example in *Helga þáttr Þorissonar* or else in *Eireks saga víðfǫrla*, but all these texts from the 13th and 14th centuries already bear marked influences from Christian visionary literature, despite the usage of native-Germanic traditions as well. Christian visions were the dominating influence on the Norwegian ballad *Draumkvæde*, which originated in the 13th century but which has continued in oral tradition until modern times.

The strong Christian element in the *fornaldarsǫgur* shows, however, that even the concepts contained in them, such as the descriptions of the fields of the Other World → Ódáinsakr or → Glæsisvellir, are the result of Christian influence and that these concepts can hardly be considered to reflect heathen thought. It is unclear how far this is true for the Eddic lays, but care should be taken here as well.

H. R. Ellis, *The Road to Hel*, Cambridge 1943; J. Simpson, 'Otherworld adventures in an Icelandic saga' (*Folklore* 77) 1966; D. Strömbäck, 'Resan till den andre världen' (*Saga och Sed*) 1976.

Jul → Yule.

Jupiter columns. In Roman Germania 800 fragments have so far been found of so-called Jupiter columns. These are cult monuments which consist of a pedestal usually with four reliefs of gods on it. Standing on this is a stone column decorated with scales crowned by a mounted Jupiter-figure who is riding away over a snake-like giant. The height of these Jupiter columns is usually 4 metres, but the Great Jupiter column in Mainz was over 9 metres high. The Jupiter columns were especially widespread in the area around Mainz and Cologne, but are also frequently found in the region of the Upper Rhine and the Neckar. The date of construction of these monuments falls in the 2nd and 3rd centuries A.D.

In older scholarship there was an intense discussion about whether the columns, which tended to be associated with the Germanic → Irminsûl, should be considered to be Germanic or Celtic. The depicted god, Jupiter, was identified as the Germanic god Zîu/Týr (Hertlein). Nowadays, on the other hand, it seems to be on the whole certain, on the basis of the population structure of the areas where the finds were made, the names found on the inscriptions, and stylistic elements, that they were predominantly the cult monuments of the Gallo-Roman inhabitants. The deity corresponding to Jupiter should therefore be sought in Celtic and not in Germanic mythology.

F. Hettner, 'Die Juppitersäulen' (*Westdeutsche Zeitschrift* 4) 1885: F. Hertlein, *Juppitergigantensäulen*, Stuttgart 1910; F. Hertlein, 'Juppitergigantensäulen' (*Hoops* 2) 1914/15; F. Drexel, 'Die Gottheiten der Equites singulares und die Juppitersäulen' (*Germania* 8) 1924; H. Birkhan, *Germanen und Kelten*, Vienna 1970; W. Müller, *Die Juppitergigantensäulen und ihre Verwandten*, Meisenheim 1975; G. Bauchhenss, P. Noelke, *Die Juppitersäulen in den germanischen Provinzen*, Köln 1981.

Kaldgrani (ON, 'cold beard'). A giant in the *Þulur*.

Kannanefates. Name of → matrons (corrected from Hiannanefates). A votive stone from Cologne, Germany (CIL XIII 8219) was dedicated to these *Matribus paternis Kannanef(atibus)* by a member of the XXX. legion. The matrons' name Kannanefates belongs to *ala Cannanefatium* (or else *Cannenefatium*). The regiment thus called is recorded fairly frequently from 74 A.D. until 149 A.D. (also in Tacitus, *Annales*) so that the name of the matron may also be dated as belonging to this period.

S. Gutenbrunner, *Die germanischen Götternamen*, Halle 1936; M. Schönfeld, *Wörterbuch der altgermanischen Personen- und Völkernamen*, Heidelberg ^{2}1965; H. Reichert, *Lexikon der altgermanischen Namen*, Vienna 1987–90.

Kára (ON). The → valkyrie who protects Helgi Haddingjaskaði according to *Helgakviða Hundingsbana* II. Kára is the re-born valkyrie → Sigrun, just as Helgi is the re-born Helgi Hundingsbani. The name Kára is only recorded in heroic poetry and could mean either 'the wild, stormy one' (cf. ON *afkárr* 'wild') or else 'curl', 'the curly one' (from ON *kárr*). According to Höfler, there is a connexion in this to the cult runic name Odinkar 'the one with the (long?) Odin's curls'.

O. Höfler, *Germanisches Sakralkönigtum*, Tübingen, Münster, Köln 1952; J. de Vries, *Altnordisches etymologisches Wörterbuch*, Leiden ^{2}1977.

Kari (ON, 'wind, gust, squall'). A giant who, according to the genealogy given in the legendary Norwegian pre-history, is one of the sons of the ancestor → Fornjótr. Frosti is said to be Kari's son in one version (*Fundinn Nóregr*), but in the other (*Hversu Nóregr byggðisk*) Jǫkull is named instead. At any rate, Kari is the grandfather of the legendary king → Snær.

Keila (ON, 'narrow fjord, gorge'). One of the giantesses who, according to Þórbjǫrn dísarskáld, was killed by Thor. However, we know nothing more of this tale.

kenning (ON, pl. *kenningar*). Poetic paraphrases of concepts in several words, which are found in both Eddic and → skaldic poetry. Because *kenningar* deliberately codify the concept, mythological kennings are mostly impossible to solve without knowledge of the corresponding myth. As a result *kenningar* on the one hand offer us an essential indication of the religious-mythological education of the poets and their public, but on the other hand they often contain references to myths about which the other sources are silent and thus serve as additional sources of information regarding Germanic mythology.

R. Meissner, *Die Kenningar der Skalden*, Bonn, Leipzig 1921; H. v. d. Merwe Scholtz, *The Kenning in Anglo-Saxon and Old Norse Poetry*, Utrecht 1927; W. Krause, *Die Kenning als typische Stilfigur der germanischen und keltischen Dichtersprache*, Halle 1930; W. Mohr, *Kenningstudien*, Stuttgart 1933; P. Trost, 'Zur Wesensbestimmung der Kenning' (*ZfdA* 70) 1933; H. Marquardt, *Die altenglischen Kenningar*, Halle 1938; A. Heusler, *Altgermanische Dichtung*, Potsdam [2]1941; H. Lie, 'Kenningar' (*KLNM* 8) 1963; T. Gardner, 'The application of the term Kenning' (*Neophilologus* 56) 1972; G. Kreutzer, *Die Dichtungslehre der Skalden*, Kronberg 1974; B. Fidjestøl, 'Kenningsystemet' (MoM) 1974 und 1979; P. Hallberg, 'Kenningsystemet' (MoM) 1978; E. Marold, *Kenningkunst*, Berlin, New York 1983; R. Frank, 'Kenning' (*DicMA* 7) 1986.

Kerlaugar (pl. of ON *kerlaug* 'bath in a tub'). Two mythical rivers in *Grímnismál* 29 (and in the *Þulur*), through which Thor must wade daily. With regard to the strange meaning of the name it is possible that it refers to an otherwise unrecorded myth about Thor.

Kíli (ON). A dwarf in *Vǫluspá* 13 and in the *Þulur*. Etymologically it belongs either to *kill* 'long, narrow bay', or more sensibly to *kíli* (borrowed from Low German) 'wedge', thus meaning 'wedge-smith'?

C. N. Gould, 'Dwarf-Names' (*PMLA* 44) 1929; S. Gutenbrunner, 'Eddastudien I' (*ANF* 70) 1955.

R: Kíli is one of the 13 dwarves on the adventurous journey related in J. R. R. Tolkien's novel, *The Hobbit*.

Kivik grave. The Bronze Age grave of Kivik on Scania (nowadays South Sweden) is made of smooth, rectangular stone plates which are decorated with drawings similar to rock carvings, but which are far more elegantly and clearly executed. It is certain that the drawings on the stone plates show us a sequence of cult scenes which can surely be considered to be processions and symbols because of the depiction of lure-players. Exactly what kind of cult this was and which gods it served – if indeed it is not connected with a cult of the dead – cannot be discovered.

J. Bing, 'Das Kivikdenkmal' (*Mannus* 7) 1915; J. de Vries, *Altgermanische Religionsgeschichte*, Berlin [3]1970.

Kjalarr (ON). The name given to Odin in *Grímnismál* 49 and twice in skaldic kennings. In *Grímnismál* the word is found in connexion with *kjalki* 'sledge', and thus Kjalarr could perhaps mean 'sledge-driver'. Another interpretation is also possible: 'the god who gives the carrion-eaters something to eat', and as such would refer to Odin as the god of war (Falk).

H. Falk, *Odensheite*, Christiania 1924; J. de Vries, *Altnordisches etymologisches Wörterbuch*, Leiden [2]1977.

Kjallandi (ON). A giantess in the *Þulur* and in a poem by the skald Þórbjǫrn dísarskáld, who reports in one stanza that she was killed by Thor. We know nothing more about her and even the name is unexplained.

Kǫr (ON, 'illness'). The bed of the goddess → Hel in Snorri's allegorizing description of her domicile (*Gylfaginning* 33).

Kǫrmt (ON, 'the protecting one', from *karmr* 'protection'?). A (mythical?) river in *Grímnismál* and in the *Þulur*. *Grímnismál* tells that Thor has to wade through the rivers 'Kǫrmt and Ǫrmt and both of the Kerlaugar' on his way to the council of the gods under the ash-tree, Yggdrasill. This could point to the fact that these were all rivers of the Other World which form the eastern border of Midgard against Jǫtunheim, where, according to the Eddic lays, Thor frequently went in order to fight against the giants. – Kǫrmt, nowadays Karmöy, is also the name of a Norwegian island between Stavanger and Haugesund.

Kǫttr (ON, 'cat'). A not particularly appropriate name for a giant given in the *Þulur*.

Kolga (ON, 'wave'). One of the nine daughters of the sea-giant → Ægir and his wife Rán (*Skáldskaparmál* 22 and 58; Einarr Skúlason; *Helgakviða Hundingsbana* I 28) who were equated with the waves of the sea in Old Norse literature.

Kráka (ON, 'crow'). A giantess in the *Þulur*.

King's luck → Sacred kingship.

Kingship → Sacred kingship.

Kvasir (ON). When the two families of gods, the Æsir and the Vanir, made their peace after the → War of the Vanir, they sealed this peace declaration by spitting into a bowl and then out of this spittle creating Kvasir who was the wisest of all creatures. Two dwarfs, Fjalarr and Galarr, murdered Kvasir and caught his blood in three vessels Boðn, Són and Óðrœrir. They mixed the blood with honey and from this came the mead, which makes a poet of anyone who drinks it (Snorri, *Skáldskaparmál* 1). This is why this mead (also known as poets' mead or the → mead of the skalds is also called 'Kvasir's blood' (*Kvasis dreyra*: Einarr Skálaglamm, *Vellekla* 1). In *Gylfaginning* 49 Snorri calls Kvasir the wisest of the Æsir. In *Ynglinga saga* 4 he calls him the cleverest of the Vanir who was kept as a hostage by the Æsir, but this diverges somewhat from the other traditions.

Originally Kvasir was probably the name given to the juice which was gained from berries and then fermented (cf. Norwegian *kvase*, Russian *kvas*). In archaic cultures the method for the production of such a drink was that the berries were chewed (as a communal practice) and then spat into a vessel – an exact correspondence to the creation of Kvasir in the Germanic myth.

The fact that Snorri indeed gives us a faithful description of an ancient myth in his tale is not only proved by the already mentioned kenning 'Kvasir's blood' from the 10th century, but close parallels with the myth of Kvasir and the theft of the mead can also be seen in the Indian myth of the theft of Soma, the god's drink, committed by the god Indra (by an eagle or by Indra himself). Common properties in both myths allow us to conclude a common myth in early Indo-European times.

The tale of Kvasir is found in Snorri at the end of the account of the war against the Vanir. The record of the mixing of spittle as an essential part of declaring peace points to the great age of the myth, since both the mixing of spittle and also the communal partaking of the intoxicating drink had a fixed place in the ceremonies of the conclusion of peace and union in numerous archaic tribes. In addition to this, Dumézil has interpreted this ceremony reflected in the myth of Kvasir as being a symbol for the union of representatives of the three mythological functions to the social and religious system of the Indo-Germanic community.

N. S. Hagen, 'On the Origin of the Name Kvasir' (*ANF* 28) 1912; A. M. Sturtevant, 'Etymological Comments' (*PMLA* 67) 1952; J. de Vries, *Altgermanische Religionsgeschichte*, Berlin [3]1970; R. Doht, *Der Rauschtrank im germanischen Mythos*, Vienna 1974; G. Dumézil, *Gods of the Ancient Northmen*, Berkeley 1977.

Kyrmir (ON). A giant in the *Þulur* whose name is obscure: either 'the pusher' or 'the screamer'.

F. Jónsson, 'Þulur' (*APhSc* 9) 1934; J. de Vries, *Altnordisches etymologisches Wörterbuch*, Leiden [2]1977.

Læraðr (ON). The name of a mythical tree. In *Grímnismál* 25 and 26 it is said to stand on the roof of Valhall and a goat (Heiðrun) and a stag (Eikþrymir) graze in its branches. According to *Gylfaginning* 38, the goat gives mead instead of milk and this nourishes the *einherjar*. Water drips from the antlers of the stag into the spring, Hvergelmir, from which all the waters in the world are fed. Both these stanzas stem from the late heathen period, when various aspects of mythology were brought into a system. This in turn is the reason why Læraðr is also usually identified as being the world tree Yggdrasill as we have no further information about Læraðr other than the above quoted, and in Norse mythology only Yggdrasill is named as a mythological tree. The meaning of the word Læraðr is also obscure. The closest interpretation is 'causer of harm' (from *læ*), but this would not be an appropriate name for a mythological tree. Sturtevant has suggested that the 'damage' refers to Odin, since Yggdrasill, too, means 'horse of the terrible one' = 'horse of Odin'. Other suggestions as to the meaning of the name are somewhat more problematic phonetically speaking: 'giver of protection' (from **hléráðr*) or else 'giver of humidity'.

A. M. Sturtevant, 'Etymological Comments' (*PMLA* 67) 1952; J. de Vries, *Altnordisches etymologisches Wörterbuch*, Leiden [2]1977.

Laessø, Danish island (ON, Hléysey), → Hlér.

Lævateinn (ON, 'damage-twig'). The name of a sword in *Fjǫlsvinnsmál* 26. In fact, it is not actually a name, but a kenning for sword.

landdísasteinar (Icelandic, 'rocks of the land-dísir'). The name by which certain rocks in North-West Iceland were known, in the vicinity of which one should neither mow grass nor let the children play, and which enjoyed a certain amount of respect, if not devotion, even as late as the 18th and 19th century. It is possible to conclude from these details and the name itself that the *landdísasteinar* were considered to be the home of the → *landdísir*, a kind of protective spirit.

K. Kaalund, *Bidrag til en historisk-topografisk Beskrivelse af Island* I, Copenhagen 1877; E. O. G. Turville-Petre, 'A Note on the Landdísir' (*Early English and Norse Studies, Pres. to H. Smith*) London 1963.

landdísir (ON, '*dísir* of the land'). A term which is not found in this form anywhere in Old Norse sources, but which can be assumed from the word → *landdísasteinar*. The *landdísir* were perhaps identical with the → *dísir*, female protective goddesses, or else are related in some way to the → *landvættir*, Icelandic protective spirits. The fact that the *landdísir* were thought to live in rocks, where they were also venerated (hence the term *landdísasteinar*), could mean that this devotion was a form of ancestor cult and that the dead were venerated here. Icelandic folklore tells of other forms of living beings from the Other World, such as dwarfs and elves, who are supposed to live in hills and rocks.

E. O. G. Turville-Petre, 'A Note on the Landdísir' (*Early English and Norse Studies, Pres. to H. Smith*) London 1963; E. O. G. Turville-Petre, *Myth and Religion of the North*, Westport 1975; J. de Vries, *Altgermanische Religionsgeschichte*, Berlin [3]1970.

landvættir (ON). Beings from lower mythology, not dissimilar to elves, who are only documentarily recorded in Medieval Icelandic sources. The main source which refers to them is the *Landnámabók*, on which the other Icelandic texts (*Egils saga* 57; Snorri, *Oláfs saga Tryggvasonar* 33) are presumably dependent. It is pointed out in Ulfljót's law in the *Landnámabók* (H 268) that in heathen times there was a law that when approaching Iceland, the dragon heads on the bows of the ship were to be removed so that the *landvættir* protecting the island would not be frightened away. Elsewhere in the *Landnámabók* the *landvættir* appear to have been thought of as spirits protecting the land (S 329; S 330 = H 289). The Icelandic settlers of the 9th and 10th centuries obviously thought the country was inhabited by such natural spirits who were quite capable of harming the farmers if they were angered in any way. To say, however, that they were demons of death is an incorrect interpretation of the source material.

S. Sohlheim, 'Landvette' (*KLNM* 10) 1965; J. de Vries, *Altgermanische Religionsgeschichte*, Berlin [3]1970.

Lanehiae. Name of → matrons, to whom a votive stone from Lechenich near Euskirchen, Germany (CIL XIII 7976) was dedicated. A link between the name Lanehiae and the place-name Lechenich is uncertain, and the latter probably derives from *Laciniacum. The Medieval name Lanehe for the present-day East Belgian town of Lasne is more similar still. None of the other attempts at interpretation (cf. Gutenbrunner) give any really satisfactory interpretation of the name.

M. Ihm, 'Der Mütter- und Matronenkultus und seine Denkmäler' (*Bonner Jahrbücher* 83) 1887; S. Gutenbrunner, *Die germanischen Götternamen*, Halle 1936; H. Reichert, *Lexikon der altgermanischen Namen*, Vienna 1987–90.

Langbarðr (ON, 'long-beard'). A name for Odin in the *Þulur*. It means exactly the same as the name Síðskeggr, which also alludes to Odin's long beard. However, a connexion with the tribal name of the Langobards would be possible, because according to Paul the deacon (*Historia Langobardorum* I, 8) Odin gave them this name.

H. Falk, *Odensheite*, Christiania 1924.

Laufey (ON, 'foliage island' ?). The name of Loki's mother (*Lokasenna* 52, *Þrymskviða* 18, 20; *Gylfaginning* 32, *Skáldskaparmál* 16; *Sǫrla þáttr* 2; *Þulur*), who is also called → Nal. In poetry Loki is always called Loki Laufeyjarson. As 'foliage island' makes little sense, the derivation is possibly from **lauf-awiaz* 'the one full of leaves', which would thus suggest a tree goddess. Perhaps, however, Laufey might mean 'the one who awakens confidence' (cf. Gothic *galaufs*)? Both suggestions are difficult to place in Loki's predominantly demonic genealogical table.

J. de Vries, *Altnordisches etymologisches Wörterbuch*, Leiden [2]1977.

laukaR → leek.

leek (ON *laukr*). In the Germanic north this plant was considered to be particularly effective for magical and healing purposes. In Medieval Iceland the expression *laukargarðr* 'leek garden' was the usual name for monastic herb gardens.

The healing properties of leek are referred to in many ON sources, in the Eddic lay *Sigrdrífumál* 8, where leek is recommended as an effective antidote against poison in mead, as well as in a whole series of runic inscriptions found almost exclusively on bracteates. On these the runic word *laukaR* (or abbreviated *lauR*, *luR*, *lkaR*) is found alone or with other magical rune words and forms an inscription which was quite clearly supposed to have a lucky or healing property. The oldest name of the l-rune is *laukaR*, sometimes also *līna*, and the connexion between leek and linen can be found in both the inscription on a bone knife from Fløsand (SW Norway, c.350 A.D.): *līna laukaR*, as well as in the High Medieval Icelandic tale of → Vǫlsi, where linen and leek were used as a means to conserve a horse's phallus for magic purposes. In this particular case the leek would appear to have been used as an antiseptic recommended in Medieval Icelandic medical works, and the linen as a bandage.

Apart from the medical-magical significance of leek, the shape of the plant led to it being used in kennings for a ship's mast and also for sword.

S. E. Eitrem, 'Lina laukar' (*Festskrift til A. Kjær*) Christiania 1924; W. P. Lehmann, 'Lin and laukr in the Edda' (*GR* 30) 1955; J. Lange, 'Løg-Laukar' (*Sprog og Kultur* 23) 1963; W. Krause, *Die Runeninschriften im älteren Futhark*, Göttingen 1966; Guðrún P. Helgadóttir, 'Laukagarðr' (*Speculum Norroenum, Studies G. Turville-Petre*) Odense 1981; W. Heizmann, *Laukr ('Lauch') in der altnordischen Literatur, Mythologie und Heilkunde*, Diss. Munich 1981.

Leiði (ON, perhaps 'the hated one'). The name of a giant who is named, together with other giants killed by Thor, in a stanza composed by Þórbjǫrn dísarskáld (10th century). We know nothing else about him.

Leifi (ON, 'heir'?). A giant in the *Þulur* and in a poem by Þórðr Kolbeinsson.

Leikn (ON). A giantess in the *Þulur*, in a stanza composed by Þórbjǫrn dísarskáld, where she is named among the giantesses whom Thor killed, and in a few stanzas by Hallfreðr (10th century) and Hallvarðr (11th century). The name is obscure but it could mean either 'the bewitched' or else, admittedly less likely, 'the playmate'.

F. Jónsson, 'Þulur' (*APhSc* 9) 1934; L. Motz, 'Giantesses and their Names' (*FmSt* 15) 1981.

Leiptr (ON, 'lightning'). A river in the catalogue of rivers in *Grímnismál* 28, and in Snorri's cosmogony (*Gylfaginning* 3) it is one of the eleven rivers called the Élivágar which flow out of Niflheim.

Leirvǫr (ON). A giantess in the *Þulur* whose name could perhaps mean 'the one with the dirty lips', but if *-vǫr* belongs to the goddess Vǫr (→ Svívǫr), it could be a kind of kenning: 'clay-goddess' = giantess.

Lejre (ON Hleiðr). According to the saga written about the Danish kings, the

Skjǫldungs, Lejre is their oldest royal residence, and → Froði is mentioned as having lived there. The OE epic *Beowulf* also reports that the great hall of the Danish kings was in Lejre and was called → Heorot, and Harald Hilditann is supposedly buried in Lejre. The German monk Thietmar of Merseburg (I, 9) reports that a heathen sacrifice was made in Lejre, the description of which is suspiciously similar to Adam of Bremen's description of the → Sacrifice at Uppsala. Admittedly Thietmar (died 1018) wrote his report at least 50 years before Adam, but both these reports could possibly go back to the same source.

In Lejre today the only remains of latter-day glory are the biggest Danish ship-setting as well as a few Iron Age burial mounds. Despite legendary suggestions that there was an important settlement at Lejre far earlier, archaeological investigations have only found the remains of buildings from the 10th century, which could substantiate Thietmar's information about Lejre as a Viking Age centre of sacrifice so that Lejre was perhaps indeed the seat of the Danish kings at that time. Traces of rich burials have been found in the burial mounds which have been dated from as early as the 4th century. However, evidence for older buildings or even traces of a Migration Age royal court have not been found and the legendary royal seat Lejre must lie somewhere else.

G. Jones, *A History of the Vikings*, Oxford 1973; O. Klose, *Handbuch der historischen Stätten. Dänemark*, Stuttgart 1982 (= KTA 327).

Lerus → Hlér.

Léttfeti (ON, 'the nimble one'). A mythical horse in the catalogue of horse names in *Grímnismál* 30 and in the *Þulur*. According to Snorri (*Gylfaginning* 14) Léttfeti is one of the horses which belongs to the Æsir.

Leudinae. An epithet for some → matrons. Three inscriptions dedicated to the *Matronis Vacallinehis* in Pesch, Germany bear the addition Leudinis. Probably another inscription (*Mercurius Leud [. . .] Janus*) from Derichsweiler near Düren, Germany, is linked with this name as well. The assumption that it comes from a place-name *Leudium (or *Leudiacum; Lüttich?) leads to the most likely interpretation of the name, which would indicate that the votive stone was erected by people who came from *Leudium, who worshipped the Vacallinehae in Pesch.

S. Gutenbrunner, *Die germanischen Götternamen*, Halle 1936; M. Schönfeld, *Wörterbuch der altgermanischen Personen- und Völkernamen*, Heidelberg [2]1965; H. Reichert, *Lexikon der altgermanischen Namen*, Vienna 1987–90.

light elves (ON *ljósálfar*). A kind of → elves. Snorri distinguishes between light elves and dark elves and says that the light elves live in Álfheimr which he obviously thought of as a sort of heaven. He describes them as being more beautiful than the sunlight which suggests that he was influenced by the concept and the appearance of Christian angels. This is especially apparent when he writes that Gimlé lies in the third heaven and at the moment is only inhabited by light elves. In fact, however, light elves are the group (or rather the aspect) of elves which lead to their conceptual relationship with the Æsir quite early on.

R: Light elves are to be found depicted as tiny fairy-like creatures in Charles P. Sainton's watercolour *The White Elves*.

Liðskjálfr (ON, perhaps: 'limb-dangler'). A dwarf in *Fjǫllsvinnsmál* 34. The interpretation 'the one who shakes because of beer and drunkenness' (Motz) is untenable. The name may well be just a corruption of → Hliðskjálf.

L. Motz, 'New Thoughts on Dwarf-Names' (*FmSt* 7) 1973.

Líf (ON, líf 'life'). One of the two people who, according to *Vafþrúðnismál* 45, survive the → Ragnarǫk and become the ancestors of a new family of man (→ Lífþrasir). This is clearly a case of a reduplication of the → anthropogeny, understandable from the cyclic nature of Eddic escatology. *Vafþrúðnismál* 45 and *Gylfaginning* 52 refer to the fact that Líf and Lífþrasir survive 'in Hoddmimir's wood' (*í holti Hoddmimis*) and feed themselves on morning dew. This wood should not be understood literally as a wood or even a forest in which the two keep themselves hidden, but rather as an alternative name for the trunk of the world-tree Yggdrasill. Thus, the creation of mankind from tree trunks (→ Askr, → Embla) is repeated after the Ragnarǫk as well. The concept of the origin of mankind from trees is ancient in Germanic regions. Legendary parallels can be found in the Bavarian legend of the shepherd who lives in a tree and whose descendants populate the land after life there has been destroyed by plague (retold by Schröder). From ON sources one may include Ǫrvar-Oddr, who is rejuvenated after living as a tree-man (*Ǫrvar-Odds saga* 24–27), as a parallel to this myth.

L. Mackensen, 'Baumseele' (*Zeitschrift für Deutschkunde*) 1924; F. R. Schröder, 'Germanische Schöpfungsmythen' (*GRM* 19) 1931; J. de Vries, *Altgermanische Religionsgeschichte*, Berlin ³1970.

Lífþrasir (ON, 'the one striving after life'). One of the two people who will survive Ragnarök, according to *Vafþrúðnismál* 45; → Líf.

A. Sturtevant, 'Semantic and Etymological Notes' (*SS* 20), 1948.

līna laukar (ON, 'linen and leek') → leek.

Litr (ON, 'the coloured one'). A dwarf in *Vǫluspá* 12 and in the *Þulur*. Snorri mentions him in the account of → Baldr's funeral (*Gylfaginning* 48) and describes how Litr gets under Thor's feet just as Thor wants to consecrate Baldr's funeral pyre with Mjǫllnir, whereupon Thor kicks him onto the pyre where he burns along with Baldr. As the dwarf in this episode fulfils no obvious function, the episode could come from an obscure name (or detail) in Snorri's original.

Living dead → draugr, → death and life afer death.

Ljómi (ON, 'splendour, lightning'). A dwarf in the *Þulur*.

Ljósálfar (ON) → light elves.

Ljóta (ON, 'the ugly one'). A typical name for giantesses in the *Þulur*.

(**Lobbon(n)us**). Supposed god's name on an inscription in Utrecht. It rests however on the imaginative interpretation of the text which was made intentionally illegible; → Hercules Alabuandus.

C. W. Vollgraff, 'Romeinsche Inscripties uit Utrecht' (*Versl.en Medel. d. Akadem. van Wetenschapen te Amsterdam, Afd. Letterk.* 70 B 5) 1930; A. W. Byvanck, 'De Inscriptionibus Traictensibus nuper repertis' (*Mnemosyne* N.S. 60) 1933; S. Gutenbrunner, *Die germanischen Götternamen*, Halle 1936; J. de Vries, *Altgermanische Religionsgeschichte*, Berlin ³1970.

Loðinfingra (ON, 'shaggy finger'). A name for a giantess (in the *Þulur*). It alludes to the hairiness of giantesses (cf. Hadda).

Loðurr (ON). A god who in *Vǫluspá* 18 is mentioned together with Odin and Hœnir. Apart from this, only one other reference to Loðurr is from the kenning for Odin, *Loðurs vinr* 'Loðurr's friend', which occurs once in Eyvind's *Háleygjatal* (10th century) and once in Haukr Valdísarson's *Íslendingadrápa* (12th century). Because Loðurr occurs in *Vǫluspá* accompanied by the same gods as Loki normally is, attempts have been made to see Loðurr as merely another name for Loki. In the myth of creation in *Vǫluspá* Loðurr gives man his good looks and his life-giving warmth (if indeed the unexplained *lá* means this). It is difficult to imagine Loki in the role of a giver of life. Attempts to find an etymological connexion of the two names Loðurr and Loki by means of the runic name of a god → logaþore (Gras, Krogmann) – are not convincing. Philippson tried to support the link Loðurr-Loki by pointing out that Loðurr gave man his good looks and that Snorri describes Loki as handsome. However, apart from the fact that Snorri was more than likely using a (Christian) literary device here to show that beauty and evil can go hand in hand, this theory is hardly likely. Recently only F. R. Schröder has spoken out in favour of identifying Loðurr as Loki in the function as a cult-hero of fire. The strongest argument for the equation Loðurr = Loki, considering the sources available, is the kenning for Odin *Lopts vinr* 'Lopt's friend' in Einar skálaglamm's *Vellekla* (9th century), since Loptr is certainly a name for Loki, and Loðurr appears in both of the previously mentioned kennings in an analogous position. – There have been numerous other attempts to interpret Loðurr (cf. de Vries). Noteworthy is the consideration of Loðurr as identical with Freyr; in this case, the etymology of Loðurr is related to Gothic *liudan* 'grow', ON *lóð* 'fruit, yield', and also to *ljóðr* 'people, community'. Thus, Loðurr would be characterized as a god of fertility, reproduction and the protection of human society.

E. J. Gras, *De noordse Loki-mythen in hun onderling verband*, Haarlem 1931; J. de Vries, *The Problem of Loki*, Helsinki 1933; W. Krogmann, 'Loki' (*APhSc* 12) 1937–38; E. A. Philippson, *Die Genealogie der Götter*, Urbana 1953; E. C. Polomé, 'Quelque notes à propos de l'enigmatique dieu scandinave Lóðurr' (*Revue Belge* 33) 1955; F. R. Schröder, 'Die Göttin des Urmeers und ihr männlicher Partner' (*PBB West* 82) 1960; E. F. Halvorsen, 'Lóðurr' (*KLNM* 10) 1965; E. C. Polomé, 'Some Comments on Vǫluspá Stanzas 17–18' (*Old Norse Literature and Mythology*) Austin 1969; J. de Vries, *Altgermanische Religionsgeschichte*, Berlin [3]1970.

Lœðing (ON). Name of the first of the fetters with which the Æsir, according to Snorri, tried to bind the wolf, → Fenrir. He tore from Lœðing as he did from the second fetter (Drómi), but he was finally properly bound by the third fetter, Gleipnir. Snorri adds a proverbial idiom to this, referring to the expression 'to free oneself from Lœðing' which means to overcome difficulties. The existence of this apparently already well-known phrase suggests that Snorri did not in fact invent the name as might otherwise be assumed. The meaning and origin of the name Lœðing are at any rate obscure.

Lofarr (ON, 'the praiser' or 'the praiseworthy warrior'?). A dwarf in *Vǫluspá* 14 and 16 and in the *Þulur*.

Lofn (ON, 'the comforter, the mild'). A goddess whom Snorri (*Gylfaginning* 34) lists as one of the Asyniur commenting: 'Lofn is so mild and benevolent to pray to that she receives permission from the Father of All (= Odin) and Frigg to bring together men and women whose marriage was previously forbidden. The expression "permission" (*lof*) derives from her name. It also suggests that she is much "praised" by men.'

Snorri used kennings to compose a short mythical tale, combining several etymologies with the female personal name Lofn. Lofn as a goddess is otherwise only found in the *Þulur*.

logaþore (Rune-Alamannic). One of the three names of gods in the runic inscription on the → Nordendorf fibula, which says:

logaþore
wodan
wigiþonar

The first name, *logaþore*, is usually linked with → Loðurr and → Loki. In this interpretation, Loki is thought of as a shortened form of Loðurr and Loðurr in turn (from **luhaþuraz*) is the same as *logaþore* (from **lugaþuraz*). However, these derivations are extremely uncertain despite the OE gloss words *logðor, logþor, logþer, logeþer* 'malicious', which support this identification since Loki is unquestionably malicious. Nevertheless, this interpretation does not fit Loðurr at all, and the final *-e* of *logaþore* is unexplained. Klingenberg (following up a similar idea from Feist) suggests that logaþore could be read backwards as well as forwards, thus giving *logaþore eroþagol*: *eorþa gol* (from pre-OHG *erþa* 'earth' and Germanic **galan* 'to shout') would mean 'earth shout' and refers to the weeping of all things after the death of Baldr, all things that is to say except Loki. However, it is at least questionable whether the (magic) rune inscription from the early 7th century can be brought so directly into relation with Snorri's (literary) text from the 13th century.

According to the most recent interpretations *logaþore* is not a name but a Christian charm offering protection against the other two gods: 'Wodan and Donar are intriguers!', but this is hardly convincing, either.

S. Feist, 'Zur Deutung der deutschen Runenspangen' (*ZfdPh* 47) 1918; J. de Vries, *The Problem of Loki*, Helsinki 1933; W. Krogmann, 'Loki' (*APhSc* 12) 1937–38; W. Krause, *Die Runeninschriften im älteren Futhark*, Göttingen 1966; W. Steinhauser, *Die Wodansweihe von Nordendorf bei Augsburg* (*ZfdA* 97) 1968; E. C. Polomé, 'Some Comments on Vǫluspá Stanzas 17–18' (*Old Norse Literature and Mythology*) Austin 1969; H. Klingenberg, 'Die Drei-Götter-Fibel von Nordendorf bei Augsburg' (*ZfdA* 105) 1976; K. Düwel, 'Runen und *interpretatio christiana*' (*Tradition als historische Kraft. [Festschrift] K. Hauck*) Berlin, New York 1982; H. Rosenfeld, 'Die germanischen Runen im kleinen Schulerloch und auf der Nordendorfer Bügelfibel A' (*ZfdA* 113) 1984.

(**Loge**). A half-god created by R. Wagner in his opera *Das Rheingold* (tenor) who is the lord of fire. Loge probably is the result of Wagner's confusion of the god Loki with the giant Logi. In Snorri Logi is the personification of fire whereas the god Loki of Germanic mythology has nothing to do with fire.

Logi (ON, 'flame, fire'). A giant who is the impersonation of fire. He is one of the three sons of the primordial ancestor → Fornjótr (*Fundinn Nóregr*; *Ynglingatal* 27) and appears as Loki's opponent in Snorri's mythological tale of Thor and → Utgarðaloki (*Gylfaginning* 45 and 46; → Skrýmir). Utgarðaloki calls upon Logi to compete against Loki. 'A trough of freshly slaughtered meat was taken and carried into the hall; Loki sat at one end and Logi at the other; both ate as quickly as they could and they met each other in the middle of the trough. Loki had then eaten all the meat from the bones, but Logi had eaten the meat together with the bones as well as the trough itself. It seemed to all, that Loki had lost the competition now.' A few pages on, Snorri puts the explanation of this spectacle in the mouth of Utgarðaloki: the gods were overcome by sorcery and Loki's opponent 'was the wild-fire, which did not only burn the meat but also the trough'.

The tale, which in this form is surely quite young, rests on the one hand upon a pun (Logi-Loki), and on the other it could derive from an old riddle ('What eats quicker than Loki? – Only wild-fire.')

Lóinn (ON, 'the lazy one'). A dwarf in the *Þulur*.

Lokasenna ('Loki's blasphemies'). A mythological poem from the Poetic *Edda* in which we are introduced to a fairly complete Pantheon and hear various things about the character of the heathen gods from Loki's insults. – The introductory prose in the Codex Regius gives an account of how the gods have met together for a drinking bout in the hall of the giant → Ægir. When everybody is praising Ægir's efficient servants, Loki kills one of them, Fimafengr, and is driven out of the hall as a result. This is where the *Lokasenna* begins. Loki tries to regain entry and is turned back first by a servant, Eldir, and then finally, after he has insisted upon his rights as Odin's blood-brother, he is reluctantly given permission to re-enter. However, he does not greet Bragi (the god of poetry) and when Idun comes to this god's defence, she herself is the butt of Loki's derision. From this point on, Loki swamps the gods with ridicule and everyone who tries to come to another's aid is immediately himself the victim of Loki's tirade. Finally, Thor returns from one of his journeys to the east and drives Loki out by threatening him with his hammer Mjǫllnir, but not without being ridiculed by Loki first. Loki's abuse of the goddesses (Idun, Gefjon, Frigg, Freyja) is restricted to imputations of infidelity and prostitution, but the abuse rained on the gods is more varied. He accuses Bragi and Byggvir (Freyr's servant) of cowardice without there being any evidence of it elsewhere in our sources. He mocks Njǫrðr by saying that his mouth has served as a chamber-pot for giants' daughters when he was a hostage with the giants, and he furthermore accuses him of incest with his own sister (→ Vanir). Týr is blamed for being a cuckold without demanding compensation after Loki has had a son with his (Týr's) wife. On the other hand, Odin is charged with injustice in the manner in which he grants victory, and also of sorcery (→ *seiðr*). Most of the reasons for these accusations, apart from the incest and sorcery, are unknown to us. B. d. Wieden pointed out that such a large lacuna in the extant sources is improbable, and that we ought to consider Loki's imputations as libellous, just as the Medieval public would have done.

However, a number of his accusations are known from other mythological tales: Týr has only got one arm because he lost the other whilst fettering the Fenris wolf (cf. *Gylfaginning* 24), and Freyr will be without a weapon at Ragnarǫk as the result of the loss of his sword (cf. *Gylfaginning* 50), whereas Heimdall must stand on guard for ever (cf. *Grímnismál* 13, *Gylfaginning* 26). Thor has to suffer hunger because he is unable to untie his rucksack which has been tied up by a giant; he has slept in a giant's mitten (cf. *Gylfaginning* 44), and will be conquered by the Fenris wolf at Ragnarǫk. Of these accusations, only the last seems to us to be incorrect, because, according to *Vǫluspá*, it is Odin who fights with Fenrir. The other charges are known at least from Snorri's *Gylfaginning*. – The position of the *Lokasenna* to the myth of Baldr is difficult to judge. It is frequently assumed that *Lokasenna* presumes Baldr's death (caused by Loki) as having already occurred, which furthermore explains → Loki's punishment at the end of *Lokasenna*. The lay itself, however, only says that Loki prevented Baldr from coming, perhaps because he could not have said anything evil about him. The punishment seems here to be the revenge for the libel.

As is true of other Eddic lays, the composition date of the *Lokasenna* is disputed. One fact in favour of a composition still in heathen times is that a Christian author would surely have staged a disparagement of the gods somewhat differently and that satirical speeches are also known between gods of Indian mythology. An early composition cannot be concluded from a supposed belief in Thor (de Boor), since Thor, even if he finally forces Loki to withdraw, does not come off any better from Loki's accusations than the other gods. The idea that such times 'hold nothing holy' and that for this reason a caricature of the gods was only possible at that time speaks in favour of b. d. Wieden's hypothesis that *Lokasenna* was composed in the heathen-Christian transition period of the 10th century. More likely is an even later composition, namely in the 12th century, since the system of a northern Pantheon as found in *Lokasenna* is closer to Snorri's ideas than to living beliefs. Schröder has gone even further and indicates possible Classical models for this, in particular the symposium of the gods at in Menippos, Seneca and Lucian. Such models, however, would be inconceivable before the 12th century. The language of the Lokasenna seems to point towards a later composition date (Kuhn), as do various allusions to other mythological tales, of which the author of Lokasenna must have known a lost lay about Thor and Skrýmir and probably also *Vǫluspá* as well as *Skírnismál.*

ED: G. Neckel, H. Kuhn, *Edda*, Heidelberg S05T1983.

LIT: A. Edzardi, 'Zur Lokasenna' (*Germania* 23) 1878; M. Hirschfeld, 'Untersuchungen zur Lokasenna', Berlin 1889; F. Niedner, 'Bemerkungen zu den Eddaliedern, 3. Lokasenna' (*ZfdA* 36) 1892; A. G. v. Hamel, 'The Prose-Frame of Lokasenna' (*Neophilologus* 14) 1929; H. de Boor, 'Die religiöse Sprache der Vǫluspá' (*Deutsche Islandforschung* 1) 1930; J. de Vries, *The Problem of Loki*, Helsinki 1933; F. R. Schröder, 'Das Symposium der Lokasenna' (*ANF* 76) 1952; H. b. d. Wieden, 'Einige Bemerkungen zum religionsgeschichtlichen Ort der Lokasenna' (*ZfdPh* 83) 1964; J. de Vries, *Altnordische Literaturgeschichte*, Berlin ²1967; A. Holtsmark, 'Lokasenna' (*KLNM* 10) 1965; G. W. Weber, 'Lokasenna' (*KLL* 4) 1968; P. N. Andersen, 'Form and Contents in Lokasenna: a Re-evaluation' (*Edda* 81) 1981; C. J. Clover, 'Lokasenna' (*DicMA* 7) 1986; R. Simek/H. Pálsson, *Lexikon der altnordischen Literatur*, Stuttgart 1987; B. Söderberg, 'Lokasenna – egenheter och ålder'. (*ANF* 102) 1987; J. McKinnell, 'Motivation in Lokasenna' (*Saga-Book* 22) 1987–88.

R: (fine art) C. Hansen, *Ægirs Gaestebud* (painting, 1857).
(literature) A. Oehlenschläger, *Ægirs Gjaestebud* (poem in *Nordens guder*, 1819); A. Strindberg, *Lokes smädelser* (poem, 1883).

Loki (ON). The god with the most different facets, but also the most negative character among the Germanic gods. He is the father of the god's enemies: the Midgard serpent, the Fenris wolf and of Hel, but equally it is he who helps the gods out of difficult situations. The sources which refer to him are numerous and ambiguous. Indeed they are just as varied as the interpretations of his person.

1. The sources.

(a) Loki, Þjazi and the abduction of Idun: Þjóðólfr ór Hvíni's poem *Haustlǫng* from the 9th century is the first source to record Loki's role in the myth of → Þjazi, but Snorri deals with the same material in his Prose *Edda* (*Skáldskaparmál* 1). In contrast to the more usual picture of Loki, in kennings used in the → *Haustlǫng*, he is called 'Odin's friend, Hœgni's friend, Thor's friend'. His role in the myth of Þjazi is altogether more positive than elsewhere: it is not malice, but his quick temper that makes him hand over Idun to Þjazi, and he makes himself useful to the Æsir both in helping to rescue her as well as in his role as jester in the subsequent myth about → Skaði.

(b) Loki and the construction of Asgard, the birth of Sleipnir: Loki's role in the building of → Asgard (*Gylfaginning* 52) can hardly be called negative, either. Not only does he evolve a plan for the Æsir, but he is also not averse to distracting the giant stallion Svaðilfari in what is for him an ignominious way, by turning himself into a mare. The outcome of this is the birth of the stallion → Sleipnir. Both *Vǫluspá* as well as *Hyndluljóð* 40 allude to this mythological tale.

(c) Loki and Thor: In the mythological tales which deal with Thor's journey to the land of the giants, there are no perjorative insinuations about Loki, and instead Loki has the occasionally humorous role of a servant, as is appropriate for the burlesque-like mode of this tale. – The fragmentary poem → *Þórsdrápa*, written at the end of the 10th century by the Icelandic skald Eilífr Góðrúnarson, records Thor's journey to → Geirrǫðargarð, a journey which was made necessary by Loki. The situation brought about by Loki releases Thor's strength, which reminds us of the → *Lokasenna* where Loki himself becomes Thor's opponent. The → *Þrymskviða* gives an account of the retrieval of Thor's stolen hammer, Mjǫllnir, in which Thor disguises himself as Freyja and Loki as a serving maid. Thus, in the *Þrymskviða*, too, Loki is more useful than malevolent for the Æsir. – Only Snorri (*Gylfaginning* 45) tells of the journey to the giant → Utgarðaloki, during which Loki competes against one of the giants, → Logi, in an eating competition and loses, just as Thor does in the drinking competition. – *Hymiskviða* 37 initially blames Loki for the laming of one of Thor's goats, but the following stanza (as in Snorri's version) then explains the incident in a way which shows that Loki had nothing to do with it.

(d) Loki and the jewels of the gods: Snorri explains various kennings in *Skáldskaparmál* 33 and imbeds these explanations in a tale in which Loki cuts off → Sif's hair. As compensation for this Loki procures golden hair for Sif at the gods' command, the spear Gungnir for Odin and Skíðblaðnir for Freyr. The dwarf Brokkr competes with him by making the ring Draupnir for Odin, the boar Gullinborsti for Freyr and the hammer Mjǫllnir for Thor, and wins the competition. Admittedly, Loki does not lose his head, but the dwarf is allowed to sew up his mouth, a clear allusion to Loki's malicious tongue. In this tale, too, Loki's ambivalent function is obvious since, despite his undeniably evil intentions, he nonetheless acquires the valuables for the Æsir. It is this function in particular which indicates, just as with the fishing net motif in the account of → Loki's punishment, that originally Loki had the role of a culture hero and only in the course of time did he increasingly become the antagonist of the gods.

(e) We know extremely little about Loki as the thief of → Brísingamen. In *Skáldskaparmál* 8 Snorri speaks of a battle between Heimdall and Loki over Brísingamen, in which both gods take on the shapes of seals. He quotes Ulfr Uggason's *Húsdrápa* (c.980 A.D.), one of whose extant stanzas does indeed speak of a battle between Heimdall and Loki in an extremely dark way, without however referring to the seal-shape and the Brísingamen. Otherwise, only *Sǫrla þáttr* ('Tale of Sǫrli') in the Icelandic *Flateyjarbók* (from the late 14th century) gives an account of Loki's theft of a jewel belonging to Freyja, but there is no mention of Heimdall. In kennings given by Snorri (*Skáldskaparmál* 16), as well as in *Haustlǫng*, Loki is called the 'thief of Brísingamen or else Brising's girdle'. It is uncertain whether there is a connexion between this and the battle between Heimdall and Loki, for they both oppose each other at Ragnarǫk.

(f) The tale of Loki and → Andvari belongs more to the area of mythologizing heroic poetry than to mythology proper. In *Reginsmál* 1–9 and *Skáldskaparmál* 37 the divine triad Odin, Loki and Hœnir appear. The golden treasure, whose origins are told here in a mythologizing way, is that of the Nibelung legend.

(g) In the myth of → Baldr's death, which is the result of Loki's urging although it occurs at the hand of the blind god Hǫðr, Loki shows himself to be a true enemy of the gods. It is also he who prevents Baldr from returning from the realm of the dead when, in the shape of a giantess, he refuses to weep for Baldr, the only thing in the whole world not to do so, and therefore the requirement laid down by Hel for Baldr's return is not fulfilled. This tale is told in detail by Snorri (*Gylfaginning* 48), and there are references to it in *Vǫluspá* 33–35 and *Skáldskaparmál* 16.

(h) Loki does not take the side of the Æsir at Ragnarǫk. *Vǫluspá* 51 tells that he is at the helm of the ship → Naglfar and moves into battle against the Æsir leading the army of monsters (which he has fathered) and the inhabitants of Hel (*Gylfaginning* 50). Loki fights against Heimdall and they kill each other.

(i) In the *Snorra Edda* (*Gylfaginning* 32) Loki and his family are introduced. The good-looking, but evil and wily god Loki is the son of the giant Farbauti. His mother is called Laufey or Nal, and his brothers are Byleistr and Helblindi. Loki's wife is called Sigyn, and one son is called Nari or Narfi. The prose framework to the *Lokasenna* names Vali as his son. Loki has three offspring with the giantess Angrboða, namely the Fenris wolf, the Midgard serpent and Hel. However, Loki does not only father children; in the shape of a mare, Loki gives birth to → Sleipnir, whose father is the stallion Svaðilfari, and a not more closely defined reproach is that Loki has also borne children himself in the shape of a woman referred to in *Lokasenna* 23, 33 and *Hyndluljóð* 41. The details of Loki's genealogy found in the *Flateyjarbók* (in *Sǫrla þáttr* 2) at the end of the 14th century are the same as given above and possibly go back to Snorri. The age of this genealogy is apparent from the names which are partly difficult to interpret.

(j) In the *Snorra Edda* (*Gylfaginning* 19, 32) Loki is also called Loptr, a name which could be interpreted as 'the airy one', but also as 'the lightening one', but neither suit Loki particularly well. Another name for Loki could be Loðurr, since the latter name is given to the god who is referred to alongside Hœnir and Odin in *Vǫluspá* 18, just as Loki is in *Haustlǫng* and in *Skáldskaparmál* 1. However, the fallacy of this hypothesis is that → Loðurr's role in *Vǫluspá* is hardly appropriate for Loki. A consideration of the etymology does not help to show a connexion between both names, either. The etymology of the name Loki has not been solved yet. It is possibly an abbreviation for Loptr or Loðurr, but it could equally well be related to ON *lúka* 'close', and as such would allude to Loki's role at Ragnarǫk. Attempts have been made which try to link Loki with the Franconian runic name → *logaþore* inscribed on the → Nordendorf fibula, but these are purely speculative. This link is extremely uncertain especially since the sources referring to Loki are limited exclusively to the northern Germanic regions.

2. The interpretations.

Loki is a god without a function. There was no cult of Loki, and place-names based on his name are equally unknown. Consequently, we must rely totally on the sources given above for information about Loki and otherwise can only draw upon non-Germanic parallels showing divine figures with similar behavioural patterns. Scholars since Grimm have attempted time and again to give Loki a function and hence he has been considered as a god of fire. This is a misinterpretation caused by the similarity of names with the giant → Logi, the personification of fire. Loki, however, has nothing to do with German *Lohe* 'blaze, flame'. Much and Gras wanted to establish an aquatic nature for Loki as the thief of fire, drawing upon his shape-changes into a seal and a salmon to do so. There has been no interpretation of Loki as yet which manages to include all of the aspects of his character as shown in the various tales. Loki is not simply the demonic being, the destructive person, whom Bugge saw as a reflection of the Christian Lucifer. Comparing him with Hermes of Greek mythology or even with the Celtic god Briciu, weakens his position and makes him the malicious, foolish, loquacious servant of the gods. It is an oversimplification to see Loki as a pure alter ego of Odin, as a personification of Odin's dark side, merely because of his closeness to Odin whose blood-brother he is said to be in *Lokasenna* (F. Ström). De Vries is somewhat fairer to his multi-faceted character when he sees him as the 'trickster' of archaic religions, who undertook the double function of culture-hero and deceiver. Dumézil has succeeded in finding a parallel for Loki in Syrdon, a mythological figure in Caucasian Ossetians. Although the Ossetians are descendants of the Scythians and accordingly are Indo-European, this kind of parallelism remains open. → Loki's punishment has led to comparisons with the Caucasian giant Amiran (Olrik) and with Prometheus. It is even possible that south-eastern concepts were superimposed onto Nordic concepts. Despite Closs' objections Amiran and Prometheus are not only both outstandingly intelligent but also have their rebellious nature in common. However, it is quite certain that both also had an original position as cult-heroes. The psychological interpretation sees Loki (since Dumézil) as the representative of an 'impulsive intelligence' linked with an unruly urge for activity and malignant attitude (de Vries).

K. Weinhold, 'Die Sagen von Loki' (*ZfdA* 7) 1849; J. Grimm, *Deutsche Mythologie*, Berlin [4]1875–78; K. Müllenhoff, 'Frija und der Halsbandmythos' (*ZfdA* 30) 1886; S. Bugge, *Studien*, Munich 1898; K. Zacher, 'Loki und Typhon' (*ZfdPh* 30) 1898; A. Olrik, 'Loke i nyere folkeoverlevering 1–2' (*DS*) 1908, 1909; A. Olrik, 'Myterne om Loke' (*Festskrift Feilberg*) Copenhagen 1911; H. Celander, *Lokes mytiska ursprung*, Uppsala 1911; H. Grüner-Nielsen, 'Efterslaet til Lokemyterne' (*DS*) 1912; H. Celander, 'Loke-problemet' (*DS*) 1914; J. Loewenthal, 'Drei Götternamen' (*ANF* 31) 1915; E. Mogk, *Lokis Anteil an Balders Tod*, Helsinki 1925; E. J. Gras, *De noordse Loki-ythen in hun onderling verband*, Haarlem 1931; J. de Vries, *The Problem of Loki*, Helsinki 1933; W. Krogmann, 'Loki' (*APhSc* 12) 1937–38; W. Mohr, 'Mephistopheles und Loki' (*DVjS* 18) 1940; E. C. Polomé, 'Quelque notes à propos de l'enigmatique dieu scandinave Lóðurr' (*Revue Belge* 33) 1955; F. Ström, Loki, *Ein mythologisches Problem*, Göteborg 1956; J. de Vries, 'Loki . . . und kein Ende' (*Festschrift F. R. Schröder*) Heidelberg 1959; A. Closs, 'Loki und die germanische Frömmigkeit' (Kairos 2) 1960; A. B. Rooth, *Loki in Scandinavian Mythology*, Lund 1961; H. Sperber, 'Der Name Loki und die Wortfamilie von german. *lukan' (*Saga och Sed*) 1962; A. Holtsmark, 'Loki – en omstridt skikkelse i nordisk mytologi' (MoM) 1962; E. O. G. Turville-Petre, *Myth and Religion of the North*, London 1964; A. B. Rooth, 'Loke' (*KLNM* 10) 1965; U. Drobin, 'Myth and Epical Motifs in the Loki-Research' (*Temenos* 3) 1968; E. C. Polomé, 'Some Comments on Vǫluspá Stanzas 17–18' (*Old Norse Literature and Mythology*) Austin 1969; J. de Vries, *Altgermanische Religionsgeschichte*, Berlin [3]1970; Å. V. Ström, H. Biezais, *Germanische und baltische Religion*, Stuttgart 1975; J. P. Schjødt, 'Om Loke endnu engang' (*ANF* 96) 1981.

R: The various ideas given in folklore in which Loki occurs are interesting in helping to determine his position in folk-belief, although useless for an interpretation of Loki in mythology itself. Numerous references have been collected together in two essays by Olrik and in Dumézil's monograph. One which is of special interest is the Faroese ballad *Lokka-táttur* in which the triad Odin, Hœnir and Loki appear. In Iceland Loki can be found in various proverbs and idioms, among them 'there's a loki in it' referring to a caught thread and *lokabrenna* for the dog-days in high summer. In Norway Loki is linked with the kitchen fire and when the fire in the stove crackles, they say that 'Lokje is beating his children'; left-overs are thrown into the fire 'for Lokje'. One figure in folklore from Flanders, Lodder, has also been connected with Loki and attempts have been made to derive a strengthening of the assumed connexion between Loki and Loðurr from this.

(Lit.) As a result of his intangible nature, Loki is one of the Germanic gods who occurs most frequently in German literature. A. Oehlenschläger's trilogy about Baldr, *Baldur der Gute*, features Loki in an important role, and Loki appears in some of Oehlenschläger's poems in *Nordens Guder* (1819). F. de la Motte Fouqué's tragedy, *Baldur der Gute* (1818) also includes a plot concerning Loki, and R. Wagner took up the incorrect interpretation of Loki as the god of fire in his *Ring of the Nibelungen* cycle (from 1848). Loki poetry was frequently written around the turn of the century: A. Kayser-Langerhanns's tragedies, *Loki* (1899), and *Balder und Loki* (1891). L. Jacobowski's symbolistic novel, *Loki. Roman eines Gottes*; K. Weiser's drama, *Loki* (1901); and A. Strindberg: *Loke God* (1882).

Loki's punishment. This is told of in a short mythological tale related in most detail in *Gylfaginning* 49, and somewhat more breifly in the prose conclusion to → *Lokasenna*. Allusions to it are found in *Lokasenna* 49 and 50 as well as in *Vǫluspá* 35. At the end of his myth about Baldr in *Gylfaginning* Snorri says that Loki fled to a mountain after Baldr's murder and during the day he changed his shape into that of a salmon and stayed in the waterfall Frananger-fors. The Æsir were finally able to corner Loki by using Loki's own invention, the fishing net, and Thor caught him. The Æsir put Loki into a cave and fetched Loki's sons, Vali and Narfi. Vali was turned into a wolf who subsequently devoured Narfi, with whose intestines Loki was then tied to three stones. Skaði fastened a poisonous snake above Loki's head and the poison dripped onto him. Loki's wife Sigyn, however, held a bowl beneath the poison, but whenever the bowl was full, the poison fell on Loki who writhed so much from it that the earth itself quaked. This is what men call an earthquake. – The similarities between this tale and the legend of Prometheus are obvious, and the legends of the 'fettered giant', Elbrus, can be found especially in Caucasian regions. Although Olrik saw the origin of the Nordic version in Caucasia, Dumézil showed in particular the differences in the details of the fettering. Nonetheless, the common traits between the Nordic and the Greek motif cannot be totally ignored, since apart from the actual binding itself, Prometheus, like Loki, appears to have counted as one of the culture-heroes. This is indicated in Loki's case even in the tale of his punishment by the reference to his invention of the fishing net. Whether a depiction on the Gosforth cross in Northumberland from the 9th century does in fact show a picture of Loki in fetters and Sigyn is not absolutely certain.

A. Olrik, *Ragnarök*, Berlin 1922; J. de Vries, *The Problem of Loki*, Helsinki 1933; G. Dumézil, *Loki*, Darmstadt 1959.

Illustrations: J. de Vries, *Altgermanische Religionsgeschichte*, Berlin ³1970; *The Vikings in England*, London 1981.

Lóni (ON). A dwarf in *Vǫluspá* 13. Possibly 'the shining one' (Gering), or else 'the lazy one' (Gould).

H. Gering, *Kommentar* 1, Halle 1927; C. N. Gould, 'Dwarf-Names' (*PMLA* 44) 1929.

Loptr (ON) A name for → Loki (*Lokasenna* 2, *Hyndluljóð* 41, *Fjǫlsvinnsmál* 26; *Þórsdrápa* 1, *Haustlǫng* 8; *Gylfaginning* 32) which probably means 'the airy one, the god of the air' to ON *lopt* 'air'. The interpretation 'the tall one' (to *lypta*) is phonetically impossible, and the derivation from *lopt-eldr 'lightning', thus 'god of lightning' rests on the incorrect supposition that Loki is the god of fire. 'The one who sends lightning', however, would fit Thor far better than Loki.

A. Olrik, 'Myterne om Loke' (*Festskrift Feilberg*) Copenhagen 1911; J. de Vries, *The Problem of Loki*, Helsinki 1933; A. M. Sturtevant, 'Etymological Comments' (*PMLA* 67) 1952.

Lubicae. The name of → matrons. A votive stone (in Cologne, Germany) is dedicated to *Matronis Lubicis* (CIL XIII 8220). Gutenbrunner relates the name to Germanic **lubja-* 'healing remedy'. The Lubicae would therefore be 'healing goddesses'.

S. Gutenbrunner, *Die germanischen Götternamen*, Halle 1936; M. Schönfeld, *Wörterbuch der altgermanischen Personen- und Völkernamen*, Heidelberg [2]1965; H. Reichert, *Lexikon der altgermanischen Namen*, Vienna 1987–90.

lundr (ON, 'grove') → sacred grove.

lures (ON, *luðar*). Germanic musical instruments which were especially popular during the Bronze Age. Lures are wind instruments made of bronze, over 6 feet long, with a curved form, and are usually discovered in archaeological excavations in pairs. This is confirmed by depictions on rock carvings where lure players usually appear in twos. The lures appear to have been at least partly cult musical instruments, as suggested by the pictorial context shown on the rock carvings and also the depictions of the Kivik grave.

Lútr (ON, 'the bent, stooped one'). A giant who is named as one of the giants killed by Thor, in a stanza written by the skald Þórbjǫrn dísarskáld (10th century). We know nothing about him apart from this.

Lyfjaberg (ON, 'healing mountain'). The mountain on which Menglǫð lives in *Fjǫlsvinnsmál*, and to which the hero Svipdagr has to gain access despite it being guarded by a giant and surrounded by a wall of flames. According to *Fjǫlsvinnsmál* 36, the mountain takes its name from its capability of healing all the sick and the lame who climb it. However, it belongs more to the world of fairy-tales than to the world of Germanic mythology.

Lyngvi (ON, 'a place overgrown with heather'). The fictitious island in the lake Amsvartnir where, according to Snorri, the Æsir have chained up the wolf → Fenrir until Ragnarǫk (*Gylfaginning* 33). The name, which first appears in Snorri's version of the myth of Fenrir, suits the island well. In the *Þulur*, however, Lyngvi is incorrectly listed among the names of sea-kings, probably the result of a misunderstanding The name probably comes from a kenning which is no longer extant and was possibly also not fully understood in the Middle Ages.

Lýr (ON). A mythological hall in *Fjǫlsvinnsmál* 32. Lýr actually means 'pike', but the correct name of the hall would appear to have been Hýr 'the shining one' (as it is called in several manuscripts).

Lytir (Old Swedish). Possibly a Swedish god, whose name is mentioned in a text from the 14th century (at the end of *Oláfs saga Tryggvasonar* according to the version given in the *Flateyjarbók*) and which may be derived also from place-names such as Lytisbergh and Lytislund(a), recorded three times. Apart from the question as to the reliability of the saga and the strength of the evidence given by place-names, another question arises, namely, who could have been meant by this name. Strömbäck assumes that it was an abusive name which the Christian author of the saga used to designate the god Freyr (from *lýta* 'dirty, bespatter, besmirch'), but the very existence of cult place-names hardly confirms this. Other interpretations consider Lytir to be a nickname for Freyr, which means either 'god who decides over fate' (from Old Swedish *liuta* 'cast lots') or as an indication of Freyr's phallic character. But Lytir could also have been the name of a 'god of destiny' in his own right (Elmevik), since this function is otherwise not recorded as being one of Freyr's.

D. Strömbäck, 'Lytir – en fornsvensk gud?' (*Festschrift til F. Jónsson*) Copenhagen 1928; L. Elmevik, 'fsv. *lytir (*Lytir)' (*NoB* 54) 1966; J. de Vries, *Altgermanische Religionsgeschichte*, Berlin ³1970.

Magic. Man's attempt to make the supernatural subservient to himself, in which the belief in the causality of supernatural powers is a prerequisite. Magic should not be seen as a pre-religious phenomenon, since it frequently occurs alongside religious concepts. Magic (roughly the same as sorcery) does not only include the mentality, but also the practices with which the mechanisms of supernatural powers are set into motion.

Snorri gives us a good insight of what he understood magic to be in the Scandinavian Middle Ages when he speaks of Odin as the master of magic (*Ynglinga saga* 7): 'Odin ruled and practised the art which is the most powerful of all and is called *seiðr* ("magic, sorcery"), and by this means he knew the fate of men and the dangers of the future, as well as how to bring death upon a man, or bring bad luck or cause illness, and how to rob man of power and understanding and give it to someone else. But so much disgrace was associated with this wisdom that men believed that they could not practise it without disgrace, and so they taught this art to the priestesses.'

From this list it is clear that we have to distinguish between two kinds of magic, namely white magic, to which prophecy belongs, and black magic which consisted of harmful sorcery (Strömbäck).

Apart from prophecy of the future, as practised by the Germanic → seeresses, fertility and weather magic also belonged to white magic although these latter two are rarely mentioned in Old Norse sources, but were probably important in runic magic. Healing magic, as manifested in the wearing of → amulets, as well as in the still extant charms was also ranked under white magic, whereas love magic appears to have counted as black magic and to have been considered to be an extremely disgraceful practice. It is, for example, only Skírnir's threat of resorting to magic which finally persuades Gerðr to marry Freyr after Skírnir has been unsuccessful in his wooing of this giantess in the *Skírnismál*, and Odin is sent into exile because of the disgrace of gaining Rinda by using sorcery (→ Odin's exile).

The victory runes which are frequently carved into weapons in order to bring about victory in battle are thought to be on the border between white and black magic. The often named Týr rune was obviously considered to be a victory rune.

The sagas repeatedly tell of certain practices of black magic, of harmful sorcery (ON *seiðr* or *gandr*), although it is admittedly extremely questionable how much really can be traced back to heathen magical rites. One frequently recorded practice was the carving of runes into bits of wood, which was supposed to have a significance in harmful magic (*Grettis saga* 79) as well as in → death magic. Runes were less used for their magical importance as letters composing individual words, but rather as concepts. Thus, the repetition of certain concept runes (such as th = *þurs* 'giant', n = *nauð* 'plight') were supposed to emphasize the message. Another form of black magic was the setting up of a → *niðstǫng* or else a → *trénið*. Originally this could have been the setting up of wooden poles with carved human faces in order to curse particular people, in which the intention was probably less to curse than to mock the person (*Gisla saga* 2). On the other hand, the setting up of a *níðstǫng* with a horse's skull on top of it and carved runes recorded in the *Egils saga* 57 should be considered to have clear magical significance. A parallel to this can be found in Saxo (*Gesta Danorum* V, 134) where a pole with a horse's head on it was supposed to scare off a hostile army.

Wherever magic is expressly referred to in Old Norse literature it is said to be disgraceful. We know from the extract cited at the beginning of this article that magic was obviously not compatible with the male code of honour and was pushed off onto women who are repeatedly referred to as sorceresses (*seiðkonur*). Another remark of Snorri's should also be mentioned here, namely that it was Freyja who first brought → *seiðr* from the Vanir to the Æsir (*Ynglinga saga* 4). The term sorcerer (ON *seiðmaðr*) was considered to be an insult, and *finnr* 'Finn' had almost the same perjorative meaning as the Finns were considered to be particularly well versed in magic. The theory that the origin of northern magic came from the Finns is nowadays generally rejected, and it would seem that Scandinavian *seiðr* was a form of shamanistic practice inherited from an archaic cultural level and could occur in different peoples totally independently.

H. Gering, *Über Weissagung und Zauber*, Kiel 1902; K. Jarausch, 'Der Zauber in den Isländersagas' (*Zeitschrift für Volkskunde* 39) 1930; F. Ohrt, 'Eddica og Magica' (*APhSc* 9) 1934/35; D. Strömbäch, *Sejd*, Stockholm 1935; A. Ohlmarks, 'Arktischer Schamanismus und altnord. seiðr' (*ARW* 36) 1939; E. Kiessling, *Zauberei in den germanischen Volksrechten*, Jena 1941; D. Strömbäck, 'Sejd' (*KLNM* 15) 1970; J. de Vries, *Altgermanische Religionsgeschichte*, Berlin [3]1970; H. R. Ellis Davidson, 'Hostile Magic' (*The Witch Figure. Studies K. M. Briggs*) London 1973.

Magni (ON, 'the strong one'). The son of the god Thor and the giantess Járnsaxa (*Skáldskaparmál* 17). In *Vafþrúðnismál* 15 Thor's sons Magni and Móði are named as the heirs of the hammer Mjǫllnir after Ragnarök, and in *Hárbarðsljóð* 9 and 53 Thor calls himself 'the father of Magni'. In the *Þórsdrápa* written in the 10th century by Eilífr the skald, Magni is called Thor's son. Thus, Magni was well known in the late heathen era. However, it seems that it was Snorri who added Járnsaxa as his mother.

In his story of Thor's fight against the giant Hrungnir Snorri included a short anecdote about Magni. When Thor kills Hrungnir, the giant falls so that one of his feet comes to lie over Thor and neither Þjalfi nor one of the Æsir is able to free him from it. 'Then Magni, Thor's and Járnsaxa's son, came on the scene; he was only three years old at the time; he threw Hrungnir's leg off Thor and said: "It is a shame, father, that I came so late; I think I would have been able to kill this giant with my fist if I had run into him," whereupon Thor got up and greeted his son in a friendly manner, saying that he would one day be strong – "and I want to give you the horse Gullfaxi which used to belong to Hrungnir". Then Odin spoke and considered that Thor was making a mistake to give the valuable horse to the giant's son and not to his father.' (*Skáldskaparmál* 17).

In this tale it is clearer than usual that Magni, like Thor's other children Móði and Þrúðr, is nothing but a personification of Thor's characteristics. Thus, Magni is Thor's embodied strength. The elevation of Magni as Thor's strength to a mythological person in his own right took place in the late heathen period when Thor became the main representative of the re-awakened interest in heathendom in its struggle against the encroachment of Christianity.

R: K. Ehrenberg, Odin, Thor and Magni (drawing, 1883).

Magusanus → Hercules Magusanus.

Mah(a)linehae. Name of some → matrons. Two votive stones from the area around Cologne, Germany are dedicated to the *matronis Mahlinehis*, and another from Deutz (CIL XIII 8492) seems to mention Mah(a)linehae as well as other deities. The Mah(a)linehae either belong to the place-name Mecheln or else to Germanic **mahl-*, **mahal* 'place of justice', and as such would be goddesses of the court or the Thing.

S. Gutenbrunner, *Die germanischen Götternamen*, Halle 1936; M. Schönfeld, *Wörterbuch der altgermanischen Personen- und Völkernamen*, Heidelberg [2]1965; H. Reichert, *Lexikon der altgermanischen Namen*, Vienna 1987–90.

Maitienae → Naitienae.

Manheimr or Mannheimr (ON, 'world of man'). The home of Skaði and Njǫrðr according to Snorri in *Ynglinga saga* 8 where he cites *Ynglingatal* 2. Elsewhere, however, Þruðheimr is said to be Skaði's home. Consequently, Snorri says that Manheimr is a name for Sweden, and Goðheimr the name for Greater Sweden (i.e. Scythia).

Manheimr is also named in Eyvind's *Háleygjatál* 3, and there it means the world of men as opposed to the world of the gods. In Snorri's euhemeristic description Manheimr = Sweden stands for the land where the mythical past goes over into the human historical past, and as such Goðheimr is the mythical land where he places the earthly Asgard from whence the gods come.

A. Y. Gurevich, 'Space and Time' (*Medieval Scandinavica* 2) 1969.

Máni (ON, 'moon'). Máni only appears in *Vafþrúðnismál* 23 and in Snorri (*Gylfaginning* 10) as a personified mythological figure, as well as in two skaldic kennings in which Máni is apparently a gigantic being in a myth of which we otherwise know nothing.

In *Vafþrúðnismál* and Snorri, Mundilfari is Máni's father and his sister is Sol. Only Snorri tells of how both the moon and the sun are drawn by horses across the sky. Just as the sun is pursued by a wolf, so Máni is pursued by Hati, who will catch him at Ragnarǫk and devour him. This is why the wolf is also called Mánagarmr 'devourer of Máni' (only in Snorri, *Gylfaginning* 11).

In connexion with this, Snorri tells a short fairy-tale about the picture in the moon: 'Máni steers the way of the moon and determines its waxing and waning. Once he took two children from earth, Bil and Hjúki, when they were coming from the spring Byrgir, and were carrying the bushel Sægr and the pole Simul on their shoulders. Viðfinnr is their father's name. These children follow the moon, as can be seen from the earth.' The names in this tale might be inventions of Snorri's, but their meaning is not quite as obvious as usual in such cases, which suggests that he may have taken them from a folk-tale.

The form of the tale of the man in the moon (a man with a pole and a woman with a bushel) as found in Snorri is also found in modern folklore in Scandinavia, England and North Germany.

The *Vǫluspá* 6, which does not contain the myth about Máni and Mundilfari etc., tells of the moon which the Æsir had set up 'in order to be able to reckon the year'. In fact Germanic computation is directed towards the moon and not towards the sun, and even shorter periods of time were given in nights and not in days.

S. Baring-Gould, *Curious Myths of the Middle Ages*, London 1884; R. Beitl, *Deutsches Volkstum der Gegenwart*, 1933; A. Holtsmark, 'Mane' (*KLNM* 12) 1967.

Mannus. The son of the mythical ancestor of the Germanic peoples, Tuisto, according to Tacitus (*Germania* 2). Mannus himself had three sons who gave their names to the Germanic tribes of the Ingaevones, Herminones and the Istaevones. The structure of this mythical genealogy (Tuisto-Mannus-3 sons) is also found in the cosmogeny of the *Edda* where Buri-Borr-Odin/Vili/Vé are said to be the ancestors of all the other gods.

Mannus corresponds to the progenitor Mánus (*manu* 'man') in the Old Indian myth of creation. The → myth of descendancy of Mannus would appear to be traceable back to Indo-Germanic times.

R: in J. E. Schlegel's play *Hermann* (1743) there is a stage direction for a 'Grove with the pictures of Thuiskon and Mannus'.

Mardǫll (ON). A name for the goddess Freyja which Snorri lists (*Gylfaginning* 34) and which occurs several times in skaldic poetry in kennings for 'gold'. The meaning of the name is not quite clear; perhaps Mannus is 'the one who illuminates the sea' (cf. Heimdallr), or else 'the one who makes the sea swell' (from *þǫll*)?

Margerðr (ON, 'sea-Gerðr'). A giantess in the *Þulur*.

Mars. The Roman god of war Mars corresponds in the *interpretatio germanica* to the Germanic god *Tīwaz (ON Týr, OHG Zîo). This can be seen quite clearly in the translation of *dies martis* by Anglo-Saxon *tīwesdæg* (Engl. Tuesday), OHG *ziestag*, ON *týsdagr*. In *Germania* 9,2, Tacitus names Mars as ranking in third place among the Germanic gods, after Mercury and Hercules, and elsewhere also includes him as being one of the gods worshipped by the Germanic peoples. The frequently quoted passage from Jordanes (*Getica* V, 41) that the Goths worship Mars as their ancestor and bring him blood sacrifice, would appear to rest on the transfer of the Thracian and Getian god Mars/Ares onto the Goths and therefore is of little importance.

It is not clear exactly why Mars was compared to Zîo/Týr. Zîo/Týr was the old Germanic god of the sky which also agrees with the linguistic correlation with Greek Zeus, Latin Jupiter. However, Mars was a god of war and no more a god of the sky than his Greek counterpart Ares. The only indication for the identification of Týr as a possible god of war is found in Snorri, who, writing in the 13th century (*Gylfaginning* 24) talks about the Æsir god Týr as follows: 'He is the boldest and bravest, and he has power over victory in battle. It is good for heroes to call upon his help.' However, as we can assume that Snorri was only too aware of the old identification of Týr and Mars as being one and the same, this evidence must be ignored, even more so since there is no further confirmation of Týr having this function in the myths. The most likely comparative possibility is given in the epithet → Mars Thingsus on a votive stone from the 3rd century which suggests that the god being called upon was the god of the Germanic Thing-council.

Another epithet for the Germanic version of Mars (= *Tīwaz) on votive stones is → Mars Halamarðus.

J. de Vries, *Altgermanische Religionsgeschichte*, Berlin [3]1970; N. Wagner, 'Der Mars der Goten' (*Volkskultur und Geschichte. Festschrift Dünninger*) Berlin 1970; O. Höfler, 'Mars Thingsus' (*Handwörterbuch zur deutschen Rechtsgeschichte*, Fasc.18) 1979.

Mars Halamarðus. A votive inscription from Horn near Roermond/Holland, which probably dates from the 1st century A.D., bears the inscription: *Marti Halamarðo sacrum* . . . The interpretation for this epithet of the Germanic Mars (= *Tīwaz) 'the murderer of men', suggested by Grienberger, explains this god as being a god of war. The etymology is however far from convincing and the evidence for Zîo/Týr does not indicate a god of war (→ Mars).

S. Gutenbrunner, *Die germanischen Götternamen*, Halle 1936; J. de Vries, *Altgermanische Religionsgeschichte*, Berlin [3]1970.

Mars Thingsus. In the 3rd century A.D. a votive altar was set up by Frisian legionaries stationed at Housesteads on Hadrian's Wall (N. England) which bears the inscription *Deo Marti Thingso Et Duabus Alaisiagis Bede Et Fimmilene.* The epithet Thingsus renders Gmc **þingsaz* and is most convincingly related to Langobardian *thinx* 'legal council', *gerthinx* 'Gerthing', ON *þing* 'meeting', and as such the god should be understood as the god of the Thing, the formal meeting. It is unclear whether **þingsaz* should be understood as an epithet for Mars, whose name is rendered in the translation of the Latin week-day name *dies martis* as Gmc Tīwaz (OHG Zîo, ON Týr), or else if **þingsaz* is a name of a god of law in his own right. It is also not certain whether the word Thing or else this god **þingsaz* survives in the German week-day name for Tuesday, *Dienstag* (Middle Low German *dingesdach*, Middle Dutch *dingsdach*). As other week-day names, Wednesday, Thursday and Friday, are all derived from the names of gods, the latter possibility would appear probable. De Vries, however, has pointed out that German *Dienstag* could possibly be a mere variant of original *diestag* which would, like English Tuesday, be derived from *Tīwaz.

K. v. See's arguments against Thingsus being a god of the Thing (and in favour of Thingsus as a god of the weather or of time) are etymologically less likely than the link with the Thing and rest predominantly on his polemic rejection of the sanctity of the Thing, for which Höfler, however, has brought convincing evidence. – The Danish place-name Tislund, which was itself a site of a Thing, speaks in favour of Thingsus as the god of the Thing; v. See considered the relatively infrequent occurrence of this place-name as indicating that the usage is coincidental. The other goddesses who are named on the inscription with Mars Thingsus and who are otherwise unkown, → Beda (2) and → Fimmilene, have also been most convincingly associated with Old Frisian legal terms: the fact that Mars Thingsus should appear on an inscription together with them also strengthens the argument in favour of him being the god of the Thing.

W. Scherer, 'Mars Thingsus' (*Sitzungsberichte der Akademie der Wissenschaften, Berlin*, Phil.-hist. Kl.) 1884; K. Weinhold, 'Tius Things' (*ZfdPh* 21) 1889; S. Gutenbrunner, *Die Germanischen Götternamen*, Halle 1936; K. von See, *Altnordische Rechtswörter*, Tübingen 1964; J. de Vries, *Altgermanische Religionsgeschichte*, Berlin [3]1970; H. Birkhan, *Germanen und Kelten*, Vienna 1972; O. Höfler, ' "Sakraltheorie" und "Profantheorie" in der Altertumskunde' (*Festschrift Gutenbrunner*) Heidelberg 1972; K. von See, *Kontinuitätstheorie und Sakraltheorie in der Germanenforschung*, Frankfurt 1972; G. Dumézil, *Gods of the Ancient Northmen*, Berkeley 1977; O. Höfler, 'Mars Thingsus' (*Handwörterbuch zur deutschen Rechtsgeschichte*, Fasc.18) 1979.

Marsacae. Name of → matrons. Two Roman votive stones from Xanten, Germany are dedicated to these matrons. The name is probably related to the tribal name of the Marsaci, which means that they were probably Germanic despite the Celtic formation of the name.

S. Gutenbrunner, *Die germanischen Götternamen*, Halle 1936; H. Reichert, *Lexikon der altgermanischen Namen*, Vienna 1987–90.

Masanae. Name of → matrons. A votive stone from Cologne, Germany (CIL XIII 8223) is dedicated to the *matribus masanabus*; the interpretation is uncertain.

S. Gutenbrunner, *Die germanischen Götternamen*, Halle 1936; H. Reichert, *Lexikon der altgermanischen Namen*, Vienna 1987–90.

Mathamod. Name of a god on a Roman votive stone from Masculula near Tunis (CIL VIII 15779) which should most likely be considered Germanic for linguistic reasons. Both elements of the name are frequently found in Germanic names, *Matha-* e.g. in Gothic Maþasuinþa, OHG Mathfrid, Anglo-Saxon Mathilda, *-mod* in ON Hermóðr. How the god's name came to Tunisia is a completely different question. As Birkhan suggests, we will probably have to assume a colony founded by Germanic veterans of the Roman army.

S. Gutenbrunner, *Die germanischen Götternamen*, Halle 1936; M. Schönfeld, *Wörterbuch der altgermanischen Personen- und Völkernamen*, Heidelberg [2]1965; H. Birkhan, *Germanen und Kelten*, Vienna 1972; H. Reichert, *Lexikon der altgermanischen Namen*, Vienna 1987–90.

Matres → Matrons. Cf. the following Matres: Annaneptiae; Atlaterv(i)ae; Aufaniae; Aumenahenae; Euthungae; Frisavae; Marsacae; Masanae; Suleviae.

Matres Germanae ('the Germanic mothers'). On the inscriptions on two Roman votive stones instead of finding the names of the *matres* worshipped, we find only their 'nationality'. This is the case on the Cologne inscription dedicated to the *[M]atribus meis [Ger]manis Suebis* (CIL XIII 12 067), and the inscription from Winchester, England (VIL VII 5) which is even dedicated to the *Matrib[us] Ital[is] Germanis Gal[lis] Brit[tis]*.

S. Gutenbrunner, *Die germanischen Götternamen*, Halle 1936; H. Reichert, *Lexikon der altgermanischen Namen*, Vienna 1987–90.

Matriarchal society. The form of society in which inheritance runs via the maternal side of the family and which also shows other matriarchal tendencies. It has been assumed for the pre-Germanic West European megalithic culture, without this theory being proved. According to the same theory, the Vanir's freedom to have incest (*Ynglinga saga* 4) reflects matriarchal conditions: the → Vanir war against the Æsir is the conflict between the patriarchal Æsir and the matriarchal Vanir. All this, however, cannot be proved, but would explain traits of proto-Germanic society, such as certain aspects of inheritance law.

Matrons (Lat. *matronae*, also *matres* and *matrae* 'mothers'). Mother-goddesses to whom votive stones and altars were set up between the 1st and 5th centuries A.D. Of more than 1100 inscriptions currently known half give Germanic → matron names. The → matron cult is not an exclusively Germanic phenomenon, but is also strongly evident in Celtic areas. The fact that the extant votive monuments are to be found exclusively in areas occupied by the Roman army, i.e. on the western bank of the Rhine, does not mean that there was no cult on the other side of the Rhine. It was the syncretism with Celtic concepts and the possibilities offered by literacy, adopted from the Romans, which allowed the setting up of the monuments to the matron cult which we still have today.

The illustrations of the matrons on the votive stones show the matrons almost exclusively in groups of three. The various modes of dress show that not only married women (recognisable by their headdresses), but also girls with loosened hair (*discriminale*) could be worshipped as matrons.

The functional aspects of the matrons, namely protection of the family, of fertility, of childbirth, sometimes also as war-goddesses, seem to correspond to the → *dísir* documented later for northern Germanic areas. There is evidence of the existence of a *dísir*-cult, beings who are possibly identical with the Idisi (mythological female beings in the First Merseburg Charm) of the southern Germanic region.

S. Gutenbrunner, *Die germanischen Götternamen*, Halle 1936; E. A Philippson, 'Mütter- und Matronenkult am Niederrhein' (*Germanic Review* 19) 1944; J. de Vries, *Altgermanische Religionsgeschichte*, Berlin [3]1970; R. L. M. Derolez, *Götter und Mythen der Germanen*, Wiesbaden 1974.

Matron cult. The worshipping of matrons (*matronae*, also *matres* and *matrae*) is a phenomenon which, apart from a minor distribution elsewhere, is basically limited to upper Italy as well as the occupied parts of Germania and eastern Gaul during the Roman Empire. Our sole source of information about the matron cult comes from inscriptions on votive stones and votive altars of which over 1100 are known up to now; of these, over half the matrons bear Germanic names. The Germanic cult of matrons is not limited to the tribal area of the Ubians, who moved to the western bank of the Lower Rhine in 38 A.D., but it is in this area where there are most finds and there are indications of numerous single individual cult centres here. The monuments of the Germanic matron cult were set up by adherents to the cult, in particular by Germanic legionaries in the Roman army, and reach as far as the borders of the empire in Scotland, Frisia, southern Spain, and also via the imperial guards even to Rome.

It is difficult to ascertain the origins of the matron cult in the Roman religion of imperial times as there is no exactly corresponding counterpart, and the origin more probably comes from Gallic matrons, upon which the other half of the extant monuments to the matron cult fall. Nonetheless, the basis of the specific Lower Rhine form of a matron cult undoubtedly rests on native-Germanic concepts of belief, such as are reflected in important later sources, namely the belief in the *dísir*, and perhaps also the belief in valkyries. On the other hand, the Germanic- Celtic-Roman mixed culture of the Lower Rhine in the first century A.D. must be accepted as the catalyst for the creation of the belief in protective mother deities, aided by the influence of literacy through the Roman troops. We have to rely exclusively on a great number of votive inscriptions as sources for our information on the matron cult, as the classical authors are silent about this aspect of Germanic belief. This may be because they saw the cult of the matrons as a religious syncretism, a consideration which would have run contrary especially to Tacitus' intentions in his description of Germanic life and beliefs.

In the cult of the matrons the terms occurring for the mother-deities are, apart from *matronae*, the terms *matres* and **matrae* (from the Dative *matrabus*). Since Gutenbrunner's work on matrons attempts have been made to define a distinction between these various descriptions and not to see them as accidental or at most regional variants. Scholars have started working out some factual differences. The geographical distribution is noteworthy: *Matronae* are to be found predominantly in the Lower Rhine and it is the only term found in Upper Italy, whereas in Britain only *matres* and in Gaul mostly *matrae* and *matres* are documented. Furthermore it is interesting to note that the *matronae*, whose epithets are based on tribal or peoples' names, are on the whole called *matres*. It is, however, very difficult to ascertain whether the *matres* should be seen as 'actually mother-deities' and the *matronae* as 'more generally as goddesses worshipped by married women', as de Vries suggested.

The temporal limitation of the matron cult can be set as the end of the 1st and 5th centuries A.D. The oldest inscription found comes from Andernach/Germany set up by a sailor in the Roman fleet (CIL XIII, 7681) from the time between 70 and 89 A.D. Although the cult of matrons was borne especially by Germanic soldiers and clerks in Roman service (as well as their families), it is clear from information on the inscriptions, as well as from the → names of the matrons themselves that the 'helper in times of need' aspect and the protective function of the *matronae* strongly predominated: *matribus paternis Kannanef.*, *Matribus [M]arsacis paternis sive maternis*, *[M]atribus meis [Ger]manis Suebis* are names given to the matrons referring directly to their personal relationship to the worshipper. Frequently they are called upon by these *pro se et suis* ('for himself and his (family)') if there is no direct petition for himself or else for a particular member of his family. Apart from this a few of the matrons have names identifying them as warrior goddesses. The stones and altars which bear the inscriptions are predominantly votive offerings which were set up after the fulfilment of a vow and to this extent do not diverge in their functon from Christian votive inscriptions.

The illustrations of the *matres* and *matronae*, also found on stones without inscriptions, are frontal depictions of them, almost exclusively in threes, either standing or sitting, with at least one of them having a basket of fruit on her lap. Sometimes the middle one is shown to be a maiden with loosened hair wearing a headband, whereas the headdresses of the other two suggest married women; all could be called *matronae*. Votive stones and altars are not monuments found singly in many cases, but rather they are grouped together with cult centres and temple buildings, as for example from Pesch, Nettersheim and Bonn as well as other places on the Lower Rhine. This link to cult centres can be clearly seen by the fact that half of the approximately 360 monuments which Gutenbrunner (1936) listed invoke only three names, Aufaniae, Suleviae, and Vacallinehae. Of these, over 60 occurrences of the name Vacallinehae are almost all documented in Pesch, approximately 70 (in 1936; now nearly 90) recordings for Aufaniae are almost exclusively found in Bonn and Nettersheim. The temple in Pesch was a processional temple with square inner cella, and recent finds have discovered more similar constructions. We know little concerning the actual forms of cult in these temples and cult centres. Apart from the fruit baskets already mentioned on the reliefs of the matrons there are sacrificial scenes, with burning of incense and sacrifice bowls filled with fruit; pigs and fish as sacrificial animals are also represented. Other decorations depicted fruit, plants and trees. Snakes (powers of the underworld, or souls of the dead?) as well as children and nappies are other attributes which indicate not only their general protective function over the family, but also their special function as midwives (a suggestion which is partly supported by the etymologies of some of the names). We have no information from the inscriptions about particular cult times, although the English historian Bede (born 673) tells that the still heathen Angles celebrated sacrificial feasts at the beginning of the year in the *mōdraniht. id est matrum noctem*, that is at Yule-tide. The undoubted connexion between the matron cult and the Anglo-Saxon → *mōdraniht* is not the only link with known Germanic cults of later times. A sacrifice, the → *dísablót*, to the → *dísir* is also said to have taken place in Scandinavia, which, according to the information of the (here very unreliable) Icelandic sagas, took place *at vetrnóttum*, i.e. at the beginning of winter in mid-October. Philippson has also presumed that the fruit baskets of the matrons point to an autumnal sacrifice; this is, however, unlikely. The Swedish

Disthing ('Thing at the time of the *dísir*-festival') is however recorded as having taken place at the beginning of February.

There is an extremely interesting reference to the cult of the Scandinavian matrons in Saxo Grammaticus (*Gesta Danorum* VI, 181) which describes a shrine of the *Parcae* (norns, *dísir*?) as follows: '[Fridlevus] approached the building of the goddesses praying, where, looking into the shrine, he saw three 'nymphs' sitting on the same number of chairs.' The temple with cella and the three seated goddesses remind us of a description of a matron shrine, as found in archaeological digs. As, however, this report was set down at least 600 years after the heyday of the cult of matrons, any evaluation of the link remains problematic.

The cult monuments to the matrons are similar to those of the worship of individual goddesses, of whom the Frisian Nehalennia is the most significant. Votive altars were also set up to male gods (Hercules, Mars Thingsus).

M. Ihm, 'Der Mütter- und Matronenkult und seine Denkmäler' (*Bonner Jahrbücher* 83) 1887; R. Much, 'Germanische Matronennamen' (*ZfdA* 35) 1891; F. Kauffmann, 'Der Matronenkult in Germanien' (*Zeitschrift des Vereins für Volkskunde* 2) 1892; S. Gutenbrunner, *Die germanischen Götternamen*, Halle 1936; H. Hempel, 'Matronenkult und germanischer Mütterglaube' (GRM 27) 1939; E. A Philippson, 'Mütter- und Matronenkult am Niederrhein' (*Germanic Review* 19) 1944; J. de Vries, *Altgermanische Religionsgeschichte*, Berlin [3]1970; H. Birkhan, *Germanen und Kelten*, Vienna 1972; R. L. M. Derolez, *Götter und Mythen der Germanen*, Wiesbaden 1974.

Matron names. There are well over a hundred different names or epithets recorded for matrons which can be called Germanic even though they are only found in Latin inscriptions. In many cases the names cannot be satisfactorily interpreted and the question whether they are Germanic or Celtic in origin is frequently equally problematical. The names which are considered to be unquestionably Germanic are those which even in their Latin context retain the proto-Germanic dative ending of the plural, such as Vatvims, Aflims, Saitchamims (in addition to Vatviabus and Afliabus). Others are obviously recognizable as coming from a Germanic base, such as Gabiae, Friagabiae, Arvagastiae. Part of the inscriptions of matron names refer directly to Germanic tribes, peoples or places, such as those dedicated to the *Matribus Suebis* ('the Suebian mothers'), *Matribus Germanis* ('my Germanic mothers'), *Matribus Frisiavis paternis* ('the paternal Frisian mothers'), as well as the Albiahenae (today's town of Elvenich), the Mahlinehae (to Mahlinium, today's Mecheln), the Nersihenae (to the river name Niers) and the Vacallinehae (perhaps to the river Waal). The frequency of the names is extremely varied: whilst many are only recorded once, others allow frequent regional concentrations to be ascertained, which partly indicate cult centres. The most frequently recorded matron names are the Austriahenae from Morken-Harff with at least 130 certain recordings, the *Matrones Aufaniae* with nearly 90 recordings, especially from Bonn and Nettersheim, the *Matronae Vacallinehae* from Pesch (over 130 recordings) and the widespread Matres Suleviae (around 40 recordings). – As far as the names can be interpreted – and in many examples this is not the case – conclusions concerning the function of the particular goddesses can be derived from the meanings of the names, for example in addition to the maternal and protective goddesses (such as Gabiae, Friagabiae, Arvagastiae) there is also another group, perhaps functionally related, of river and spring goddesses (Aumenahenae, Vacallinehae).

The following matron names are expressly called *matronae*: Chuchenehae; Et(h)rahenae; Fachine(i)hae; Fernovinae; Gabiae; Gavadiae; Gavasiae; Gesahenae; Gratich(iae); Guinehae; Hamavehae; Havae; Hiheraiae; Ineae; Iulineihiae;

Lanehiae; Lubicae; Mah(a)linehae; Naitienae; Octocannae; Ollogabiae; Ratheihiae; Renahenae; Rumanehae; Saitchamiae; Seccanehae; Suebae; Teniavehae; Tummaestiae; Udravarinehae; Ulauhinehae; Vaccalinehae; Vallabneihiae; Vataranehae; Vativiae; Vesuniahenae; Veterahenae; Veteranehae; Vocallinehae.

M. Ihm, 'Der Mütter- und Matronenkult und seine Denkmäler' (*Bonner Jahrbücher* 83) 1887; R. Much, 'Germanische Matronennamen' (*ZfdA* 35) 1891; Th. v. Grienberger, 'Germanische Götternamen auf rheinischen Inschriften' (*ZfdA* 35 & 36) 1891 & 1892; Th. v. Grienberger, 'Niederrheinische Matronen' (*Eranos Vindobonensis*) 1893; S. Gutenbrunner, *Die germanischen Götternamen*, Halle 1936; E. A Philippson, 'Mütter- und Matronenkult am Niederrhein' (*Germanic Review* 19) 1944; J. de Vries, *Altgermanische Religionsgeschichte*, Berlin [3]1970; H. Birkhan, *Germanen und Kelten*, Vienna 1972; R. L. M. Derolez, *Götter und Mythen der Germanen*, Wiesbaden 1974; K.-E. Westergaard, 'Die vergessenen Göttinnen der Fruchtbarkeit' (*Frauen und Frauenbilder dokumentiert durch 2000 Jahre*) Oslo 1983; G. Neumann, 'Germani cisrhenani – die Aussage der Namen' (*Germanenprobleme in heutiger Sicht*) Berlin, New York 1986; M. Gysseling, 'Nordostgallische Götternamen' (R. Bergmann: *Althochdeutsch*) Heidelberg 1987.

máttr ok megin (ON, 'power and strength'). The ON formula *trua á mátt sitt ok megin* frequently occurs and denotes somebody trusting solely in his own might and strength, only in himself and not in the gods and other supernatural powers. For a long time this formula was thought to reflect a basic attitude of the heathen Germanic peoples. Indeed, the alliteration of the formula seemed to indicate its great age. However, Weber has shown that the phrase is merely a motif in ON literature from the 13th century onward with which Christian authors worked in order to illustrate the way in which their heathen heroes renounced the heathen gods, and thus simplified the transition of such heroes into the Christian context. Therefore, the *máttr ok megin-* formula should not be seen as evidence of a kind of atheism among the heathen Germanic peoples.

C. L. Wrenn, 'Some earliest Anglo-Saxon Cult Symbols' (*Franciplegus. Studies F. P. Magoun*) New York 1965; J. de Vries, *Altgermanische Religionsgeschichte*, Berlin [3]1970; G. W. Weber, 'Irreligiosität und Heldenzeitalter' (*Speculum Norroenum. Studies G. Turville-Petre*) Odense 1981.

mead of poetry. A mythological mead brewed from the blood of → Kvasir, which gives the gift of poetry.

The Norse myth of the acquisition of the mead is given in most detail in Snorri's account (*Skáldskaparmál* 1), which diverges slightly from *Hávamál* 104–110, and finally in a number of scaldic kennings from the 10th century which refer to the essential contents of the myth. Apart from this, there is a clear reference to this myth in the depiction on the Gotland pictorial sone from Lärbro St Hammars III (c.700 A.D.).

Snorri tells that after the wars against the Vanir, the Æsir and the Vanir sealed their peace not only by exchanging hostages but also by spitting into a vessel. From this spittle they created a being called Kvasir who was extraordinarily wise. However, two dwarfs Fjalarr and Galarr murdered Kvasir and caught his blood in a cauldron (Óðrœrir) and two other bowls (Són and Boðn); they mixed this blood with honey and then from this they brewed the mead which makes a poet of everyone who partakes of it. After this account comes the tale of how the two dwarfs kill the giant Gillingr and his wife. The giant's son Suttungr takes revenge by marooning them on a skerry which is flooded every high tide; they are only able to save their lives by offering Suttungr the precious mead as compensation. Suttungr then keeps the mead in Hnitbjǫrg and lets his daughter Gunnlǫð guard it.

Odin sets out to gain the mead for the gods (afterwards he, as the god of poetry, can be thought of as the keeper of the mead); he meets nine serfs of the giant → Baugi who are mowing the hay, and manages to make them kill each other by entangling them in an argument about his good whetstone. Odin then enters into service with Baugi as a mower himself, under the name of → Bǫlverkr, and works for a whole summer doing the same amount of work as nine people would; he is promised that his reward will be a sip of the mead. When Baugi comes with Odin to the giant, → Suttungr refuses even to give up a few drops of the mead so that Odin has to resort to a ruse. Using the drill called Rati, Baugi drills a hole through the mountain through which Odin can creep up to the giant's daughter Gunnlǫð in the shape of a snake. After he has slept with her for three nights, she allows him three sips of the mead. With each of these sips, however, he empties one of the three bowls Són, Boðn and Óðrœrir, and then, changing into the shape of an eagle, he escapes to Asgard, pursued by Suttungr, also in the shape of an eagle. Once in Asgard, he regurgitates the mead into the bowls put ready there by the gods. During this flight, however, Suttungr comes so close to catching him that Odin lets a few drops fall, which nobody worries about and which anybody can have; these drops are called 'the part of the would-be poets'.

The Eddic *Hávamál* (104–110) also records the theft of the mead in great detail; the description here diverges in several points from Snorri's: in *Hávamál* 109 the frost giants organize a search for the escaped Odin/Bǫlverkr, and there is no mention of either changing into an eagle or into a snake. Óðrœrir (in Snorri the cauldron of mead) is the name given to the mead itself, which seems more fitting for the etymology, and Hnitbjǫrg does not occur in *Hávamál* at all; on the other hand *Hávamál* 13 and 14 refer to the fact that Odin got drunk on the mead at Gunnlǫð's (who is called the daughter of Fjalar here), whereas this is not mentioned in either Snorri or in *Hávamál* 104–110.

It seems quite clear that there are two (in consideration of *Hávamál* 13f. perhaps even three) different versions of the myth of the mead. Snorri's version in particular appears to reveal truly old characteristics; most of the details in his tale are substantiated by old kennings: the mead as 'Kvasir's blood' (*Kvasis dreyri* in Einarr skálaglamm), as a life-saving 'vehicle of the dwarfs' (*dverga farkostr* in Arnorr jarlaskáld), 'drink of the dwarfs' (*dverga drykkr* in Gisli), 'the flood of dwarfs hidden in the mountain' (*bergs geymilǫ dverga* in Einarr skálaglamm), 'Odin's theft' (*Viðurs þýfi* in Egill, *Sonatorrek* 1) and 'seed of the eagle's beak' (*arnar kjapta órð* in Egill, *Berudrápa*). Consequently, even the episode of → Gilling's murder by the dwarfs and their payment for release, which is mostly considered to be an 'unorganic insertion', is at least partially covered by a kenning.

The already mentioned pictorial stone on Gotland also shows a woman (Gunnlǫð), who is offering a human figure in eagle costume (Odin) a drinking horn, whilst behind him a sword-bearing man (Suttungr) moves towards a symbolised snake (Odin/Bǫlverkr?). Thus, a continuity in the knowledge of this myth is documentarily evident over a period of 500 years, and its popularity is evident in the numerous references in skaldic poetry; the picture stone might presuppose an already embellished myth which agrees in most cases with the version which Snorri give us.

The myth of the mead can be traced far further back with the role of Odin as a culture hero. The theft of the intoxicating drink Soma by the god Indra in the Indian mythology of the Rigveda points to basic similarities with the Germanic myth: Soma is also a cult drink of the poets; Indra steals it with the help of a bird (or even in the shape of a bird himself) from a hideaway in the mountain, and the thieving bird also escapes by the skin of his teeth. Even if differences between the Germanic and Indian versions cannot be totally ignored, with regard to the myth of the theft of the divine potion a common heritage from Indo-Germanic times may be assumed.

A. Olrik, 'Skjaldenmjøden' (*Edda* 24) 1626; A. G. v. Hamel, 'Gods, Skalds and Magic' (*Saga-Book* 11) 1928–36; A. G. v. Hameln, 'The Mastering of the Mead' (*Studie Germanica till. E. A. Kock*) Lund 1934; R. Doht, *Der Rauschtrank im germanischen Mythos*, Vienna 1974; G. Dumézil, *Gods of the Ancient Northmen*, Berkeley 1977.

R: pictorial stone from Lärbro St Hammars III (Gotland) in: K. Hauck, 'Germanische Bilddenkmäler des frühen Mittelalters' (*DVjS* 31) 1957.
E. Doepler d. J., *Odin bei Gunnlöd* (in: E. Doepler, W. Ranisch, *Walhall*, 1901).

Mead. An alcoholic drink made from honey, water and spices which was considered to be the drink of the gods in Germanic mythology. The → mead of poetry is a mythological intoxicating potion which made a poet out of whoever drank it, and which was in Odin's possession (*Skáldskaparmál* 1).

Mediotautehae. → Matron name on an inscription from Cologne/West Germany (CIL XIII 8222). The (probably Celtic) name can be interpreted as 'goddesses of the midland'.

S. Gutenbrunner, *Die germanischen Götternamen*, Halle 1936; H. Reichert, *Lexikon der altgermanischen Namen*, Vienna 1987–90.

Meduna. Name of a goddess. An inscription on a Roman Age votive stone from Bad Betrich, Germany (CIL XIII 7667) names the two goddesses, Meduna and Vercana, who were probably goddesses of springs. Whether the name Meduna may really be considered as Germanic (and not perhaps as Celtic) is debatable.

S. Gutenbrunner, *Die germanischen Götternamen*, Halle 1936; H. Reichert, *Lexikon der altgermanischen Namen*, Vienna 1987–90.

megingjǫrð (or plural *megingjarðar*, ON, 'belt of power'). One of the attributes belonging to the god Thor, in addition to his hammer Mjǫllnir and his iron gauntlet (*járngreipr*; *Gylfaginning* 20, *Skáldskaparmál* 18). As Snorri is the first to refer to this belt, it is probaby a fairy-tale addition of the 13th century. In his tale of Thor's journey to → Geirrǫðargarð, Snorri gives an account of how Thor has to free Loki from Geirrǫð's custody without his hammer, *megingjǫrð* and *járngreipr* in accordance with Loki's promise to his captor. However, when Thor stays overnight with the giantess Gríðr, she gives him a stave called Gríðarvǫlr, a belt of power and an iron gauntlet. As these objects are basically the same as those which he – according to Snorri – already possessed, there would appear to be some confusion in Snorri's account.

Meili (ON, 'the lovely one'). The name of one of Odin's sons in the *Þulur*, and in *Hárbarðsljóð* 9 Thor is called Meili's brother. Thor is repeatedly named as Odin's son, so it would seem that Meili is indeed another of Odin's sons.

Menglǫð (ON, 'the one who takes pleasure in jewels'). In → *Svipdagsmál* → Svipdagr sets out to win the hand of the maiden called Menglǫð. The *Fjǫlsvinnsmál* describes how she lives on the Lyfjaberg which is surrounded by a wall of fire and a clay wall and is guarded by a giant called Fjǫlsviðr and two dogs.

Menglǫð is usually considered to be identical with the goddess Freyja who owns the necklace Brísingamen, but the pun in the name is the only clue which suggests this.

The remainder of the myth of the wooing of the bride, which is the basis of the *Fjǫlsvinnsmál*, in which the god Svipdagr woos Menglǫð, does not help us any further in trying to determine Menglǫð's true identity as Svipdagr was extremely insignificant at the end of Germanic heathendom and otherwise we know very little about him.

J. de Vries, *Altgermanische Religionsgeschichte*, Berlin [3]1970.

Menja (ON, 'slave-girl' or 'wearer of the necklace'). One of the two giantess serving girls who turn the mill-stone of the mythical mill → Grotti in the Eddic lay *Grottasǫngr* (cf. Fenja). Snorri also records this mythical-legendary tale (→ *Grottasǫngr*) in detail (*Skáldskaparmál* 40).

Menmanhia. Name of a goddess. A votive stone in Rome bears an inscription which dedicates it to the *deae Menmanhiae* (CIL VI 31 158). Although the name seems to be Germanic this is by no means certain.

Th. Siebs, 'Beiträge zur deutschen Mythologie' (*ZfdPh* 24) 1892; S. Gutenbrunner, *Die germanischen Götternamen*, Halle 1936; H. Reichert, *Lexikon der altgermanischen Namen*, Vienna 1987–90.

Mercurius → Mercury.

Mercury. The Roman god of trade replaced Wodan/Odin in the *interpretatio romana*. The first references to this can be found in Tacitus (*Germania* 9,1) and in Caesar (*De bello gallico* 6,17), who call Mercury the chief god of the Germanic peoples. Accordingly, many Roman votive stones dedicated to Mercury have been found on Germanic soil. It is thought that the Mercury intended is the Germanic Mercury, i.e. Wodan, although only a few of the names used on the inscriptions for Mercury are unquestionably Germanic (Mercurius Cimbrianus, *Leudisius, *Eriausius). The fact that in the subsequent centuries Mercury was certainly used instead of Wodan, can be proved by the translations of the Latin week-day names *dies Mercurii* into Anglo-Saxon *Wōdnesdæg* (English Wednesday), Middle Dutch *Wōdensdach* (Dutch *Woensdag*), ON *Oðinsdagr* (Danish *Onsdag*), OHG *wôdanestag*. Christian authors of the early Middle Ages also confirm that Mercury was identified as Wodan: Jonas of Bobbio (*Vita Columbani* I, 27; composed around 642 A.D.) and Paul the Deacon (*Historia Langobardorum* I, 8; composed in the second half of the 7th century), as well as the *Origo gentis Langobardorum*. In Geoffrey of Monmouth's *Historia Regum Britanniae* VI, 10 (finished c.1136) there is a detailed passage about the identification of Mercury and Wodan, but even Aelfric's homilies from the second half of the 10th century already allude to the heathen god, Mercury, 'who is called Odin in Danish' (*Annaler f. Nord. Oldkyndighed* 1846). Thus it appears that Mercury is well-documented as a Latin term for the Germanic god Wodan/Odin from the first century A.D. to the High Middle Ages.

The identification was based on the external attributes of the two gods, Mercury and Wodan/Odin: Mercury's broad-rimmed hat, cloak and staff (the Greek god Hermes had the same attributes; a fusion of the Roman and Greek gods had already begun at the beginning of the Christian era) corresponding to the hat, cloak and spear belonging to Wodan/Odin. Admittedly, Odin is only described in this way in the literary works of the Middle Ages, and the image of the classical god was almost certainly not without influence here. The two gods must have had more in common apart from these external details which led to them being identified as the same god, for Mercury was by no means as important a god for the Romans as Odin was for the

Scandinavians. Odin's main role was certainly not that of a god of trade, as Mercury was, even despite the ON name for Odin, Farmatýr 'god of burdens'. One convincing parallel between Odin and Mercury is that both had the function of being the companion of the soul in death. Another similarity, taking into consideration the already progressed Hellenization of Mercury, was that the Greek god Hermes was also the god of speech and as such could be linked with Wodan/Odin, if Odin/Wodan was indeed thought to be a god of poetic art so early on.

J. Grimm, *Deutsche Mythologie*, Berlin [4]1875–78; H. Collitz, 'Wodan, Hermes und Pushan' (*Festskrift Pipping*) Helsingfors 1924; L. Deubner, 'Die Römer' (Chantepie de la Saussaye, *Lehrbuch der Religiongeschichte*) Tübingen [4]1925; J. de Vries, *Altgermanische Religionsgeschichte*, Berlin [3]1970; H. Hunger, *Lexikon der griechischen und römischen Mythologie*, Tübingen [6]1974.

Merseburg Charms → First Merseburg Charm, → Second Merseburg Charm.

Mercurius Arvernorix. Name of a Germanic god (= Wodan/Odin?). The inscription with this god's name on it, as in the case of Mercurius Arvernus, was found on the hill Greinberg near Würzburg/Germany next to the inscription of Mercurius Cimbrianus, who is most likely Germanic. However, Mercurius Arvernorix is probably a Celtic god. Admittedly, the fact that the inscription stones lay next to each other could suggest an adoption of the cult of Wodan by parts of the Celtic population, but the parallel existence of two different cults which influenced each other is just as likely.

J. de Vries, *Altgermanische Religionsgeschichte*, Berlin [3]1970.

Mercurius Arvernus. Name of a Germanic god (= Wodan/Odin?). Even though the epithet suggests that the name is Celtic (from the tribe of the Arvernians), in the main shrine belonging to the tribe only one inscription has been found, and that was dedicated to Mercurius Dumiatus. On the other hand, all seven of the inscriptions dedicated to *Mercurio Arverno* are found on Germanic soil so that it is possible that Mercurius Arvernus was a Germanic god. In this case, however, the additional name cannot be explained. If this Mercury is a Gallic god, then we would have to assume a closer relationship between the Arvernians and the Rhineland (Gutenbrunner).

S. Gutenbrunner, *Die germanischen Götternamen*, Halle 1936; J. de Vries, *Altgermanische Religionsgeschichte*, Berlin [3]1970.

Mercurius Channin(i)us (or Hannin(i)us). An inscription from the vicinity of Blankenheim, Germany (CIL XIII 7781) is dedicated to this Germanic Mercury. It is, however, extremely uncertain whether Channinus is indeed an epithet for the god Mercury or not. The name could perhaps come from the tribe of the Kannanefates, but it is possibly simply the name of the person who had the stone set up.

R. Much, 'Mercurius Hanno' (*ZfdA* 35) 1891; S. Gutenbrunner, *Die germanischen Götternamen*, Halle 1936; J. de Vries, *Altgermanische Religionsgeschichte*, Berlin [3]1970.

Mercurius Cimbrianus. As yet five of the votive inscriptions dedicated to *Mercurio Cimbriano* have been found on German soil: two on a hill, Greinberg, near to Miltenberg (near Würzburg; CIL XIII 6604, 6605), two on the Heiligenberg near Heidelberg (one of which (CIL XIII 6402) has Cimbrio) and one near Mainz (CIL XIII 6742). All of these inscriptions date from the time between 150–210 A.D. This epithet of Mercury is usually thought to belong to the Germanic tribe of the Cimbri. Although four of the inscriptions were not found in a Germanic area of settlement at this time, we should not exclude the possibility of the migration of scattered groups to these areas. These migrants could well have brought the cult of their main god, the 'Wodan of the Cimbri', with them from their homeland, and this appears in the *interpretatio romana* on votive stones as Mercurius Cimbrianus. It is possible that the epithet Cimbrianus only originated in foreign parts in order to show the distinction from a Celtic god, who might also have been rendered by the name of Mercury.

F. Kauffmann, 'Mercurius Cimbrianus' (*ZfdPh* 38) 1906; S. Gutenbrunner, *Die germanischen Götternamen*, Halle 1936; J. de Vries, *Altgermanische Religionsgeschichte*, Berlin ³1970.

Mercurius Dumiatus ('Mercury of Puy de Dôme'). Unlike the previously named ones, this is not a name for the Germanic Mercury, i.e. Wodan, but is most likely the Latin form of a Celtic god who was worshipped at the main shrine of the Gallic tribe of the Arvernes, in the Puy de Dôme area in southern France.

J. de Vries, *Altgermanische Religionsgeschichte*, Berlin ³1970.

Mercurius *Eriausius? (or Mercurius Friausius?). Name of a Germanic god (= Wodan/Odin?). A fragmentary inscription on a Roman votive stone from Ubbergen near Nijmegen, Holland (CIL XIII 8726). Of the text only *Mercurio . . . iausio* still exists and this could perhaps be extrapolated to Eriausius (cf. the Gothic personal names Eriulfus, Erilieva), or perhaps to Friausius (from **frija* 'kind', or from **fri(h)alsio* 'free'?).

S. Gutenbrunner, *Die germanischen Götternamen*, Halle 1936; J. de Vries, *Altgermanische Religionsgeschichte*, Berlin ³1970.

Mercurius Gebrinius. Name of a god on ten Roman votive stones from Bonn. As none of the dedicators is Germanic and even the attempts to interpret the name are all extremely uncertain, Gutenbrunner's explanation that Mercurius Gebrinius is a Germanic Mercury (i.e. Wodan/Odin) is not convincing. He relates the epithet to ON *gífr* 'monster') (from Gmc **gibria-*) and explains the Germanic root of the name **gebrinio-* as 'lord of the monsters' which he considers refers to Odin as the leader of the Wild Hunt.

The link to Celtic *gabros* 'ram' is far more likely despite the constantly occuring -e- of the root syllable, as on half of the votive stones the attribute of the god is a ram. Thus, Mercurius Gebrinius is a Celtic version of Mercury.

S. Gutenbrunner, 'Gallisches 1. Mercurius Gebrinius' (*Zeitschrift für Celtische Philologie* 20) 1936.

Mercurius *Leudisius (?). On a Roman votive stone from Weisweiler (near Düren, West Germany; CIL XIII 7559) there is a mutilated inscription, the beginning of which is:

CURIO LEUD
ANO C. AMRT

It is impossible to ascertain whether a Mercurius *Leudisianus, *Leudcianus or *Leudiacanus would have been the complete version, if the three missing letters at the beginning of the line are added. *Leudisianus could be related to a verb ***leudisjan** 'rule, dominate', but other interpretations link it more convincingly to a Latin form of the town name Lüttich: Leudicum (or *Leudiacum), in which case the inscription would have been dedicated to the 'Mercury = Wodan of Lüttich'.

S. Gutenbrunner, *Die germanischen Götternamen*, Halle 1936; J. de Vries, *Altgermanische Religionsgeschichte*, Berlin ³1970.

Mercurius Mercator. ('Mercury the trader'). Epithet for the Germanic Mercury (i.e. Wodan) on a Roman votive stone from Metz, Germany (CIL XIII 4308). The epithets *mercator*, *nundinator*, *negotiator* could of course be epithets for the Roman Mercury, but nonetheless the name for Odin → Farmatýr 'god of burden' allows for speculations about the meaning of Mercurius Mercator as Wodan/Odin, as does the predominantly Germanic population of the area. If the devotion to Odin (via the bands of warriors) was indeed carried abroad by traders, here would be a further reason for the *interpretatio romana* to identify Odin as Mercury.

H. Falk, *Odensheite*, Christiania 1924; O. Höfler, *Kultische Geheimbünde der Germanen*, Frankfurt 1934; J. de Vries, *Altgermanische Religionsgeschichte*, Berlin ³1970.

Mercurius Negotiator ('Mercury the dealer'). Possibly the epithet for the Germanic Mercury, i.e. Wodan. It appears on a Roman inscription from Heddernheim, W.Germany (CIL XIII 7360); → Mercurius Mercator.

Mercurius Nundinator ('Mercury the trader'). Possibly an epithet for the Germanic Mercury, i.e. Wodan. It is inscribed on a Roman votive stone found near Wiesbaden (CIL XIII 7569); → Mercurius Mercator.

Mercurius Rex. The name 'King Mercury' on a Roman inscription from Nijmegen, Holland (CIL XIII 1326) refers, as do most of the other namings of Mercury on the Lower Rhine, to the Germanic → Mercury (= Wodan/Odin). This is quite clearly confirmed here by the epithet *rex*, because the Roman Mercury did not have such an exalted position among Roman gods, whilst Wodan/Odin certainly could have received this title within the world of the Germanic gods.

J. de Vries, *Altgermanische Religionsgeschichte*, Berlin ³1970.

Midgard (ON *Miðgarðr*, Gothic *midjungards*, OHG *mittilgart*, *mittangard*, Old Saxon *middelgard*, OE *middangeard* 'dwelling place in the middle'). The name the Germanic people gave to the centre of the world, the earth inhabited by men. In the *Edda* Midgard does not only seem to be the place where men lived, but was also used to denote the protective wall surrounding it (*Vǫluspá* 4 and 56); the expression *undir miðgarði* (*Hárbarðsljóð* 23, *Hyndluljóð* 11 and 16) speaks in favour of this, as does the tale in *Grímnismál* 41 in which Midgard was created from the eyebrows of the protogiant → Ymir. Snorri also speaks in *Gylfaginning* 8 of the fact that the descendants of the first humans, Ask and Embla, were given *undir Miðgarði* as their dwelling place. Otherwise, in Snorri too, Midgard is the actual world in which not only men but also the gods live, and the following terms for Midgard in other Germanic languages are used throughout as synonyms for 'earth, world': Gothic *midjungards* stands for Latin *orbis terrarum*, the Anglo-Saxon *middangeard* is a gloss for *chosmos*. Despite the fact that the earliest Scandinavian sources we have for Midgard are from the 11th century skalds Þórleikr fagri and Arnórr Þórðarson, Midgard is unquestionably an old Common Germanic designation.

E. F. Halvorsen, 'Midgard' (*KLNM* 11) 1966; J. de Vries, *Altgermanische Religionsgeschichte*, ³1970.

R: Midgard is apparently of symbolic value for people who still attach religious importance to Germanic beliefs: Midgardbund was the name of such a 'Neo-Germanic' pseudo-religious movement in the mid-thirties, and *Midgards Morgen* is the name of a 'Book for the Germanic Faith' by H. W. Hammerbacher, published as late as 1977.

Midgard serpent (ON, *Miðgarðsormr* 'world serpent'). The monster in Nordic mythology which lives in the primeval ocean surrounding the world and which winds itself around the world. The name, Midgard serpent, appears neither in the Eddic lays nor in skaldic poetry; only Jǫrmungandr, Ormr, Naðr 'serpent, dragon' are found in the *Edda*. It is only in Snorri (*Gylfaginning* 33, 46, 47, 50, 52) that the widely spread information is systematically ordered. Kennings in poetry which describe the fight between → Thor and the Midgard serpent (Bragis *Ragnarsdrápa* 16 from the 9th century, and the *Húsdrápa* by Ulfr Uggason from the 10th century) prove that the ancient mythological concept of the cosmic being winding itself around the world had already, at the beginning of literary time, been personified as the legendary sea-serpent. The same scene (which shows Thor having baited his fishing line with an ox's skull in order to catch the Midgard serpent and about to kill the monster with his hammer when the terrified giant, Hymir, cuts through the line) can be seen on three Viking Age pictorial stones and is retold in literature by Snorri (*Gylfaginning* 46, 47) as well as in *Hymiskviða*. At Ragnarǫk the Midgard serpent and Thor meet with each other (*Gylfaginning* 50; *Vǫluspá* 56). Thor kills the monster, but dies himself because of its poisonous breath. Snorri also reports (*Gylfaginning* 33) that the father of the Midgard serpent (like the father of the Fenris wolf and of Hel) is Loki, who fathered this monster with the giantess, Angrboða. This is not merely Snorri's invention, but is already mentioned in Eilíf's *Þórsdrápa* 1 (10th century) and in the *Hymiskviða* 22, 23. Loki's role as the father of the monster is unquestionably ancient. In the Christian Middle Ages the Midgard serpent is naturally enough associated with Leviathan from the Old Testament, and the Midgard serpent serves throughout as a gloss for this Biblical sea-serpent.

The world serpent, if not known by this name, was also known in Germanic areas outside Scandinavia. German folk-belief even in the Middle Ages attributed earthquakes to its writhings (Konrad von Megenberg, *Buch der Natur* II, 33; *De mundi constitutione* I, 52ff.).

E. F. Halvorsen, 'Miðgarðsormr' (*KLNM* 11) 1966; J. de Vries, *Altgermanische Religionsgeschichte*, [3]1970.

R: → Thor and the Midgard serpent.

Miði (ON, cognate to *miðr* 'the middle one'). A giant in the *Þulur*.

Miðjungr (ON, 'being of the middle'). A giant in the *Þulur*. In the interpretation of Miðjungr it is less a question of beings which stand 'in the middle' between the gods and the giants, but rather of beings which live in the middle of the cosmos, in Midgard, that is, basically all living beings. This interpretation is, however, not fully convincing, as elsewhere in Germanic mythology the giants are housed in Utgarð, that is outside the world inhabited by men.

F. Jónsson, 'Þulur' (*APhSc* 9) 1934.

Miðviðr (ON, 'middle board'?). A dwarf in the *Þulur*.

Miðvitnir (ON). A giant in *Grímnismál* 50, where Odin boasts about having killed him when he was at the home of the giant's son, Sǫkkmimir. Apart from this reference we know nothing about a myth of Odin, Miðvitnir and Sǫkkmimir, and even the name Miðvitnir is unexplained. In its present form it could mean 'wolf of the middle', but 'sea-wolf' would also be possible, whereas 'mead-robber' (from Mjǫð-vitnir) is more unlikely as this is the name of a dwarf in *Vǫluspá*. Apart from this neither dwarfs nor giants are the thieves of the mead of poetry, but rather Odin is. However, if one assumes that Miðvitnir means 'Odin', then not only the name but also the entire strophe must be corrupt. This latter explanation is not impossible because the name occurs among the stanzas in which Odin lists his various names.

A. M. Sturtevant, 'Semantic and Etymological Notes' (*SS* 20) 1948.

Mímameiðr (ON, 'Mimi's tree'). A tree mentioned in *Fjǫlsvinnsmál* 20 and 24. Mímameiðr presupposes a name-form Mími, but nonetheless → Mímir must be meant, whose well (→ Mímir's well) lies under one of the roots of the World-Tree Yggdrasill, at least according to Snorri. Therefore, Mímameiðr is probably another name for Yggdrasill.

(**Mime**). Name of a dwarf (tenor) from the Nibelung family in R. Wagner's operas *Das Rheingold* and *Siegfried*. Mime is Siegfried's teacher in Wagner's works, just as Mímir is in the Old Norse *Vilkina saga*. In the MHG legend of *Biterolf*, Mímir is found as Mîme, in which form Wagner adopted the name for his own purposes.

Mímir (also Mímr; ON). A wise person in Nordic mythology. In Snorri's *Ynglinga saga* 4 he appears to be one of the Æsir, whereas in the *Þulur* Mímir is found among the names of giants. The form of the name in the formula → Mímir's head is always Mímr, otherwise the form is Mímir. This has led to speculation that there are two different myths, one about Mímir's head, the other about Mímir's well (de Vries). However, Mímir and Mímr were already thought to be identical in the 12th century by Snorri, and more recent investigations about the origin of the myths of the prophesying head in the spring in Celtic regions (J. Simpson) confirm this identification. The kenning *Míms vinr* 'Mímir's friend' for Odin in Egill Skalagrímsson: *Sonatorrek* 23 and Vǫlu-Stein 1 proves that the myth about Mímir is not limited to late Eddic poetry and Snorri's mythography (*Gylfaginning* 14 and 50; *Ynglinga saga* 4 and 7), but was already known in the 10th century. *Vǫluspá* 46 mentions Mímir's sons, too, but their identities are never revealed.

Mímir probably means 'the rememberer, the wise one' and is etymologically related to Latin *memor*. → Hoddmímir, → Sǫkkmímir.

G. Sverdrup, *Rauschtrank und Labetrank im Glauben und Kultus*, Oslo 1940; J. Simpson, 'Mímir: Two Myths or One?' (*Saga Book* 16) 1962; E. F. Halvorsen, 'Mímir' (*KLNM* 11) 1966; J. de Vries, *Altgermanische Religionsgeschichte*, Berlin ^{3}1970.

R: H. E. Freund, *Mimer og Balder raadspørger Nornerne* (relief, 1822); D. Werenskiold, *Odin og Mime* (relief in the Oslo town hall, 1938).

Mímir's well (ON, *Mímis brunnr*). The spring of wisdom mentioned in *Vǫluspá* 28 from where Odin gets his advice. According to Snorri's version of the passage in *Vǫluspá* (*Gylfaginning* 14), the spring lies under the roots of the world-tree Yggdrasill which stretches out to the Hrímþursar. 'Mímir is the one who owns the spring. He is full of wisdom, because he drinks from the spring using the horn Gjallarhorn' (*Gylfaginning* 14). In *Gylfaginning* 50 Snorri tells how at the Ragnarǫk Odin gets advice from Mímir at the spring. He follows *Vǫluspá* 46 for this information where only Mímir's head is mentioned and not the spring itself. The link between Mímir's well and → Mímir's head is difficult to define with any certainty. It has generally been thought among scholars that there were either two different myths (de Vries) or else that the head referred to was in fact 'the head of the spring' (Sverdrup), but neither of these explanations make very much sense. In Celtic mythology and folklore a prophesy-giving head in a spring is by no means a rare occurrence, and the origin of the Nordic myth is probably to be found in this area (Simpson). On the other hand, names for waters such as the German Mimling, Swedish Mimesøa and Mimesjöen deserve consideration as they too appear to indicate a belief in a wise, prophesying being living in the waters.

→ Mímir.

Mímir's head (actually Mímr's head: ON *Míms hǫfuð*). A wise adviser mentioned twice in the Eddic lays (*Vǫluspá* 48, *Sigrdrífumál* 14). The form of the name used in these Eddic passages is actually Mímr and there is a debate whether Mímr and Mímir are the same person or not. Snorri quite clearly considers Mímir and Mímr to be identical and although he mentions that Odin gets advice from Mímir (*Gylfaginning* 14 and 50), he does not refer to the prophecy being given only by a head. On the other hand he reports Mímir's decapitation in detail in *Heimskringla* (*Ynglinga saga* 4 and 7): Mímir was 'a very wise man' and the Æsir provided him as one of the hostages after the wars against the Vanir where he was to serve → Hœnir as an adviser. When the Vanir recognised that Hœnir was helpless without his adviser, they decapitated Mímir and sent the head to the Æsir where Odin with the help of healing herbs and charms is able to keep him from decay, so that he can continue to give secret information and such things which he gets 'from the Other World'. – In the sagas of the Icelanders speaking heads are known but written of in different contexts. They are particularly well known from shamanistic practices, but they are also known in Celtic areas where the link can be found between an oracle-speaking head and a spring (Simpson). Therefore, it is not necessary to try to separate the tales of the speaking head Mímr and the wise Mímir into two distinct myths (de Vries).

→ Mímir

Mímir's sons (ON, *Míms synir*). These are mentioned in *Vǫluspá* 46 at the beginning of the Ragnarǫk, but their names are not given and no further information about them is available.

minni (ON, 'remembrance drink, toast'). According to Snorri, the *minni* was drunk at the sacrificial meal after the toasts to the gods and the → *bragafull* had been drunk. It frequently occurs as a 'memory drink; toast' in saga literature. Presumably the custom of 'drinking in memory of someone' only reached Scandinavia in the High Middle Ages from Germany, and therefore it should not be seen as a heathen custom.

K. Düwel, *Das Opferfest von Lade*, Göttingen 1971.

Miskorblindi (ON). The father of the giant → Ægir. He is only called by this name in *Hymiskviða* 2, elsewhere Ægir's father is said to be Fornjótr. Consequently, it is not certain whether the two are identical and it is another name for Fornjótr, or if it is a separate name. The meaning of the name is equally uncertain: either 'the one who stirs the brewing mixture' (Gutenbrunner) or else 'the ugly one' (Sturtevant). The lack of any further information about Miskorblindi means that neither explanation is totally convincing.

S. Gutenbrunner, 'Eddica' (*ZfdA* 77) 1940; A. M. Sturtevant, 'Etymological Comments' (*PMLA* 66) 1951; J. de Vries, *Altnordisches etymologisches Wörterbuch*, Leiden [2]1977.

Mist (ON). One of the → valkyries (*Grímnismál* 36, *Þulur*) who reminds us of the way in which valkyries can ride through the air and over water (*Helgakviða Hjǫrvarðssonar* 9 Pr, *Helgakviða Hundingsbana* II 4 Pr), since her name is probably related to ON *mistr* 'cloud, mist'.

mistletoe (ON *mistilteinn*). This plant plays an important role in the Icelandic tradition of the myth of → Baldr. Loki tricks the blind god, Hǫðr, into throwing a sprig of mistletoe at Baldr. This then changes into a spear in mid-flight and kills the otherwise invulnerable god. The word *mistilteinn* also occurs in *Vǫluspá* 31. In the *Þulur*, in *Hervarar saga ok Heiðreks* and the *Hrómundarsaga Gripssonar* it is a name given to a sword. This suggests that there might be a connexion with the Danish version of the Baldr-myth in Saxo where Baldr is killed by a special sword.

The apparently strange idea of mistletoe being a weapon and as such the direct cause of Baldr's death, is not only the result of the seemingly harmless appearance of the plant but also of its magical powers which are attributed to evergreen plants in most old European cultures. However, the mistletoe was usually thought to protect people from harm.

A. Kabell, *Balder und die Mistel*, Helsinki 1965; O. A. Hœg, 'Misteltein' (*KLNM* 11) 1966; W. H. Wolf-Rottkay, 'Balder and the Mistletoe: A Note' (*SS* 39) 1967; J. de Vries, *Altgermanische Religionsgeschichte*, Berlin [3]1970.

Mithotyn. A sorcerer in Saxo Grammaticus' *Gesta Danorum* I, 25f. who usurped the rule over the Æsir during → Odin's exile. He introduced a new form of cult which meant that the gods were not sacrificed to collectively, but rather individually. After Odin's return he fled to the Danish island Fyn but was killed by the inhabitants there. His corpse caused diseases even in its grave, and only after the body had been dug up again, decapitated and impaled through his chest, could they free themselves from his posthumous evil influence. The circumstances surrounding Mithotyn's death and second killing are a clear reflection of Nordic concepts of the → living dead. His role in the story of Odin's exile causes greater problems.

The most convincing interpretation of the name Mithotyn relates it to ON *mjǫtuðr*, a term which describes in a very diffuse way the ordering, divine, but mostly impersonal omnipotence. The explanation 'false Odin' (from Old Indian *mithu* 'false') is not impossible, but Saxo's version supports the theory that the new order of cult customs supposedly declared by Mithotyn is an action 'of an ordering power who considers every individual sphere of human action, whilst Odin embodies a form of governing which takes everything into a single grasp, a 'totalitarian rule' (de Vries). It is not unlikely that an antagonism surfaces here which might well be connected with the story of Odin's exile and the usurpation of the divine rule by other gods, perhaps even with the war against the Vanir.

P. Herrmann, *Die Heldensagen des Saxo Grammaticus*, Leipzig 1922; J. de Vries, *Altgermanische Religionsgeschichte*, Berlin [3]1970; G. Dumézil, *From Myth to Fiction*, Chicago and London 1973.

Mjǫðvitnir (ON, 'Mead-wolf', 'Mead-robber'). A dwarf in *Vǫluspá* 11 and in the *Þulur*. The name perhaps refers to the myth of Kvasir, from whose blood the dwarfs Fjalarr and Galarr brewed the mead of the skalds, according to Snorri. Odin, not dwarfs, however, is the robber of the mead: → Miðvitnir.

Mjǫklituðr (ON, 'the strongly coloured one'). A dwarf in the *Þulur*.

Mjǫll (ON, 'powder snow'). A giantess (?) in the genealogy of the mythical ancestor → Fornjótr in the version of *Hversu Nóregr byggðisk*, where Þorri, Fǫnn, Drífa and Mjǫll are said to be the children of King Snær. As all these names personify aspects of winter, it would seem possible that originally it had to do with a genealogy of frost giants.

Mjǫllnir (ON, Mjǫllnir or Mjollnir). The hammer belonging to the god → Thor. Just like the divine attributes of Freyr and Odin, it was made by the dwarfs Sindri and Brokkr and brought to the Æsir by Loki. In the shape of a fly Loki disturbed → Sindri (or Eitri) at his work so that the handle of the hammer turned out too short (*Skáldskaparmál* 33). According to Saxo (*Gesta Danorum* III, 73) the handle was broken off in a battle. Mjǫllnir produces thunder and lightning (*Skáldskaparmál* 17) when it is thrown, and then it returns like a boomerang to Thor's hand (*Skáldskaparmál* 33); in order to hold the hammer he needs iron gauntlets (*Gylfaginning* 20). Mjǫllnir is Thor's weapon in his fight against Skrýmir (*Gylfaginning* 44), Hrungir (*Skáldskaparmál* 17), Hymir (*Hymiskviða* 36), Þrymr (*Þrymskviða* 30), perhaps also against Þjazi (*Hárbarðsljóð* 19) and other giants (*Gylfaginning* 41). The theft of the hammer and the way it was fetched back from the giant Þrymr by Thor, disguised as Freyja, is told in the comic tale → *Þrymskviða*. After Thor's death at the Ragnarǫk his sons Móði and Magni inherit the hammer (*Vafþrúðnismál* 51; *Gylfaginning* 52).

Mjǫllnir does not only serve as a mythical divine weapon. As the Bronze Age rock carvings of axe or hammer-bearing god-like figures show, it played a role as a consecratory instrument early on, probably in the fertility cult, which is connected with the shift of Thor's function from strength (as the god of war) to the fertility cult. Similarly, it would be unwise to interpret the consecration of Viking Age runes on ten Danish and Swedish rune stones, which either bear the formula 'May Thor bless these runes' or else, even more frequent, merely show a picture of the hammer alone, as evidence for Thor as a consecratory god; these only seem to confirm the cult function of the hammer as a consecratory instrument. Mjǫllnir plays this role in the blessing of marriages on Bronze Age rock carvings as well as in the consecration of marriage in the Eddic *Þrymskviða* and in medieval German poetry (the poem *Marienleich* by Frauenlob, and verses by Muskatplüt). Its wondrous properties are also mentioned in the *Snorra Edda* when Thor brings his goat back to life with it.

In the Viking Age Thor's hammer Mjǫllnir became the most important symbol for Scandinavian heathendom in its opposition to Christianity; this is confirmed by the previously mentioned pictures of hammers on runic grave stones of the Viking Age, as well as the numerous little silver amulet-hammers (pictured in J. Graham-Cambell and D. Kidd, *The Vikings*, London 1980); late Viking Age casting moulds, which could be used either for the production of Christian crosses or else for Thor's hammers, emphasize the symbolic significance. Whether a statuette of a sitting god with a hammer-like object found in Iceland really represents Thor with Mjǫllnir has been called into question again recently, as the shape of the symbol differs too drastically from the shape of other Thor's hammers found so far.

Not only does Thor's projectile Mjǫllnir have its counterpart in the whetstone thrown by his giant opponent, → Hrungnir (*Skáldskaparmál* 17), but also in the weapons of the gods outside Germanic areas: the Gallic hammer-god Sucellos, the Irish Dagda, the old Slavic Perkunos, the Indian Indra. The thunder-god's hammer-shaped weapon of lightning would therefore seem to go back to Indo-Germanic concepts.

The etymology of Mjǫllnir (from Proto Norse **melluniaR*) is controversial; it may be related to Old Slavic *mlunuji*, Russian *molnija*, 'lightning' (either borrowed from there or else from an early stage) which would allow an interpretation of 'the one who makes lightning'; another attempt to explain it, however, relates Mjǫllnir to ON *mjǫll* 'new snow', Icelandic *mjalli* 'white colour', and as such would mean 'the shining lightning weapon'. In earlier scholarship Mjǫllnir had been connected with Gothic *malwjan* and ON *mala* 'to grind' and interpreted as 'the grinder'.

A. Kock, 'Etymologisch-mythologische Untersuchungen' (*IF* 10) 1899; F. Ohrt, 'Hammerens lyde – Jaernets last' (*Festskrift t. F. Jónsson*) Copenhagen 1928; O. Bø, 'Hammarseng' (*KLNM* 6) 1961; H. R. Ellis Davidson, 'Thor's Hammer' (*Folklore* 76) 1965; J. de Vries, *Altgermanische Religionsgeschichte*, Berlin [3]1970; M. Puhvel, 'The Deicidal Otherworld Weapon in Celtic and Germanic Mythic Tradition' (*Folklore* 83) 1972; E. Marold, ' "Thor weihe diese Runen" ' (*FmSt* 8) 1974; O. Bø, 'Torshamrar' (*KLNM* 18) 1974; Kristján Eldjárn, 'The Bronze Image from Eyrarland' (*Speculum Norrœnum. Studies G. Turville-Petre*) Odense 1981.

R: Thor is almost always depicted along with Mjǫllnir: in fine art the illustration of Mjǫllnir varies between a hammerlike version of Hercules' club (Fogelberg), an oversized sledge hammer (Dollman) or an attempt to make a reconstruction of the heathen god's weapon from archaeological finds of the little amulet hammer (Winge).

The hammer is still considered to be the symbol of Germanic heathendom even today, as one of the so-called 'Neo-Germanic Faith Federations' of the thirties, the '*Hammerbund*', confirms.

Móðguðr (ON, 'furious battle'). The name of the female warden of the bridge to the Other World → Gjallarbrú which leads to Hel (*Gylfaginning* 48). As this maiden Móðguðr is recorded nowhere else, she appears to be one of Snorri's additions to the tale of → Hermód's Ride to Hel. The allegorical name rather speaks in favour of such an interpretation.

Móði (ON, 'the angry one'). One of Thor's sons. He is only expressly named as son of the god in *Hymiskviða* 34 and in Snorri (*Gylfaginning* 52, *Skáldskaparmál* 4), but in *Vafþrúðnismál* 52 Móði and → Magni are also named as the heirs of Thor's hammer Mjǫllnir after the Ragnarǫk. The name can be found frequently in kennings in skaldic poetry.

Like Thor's other children, his son Magni and his daughter Þrúðr, Móði is a personification of one of Thor's characteristics, which was given its own mythological form in the literature of the late heathen period.

Mōdraniht (Anglo-Saxon, 'Mothers-night'). The medieval English historian, The Venerable Bede (born 673), mentions in *De temporum ratione* 13 that the still heathen Angles hold a sacrifice at New Year in the *modraniht id est matrum nocturum* ('the Mōdraniht, that is, in the night of mothers (= matrons)'). Thus it corresponds to other Germanic Yule-tide festivals; the idea that it might have been a Celtic festival is largely refuted nowadays. The *Mōdraniht* as a Germanic sacrificial festival should be associated with the → Matron cult of the West Germanic peoples on the one hand, and to the *dísablót* and → Disting already known from medieval Scandinavia on the other hand and is chronologically to be seen as a connecting link between these Germanic forms of cult.

F. Kauffmann, 'Der Matronenkultus in Germanien' (*Zeitschrift des Vereins für Volkskunde* 2) 1892; S. Gutenbrunner, *Die germanischen Götternamen*, Halle 1936; J. de Vries, *Altgermanische Religionsgeschichte* Berlin [3]1970; R. L. M. Derolez, *Götter und Mythen der Germanen*, Wiesbaden 1974.

Móðsognir, or Mótsognir (ON). A dwarf in *Vǫluspá* 10 (also *Gylfaginning* 13). The meaning of the name is controversial: most likely it means 'the tired one, the powerless one', cognate to ON *móðr* and *súga*, cf. Swedish dialect *modsugen* 'apathetic'; possibly however 'the tired sigher' is meant, but it could mean also 'the moth sucker' (according to Gutenbrunner), however unlikely this may seem. Another possible interpretation is the 'furious sucker' (Motz).

S. Gutenbrunner, 'Eddastudien I' (*ANF* 70) 1955; L. Motz, 'New Thoughts on Dwarf-Names' (*FmSt* 7) 1973; B. Ejder, 'Eine Vǫluspá-Stelle' (*Die Sprache* 22) 1976; J. de Vries, *Altnordisches etymologisches Wörterbuch*, Leiden ²1977.

Móðvitnir (ON, 'angry wolf'). A dwarf in one version of *Vǫluspá* 11.

Mǫgþrasir (ON). A giant (?) in *Vafþrúðnismál* 49, where the norns are called his girls (*Mǫgþrasis meyjar*). Exactly why this is so is unknown. The name is not clear but 'the one striving for sons' would seem to give more or less the correct meaning. The supposition that Mǫgþasir and Lífþrasir are one and the same mythological person has little to be said for it; Odin's name Þrasarr and the dwarf's name Þrasir are closely related.

A. M. Sturtevant, 'Semantic and Etymological Comments' (*SS* 20) 1948.

Mǫkkurkálfi (ON, 'fog-leg, fog-shin'). The name of an artificial giant, formed by the giants out of clay and given the heart of a mare, who according to Snorri (*Gylfaginning* 17) is supposed to stand by the giant → Hrungnir in his fight against Thor; he was nine miles high and three miles wide across his shoulders; when Thor attacked with thunder and lightning, however, even this clay giant began to quake and was finally beaten by Thor's servant Þjálfi without any great difficulty.

Dumézil compared this clay giant to the artificially constructed monsters within the framework of initiation rites of archaic cultures, with which the mythical tale of Thor and Hrungnir has parallels; nonetheless the real hero of the initiation rite would then be → Þjálfi. In the tradition of this myth Þjálfi had been so much forgotten, however, that he does not even appear in the version given in *Haustlǫng*, and Snorri had to go back to a different, perhaps older source; this, however, is not particularly convincing.

Mǫkkurkalfi seems to be a Scandinavian counterpart to the Jewish Golem of the *Cabbala*, but an adoption of this motif on the part of Snorri is most unlikely, even if it is only found in his writings.

J. de Vries, *Altgermanische Religionsgeschichte*, Berlin ³1970; G. Dumézil, *Gods of the Ancient Northmen*, Berkeley 1977.

Mǫrn (ON, 'the grinding one'?). Frequently used as the name of giantesses in the kennings in skaldic poetry.

Mǫrnir (ON) → Vǫlsi.

Mogk, Eugen (1848–1939). A Scandinavian scholar from Leipzig who in his writings between 1879 and 1932 repeatedly attacked the credibility of the Old Norse sources of mythology, especially on the *Snorra Edda*, and as such introduced misgivings about the overly credulous attitude of scholars towards Snorri's teaching about the gods. Mogk's Eddic criticism went too far, as he did not even want to see Snorri as a collector of old myths, but his attitudes resulted in a general critical re-consideration of Old Norse prose literature as source material for mythological studies, which in turn led to the justified rejection of saga literature as a totally reliable source for the history of religion. Despite much rejection (from H. Kuhn, for example) Mogk's theories met with wide acceptance and W. Baetke defended them well into the recent past.

Móinn (ON, probably 'moor-animal'). One of the snakes which live beneath the roots of the world-ash Yggdrasill (*Grímnismál* 34). According to Snorri (*Gylfaginning* 15) these snakes live in the spring Hvergelmir. Móinn and Góinn are called the sons of Grafvitnir in *Grímnismál*.

Moon → Máni.

Mopates. The name of → matrons on a votive stone from Nijmegen/Holland (CIL XIII 8725) which probably has something to do with the wood *forestum Moffet* which was first referred to in 996. The name is however Celtic.

S. Gutenbrunner, *Die germanischen Götternamen*, Halle 1936; H. Birkhan, *Germanen und Kelten*, Vienna 1970; H. Reichert, *Lexikon der altgermanischen Namen* I, Vienna 1987.

Mundilfari (ON, 'the one moving according to particular times'?). The father of the moon (Máni) and the sun (→ Sól), according to *Vafþrúðnismál* 23 and Snorri (*Gylfaginning* 10). Mundilfari is possibly a name for the moon itself.

J. de Vries, *Altgermanische Religionsgeschichte*, [3]1970

Muninn (1) (ON, 'the thought'). One of Odin's two ravens; the other is called → Huginn. In the *Edda*, Muninn is recorded only in *Grímnismál* 20 as well as a fragment of a stanza, whereas Huginn is far more prominent in the sources. Snorri (*Gylfaginning* 37) tells of the two ravens which sit on Odin's shoulders and tell him everything that they have seen or heard on their flights over the whole world. In skaldic poetry the names Huginn and Muninn are used as a general term for 'raven'.

Muninn (2) (ON, 'the one who remembers'). A dwarf in the *Þulur*.

Munnharpa ('shrivelled mouth'). One of the names of giantesses which refers to their ugly appearance (only in the *Þulur*).

Munnriða (or else more correctly Myrkriða, Munnrifa? ON). A giantess in the *Þulur*. The manuscripts give widely diverging variants of her name; Munnriða could mean 'mouth mover', 'chatterbox', if this form is at all correct.

F. Jónsson, 'Þulur' (*APhSc* 9) 1934.

Muspell. Probably a Germanic term for the 'world conflagration causing the end of the world'. The recorded forms of the word are: the dative sg. *muspille* in the OHG poem *Muspilli*; the nominative sg. *mutspelli*, genetive sg. *mutspelles*, *mudspelles* in the Old Saxon *Heliand*. It is recorded several times in the genetive sg. in ON, in *Muspellz lýðir* ('Muspell's people' *Vǫluspá* 51), *Muspellz synir* ('Muspell's sons' *Lokasenna* 42; *Gylfaginning* 12, 36 and 50), *Muspellz heimr* (*Gylfaginning* 4, 7 and 10), *Muspellz megir* ('Muspell's powers' *Gylfaginning* 12 and 50) and in the nominative sg. *Muspell*, dative sg. *Muspelli* (*Gylfaginning* 3, 4 and 42). The meaning of the word in these texts varies.

In OHG and Old Saxon the word means roughly 'end of the world', whereas in ON it is probably the name for a giant, even if it is identical with Muspellz heimr (the name given in Snorri's cosmogeny to the hot counterpart – in the south of Ginnungagap – to the icy Niflheim) as Snorri understands it at one point (*Gylfaginning* 3 and 4). On the other hand Snorri also seems to think of Muspell as a giant. The information given in *Gylfaginning* 42 that Muspell is the owner of the ship called → Naglfar speaks in favour of this, as well as the expression 'Muspell's sons'. In Snorri's case it would appear to be an identification of the ruler over *Muspellz heimr* (**Muspellr*) as being the fire giant → Surtr, which is an identification which comes from Snorri himself and nowhere else. The crowds known as the people of Muspell, Muspell's powers, Muspell's people are the followers of Muspell. His sons are named in *Lokasenna* 42, *Gylfaginning* 36 and 50. At the Ragnarǫk, at the end of the world, these crowds will set out together against the gods (*Gylfaginning* 50) together with Surtr who will finally kindle the world conflagration. Loki will be the helmsman of the ship Naglfar according to *Vǫluspá* 51 and with this ship the powers of Muspell will cross the sea. It is not certain whether, because of this, Loki should be seen as their leader.

Despite numerous attempts to interpret Muspell (mainly by Braune, Helm, Ebbinghaus) on the one hand as a Germanic word deriving from the elements *spell* 'damage, spoil' and *mu-* 'earth' or 'people' or 'moisture' and on the other hand as a Christian expression, with *spell* meaning 'speech' and *mu-* related to 'mouth' or *mundus* 'world', the etymology has still not been solved. The basic meaning, if we go along with what Braune suggested, is roughly 'end of the world through fire', an idea which according to de Vries could reach back into the Migration Age. Nowadays the generally accepted idea is that the concept was taken over from the continent by the North Germanic peoples and the shift in meaning resulted from the belief in the north that Muspell was a mythological person. → Ragnarǫk, → Surtr.

T. v. Grienberger, 'Múspell' (*IF* 16) 1904; W. Braune, 'Muspilli' (*PBB* 40) 1915; W. Krogmann, 'Mûdspelli' (*WuS* 14) 1932; W. Krogmann, *Mudspelli auf Island*, Wismar 1933; W. Krogmann, 'Muspilli and Muspellsheim' (*Zeitschrift für Religions- und Geistesgeschichte* 5) 1935; E. F. Halvorsen, 'Muspell' (*KLNM* 12) 1967; J. de Vries, *Altgermanische Religionsgeschichte*, Berlin [3]1970; W. Mohr/W. Haug, *Zweimal "Muspilli"*, Tübingen 1977; W. Braune, K. Helm, E. A. Ebbinghaus, *Althochdeutsches Lesebuch*, Tübingen [16]1979; S. Nordal, *Vǫluspá*, Darmstadt 1980.

Muspellzheimr (ON, 'world of Muspell'). The term for a fiery world which forms the southern pole in the creation myth as Snorri describes it in *Gylfaginning* 4 (→ Cosmogeny). The sparks flying from Muspellzheimr melt the ice in Niflheim which leads to the creation of the primeval giant Ymir. The heavenly bodies are also created from sparks from Muspellzheimr. The name is, however, found neither in Eddic lays nor in skaldic poetry, and presumably Snorri derived it himself from → Muspell.

Muspell's sons (ON *Muspellzsynir*). The sons, or rather the followers of → Muspell who was obviously the ruler of Muspellsheimr in Snorri's account of Old Scandinavian mythology and who, with the possibly identical fire giant → Surtr, will kindle the world conflagration at the Ragnarǫk. The fact that in Snorri's description (*Gylfaginning* 50) Surtr is called the leader of Muspell's sons supports this. In Snorri, the phrase *þá er Muspellz-synir herja* 'when the Muspell's sons move into battle' is another term for the Ragnarǫk (*Gylfaginning* 12 and 36); the bridge Bifrǫst falls down beneath them (*Gylfaginning* 12 and 50); then they move to the battle field Vígríðr. – The only reference to Muspell's sons outside the *Snorra Edda* is in *Lokasenna* 42 ('when the Muspell's sons ride through the Mirkwood'). In Snorri the Muspell's sons seem to be synonymous with the *Muspells megir* (*Gylfaginning* 12 and 50) and this has a literal counterpart in the 400 years older Old Saxon *Heliand* (*mūdspelles megin*, line 2591). As, apart from the short reference in *Gylfaginning* 42 that Muspell is the owner of the ship Naglfar, there is no reference to the idea that Muspell was a mythological person, the expression *Muspell's megir* could be the key to the transmission history of the borrowing of the word → Muspell from the continent to Scandinavia.

Muspilli. The usual title now of an OHG poem which deals with the Christian teaching of the end of the world. The title comes from the first editor of the poem (Schmeller 1832) and refers to the 57th line: *dar ni mac denne mak andremo helfan vora demo muspille*; this word obviously refers to the end of the world caused by fire, and has been associated with → Muspell. The poem *Muspilli* appears in a manuscript from the late 9th century or else in the 10th century was written into an earlier manuscript of the 9th century or older.

G. Ehrismann, *Geschichte der deutschen Literatur*, Vol. 1, Munich 1915; H. de Boor, R. Newald, *Geschichte der deutschen Literatur*, Vol. 1, Munich [10]1979; W. Mohr, K. Haug, *Zweimal "Muspilli"*, Tübingen 1977.

Myrkriða (ON, 'the one who rides about in the dark'). A giantess in the *Þulur*, whose name is however only a manuscript variant of Munnriða.

Myrkviðr (ON, 'mirky wood', 'dark wood'). A wood which comes more likely from the legendary world than mythical geography, even if *Lokasenna* 42 includes it in a reference to the Ragnarǫk, when it speaks of 'Muspell's sons riding through Myrkviðr'. Otherwise Myrkviðr only occurs in heroic poetry (*Atlakviða*; *Helgakviða Hundingsbana* I 51; *Hlǫðskviða*).

R. Much, 'Myrkviðr' (J. Hoops, *Reallexikon der Germanischen Altertumskunde* 3) 1915–16; T. A. Shippey, 'Goths and Huns' (*The Medieval Legacy*) Odense 1982.

R: J. R. R. Tolkien used Myrkviðr in his novel, *The Hobbit* (1937), calling it Mirkwood.

Myth of descendency. Myths such as these about the Germanic peoples are recorded in written form from the times of Tacitus to the High Middle Ages and are a mixture of myths, legends and historical facts. It is not necessary to differentiate between the different levels as the mythical function remains unaltered. Characteristic of all branches of Germanic myths of descendency is the element of sacral descendency whether the myths refer to peoples, tribes or ruling families.

The oldest information about Germanic myths comes from Tacitus (*Germania* 2): 'In old lays, the only way of passing down history they have, they worship → Tuisto, the earth-born god. They say that his son Mannus, the ancestor and founder of the people, had three sons from whom the different tribes derive their names: the Ingaevones on the coast, the Hermiones in the middle and finally the Istaevones. Some assure us – since primeval times allow lots of different suppositions – that this son had more descendants from whom the names of the peoples derive: Marsis, Gambriviis, Suebi, Vandiliis, which were the old and true names.' Attempts have been made to read the gods *Yng (= Freyr), *Ermin (→ Irmin = *Tīwaz?) and an unidentifiable *Ist from the three unnamed ancestors of the three peoples; of these, only *Yng stands up to critical examination. On the other hand the formal structure of these myths of descendency, Tuisto ('hermaphrodite') – Mannus ('man') – three sons, can also be found in the Scandinavian tradition of the Edda (→ Cosmogony) where three sons of

Buri (Borr), Odin, Vili and Vé are the ancestors of the gods. This structure can be found in the myths of descendency of other Indo-Germanic peoples, for example the Greeks. The hermaphrodite Tuisto seems to correspond to the gigantic primeval hermaphrodite Ymir in Nordic mythology who in turn corresponds to the Old Indian proto-couple Yama – Yamî, Avestic Yima. The Germanic myth about Mannus according to Tacitus corresponds in Old Indian to Mânus as the ancestor of the human race. Essential characteristics of this myth appear to be traceable back to the third millenium B.C. in Indo-European areas.

However, as we know from the passage in Tacitus, the individual Germanic tribes thought greatly about their sacred descendency, which is confirmed by the Germanic tribes' myths of descendency as recorded in later times. Bede's genealogy of the Anglo-Saxon leaders from 731 A.D. (*Hist. Eccl.* I, 15) traces the origins of Hengist and Horsa via Wictgils, Witta and Wecta back to Wodan 'from whom the royal families of many other provinces also hale.' This genealogy in the lengthier versions made by medieval historians contains numerous other mythological names including Geat (which corresponds to Gaut, the ON name for Odin).

According to *Historia Langobardorum* 5, a Langobardian royal family, to which Audoin and Alboin belonged, traces itself back to a mythical ancestor called Gaus (from *Gaut). Similarly, Jordanes tells (*Getica* 13, 78) of the Goths whose royal family, the Amales, can be traced back to Gapt (from *Gaut). Jordanes calls this family 'Anses' (probably identical with the Æsir) which he translates as *semideos* (half-gods).

In medieval Old Norse literature the tales about the sacral descendency reflect the purpose of the legitimization of royal and noble genealogies. Whereas the Swedish Ynglingar traced themselves back to Yngvi-Freyr (*Ynglingatal*), in the *Ynglinga saga* Snorri considers them to be Odin's descendants, as did Eyvindr in the *Haleygjatal* in the 10th century with the genealogy of earls of Hlaðir. The Danish Skjoldungs and the Nordic Skilfings link their claims to descendency from gods with other, older genealogies.

There is proof that in Germanic areas royal families, individual tribes and peoples believed in descendency from gods just as the Eddic sources prove this to be the case for the origins of the human race (→ Anthropogeny).

J. Grimm, *Deutsche Mythologie*, Berlin [4]1875–78; O. Höfler, 'Abstammungstraditionen' (*Hoops* 1) [2]1972; A. Faulkes, 'Descent from the Gods' (*Medieval Scandinavia* 11) 1978/79.

Mythological poetry. The poetic → *Edda* contains mythological lays as well as heroic poetry. This include particularly → *Vǫluspá*, → *Hávamál*, → *Vafþrúðnismál*, → *Grímnismál*, → *Skírnismál*, → *Lokasenna*, → *Hymiskviða*, → *Þrymskviða*, → *Hárbarðsljóð* and *Alvíssmál*. The main manuscript for these lays is the Codex Regius (written in Iceland c.1170). However, the mythological lays → *Rígsþula* and → *Baldrs draumar* are not in this manuscript. The form of the mythological poetry is the stave rhyming long line of Germanic poetry. Dating is extremely difficult as both the form and the mythological content of poetry was kept up, long after Christianization, as a traditional literary genre as shown by the mythological poems *Grógaldr* and *Fjǫlsvinnsmál* (usually put together under the title → *Svipdagsmál*), probably written in the late Middle Ages. The dating of the lays varies from lay to lay, but can be roughly assumed to be between the 9th and 12th centuries. As such, mythological poetry is, together with → skaldic poetry, the oldest literary documentation of northern Germanic mythology.

H. Schneider, 'Über die ältesten Götterlieder der Nordgermanen' (*PBB* 69) 1947; A. Holtsmark, 'Eddadiktning' (*KLNM* 3) 1958; J. de Vries, *Altnordische Literaturgeschichte*, Berlin [2]1970;

K. v. See, 'Altnordische Literatur' (*LexMA* 1) Munich 1980; K. Schier, 'Die Literaturen des Nordens' (*Neues Handbuch der Literaturwissenschaft* 8) 1981.

Nabbi (ON, probably 'bump') is the name of a dwarf in *Hyndluljóð* 7 who prepared the wild boar → Hildisvini together with Dáinn.

Næfi (ON, 'the capable one' as in Næfr, or rather Nefi 'relation'?) is the name of a dwarf in the *Þulur*.

Næfr (ON, 'the capable one') is the name of a dwarf in the *Þulur*.

Naglfar (ON, 'nail ship', 'ship of the dead') is the ship of the dead in northern mythology which puts to sea at → Ragnarǫk and which is helmed by the giant Hrymr (by Loki, according to *Vǫluspá* 51) and takes the sons of → Múspell to their fight with the gods (*Gylfaginning* 42 and 50); it is the biggest of all ships (whereas Skíðblaðnir is described as the best of all ships: *Gylfaginning* 42) and is said to be built from the uncut nails of the dead which is the reason why the nails of corpses should always be cut so that the arrival of Naglfar and with it the end of the world may be delayed (*Gylfaginning* 50).

In post-medieval folklore the ship of the dead Naglfar is found everywhere from Iceland (mod. Icel. *náskipið*) to eastern Europe, and there is always the command to cut the nails of the dead since otherwise the devil would build a ship out of them to convey people to hell.

There is a possible connexion between the ship Naglfar and the widespread custom in the Migration and Viking Ages of → boat burial, as the name originally meant 'ship of the dead'. Admittedly there is a clear difference between the journey of the dead to the Other World in the death-ship and the journey of the sons of Múspell in Naglfar to the Ragnarǫk. It is possible that the ship of the dead Naglfar in the description of the Ragnarǫk was a literary appropriation; however, this being the case, the Medieval popular belief must then have referred to the death-ship of the individual rather than to the ship associated with the end of the world.

The interpretation of Naglfar as 'nail ship' (*naglafar* from ON *nagli* 'nail') is surely a folk-etymology; Naglfar (Nagl from *nā*) is however related to Gothic *naus* 'dead', Greek *nékus* 'corpse'; thus, it originally meant 'corpse ship', 'ship of the dead'.

K. Krohn, 'Das schiff Naglfar' (*FuF* 11) 1911; K. Krohn, 'Zum schiffe Naglfar' (*FuF* 11) 1911; H. Lie, 'Naglfar og Naglfari' (*MoM*) 1954; E. F. Halvorsen, 'Naglfar' (*KLNM* 12) 1967; R. Simek, *Die Schiffsnamen*, Vienna 1982.

Naglfari (ON) is the name (according to Snorri: *Gylfaginning* 9) of the first husband of → Nótt, who personifies night; both sons are called Auðr. What could have made Snorri invent the otherwise unmentioned husband of Nótt is unknown.

Nágrind (ON, 'Death-fence') is the name of the fence surrounding the underworld Hel (*Skírnismál* 35, *Lokasenna* 63); in other places it is also called → Helgrind or Valgrind.

Náinn (ON) is the name of a dwarf (*Vǫluspá* 11: *Gylfaginning* 19, *Þulur*). For an interpretation of his name → Náli.

Naitienae (or Maitienae?) is the name of → matrons on a votive stone from Thorr near Cologne (CIL XIII 12 068) from the 3rd or 4th century A.D.; the interpretation is uncertain. Possibly the name could be derived from the name of a river.

S. Gutenbrunner, *Die germanischen Götternamen*, Halle 1936; H. Reichert, *Lexikon der altgermanischen Namen*, Vienna 1987–90.

Nal (ON) is the name given to Loki's mother, otherwise known as Laufey, in *Gylfaginning* 32, *Skáldskaparmál* 16 and *Sǫrla þáttr* 2, but not in all of the Eddic lays. It is extremely doubtful whether the same person is meant by both of these names although the *Sǫrla þáttr* gives the explanation that Laufey was so slender and nimble that she was called Nal ('needle'), but this interpretation is obviously secondary. The fact that in the sources mentioned above both names are given suggests that there were two different traditions. On the other hand Nal is not found either in the *Edda* or in skaldic poetry. The name either means the same as ON *nal* 'needle' or else refers to a connexion with the realm of the dead (→ Náli, → Naglfar).

J. de Vries, *Altnordisches etymologisches Wörterbuch*, Leiden [2]1977.

Náli (ON) is the name of a dwarf (*Vǫluspá* 13). It is related either to ON *nal* 'needle' or else 'the one as small as a needle'. Originally Náli was possibly a demon of the dead (from Gothic *naus* 'dead person', cf. → Náströnd, → Naglfar) as well as the dwarf names Nár and Náinn.

S. Gutenbrunner, 'Eddastudien I' (*ANF* 70) 1955; J. de Vries, *Altnordisches etymologisches Wörterbuch*, Leiden [2]1977.

Nanna (ON) is → Baldr's wife according to the Icelandic tradition of the Baldr myth; however, according to Saxo, she is the wife of Baldr's opponent and killer Hötherus/→ Hǫðr.

In Snorri Nanna is Nepr's daughter (who however is named in the *Þulur* as one of Odin's sons), Baldr's wife and Forseti's mother; in his description of → Baldr's Funeral he remarks that Nanna dies of her grief and is burned on the same pyre as her husband. Snorri includes her among the Asyniur goddesses in *Skáldskaparmál* 1 and he probably invented the idea that Frigg is Nanna's sister-in-law. In skaldic poetry, the name Nanna occurs relatively frequently, but the passages do not allow any conclusions as to who Nanna was. Of all the Eddic lays, only *Hyndluljóð* 20 names a certain Nanna who is here the daughter of a similarly undefined Nǫkkvi.

Despite the sparsity of the ON sources Snorri is not alone in his association of Nanna with the myth of Baldr since Saxo Grammaticus (*Gesta Danorum* III, 63ff.) also repeatedly names Nanna in his version of the myth. Admittedly here she is the daughter of the Norwegian king Gevarus and marries Hötherus, but she is also loved by Baldr and this is the circumstance which leads to the battle between the two and to the death of Baldr.

The similarity between the names of Nanna and the Sumerian Inanna, Nannar (Babylonian Ishtar) or Nana, the mother of the Phrygian Attis, has repeatedly led to the opinion that Nanna was identical with one of these goddesses but this is hardly likely because of the great distances both temporally and geographically between them.

The meaning of the name is not totally clear, but the origin from a babble word *nanna* 'mother' would be possible. De Vries, however, relates it etymologically to the Germanic root '*nanþ*-; in this case Nanna would mean 'the daring one'.

F. R. Schröder, *Germanentum und Hellenismus*, Heidelberg 1924; A. Sommerfelt, 'Har syden og vesten vaert uten betydning for nordisk hedenskap?' (*MoM*) 1962; J. de Vries, *Altnordisches etymologisches Wörterbuch*, Leiden [2]1977; J. de Vries, *Altgermanische Religionsgeschichte*, Berlin [3]1970.

Nár (ON, 'corpse') is the name of a dwarf (*Vǫluspá* 11, *Gylfaginning* 13, *Þulur*), cf. also → Náli and → Náinn.

Narfi 1 (ON) is the name of Loki's son and indeed not only in 13th century sources (*Lokasenna* 65 Pr; *Gylfaginning* 32, 49, *Skáldskaparmál* 16) but also in 9th century sources (Þjóðólfr ór Hvíni, *Ynglingatal* 7). Narfi, which alternates with the form Nari, is also recorded as a personal name. The kenning for → Hel *jóðis Ulfs ok Narfa* ('sister of the wolf and Narfi') puts Narfi in the region of the realm of the dead. The name of the giant →Nǫrr (also Nǫrfi, Narfi) who is said to be the father of the night, speaks in support of this. The name possibly means 'narrow' but, if Narfi was originally a demon of the dead, despite the vowel quantity an association with ON, *nár*, Gothic *naus* 'corpse' (→ Nástrǫnd, → Náli, → Naglfar) would also be conceivable.

J. de Vries, *The Problem of Loki*, Helsinki 1933; J. de Vries, *Altgermanische Religionsgeschichte*, Berlin [3]1970.

Narfi 2 → Nǫrr.

Nari → Narfi, Loki's son.

Narr (ON) is the name of a dwarf in the *Þulur*; the name is possibly a borrowing from MHG *narre* 'fool'.

L. Motz, 'New Thoughts on Dwarf-Names' (*FmSt* 7) 1973.

Násheimr (ON, 'world of the dead') occurs only once in the Sturlunga saga (II, 220) in the 13th century and is certainly not the name for any particular place in heathen mythology, but could be the name for the Christian Other World; the word is a new formation based on mythological concepts such as → Nástrǫnd.

Nástrǫnd (ON, 'shore of death') is the name given to a mythological place in *Vǫluspá* 38 where, far away from the sun, there is a hall with its gate facing north and from whose roof poison drops and in which snakes curl. In Snorri (*Gylfaginning* 51) this hall is described in more detail, but otherwise quite similarly. Nástrǫnd lies in the north, as does Hel, and is already marked as a place of the dead by this geographic situation; the details of the hall remind us, however, of Christian visions of the Other World.

F. Ström, 'Döden o. de döda' (*KLNM* 3) 1958.

Nati (ON) is the name of a giant in the *Þulur*. The meaning of the name is obscure.

Neck (German; Swedish *Nekk*, ON *nykr*) is a kind of water spirit as found in German *Nix*, *Nixe*. All these names go back to a common Indo-Germanic root *nig-* 'bathe, wash'.

J. de Vries, *Altgermanische Religionsgeschichte*, Berlin [3]1970.

Nefi (ON, 'nephew, relation') is the name of a dwarf in the *Þulur*.

Nehalennia is the name of a Germanic goddess who is named in numerous votive altars from the 3rd century.

28 inscriptions come from Domburg on the Dutch island of Walcheren and a similar number were found in new finds made in 1971/72 at Colijnsplaat on the island of Noord-Beveland; 2 others come from the Cologne-Deutz area.

The goddess is depicted on these votive altars and her attributes are mostly baskets of fruit, like those we know from the monuments of the → matron cult, often a dog; several times she is resting against the bow of a ship, partly even on an oar. Whereas the fruit could point to a fertility function, as is the case with the matrons, the dog would be more characteristic for a goddess of the dead, and an attempt to etymologize Nehalennia has related it to Latin *nex*, *necare* 'to kill'). The connexion with the ship and the rudder is also further supported by the inscriptions themselves in which merchants are named so that we may perhaps have to reckon with a goddess of seafaring. All of the attributes mentioned are also those belonging to Isis. With the adoption of Roman forms of inscriptions and altars iconographic detail such as the attributes of the goddess were also adopted. Tacitus's reference (*Germania* 9) to the fact that the Germanic Suebi made sacrifices to the goddess Isis whose symbol was a ship is even more important in these circumstancs. This Germanic Isis in Tacitus has been associated in various ways with the cult of → Nerthus. There is the possibility – as de Vries and Much supposed – that Nehalennia is the local special form of a Germanic goddess of fertility and seafaring as whose representative also Nerthus should be understood. The illegibility of the inscription (CIL XIII 8798) does not allow it to be said with any degree of certainty that on a particular altar to Nehalennia Isis is also named.

The etymology of the name Nehalennia is uncertain; apart from the already mentioned 'goddess of death' (from Latin *necare* 'to kill', or also from the verb *helan* 'hide') Kaufmann's derivation of it from **nēu-* is worth thinking about as it would also fit the explanation of 'goddess of seafaring'. On the other hand Much interpreted Nehalennia as meaning 'the helpful goddess coming close'.

T. v. Grienberger, *Über germanische Götternamen auf Inschriftsteinen des Niederrheins*, Diss. Vienna 1890; R. Much, 'Nehalennia' (*ZfdA* 35) 1891; F. Kauffmann, 'Dea Nehalennia' (*PBB* 16) 1892; S. Gutenbrunner, *Die germanischen Götternamen*, Halle 1936; A. Hondius-Crone, *The Temple of Nehalennia at Domburg*, Amsterdam 1955; M. Schönfeld, *Wörterbuch der altgermanischen Personen- und Völkernamen*, Heidelberg [2]1965; J. de Vries, *Altgermanische Religionsgeschichte*, Berlin [3]1970; S. J. de Laet, 'Nehalennia, déesse germanique ou celtique?' (*Helinium* 11) 1971; E. Cramer-Peters, 'Zur Deutung des Namens Nehalennia', and: 'Frija-Isis-Nehalennia' (*Amsterdamer Beiträge zur älteren Germanistik* 3) 1972; H. Reichert, *Lexikon der altgermanischen Namen*, Vienna 1987–90.

neorxnawang (OE, 'paradise') is a frequently recorded term for the Christian concept of paradise in OE literature. The word belongs to Gmc *wang* 'meadow' (similarly Gothic *waggs* 'paradise'), but the first part of the word remains obscure even today although there have been over a dozen different attempts to interpret it. It is possible to consider that it was already an Old Germanic term for the 'Other World; Asgard' on the basis of the dark meaning (which certainly was not understood any better by the Christian authors using it) and as such it corresponds to North Germanic Iðavǫllr or Glæsisvellir.

A. Leitzmann, 'Ags. neorxnawang' (*PBB* 32) 1907; R. Jente, *Die mythologischen Ausdrücke im altenglischen Wortschatz*, Heidelberg 1921; E. A. Philippson, *Germanisches Hedientum bei den Angelsachsen*, Leipzig 1929; W. Krogmann, 'Neorxna wang und Iða vǫllr' (*Archiv* 191) 1955.

R: K. H. Strobl, *Die Runen und das Marterholz* (novel, 1942).

Nepr (ON) is in Snorri the otherwise unnamed father of Nanna; in the *Þulur* he is said to be one of Odin's sons. The origin of the name is obscure, as is its place in the myth.

Nersihenae is a → matron name on a votive stone from Jülich (CIL XIII 7883); the name is probably derived from the river name Niers (recorded in 856 as Nersa).

S. Gutenbrunner, *Die germanischen Götternamen*, Halle 1936; J. de Vries, *Altgermanische Religionsgeschichte*, Berlin [3]1970; H. Reichert, *Lexikon der altgermanischen Namen*, I. Vienna 1987.

Nerthus is a Germanic goddess about whose cult on a Baltic island in the 1st century A.D. Tacitus (*Germania* 40) reported in detail. He lists seven Germanic tribes who congregated to worship Nerthus as Mother Earth (*Terram Matrem*). On an island in the ocean there is a covered dedicated cart which stands in a sacred grove and which only a priest is allowed to touch. He receives the goddess in the sanctum and walks next to her cart which is drawn by cows. During the days in which she drives in procession, there is a festive peace and weapons are shut away. When the goddess returns to her shrine, the cart, cloths and the goddess herself are washed in a secluded lake and the slaves who helped with this ritual washing are then drowned in the same lake and this means that her shrine is surrounded by a holy secret.

The island mentioned must be an island in the Baltic since the tribes whom Tacitus counts as belonging to the Suebi settled to the east of the river Elb. Considering the proximity of the island to the mainland Als or Fyn have been thought to be the island in question. The cult of Nerthus, who is surrounded by a divine peace, most likely includes the execution of a *hierós gámos* as the washing of the goddess would suggest. Remains of cult carts and models of the same are known from finds from the Iron Age and rock carvings confirm the tradition of cult processions as early as the Bronze Age in southern Scandinavia. The draping of the cart suggests that it was only used in the Nerthus cult for sacred purposes.

The earth mother Nerthus in Tacitus, Gmc *Nerþus, is exactly the same form of the name which would correspond to the ON god Njǫrðr. The change of sex here from Nerthus to Njǫrðr can be explained in various ways. It seems to be perfectly possible that even in *Nerþus a male and a female goddess were worshipped, as is the case in the (probably younger) brother and sister Freyr/Freyja. Another possibility would be that *Nerþus was a hermaphrodite deity. The usage of the plural of the god's name Njǫrðr, which occurs in several skaldic poems, points to the first solution. The fact that the masculine and feminine of the grammatical u-stems fall together means that a formal differentiation according to gender becomes impossible.

Whilst Nerthus occurs in the 1st century on a Danish island, Njǫrðr is documented in Middle Swedish and West Norwegian place-names as well as in late heathen myths. The questions as to whether this could suggest a migration of the cult from the south to the north must remain open, although the distribution of the place-names speaks rather in favour of an expansion from around several Scandinavian cult centres.

A. Kock, 'Die Göttin Nerthus und der Gott Njörðr' (*ZfdPh* 28) 1896; G. Schütte, 'The Cult of Nerthus' (*Saga-Book* 8) 1913–14; E. Bickel, 'Die Glaubwürdigkeit des Tacitus' (*Bonner Jahrbücher* 139) 1934; E. C. Polomé, 'A propos de la déesse Nerthus' (*Latomus* 13) 1954; H. Kirchner, 'Eine steinzeitliche "Nerthus"-Darstellung' (*Studien aus Alteuropa* I) Köln, Graz 1964; R. Much, Die *Germania* des Tacitus, Heidelberg [3]1967; J. de Vries, *Altgermanische Religionsgeschichte*, Berlin [3]1970; G. Dumézil, *Gods of the Ancient Northmen*, Berkeley 1977; E. C. Polomé, 'Some aspects of the cult of the mother goddess in Western Europe' (*Vistas and Vectors, Festschrift H. Rehder*) Austin 1980.

R: E. Doepler d. J., *Nerthus* (E. Doepler, W. Ranisch, *Walhall*, 1901).

Nervinae. → Matron name (?). The name is found on a votive stone from Bavay,

North France and is derived from the name of the probably Germanic tribe of the Nervii.

S. Gutenbrunner, *Die germanischen Götternamen*, Halle 1936; H. Reichert, *Lexikon der altgermanischen Namen*, Vienna 1987–90.

Niðafjǫll (ON, 'dark mountains') are mountains in the underworld from which the dragon of death Níðhǫggr comes (*Vǫluspá* 66). In Snorri (*Gylfaginning* 51) the Niðafjǫll are the same as the Niðvellir in *Vǫluspá* 37. According to his information there was a golden palace there called Sindri, but this is probably based on a misunderstanding as in *Vǫluspá* 37 the palace is the residence of Sindri's family, i.e. the dwarfs. Snorri further comments that this palace will be inhabited in the new world following the Ragnarǫk by good and virtuous people. This re-interpretation, which, despite its proximity to Hel, apparently causes Snorri no problem whatsoever, shows that the northern Other World landscapes (such as Niðafjǫll, Niðavellir, Glæsisvellir, Oðáinsakr and others) were never understood as places of punishment in the sense of the Christian hell.

Niðavellir (ON, 'dark fields') is the name of the mythological place in the north where the golden hall of Sindri's family is situated (*Vǫluspá* 37). Sindri's family are the dwarfs and only in this passage do we hear of their golden hall in the north; otherwise they live in rocks and in the mountains. The information that the Niðavellir lie in the north pushes them into the vicinity of the underworld Hel which was similarly thought of being situated in the north. In Snorri (*Gylfaginning* 51) Niðavellir and → Niðafjǫll would appear to mean the same place, also in *Vǫluspá* 66, although in both cases events and places after the Ragnarǫk are being spoken of. Snorri is more detailed and in his version the golden hall itself is called Sindri, and in the new world the good and virtuous will live there – a picture heavily influenced by Christian concepts of paradise.

Níðhǫggr (1) (ON, 'the one striking full of hatred') is a dragon of death in *Vǫluspá* which drinks the blood of the dead and eats corpses (*Vǫluspá* 39). *Vǫluspá* 66 describes how it will live in Niðavellir in the new world after the Ragnarǫk. In *Grímnismál* 32 and 35 it lives under and gnaws at the roots of the world-ash Yggdrasill. A squirrel → Ratatoskr is a go-between messenger between Níðhǫggr and the eagle who sits in the branches of the ash bringing discord. Snorri repeats this information from *Grímnismál* in *Gylfaginning* 14 and 15 whilst in *Gylfaginning* 51 he repeats the passage from *Vǫluspá* 39 in a different form in which Níðhǫggr torments the dead in the spring Hvergelmir and thus becomes like the dragon in Christian visionary literature, with elements of hell-like places of punishment.

R: D. Werenskiold, *Nidhogg* (wooden relief in the town hall in Oslo, 1938).

Níðhǫggr (2) (ON) is the name of a dwarf in the *Þulur*.

Niði (ON, 'the dark one', from *nið* 'new moon'?) is the name of a dwarf in *Vǫluspá* 11 and in the *Þulur*.

Niðǫtr (ON) is the name of a dwarf in the *Þulur*. It is probably a misspelling of → Níðhǫggr.

níðstǫng (ON, 'derision pole') → magic.

Nifengr (ON) is the name of a dwarf in the *Þulur*. It is possibly only a variant of → Nipingr, but Fengr is also a name for Odin, or perhaps comes from *ný-fengr* 'recently acquired'? Motz considers that Nifengr is related to *níu* 'nine', i.e. 'the one who can catch nine' and supposes that this refers to a game, but this is hardly very convincing.

L. Motz, 'New Thoughts on Dwarf-Names' (*FmSt* 7) 1973.

Niflheim (ON, 'the dark world') is a mythical place in the icy north. The name is not given in the mythological Eddic lays but is a standard element in Snorri's cosmogony. He reports that Niflheim existed even before the creation of the world (*Gylfaginning* 3) and that Niflheim is separated from the heat of → Muspell by → Ginnungagap (*Gylfaginning* 4). One of the roots of the world-ash Yggdrasill stretches out towards Niflheim and beneath it also lies the spring → Hvergelmir from which the Élivágar rivers begin (*Gylfaginning* 3, 14). Snorri identifies Niflheim in *Gylfaginning* 33 however with Hel (probably under the influence of the name Niflhel), and this is apparent also in *Gylfaginning* 43; in the individual manuscripts the terms Niflheim and Niflhel actually alternate. If the concept itself does not come from Snorri, the name certainly does.

J. de Vries, *Altgermanische Religionsgeschichte*, Berlin [3]1970.

Niflhel (ON, 'the dark Hel') is part of the underworld → Hel. Niflhel, originally probably only a poetic intensification to Hel (*Baldrs draumar* 2), was understood by Snorri in connexion with *Vafþrúðnismál* 43 in such a way that it is the ninth world under the earth, i.e. the deepest and darkest hell (*Gylfaginning* 2), and it is where the people from Hel die (*Vafþrúðnismál* 43). As Hel is only the resting place of shadows and not a place of punishment, this strengthening of Niflhel was brought about by Snorri as a result of the Christian concept of hell (cf. *Gylfaginning* 41). – Niflhel probably belongs etymologically rather to OE *nifol* 'dark', OHG *nebul*, Latin *nebula* 'fog, mist' (thus meaning 'dark Hel') than to OE *neowal* 'low'?, i.e. 'deep Hel'. The first explanation is also supported by → Niflheim.

J. de Vries, *Altgermanische Religionsgeschichte*, Berlin [3]1970; J. de Vries, *Altnordisches etymologisches Wörterbuch*, Leiden [2]1970.

Night. In Germanic mythology the personification of night occurs in the figure of the ON giantess → Nótt.

As the Germanic peoples used the lunar month for their computation, they counted in nights rather than days and also in winters and not summers; a man would thus be said to be so many winters old. In religious areas, however, the night did not play a particularly important role even though the nightly ride of the Wild Hunt (during Twelfth night, ON *hǫkunótt*) and the sacrifices to the mothers (matrons? *dísir*?), OE *mōdraniht*, should not be forgotten. In folklore the night was considered to be a time of particular activity of the beings of lower mythology such as dwarfs and trolls, but this is a phenomenon that is not limited only to Germanic religion.

J. Grimm, *Deutsche Mythologie*, Berlin [4]1875–78.

Nine. Apart from the number three which played a role in many other cultures, nine is the mythical number of the Germanic tribes. Documentation for the significance of the number nine is found in both myth and cult. In Odin's self-sacrifice he hung for nine nights on the windy tree (*Hávamál*), there are nine worlds to Niflhel (*Vafþrúðnismál* 43), Heimdallr was born to nine mothers (*Hyndluljóð* 35), Freyr had to wait for nine nights for his marriage to Gerd (*Skírnismál* 41), and eight nights (= nine days?) was the time of betrothal given also in the *Þrymskviða*. Literary embellishments in the Eddas similarly use the number nine: Skaði and Njǫrðr lived alternately for nine days in Nóatún and in Þrymheimr; every ninth night eight equally heavy rings drip from the ring Draupnir; Menglǫð has nine maidens to serve her (*Fjǫlsvinnsmál* 35ff.), and Ægir had as many daughters. Thor can take nine steps at the Ragnarǫk after his battle with the Midgard serpent before he falls down dead.

Sacrificial feasts lasting nine days are mentioned for both → Uppsala and Lejre and at these supposedly nine victims were sacrificed each day.

Like the number three, nine was one of the important numbers for magic. With the 27 they belong to the lunar calender.

Nipingr (ON, 'the sorrowful' from *hnipinn*?) is the name of a dwarf in the *Vǫluspá* 11.

Nipt (ON, 'sister') is a name for a valkyrie which only occurs once in the *Þulur*. Although the meaning from ON *nipt* 'sister, niece' is not sufficient for an interpretation as the name of a valkyrie, it is interesting that the same word root was used to form the Old Germanic matron name → Annaniptiae.

Nisse (Norwegian, Danish, Swedish) is a kind of brownie or house spirit. Linguistically speaking it is not related to German *Nix*, but is rather derived from the personal name Nils (from Nicolaus).

H. Feilberg, 'Der Kobold in nordischer Überlieferung' (*Zeitschrift für Volkskunde* 8) 1898.

Njarðarlǫg was the name of the tiny West Norwegian island Tysnesö in Hardanger until early modern times. The name Njarðarlǫg means 'Njǫrð's cult area' and belongs to the place-names which point to a cult of the god → Njǫrðr (as do Naervik, Naereim, Nerland). The place-names found on the island Njarðarlǫg, Vevatne and Ve ('holy lake' and 'shrine', both from ON *vé* 'shrine') as well as Hovland ('temple land') and also Tysnes ('Týr's ness') from which the modern name of the island is derived, point to the fact that there was an important cult centre here. Vevatn, the lake on the island, reminds us strongly of the cult of → Nerthus described by Tacitus (*Germania* 40). It is impossible to decide whether the occurrence of the god of the heavens, Týr, in one of the place-names allows the assumption of the celebration here of a *hierós gámos* between the god of the sky and the mother of the earth (Nerthus/Njǫrðr). Olsen sees in Njarðarlǫg the place where the Nerthus cult was practised for the first time in Scandinavia.

M. Olsen, *Det gamle norske ønavn Njarðarlǫg*, Christiania 1905; M. Olsen, *Ættagård og Helligdom*, Oslo 1926; F. R. Schröder, *Ingunar-Freyr*, Tübingen 1941; J. de Vries, *Altgermanische Religionsgeschichte*, Berlin ^{3}1970; G. Dumézil, *From Myth to Fiction*, Chicago, London 1973.

Njǫrðr (ON). A Scandinavian god who belongs to the Vanir family of gods and is the father of the twins Freyr and Freyja (*Grímnismál* 43, *Skírnismál* 41, *Þrymskviða* 22). He lives by the sea in Nóatún (*Grímnismál* 16) and is married to the giant's daughter → Skaði who was allowed to choose a husband from among the gods. This marriage is not a success since Njǫrðr wants to live by the sea and Skaði is drawn towards the mountains (*Gylfaginning* 22, *Skáldskaparmál* 1). Snorri adds that Njǫrðr rules over the wind and the sea as well as controlling fire and he is called upon to aid seafarers and fishermen. He is also rich and can grant wealth. Only Snorri says that Njǫrðr is one of the Vanir and that he came to the Æsir as a hostage, in exchange for Hœnir, after the Vanir wars (*Gylfaginning* 22). Njǫrðr only occurs occasionally in skaldic poetry and is only found in the above mentioned Eddic lays, so that apart from the fact that he is the father of Freyr and Freyja and his home is at Nóatún we know very little about him. The reference in *Lokasenna* 34 that he had problems with Hymir's daughters who used his mouth as a chamber pot is probably a late jocular addition and is not found in the original myth itself.

Snorri tells of a sacrifice made to Njǫrðr in the *Hákonarsaga* 14 where a toast is drunk to Njǫrðr and Freyr as a harvest blessing.

Dumézil considered that Njǫrðr is at least reflected in other works of literature, namely in Snorri's extensive tale of → Haddingus. The tales of Njǫrðr and Haddingus have traits in common but Dumézil is unable to give a satisfactory answer as to why the adventure of the god should have been transferred to Haddingus, particularly as all the names have been changed.

Despite the extremely poor picture we have of Njǫrðr as reflected in Old Norse literature Njǫrðr would appear to have had a significant position in the cult of the Vanir in Germanic antiquity. This is not only confirmed by the considerable number of cult place names, which occur particularly in middle Sweden and western Norway, but also by the linguistic identity of the name Njǫrðr with proto-Gmc *Nerþuz, → Nerthus, an earth goddess, for whom Tacitus describes a cult as taking place on an island in the Baltic in the 1st century A.D. The change of sex from Nerthus to Njǫrðr can presumably be explained by the fact that with *Nerþuz either a hermaphrodite deity was meant or else, more likely, a divine brother and sister (like Freyr and Freyja).

Njǫrð's association with seafaring which he shares with his son → Freyr and which is confirmed by his home at Nóatún, not only allows the Vanir god Njǫrðr to be seen as a god of fertility but also as the god of seafaring. As such he was, together with the other Vanir, perhaps a relic of the divine world of the pre-Germanic megalithic culture who were quite definitely seafarers. On the other hand seafaring played an important role among the Bronze Age Germanic peoples and therefore it would be conceivable that the numerous cult pictures of ships on Bronze Age rock carvings in south Scandinavia played a role in the cult of the seafarer god Njǫrðr. However, the distribution of the Scandinavian place-names based on Njǫrðr shows that the problem was more complex in historical times. Whereas the Norwegian place-names are always found near the coast, as would be expected for a seafaring god, the Swedish place-names are always found in inland agricultural areas so that the supposition seems true that Njǫrðr was worshipped here as god of fertility (Wessén), and that the deity may even have been a female Nerthus. This would also point to the existence of a dual function divine brother and sister of the same name, and not, as Wessén suggested, two gods Njǫrðr (female) and Ullr (male).

Elgquist has postulated a migration of the cult of Njǫrðr from the south to the north, but this is by no means substantiated by the material from place-names, and it would seem more likely that there was a slow expansion from certain cult centres.

A. Kock, 'Die Göttin Nerthus und der Gott Njǫrðr' (*ZfdPh* 28) 1896; S. Konow, 'Njord und Kali' (*Festskrift A. Kjær*) Oslo 1924; F. R. Schröder, 'Njǫrðrs nackte Füße' (*PBB* 51) 1927; E. Wessén, 'Schwedische Ortsnamen und altnordische Mythologie' (*APhSc* 4) 1929; H. Schück, 'Ingunar – Freyr' (*Fornvännen* 35) 1940; E. Elgqvist, *Studier rörande njordkultens spridning bland de nordiska folken*, Lund 1952; F. R. Schröder, 'Die Göttin des Urmeeres und ihr männlicher Partner' (*PBB West* 82) 1960; E. F. Halvorsen, 'Njǫrðr' (*KLNM* 12) 1967; J. de Vries, *Altgermanische Religionsgeschichte*, Berlin [3]1970; G. Dumézil, *From Myth to Fiction*, Chicago 1973.

R: K. Ehrenberg, *Freyr und Gerda; Skade und Niurd* (drawing, 1883); E. Doepler d. J., *Skadi* (E. Doepler, W. Ranisch, *Walhall*) 1901.
Njördr, Swedish ice-breaker, built 1969.

Njótr (ON). A name for Odin in the *Þulur* which should probably also be understood as such in numerous kennings in skaldic poetry. Njótr actually means 'user, enjoyer' and is perhaps closely related to the mythical name Fornjótr, but it might be a borrowing from West Germanic and as such it could be associated with the Saxon god's name Sahsnôt, Anglo-Saxon Saxneat.

H. Falk, *Odensheite*, Christiania 1924; J. de Vries, *Altnordisches etymologisches Wörterbuch*, Leiden [2]1977.

Nóatún (ON, 'place for ships', 'ship-town'). Home of the god → Njǫrðr in *Grímnismál*. Most of Snorri's references to Nóatún (*Gylfaginning* 22, 23, *Skáldskaparmál* 1) are in connexion with Njǫrðr's marriage to Skaði. The ill-matched couple cannot agree on a permanent home, as Njǫrðr wishes to live in Nóatún beside the sea, but Skaði wants to live in the snow-covered mountains and go hunting.

Nóatún is related to the Indo-European **nāus-* 'ship' (ON *nór*, Old Indian *nāu*, Latin *navis*) and to ON *tún* 'town, yard' and provides an important indication of the link between Njǫrðr and seafaring of which he and his son Freyr are the patrons.

R: W. Heinesen, *Noatun* (novel, 1951).

Nǫkkvi (ON, actually 'boat, skiff'). Nanna's father in the Eddic lay *Hyndluljóð* 20. However, this Nanna can hardly be identified as the wife of Baldr, as she is said to be the daughter of a certain Nepr.

Nǫnn (ON, 'the strong one'). One of the (mythical?) rivers in the catalogue of rivers in *Grímnismál* 28.

Nǫrfi → Nǫrr.

Nǫrr (ON, 'slight, narrow'). The name given in *Vafþrúðnismál* 25 and *Alvíssmál* 29 to the father of the night. In Snorri (*Gylfaginning* 9) he is called Nǫrfi or Narfi and is a giant in Jǫtunheim. The name Nǫrr is used in the Eddic lay predominantly as an embellishment since it complies with the rules of alliteration. It is however striking that an OE term for night *narouua* is related to Nǫrr.

Nǫt (ON, 'the stinging one'). One of the (mythical?) rivers in the catalogue of rivers in *Grímnismál* 28 and in the *Þulur* The name possibly refers to the stinging cold of the water.

Nordendorf fibula I. The silver gilded curved fibula, nearly 13 cm long, was found in 1843 in the vicinity of Nordendorf (near Augsburg, Germany). It comes from the Alamannic region dating from the first half of the 7th century and has a runic inscription engraved into it which was only discovered in 1865. This inscription is especially interesting with regard to the mythology of the South Germanic area because of the names of the gods mentioned in it. Together with the Second Merseburg Charm and the Saxon baptismal vow it is one of the few sources which record the South Germanic belief in the gods. The inscription is:

logaþore
wodan
wigiþonar (or: wiguþonar)

and then written at an angle of 180° to this, is:

awaleubwini.

This last part contains the woman's name Awa and the man's name Leubwini. Of the other names, which obviously give the names of gods, only the name → Wodan brings no further problems with it. → wigiþonar should probably be interpreted with → Vingthor as 'battle-Thor', and not as 'dedication-Donar'. The suggestion that the correct reading is 'dedicate, Donar!' is absurd. → *logaþore* is usually interpreted to be connected to Loðurr despite considerable problems there and as such is understood to be a name for Loki. The traditional interpretation is that the three gods named in the inscription are called upon to bring happiness to the two people named who are giving the fibula.

Klingenberg's somewhat different explanation is that the three gods' names are connected with Snorri's version of → Baldr's death (*Gylfaginning* 48), whereby Loki (= *logaþore?*) instigates the murder, Odin (= *wodan*) mourns for Baldr, and Thor (= *wigiþonar*) dedicates the funeral pyre with his hammer. Admittedly, 'myth-abbreviations' like this are indeed recorded for this time on pictorial representations on bracteates, but a magical meaning for a runic inscription seems more likely.

Recently Düwel (and following him Rosenfeld) have interpreted the inscription as a Christian protection against the heathen gods, and thus, it should be interpreted: 'Wodan and Donar are intriguers!' (→ *logathore*).

But is it really likely that the heathen gods were inscribed in runes onto the fibula only to refer to the 'tabu-figure' of Christ (Rosenfeld)? This hardly seems to correspond to the practise in a missionary era, and therefore it seems that the inscription is indeed a heathen monument, even if the final interpretation has not yet been made.

S. Feist, 'Zur Deutung der deutschen Runenspangen' (*ZfdPh* 47) 1918; W. Krause, *Die Runeninschriften im älteren Futhark*, Göttingen 1966; W. Steinhauser, 'Die Wodansweihe von Nordendorf' (*ZfdA* 97) 1968; A. Kabell, 'Nordendorf A' (*PBB West* 92) 1970; K. Hauck, *Goldbrakteaten aus Sievern*, Munich 1970; O. Höfler, 'Brakteaten als Geschichtsquellen' (*ZfdA* 101) 1972; E. Marold, '"Thor weihe diese Runen"' (*FmSt* 8) 1974; H. Klingenberg, 'Die Drei-Götter-Fibel von Nordendorf' (*ZfdA* 105) 1976; U. Schwab, 'The Inscription of the Nordendorf Brooch I' (*Michigan Germanic Studies* 7) 1981; K. Düwel, 'Runen und interpretatio christiana' (*Tradition als historische Kraft. [Festschrift] K. Hauck*) Berlin, New York 1982; H. Rosenfeld, 'Die germanischen Runen im kleinen Schulerloch und auf der Nordendorfer Bügelfibel A' (*ZfdA* 113) 1984.

Norðri (ON, from *norðr* 'north'). A dwarf in *Vǫluspá* 11. Norðri supports the vaults of heaven in the north, which are formed from Ymir's skull (*Gylfaginning* 7). → Vestri.

Nóri (ON, 'tiny person' from Icelandic *nori* 'little piece'?). A dwarf in *Vǫluspá* 22. In the *Þulur* Nóri is found among the names of sea-kings.

R: Nóri is one of the 13 dwarfs in J. R. R. Tolkien's novel, *The Hobbit* (1937).

Norns (ON, sg. *norn*, pl. *nornar*). Women of destiny in Nordic mythology. In *Gylfaginning* 14 Snorri writes: 'Under the ash near the spring stands a beautiful hall; three maidens come out of this hall whose names are Urd, Verdandi, Skuld; these maidens determine the life of men; we call them norns. But there are other norns who come to each child that has been born in order to determine its life, and they are of divine descent; others, however, are descended from the elves and the third kind from dwarfs [. . .] The good norns from good families grant good lives, but men who encounter misfortune have had their lives determined by malevolent norns'. The concept of norns is well documented both in the Eddic lays (and in other heroic poetry; *Reginsmál* 2, *Sigrdrífumál* 17, *Hlǫðskviða* 34, *Hamðismál* 29, 30, *Fáfnismál* 11, 12, 44) as well as in skaldic poetry from the 10th century onwards and in prose texts. In the *Barlaams saga ok Josaphats* nine norns are said to be Thor's daughters. Snorri's reference to good and malevolent norns is confirmed by other sources: on the one hand in heroic poetry the 'decision of the norns' (*norna domr*) is identical to 'misfortune' whereby the norns move closer to valkyries in their function (*Hamðismál* 29), but on the other hand they have powers which are helpful in child-birth and their association with the spring at the foot of the world-ash Yggdrasill similarly indicates a life-enhancing aspect which they share with the dísir and the matrons. – A runic inscription from the High Middle Ages from the stave church at Borgund in Norway confirms the dual function of the norns: 'The norns determine good and bad things and they have brought great sorrow to me.' – De Vries writes: 'The idea that the norns were partly good and partly evil could originate from the experience that fortune and misfortune are mixed together in the lives of men.'

The opinion that the three norns referred to by Snorri are derived from one older norn → Urd who originally represented a personified power of destiny is unlikely since the name of this norn is probably derived from the so-called Urd's well, the well of destiny, and not vice versa.

The meaning of the names of the three norns Urd, Verdandi, and Skuld as past, present and future (as forms of the verb *verða: urðr* to *urðum* 'became', *verdandi* 'becoming', *skuld* to *skulu* 'become, intend') possibly also first comes from the poet of the *Vǫluspá*, since Skuld is elsewhere recorded as being a name of a valkyrie and Verdandi is a telling new formation.

The norns as a triad of women of fate have been compared with the *Moĩrai* of Greek and the *Parcae* of Roman mythology, and indeed the distinct number of norns, three, as referred to in Snorri, could be influenced by classical ideas; nevertheless with the norns the typical motif of the *Parcae*, namely spinning or weaving fate which is only recorded in Scandinavia for the valkyries (→ *Darraðarljóð*) is missing with regard to the norns. In his opera, *Götterdämmerung*, Wagner also confuses the various characteristics of the valkyries and the norns.

The concept of a plurality of women of fate in Germanic religion is however certainly older than the Middle Ages and is certainly based to some degree on the Germanic → matron cult in Roman times. The norns also represent the fateful aspect of the → *dísir* in which life-giving aspects are united with those of battle and death.

E. Mogk, 'Nornen' (J. Hoops, *Reallexikon der Germanischen Altertumskunde* 4) 1913–16; F. Ström, *Diser, Nornor, Valkyrjor*, Stockholm 1954; G. W. Weber, *Wyrd*, Bad Homburg 1969; E. F. Halvorsen, 'Norner' (KLNM 12) 1967; J. de Vries, *Altgermanische Religionsgeschichte*, Berlin [3]1970.

R: (fine art) H. Natter, *Group of Norns* (marble statues on the graveyard of Ober-St Veit, Vienna, 1886); K. Donndorf, *Nornenbrunnen* (fountain in Stuttgart); K. Ehrenberg, *Die Nornen* (oil painting, 1888); H. Thoma, *Die Nornen* (oil painting, 1889);
(literature) E. Bertram, *Nornenbuch* (poems, 1925);
(folklore) The norns are probably reflected in the numerous prophecies by old women in fairy-tales, such as 'Snow-White'.
(other) Nornen, Norwegian fishery protection vessel, built 1963.

Nótt or Nǫtt (ON, 'night'). The personification of night in the Eddic lays *Vafþrúðnismál* 25 and *Alvíssmál* 29. The father of Nótt is said to be Nǫrr (only recorded in the dative form Nǫrvi). Snorri (*Gylfaginning* 9) builds on this sparse information and tells of the following: 'Nǫrfi or Narfi is the name of a giant who lived in Jǫtunheim. He had a daughter called Nótt who was black and dark as was typical in her family. She was married to a man called Naglfari and their son was called Auðr. Next she married Annar and their daughter was called Jǫrð. Finally, she married Dellingr who came from the race of the Æsir and their son was called Dagr ('day') and he was bright and beautiful as was the rest of his father's family. Then Alfaðir ('Allfather' = Odin) took Nótt and Dagr, her son, and gave them two horses and two chariots and sent them into the sky so that they should always ride in two days around the entire earth. Nótt rides in front on the horse called Hrímfaxi and early each day it makes dew fall to the earth from foam dripping from its bit. Dagr's horse is called Skinfaxi and it illuminates the whole sky and the earth with its mane.' Snorri has harmonized various concepts which he knew from Eddic and skaldic poetry and formed them into one myth in which elements from classical mythology also appear to have been included.

Nýi (ON, 'the dark' from *ný* 'new moon'? or simply 'the new one'?). A dwarf in the *Vǫluspá* 11 and in the *Þulur*.

Nýr (ON). A dwarf in the *Vǫluspá* 11 (*Gylfaginning* 13); for the meaning of the name see → Nýi. In the main manuscripts apart from the *Snorra Edda* this dwarf is, however, called Nár.

Nýráðr (ON, 'the new-advising one'). A dwarf in the *Vǫluspá* 12 and in the *Þulur*.

Nyt (ON, 'use'). One of the (mythical?) rivers in the river catalogue in *Grímnismál* 28 and in the *Þulur*.

Oak. The Germanic peoples not only worshipped sacred groves in their tree-worship (→ tree), but also considered lone-standing trees to be sacred. One of these trees was perhaps the oak in Geismar, presumably dedicated to Thor, as it was known as *rubor jovis* ('Jupiter's = Thor's oak'), which the missionary Boniface found necessary to fell at the beginning of the 8th century. However, apart from this example, the oak was by no means the 'sacred tree' of Germanic antiquity, as modern day folklorists would like to have us think; even the world-tree Yggdrasill was actually an ash tree.

Oath. The oath, namely the appeal to sacred powers to witness the truth of a statement, was characterized as early as Germanic times by particular formalities. The curse upon himself made by the oath-taker, should he break it, also belonged to the oath as such. Oaths were taken on weapons, but apparently mostly on rings (→ ring oath). Heathen oath formulae have only passed down to us from Christian times, for instance the invocation of Freyr and Njǫrðr and the → *almáttki áss* in the *Landnámabók*, both of which, however, appear to have been influenced by Christian formulae.

A formal heathen oath seems to find an echo in a truce formula recorded in several ON texts (*Heiðarvíga saga* 33, *Grettis saga* 72; more briefly in *Grágás* 114): 'A traitor is he who breaks the peace . . . and he should be driven out . . . and should be rejected everywhere like a wolf is, where Christians go to church, where heathens make their sacrifices, where fire burns, where the earth allows anything to grow, where a child calls his mother and a mother bears a son, where men make fire, ships sail, shields flash, the sun shines, snow falls, Finns go skiing, the firs grow, the falcon flies on a long spring day carried by a gentle wind under both wings, where the skies are vaulted above, where houses are lived in, where the wind shows the waters the way to the sea and where men sow seed. He should avoid churches and Christians and sacrifices made by the heathens, house and cave, every dwelling except for the underworld.' (Quoted from the *Grettis saga* 72).

W. Baetke, 'guð in den altnordischen Eidesformeln' (*PBB* 70) 1948; A. Kabell, 'Baugi und der Ringeid' (*ANF* 90) 1975.

Oberon. The Elf king Oberon is a literary figure who originated in the 13th century in the French novel by Huon de Bordeaux, but developed from the dwarf king Alberich of German heroic epos. In England Oberon became the king of elves or fairies (probably due to the influence of the concept of light elves in English folklore) and as such he achieved fame through Shakespeare's play, *A Midsummer Night's Dream.*

R: Oberon achieved growing popularity in England after the translation (1525–33) of the French chapbook by Huon de Bordeaux (1513), subsequently appearing in R. Greene's play, *James IV* (1590), in E. Spenser's poem (1590–96) which gives Oberon Titania as a wife, W. Shakespeare's *A Midsummer Night's Dream* (1595/96) and B. Jonson's *Oberon the Fairy Prince* (masque, 1610). In Germany Oberon was introduced by C.M. Wieland's *Oberon* (verse epic, 1780); Wieland was acquainted with both Huon's Old French version and Shakespeare's play.

(music) Wieland's *Oberon* begged to be turned into an opera and F. Schiller planned an opera text in 1797; a fragment by F. Grillparzer (1808) *Der Zauberwald* deals also with the matter. C. M. Weber's opera *Oberon* was the most successful (1826).

(other) Weber's music appears to have been decisive in the naming (in 1827) of a satellite Oberon orbiting Uranus.

Octocannae. Name of matrons. These matrons are recorded seven times in Gripswald (Krefeld, Germany) (CIL XIII 8571–77), where therefore a cult centre can be assumed. The name is most likely Celtic and could be derived from a place-name *Octocanna (from Celtic **uktā* 'spruce').

S. Gutenbrunner, *Die germanischen Götternamen*, 1936; H. Birkhan, *Germanen und Kelten*, Vienna 1970.

Ódáinsakr (ON, 'field of the living') is a kind of Elysian fields in the Old Icelandic *fornaldarsǫgur* (*Hervarar saga* 1, *Halfdanar saga Eysteinssonar* 1, *Eireks saga víðfǫrla* 1–4) which also appears in Saxo (*Gesta Danorum* IV, 105) in the form Undersakre/Undensakre; these forms in Saxo could point to the fact that Ódáinsakr meant originally either 'land in the south-east' or 'Underworld' (Much).

Ódáinsakr is only described in more detail in *Eireks saga.* The saga follows medieval visionary literature in its description and does not help us any further in the question of whether Ódáinsakr had an actual place in heathen concepts of the Other World or if it was merely a Christianized concept transferred onto a heathen context. References to Ódáinsakr in all of the named sagas only come from the 14th century; admittedly, Saxo's naming of Undensakre proves that the name already existed before 1200, but there is no documentary evidence for the heathen period. As with similar paradisiacal descriptions, OE *neorxnawang* and ON *Glæsisvellir*, it is possible that the concept Ódáinsakr comes from the heathen period, but by the time it was written down the contents of the concept were already totally Christian.

R. Much, 'Undensakre-Untersberg' (*ZfdA* 47) 1904; E. Lidén, 'Om några ortnamn' (*ANF* 23) 1907; H. Rosén, *Om dödsrike och dödsbruk*, Lund 1918; P. Herrmann, *Die Heldensagen des Saxo Grammaticus*, Leipzig 1922; H. R. Ellis, *The Road to Hel*, Cambridge 1943; K. Strauberg, 'Zur Jenseitstopographie' (*Arv* 13) 1957.

Odensjakt (Swedish, 'Odin's hunt') → Wild Hunt.

Odin (ON, Oðinn, Anglo-Saxon Wōden, Old Saxon Woden, Old Franconian Wodan, OHG Wutan, Wuotan). The chief god of Eddic mythology and the most versatile of all the gods. He is the father of the gods, the god of poetry, the god of the dead, of war, of magic, of runes, of ecstasy. The numerous names for Odin in Old Norse literature exemplify his diversity.

1. Myths about Odin.

According to Snorri (*Gylfaginning* 5) Odin and his brothers Vili and Vé are the first gods to be created. They are the sons of the giants → Burr and the giantess → Bestla. Odin is Frigg's husband and his sons are Baldr (from Frigg), Thor (from Jǫrð), Vali (from Rindr). In addition to this genealogy which is already documented in skaldic poetry, Snorri also names Heimdall, Týr, Bragi, Víðar and Hǫðr as Odin's sons.

Snorri has the following to say about Odin: 'Odin is the highest and oldest of the gods; he rules over everything and however mighty the other gods may be, they all serve him like children serve their father.' 'Odin is called Alfǫðr ("Father of All"), because he is the father of all the gods.' (*Gylfaginning* 19).

He lives in Asgard in → Hliðskjálf from where he can look over the whole world. He is considered to be omniscient and because of this he is also known as Fjǫlsviðr ('the extremely wise one').

Odin's attributes are his spear → Gungnir, his blindness in one eye, his hat and cloak. All of these belong to his stereotypical appearance as shown in the *fornaldarsǫgur* of the 13th and 14th centuries to texts from modern times. Another, much older, attribute is Odin's ring → Draupnir from which every nine nights another eight equally heavy rings drip (*Skáldskaparmál* 33). Odin's two ravens, Huginn and Muninn, are likewise firmly established attributes from the end of the Migration Age onwards (as illustrations on bracteates and picture-stones prove). The two ravens fly over the whole world and return before breakfast bringing Odin news of many things: 'this is why he is also called "the raven-god" (Hrafnaguð)' (*Gylfaginning* 37). Odin's eight-legged horse → Sleipnir is mentioned quite early in Old Norse literature; according to Snorri, the amazing horse was the offspring of the giant stallion Svaðifari and Loki (in the shape of a mare).

Odin acquires his knowledge from → Mímir's head (*Vǫluspá* 46; *Ynglinga saga* 4 and 7) or else by drinking from Mímir's well but, according to Snorri (*Gylfaginning* 14), he has to sacrifice an eye in order to do so. Despite his position as chief god Odin is the hero of far fewer mythical adventures than Thor. There are several accounts of Odin proving his immense knowledge. In the Eddic *Vafþrúðnismál* he challenges the giant → Vafþrúðnir to a battle of wits and is victorious. In *Grímnismál* he is forced to reveal his mythical knowledge to → King Geirrǫðr, and gives a long list of → Odin's names which are only preserved in this poem and in the *Hervarar saga* we hear of another battle of wits in which Odin takes part. Snorri records the probably older myth of Odin's theft of the → mead of the skalds in which he has to seduce the giant's daughter Gunnlǫð in order to acquire the mead. The so-called second → Odin's example in *Hávamál* (103–110) alludes to this episode, whereas the first Odin's example (*Hávamál* 96–102) refers to an adventure of Odin's with the daughter of a certain Billingr (further details of which are no longer extant). Furthermore, Odin is mentioned in connexion with many love-adventures (perhaps modelled on those enjoyed by Zeus of classical antiquity?), such as with Rindr who subsequently bears him a son, Váli. In a battle of words with Thor, Odin boasts repeatedly about his affairs (*Hárbarðsljóð* 16/18, 20, 30/32) which he compares to Thor's heroic deeds.

In *Hávamál* the myth of → Odin's self-sacrifice is told in which he hung on a 'wind-swept gallows' for nine nights, sacrificing himself and thus acquiring the knowledge of the runes.

In 10th century skaldic poetry Odin is frequently called the guardian of warriors and the god of those slain in battle. He is also said to be the god of the → *einherjar* whom he gathers around himself in Valhall so that they can support him at the Ragnarǫk in the battle against the forces of the Underworld (*Eireksmál*). The valkyries (*Oðins meyjar* 'Odin's maidens') fetch the slain from the battle-field and lead them to Valhall where they attend to their needs (*Gylfaginning* 37, 38, 40). Valhall takes the characteristics of a warrior paradise here.

A euhemeristic interpretation of the gods occurs in the tale of the migration of the Æsir during the rule of their king Odin, as is told, somewhat variedly, in Snorri (Prologue to his *Edda, Ynglinga saga*) and in Saxo (*Gesta Danorum* I–III). The generally accepted opinion among scholars in Iceland of the 12th and 13th centuries was that the gods were 'long dead kings and priests, well-versed in sorcery who were mortal men, but who possessed magical powers and instruments. They allowed themselves to be worshipped as gods, but their supernatural deeds were in fact mere illusion' (Herrmann). (→ Euhemerismus).

Snorri refers to Odin's leading of the migration of the Æsir to Sweden via Germany and Jutland. He mentions here that Vegdeg, Baldr, Sigi, Skjǫld, Sæmingr, Yngvi are Odin's sons. Both Snorri and Saxo tell of → Odin's exile, and record that during this time other gods ruled over the Æsir, namely Mithotyn and Ollerus (= Ullr) according to Saxo, but Vili and Vé according to Snorri.

2. Odin's functions.

(a) Odin personifies the function of sovereignty in Germanic mythology, and in the literary period the role of the father of the gods. As such he is called Alfǫðr ('Father of All') in the literary sources where both this name and also the term *almáttki áss* ('Almighty As') appear to be influenced by Christian names for God since it is certain that Odin did not have such a dominant position in the cult and folk-beliefs of the Viking period as the literary sources would have us believe. Snorri's aforementioned comments that Odin is the father of a long line of gods ought not to be taken literally either. Nevertheless, Odin appears in a myth before the creation of mankind in which he is named along with Hœnir and Loðurr (in *Vǫluspá* 17/18), and with Vili and Vé in Snorri's version (*Gylfaginning* 5). According to this myth, the three gods created the first people Ask and Embla (→ Anthropogeny). Odin appears not only as the creator of mankind, but also as the ancestor of royal dynasties, such as the Vǫlsungs, the Skjǫldungs and the Ynglings as well as the Anglo-Saxon royal houses (→ Myth of Descendency.

(b) In the process of the 'shift' in the functions originally held by the Germanic gods, as suggested by Dumézil → Three-Function-Theory, Odin emerges increasingly as the god of war. According to this theory Odin first won esteem as the god of warriors and poets during the Viking Age. This is reflected in literature, particularly in heroic poetry. This view is however not necessarily correct as in southern and western Germanic sources Odin was considered to be the god who granted victory: Wodan is able to decide the fate of the battle among the Langobards (*Origo* 1, Paul the Deacon, *Hist. Lang.* I, 8) and the heathen Anglo-Saxons made sacrifices to Uuoddan before battle (Æthelweard, *Chronicorum libri* IV, 1). In the north from the Viking Age on it is always Odin who gives victory (*Hyndluljóð* 3), and hence he is also known as Sigfaðir, Sig-Gautr, Sigtýr and so on.

According to *Ynglinga saga* 4, it was Odin who first brought war into the world, and battles are begun by a spear being thrown into the hostile army to dedicate it to Odin. Odin is also responsible for the personal fate of the individual in battle, and death in battle was even understood as being betrayed by Odin (Egill, *Sonatorrek* 22; Eyvindr, *Hákonarmál* 15). In heroic poetry Odin is frequently referred to as the protector of individual heroes (Sigurd, Starkaðr, Haddingus), but it is he who time and again instigates the argument which leads to war (as in the Battle of Bravalla: Saxo, *Gesta Danorum* VII, 246 – VIII, 264, or the war between Agantýr and Hlǫð: *Hervarar saga* 10).

(c) Odin's close connexion with the dead, in particular those slain in battle, fits in with his role as the god of war. He awaits them in → Valhall, where they become his special followers, the → *einherjar*. In the concept of the Wild Hunt Odin also emerges as the leader of a band of warriors who are related to the army of the dead.

(d) The form of the → dedication to Odin is found in → Odin's sacrifice, in which Odin acquires the knowledge of runes (*Hávamál* 138–145) by hanging on the 'wind-swept gallows' and being pierced by a spear. The names used in skaldic poetry for Odin, such as Hangaguð, Hangatýr, Hangi, show that even the skalds knew Odin as the god of the gallows. As a result of Odin's sacrifice ('myself to myself'), *Hávamál* links the gain of the runic knowledge to the acquisition of the art of poetry, which is described, however, elsewhere in Old Norse literature quite differently: *Skáldskaparmál* 1 Odin steals the → mead of the skalds (→ Oðrœrir), which has been brewed by the giant Suttungr and his daughter Gunnlǫð from the blood of → Kvasir, by drinking it and then bringing it back to Asgard for the good of the gods and man in the guise of an eagle. This is why, according to Snorri, poetry is also called *farmr Oðins* 'Odin's burden'. The name for Odin, Farmatýr, probably comes from this.

(e) Odin's role as the god of sorcery and magic is connected with his acquisition of the art of poetry and his knowledge of the runes. Although the Vanir are especially associated with → magic (*seiðr*) in Nordic mythology, Odin is considered to be the one among the Æsir most versed in magic. In *Hávamál* he boasts about his knowledge of magic formulae. In the Second Merseburg Charm Wodan heals by magic and in the Eddic *Baldrs draumar* 3 he is called 'Father of the magic chant'.

Parallels with shamanistic practices in which ecstatic states play an essential role may be assumed as a result both of Odin's acquisition of runic knowledge and poetic art and his particular kind of magic. Ecstatic states are also an integral part of Odin's cult according to our sources: *Wodan id est furor* ('Wodan, that is to say fury') records Adam of Bremen in the 11th century (*Gesta Hammaburgensis ecclesiae Pontificum* IV, 26) and documents with this what the etymology of Odin's name also tells, namely that Odin is related to ON *óðr* 'furious' and German *Wut* 'excessive anger'. This ecstatic fury which manifests itself in Odin's warriors, such as → berserks and → Ulfheðnar, as well as in cult traditions still reflected in the concepts of the Wild Hunt, is an essential factor in Odin's being and points to the shamanistic origin of the god.

(f) A further hint of Odin as a shaman is his repeatedly recorded function as a god of healing. Odin's role in this function is best known from the → Second Merseburg Charm where Wodan heals the dislocated leg of Baldr's horse. This mythical deed is supposed to be repeated and a healing brought about if the charm is said again. Hauck has been able to show that Odin's/Wodan's veterinary function is also recorded in the pictorial representations on the Germanic golden → bracteates (Group C) of the Migration period, which depict a (god's) head above a horse usually shown to have dislocated forelegs.

3. The cult of Odin and belief in Odin.

(a) Considering that Odin is named as the main god of Nordic mythology in Old Norse literary sources, in particularly by Snorri, it is perhaps surprising that in comparison with the god Thor there are only a few indications of a cult veneration of Odin during the 130 years between the settlement and the end of heathendom. There are neither place-names nor personal names which point to a cult of Odin and the relatively few myths told about Odin would not suggest that Odin was the chief god. Indeed, it seems likely that the literary sources considered him to have such an elevated position from their own point of view, since there can be no doubt that Odin was the god of poetry (and poets), and our sources, which come either directly or indirectly – via Snorri's systematization – from the skalds of heathen times not surprisingly show a particular inclination in favour of the god of their own craft.

Even in mainland Scandinavia cult place-names based on Odin are by no means common, and do not even constitute 10% of the actual theophorous ('formed with a god's name') place-names. In his description of the great temple at Uppsala (Sweden), Adam of Bremen refers to a devotion to Odin in the form of idols in the temple. He writes that the temple at Uppsala contained statues of Thor, Wodan and Fricco (*Gesta Hammaburgensis Ecclesiae Pontificum* IV, 26–27). In the same passage Adam of Bremen reports sacrifices which were held every nine years and during which both animals and men were sacrificed. He does not explicitly mention that these → human sacrifices were dedicated to Odin, but human sacrifice is elsewhere exclusively linked to Odin (Snorri, *Ynglinga saga* 25 and 43; Tacitus, *Germania* 9). A sacrifice to Odin related to his self-sacrifice by hanging on a tree and being pierced by a spear is obviously also the case in the death of King → Víkarr (Saxo, *Gesta Danorum* IV, 184). The aforementioned and frequently documented dedication of a hostile army to Odin by a spear being thrown over them should be counted as a sacrifice to Odin in the widest meaning of the word. Even though the skaldic poems *Eireksmál* and Eyvind's *Hákonarmál* do not give details of an actual cult, they do regard Odin as the god of the dead and as the ruler over Valhall, and as such are evidence of a belief in Odin in the 10th century.

(b) Place-names containing the name Odin are not found in Iceland at all, are seldom found in south Norway, but are more frequent in south Sweden and Denmark. This has been interpreted as meaning that Odin's cult in Scandinavia was comparatively young and, spreading from the southern Germanic parts during the Viking Age, was unable to extend far enough in order to reach Iceland before it was overtaken by Christianity. Among the place-names based on Odin are a number which are clearly ancient, namely those based on *-vin* and *-akr*, and these contradict the theory that devotion to Odin was a young development. In the whole of *Germania* it is clear from the standard translation of the Latin weekday name *dies Mercurii* with Germanic **Wodanesdag* (OE *Wodnesdag*, Eng. Wednesday; ON *Ოðinsdagr*, Danish *Onsdag*). Since the translation of the weekday names was concluded in the 4th century, the cult centering on Odin must have been very widespread in all of the western and probably in the northern Germanic regions.

Personal names based on Odin are extremely rare. In Sweden the name Uþintisa

(Oðindís) occurs on a rune stone, and in Denmark the male personal name Uþinka(ur) (Oðdinkár) is recorded several times which points to a personal dedication to Odin.

(c) The translation of the Latin Mercury by Wodan/Odin both in the *interpretatio romana* as well as in the *interpretatio germanica* points to clear parallels in the understanding of the essence of these gods in the first centuries A.D. External attributes (staff and hat) as well as the role as the wandering god, and perhaps the god of traders, were determining factors but were not, however, sufficient reason alone for considering the two gods to be one and the same within two different cultures. Tacitus reported that the Germanic peoples only made human sacrifice to Mercury (= Wodan/Odin), whereas other gods received animal sacrifices. He was also informed already about the high rank that Odin took among the Germanic peoples, a position which is hardly comparable with that of the god Mercury among the Romans.

The Germanic Mercury can only be distinguished on votive inscriptions from the Roman god Mercury by his epithets; at least Mercurius Cimbrianus and Mercurius *Leudisius point to the Germanic god.

(d) Pictorial monuments: it is possible to trace depictions of Odin back to the Bronze Age if the large spear-bearing god-figures on some southern Swedish rock carvings may be interpreted as representing Odin. These depictions are without exception found overlaying older rock carvings and ought therefore to be seen in connexion with the religious changes during the later Bronze Age. In a Roman quarry near Bad Dürkheim (Germany) there is one such pictorial representation of a spear-god which bears witness to a cult in the Iron Age.

The pictorial material is far more substantial and circumspect about Odin during the Migration period. K. Hauck has been able to show in a number of studies that there is a depiction of Odin in the pictures of gods on the golden bracteates of group C (god's head over four-legged animal) which forms the largest group of gold bracteates (numbering around 350 examples). This is clearly Odin as the god depicted is also accompanied by birds (cf. Odin's ravens Huginn and Muninn) on the one hand, and also is shown to have a distinct medical function on the other. There are identifiable parallels here to the healing referred to in the Second Merseburg Charm.

Depictions of Odin and Odin's warriors (as well as the *dioskuri* who possibly also belong to Odin's followers?) are most likely the case in the Vendel Age Swedish metal mounts which were used as helmet decorations. Without exception all these show cult scenes quite clearly.

Odin is repeatedly depicted on Viking Age pictorial stones, at times accompanied by birds, more commonly however riding his eight-legged horse Sleipnir. It is extremely unlikely that in this case, as de Vries assumed, it is not Odin himself who is illustrated, but rather a dead man riding to Valhall. On the contrary it could be seen to be Odin in his role as leader of the dead. It is doubtful whether a stone relief of a rider armed with a spear found outside Scandinavia, such as on the Hornhaus rider's stone in Magdeburg, can be interpreted as Odin because of a typologically very similar relief of two spear-bearing riders (found in Sockburn, Co. Durham, North England). The English relief should probably be interpreted as depicting Odin's warriors, but not Odin himself. Whatever the answer to this particular problem it would be going too far to try to see depictions of Odin in all Viking Age pictures of riders.

4. Odin's/Wodan's name is, as already mentioned, etymologically related to ON *óðr*, German *Wut* 'fury', Gothic *wods* 'possessed', which alludes to the poetic cult frenzy

which was a characteristic of this god and his cult. Non-Germanic etymological parallels can be found in Latin *vates*, Old Irish *faith* 'seer'.

Theologically speaking, Odin is related the Indian god Varuna, who has sorcery, the gift of shape-changing and the directing of the fortunes of battle in common with the Germanic god. Both are the gods of rulers and poets, both receive human sacrifice. Dumézil has identified the Indian ruling pair of gods Mithra – Varuna with both the representatives of sovereignty in Germanic mythology, Týr and Odin, whereby both these gods can be traced back to Indo-Germanic times. Týr, however, faded more and more in status over the years so that in the literary period he was totally subordinate to Odin. This theory is unquestionably more convincing than that of the slow expansion of a belief in Odin northwards.

A. Mahr, 'Wodan in der deutschen Volksüberlieferung' (*Mitteilungen der anthropologischen Gesellschaft in Wien* 58) 1928; O. Höfler, *Kultische Geheimbünde der Germanen*, Frankfurt a.M. 1934; K. Helm, *Wodan*, Gießen 1946; G. Turville-Petre, 'Prof. Georges Dumézil' (*Saga-Book* 14) 1953–55; K. Hauck, 'Herrschaftszeichen eines wodanistischen Königtums' (*Jahrbuch für fränkische Landesforschung* 14) 1954; J. S. Ryan, 'Othin in England' (*Folklore* 74) 1963; Kr. Hald, 'The Cult of Odin in Danish Place-names' (*Early English and Norse Studies Presented to H. Smith*) London 1963; A. L. Meaney, 'Woden in England' (*Folklore* 77) 1966; E. F. Halvorsen, 'Óðinn' (*KLNM* 12) 1967; O. Höfler, 'Die nordischen Kultortsnamen' (*Disputationes ad montium vocabula* 1) Vienna 1969; J. de Vries, *Altgermanische Religionsgeschichte*, Berlin [3]1970; H. E. Davidson, *The Battle God of the Vikings*, York 1972; K. Hauck, 'Zur Ikonologie der Goldbrakteaten IV' (*Festschrift S. Gutenbrunner*) 1972; O. Höfler, 'Brakteaten als Geschichtsquelle' (*ZfdA* 101) 1972; G. W. Weber, 'Das Odinsbild des Altunasteines' (*PBB* 94) 1972; G. W. Weber, 'Odins Wagen' (*FmSt* 7) 1973; O. Höfler, 'Zwei Grundkräfte im Wodankult' (*Antiquitates Indogermanicae. Gedenkschrift H. Güntert*) 1974; E. O. G. Turville-Petre, *Myth and Religion of the North*, Westport 1975; Å. V. Ström, H. Biezais, *Germanische und baltische Religion*, Stuttgart 1975; P. Renauld-Krantz, 'Odin' (*Les Vikings et leur civilisation*) Paris 1976; K. Hauk, 'Zur Ikonologie der Goldbrakteaten XII' (*Archäologisches Korrespondenzblatt* 6) 1976; K. Hauck, 'Zur Ikonologie der Goldbrakteaten XV' (*Festschrift H. Beumann*) 1977; G. Dumezil, *Gods of the Ancient Northmen*, Berkeley 1977; K. Hauck, 'Bildforschung als historische Sachforschung' (*Festschrift H. Löwe*) 1978; K. Hauck, 'Gott als Arzt' (*Text und Bild*) Wiesbaden 1980; E. Haugen, 'The Edda as ritual: Odin and his masks' (*Edda: a collection*) Winnipeg 1983.

R: (fine art) P. Hörberg, *Odin byggande Sigtuna* (pen and ink drawing, 1812); P. Hörberg, *King Gylfe receives Oden on his arrival in Sweden* (sketch, 1816); B. E. Fogelberg, *Odens möte med Gylfe* (relief on a drinking horn, 1818); H. E. Freund, *Odin* (statue, 1821/22); H. E. Freund, *Odin* (seated statue, 1924/25); B. E. Fogelberg, *Odin* (marble statue, 1830); B. E. Fogelberg, *Odin* (colossal bust); R. Krausse, sgraffito over the entrance to Villa Wahnfried Bayreuth (1874); Sir E. Burne-Jones, *Odin* (painting, c.1880); K. Ehrenberg, *Odin; Thor und Magni* (drawing, 1883); H. Natter, *Wodan* (marble statue, c.1887); K. Dielitz, *Odin und Brunhilde* (painting, c.1890); H. Thoma, *Odin als Kriegsgott* (graphic drawing, 1896); D. Hardy, *Odin and Fenris* (painting, c.1900); K. Moser, *Wotan und Brünhilde* (oil painting, 1914); S. Nilsson, *The Road to Walhall* (painting); D. Werenskiold, *Odin og Mime* (wooden relief in the town hall in Oslo, 1938; D. Werenskiold, *Odin på Sleipnir* (coloured wooden relief in the courtyard of the town hall in Oslo, 1945–50); B. Marklund, *Odin* (in the bronze relief on the doors of Statens Historiska Museum Stockholm, c.1950);

(literature) F. v. Hagedorn, *Der Wein* (poem, 1745); F. G. Klopstock, *Hymne an Wodan* (in: *Hermanns Schlacht*, drama, 1769); P. F. Suhm, *Om Odin* (1771); K. G. Leopold, *Odin eller Asarnes invandring* (tragedy, 1790); J. Baggesen, *Odin eller Danrigets Stiftelse* (epic poem, 1803); N. F. S. Grundtvig, *Maskeradenball* (poem, directed to Odin and Christ, 1808); N. F. S. Grundtvig, *Optrin af Nomers og Asers*

Kamp: Odins komme til Norden (part of a trilogy, 1809); A. Oehlenschläger, *Nordens Guder* (poems, 1819); C. J. L. Almqvist, *Sviavigamal* (novel in four parts, 1833, about Odin's migration); W. Wordsworth, *Prelude* (poem, 1850); R. Hamerling, *Germanenzug* (canzone, 1864); R. Wagner, *Zum 25. August 1870* (poem, 1870); F. Schanz, *Rolf Krake* (ballad, 1910); O. Duun, *Juvikingerne* (novel, 1918–23); E. Toller, *Der entfesselte Wotan* (comedy, 1923); K. H. Strobl, *Wotan* (novel); H. F. Blunck, *Herrn Wodes Ausfahrt* (in: *Märchen und Sagen*, 1937); H. Burte, *An das Ich* (poem in: *Anker am Rhein*, 1938); H. F. Blunck, *Sage vom Reich* (Roman, 1941–42). (music) J. H. Stuntz, *Odins Schwert* (ballet, 1818); J. H. Stuntz, *Orfa* (ballet, 1852); R. Wagner, *Der Ring des Nibelungen* (opera, 1848–1874).
(other) Odin is the name of a bulk freighter belonging to the German shipping company Frigga (1965); Oden is a Swedish ice-breaker (1958); Odinn is an Icelandic coastal patrol boat (1960); Wotan is a naval repairs ship belonging to the German navy.

Odin's examples. The so-called Odin's examples are episodes in *Hávamál*, which tell about Odin's romantic adventures. The first Odin's example (*Hávamál* 96–102) speaks of Odin's unsuccessful attempt to seduce Billing's daughter (→ Billingr 2); the second Odin's example records Odin's seduction of → Gunnlǫð in the myth of the theft of the mead (*Hávamál* 103–110), a possible third Odin's example (*Hávamál* 12–14) refers perhaps to the same myth.

R: F. D. Gräter, *Nordische Blumen* (translation, 1789).

Odin's exile. In the euhemeristic description of the Æsir as found in Saxo Grammaticus, *Gesta Danorum*, and in Snorri's Prologue to his *Edda* as well as in the *Ynglinga saga*, there are altogether three different tales telling of Odin's exile. The shortest version is in *Ynglinga saga* 3: 'Odin had two brothers, one of whom was called Vé, the other Vili. The brothers ruled over his lands whenever he was absent. Once, when Odin was far away and had been gone for so long that the Æsir doubted that he would ever return, the brothers began dividing up his property between themselves, everything that is apart from Odin's wife Frigg whom they shared with each other. Not long afterwards Odin returned home and took his wife back again.' The two divergent descriptions which Saxo relates are extensive and illuminating: the first one (*Gesta Danorum* I, 25f.) records the voluntary nature of Odin's exile: Nordic kings send Odin, a well-respected man in the whole of Europe, a heavily gilded statue of himself to his home in Byzantium (repeatedly stipulated to be the home of the Æsir by Saxo) as an expression of their respect. His wife Frigg has the gold taken off by smiths out of pure jealousy; Odin has the smiths hung and then using magic makes the statue speak whenever it is touched by someone. Frigg then gives herself to a servant and seduces him to make him destroy the statue and steal the gold. Because of this disgrace Odin goes into voluntary exile. During his absence Mithotyn the Sorcerer takes over his rule but he flees to Fyn after Odin's return and is killed there by the local inhabitants. Odin's honour is thus restored by Mithotyn's death.

Odin's second exile according to Saxo (*Gesta Danorum* III, 80–82) is the most extensive version of the tale and was worked into the tale of Odin's wooing of → Rinda/Rindr. After several disappointments due to Rinda's total unwillingness to accept his advances, Odin is at last able to seduce her by using devious deception. The other Æsir react by sending Odin into exile for ten years because of the ignominy of his actions and during this period of time his lands are ruled over by a 'certain Ollerus'

(= Ullr). When Odin returns to Byzantium, Ollerus withdraws to Sweden, but is finally killed there by the Danes. Odin, on the other hand, is able to reinstate himself in his former glory. Rinda bears him a son, Bous, who becomes Baldr's avenger.

As in the case of Odin, an exile is also reported of the god → Oðr, who is surely closely related to Odin. Attempts have been made to trace the tale of Odin's exile to various stories of classical or Russian origin, or even, in the version with the conquest of Rinda, from a fairy-tale about the taming of the shrew, and in Saxo the description has certainly been enriched by such motifs. The core of the story appears nonetheless to have its origin in a myth which occurs in Indian, Greek and (as Schröder has shown) also in Sumerian mythology, namely the dethronement of the ruling god by his sons or brothers (here Vili and Vé).

P. Herrmann, *Die Heldensagen des Saxo Grammaticus*, Leipzig 1922; F. R. Schröder, 'Odins Verbannung' (GRM 17) 1967; J. de Vries, *Altgermanische Religionsgeschichte*, Berlin [3]1970; H. E. Davidson, P. Fisher, *Saxo Grammaticus: The History of the Danes*, Cambridge 1980.

Odin's migration or the migration of the Æsir to Scandinavia is an explanation for the origin of the Nordic belief in the Æsir in the euhemeristic writings of Christian Scandinavian authors of the 12th and 13th centuries, especially by Snorri Sturluson.

The Nordic historians link heathen traditions of genealogies of gods with scholarly European chronicle historiography, for which among others the *Gesta Francorum* and Geoffrey of Monmouth's *Historia Regum Britanniae* (c.1130) or works influenced by these, served as sources in order to make possible the uninterrupted descent of Nordic royal houses and thus divine dynasties from Trojan and also finally from Old Testament families; the aim of this was to acquire a historical legitimization of sovereignty for Nordic kingship within Christian history, at the same time allowing for indigenous heathen traditions.

Ari's *Libellus Islandorum*, completed before 1133, begins with a reference to (1) Yngvi, the Turkish king, (2) Njǫrðr, the Swedish king, (3) Frayr (= Freyr). As here in the tracing of the Vanir gods, all subsequent sources writing about Scandinavian prehistory report the descent of the Æsir from Asia which appears to have found welcome support in the supposed etymology of the name Æsir.

The migration of Odin and the Æsir to Scandinavia is referred to in a number of Icelandic texts of the 12th and 13th centuries (collected by Heusler). The most detailed is the description by Snorri, of which there are two divergent versions still extant: the first is in the Prologue to the *Snorra Edda*, the other is in the *Ynglinga saga*. The version in the prologue to the *Edda* contains the following facts: King Memnón of Troja ('which we call Tyrkland (= Turkey)') married the daughter of King Priamus, and they had a son called Trór, 'who we call Thor'; he ruled in Trákíá, which is called Þrúðheim in Scandinavia, and married the sibil Sif. A genealogy follows, the majority of which is names for Thor, ending with Voden = Odin, who is married to Frígíðá = Frigg. They leave Turkey with a large number of followers and move first towards Saxony, where Odin sets up some of his sons as kings over the German kingdoms, and then move on to Sweden where Gylfi ruled at that time. Gylfi offers Odin his sovereignty and so he settles in Sigtuna whereupon he appoints 12 chieftains 'according to Trojan custom'.

The description given in the *Ynglinga saga* (2–5) differs slightly: Odin was lord over Asgard, the land that lies east of the Don in Asia; the stories of Odin's exile and the war with the Vanir are interposed here; then follows the tale of the actual migration during which Odin places his brothers Vili and Vé as rulers over Asgard, then over

Russia and Saxony, where he appoints his sons again as kings, via Fyn to Sweden where he settles in Sigtuna.

The differences in Snorri's two descriptions can be explained by the fact that at the beginning of the 13th century Snorri was faced with two differing hypotheses regarding the migration, and in the Prologue to the *Edda* he followed the tradition set up by the scholar Ari more than the tradition of the Skjǫldunga saga (which he followed in the *Ynglinga saga*).

Although the sources for the migration tales can be traced back to Continental European historiography, the teaching of the original home of the Scandinavian gods and royal houses as being in Asia is an Icelandic construction: neither the Norwegian historian Theodoricus in his *Historia Norwegiae* nor the Dane Saxo Grammaticus record the theory which was so widespread in Iceland.

The tales of Odin's migration have led to an assumption among scholars of a relatively young expansion of Odin's cult, which is supposed to have reached Scandinavia via Germany, but no credible evidence has been produced.

A. Heusler, *Die gelehrte Urgeschichte*, Berlin 1908; F. Wild, *Odin und Euemeros*, Vienna 1941; K. Helm, Wodan, *Ausbreitung und Wanderung seines Kultes*, Gießen 1946; G. Dumézil, *Gods of the Ancient Northmen*, Berkeley 1977.

R: (fine art) P. Hörberg, *Oden byggande Sigtuna* (coloured pen drawing, 1801); P. Hörberg, *König Gylfe empfängt Odin bei seiner Ankunft in Schweden* (sketch, 1814); B. E. Fogelberg, *Odens möte med Gylfe* (relief on a drinking horn, 1818); M. W. Winge, *Asarnes invandring* (painting).
(literature) K. G. Leopold, *Odin eller Asarnes invandring* (tragedy, 1790); J. Baggesen, *Odin eller Danrigets stiftelse* (epic poem, 1803); N. F. S. Grundtvig, *Optrin af Norners og Asers kamp: Odins komme til Norden* (Roman, 1809); J. L. Almqvist, *Sviavigamal* (novel in four parts, 1833).

Odin's names. Names for the god Odin are more numerous than for any other god. Over 170 have been passed down to us which Odin uses either as a pseudonym (Hárbarðr, Hnikarr, Grímnir), or which are a poetic coinage for the god (Alfaðir, Fimbultýr, Fjǫlsviðr), or were used much earlier by the individual Germanic tribes for the chief god (Gautr, Viðurr, Skilfingr, Jǫrmunr). In Snorri (*Gylfaginning* 19), Gangleri is surprised at the large number of Odin's names (which are quoted by Snorri from the lists given in *Grímnismál* 46–50) and receives the answer: 'It takes great wisdom to explain them all; but to put it in a word, it should be said that most names were given to him because everyone in the world, who speaks different languages, wanted to translate his name into their own tongue in order to speak to him and worship him. But some of his names have arisen from events which have occurred on his travels, which are dealt with in tales, and you cannot be called a scholar if you are unable to retell these great deeds.'

The second group of names which Snorri mentions are the names which refer directly to a myth or to Odin's role in it: Hangi and Handaguð to Odin's (self-) sacrifice, Sigfaðir and Hertýr to his role as the manipulator of battles, Arnhǫfði to his shape-change into an animal in the myth of the theft of the mead, Grímnir, Blindr, Tvíblindi to Odin the one-eyed god, Hárbarðr and Siðskeggr to his beard, Síðhǫttr and Hjalmberi to his clothing, Gangraðr, Gangleri, Vegtamr to his appearance as a wanderer.

Odin's names enlighten many aspects of his personality as seen from literary sources, but they also allude to cult and devotion among the various Germanic tribes in the pre-literary age.

H. Falk, *Odensheite*, Kristiania 1924; E. O. G. Turville-Petre, *Myth and Religion of the North*, Westport 1975.

Odin's (self-)sacrifice is recorded in the famous passage in *Hávamál* 138–141 where it says:

138: I know, I hung on the wind-swept tree
for nine nights in all
wounded by a spear and dedicated to Odin
Given myself to myself
on the tree, of which nobody knows
from which root it grows.

139: With nothing to eat and nothing to drink
I bent my head down
and groaning took the runes up
and fell down thereafter.

The stanzas speak about Odin acquiring the knowledge of the runes by offering himself to himself; the mode of sacrifice through hanging and wounding with a spear is also recorded for other sacrifices to Odin, such as the sacrifice of King → Víkarr, or Odin's self-mutilation in Snorri's euhemeristic description in *Ynglinga saga* 9.

The motifs in this myth reminiscent of Christ's crucifixion have led to a theory that this is merely an adoption of Christ's Sacrifice of the Cross by the ancient Scandinavians who, having heard of Christ's sacrifice on their travels to the British Isles, subsequently transferred it to their chief god, Odin (Bugge). However, this form of sacrifice is also well-known from initiation rites in archaic cultures, and has sufficient parallels in Indian (Prajāpati, Krsna) and in Greek mythology (Dionysius) to warrant its acceptance as an Indo-Germanic motif.

Consequently, the origin of Odin's self-sacrifice should be seen as one of the shamanistic initiation rites into the knowledge of poetry and magic (connected with the knowledge of runes).

The world-tree, on which Odin hung, is Yggdrasill 'Yggs = Odin's horse' = 'gallows'; because of Odin's (self-)sacrifice by hanging, he is also the god of the hanged (Hangaguð, hagatýr) and is even called 'lord of the gallows' (*gálga valdr*: Helgi traust, 10th century); Hangi ('the hanged') is also one of Odin's names, and Eyvindr calls him 'the gallow's burden' (*gálga farmr*). According to *Hávamál* 157 and Snorri (*Ynglinga saga* 7) Odin was able to awaken hanged men to life and to make them speak using rune-magic, a kind of magic peculiar to him alone.

Thus, hanging is seen to be a typical kind of sacrifice to Odin, and as such Adam of Bremen's information about the great sacrifice of human victims as sacrifices to Odin in → Uppsala should be understood.

S. Bugge, *Studien über die Entstehung der nordischen Götter- und Heldensagen*, Munich 1889; F. Kauffmann, *Oðinn am Galgen*, Helsingfors 1928; A. G. v. Hamel, 'Oðinn Hanging on the Tree' (*APhSc* 7) 1932/33; J. de Vries, 'Odin am Baume' (*Studia Germanica till. E. A. Kock*) Lund 1934; F. Ström, *Den döendes makt och Odin i trädet*, Göteborg 1947; J. de Vries, *Altgermanische Religionsgeschichte*, Berlin [3]1970; J. Fleck, 'Oðinn's Self-Sacrifice – A New Interpretation' (*SS* 43) 1971; Å. V. Ström, H. Biezais, *Germanische und baltische Religion*, Stuttgart 1975.

Odin's warriors → Dedication to Odin.

Óðr (ON). A god in Eddic mythology, according to Snorri (*Gylfaginning* 34, *Skáldskaparmál* 20 and 35) Freyja's husband and the father of Hnoss. Óðr is alluded to already in a kenning used by the skald Einarr Skulason (11th century) as well as in *Vǫluspá* 25 and *Hyndluljóð* 46 and 47, and so he is not a late invention. In his discussion of Freyja, Snorri says that Óðr was once absent for a long time, and Freyja had wept for his absence and had gone out in search of him.

The most obvious explanation is to identify Óðr with Odin; the similarity of the names (which show a parallel with Ullr/Ullinn), the long absence (cf. Odin's exile) and his marriage with Freyja (whom *Grímnismál* 14 identifies with Frigg, Odin's wife) support this suggestion.

Admittedly, there are several things which speak against it: Freyja's tears for Odin and her search are unmotivated, and the reference to Hnoss as being their only child is surprising – why, for example, should Baldr not be mentioned? These incongruities have led to various, at times quite divergent, explanations; Bugge and Falk saw Adonis reflected in Óðr, Much the Near Eastern name of a god Attis, and Hollander even sees a reflection of the fairy-tale about Amor and Psyche in Snorri's tale about Óðr and Freyja.

If the two gods were indeed identical, then Snorri would surely not have mentioned them separately; on the other hand, the names Óðr and Odin are so close that a complete differentiation between the two gods can hardly be achieved. The investigation into the relationship between the two and the division of them into older and younger 'layers' (Helm, Philippson, de Vries) has as yet not brought forward any convincing result because of the sparsity of the sources referring to Óðr.

K. Helm, *Wodan*, Gießen 1946; E. A. Philippson, *Die Genealogie der Götter*, Urbana, Ill. 1953; J. de Vries, 'Über das Verhältnis von Oðr und Oðinn' (*ZfdPh* 73) 1954; L. M. Hollander, 'The Old Norse God Oðr' (*JEGPh* 49) 1956; E. F. Halvorsen, 'Oðr' (*KLNM* 12) 1967.

Óðrœrir (ON, approximately: 'the one that stimulates to ecstasy'). The → mead of the skalds. According to Snorri (*Skáldskaparmál* 1), however, Óðrœrir is the cauldron in which the dwarfs Galarr and Fjalarr caught the blood of the giant → Kvasir whom they had killed. Snorri came to this interpretation because of an obscure passage in *Hávamál* 140, but *Hávamál* 107 and a number of kenning in skaldic poetry prove quite clearly that Óðrœrir originally meant the name for the mead itself, which, as the name implies, was understood to be an intoxicating drink. The myth of Kvasir (even in the version passed on by Snorri) confirms the significance of the intoxicating drink in the cult which reached back far into the heathen past.

The name Óðrœrir is nicely appropriate to the mead so that an improved reading in Ohrœrir, 'rejuvenating potion', is unnecessary.

H. Lindroth, 'Boðn, Són och Oðrœrir' (MoM) 1915; J. de Vries, *Altgermanische Religionsgeschichte*, Berlin [3]1970.

R: Óðrœrir is the title of the paper published by a 'new-Germanic' religious group, founded in 1976.

Öflugbarða (ON, 'strong-beard' or 'strong-axe'). A giantess in the *Þulur*. However, if the first meaning of the name is correct, then it would naturally enough be more a case of a giant Öflugbarði and indeed there is a giant of this name in Bragi's *Ragnarsdrápa* 15. It would thus appear that the compiler of the *Þulur* listed the name among the giantesses because of the genitive ending *-a* by accident.

F. Jónsson, 'Þulur' (*APhSc* 9) 1934.

Œgishjálmr → Ægir's helmet.

Ǫku-Thor (ON, Ǫku-Þórr, 'driving Thor') is only used by Snorri as a name for the god Thor (*Gylfaginning* 20, 43, 45, 53), and is to be found nowhere else in Old Norse literature. He derives the name from *aka* 'to drive a chariot', as Thor does indeed drive a chariot pulled by two he-goats; the origin of the idea of Thor's chariot driving could be the rumbling noise of thunder.

The opinion that Ǫku- is a mere folk-etymological derivation from *aka*, but was originally borrowed from the Finnish thunder-god Ucco (Finn Magnusson, Cleasby-Vigfusson) is unlikely considering that the opposite direction of cultural transfer is more usual.

Ǫlnir. A dwarf in the *Þulur* where he is also called Odin's son; Odin's son is Thor, however, and therefore F. Jónsson assumes that Ǫlnir is a name for Thor which was later transferred onto Odin and had Geir- added to it (→ Geirölnir), as Ölnir suits Thor much better than Odin. – The name probably belongs to ON *ala* and therefore might mean 'nourisher'? A connexion to the magic rune-word *alu* would also be possible.

F. Jónsson, 'Gudenavne – dyrenavne' (*ANF* 35) 1919; F. Jónsson, *Lexicon Poeticum*, Copenhagen ²1966; J. de Vries, *Altnordisches etymologisches Wörterbuch*, Leiden ²1977.

Ǫlrun. A → valkyrie, who is only mentioned in heroic poetry (*Vǫlunðarkviða*). She is described as the daughter of a certain King Kiarr from Valland and like → Hervǫr and → Hlaðguðr as a swan-maiden. The name could actually mean 'beer-rune', but whether it really belongs etymologically to ON *ǫl* 'beer' is doubtful.

Ǫlvaldi (ON, 'the keeper of the beer'). The giant, according to Snorri (*Skáldskaparmál* 1), who is the father of Þjazi, Iði and Gangr. Ölvaldi, who is extremely rich, shares his inheritance out between his sons so that each may take a mouthful of gold; this is why gold could also be called 'Þjazi's mouthful' (or Ið's or Gangr's) in kennings. As these three giant's sons do indeed frequently occur in kennings for gold, it appears that the whole story is not merely an invention of Snorri's, but is actually the remains of an old myth. However, of all Eddic lays only *Hárbarðsljóð* 19 refers to the giant Ölvaldi (in the form Allvaldi) as being the father of Þjazi, namely in the passage relating Thor's killing of Þjazi; there is nothing else still extant of the rest of the myth.

Ǫnduðr or Ǫndóttr (ON). A giant in the *Þulur*. Önduðr is also a personal name, but the manuscript variant Öndóttr 'the terrible' for a giant appears to be the original.

ǫndvegissúlur (ON, 'high-seat pillars') play a particular role in pagan Scandinavian religion; the significance of these pillars of the high seat on the north side of the house comes most likely from a link between the cult of the ancestors and the cult of the world-pillar, represented by the pillars supporting the house roof.

The sagas relate that Icelandic settlers threw their *ǫndvegissúlur* into the sea in sight of land and then settled wherever the *ǫndvegissúlur* were washed ashore. *Eyrbyggja saga* tells of *ǫndvegissúlur* which had pictures of Thor carved into them, saying that they came from a Norwegian temple. Even if this information does indeed have any claim to factual relevance, the position of such pillars and seats in the temple were at best secondary.

V. Kiil, 'Fra andvegissula til omnkall' (*Norveg* 7) 1960; J. de Vries, *Altgermanische Religionsgeschichte*, Berlin ³1970.

Ǫnn or Ǫnni (ON, 'work'?). A dwarf in the *Þulur*.

Ǫrmt (ON, 'the one dividing into arms'?). A (mythical?) river in *Grímnismál* 29 and in the *Þulur*. *Grímnismál* says that Thor has to wade through the rivers 'Kǫrmt and Örmt and both of the Kerlaugar' every day on his way to the council of the gods beneath the world-tree Yggdrasill. This could point to the idea that all these Other World rivers form the borders of Midgard in the East against Jǫtunheim, where Thor, according to Eddic lays, could often be found fighting the giants.

Ǫrnir (or Aurnir, ON). The father of one of the giant maids in *Grottasǫngr* 9, who is mentioned in later kennings and in the *Þulur*, like the other giants of this stanza (Hrungnir, Þjazi, Iði). Elsewhere, Örnir usually appears in the form Aurnir. The name in this form could then mean 'rock or earth-dweller', similar to the giants' names Aurgelmir, Aurboða.

Ǫsgrúi (ON, 'heap of ashes '). A giant in the *Þulur*.

Ǫskruðr (ON, 'bellower'). A giant in the *Þulur*. Numerous giants' names seem to have a similar meaning.

Ófnir (1) (ON, 'the instigator') is one of Odin's names in *Grímnismál* 54 and in the *Þulur*.

Ófnir (2) (ON, 'the winding one, the twisting one'). One of the snakes which live under the roots of the world-tree Yggdrasill (*Grímnismál* 34), or, according to Snorri, live in the spring, Hvergelmir (*Gylfaginning* 15).

Ófóti (ON, 'the legless one'). The giant in the *Þulur* who was possibly understood to be the eponymous figure whose name is to be found in the Norwegian Ofótansfjord.

Óglaðnir (ON, 'the cheerless one'). A giant in the *Þulur*.

Óinn (ON, 'the fearless' from *óast*). A dwarf in *Vǫluspá* 11.

R: under the Anglicized form of his name, Oin, this dwarf is one of the 13 dwarfs in J. R. R. Tolkien's novel, *The Hobbit* (1937).

Ókolnir (ON, 'the uncold place'). A mythical place in which, according to *Vǫluspá* 37 (and *Gylfaginning* 51), the drinking hall of the giants is situated. As the giants' homes are usually considered to be cold, it has been read as Of-kolnir, 'the very cold place'. It is more probable, however, that Ókolnir was originally thought of as another name or kenning for the (heated) drinking hall which was only understood by the poet of *Vǫluspá* as a mythical place, and as such has little to do with a giants' abode.

A. M. Sturtevant, 'Comments on Mythological Name-Giving in Old Norse' (*Germanic Review* 29) 1954.

Óláfr Pá → *Húsdrápa*.

Olgr (ON). A name for Odin in the *Þulur*, which can most likely be interpreted to mean 'the roaring one', thus the god of the stormy sea.

H. Falk, *Odensheite*, Kristiana 1924.

Ollerus. One of the Æsir gods who, according to Saxo (*Gesta Danorum* III, 81), ruled over the Æsir during → Odin's exile; in this function he was also called 'Odin'. Ollerus is clearly the northern god → Ullr/Ulinn.

Ollogabiae. Matron name. Two votive stones from the area around Mainz are dedicated to the *Matronae Ollogabiae* (CIL XIII 6751 and 7280); the name is a Celtic counterpart to the Germanic Alagabiae and as such means roughly the 'bountiful donors'.

R. Much, 'Baudihillia und Friagabis' (*Festschrift Jellinek*) 1928; S. Gutenbrunner, *Die germanischen Götternamen*, Halle 1936.

Olsen, Magnus (1878–1963) was a Norwegian researcher of place-names who at the beginning of this century first drew attention to the significance of theophorous place-names for Germanic history of religion. Furthermore, in his investigations he attempted to conclude the age and kind of cult – whether private or public – from the form of composition of the god's name and geographical elements. However, although since Olsen's works *Hedenske Kultminder i norske Stedsnavne* (Kristiana 1915) and *Ættegård og Helligdom* (Kristiana 1926) there have been numerous essays on the relationship between place-names and the history of religion, there is still no revised conspectus of the matter, although J. de Vries did take it up in his history of Germanic religion (*Altgermanische Religionsgeschichte*).

Ómi (ON) is a name for Odin in *Grímnismál* 49, the *Þulur* and in Snorri (*Gylfaginning* 2). It could mean 'the noisy one' (from *ómun* 'loud'); an explanation as 'the superior one' (from **auhuma*) is, however, more meaningful.

H. Falk, *Odensheite*, Kristiania 1924; J. de Vries, *Altnordisches etymologisches Wörterbuch*, Leiden [2]1977.

Ónarr (ON). A dwarf. In *Reginsmál* 2 he is said to be the father of the dwarf Andvari; it is debatable whether the Ónarr named in *Skáldskaparmál* 22 is identical with this dwarf.

Oracles. Various ways of divination seem to have played a role among the Germanic peoples at least in the early period, if we are able to believe Tacitus who names different kinds of Germanic oracles. According to *Germania* 10 the Teutons prophesied the future from the flight of birds (like the Romans did), and also from the behaviour of horses. Tacitus also named single-handed combat as a kind of divine judgement, and he notes in addition the throwing of little pieces of wood in which *notae* (probably runes) were carved.

This kind of throwing of lots is mentioned sporadically in Celtic sources, too. On the other hand the term for a similar kind of divination in ON sources, the 'felling of the sacrificial twig' (*fella blótspán*) is described (*Landnámabók* S 196 = H 166; *Ynglinga saga* 38; *Gautreks saga* 7; *Hervarar saga* 6 and 7). The single twig points out that a different kind of oracle is meant here, especially as the casting with pieces of wood by throwing them up into the air (*taka upp hlutir*) is described in a quite different way (*Egils saga* 48). However, a reflection of heathen-religious acts of divining the future may have been reproduced in a very distorted way by Christian authors. The *Eyrbyggja saga* shows how far heathen practices and concepts could be misunderstood: it describes a *hlautteinn* as if it were a Christian sprinkler (*asperges*) even though the *hlautteinn* was probably identical with the *blótspánn* mentioned above, as the actual term for the sticks for casting lots is ON *teinn* (*Hymiskviða* 1), OE *tan*, and is given in the Frisian law books, written in Latin, as *tenos* (*Lex. Fris.*, 14,1).

The throwing up of pieces of wood marked with (pre-runic?) signs, as described by Tacitus, appears to have really existed as a form of divination. However, the different descriptions of the Nordic sources hardly reflect the true circumstances concerning divination and oracles.

R. Meissner, 'Ganga til fréttar' (*Zeitschrift für Volkskunde* 27) 1917; L. Elmevik, 'fsv. *lytir (L*ytir)' (*NoB* 54) 1966.

R: E. Doepler d. J., *Losungen* (E. Doepler, W. Ranisch, *Walhall*, 1901).

Orendel (MHG). The eponymous hero of the MHG poem of that name, whose name corresponds to the ON → Aurvandill.

Óri (ON, 'the man one' from *œrr*?). A dwarf in the *Vǫluspá* 15 (*Gylfaginning* 13). As with the dwarf's name Onarr, Ori too appears in the *Þulur* as a name for 'snake'; → Orinn.

R: Ori is one of the 13 dwarfs in J. R. R. Tolkien's novel, *The Hobbit* (1937).

Órinn (ON, 'the quarrelsome'). A dwarf in the *Vǫluspá* 11; → Óri.

(**Ortlinde**). The name of a valkyrie (mezzo soprano) in R. Wagner's opera *Die Walküre*. The name is an invention of Wagner's.

Óski (ON) is a name for Odin in the *Grímnismál* 49, in Ottar svarti and in the *Þulur*; Snorri also includes it. Oski could mean roughly 'wish fulfiller' – as the valkyries are called *óskmeyjar* – and thereby refers to the fact that he receives the slain warriors in Valhall.

H. Falk, *Odensheite*, Christiana 1924.

óskmey (ON, 'wish-girl') is a synonym for → valkyrie (*Oddrúnargrátr* 16) as the valkyries were girls who brought those slain in battle to Valhall. They were chosen by Odin and longed for by the slain warriors.

Óskópnir (ON) is the name of the battlefield (*Fáfnismál* 14 and 15) which is otherwise known as Vígríðr, on which the Æsir at Ragnarǫk will fight against Surtr and his powers of Muspell. The meaning of the name has not yet been satisfactorily explained, but possibly means 'the (not yet) created'.

Oskoreidi (Norwegian) is the name given in the south and west of Norway to the → Wild Hunt. The name has been interpreted as Asguðsreið ('ride of the Æsir god = Odin') which would suit Odin's role in the Wild Hunt in heathen times well; but purely linguistically speaking, an interpretation of Oskoreidi as 'ride of terror' would be equally likely.

M. Hægstad, 'Um namnet Oskoreidi' (MoM) 1912; J. de Vries, *Altgermanische Religionsgeschichte*, Berlin [3]1970.

***Ostara** (OHG) was perhaps a heathen goddess of the Spring (proto-Gmc *Austrō) which could be derived from the OHG name of the Easter festival Ôstarûn and the reference to an Anglo-Saxon goddess → Ēostra in Bede (Grimm).

It is uncertain whether the goddess derived her name from the Easter month or vice versa. In any case, the Christian Easter festival has received a heathen name via the name of the month.

Lit. → Ēostra.

R: the name of Ostara was used from 1905 as the name of a German nationalist publishing house and book series ('Bücherei der Blonden und Mannesrechtler') with its headquarters in Mödling near Vienna.

Other World. The Germanic concept of the Underworld and of the Other World are by no means homogeneous. In Eddic cosmology the Underworld is → Hel, the place where people go who have died from illness or old-age; the drowned belong to → Rán; the warriors who have fallen in battle come to Odin in → Valhall. Hel and the other places of the dead Niðavellir, Nástrǫnd were thought to lie in the north, which agrees with the north-south alignment of graves, from the passage graves of Stone and Bronze Age megalithic cultures to the late heathen Viking Age. But the burial customs of these three milleniums also prove that the way to the Underworld, → *helvegr*, was usually thought to lead over the sea, further evident in the numerous examples of ship's graves and ship settings. Other concepts of the Other World, which were already influenced by Christian ideas and indeed given in a Christian context, are reflected in the OE *neorxnawang* as well as ON → Glæsisvellir and → Óðáinsakr, both of which are handed down in sagas of the 14th century. Another possible term for the Other World is Hvitramannaland, situated in the west. One Other World realm which is not populated by the dead, but by giants and demons, is Utgard which was thought of as being on the other side of the sea in the Arctic north. The later descriptions of the Other World and of journeys there are certainly heavily marked by the Christian ideas of paradise, but even the Eddic lays are not free from Christian influences, which however took their effect probably in early times, during the first Christian millenium. One aspect of Germanic concepts of the Other World continued, however, until the High Middle Ages: Hel and the other places in the Other World are never thought of as places of punishment, as they are in Christianity.

Ottarr (ON, mostly as Ottarr heimski 'Ottar the stupid') is the name of the person about whom the mythologizing frame story of the → *Hyndluljóð* deals.

Paul the Deacon (Lat. Paulus Diaconus, c.720–799). A cleric from a Langobard noble family who, after being educated at the royal seat of the Langobard kings in Pavia, was ordained a deacon in Aquilea and subsequently lived as a monk in Monte Cassino. In 782–786 he was at the court of Charlemagne. He wrote several books but the work which is particularly interesting for Germanic studies is his *Historia Langobardorum* (c.790), in the first book of which he refers to the origin and mythical legends of the Langobards. It is this which is of value for Germanic mythology.

The other important source for the history of the Langobards, the anonymous *Origo gentis Langobardorum*, dates from a century before Paul's work, and he agrees with it in most cases.

Peace. 'The entirety of that legal-ethical system which guarantees a peaceful and fruitful co-habitation in the political community' (Baetke). This concept of peace is met in the sources in the ideal picture of a golden age at the time of → Fróði's peace, as well as in the sacrifice for → *ár ok friðr*, which cannot only be seen as a sacrifice to the fertility god Freyr, but must be seen as a religious as well as a legal matter in connexion with the healing powers of the king; → sacred kingship.

W. Baetke, 'Der Begriff der "Unheiligkeit"' (*PBB* 66) 1942; A. Ebenbauer, 'Fróði und sein Friede' (*Festgabe* O. *Höfler*) Vienna 1976; F. Ström, 'År och fred' (*KLNM* 29) 1976.

Peace of Fróði → Fróði's peace.

peat bog bodies → bog corpses.

Phol (presumably instead of Fol). A god mentioned at the beginning of the → Second Merseburg Charm. This god's name is not recorded anywhere else and it can probably only be interpreted in connexion with the name of the goddess Volla (for Folla?) who is mentioned in the same charm. The most likely explanation is that Phol and Volla are divine brother and sister who are identical or at least closely related to the Scandinavian deities Freyr and Freyja. The Nordic equivalence of the goddess Volla, → Fulla, is described in Eddic mythology as a goddess in her own right, but the meaning of the name itself, 'goddess of fullness', suggests that it could indeed be another name for Freyja. Therefore, Phol should probably be interpreted etymologically in a similar way, which would speak in favour of a close connexion to the fertility god, Freyr.

This interpretation is, however, not entirely undisputed, and sporadically there have been suggestions that Phol is not the name of a god but that it actually refers to the later named *volon* 'foal' (Steller, Warnatsch).

The unconvincing theory found in older scholarship is that Phol is actually identical with Baldr.

E. Brate, 'Andra Merseburg-besvärjelsen' (*ANF* 35) 1919; W. Steller, 'Phol ende Wodan' (*Zeitschrift für Volkskunde* 40) 1930; O. Warnatsch, 'Phol und der 2. Merseburger Zauberspruch' (*ZfdPh* 64) 1939; S. Gutenbrunner, 'Der zweite Merseburger Spruch' (*ZfdA* 80) 1944; F. Genzmer, 'Die Götter des zweiten Merseburger Zauberspruchs' (*ANF* 63) 1948; F. R. Schröder, 'Balder und der zweite Merseburger Zauberspruch' (*GRM* 34) 1953; A. Spamer, 'P(h)ol ende uuodan' (*Deutsches Jahrbuch für Volkskunde* 3) 1957; J. de Vries, *Altgermanische Religionsgeschichte*, Berlin [3]1970.

Place-names had already been recognized in the 19th century as a source for the history of Germanic religion, but the first systematic research of this source material was begun by the Norwegian place-name researcher Magnus → Olsen at the beginning of the 20th century.

Theophorous ('formed with a god's name') place-names can be divided into those whose second element is a toponymic name (for instance, *-nes* 'spit (of land)', *-ey* 'island', *-berg* 'mountain') and those whose second element refers to cult places: the latter include all theophorous place-names based on *-hof* 'temple?', *-hǫrgr* and *-vé* 'cult place', *-lund* 'grove', perhaps also those based on *-vin* 'meadow' and *-akr* 'field'. Naturally enough, the place-names of this second group are of substantially more importance as evidence for a god's cult. Apart from actual theophorous place-names there is also a greater number of those which point to a cult place in general without naming the particular deity worshipped there; such names as Vi (from *vé* 'shrine') or Guðakr 'gods' field', perhaps also Hof 'temple?; farm' belong to this group.

In this most extensive meaning there are great numbers of sacred place-names in Scandinavia (Olsen refers in Norway alone to over 600), and even in the limited meaning around 1050 theophorous place-names are to be found in Scandinavia, including Iceland. Of these, there are approximately 225 in Norway, 270 in Denmark, 510 in Sweden, just 30 in Finland and around 40 in Iceland.

M. Olsen pointed out the remarkable fact that the frequency of the gods appearing in place-names does not correspond with the importance of these gods in the mythology of the literary sources. Odin appears in the *Eddas* as the main god and yet in Iceland where these works originated there are no place-names recorded which are based on Odin, and even in Norway where the cultural background of the Old Icelandic heathen religion should be sought, there are only 12 such theophorous place-names based on Odin (that is 5.3%: Höfler); similarly in Denmark and Sweden they are by no means frequent (32 and 72 occurrences respectively). On the other hand, the god Thor is well documented in place-names, although there is a problem with regard to place-names based on Thor in that it is difficult to distinguish between theophorous place-names and those which are based on bearers of Thor-names (Þorbjǫrn, Þorleif, Þorstein, Þorkel, Þorgil etc.); this is also true for the frequent place-names based on Thor in Britain.

The name of the god Ullr (or the other form Ulinn) is found surprisingly often in place-names in Norway and Sweden, although this god appears hardly anywhere else and seems particularly insignificant in the literary sources. This fact must lead to the supposition that Ullr must have played a much greater role at the time that the place-names were formed than in the late heathen period when our oldest literary sources were written.

As would be expected, place-names which are formed with the names of the Vanir, that is the fertility gods Njǫrðr, Freyr and Freyja, are very widespread in Norway and Sweden, and yet are missing almost totally in Denmark, and in Iceland only three place-names based on Freyr can be found. Nonetheless, altogether the number of place-names using names of the Vanir are as frequent as those based on Ullr.

Apart from theophorous place-names with names of these known gods there is also a number of them with names of deities which we do not know at all from literature, such as Hǫrn and *Vrindr. However, it is almost impossible to draw conclusions about such gods from the place-names alone.

Place-names tell something about the distribution of the cults of gods; for example, it is striking that several gods were obviously worshipped in connexion with another god; there seems to have been a connexion in cult between Njǫrðr and Týr, Ullr and Freyr, Ullr and Njǫrðr, and yet it is difficult to draw conclusions concerning the system of gods from this. The discrepancy between the data of the place-names on the one hand and the didactic teaching of the Eddas on the other does not prove of course that one of these sources has not passed down incorrect information, but only that we are faced with relationships from widely separated epoches; for, whereas the Eddas refer to the religion of the late Viking era, the place-names give information about the situation over several centuries during the whole of the Migration period.

The way and distribution of shrines can also be read from the distribution of place-names and could, in relation to the distribution of the names of settlements, undoubtedly give explanation about the temporal layers of different types of shrines; proper investigations of this are still needed.

J. C. H. R. Steenstrup, 'Nogle Undersøgelser om Guders Navne i de nordiske Stedsnavne' (*Historisk Tidsskrift* R. 6) 1895; M. Olsen, *Det gamle norske ønavn Njarðarlǫg*, Christiania 1905; E. Brate, 'Thor(s)hugle' (*ANF* 29) 1913; M. Olsen, *Hedenske Kultminder* 1, Kristiania 1915; E. Noreen, 'Ett hedniskt Kultcentrum i Värmland' (*NoB* 8) 1920; A. Olrik, H. Ellekilde, *Nordens Gudeverden*, Copenhagen 1926–51; M. Olsen, *Ættegård og Helligdom*, Kristiania 1926; M. Olsen, *Farms and Fanes of Ancient Norway*, Oslo 1928; E. Wessén, 'Schwedische Ortsnamen und altnordische Mythologie' (*APhSc* 4) 1929; R. Knudsen, 'Vi og Vis i Stednavne' (*Studier til V. Dahlerup*) Aarhus 1934; S. K. Amtoft, 'Stednavna' (*Aarbøger för nordisk Oldkyndighed og Historie*) 1941; S. K. Amtoft, *Nordiske Gudeskikkelser i bebyggelseshistorisk Belysning*, Copenhagen 1948; E. Elgqvist, *Studier rörande njordkultens spridning*, Lund 1952; N. Lid, 'Scandinavian Heathen Cult Places' (*Folk-Liv* 21/22) 1957/58; K. Hald, 'The Cult of Odin in Danish Place-Names' (*Early English and Norse Studies. Pres. to H. Smith*) London 1963; O. Höfler, 'Die nordischen Kultortsnamen und die Edda' (*Disputationes ad montium vocabula*) Vienna 1969; J. de Vries, *Altgermanische Religionsgeschichte*, Berlin [3]1970; G. Turville-Petre, 'Thurstable' (in: *Nine Norse Studies*) London 1972; G. Turville-Petre, *Myth and Religion of the North*, Westport 1975; K. Bondevik, 'Truer og førestellingar i stadnam' (*Norske stedsnavn/stadnamn*) Oslo 1975.

Pole gods. Worship of wooden carved images of gods or else poles is one of the oldest recorded forms of belief in gods. Poles were erected in heaps of stones and worshipped among the Germanic tribes of the Bronze Age, and also as early as the European Stone Age. Anthropomorphic pole gods are known from the Iron Age, namely posts up to one metre high or else forked branches with roughly carved human features. Such pole gods are known from Germany as well as from Denmark and England. These pictures of gods of the late heathen period, for example the statue of the god → Freyr in *Gunnar þáttr helmings*, were decried as being wooden 'idols' in Christian sources.

The origin of pole worship in a narrow sense has been interpreted on the one hand as being part of a phallus cult, which however would seem to have played only a minor role for the Germanic peoples, or on the other hand it could come from an archaic tree cult, or else from ideas to do with the world pillar (→ Irminsûl) possibly associated with it.

R. Meringer, 'Wörter und Sachen III. Der verehrte Pflock' (*IF* 18) 1905/06; R. Meringer, 'Wörter und Sachen V. Die Pflock- und Säulenverehrung' (*IF* 21) 1907; R. Meringer, 'Indogermanische Pfahlgötzen' (*Wörter und Sachen* 9) 1926; J. Trier, 'Irminsul' (*Westfälische Forschungen* 4) 1941; G. Behn-Blancke, 'Germanische Mooropferplätze' (*Ausgrabungen und Funde* 2) 1957; H. Jankuhn, *Archäologische Bemerkungen*, Göttingen 1966.

Priests. Tacitus mentioned Germanic priests as early as the first century A.D. (*Germania* 7, 10, 11, 40). OHG *êwart* (Anglo-Saxon *æweweard*) could have referred to such priests, since it sometimes glosses the Latin word *sacerdos*, although the word actually means 'law-guardian'.

In Scandinavia, *goði* is the most usual term for the heathen priests, a word which is recorded on rune stones from the 5th century as Runic Norse *gudija* and corresponds to Gothic *gudja*. The Scandinavian → goði also had increasingly secular functions, particularly in Iceland, and these priests developed into a kind of district chieftain.

In Germanic antiquity the → seeresses appear to have fulfilled a priestly function, but for the late heathen period our sources hardly give any information about priestesses, apart from the ON epithet *gyðja* (from *goði*) for several Icelandic women.

Ráðgríðr (ON, 'the bossy'?). A → valkyrie in *Grímnismál* 36.

Ráðseyjarsund (ON, 'council island sound'). A fictitious place-name in *Hárbarðsljóð* 8 where Hildólf the ferryman lives.

Ráðspakr (ON, 'the quick-witted one'). A dwarf in the *Þulur*.

Ráðviðr (ON, 'the wise giver of advice'). A dwarf in the *Vǫluspá* 12 and in the *Þulur*.

Ragnarǫk (ON, pl., 'final destiny of the gods'). The term for the Nordic eschatology in the *Edda*, whilst the *Snorra Edda* (like *Lokasenna* 39) uses throughout the term → *ragnarǫkr* 'twilight of the gods' which is, however, a late re-interpretation.

The main source for the concept of the end of the world is *Vǫluspá* 44–66 and its prose version with commentary given by Snorri in *Gylfaginning* 50.

Nordic cosmology includes a destruction of the world which involves the gods as well as man. Thus, the presence of the gods is limited and not without reason: like man they have much to be blamed for because of crimes and wars.

The Ragnarǫk is characterized by four great eschatological events which are described in detail in *Gylfaginning* 50: the → Fimbulwinter; the world-fire with which Surtr destroys the whole world; the sinking of the earth into the ocean which has been whipped up by the → Midgard serpent; and finally the darkening of the sun which has been devoured by the → Fenris wolf. Other natural catastrophes then follow: the earth quakes, rocks fall, the world-tree Yggdrasill shakes (*Vǫluspá* 47), the bridge Bifrǫst collapses (*Gylfaginning* 50). Heimdall blows the Gjalarhorn to warn the gods of the coming events. Odin asks Mímir's head for advice (*Vǫluspá* 46) and the gods hold a council. The powers of the underworld approach on all sides: the ship → Naglfar is set afloat and arrives with the giants, steered by Hrymr (*Gylfaginning* 50; by Loki according to *Vǫluspá* 51); Surtr leads the → Muspell sons into battle against the gods. The battle of the gods, in which the gods supported by the → *einherjar* fight against the powers of the underworld, takes place on the battlefield called Vígríðr (*Vafþrúðnismál* 18) and is described in especial detail (*Vǫluspá* 53–58; *Gylfaginning* 50). Odin fights against the Fenris wolf and falls, but is avenged by Víðarr. Thor kills the Midgard serpent but dies from its poison. Freyr fights with Surtr but dies because he has no sword. Týr and the hound of hell, Garmr, and Heimdallr and Loki kill each other. Finally Surtr kindles the world-fire which will destroy everything.

The destruction is, however, not total; according to a cyclic concept of the world a new pure world arises out of the sea. The surviving gods Víðarr and Váli, Móði and Magni meet each other on the plain called Iðavǫllr, the site of the former Asgard; Baldr and Hǫðr return from Hel. The last stanza of the *Vǫluspá* speaks of the final destruction of the dragon of death Níðhǫggr.

The stanzas *Vǫluspá* 59–66 with the description of the new world, as well as 37, which Snorri quotes in connexion with the Ragnarǫk (*Gylfaginning* 51) and interprets within the description of heaven and hell, have led to the question about Christian elements in the description of the Ragnarǫk in *Vǫluspá* as they partly remind us very much of the description of the heavenly Jerusalem in Revelations. Olrik has tried to divide the elements of this myth and sees the moral state of the world, the blowing of the Gjallarhorn, the disappearance of the sun, the world-fire and the description of the new world as being influenced by Christianity.

Other terms for the destruction of the world apart from Ragnarǫk in the Eddas are *aldar rǫk* ('end of the world', *Vafþrúðnismál* 39), *tíva rǫk* ('fate of the gods', *Vafþrúðnismál* 38, 42), *þá er regin deyja* ('when the gods die', *Vafþrúðnismál* 47), *unz um rjúfask regin* ('when the gods will be destroyed', *Vafþrúðnismál* 52; *Lokasenna* 41; *Sigrdrífumál* 19), *þá er Muspellz-synir herja* ('when the sons of Muspell move into battle'; *Gylfaginning* 18, 36), *aldar rof* ('destruction of the world', *Helgakviða Hundingsbana* II 41) and *regin þrjóta* ('end of the gods', *Hyndluljóð* 42).

A. Olrik, *Ragnarök*, Berlin 1923; R. Reitzenstein, 'Weltuntergangsvorstellungen' (*Kyrkohistorisk Årsskrift* 24) 1924; R. Reitzenstein, 'Die nordischen, persischen, und christlichen Vorstellungen vom Weltuntergang' (*Vorträge der Bibliothek Marburg* 26) 1923–24; A. Holtsmark, 'Ragnarök'

(*KLNM* 13) 1968; J. de Vries, *Altgermanische Religionsgeschichte*, Berlin [3]1970; J. S. Martin, *Ragnarök*, Assen 1972; S. Nordal, *Vǫluspá*, Darmstadt 1980.

R: (fine art) P. N. Arbo, *The Dusk of Gods* (oil painting); H. E. Freund, *Ragnarok* (frieze, 1825); K. Ehrenberg, *Beginn der Götterdämmerung* (charcoal drawing, 1881). (music) R. Wagner: *Die Götterdämmerung* (opera, 1876); D. Bedford, *Ragnarok* (opera, 1983).

ragnarǫkr (ON, 'twilight of the gods'). The name used wrongly in *Lokasenna* 39 and in Snorri for the older term → Ragnarǫk 'destiny of the gods' as the name for the Nordic concept of the downfall of the world. This corrupt form in Snorri has led to the usage of the modern translation usually of 'twilight of the gods' rather than 'destiny of the gods' for the Germanic apocalypse.

K. Müllenhoff, 'Um Ragnaröckr' (*ZfdA* 16) 1873.

Ragnarsdrápa (ON, 'the poem about Ragnarr'). This is the oldest skaldic poem still in existence today. It was written in the 9th century by Bragi enn gamli and is a shield-poem which means that it describes legendary and mythological scenes which had been carved or painted on a shield which Bragi had received from a certain Ragnarr, who was, according to *Skáldatal*, the Danish king Ragnarr Loðbrók. In his *Edda*, Snorri has retained 20 stanzas and half-stanzas of the poem, which was probably originally somewhat longer.

The *Ragnarsdrápa* obviously describes four pictorial scenes: the fight of Hamðir and Sǫrli in Ermanarich's hall (8½ half-stanzas); the myth of Gefjon (2 half-stanzas); → Thor and the Midgard serpent (7 half-stanzas); two other half-stanzas deal with the giver and bringer of the shield.

Like another early shield-poem, Þjóðólf's *Haustlǫng*, Bragi's *Ragnarsdrápa* belongs to the oldest literary sources of Nordic mythology. Although the genuineness of the *Ragnarsdrápa* has been doubted, partly because of the developed technique of kennings used, the arguments in favour of it being Bragi's work, and thus one of the oldest skaldic poems, predominate.

LIT: F. Detter, 'Zur Ragnarsdrápa' (*ANF* 13) 1897; V. Kiil, 'Gevjonmythen og Ragnarsdråpa' (MoM) 1965; H. Lie, 'Ragnarsdrápa' (*KLNM* 13) 1968; E. O. G. Turville-Petre, *Scaldic Poetry*, Oxford 1976; E. Marold, 'Ragnarsdrápa und Ragnarssage' (*Germanic Dialects*) Amsterdam/Philadelphia 1986.

Rán (ON). In Eddic mythology, Rán is the wife of Ægir, the sea god (or giant). Thus, she is the mother of → Ægir's daughters, the waves (*Skáldskaparmál* 22, 31, 58). In mythological poetry Rán does not occur at all, but in skaldic poetry (Egill, *Sonatorrek* 7) and in the sagas (*Friðþjófs saga* 6) drowning is more or less idiomatically equated with 'falling into Rán's hands'. Therefore, Rán is the ruler over the realm of the dead at the bottom of the sea to which people who have drowned go. Whilst Ægir personifies the sea as a friendly power, Rán embodies the sinister side of the sea, at least in the eyes of the late Viking Age Icelandic seafarers.

Although the meaning of the name has not been fully clarified, Rán was probably understood as being 'robber' (from *rán* 'theft, robbery'), and has nothing to do with *ráða* 'rule'.

F. R. Schröder, 'Die Göttin des Urmeeres' (*PBB* West 82) 1960; A. Holtsmark, 'Rán' (*KLNM* 13) 1968; J. de Vries, *Altnordisches etymologisches Wörterbuch*, Leiden [2]1977.

R: M. E. Winge, *Ran* (painting); E. Dopler d. J., *Ran* (E. Doepler, W. Ranisch, *Walhall*, 1901).

Randgrid (ON). A valkyrie in the *Þulur*, → Randgríðr.

Randgríðr (ON, 'the shield destroyer'?). One of the 13 → valkyries in *Grímnismál* 36.

Rangbeinn (ON, 'crooked leg'). A giant in the *Þulur* whose name is one of the young giants' names which play on the ugliness of giants.

Rani (ON, 'snout'?). A female mythological figure in *Grógaldr* 6, perhaps identical with the goddess Rán, although the vowel quantity speaks against this. Rani is very unlikely even as an additional name for Vali.

H. Gering, B. Sijmons, *Kommentar zu den Liedern der Edda*, Halle 1927.

Ratatoskr (ON, 'drill-tooth'). A squirrel in *Grímnismál* 30 who runs up and down the trunk of the world-ash Yggdrasill and conveys the words of the eagle, who sits in the branches above, to the dragon Níðhǫggr, who lives under the roots, in order (according to Snorri, *Gylfaginning* 15) to bring discord between the two. The squirrel probably only represents an embellishing detail to the mythological picture of the world-ash in *Grímnismál*.

S. Bugge, **Studien**, Munich 1889; A. Holtsmark, 'Ratatoskr' (*KLNM* 13) 1968.

R: the name Ratatöskr was used as a pseudonym by the German writer Hans Erich Blaich (1873–1945).

Ratheihiae. A → matron name on a (now lost) votive inscription from Euskirchen, Germany. There are numerous interpretations of the name. Birkhan interpreted it rather convincingly as being related to proto-Gmc **raþa* 'wheel' and understood Ratheihiae as being 'goddesses of fate' (actually 'wheel goddesses'). The concept of the wheel of fate came to the Germanic peoples either from the Celts or from the Roman belief in the Parcae (who are identical with the matrons on some monuments).

S. Gutenbrunner, *Die germanischen Götternamen*, Halle 1936; M. Schönfeld, *Wörterbuch der altgermanischen Personen- und Völkernamen*, Heidelberg [2]1965; H. Birkhan, *Germanen und Kelten*, Vienna 1970; H. Reichert, *Lexikon der altgermanischen Namen*, Vienna 1987–90.

Rati (ON, 'drill'). According to Snorri (*Skáldskaparmál* 1) and the *Hávamál* 106, Rati is the name of the drill in the myth of the theft of the skaldic mead, with which Baugi the giant drilled a hole into the mountain through which Odin, in the shape of a snake, slunk through to the giant's daughter Gunnlǫð who guarded the mead. The fact that the drill has a name probably only rests on a misunderstanding made by Snorri who understood the word at the beginning of the stanza in *Hávamál* 106 to be a name.

Raven → Huginn.

Realm of the dead → Hel (1). → Other World.

regin (ON, 'gods', actually 'the advising ones'). An old name for the gods in Scandinavia (*raginakuðo* has been found on a Swedish rune stone from Fyrunga, which dates from c.600 A.D.). It is used especially wherever the gods come together in council (e.g. *Vǫluspá* 6). The runes are also called *reginkunnar* (*Hávamál* 80) as they are sent from the gods. Regin, meaning 'gods', can be found in many personal names, such as Ragnarr, Rǫgnvald, Reginn.

H. de Boor, 'Die religiöse Sprache der Vǫluspá' (*Deutsche Islandforschung* 1) Breslau 1930; J. de Vries, *Altgermanische Religionsgeschichte*, Berlin [3]1970; J. de Vries, *Altnordisches etymologisches Wörterbuch*, Leiden [2]1977.

regindómr (ON, 'sentence, court of the gods'). This term in *Vǫluspá* 65 possibly means the 'rule of the gods', but it could also have been another expression for → Ragnarǫk.

Reginleif (ON, 'daughter of the gods'). One of the 13 → valkyries in the *Grímnismál* 36.

Reginn (1) (ON, 'the mighty one'). The foster father of Sigurð in Germanic heroic poetry. He is called the brother of Fafnir, Otr (*Reginsmál* 9 Pr; *Fáfnismál* 25, 36, 39), Lyngheiðr and Lofnheiðr (*Reginsmál* 10, 11 Pr), and the son of Hreiðmarr (*Reginsmál* Pr; *Vǫlsunga saga* 13). He is a skillful but evil dwarf. He forges the sword Gramr for Sigurð and provokes him to kill his brother Fafnir (the dragon) (*Fáfnismál*). Sigurð is warned about Reginn, however, and finally chops off his head (*Fáfnismál* 39 Pr; *Vǫlsunga saga* 19).

Reginn (2) (ON). A dwarf in *Vǫluspá* 12; → Reginn 1.

Reginnaglar (ON, 'gods-nails'). These are mentioned twice in Old Norse literature in a religious context, without their exact function or significance becoming clear. *Eyrbyggja saga* 4 is most detailed about *reginnaglar*. The Christian author of this saga, written at the earliest c.1250, shows repeated interest in the religious customs of the heathens. In a description of the landfall of the settler Þórólfr Mostrarskegg, he tells of how Þórólfr took the pillars of the high-seat along with him on his journey from Norway. He threw them overboard off the coast of Iceland and then settled where they were washed ashore. Later he built a temple in which the high-seat pillars, on which the image of the god Thor had been carved, were set up. It was into these pillars that the *reginnaglar* had been hammered. The extremely detailed description of the pagan temple which follows is probably on the whole the creation of the saga author's imagination. Only the word *reginnaglar* is obviously older because of the form *regin-*. It is possible that the author knew that there was some connexion between the *reginnaglar* and the high-seat pillars (which he said had come from a temple, but this can hardly be true); however, this is by no means certain.

The second allusion to *reginnaglar* is much older and comes from *Glælognskviða*, composed in 1032 by the skald Þórainn Loftunga who praises the miracles occurring at the grave of St Olaf. The context of the word *reginnaglar* here is totally obscure, but it could be seen to have some connexion with Christ having been nailed to the Cross.

Two kennings for 'nail' in a version of the *Þulur* (AM 758 I, 4to) confirm that *reginnaglar* did indeed have a religious function: *regingaddi* 'gods' sting' and *veraldarnagli* 'world-nail', both of which come from poetry no longer extant.

The details in *Eyrbyggja saga* have led to comparisons between the nails hammered into a picture of Thor with the nail on pole idols from Lappland which is knocked in together with a whetstone. This could at best find a correspondence in Germanic paganism, if the nails in the picture of Thor are compared to the myth of Thor and

Hrungnir's whetstone, where a piece from Hrungnir's whetstone remains in Thor's head.

Apart from these suppositions we only know that the *reginnaglar* played a role in early Medieval Scandinavian religion, but whether they can really be ascribed to heathendom is uncertain.

J. Trier, 'Irminsul' (*Westfälische Forschungen* 4) 1941; A. Holtsmark, 'Reginnaglar' (*KLNM* 13) 1968; J. de Vries, *Altgermanische Religionsgeschichte*, Berlin [3]1970.

Rekkr (ON, 'warrior'). A dwarf in *Vǫluspá* 12.

Renahenae. Name of a matron on a Roman Age votive inscription from Bonn which can without doubt be compared to the other river goddesses among the matronae (Aumenahenae, Nersihenae, Vatviae, Veteranehae) and mean 'Rhine goddesses'.

E. A. Philippson, 'Neues über den Mütter- und Matronenkult am Niederrhein' (*MLN* 65) 1950; H. Birkhan, *Germanen und Kelten*, Vienna 1970.

Rennandi (ON, 'the running one). A mythical river in the catalogue of rivers in *Grímnismál* 27 and in the *Þulur*.

Requalivahanus. Name of a god on a votive inscription from Blatzheim a. d. Neffel, Germany from the time between the 2nd/4th centuries (CIL XIII 8512); the votive stone comes from the area of the Germanic tribe of the Ubii and the etymology of the name also suggests a Germanic god since it can best be related to a Germanic word **rehwaz* 'darkness'. This could indicate a god of the underworld although from the inscription we know that fruit was dedicated to him.

R. Much, 'Requalivahanus' (*ZfdA*35) 1891; F. Holthausen, 'Requalivahanus' (*PBB* 16) 1892; F. Kauffmann, 'Mythologische Zeugnisse aus römischen Inschriften. 5. Deus Requalivahanus' (*PBB* 18) 1894; S. Gutenbrunner, *Die germanischen Götternamen*, Halle 1936; M. Schönfeld, *Wörterbuch der altgermanischen Personen- und Völkernamen*, Heidelberg [2]1965; J. de Vries, *Altgermanische Religionsgeschichte*, Berlin [3]1970; H. Reichert, *Lexikon der altgermanischen Namen*, Vienna 1987–90.

Residences of the gods. Some of these are individually named, in particular in the heroic poetry of the *Edda*, especially in *Grímnismál*, and these 12 residences are to be found in the *Snorra Edda*, too: → Þrúðheimr is Thor's home, → Ydalir is Ullr's, → Alfheimr belongs to Freyr. According to Snorri (*Gylfaginning* 16), both → Valaskjálf and → Glaðsheimr belong to Odin; Saga lives in → Sǫkkvabekkr and Njǫrð's giant wife Skaði lives in → Þrymheimr, her father's fortress in the mountains, whereas Njǫrðr himself lives by the sea in → Nóatún; → Breiðablik is Baldr's home and → Himinbjǫrg Heimdall's; Folkvangr belongs to Freyr and Glitnir to Forseti. Most of these residences have expressive names and therefore appear to be young formations. It seems to be more the case that the poet of *Grímnismál* proffers word material to the skalds by giving these names, but it is possible that the tendency towards systematization of the late heathen period plays a role here. Despite concurring with *Grímnismál* in his *Gylfaginning*, Snorri deviates in his naming of the residences in two cases in the *Ynglinga saga* 5: in the saga Odin lives in 'old Sigtúnir' (near Sigtuna) where, according to Snorri, there was a temple, and Freyr's residence is localized as being at Uppsala, no doubt as a result of the knowledge of a cult of Freyr there.

(**Rhine daughters**). Three water-beings from R. Wagner's operas *Das Rheingold* and *Die Götterdämmerung* who were created from the example of the river women

Hadeburc and Sigelint in the Lay of the Nibelungs (1535–1549). However, even these river-women from the Lay of the Nibelungs belong more to the world of Medieval legend than anywhere else and they are otherwise not recorded in Germanic mythology.

Ricagambeda. Germanic goddess. A Roman votive inscription from Birrens on Hadrian's Wall, N. England, is dedicated to this *deae Ricagambedae* (CIL XIII 1072). Several interpretations of the name would be conceivable but 'the strong lady' would seem to convey the sense best.

S. Gutenbrunner, *Die germanischen Götternamen*, Halle 1936; H. Reichert, *Lexikon der altgermanischen Namen*, Vienna 1987–90.

(**Ricen**). Supposedly the name of a goddess according to J. Grimm who assumed a goddess Ricen from a wrong assignment of the goddess Diana's name in an OHG gloss.

E. Sievers, 'Die angebliche Göttin Ricen' (*PBB* 16) 1892.

Rifingafla (ON, 'with the forked gable'?). A giantess in the *Þulur*. The name is not totally clear, but contains possibly a hidden insult, cf. Bakrauf.

Rígr (ON). The god who begets the descendants of the three social orders in the → *Rígsþula*, namely the slaves, the farmers and the nobles. The prose introduction to the *Rígsþula* in the *Codex Wormianus* (14th century) records that it was the Æsir god Heimdall who took on the name Rígr. The first stanza of the *Vǫluspá* is also drawn in to support this interpretation where the people *meiri oc minni mǫgo Heimdalar* ('Heimdall's high and the low relations') are named, but this could also have a totally general meaning. The picture of the god who wanders about under a pseudonym visiting people and finally conveying the knowledge of the runes to a chosen one among them fits better with Odin who was probably originally meant by Rígr.

Rígr comes from the Irish word *rí*, acc., dat., gen. *ríg* 'king', but had already lost this meaning at the time of the composition of the *Rígsþula* since the play on words of konr ungr/konungr in the *Rígsþula* could otherwise hardly have formed the pun. Sturtevant's interpretation of Rígr as being a native word to an ON *rigr* 'stiffness' is unlikely.

E. Mogk, 'Nordische Literaturen' (*Grundriß der germanischen Philologie*, hrsg. v. H. Paul, Bd. 2) Straßburg 1901–09; R. Meissner, 'Rígr' (*PBB* 57) 1933; A. M. Sturtevant, 'Etymological comments' (*PMLA* 67) 1952.

Rígsþula (ON, 'didactic poem about Rig'). An Eddic lay which can be counted among the → mythological poetry. Although a god called → Rígr appears as the protagonist in the first part of the lay, and the lay appears to be a myth about the pre-history of man, nevertheless it is in fact an example a poem teaching the origins of the three social orders. As the name of the lay suggests, it contains lists of names (→ *Þulur*), but *Þula* here probably refers to didactic literature in general.

The *Rígsþula* tells of how the god Rígr came to earth and visited three (childless) couples with whom he stayed for three days each. From the first pair, Ai and Edda ('great grandfather and great grandmother') a son called Þræll ('farm-labourer') is the result of his visit, who begets with his wife Þír ('maid') children with names such as Kleggi, Fjósnir, Arinnefja ('hay stack, cow shed, eagle-nose') etc. Ríg's second visit is to Afi and Amma ('grandfather and grandmother') and the son conceived at this visit is called Karl ('man, farmer, churl'). His children by his wife Snør ('string') have names such as Smiðr, Drengr, Bondi ('smith, chap, farmer') etc. Ríg's third visit is to the couple called Faðir and Móðir ('father and mother') and their son is called Jarl here ('warrior, earl'). Rígr teaches him the wisdom of the runes, takes him as his son and calls him Jarl-Rígr. Jarl's children from his marriage with Erna ('the capable one') are called names such as Aðal, Barn, Sonr ('noble, child, son') and the youngest is called Konr ungr ('young descendant'?). This latter child surpasses even his father in wisdom and takes over the name of Rígr. The lost end to the lay would appear to have been the pun on the transition from Konr ungr to *konungr* ('king'). – Rígr also means 'king', however (from Irish *rí*, acc., gen., dat. *ríg*). Different motifs in the lay have been considered to be Celtic and it is thought that the *Rígsþula* was written in the 10th century. Since Heusler, however, *Rígsþula* has been understood as a scholarly piece of work from the 13th century in which an educated Icelandic author gave an aetiological interpretation to the origins of the different orders. Thus, the *Rígsþula* would be a kind of artistic rewriting of a myth, a '*mythos philosophicus*' (Heusler). – In contrast to this Fleck considers the *Rígsþula* to be cult-functional poetry which reflected the consecration of the individual and the passing on of knowledge involved in this in the succession of the sacred kingship, a somewhat far fetched hypothesis. – It is extremely doubtful whether Rígr can be identified with the god Heimdall, as occurs in the prose introduction added later to the lay. The picture of a god wandering about and spreading the knowledge of the runes would appear to fit Odin more than Heimdall.

ED: G. Neckel, H. Kuhn, *Edda*, [5]1983.

K. Lehmann, 'Die Rígsþula' (*Festschrift Amsberg*) Rostock 1904; A. Heusler, 'Heimat und Alter der eddischen Gedichte' (*Archiv* 116) 1906; F. Jónsson, 'Rígsþula' (*ANF* 33) 1917; R. Meissner, 'Rígr' (*PBB* 57) 1933; J. I. Young, 'Does Rígsþula betray Irish Influence?' (*ANF* 49) 1933; E. O. Sveinsson, 'Celtic Elements in Icelandic Tradition' (*Béaloideas* 15) 1959; K. v. See, 'Rígsþula Str. 47 u. 48' (*PBB* West 82) 1960; K. v. See, 'Das Alter der Rígsþula' (*APhSc* 24) 1961; S. P. Scher, 'Rígsþula as Poetry' (*MLN* 78) 1963; B. Nerman, 'Rígsþulas ålder' (*ANF* 84) 1969; A. Holtsmark, 'Rígsþula' (*KLNM* 14) 1969; J. Fleck, 'Konr-Ottar-Geirroðr: A Knowledge Criterion for Succession to the Germanic Sacred Kingship' (*SS* 42) 1970; H. Gimmler, 'Rígsþula' (KLL 6) 1971; T. D. Hill, 'Rígsþula: Some Medieval Christian Analogues' (*Speculum* 61) 1986.

R: A. Edelfelt, *Jarl* (painting).

Rín (ON, 'the Rhine'). One of the rivers in the catalogue of otherwise mythical rivers in *Grímnismál* 27.

Rinda. The name given in Saxo (*Gesta Danorum* III, 78–82) to Váli's mother, otherwise known as → Rindr.

Rindr (ON). The mother of Odin's son Váli who avenges the death of Baldr. According to *Gylfaginning* 35, she is one of the Asyniur. She is repeatedly mentioned as being Váli's mother in skaldic poetry as well as in the Eddic lays *Baldrs draumar* 11 and *Grógaldr* 6.

In his *Gesta Danorum* (III, 78–82), Saxo tells the story of Odin's wooing of Rinda (as Rindr is called in his version) in great detail, a tale which is only told in passing elsewhere in ON literature: after Baldr's death Odin is given a prophesy by a Finnish soothsayer that only Rinda, the daughter of the Rutenian king, would bear him a son who would be able to avenge Baldr. Therefore, Odin approaches the uninterested king's daughter in four different disguises, as a general, a goldsmith, a warrior-hero and finally as a healing woman called Vecha. This last disguise enables him to rape Rindr, deceived and threatened with madness and illness by Odin. The disgracefulness of what Odin did leads to the second → Odin's exile, but also to the birth of the warrior Bous who finally avenges Baldr.

In Old Norse literature only the verse by Kormakr the skald, quoted by Snorri as mentioned above, plays on Odin's wooing of Rindr: *Seið Yggr til Rindar* ('Odin enchanted Rindr'). This obviously refers to the madness Odin caused in Rindr; Saxo says that he caused it through a piece of bark with runes written on it.

Despite the sparse Icelandic sources, Saxo gives us a fairly complete picture of the myth of Rindr, which belongs to the Baldr myth.

Various etymologies have been suggested for the name Rindr, but none of them are fully convincing; even the form **Vrindr* which is suggested by the alliteration in *Baldrs draumar* 11 does not help us much. On the other hand, **Vrindr* has led to an association with the Swedish place-name Vrinnevi (from *Wrindawi), the 'shrine of (V)Rind' (Brate). However, *-vi* can also be derived from *viþi* 'wood' so that it is not indubitably a cult place-name.

E. Brate, 'Wrindawi' (*ANF* 29) 1913; P. Herrmann, *Die Heldensagen des Saxo Grammaticus*, Leipzig 1922; A. Holtsmark, 'Rindr' (*KLNM* 14) 1969; J. de Vries, *Altgermanische Religionsgeschichte*, Berlin [3]1970; J. de Vries, *Altnordisches etymologisches Wörterbuch*, Leiden [2]1977.

Ring → temple ring; → Draupnir.

Ring oath. Numerous literary sources mention the Germanic custom of swearing an oath upon a ring (like Christians do on a crucifix or on a Bible). According to *Alvíssmál* 30 the ring oath is sworn on a ring dedicated to the god Ullr, whereas in the Old Icelandic *Landnámabók* the ring oath is sworn in the name of Freyr and Njǫrðr and the almighty As, and in *Hávamál* 110 even the god Odin himself swears a ring oath. All the Icelandic sagas which mention a ring oath are dependent on the *Landnámabók*, but they refer to Thor as the god of oaths. The Anglo-Saxon Chronicle is a most reliable source which refers to an oath made on a ring between the Anglo-Saxons and the Danes in 876.

Even if the information about the oath on a → temple ring given in the sagas is to be treated with care, the cult significance of the ring for the Germanic tribes is so well recorded that we may also assume the existence of a ring oath.

H. Vordemfelde, *Die germanische Religion in den deutschen Volksrechten. 1. Der religiöse Glaube*, Gießen 1923; F. P. Magoun, 'On the Old-Germanic Altar- or Oathring (stallhringr)' (*APhSc* 20) 1947/49; J. de Vries, *Altgermanische Religionsgeschichte*, Berlin [3]1970; J. Jóhannesson, *A History of the Old Icelandic Commonwealth*, Winnipeg 1974; A. Kabell, 'Baugi und der Ringeid' (*ANF* 90) 1975.

Rock carvings. Rock carvings are valuable sources for the religion of the pre-historic Germanic tribes, especially those of the Bronze Age in Scandinavia. They are found particularly in the coastal areas of South Norway and South Sweden, the greatest concentration of them being in the border district of Bohuslän, Sweden. The rock carvings were probably made over a period of 1500 years up until the end of the Bronze Age (c.500 B.C.). They consist mostly of flat carvings, only a few centimetres deep, on flat stone surfaces in the open countryside, and were possibly coloured in with chalk or ruddle as they would otherwise be hardly visible. The most frequent motif on the rock carvings, apart from the depictions of people who are often dancing or worshipping, is the ship as well as trees or discs. There are animals, scenes of ploughing, carts pulled by oxen, battle and wedding scenes. The carvings are by no means realistic and the proportion between individual details varies greatly, and we occasionally find an extra-dimensional figure next to other (or even partially covering older) scenes. In addition to these less abstract carvings, there are also cup-like indentations of varying size, discs, spirals, net-like structures and footprints.

Nowadays it is generally accepted that the rock carvings depict religious scenes and symbols and it is in this that the ship can be seen playing a role in the cult of a sun god, prayed to for protection in seafaring. Ploughing and wedding scenes would appear to preserve the cult of a fertility god. Several symbols, however, remain enigmatic, for example the cup-like indentations, known in folklore as elf-mills (Swedish *älvkvarnar*), or else the footprints, although these perhaps are supposed to symbolise the earthly presence of the worshipped god.

Despite the fact that it is obvious that the illustrated processions and cult scenes on ships deal with the worship of certain gods, we nonetheless do not know which gods are meant. It is most likely to have been a cult of fertility gods, such as the Vanir Njǫrðr and Freyr although some scholars consider the figures with raised axes to be early forms of the god of the hammer, Thor, or see Odin in spear-bearing men. Despite the long continuity in the cult traditions of rock carvings it is very difficult, and not particularly sensible, to try and match the gods of the Bronze Age rock carvings directly with the world of the gods dealt with in the Eddas 3000 years later.

A. W. Persson, 'Åkerbruksriter och hällristningar' (*Fornvännen* 25) 1930; O. Almgren, *Nordische Felszeichnungen als religiöse Urkunden*, Frankfurt 1934; F. Behn, 'Die nordischen Felsbilder' (*ARW* 34) 1937; J. de Vries, *Altgermanische Religionsgeschichte*, Berlin [3]1970.

Rǫkstólar (ON, 'fate-chairs'). This name is given (only in *Vǫluspá* 7ff.) to the chairs on which the gods sit in their role of rulers and judges. Instead of *rǫkstólar* Snorri uses *dómstólar* 'court chair', perhaps because the concept of *rǫkstolar* was no longer current even in his day.

The finds of tiny throne-like amulets made in Scandinavia, and which are probably supposed to represent the thrones of the gods, should possibly be seen in connexion with the *rǫkstólar*, but see also → Hlíðskjalf.

A. Holtsmark, 'Rǫkstólar' (*KLNM* 14) 1969; H. Drescher, K. Hauck, 'Götterthrone des heidnischen Nordens' (*FmSt* 16) 1982.

Rǫskva (ON). Þjálfi's sister, according both to Snorri and his source, *Þórsdrápa*. Thor takes Rǫskva and Þjálfi, the children of a farmer, with him as his servants in compensation after Þjálfi brought about the laming of one of Thor's two he-goats while he was staying overnight at their home farm on his way to Utgarðaloki. Snorri (*Gylfaginning* 43ff. and *Skáldskaparmál* 4) says that his source for this is *Þórsdrápa* written by the skald Eilífr Goððrunarson. We know nothing else about Rǫskva apart from this.

The etymology of the name (from ON *rǫskvast* 'grow, mature') could refer to a role in some fertility rite, but the interpretation that Rǫskva was an ancient fertility goddess is somewhat bold, considering the scarcity of the source material concerning her.

A. Olrik, 'Tordenguden og hans dreng' (*DS*) 1905; J. de Vries, *Altgermanische Religionsgeschichte*, Berlin [3]1970.

Rolf → Hrolfr.

Romanehae → Rumanehae.

(**Roßweiße**). A valkyrie (mezzo-soprano) in R. Wagner's opera *Die Walküre*. The name is a pure invention of Wagner's and is possibly the pseudo-Germanization of the OHG female name Hrosvita.

Rosterus or Rostarus (Middle Latin). A name for Odin in Saxo (*Gesta Danorum* IX, 304; III, 79). It is probably identical with → Hroptr. Rosterus appears in disguise, once as a goldsmith and once as a doctor.

S. Bugge, *Studien*, Munich 1889.

Ruðr (ON, 'the red one'?). A river (?) in *Grógaldr* 8.

Rumanehae (or Romanehae). A matron name. Over a dozen votive inscriptions on the Lower Rhine from the period around 200 A.D. are dedicated to the *matronis Rumanehis*. These goddesses are not 'Roman goddesses', but rather the 'goddesses of the Roman settlement' who were of course also important for the Germanic people living there.

S. Gutenbrunner, *Die germanischen Götternamen*, Halle 1936; M. Schönfeld, *Wörterbuch der altgermanischen Personen- und Völkernamen*, Heidelberg [2]1965; H. Reichert, *Lexikon der altgermanischen Namen*, Vienna 1987–90.

Runes. Germanic letters which began to be used by the Germanic tribes in the first century A.D. as they came into contact with the Romans in the south of their territories. The formation of letters was based on the alphabets used by the Mediterranean languages but also included older Germanic symbolic signs. By the 5th century an extensive and fairly standardized runic alphabet consisting of 24 letters had developed which was known by its first six letters as the (older) Futhark. Towards the mid 8th century alterations in the runic system began to occur and most of the Viking Age, Medieval Scandinavian and British runic inscriptions are composed in the younger Futhark which comprises only 16 symbols.

The length, type and purpose of the → runic inscriptions are very varied and encompass single concept runes on weapons and amulets as well as extensive inscriptions, such as on the Swedish runestone at Rök which contains over 750 signs. Runes are found almost everywhere where the Germanic tribes went, from Iceland to Constantinople, and were the normal form of writing used especially among Scandinavians in the Viking era.

However, runes were not merely letters in today's sense. Every rune had a particular name and could represent the concept indicated by the name on its own, especially in a magical context. Thus, the inscription of the three repeated t-runes (Týr-runes) on the bracteate Zealand II represent the three-fold repetition of the name of the ancient god of war, Týr, who was called upon to help the warriors to victory through these runes. In the *Edda*, too, in *Sigrdrífumál* 6 a recommendation is given to call upon Týr twice whilst carving the 'victory rune'. The three-fold carving of the f-rune (fe-rune; *fé* 'possession, wealth') as a wish for happiness and wealth has a similar magical character.

Runes could also be used in black magic. For instance, in *Skírnismál* 6 Freyr's servant Skírnir threatens Gerðr by saying that he 'will carve a *thurs* for her', by which he means the th-rune (Thurs-rune). He then continues to impress upon her that the three-fold carving of this rune will bring about disgrace, madness and restlessness for her. There are numerous examples of this kind and they show quite clearly the magical-religious significance of runes.

Klingenberg has shown that occasionally the runes probably also had a specific numerical value which could give an inscription a further hidden significance. However, he possibly overestimates somewhat the influence of this numerical symbolism on the runic inscriptions.

Odin is the god of runic knowledge and of runic magic. According to mythological poetry (*Hávamál*) he acquired the knowledge of the runes in → Odin's self-sacrifice by hanging for nine nights without food or drink on the 'windy tree'. Not only the corresponding usage but also the acquisition of runic knowledge were considered to be magical in some way and Odin as the god of magic was therefore the first who possessed the art of the runes, just as he also acquired the skill of poetry for mankind. The Swedish runic stone from Noleby (c.600) speaks in favour of this, as does the younger stone from Sparlösa which refers to the fact that the 'runes come from the gods' (*rûnaR raginu-kundu*), a formula which is also found in the Eddic *Hávamál* 80.

Attempts to see the older runes as being a completely secular mode of writing which has no magical or religious significance whatsoever have been made recently (Moltke) but these can hardly be taken seriously.

R. W. V. Elliott, 'Runes, Yews and Magic' (*Speculum* 32) 1957; W. Krause, *Die Runeninschriften im älteren Futhark*, Göttingen 1966; O. Höfler, 'Herkunft und Ausbreitung der Runen' (*Die Sprache* 17) 1971; E. Moltke, 'The Origins of the Runes' (*Michigan Germanic Studies* 7) 1981.

R: K. H. Strobl, *Die Runen Gottes* (novel, 1919); K. H. Strobl, *Die Runen und das Marterholz* (novel, 1942).

Runic inscriptions. These are found from the first century A.D. to late Medieval times on all possible objects and for a variety of purposes. Among the oldest runic inscriptions are the inscriptions on the helmets from Negau, Slovenia, which bear the names either of individuals or of gods (→ Harigast, Heruli). Inscriptions from the Migration era frequently include bear magical runes, among which the runic words → *alu* and *laukaR* (→ Leek) frequently occur. Magical runic inscriptions such as these are also found on bracteates, weapons and fibulae. The Nordendorf fibula is of particular importance for the study of Germanic religion as it names three gods, which seldom occurs on runic inscriptions. The Scandinavian runic stones of the Viking era, which were predominantly monumental or grave stones, often bear longer runic inscriptions which occasionally also give information concerning religious beliefs, for example, the repeatedly recorded formula 'Thor, consecrate these runes' (→ Mjǫllnir) or else in the form of mythological scenes on pictorial stones. In the Middle Ages the runes took on all the features of a secular script which was used for private and business purposes and was even used in Christian contexts, as crucifixes inscribed with runic prayers indicate.

Even if gods' names do not occur frequently in heathen runic inscriptions, the runic inscriptions are nevertheless of prime importance for the study of Germanic religion as they allow us a view into the living belief of Germanic antiquity.

Rýgr (ON, 'woman, lady'). One of the few polite names for a giantess given in the *Þulur*.

Rymr (ON, 'noise'). A name for the god Thor in the *Þulur*, the mythological significance of which is unknown.

Sacred kingship. Despite a few voices rejecting it (Kuhn, v. See) it is nowadays generally accepted that among Germanic tribes kings derived their legitimate right of power from the gods.

Baetke summarized the essence of Germanic sacred kingship in three theories:

(1) The king's fortune which is associated with his sacred position as a gift.

(2) The position of the king in the cult, but also as a cult object.

(3) The belief in the divine descendency of the Germanic kings.

ad (1) The king's sacred position resulted in his being held personally responsible for the weather and the harvest as well as for external and internal peace. The Swedish rune stone from Stentoften (7th century) and possibly also the one from Sparlösa (c.800) show that the Swedish kings 'gave the annual harvest' and even in Christian times skaldic poetry refers to St Olaf as the mediator, if not indeed the guarantor, of *ár ok friðr* ('good year and peace'). Sacrifices (→ Geirstaðaálfr) were made to the Norwegian kings Oláf Guðroðarson and Oláf Haraldsson even after their deaths in order to bring about a good harvest *til árs* ('for a good year'), as well as to the former's brother, Halfdan (*Heimskringla*). The Burgundians deposed a king in the 4th century blaming him for a series of poor harvests (Amminanus Marcellinus XXVIII, 5) and the reduction of the king's benefactory powers as a result of illness or old age could even lead to the ritual sacrifice of the king. Snorri reports in the *Ynglinga saga* 15 that the Swedish kings were sacrificed in order to free the people from a danger of some kind. A stanza in the *Ynglingatál* confirms this for → Dómaldi and Snorri names Sveigðir, Jǫrundr and perhaps also Fjǫlnir and Agni as being other kings who were sacrificed. In the case of Óláfr trételgja (*Ynglinga saga* 43) Snorri appears to have misunderstood his source, as according to the *Ynglingatál* the king was probably burned only after his death.

Sacrifices were held not only to assure good harvests, but also for the victory of the king: in Sweden with a battle sacrifice (*sigrblót: Ynglinga saga* 8; *til friðar ok sigrs konungi: Oláfs saga hins helga* 77), in Norway with a sacrificial drink (*til sigrs ok ríkis konungi: Hákonar saga goða* 28), and even the physical participation of the king in the battle was so important for the West Germanic peoples (evidence in Grönbech) that the sacred position of the king is not disputed here (Kuhn's objections are unfounded).

ad (2) The significance of the king is already mentioned in Tacitus (*Germania* 10), specifically referring to prophesies. In the euhemeristic presentation of the gods as kings in the *Ynglinga saga* (8 and 9) Odin and Njǫrðr are described as kings making sacrifices. When, during Odin's exile, other kings usurp his position, they legitimise themselves by certain forms of sacrifice. The Yngling kings are always described as being great believers in sacrifice; even in a gloss (140) to Adam of Bremen emphasis is put on the fact that it was the duty of the kings in → Uppsala to hold sacrifices. *Hákonar saga goða* 17 tells of the way that King Hákon forced the farmers to participate in the sacrifice. On the Danish rune stone at Glavendrup (c.900) the identity between sacrificial priest and lord is confirmed (Ström 1975).

ad (3) The belief in the divine descendence of the old royal houses is documented for the whole of Germanic areas (→ Myth of descendency). In the genealogies of Anglo-Saxon royal houses in particular Wodan and Geat are named as being mythical ancestors, and in the case of the East Gothic royal family of the Amales it is Gapt/Geat. The Swedish Ynglings trace themselves back to Yngvi-Freyr, and the Skjǫldungs and the Norwegian earls from Hlaðir to Odin. The mythical genealogies of the gods' descendency continued in those of the earthly royal houses whereby the name of the divine ancestor of the kings could also be born as an honorary name, such as Yngvi in the case of the Yngling kings.

Although many of the documents mentioned above for sacred kingship come from Christian times and there is therefore a danger that the concepts might have been influenced by Christian thought with regard to kingship by the grace of God, it is the sacred descendency itself, as well as the cult significance of the Germanic kings, which makes clear the differences between heathen and Christian concepts and which allows the supposition of a heathen sacred kingship.

W. Baetke, *Das Heilige im Germanischen*, Tübingen 1942; O. Höfler, *Germanisches Sakralkönigtum*, Münster, Köln 1952; K. Hauck, 'Herrschaftszeichen eines wodanistischen Königtums' (*Jahrbuch für fränkische Landesforschung* 14) 1954; W. Grönbech, *Kultur und Religion der Germanen*, Darmstadt [5]1954; W. Baetke, 'Zur Religion der Skalden' (*Atti dell' VIII congresso internationale di storia delle religione*) Firenze 1956; B. Kummer, 'Sverre und Magnus' (*Atti dell' VIII congresso internationale di storia delle religione*) Firenze 1956; H. Ljungberg, 'Das sakrale Königtum im Norden' (*Atti dell' VIII congresso internationale di storia delle religione*) Firenze 1956; M. A. Murray, 'The Divine King in England' (*Atti dell' VIII congresso internationale di storia delle religione*) Firenze 1956; J. de Vries, 'Das Königtum bei den Germanen' (*Saeculum* 7) 1956; O. Höfler, 'Der Sakralcharakter des germanischen Königtums' (*Sacral Kingship*) Leiden 1959; Å. V. Ström, 'The King God and his Connection with Sacrifice' (*Sacral Kingship*) Leiden 1959; K. Hauck, 'Die geschichtliche Bedeutung der germanischen Auffassung von Königtum und Adel' (*Rapports du XIe Congrès Internationale des Sciences Historiques*), Stockholm 1960; A. Closs, 'Die Heiligkeit des Herrschers' (*Anthropos* 56) 1961; W. Baetke, *Yngvi und die Ynglinger*, Berlin 1964; W. A. Chaney, *The Cult of Kingship*, Manchester 1970; J. de Vries, *Altgermanische Religionsgeschichte*, Berlin [3]1970; K. von See, *Kontinuitätstheorie und Sakraltheorie*, Frankfurt 1972; Å. V. Ström, H. Biezais, *Germanische und baltische Religion*, Stuttgart 1975; E. Hoffmann, *Die heiligen Könige bei den Angelsachsen*, Neumünster 1975; O. Höfler, 'Staatsheiligkeit und Staatsvergottung' (*Festschrift A. Erler*) Aalen 1976; H. Kuhn, 'Germanisches Sakralkönigtum?' (in: *Kleine Schriften* 4), Berlin, New York 1978; E. Picard, *Germanisches Sakralkönigtum?*, Heidelberg 1991.

Sacrifices. The Germanic tribes offered sacrifices both to sacred places as well as to personified deities. The sacrifices served the purpose of influencing the powers of the underworld in order to achieve the desired effect not through magical manipulation but rather through the bringing of gifts. Mythical rites could be performed at the same time.

Votive gifts – in particular deliberately broken weapons – were possibly also a gift of gratitude: sacrifices of petition are also recorded.

Among the oldest attestable forms of sacrifices in Germanic tribes is the laying down of votive gifts at sacred places such as moors, springs, waterfalls, stones and trees. The kind of gift depends on the response required from the deity: the approximately 100 tiny golden miniature boats from one moor near Nors in Jutland were certainly linked to the desire for a safe sea journey, and deliberately broken weapons from other Danish moor finds (e.g. Hjørtspring on the island of Als) are undoubtedly connected with the desire (or thanks) for victory in war; in addition to these there are also gifts of food and domestic implements in votive gifts.

The sacrifice of food was one of the most important forms of sacrifice among Germanic peoples, in which the slaughtered animal was eaten by the sacrificing community. The sparse and unfortunately not very reliable literary sources about Viking Age sacrifices (compiled by Ström in 1966) also point to predominantly slaughter and food sacrifices.

The ON word for sacrifice is *blót* (*blóta* 'to sacrifice', Gothic, OE *blōtan*) and probably originally meant 'strengthen (the god)' and does not belong etymologically to the word blood. In Heimskringla (*Hákonar saga góða* 14) Snorri gives a description of a sacrifice in Norway: Sigurð, Jarl of Hlaðir, was keen on making sacrifices and he kept up a sacrifice according to ancient tradition in Thrandheim. All the farmers had to participate in it and had to look after their own requirements for the duration of the sacrifice festival. Various small animals, and also horses, were slaughtered and the sacrifical blood (*hlaut*) was caught in special bowls (*hlaut-bollar*) and then sprinkled using a twig (*hlautteinn*) like a sprinkler on the altar and the walls and the guests; cauldrons were hung over the long fires. The chieftain who organized the sacrifice then dedicated the beakers (*full*) and the first was drunk to Odin, the next to Njǫrðr and Freyr 'for a good harvest and peace', then the → *bragafull* and then the → *minni* (the beaker to commemorate the dead). An even more detailed description of such a sacrifice festival in Iceland is related in *Eyrbyggja saga* 4, but this is most probably based on Snorri. At any rate, both depictions are obviously an imaginative reconstruction of Christian liturgy onto heathen practices, and as such have only little value as sources (Düwel, Walter). The *hlautteinn* for example was in heathen times in reality a stick used for divination (cf. *Hymiskviða* 1; Þorvaldr Koðránsson) which the Christian authors however interpreted as a kind of ecclesiastical sprinkler (*aspergium*).

In fact only the reddening (of an altar? of a → Hǫrgr?) and the ritual meal of the sacrificial meat can be traced back to Viking Age heathen practices (Ström 1966). These should be considered as the main forms of the late heathen communal sacrifices. It would seem that the gods to whom these sacrifices were dedicated differed both temporally and regionally. The sacrificial rites were, however, probably more complex than we can recognise from the sources available and characterized by secret knowledge about the cult regulations, if we are to trust stanza 144 of the *Hávamál*:

'If you know how to carve (*rísta*),
Do you know how to advise (*ráða*),
Do you know how to colour (*fá*),
Do you know how to ask (*freista*),
Do you know how to bid (*biðja*),
Do you know how to send (*senda*),
Do you know how to slaughter (*sóa*)?'

Presumably all the ritual acts are listed here and presumably even the word *senda* (otherwise 'send') should probably be understood here as 'sacrifice, offer' (Liberman; Düwel 1970).

Snorri mentions the main times of sacrifices in *Ynglinga saga* 8: at the beginning of the winter half-year for good harvests, at mid-winter (Yule?) for fertility, at the beginning of summer for victory. This systemization probably does not correspond to reality as the Spring sacrifice was undoubtedly a sacrifice of fertility.

The highest form of sacrifice was → human sacrifice which appears to have been reserved for Odin, as Tacitus tells us (*Germania* 9). The form of Odin's sacrifice was hanging and piercing with a spear, although the carving of the → blood eagle also possibly represented a sacrifice to Odin. There are only pictures of human sacrifice in the Migration era, and human sacrifice was also offered at the great sacrificial festival in → Uppsala.

E. Klein, 'Der Ritus des Tötens bei den nordischen Völkern' (*ARW* 28) 1930; F. Ström, 'Tro och Blot' (*Arv* 7) 1951; W. Grönbech, *Kultur und Religion der Germanen*, Darmstadt [5]1954; Å. V. Ström, 'Die Hauptriten des wikingerzeitlichen nordischen Opfers' (*Festschrift W. Baetke*) Weimar 1966; E. Walter, 'Quellenkritisches und Wortgeschichtliches zum Opferfest von Hlaðir' (*Festschrift W. Baetke*) Weimar 1966; J. Simpson, 'Some Scandinavian Sacrifices' (*Folklore* 78) 1967; O. Nordland, 'Offer' (*KLNM* 12) 1967; K. Düwel, 'Germanische Opfer und Opferriten' (H. Jankuhn, *Vorgeschichtliche Heiligtümer*), Göttingen 1970; H. Beck, 'Germanische Menschenopfer' (H. Jankuhn, *Vorgeschichtliche Heiligtümer*), Göttingen 1970; J. de Vries, *Altgermanische Religionsgeschichte*, Berlin [3]1970; J. L. Sauvé, 'The Divine Victim' (*Myth and Law among the*

Indo-Europeans) Austin, 1970; K. Düwel, *Das Opferfest von Lade*, Göttingen 1971; K. Hauck, 'Zur Ikonologie der Goldbrakteaten VIII' (*Festgabe für* O. *Höfler*) Vienna 1976; A. Libermann, 'Germanic sendan' (*JEGPh* 77) 1978; P. C. Bauschatz, 'The Germanic Ritual Feast' (*The Nordic Languages and Modern Linguistics*) Stockholm 1978.

Saðr or Sannr (ON, 'the true one'). A name for Odin in the *Grímnismál* 47, in Einarr Gilsson and in the *Þulur*. As the name Saðr certainly has no bearing on Odin's character, it possibly means 'the true Odin' (as opposed to Odin in one of his many disguises during his appearances on earth). This interpretation is not totally convincing.

H. Falk, *Odensheite*, Kristiania 1924.

Sægr or Sœgr (ON, 'noise' or 'sea') A vat. In the tale of the picture in the moon told by Snorri in *Gylfaginning* 10, the two figures depicted, Bil and Hjuki, carry a vat called Sægr. → Máni.

A. Holtsmark, 'Bil og Hjuke' (MoM) 1945.

Sæhrímnir (ON, 'sooty sea-animal'?, perhaps from *seyðir* 'cooking ditch'). A boar in *Grímnismál* 18 which is prepared nightly in Valhall by Andhrímnir the cook in the cauldron called Eldhrímnir (*Gylfaginning* 37): 'But there are never so many people present in Valhall that there is not enough meat on the boar Sæhrímnir to feed them. Sæhrímnir is cooked every day and in the evening he is whole again [. . .]. The cook is called Andhrímnir, but the cauldron Eldhrímnir.' The motif of the ever-renewed animal can also be found in the tale of Thor's goats and probably refers to a sacrificial rite related to shamanistic practices. Snorri's embellishment, however, bears more the characteristics of a medieval paradise.

J. de Vries, *Altgermanische Religionsgeschichte*, Berlin [3]1970; A. Holtsmark, 'Sæhrímnir' (*KLNM* 17) 1972.

Sækarlsmúli (ON). A giant in the *Þulur*. The peculiar name could mean 'sailor's snout', but *sækarl* is not recorded anywhere else despite its obvious meaning, and also what, apart from a joke, is 'seaman's snout' supposed to be? Another explanation, equally unfounded but semantically somewhat more likely, is to to read *sækarl* as another form of *hákarl* 'shark' in which case the name would mean 'shark's mouth'.

Sæmingr (ON). One of Odin's sons, according to the prologue to Snorri's *Edda* and the *Þulur*. According to Snorri's *Ynglinga saga* he was Yngvi-Frey's son and the earls of Hlaðir were supposed to be descended from Sæmingr.

The meaning of the name is uncertain: either 'the grey one' (from ON *sámr*), or else 'son of the seed god' (cf. Latin *Sēmen*)?

Sæmundar Edda. An incorrect name for the → Poetic *Edda*. When Bishop Brynjólfr Sveinsson of Skálholt discovered and acquired the most important manuscript of the *Edda*, the *Codex Regius*, in 1643, he was under the incorrect impression that the collection was the work of the Icelandic historian Sæmundr Sigfússon enn fróði ('the wise', 1056–1133). This mistake continued to be made by scholars even as late as the 18th century.

Sága (ON). A goddess, mentioned in *Grímnismál* 37, and said to drink with Odin in → Sǫkkvabekkr. Snorri interpreted this to mean that Sǫkkvabekkr is the heavenly residence of Sága (*Gylfaginning* 34). Despite several references to Sága in skaldic poetry we know nothing more about the nature of this goddess.

It has been suggested that the name Sága is related to ON *sjá* (Gmc **sehwan*) 'see'. As Frigg is called a seeress in *Lokasenna* 21, and the names of Sǫkkvabekkr and Frigg's residence, Fensalir are also similar in meaning, it would appear that Sága is merely another name for Frigg. However, apart from the phonetic problems – despite the vowel quality a link is more likely with *saga* and *segja* 'say, tell', an identification such as this is somewhat problematic. Sága should be thought of as one of the not closer defined Asyniur (Hlín, Sjǫfn, Snotra, Vár, Vǫr) who should probably be seen as female protective goddesses. These goddesses were all responsible for specific areas of the private sphere, and yet clear differences were made between them so that they are in many ways similar to the matrons.

A. M. Sturtevant, 'Etymological Comments' (*PMLA* 67) 1952; A. Holtsmark, 'Saga' (*KLNM* 14) 1969; J. de Vries, *Altgermanische Religionsgeschichte*, Berlin [3]1970.

Sagas (ON, *saga*, pl. *sǫgur*). General term denoting lengthy Icelandic prose works. The oldest sagas were written around the year 1200 and saga writing reached its peak in the 13th and 14th centuries. Because the *Íslendinga sǫgur* ('Sagas of the Icelanders') are still partly set in the times before Iceland's Christianization in the year 1000, and the *fornaldarsǫgur* ('Sagas about Pre-History') always refer to a legendary pre-history, there are numerous references in the sagas to Germanic religion. However, the sagas are by no means always based on an unbroken oral tradition over three centuries, as was previously generally supposed, and therefore the information they give concerning heathen Germanic religion should only be accepted insofar as the information is supported by other sources.

K. Schier, *Sagaliteratur*, Stuttgart 1960; P. Hallberg, *The Icelandic Saga*, Lincoln 1962; J. de Vries, *Altnordische Literaturgeschichte*, Berlin [2]1967; W. Baetke, *Die Isländersaga*, Darmstadt 1974; R. Simek, H. Pálsson, *Lexikon der altnordischen Literatur*, Stuttgart 1987.

Sagas of the Icelanders (Icel. *Íslendinga sǫgur*). This small group of sagas has become the most famous genre of Icelandic literature because of their Viking Age Icelandic material, their brief, realistic 'saga style' and their high literary quality.

Because of their realistic presentation, these sagas give the impression of historical accuracy, so that it was thought for a long time that the tales had been handed down orally at least partly from the time of their origin in the 10th and 11th centuries until they were finally written down in the 13th century (free prose theory). In fact, they were the literary masterpieces of 13th-century authors (book prose theory) into which admittedly historical sources, genealogies and short episode-like tales flowed, and in which partly also real orally transmitted skaldic verses were used. They are equally marked by Medieval scholarship, Christian education and political thought of the 13th century.

Consequently, stringent critical attitudes with regard to the sources should be adopted, if the Icelandic sagas are to be used as sources for the history of Germanic religion, as with any other High Medieval scholarly texts, such as the *Snorra Edda*. Uncritical acceptance of the few descriptions of pagan customs and cults in the Sagas of the Icelanders could lead to dangerously wrong conclusions: they reveal more about the historical interest of their authors than about actual conditions in heathen times. An example of this is the description of a heathen temple in Iceland in the fanciful *Eyrbyggja saga*. This has frequently been called upon as a source for a history of a Germanic temple, although it most likely does not possess the slightest value as a source. Nonetheless, traces of the old heathen religion are certainly preserved in the sagas, which are increasingly reliable the lower the religious plane is, because simple magical practices were surely continued even after Christianization.

E. O. G. Turville-Petre, *Myth and Religion of the North*, Westport 1975; R. Boyer, 'Paganism and Literature' (*Gripla* 1) 1975; B. McCreesh, 'How pagan are the Icelandic family sagas?' (*JEGPh* 79) 1980.

Saitchamiae. Matron name found on two inscriptions on votive stones from Hoven near Zülpich (CIL XIII 7915–6). The name is considered to be unquestionably Germanic because of the dative ending *-ms*, and the first part is usually related to ON → *seiðr*; thus, the Saitchamiae would be perhaps 'goddesses of magic'.

S. Gutenbrunner, *Die germanischen Götternamen*, Halle 1936; H. Birkhan, *Germanen und Kelten*, Vienna 1970; H. Reichert, *Lexikon der altgermanischen Namen*, Vienna 1987–90.

Salfangr or Svalfangr (ON). A giant in the *Þulur*. The name is obscure, although 'catcher of payment' would be possible.

Sámendill (ON). A giant in the *Þulur*. The name literally means 'the dark Endill', but Endill is not a giant, but rather the name of a sea-king. Therefore, what Sámendill really refers to is unclear.

Sandraudiga. Name of a goddess on a Roman votive altar from Zundert, Holland (CIL XIII 8774). The inscription reads: *Deae Sandraudigae cultores templi*. The name Sandraudiga used to be related to the place name Zundert, but Gutenbrunner's explanation as 'the truly rich one' (cf. ON *sannr* 'true' and Gothic *audags* 'rich') seems to be more likely.

R. M. Meyer, 'Beiträge zur altgermanischen Mythologie' (*ANF* 23) 1907; S. Gutenbrunner, *Die germanischen Götternamen*, Halle 1936; H. Reichert, *Lexikon der altgermanischen Namen*, Vienna 1987–90.

Sanngetall (ON, 'the one who guesses the truth'). A name for Odin in the *Grímnismál* 47 and in the *Þulur* which refers to the fact that Odin is repeatedly the winner of contests of knowledge (in *Vafþrúðnismál*, *Baldrs draumar* and *Hervarar saga*), as indeed he should be as the wisest of the gods.

H. Falk, *Odensheite*, Kristiania 1924.

Sanngriðr or Sangriðr (ON, 'very violent, very cruel'). The otherwise undocumented name of a → valkyrie in *Darraðarljóð* 3.

Saxo Grammaticus (c.1150–1220). A Danish cleric and scholar, employed at the court of the archbishops of Lund at the beginning of the 13th century, who composed there his Latin *Gesta Danorum*, a history of Denmark in 16 books, which records Danish history from its beginnings to 1202.

The first nine books deal with the legendary past of Denmark from the beginning to the rule of Harald Bluetooth (936) and books 10–16 with the historical period from 936–1202. The first part of this work has interested scholars far more than the rest, and most editions and translations only give books 1–9.

Saxo's work is of particular value not only because of his detailed retelling of old legends and myths but also because he used Icelandic informants and sources, thus giving us a large number of Old Norse mythological and heroic tales to which we would otherwise no longer have access to today. Admittedly, Saxo dealt with his sources fairly freely in his Latin version so that their original form has mostly been lost. He adhered to the understanding of Germanic mythology prevalent among Icelandic scholars during the 12th and 13th centuries which is marked by a definite → euhemerism.

Saxo's work was recognised early on by literary historians as the oldest source for the Hamlet material (Amlethus) and his history of the Danes is a treasure trove for tales about mythical-heroic figures of the Scandinavians such as Hading, Starkaðr, Fróði, Guðmundr, Ragnar Loðbrok and many more. He is also one of the most valuable sources for legendary history and after the Poetic *Edda* and Snorri's works also one of the most important sources for Germanic mythology.

ED: C. Knabe, P. Herrmann, *Saxonis Gesta Danorum* 1–2, Hauniae 1831–57; A. Holder, *Saxo Grammaticus, Gesta Danorum*, 1886.

Transl.: P. Herrmann, *Erläuterungen zu den ersten neun Büchern der dän. Geschichte des Saxo Grammaticus* 1–2, 1901–22; H. E. Davidson, P. Fisher, *Saxo Grammaticus: The History of the Danes*, Cambridge 1980.

Lit.: I. Skovgaard-Petersen, 'Saxo' (*KLNM* 15) 1970; C. Weibull, 'Knytlingasagan och Saxo' (*Scandia* 42) 1976; K. Friis-Jensen, *Saxo Grammaticus. A medieval author between Norse and Latin Culture*, Copenhagen 1981; K. Friis-Jensen: *Saxo Grammaticus as Latin poet*, Rome 1987.

Saxon baptismal vow. The baptismal vow (Lat. *abrenuntiatio*) is one of numerous ecclesiastical formulas which have been passed down to us in the language of the country from the time of Christianization. The Saxon baptismal vow, which is preserved in a codex from a monastery library in Mainz from the 9th century (now Cod. pal. 577 of the Vatican), contains the names of three Germanic gods and is therefore interesting as a source for the history of Germanic religion: *end ec forsacho allum dioboles uuercum and uuordum, Thunaer ende UUôden ende Saxnôte ende allum thêm unholdum thê hira genôtas sint* ('I renounce all deeds and words of the devil, Thor, Wodan and Saxnôt and all fiends which are their companions'). → Saxnôt is of especial interest here as he is only named in this one place in a religious context.

Saxnôt. A Germanic god who is named in a → Saxon baptismal vow from the 9th century. As Saxnôt occurs also in the genealogies of Anglo-Saxon royal houses (Essex) in the forms Seaxnet, Saxnêat, Saxnat, he was also considered to be the eponymous ancestor of the Saxons, which is certainly correct whether his name actually means 'friend of the Saxons' or 'sword-companion'.

In the baptismal vow, Saxnôt is named in a divine triad together with Thor and Wodan and as such we may assume that he must have been an important god. As a result, some scholars (de Vries, Philippson) have wanted to identify him with *Tīwaz/Týr, but an identification with Freyr (Turville-Petre) would seem to be more likely according to the Indo-Germanic → three-function-system. The possibly etymologically related ON *Njótr*, recorded as a name for Odin, does not make matters any easier.

A. Leitzmann, 'Saxonica I' (*PBB* 25) 1900; R. Jente, *Die mythologischen Ausdrücke im altenglischen Wortschatz*, Heidelberg 1921; E. A. Philippson, *Germanisches Heidentum bei den Angelsachsen*, Leipzig 1929; J. de Vries, *Altgermanische Religionsgeschichte*, Berlin [3]1970; E. O. G. Turville-Petre, *Myth and Religion of the North*, Westport 1975.

Sax(s)anus, Saxsetanius → Hercules Saxanus.

Sceaf (OE, 'sheaf'). One of the mythical ancestors of the Anglo-Saxon line of kings.

Whereas Sceaf appears in the genealogies of the English royal houses as one of the many names of Voden's (= Odin's) mythical ancestors, the medieval historians gave detailed accounts of him. Æthelweard (*Chronic*. 3, 3; 10th century) tells of the miraculous arrival of the child, Sceaf, on the island of Scania in a ship full of weapons. Later Sceaf becomes king of the Scania and ancestor of Odin's dynasty. William of Malmesbury (*Gestis regum Anglorum* 2, 116) gives additional information about the arrival of a sleeping boy in a boat without oars and explains Sceaf's name by saying that he was lying in the boat asleep on a sheaf. In the OE *Beowulf* (4–31) Scyld Scefing (= Scef's son) is the hero of a very similar episode, but the name Sceaf is probably the more original. William's explanation of the name can easily be explained away as being an additional Medieval interpretation, if the genealogies and *Beowulf* name another ancestor, Beow, Beav ('barley'). Hence, some scholars have understood Sceaf to be a corn spirit or a corn demon of a fertility cult, but there is too little evidence to substantiate this. It is more likely that Sceaf should be thought of as a culture hero, as the bringer of agriculture.

J. Grimm, *Deutsche Mythologie*, Berlin [4]1875–78; P. Herrmann, *Die Heldensagen des Saxo Grammaticus*, Leipzig 1922; E. A. Philippson, *Germanisches Heidentum bei den Angelsachsen*, Leipzig 1929.

Schröder, Franz Rolf (1893–1979). A scholar in German and Scandinavian Studies whose research turned increasingly towards the study of Germanic religious history and who was especially interested in the relationship of other Indo-European religions to the Germanic religion. On the one hand he was always cautious in his theories and carefully tried to determine the influence of south-eastern Hellenistic thought on Germanic religion, and on the other hand he was constantly investigating parallels between the myths and gods of the Germanic peoples with the other Indo-Germanic peoples. Thus he introduced a new era of comparative mythology, an important step in the history of scholarship in this particular field which has been continued in the middle of the 20th century by G. Dumézil's research.

(**Schwertleite**). A valkyrie (alto) in R. Wagner's opera, *Die Walküre*, whose name he invented himself.

Scyld Scefing (Anglo-Saxon, 'Scyld, Scef's son'). The ancestor of the Scyldingas (= Skjǫldungs?) in the OE *Beowulf* (4ff.). In *Beowulf* an account is given of his miraculous arrival on Scania as a child in an oarless boat filled with weapons. Elsewhere, however, the name is said to be → Sceaf, probably the more original version. According to Scandinavian tradition, Scyld Scefing ('shield') is Odin's son and the ancestor of the Skjǫldung dynasty whereas in the OE tradition he only plays an important role in *Beowulf* as being the hero's father, and in the genealogies of the Anglo-Saxon royal houses Scyld Scefing (also Sceldva) is named without any further commentary as the name of the man coming between Beav and Sceaf.

J. Grimm, *Deutsche Mythologie*, Berlin [4]1875–78; P. Herrmann, *Die Heldensagen des Saxo Grammaticus*, Leipzig 1922; C. W. v. Sydow, 'Scyld Scefing' (*NoB* 12) 1924; E. A. Philippson, *Germanisches Heidentum bei den Angelsachsen*, Leipzig 1929.

Scyldingas. The Anglo-Saxon name for the royal line of the Danish kings, the → Skjǫldungs. In the OE *Beowulf* Scyld is the ancestor of the Scyldingas from which line Beowulf himself is descended.

Scylfingas (Anglo-Saxon, identical with ON → Skilfingar). The Anglo-Saxon name of the Swedish royal house of Ynglings.

Seccanehae. Matron name on a votive inscription from Blankenheim near Aachen, Germany (CIL XIII 8846); perhaps related to the personal name Seccus?

S. Gutenbrunner, *Die germanischen Götternamen*, Halle 1936; M. Schönfeld, *Wörterbuch der altgermanischen Personen- und Völkernamen*, Heidelberg [2]1965; H. Reichert, *Lexikon der altgermanischen Namen*, Vienna 1987–90.

Second Merseburg Charm. OHG charm. This charm is recorded in a manuscript from the 10th century, but it is certainly older. The words are as follows:

Phol ende Uuodan vuorun zi holza.
du uuart demo Balderes volon sin vuoz birenkit.
thu biguol en Sinthgunt, Sunna era suister;
thu biguol en Friia, Volla ers suister;
thu biguol en Uuodan, so he uuola conda:
sose benrenki, sose bluotrenki, sose lidirenki:
ben zi bena, bluot zi bluoda,
lid zi giden, sose gelimida sin!

Phol and Wodan rode into the wood; the foreleg of Baldr's horse was dislocated; then Sintgunt and Sunna, her sister, sang over it, then Friia and Volla, her sister, sang over it, then Wodan sang over it, for he could do that well: be it dislocation of bone, be it an ailment of the blood, be it dislocation of the limbs: bone to bone, blood to blood, limb to limb, as if they were glued.

The meaning of the healing magic itself is obvious and corresponds to the mythical treatment of other charms. Some of the gods' names, however, have created some difficulties, and the ensuing discussion is still ongoing. Wodan and his wife Frîja are the only gods who can be identified. Sinthgunt, Sunna and Volla are only known from this one brief reference, and the names Phol and Baldr have caused dispute since it is unclear whether these are in fact gods' names or whether, for example, Baldr might simply be mean 'lord' and as such refer back to the god Wodan in the first line. However, this is difficult to prove and therefore the Second Merseburg Charm should continue to be regarded as the first recording of the name Baldr. The name Phol (= Fol? Vol?) is also not undisputed. The most elegant solution, although admittedly little more than a hypothesis, was made by Brate who interpreted Fol and Fulla (= Volla) as brother and sister, thus corresponding to the Scandinavian gods Freyr and Freyja.

The scene of the horse being healed described in the Second Merseburg Charm, which is supposed to occur through the magical recitation, is depicted on bracteates from the 5th and 6th centuries, where the head of a god, most likely Wodan, frequently appears above a horse with quite obviously dislocated forelegs. These bracteates (Group C) with Wodan as the magical doctor probably had the function of tallismen.

H. Gering, 'Der Zweite Merseburger Zauberspruch' (*ZfdPh* 26) 1894; R. Th. Christiansen, *Die finnischen und nordischen Varianten*, Helsinki 1914; E. Brate, 'Andra Merseburg-besvärjelsen' (*ANF* 35) 1919; W. H. Vogt, 'Zum Problem der Merseburger Zaubersprüche' (*ZfdA* 65) 1928; S. Gutenbrunner, 'Der Zweite Merseburger Zauberspruch' (*ZfdA* 80) 1944; H. W. J. Kroes, 'Die Balderüberlieferung und der Zweite Merseburger Zauberspruch' (*Neophilologus* 35) 1951; F. R. Schröder, 'Balder und der Zweite Merseburger Zauberspruch' (*GRM* 34) 1953; W. Betz, 'Sose gelimida sin' (*Rheinische Vierteljahresblätter* 21) 1956; L. Forster, 'Zum Zweiten Merseburger

Zauberspruch' (*Archiv* 192) 1956; A. Schirokauer, 'Der Zweite Merseburger Zauberspruch' (in: *Germanistische Studien*) Hamburg 1957; K. Northcott, 'An Interpretation of the Second Merseburg Charm' (*MLR* 54) 1959; F. Wrede, 'Zu den Merseburger Zaubersprüchen' (In: *Kleine Schriften*), Marburg 1963; J. de Vries, *Altgermanische Religionsgeschichte*, Berlin [3]1970; K. Hauck, 'Text und Bild in einer oralen Kultur' (*FmSt* 17) 1983.

Seeresses. There is evidence from Germanic antiquity to the High Middle Ages that the Germanic peoples believed that women had prophetic gifts and that they quite clearly worshipped some women as seeresses. In *Germania* 8 Tacitus records: 'The Germans even believe that there is something sacred and prophetic inherent to women' and he mentions the seeresses Veleda and Albruna. Other seeresses known to us by name from antiquity are Waluburg and Ganna who both lived in the first century A.D. However, other classical authors also mention the Germanic people as having seeresses apart from the ones named above: Strabo (7, 2) mentions old women in white garments who went to war with the armies and who prophesied the future from the blood of the captives, and Dio Cassius (*Roman History* 55, 1) reports of a woman with supernatural powers who faced Drusus in the region of the Cherusci. From the descriptions of Veleda in Tacitus (*Historiae* 4 and 5) and of Ganna in Dio Cassius (*Roman History* 67, 5) it appears that the seeresses were supposed to be virgins. Evidence given by the Medieval Nordic sources as well as the old names (Waluburg, Gambara), reveals that a further attribute was the wand (ON *vǫlr*), from which the seeresses received their name in ON (*vǫlva*, actually 'wand-bearer', then 'seeress').

In the Eddic lays important knowledge is repeatedly put into the mouths of seeresses (*Vǫluspá*, *Baldrs draumar*), and even the sagas name several seeresses: Þorbjǫrg lítilvǫlva (*Eireks saga*), Þordís spákona (*Vatnsdœla saga*), Heimlaug vǫlva (*Gull-Þóris saga*), Þuríðr sundafyllir (*Sturlunga saga* 145).

All our sources about seeresses have however been influenced by the *interretatio romana* or *christiana*. The Roman authors projected experiences with their own augurs onto the 'barbarians', and the Christian Medieval Icelandic saga authors considered the seeresses to be more or less witches who practised sorcery (→ seiðr). The frequent other name for seeresses *heiðr* (approximately: 'witch') found in ON texts points in this direction, too.

From various accounts about Veleda and Ganna, it is clear that the Germanic seeresses had occasionally a remarkable political influence in Roman times, and indeed even the Romans themselves were not backward in making use of the services of the Germanic seeresses (Tacitus, *Historiae* 5, 24; Sueton, *Aulus Vitellius* 14).

Despite the fact that some of the seeresses and their effectiveness have a very definite place in history (→ Veleda, → Waluburg), we are nonetheless somewhat in the dark with regards to the actual practice of their prophecy, in particular for the earlier times, even if a few sparse hints (such as Veleda's tower) suggest a continuity of the procedures mentioned in the ON sources. The practices described in the sagas (*Gisla saga* 18, *Vatnsdœla saga* 10, *Örvar-Odds saga* 2 and especially *Eireks saga rauða* 4) are called → *seiðr* ('magic') and are only slightly different from the black magic found elsewhere. A 'magic platform' (*seiðhjallr*) seems to play an important role in these practices on which the seeress sat and made her prophesies. *Eireks saga rauða* mentions in addition to this sung incantations. Additional attributes are a magic wand and the animal-skin clothes of the seeresses among other details which, however, probably originate more in the fantasy of the narrator than from his knowledge of actual magical practices.

The magic of prophesy is undoubtedly a form of shamanism but it is unlikely to have been adopted from the Finns (as Strömbäck assumes) since early Germanic sources already refer to it. Therefore, it is probably the reflection of a shamanistic stage of development since it can be found in the cultural history of numerous peoples.

D. Strömbäck, *Sejd*, Uppsala 1935; H. Volkmann, *Germanische Seherinnen in römischen Diensten*, Krefeld 1964; Å. V. Ström, H. Biezais, *Germanische und baltische Religion*, Stuttgart 1974.

seiðkona (ON, 'sorceress') → magic, → seeresses.

seiðlæti (ON, approximately 'magical tune') → Varðlokkur.

seiðmaðr (ON, 'sorcerer') → magic.

seiðr (ON, 'magic, spell, incantation'). The specific Scandinavian form of magical practices; → magic.

Semnones' grove. Tacitus (*Germania* 39) says that the Semnones are the oldest and the most well-known tribal group of the Suebi and records that they made a public human sacrifice performed by delegates from the individual tribes in a sacred grove. They showed great reverence for this grove and only entered the grove in fetters so that they could acknowledge their own inferiority and the superiority of the god. If one of them were to fall whilst in the grove, then he had to roll over the ground, but might not get up himself or be picked up within its limits. According to Tacitus, the cult went back to the belief that the grove was the cradle of their race and that the supreme god (*regnator omnium deus*) lived there.

The rule of wearing fetters in the Semnones' grove was compared quite early on in scholarly research with the grove of Fjǫturlundr ('fetter-grove') referred to in the Eddic lay *Helgakviða Hundingsbana* I 30 where Helgi is killed by → Dagr using a spear. The divine ancestor who was worshipped in the Semnones' grove would probably have been Odin since he was still considered to be the god of fetters in late ON religion, and not *Tīwaz, as Much assumed. Analogous Germanic religious beliefs and cults are present in any case in the Eddic Fjǫturlundr and in the Semnones' grove whereby the human sacrifice in the Semnones' grove could quite possibly be thought of as a kind of cult imitation of Odin's self-sacrifice (Höfler). In addition to this Höfler tried to show that in the case of the groves it was not only a case of analogy but identity so that the Eddic poetry about Helgi contained the reflection of Suebian religious concepts, but in particular cult forms.

O. Höfler, 'Das Opfer im Semnonenhain und die Edda' (*Edda, Skalden, Saga. Festschrift F. Genzmer*) Heidelberg 1952; R. W. Fischer, 'Vinculo ligatus' (*Antaios* 5) 1963; R. Much, *Die Germania des Tacitus*, Heidelberg ³1967; J. de Vries, *Altgermanische Religionsgeschichte*, Berlin ³1970.

Sessrumnir (ON, actually 'seat-roomer'). A ship with many rowers' seats in each thwart. Sessrumnir is the name of a ship mentioned in the *Þulur* but nowhere else. However, in Snorri (*Gylfaginning* 23) Sessrumnir is used as a name for Freyja's hall in her heavenly home Fólkvangr. One of the two interpretations probably comes from a misunderstanding as the meaning can be understood in both cases as 'space with many or roomy seats'.

R. Simek, *Die Schiffsnamen*, Vienna 1982.

Shamanism. Traces of shamanistic practises are repeatedly found in Germanic religion, especially in the myths recorded about Odin. One of the most obvious cases is Odin's acquisition of runic knowledge through his self-sacrifice, itself reminiscent of the ordeals of shamanistic initiation rites. Similarities of this type have also led to the → *Grímnismál* being interpreted as reflecting initiation rites connected with knowledge acquisition, although this assumption is not uncontended.

Another aspect of shamanistic initiation ceremonies, namely death, Other World voyage and resurrection, may be inherent in the → Baldr myth, although Baldr's failure to return from the dead deviates from the shamanistic pattern.

Most importantly, many aspects of the Odinic religion show parallels to the ecstatic states in which shamans perform both healings and prophecies. Trances in which neither pain nor fire are felt are typical of Odin's warriors, especially → berserks and *ulfheðnar*, and both Odin's name and his role in the Wild Hunt show his affiliation with extraordinary states of consciousness. Odin is also linked with details in magic which may well date back to a shamanistic level of Germanic religion: he uses Mímir's talking head for divination, and his seat → Hliðskjálf is reminiscent of the towers and platforms used by shamans for their visions. Such constructions were also used by Germanic seeresses and called → *seiðhjallr*.

The shamanistic traces found in Germanic religion seem to date back to an archaic religious level which occurred for different peoples at different times in history and which survived most obviously in the practises of the Scandinavian magic, the → *seiðr*, and seems closely connected to the god of magic, Odin.

A. Ohlmarks, 'Arktischer Schamanismus und altnord. seiðr' (*ARW* 36) 1939; V. Kiil, Hilðskjálf og seiðhjallr (*ANF* 75) 1960; P. Buchholz, *Schamanistische Züge in der altisländischen Überlieferung*, Münster 1968; J. Fleck, 'The "Knowledge-Criterion" in the Grímnismál: The Case against "Shamanism" ' (*ANF* 86) 1971.

Ship. The ship played a major role in the Germanic cult of the older period as can be seen from the Bronze Age rock carvings and other pictorial representations from this time (Kivik grave; ritual razors) on which, apart from human figures, the ship is the most frequent motif.

As the rock carvings are generally accepted today as being religious documents, the question arises about the cult in which the ship played such a major role. The form of the cult emerges from the representations themselves: it is concerned with processions with a ship (sometimes carried) which is manned with figures who are dancing, worshipping and occasionally blowing lures. The ship is also frequently linked with the symbol of the sun. The ship depicted is not one in practical use, but one used as a cult ship which had little or nothing to do with secular needs.

Since Almgren it has been accepted that such cult ships were only built on land for the duration of a festival, an idea which perfectly fits the name of Freyr's ship → Skíðblaðnir. It is obvious from the decorations on the Iron Age golden votive boats from Nors, Jutland that the ship is still associated with the sun in the religion of the Iron Age, as well as in the Middle Ages, → Hringhorni. Quite clearly, the ship also played a role in the cult of a sun or fertility god (Njǫrðr/Freyr), to whom not only the farming population prayed for good harvests, but also the seafarers to ensure good sailing weather and successful fishing (Simek 1977). It is uncertain whether the non-Germanic concept of a sun-god who sailed his ship across the sky had any influence on this cult. The ship has maintained its significance in the devotion to the sun god in folk customs up to the present day, for example in western European processions with a ship-chariot (where the sun is understood as the 'wheel of fortune'), and also in the Scandinavian boat burning at midsummer, with its counterpart in the Alpine midsummer custom of the burning wheel, both clearly connected to sun-god worship.

In addition, the ship had an important role in burial customs from the Iron Age to the Viking Age. During this entire period the custom of → boat burial was common in Scandinavia; similar ideas might be reflected in the stone → ship-settings, at least insofar as they are identified as being graves. In Eddic mythology the ship of death is called → Naglfar.

O. Almgren, *Nordische Felszeichnungen*, Frankfurt 1936; R. Simek, *Skíðblaðnir* (*Northern Studies* 9) 1977; R. Simek, *Die Schiffsnamen*, Vienna 1982.

Ship burial → Boat burial.

Ship grave → Boat burial.

Ship-settings is the usual name for stone settings whose form suggest the outline of a ship: they consist of standing stones, set at short distances apart, gradually increasing in size to a prow at both ends. Ship-settings are found in Middle and South Scandinavia, mostly in Sweden; over 1,500 ship-settings are still in existence, of which the majority belong to the Migration and Viking period, but some are from the late Bronze Age; it is however not possible to identify any ship-setting as coming from the 800-year period in between with any certainty. The majority of ship-settings contain graves and therefore are associated with the custom of → boat burial. However, some Bronze Age ship-settings without graves point to the possibility of their being cult monuments, either in connexion with burial customs or within a cult which manifests itself in the depictions of ships on Bronze Age rock carvings.

A. Ohlmarks, *Gravskeppet*, Stockholm 1946; M. Müller-Wille, 'Bestattung im Boot' (*Offa* 25–26) 1970; R. Simek, *Die Schiffsnamen*, Vienna 1982.

Síarr → Svíurr.

Sibulca. Name of a goddess. A Roman Age votive stone from Bonn, found in 1958, is dedicated to this *Deae Sibulcae*; the name has not yet been explained.

H.-G. Kolbe, 'Neue Inschriften aus Bonn' (*Bonner Jahrbücher* 161) 1961.

Sið (ON, 'the slow one'). A mythical river in the catalogue of rivers in *Grímnismál* 27 and in the *Þulur*.

Síðgrani (ON, 'the one with the long moustache'). A name for Odin recorded in *Alvíssmál* which refers to Vingthor (= Thor) as being Síðgrani's son; cf. the similarly formed names for Odin Síðskeggr and Langbarðr. In *Örvar-Odds saga* (ch. 35) Odin is described as having a long beard and moustache.

H. Falk, *Odensheite*, Kristiania 1924; S. Gutenbrunner, 'Über die Redewendung "láttu grǫn sía þá" ' (*ZfdA* 72) 1935; J. de Vries, *Altnordisches etymologisches Wörterbuch*, Leiden [2]1977.

Síðhǫttr (ON, 'long hat'). A name for Odin in *Grímnismál* 47 and in the *Þulur*, which suits the usual description of Odin with a wide-brimmed hat pulled far down over his face.

Síðskeggr (ON, 'long beard'). A name for Odin in the *Grímnismál* 47 and in the

Þulur. In his appearances on earth Odin is described as having a long, grey beard (cf. the names Hárbarðr, Langbarðr, Síðgrani).

(**Siegrune**). A valkyrie (mezzo-soprano) in R. Wagner's opera *Die Walküre*. The name is a Germanized form of the valkyrie's name Sigrun.

Sif (ON). A goddess. Sif is one of the Æsir, Thor's wife and the mother of the god Ullr, who she apparently gave birth to before her marriage with Thor (*Gylfaginning* 30; *Skáldskaparmál* 4, 14, 22; *Hymiskviða* 3, 15, 34; *Hárbarðsljóð* 48; *Þrymskviða* 24). Despite frequent references to her in the younger Eddic lays, and also in skaldic poetry, she seems to have been without a particular function. The most likely interpretation is to see her as a goddess who originated as a complement to Thor when he played an increasingly important role as a god of fertility; the name Sif can be seen to support this view as Sif can hardly mean anything else but 'relation by marriage', originally therefore simply 'the wife (of Thor)'. N. Å. Nielsen diverges from this view, considering that Sif was originally married to Njǫrðr and only became Thor's wife after the war against the Vanir. This would take an extremely speculative identification of Ullr = Freyr for granted, and is as such very precarious.

Snorri relates the only myth we know of Sif as an explanation for the kenning 'Sif's hair' = 'gold'; although this kenning does not occur in any extant skaldic poetry, it gives the impression of being real as Sif is also to be found in *Bjarkamál* 5 in a kenning for gold. Snorri's account (*Skáldskaparmál* 33) relates: 'that Loki Laufeyjarson once cut off all Sif's hair out of pure malice. When Thor noticed what had happened, he took Loki and would have broken every bone in his body if he had not sworn to get the black-elves to make hair which would grow like real hair for Sif out of gold.' Loki then goes to the dwarfs, Ivald's sons Brokkr and Sindri, who have not only forged Sif's hair, but also Odin's spear Gungnir, the ship Skíðblaðnir, Freyr's golden boar Gullinborsti, the ring Draupnir and Thor's hammer Mjǫllnir.

Since Uhland first suggested it, Sif's golden hair has been seen mostly as a mythical picture for the gentle waves of a cornfield, which is cut every year and yet grows again the year after; but even Grimm was sceptical of this interpretation; the fact that a particular kind of moss (*polytrichum aureum*) is called *haddr Sifjar* 'Sif's hair' in Old Norse also clearly contradicts this hypothesis. Therefore, it seems that the vegetation cult, which various scholars (de Vries, Å. V. Ström) wanted to assume for Sif, deriving from the connexion with her golden hair, is the mere product of an over-zealous interpretation of Snorri's anecdote which has added the fairy-tale motif of the golden hair to the tale of the creation of the various attributes of the gods; otherwise there is no reason to assume a cult of Sif.

L. Uhland, *Der Mythus von Thôr*, Stuttgart 1836; J. Grimm, *Deutsche Mythologie*, Berlin [4]1875–78; E. Mogk, 'Das angebliche Sifbild' (*PBB* 14) 1889; J. de Vries, *Altgermanische Religionsgeschichte*, Berlin [3]1970; Å. V. Ström, H. Biezais, *Germanische und baltische Religion*, Stuttgart 1975; N. Å. Nielsen, 'Mythen om Krigen' (*Nordiska Studier i filologi och linguistik. Festskrift* G. *Holm*), Lund 1976.

Sigfaðir (ON, 'father of battles, father of victory'). A name for Odin (*Vǫluspá* 55, *Lokasenna* 58), which refers to Odin as the god of war and as the ruler of the fate of battles. Apart from Sigfaðir, the possibly archaic form → Sigfǫðr is recorded twice; other names for Odin are also formed on the base Sig- 'victory', such as Sigtýr and Siggautr.

H. Falk, *Odensheite*, Christiania 1924; H. Kuhn, 'Das nordgermanische Heidentum' (*ZfdA* 79) 1942.

Sigfǫðr (ON, 'father of victory, father of battle'). A name for Odin in the *Grímnismál* 48 and in the *Þulur*, both times in mnemonic poetry. Apart from this form, Sigfaðir is also recorded. It appears that didactic poetry favoured the use of the apparently archaic forms on *-fǫðr* for names which are alternating between *-fǫðr/-faðir*: *Grímnismál* 48 names both Alfǫðr and Sigfǫðr, as do the *Þulur*, which admittedly have Valfǫðr and Herjafǫðr as well, but do not have Alfaðir and Sigfaðir.

H. Falk, *Odensheite*, Christiania 1924; H. Kuhn, 'Das nordgermanische Heidentum' (*ZfdA* 79) 1942.

Siggautr (ON, 'victory-Gautr'). A name for Odin in the *Þulur*; the name represents an extension to Gautr following the pattern of Sigtýr and Sigfaðir.

Sigi (ON, 'victor'). One of Odin's sons, who is only mentioned in the *Þulur* and in Snorri's prologue to his *Edda*. Apart from this, nothing is known about him.

Sigrdrífa (ON, 'inciter to victory'). The name of the valkyrie in *Fáfnismál* 44 and *Sigrdrífumál* who otherwise (even in the *Edda*) is called Brynhildr.

Sigrún (ON, 'victory-rune'). A → valkyrie in Norse heroic poetry (*Helgakviða Hundingsbana* I, *Helgakviða Hundingsbana* II), who is called the daughter of King Hǫgni and the mistress of Helgi Hundinsbani. After her death she will be reborn as → Kára.

Sigþrór (ON, 'victory-Þrór'). A name for Odin in the *Þulur*, which is an extension of → Þrór.

Sigtýr (ON, 'battle-god, victory-god'). A name for Odin in Glumr Geirason (*Gráfeldardrápa* 12) and in *Atlakviða* 30. It is one of the names for Odin basied on *-týr*, which flourished at the end of the 10th century (Hertýr, Gautatýr, Hroptatýr etc.). The plural of the word, *sigtívar*, is however far more frequent as a kenning for 'gods' (*Vǫluspá* 44 and 49, *Grímnismál* 45, *Lokasenna* 1 and 2, *Fáfnismál* 24, *Atlakviða* 29).

H. de Boor, 'Die religiöse Sprache der Vǫluspá' (*Deutsche Islandforschung* 1) 1930.

Sigyn (ON). Loki's wife (*Vǫluspá* 35; *Gylfaginning* 32, 49, *Skáldskaparmál* 16), who is on the list of Æsir given by Snorri (*Skáldskaparmál* 1; *Þulur*). She mostly occurs in connexion with the tale of → Loki's punishment, where she catches the poison, which drops from a snake onto Loki's chained body, in a bowl. – Although Sigyn is recorded as a female personal name (ON *sigr* 'victory' and *vina* 'girl-friend'), she was already known to be Loki's wife by Þjóðólfr ór Hvíni in the 9th century (*Haustlǫng* 7) and as such probably belongs to the Germanic Pantheon of earlier times, and is thus not merely a mythographical creation of later ages.

J. de Vries, *The Problem of Loki*, Helsinki 1933; J. de Vries, *Altgermanische Religionsgeschichte*, Berlin [3]1970.

R: N. J. O. Blommér, *Loke och Sigyn* (painting, c.1850); M. E. Winge, *Loke och Sigyn* (painting, 1863); O. Wergeland, *Loki och Sigyn* (painting, 1879); K. Ehrenberg, *Loki und Sigyn; Hel mit dem Hunde Garm* (drawing, 1883).

Silfrintoppr (ON, 'silver mane'). A mythical horse in *Grímnismál* 30 and in the *Þulur*; in Snorri (*Gylfaginning* 14) Silfrintoppr is a horse belonging to the Æsir.

Simul (1) (ON, 'female reindeer'). A giantess in the *Þulur*.

Simul (2) (ON). The name of the pole which the two men in the moon Bil and Hjuki carry in an aetiological (fairy-?)tale about the picture in the moon, told by Snorri (*Gylfaginning* 10); → Máni.

A. Holtsmark, 'Bil of Hjuke' (MoM) 1945.

Sindri (ON, 'the spark sprayer', 'blacksmith'). A dwarf in *Vǫluspá* 37. According to Snorri (*Skáldskaparmál* 33), it is Sindri who forged the golden boar Gullinborsti, the ring Draupnir, the ship Skíðblaðnir, and the hammer → Mjǫllnir. Sindri's brother and assistant is called Brokkr.

Singasteinn (ON). The name of a mythological object or place which Snorri (*Skáldskaparmál* 8) mentions in a kenning for Heimdall (*tilsækir Singasteins* 'Singastein's visitors') and which comes from Ulfr Uggason's *Húsdrápa*. The construction in *Húsdrápa* 2 makes it more likely that is is a place-name (at Singasteini), and apparently Snorri understood it as being the name of an island (Jónsson, Schier). From the semantic context Singastein might be considered to be the name of an object, on the other hand, over which Loki and Heimdall fight (de Vries, F. Ström). The name Singastein is difficult to interpret: it has been interpreted etymologically as 'old stone' (from Gothic *sineigs* 'old'; Jónsson), but also as 'magic stone, amulet' (from **signasteinn*, Pering; or else from OE *sincstān*, de Vries). It seems to me to be hardly less likely, if Singastein in Húsdrápa does indeed refer to a kenning for a piece of jewelry, that the name Singastein could be interpreted as *sǫngvastein* 'stone of songs', thus 'the much praised stone'. It is therefore extremely doubtful if Singstein is indeed a mythological name at all.

→ Brísingamen.

Sinir (ON, 'the sinewed one'). A mythical horse in the catalogue of horse names in *Grímnismál* 30 and in the *Þulur*. In Snorri (*Gylfaginning* 14) Sinir is one of the horses belonging to the Æsir.

Sinmara (ON). The female companion of the giant Surtr in *Fjǫlsvinnsmál* (26, 30). The name is obscure; *mara* is '(night-)mare', but *sin* can hardly be related to *sindr* 'cinders' (Gutenbrunner), even if it would be a meaningful interpretation with regard to the colour. A more likely interpretation is: 'the pale (night-)mare', which might fit the wife of a fire-giant well.

S. Gutenbrunner, 'Eddica' (*ZfdA* 77) 1940; J. de Vries, *Altnordisches etymologisches Wörterbuch*, [2]Leiden 1977.

Sinthgunt (in the manuscript: Sinhtgunt). A goddess who is only named in the → Second Merseburg Charm, and is called there Sunna's sister.

The significance of this goddess is unknown, and even her name has remained unexplained up to today: if one sticks to the manuscript form Sinhtgunt, then an interpretation 'the night-walking one', that is to say the moon, would be possible (Brate, Ström); other interpretations (reading Sinthgunt) have resulted in 'the one moving into battle' (Gering) or 'heavenly body, star' (Grimm). The explanation as 'moon' (because she occurs in the charm as the companion of the sun) is unlikely as the Germanic peoples usually considered the moon to be a male being (→ Máni), and Schröder's interpretation as 'the all-night changing one', that is the moon-god, stands in contradiction to the statement given in the charm, 'Sunna's sister'. Thus, it is clear that the etymology is by no means satisfactorily explained and the semantic interpretation of the goddess depends on it.

J. Grimm, *Deutsche Mythologie*, Berlin [4]1875–78; S. Bugge, *Studien über die Entstehung der nordischen Götter- und Heldensagen*, Munich 1889; H. Gering, 'Der zweite Merseburger Spruch' (*ZfdPh* 26) 1894; E. Brate, 'Andra Merseburg-besvärjelsen' (*ANF* 35) 1919; F. R. Schröder, 'Balder und der zweite Merseburger Spruch' (*GRM* 34) 1953; S. Gutenbrunner, 'Ritennamen – Kultnamen Mythennamen' (*Namenforschung. Festschrift A. Bach*) Heidelberg 1965; J. de Vries, *Altgermanische Religionsgeschichte*, Berlin [3]1970; Å. V. Ström, H. Biezais, *Germanische und baltische Religion*, Stuttgart 1975.

Sívǫr (ON). A giantess in the *Þulur*; the name could possibly mean 'the one with the hanging down lips' or else even 'hemp-lip'; cf.→ Svívǫr.

Sjǫfn (ON). A goddess of whom Snorri (*Gylfaginning* 34) tells that she turns people's senses to love, and therefore love is also known as *sjafni*. Thus, Snorri interprets this goddess's name etymologically (either from *sefi* 'sense' or from *sefi* 'relation'?); the few references to Sjǫfn as a mythical figure in skaldic poetry do not allow any better explanation; accordingly then, Sjǫfn is a goddess of marriage and love, or else one of relationships, and is one of several goddesses named by Snorri who are matron-like guardian-goddesses.

Skaði (ON). The daughter of the giant Þjazi, the wife of the god → Njǫrðr and the mother of Freyr, a goddess of hunting and skiing. The Eddic lays only say that Skaði is the daughter of the giant Þjazi (*Hyndluljóð* 30) and that she lives in Þrymheimr (*Grímnismál* 11); *Lokasenna* (49, 51, Pr) names her as the wife of Njǫrðr and one of the Æsir.

Snorri is more detailed in his account: in *Skáldskaparmál* 1 he reports how Skaði arms herself in order to avenge her father → Þjazi who has been killed by Thor. When she arrives at Asgard fully armed, the gods ask her to accept compensation: she should look for a husband among the Æsir, but she will only see his feet before her choice is made. She chooses the obviously most beautiful (or cleanest?) feet, expecting them to be Baldr's, but she chooses the god of the sea Njǫrðr. In addition it is agreed that as a further atonement the gods must make her laugh; Loki manages this by tying a piece of rope around the beard of a goat and around his testicles and the resulting spectacle makes even Skaði laugh. – From *Gylfaginning* 22 we learn that the marriage between Skaði and Njǫrðr is not successful: whilst Njǫrðr is only happy in his domicile Nóatún beside the sea, Skaði longs to hunt in the snow-covered mountains; therefore, they make an agreement whereby they spend nine days alternately in Nóatún and in Þrymheimr; but Skaði cannot bear Nóatún at all and moves back to the mountains. Njǫrðr's children, Freyr and Freyja, appear nonetheless to be hers.

According to the tradition in Snorri's *Ynglinga saga*, after her separation from Njǫrðr Skaði had numerous sons by Odin, from whom Earl Hakon is descended. Here again it is a case of one of the frequent attempts to trace divine ancestors in personal descendency myths and as such it is certainly a construction from the High Middle Ages.

Skaði is called *ǫndurdís* 'ski-goddess' by the skalds (Eyvindr, *Háleygjatal* 4 and Bragi, *Ragnarsdrápa* 20); she goes hunting armed with a bow and arrow, and as such she is the counterpart to the Greek goddess Artemis. On the other hand, the comparison with the Nordic god Ullr, similarly a 'ski-god' (*ǫnduráss*), suggests itself; Schröder wanted to interpret Skaði and Ullr as a couple (or brother and sister?), but the Old Norse sources do not give any indication of this.

Skaði's relationship to Loki is strange: he is partly to blame for her father's death, and he must also make her laugh. In the prose text of *Lokasenna* it is Skaði of all people who hangs the poison-dripping snake over the shackled Loki, yet on the other hand she is accused of adultery with Loki in *Lokasenna* 52. Perhaps there was a relationship between them in an older myth, but whatever the case, the statements made in *Lokasenna* are not of great significance because most of the goddesses are accused of adultery or whoring in this lay.

Similarly in *Lokasenna* (51) there is an obvious reference to cult places connected to Skaði, which could find substantiation in the various Swedish, less frequently Norwegian, place-names which might be derived from Skaði: Skedevi, Skedvi, Skea and place-names based on Ska- and Skada-; admittedly, it is by no means certain that these are really names of cult places. Because of her name, Skaði has even been considered as the eponymous mistress of Sca(n)dia (= Schonen) and thus of Scandinavia, but this is, however, not totally convincing.

H. Lindroth, 'En nordisk gudagestalt i ny belysning genom ortnamn' (*Antikvarisk tidskrift för Sverige* 20) 1915; G. Schütte, 'Eponyme Götter und Heroen' (*ZfdA* 69), 1932; F. R. Schröder, *Skadi und die Götter Skandinaviens*, Tübingen 1941; J. de Vries, *Altgermanische Religionsgeschichte*, Berlin [3]1970; A. Holtsmark, 'Skaði' (*KLNM* 15) 1970.

R: (literature) A. Oehlenschläger, *Skades Giftermaal* (poem in: *Nordens Guder*, 1819).
(fine art) K. Ehrenberg, *Skadi und Niurd* (drawing, 1883); E. Doepler d. J., *Skadi* (in: E. Doepler, W. Ranisch, *Walhall*, 1901).

Skærir (ON). A giant in the *Þulur*, whose name possibly means 'shearer, cutter'; admittedly, the form of the name is not totally certain.

Skaldic mead → Mead of the skalds.

Skaldic poetry is conventionally considered to be the part of Old Norse poetry which (in contrast to the anonymous Eddic poetry) may be connected with the authorship of a particular poet (skald) and which is composed in the courtly verse form of the *dróttkvætt*. Skaldic poetry is the name for Medieval Norwegian court poetry and subsequently poetry related to it in form and composed in Old Norse. The difference between skaldic poetry and Eddic poetry has not been totally satisfactorily defined and the *dróttkvætt* alone cannot be considered to be the main constituent of a whole genre. Originally skaldic poetry was not actually epic poetry, but served as a eulogy on living, less often dead chieftains. Because of the close interaction between alliteration, internal rhyme, syllable-counting meters and the use of → kennings, skaldic poetry allows little freedom, but the emphasis on skilful composition within this formal system is all the greater.

Skaldic poetry is a very important source material for the mythology of the Germanic north for two reasons: firstly, the skalds liked using mythological metaphors for their → kennings, which are often the sole extant indications of an otherwise unrecorded myth from heathen Scandinavia; this is not only limited to the early period of the 9th and 10th centuries, but is still applicable to the Christian High Middle Ages. Secondly, apart from runic inscriptions, skaldic poems are the oldest datable literary sources in Scandinavia which can be ascribed to an early period because of the mostly historically definable persons of the skalds themselves, even if the recording of the poems only occurred several centuries later in the 13th century. Admittedly, consideration should be given to the fact that in the skaldic verses recorded frequently in the Icelandic family sagas fakes from later times might have crept in. – Especially at the end of the heathen time, at the end of the 10th century, a strong heathen reaction against the Christian kingship in Norway had set in around the Norwegian earls of Hlaðir in Trondheim. This reaction was carried mostly by the (Icelandic) skalds (such as Einarr Skálaglamm, Tindr Hallkelsson, Eyvindr Skáldaspillir and Hallfreðr Ottarsson), and as a result of this their poetry preserves for us a collection of heathen- religious concepts (in the form of myth abbreviations given through kennings) from the end of the pre-Christian period, even if these might be influenced by the new religion of Christianity, partly by the reaction against the strengthening Christianity.

M. Kristensen, 'Skjaldenes Mytologi' (*APhSc* 5) 1930/31; L. M. Hollander, *Bibliography of Scaldic Studies*, Copenhagen 1958; J. de Vries, *Altnordische Literaturgeschichte*, Berlin [2]1964–67; A. Holtsmark, 'Skaldediktning' (*KLNM* 15) 1970; E. O. G. Turville-Petre, *Scaldic Poetry*, Oxford 1976; G. Kreutzer, *Die Dichtungslehre der Skalden*, Meisenheim [2]1977; R. Frank, *Old Norse Court Poetry. The Dróttkvætt Stanza*, Ithaca, N.Y. 1978 (= *Islandica* 42); K. v. See, *Skaldendichtung*, Munich 1980; F. Ström, 'Poetry as an instrument of propaganda' (*Speculum Norrœnum, Studies G. Turville-Petre*) Odense 1981; B. Fidjestøl, *Det norrøne fyrstediktet*, Øvre Ervik 1982.

Skáldskaparmál ('treatise on poetic art; poetics of skaldic poetry'). The second section of the → *Snorra Edda*. In this handbook for the study of skaldic poetry Snorri tells of numerous myths in order to explain the mythological → kennings which occur in ON poetry.

Skalli (ON, 'bald-headed one'). A giant in the *Þulur*.

Skalmǫld (ON, 'sword-time' = battle). A valkyrie in the *Þulur*.

Skaværr (ON, either 'the good-natured one' or 'the crooked one'). A dwarf in the *Þulur*.

Skáviðr (ON, also Skáfiðr, Skafiðr 'good tree' or 'slanting tree'?). A dwarf in *Vǫluspá* 15 and in the *Þulur*.

Skeggǫld or else Skeggjǫld (from ON *skeggja* 'battle-axe' and *ǫld* 'age, time', thus, 'axe-age' = 'battle'). The kenning-like name of a → valkyrie in *Grímnismál* 36, which like numerous other valkyrie names is actually a synonym for 'battle'.

Skeiðbrimir (ON, 'the one shining in contest' or 'the one puffing in the race'?). A mythical horse in the catalogue of horse-names in *Grímnismál* 30 and in the *Þulur*. Snorri (*Gylfaginning* 14) mentions Skeiðbrimir as being among the horses belonging to the Æsir.

Skelfir (ON). According to Snorri (*Skáldskaparmál* 62), this is the mythical ancestor of the royal house of the → Skilfingar; Skelfir is probably an aetiological invention of Snorri's.

Skerkir (ON 'noise-maker'). A giant in the *Þulur*.

Skíðblaðnir (ON). The ship of the god → Freyr; only in the *Ynglinga saga* 7 does it belong to Odin. It was built by dwarfs, the sons of Ivaldi (*Grímnismál* 43; *Gylfaginning* 42); Skíðblaðnir is not as big as the death-ship → Naglfar, but it is more cleverly built and has wonderful properties: it always has fair wind as soon as the sails are set, and it allows itself to be folded up like cloth and put into a bag; moreover, there is space for all the Æsir in full battle dress on board (*Gylfaginning* 42, *Skáldskaparmál* 35) and it is the very best of all ships.

In the religion of Bronze Age Scandinavia → ships played a central role, as can be seen on the rock carvings where the most frequent motif, apart from human figures, is the ship itself, at this time most likely a cult ship from the cult of one of the Vanir gods who were not only responsible for fertility but also for seafaring. The name Skíðblaðnir, which means 'assembled from pieces of thin wood', would fit well for a cult ship which was only built for the duration of festivities; a continuity between the ships of the rock carvings and the ship Skíðblaðnir of Eddic mythology is not unlikely as links are indeed traceable, and even Snorri's assignment of the ship to the fertility god, Freyr, speaks in favour of this connexion. Thus Skíðblaðnir is distinct from the non-Germanic concept of the ship of the gods in which the sun-god crosses the skies; the name of the ship → Hringhorni points to another link between ships and the sun. – However, if one were to associate the origin of the name Skíðblaðnir with the invention of a boat made of planks, then the ships on the rock carvings would be of no relevance, as plank-built boats are much younger. Skíðblaðnir's wonderful properties described in the *Snorra Edda* most likely arose from folklore. A ship with the same fairy-tale elements occurs in the very late *Samsons saga fagra* (14th century) which appears to have taken its ideas about this ship from Snorri.

B. Kahle, 'Altwestnordische Namensstudien' (*IF* 14) 1903; E. Magnússon, 'Notes on Ship-Building' (*Saga-Book* 4) 1905; O. Almgren, *Nordische Felszeichnungen*, Frankfurt 1936; J. de Vries, *Altgermanische Religionsgeschichte*, Berlin [3]1970; E. O. G. Turville-Petre, *Myth and Religion of the North*, Westport 1975; R. Simek, 'Skíðblaðnir' (*Northern Studies* 9) 1977; R. Simek, *Die Schiffsnamen*, Vienna 1982.

Skilfingar. The ON form of the Anglo-Saxon Scylfingas, which, in turn, is the name for the Swedish royal house of the Ynglings. Snorri (*Skáldskaparmál* 62) traced the Skilfingar back to an ancestor called Skelfir who is not mentioned elsewhere, although there may be a connexion with the name Skilfingr, which is one of Odin's names. Therefore, the question arises as to whether the Skilfingar are 'those coming from Skilfingr' = 'Odin's descendants'? As the Ynglings trace their own line back to Yngvi = Freyr, it is possible that the identification of Skilfingar = Ynglings is secondary; the Skilfingar are also mentioned in *Hyndluljóð* 16 and in the *Flateyjarbók* as a dynasty, but the connexion is unclear in both cases.

Skilfingr (ON, 'the one who lives on a mountain'). A name for Odin in *Grímnismál* 54. It may be that Skilfingr has some ancestral connexion with the legendary royal house of the Skilfingar (= Ynglings?). If the name Skilfingr is present in the names → Hliðskjálf and Válaskjálf (a cult place-name to Odin's son Váli?) then these names could refer to a cult centred on Odin and his descendants (Turville-Petre).

D. v. Kralik, 'Niblung, Schilbung und Balmung' (*Wiener Prähistorische Zeitschrift* 19) 1932; E. O. G. Turville-Petre, *Myth and Religion of the North*, Westport 1975.

Skinfaxi (ON, 'light-horse'). The horse which pulls daylight, according to *Vafþrúðnismál* 12, whereas the horse which brings the night is called Hrímfaxi. In *Gylfaginning* 9

Snorri tells the mythological fable of day and night (Dagr and Nótt): 'Nótt rides on the horse called Hrímfaxi, and every morning it drops dew onto the earth from its bit dripping with spittle; Dag's horse is called Skinfaxi and all the air and earth is lit up by his mane.'

Skírnir (ON). Servant and messenger of the god, Freyr. Skírnir is the protagonist of the Eddic lay → *Skírnismál* in which Skírnir woos the beautiful giant's daughter → Gerðr for Freyr. In the *Snorra Edda* (*Gylfaginning* 36) Skírnir is said to be Freyr's messenger and the mythical lay of Gerðr's wooing is retold (*Gylfaginning* 33). The name Skírnir, actually 'shining one' (from ON *skírr* 'clean, clear'), is certainly connected to his function as the messenger of the sun-god, Freyr.

Skírnismál (ON, 'lay of Skírnir'), also *Skírnisfǫr* (or *Fǫr Skírnis* 'Skírnir's journey'). A mythological lay in the *Codex Regius* which tells of Freyr's wooing of the giant's daughter, Gerðr. Freyr has fallen in love with Gerðr and sends his servant Skírnir, to whom he gives his horse and sword, to woo her for him. As her reactions to his advances leave much to be desired and she does not even rise to Skírnir's bait of 11 golden apples (*epli ellifo allgullin*) and the ring Draupnir, he has to force her to agree with the threat of magic runes (*Þurs ríst ec þér oc þriá stafi, ergi oc œði oc óþola* 'I will carve a Þurs (= *th*-rune) for you and three staves, shame, madness and restlessness': stanza 36). After ten days the first meeting with Freyr is to take place in the grove called Barri, and Freyr complains longingly in the last stanza about the length of this interval. The lay is introduced by a short prose passage and the 42 stanzas which are composed in the *ljóðaháttr* metre and present the whole chain of events in dialogue form. Ever since Niedner's and Olsen's considerations, the *Skírnismál* has been interpreted as being the poetic presentation of the → *hierós gámos* in which the sun and fertility god Freyr united with the earth goddess Gerðr. According to this, the *Skírnismál* would be a cult lay which was possibly even enacted dramatically at Freyr-festivals at the beginning of spring. Olsen's interpretation rests predominantly on a chthonic interpretation of the names of Gerðr and her father Gymir in which he relates Gerðr to ON *garðr* 'fenced in field'. Sahlgren and others since have repeatedly doubted this, since the name Gerðr cannot be traced back to an earth goddess (Sahlgren) and *garðr* and its cognates do not mean the 'fertile field' but rather a 'fenced in place' (Motz). Sahlgren's interpretation of *Skírnismál* as the myth of the daughter of the sea giant is not convincing, however, and even Lönnroth's theory of his one-sided, profane understanding of the myth should be similarly rejected. Motz, on the other hand, sees the *Skírnismál* as the representation of a conflict between the masculine dynasty of the Æsir and a dynasty of giants symbolizing the female powers. Nevertheless, this interpretation fails basically because Freyr does not appear as a warlike conqueror anywhere else, a stance which also totally contradicts the languishing tone of the *Skírnismál*. Thus, despite the etymological problems, Olsen's interpretation of the mythical marriage between the fertility god and earth seems to be the most illuminating. – The dating of the lay differs, depending on the interpretation of the mythical-cult function of the lay, between the late heathen period and the 12th century. *Lokasenna* 42 and *Hyndluljóð* 30 refer to the *Skírnismál*. In the *Ynglinga saga* 10 Gerðr is called Frey's wife and Fjǫlnir is listed as her son. The *Snorra Edda* refers to *Skírnismál* in its account of Ragnarǫk (*Gylfaginning* 50) because of Freyr's lost sword; in *Gylfaginning* 36 Snorri relates the content of the myths in which he cites the last stanza, the only recording of this in extant sources. Snorri surely added the name of Gerð's mother → Aurboða according to a probably more complete version of the *Skírnismál*, as this information is also referred to in *Hyndluljóð* 30, although again, this is the only source for it.

ED: G. Neckel, H. Kuhn, *Edda*, Heidelberg [5]1983.
Lit.: F. Niedner, 'Skírnis Fǫr' (*ZfdA* 30) 1886; M. Olsen, 'Fra gammelnorsk mythe og kultus' (MoM) 1909; J. Sahlgren, 'Skírnismál' (in: *Eddica et scaldica*) Lund 1928; U. Dronke, 'Art and Tradition in Skírnismál' (*English and Mediaeval Studies, pres. to Tolkien*) Oxford 1962; A. Holtsmark, 'Skírnismál' (*KLNM* 15) 1970; L. Lönnroth, 'Skírnismál och den fornisländska äktenskapsnormen' (*Opuscula Septentrionalia, Festskrift O. Widding*), Copenhagen 1977; L. Motz, 'Gerðr' (MoM) 1981; S. A. Mitchell, 'Fǫr Scírnis as Mythological Model: frið at kaupa' (*ANF* 98) 1983; J. Randlev, 'Skírnismál' (MoM) 1985; P. Bibire, 'Freyr and Gerðr: the story and its myths' (*Sagnaskemmtun. Studies H. Pálsson*) 1986; G. Steinsland, *Det hellig bryllup og norrøn kongeideologi*, Oslo 1991.

R: J. Møller, *Skirners Reise* (Gedicht, 1806); A. Oehlenschläger, *Skirnirs Reise* (Gedicht in *Nordens Guder*, 1819).

Skírnis fǫr *Skírnismál*.

Skirvir, also Skirfir or Skirpir (ON, 'the spitter' from *skirpa?*). A dwarf in the *Vǫluspá* 15 and in the *Þulur*.

Skjalf (ON). The daughter of a Finnish king in Snorri's *Ynglinga saga* 14 who marries the legendary king Agni whom she strangles with a necklace. According to the *Þulur*, Skjalf is one of the names for Freyja. Apart from this, nothing else is told about her in the extant sources but the tale of the strangling of Agni with a necklace suggests a parallel with Freyja's necklace → Brísingamen, which was perhaps the reason for Skjalf's inclusion as a name for Freyja in the *Þulur*. Schröder's interpretation that Agni's strangling and subsequent hanging suggested 'a tree-sacrifice' to the goddess Skjalf-Freyja is totally unfounded. Similarly, although he identifies Skjalf with Skaði, thus trying to trace the dynasty of the Skilfingar back to Skjalf, this identification is not convincing.

E. Björkman, 'Skjalf och Skilfing' (*NoB* 7) 1919; F. R. Schröder, *Skadi und die Götter Skandinaviens*, Tübingen 1941; K. E. Gade, 'Skjalf' (*ANF* 100) 1985.

Skjǫldr (ON, 'shield'). According to Scandinavian tradition, Skjǫldr is the mythical ancestor of the dynasty of the Skjǫldungs (OE *Scyldingas*). In Snorri (Prologue to his *Edda*) a Skjǫldr is named as Odin's ancestor (probably in accordance with the OE and Danish tradition of Odin's ascendency), but otherwise, even in Snorri's writings (Prologue 4, *Skáldskaparmál* 40 and 62), Skjǫldr is Odin's son and the first Danish king. Saxo (*Gesta Danorum* I, 11f.) gives a detailed account of Skjǫldr's life and thereby shows certain parallels to the description of → Scyld in OE *Beowulf*: both distinguish themselves in their youth, are great plunderers, subdue other kings and both have a famous son, Gram and Beowulf respectively. In the *Ynglinga saga*, Snorri makes Skjǫldr the husband of the giantess Gefjon. Despite the age and popularity of the tradition of Skjǫldr as the ancestor of the Skjǫldungs, it is nonetheless likely that the name Skjǫldr is an aetiological derivation from the name of the Danish royal house of the Skjǫldungs/Scyldingas which probably originally only meant 'shieldmen, Danish warriors'.

P. Herrmann, *Die Heldensagen des Saxo Grammaticus*, Leipzig 1922; H. E. Davidson, P. Fisher, *Saxo Grammaticus: The History of the Danes*, Cambridge 1980.

Skjǫldungs. The dynasty of Danish kings during the Migration Age of the 4th and

5th centuries A.D. whose historical significance and fame have been glorified in heroic poetry. In spite of the old Danish heroic lays no longer being extant, the tales have been passed down through the OE *Beowulf* and *Widsith* as well as Saxo's Latin history of the Danes and the ON *Skjǫldunga saga.* In all the various branches of the tradition, Skjǫldr is the eponymous ancestor of the line which can be traced back to Odin which suggests the predominating tendency of Germanic dynasties to a legitimization of their rule by means of divine descendency.

Skǫgull (ON). A → valkyrie (*Vǫluspá* 30, *Grímnismál* 36) whose name means 'battle' as so many other names of valkyries do.

Skǫll (ON, 'mockery'). The name given in *Grímnismál* 39 and Snorri (*Gylfaginning* 11) to the wolf who pursues the sun in its course across the sky and will finally devour it. Whereas it is possible that Skǫll is merely another name for → Fenrir, there could be a nature-mythological interpretation in the case of Skǫll and Hati (who pursues the moon). Such an interpretation would see the phenomen of parhelions reflected in the wolves as these are called 'sun-wolf' in Scandinavian languages (Norwegian *solvarg*, Swedish *solulv*).

J. de Vries, *Altgermanische Religionsgeschichte*, Berlin [3]1970.

R: the mythological scene of the sun and the moon being pursued by Skǫll and Hati is illustrated in J. C. Dollmann's painting *The wolves pursuing Sol and Mani.*

Skrati (ON, 'troll'). A giant in the *Þulur.*

Skríkja (ON, 'the screamer'). The name of a giantess in the *Þulur.*

Skrýmir (ON, 'boaster'). A giant who is the opponent of Thor on his journey to → Utgarðaloki (who is identical with Skrýmir). Snorri retells the myth about Thor and Skrýmir in some detail (*Gylfaginning* 44): Thor and Loki are on their way to Jǫtunheim, accompanied by the peasant children, Þjálfi and Rǫskva, who are Thor's servants. In search of a night's accommodation, they find a gigantic hall with a mighty entrance where they spend the night. On being woken up around midnight by an earthquake, they go further into the hall until they reach a room just off the hall in which they finally go to sleep again. In the morning they leave the building and see a giant sleeping not far away who calls himself Skrýmir and tells them that they spent the night in his mitten and that the side-room was the thumb. Skrýmir offers to accompany them and carries all their provisions in his rucksack. In the evening when the giant is asleep, Thor tries in vain to undo the knapsack with the food and is so angry at his lack of success that he decides to kill the giant with his hammer Mjǫllnir; the giant wakes up, however, and thinks that a leaf has fallen onto his head; two further attempts during the night remain similarly unsuccessful. Early in the morning Skrýmir leaves the travellers and heads northward while Thor and his companions go east, making for Utgarðaloki. When they arrive at the home of Utgarðaloki and his giants they are urged to take part in some contests, during which Loki is challenged to an eating competition by the giant → Logi, Þjálfi to a race by the giant → Hugi. Thor himself is unable to empty Utgarðaloki's drinking horn in three draughts, cannot pick up his cat from the ground and loses the wrestling match with his old wet-nurse Elli. Only on the next day does Utgarðaloki explain to Thor that he was beaten by magic and that Utgarðaloki himself was the giant Skrýmir. Thor's failures are now explained:

the rucksack was fastened with iron wire and Thor's three blows with the hammer did not hit Skrýmir's head, but three hills in which he left deep valleys; Loki was beaten at eating by Logi, the 'wild fire' which eats everything, and Þjálfi was beaten in the race by Hugi ('thought'); the drinking horn reached down to the sea and Thor's draughts merely caused the ebb to occur; the cat was really the Midgard serpent surrounding the earth and Thor was beaten in the wrestling match by Elli 'age' since everyone is overcome by age at some point. When Thor wants to take revenge on Utgarðaloki for these tricks, he and his castle suddenly disappear into thin air.

Apart from Snorri's detailed account, only *Lokasenna* (60 and 62) and *Hárbarðsljóð* (26; here the giant is called Fjallarr) refer to the story of Skrýmir, his rucksack and his mittens which is, however, no absolute proof for the great age of the mythical tale. The great significance of the fairy-tale elements and the word-play could point to the fact that the story was only later (perhaps even originally from Snorri) compiled out of older fairy-tales and mythical remnants. On the other hand there are non-Germanic parallels in Russian and Ossetic legends (→ Utgarðaloki) which have a very similar sequence of events so that the possibility cannot be excluded that Snorri's tale about Skrýmir was indeed based on a pagan myth.

C. W. v. Sydow, 'Jättarna i mytologi och folktro' (*Folkminnen och Folktankar* 6) 1919; G. Dumézil, 'Legendes sur les Nartes' (*Rev. d l'hist. des religiones* 125) 1943; N. K. Chadwick, 'The Russian Giant Svyatogor and the Norse Utgarða-Loki' (*Folklore* 75) 1964; J. de Vries, *Altgermanische Religionsgeschichte*, Berlin ^{3}1970.

R: (literature) A. Oehlenschläger: *Thors Reise til Jotunheim* (epical poem, 1807); W. Hertz, *Thor kam als Gast ins Riesenland* (1859), W. Hertz, *Thors Trunk* (1859).
(fine art) E. Doepler d. J., *Thor bei Skrymir* (E. Doepler, W. Ranisch, *Walhall*, 1901); J. C. Dollman, *Thor and the mountain* (painting).

Skuld (1) (ON, 'blame'; perhaps 'future'?). One of the three → norns in Snorri (*Gylfaginning* 14) following *Vǫluspá* 20; the other two are called Urd and Verdandi.

R: Klopstock composed an ode, entitled *Skulda*, to this norn in 1766.

Skuld (2) (ON, 'blame'). A → valkyrie in *Vǫluspá* 30.

Sleipnir (ON, 'Slipper, Sliding one'). Odin's eight-legged horse. According to Snorri in his tale of → the giant master builder (*Gylfaginning* 41; cf. *Hyndluljóð* 40) Loki (as a mare) conceived Sleipnir from the giant stallion Svaðilfari. Snorri calls Sleipnir the best of all the gods' horses (*Gylfaginning* 14; cf. *Grímnismál* 44), on his ride to Hel, → Hermóðr is able to jump over the fence around Hel riding on Sleipnir (*Gylfaginning* 48). Odin also is said to ride the horse to Hel (*Baldrs draumar* 2). When Haddingus rides with Odin on Sleipnir, he sees the sea lying beneath him (Saxo, *Gesta Danorum* I, 24). *Sigrdrífumál* 15 refers to runes on Sleipnir's teeth. Although Sleipnir is repeatedly referred to in the Eddic lays the horse is rarely mentioned in skaldic poetry which suggests that the name is quite young, perhaps only originating as the name of Odin's horse towards the end of the 10th century. The story of Loki giving birth to Sleipnir was probably only an invention of Snorri's.

Sleipnir is grey and has eight legs, as later sources all record (Snorri, *Gylfaginning* 41; *Hervarar saga*, stanza 72). However, Odin is portrayed astride an eight-legged horse on Gotland pictorial stones from as early as the 8th century (Tjängvide; Ardre), although this is not the case with other pictures of Odin on horseback. It might, therefore, be supposed that on the Gotland stones the eight legs merely serve to give the impression of speed, and that the pictorial tradition paved the way for the eight-legged horse in literary tradition.

Not only is Odin frequently portrayed pictorially on horseback, but also two of his numerous pseudonyms point to his connexion with horses: Hrósshársgrani ('Horse-hair beard') and Jálkr ('gelding'). It is questionable whether these might point to a cultic significance of the horse. The cultic origin of the eight legged Sleipnir (because he was represented by four young men: Höfler) is not totally convincing. Nevertheless, the traditional natural-mythological interpretation of Sleipnir as being the wind, whose eight legs represent the eight directions of the heavens, and which grazes in the branches of the world-tree Yggdrasill (e.g. Magnusson), is dismissable.

E. Magnússon, *Odin's Horse Yggdrasil*, London 1885; E. Magnusson, 'Yggdrasil' (*ANF* 13) 1897; F. Detter, 'Erwiderung' (*ANF* 13) 1897; G. Gjessing, 'Hesten i førhistorisk kunst og kultus' (*Viking*) 1943; J. de Vries, *Altgermanische Religionsgeschichte*, Berlin ³1970; A, Holtsmark, 'Sleipnir' (*KLNM* 16) 1971; E. O. G. Turville-Petre, *Myth and Religion of the North*, Westport 1975.

R: Odin is rarely shown riding on Sleipnir in artistic representation. An exception is Dagfinn Werenskiold's wooden relief *Odin på Sleipner* (1945–50) in Oslo town hall.
(literature) R. Kipling, *'Sleipnir' late 'Thurinda'* (short story, 1888).
(other) In Icelandic folklore the horseshoe-shaped gorge Asbyrgi in northern Iceland is an imprint of Sleipnir's hoof. Rather surprisingly, Sleipnir was and is still frequently used in naming ships (cf. Kipling's story quoted above), especially in Germany and Norway. One of the oilfields between Norway and Scotland was also called Sleipner (1983/84).

Slíðr (ON, 'dangerously sharp'). One of the rivers of the underworld in *Vǫluspá* 36 (and in the catalogue of rivers in *Grímnismál* 28). It is described as follows: 'A river called Slíðr, which is full of daggers and swords, flows from the east out of the valley of poison.' According to Snorri, Slíðr is one of the mythical Élivágar rivers (*Gylfaginning* 3). Weapon-bearing rivers such as this are also found in Saxo, *Gesta Danorum* I, 31 and in the river name Geirvimull ('river bubbling with spears': *Grímnismál* 27) and come from the influence of Christian visionary literature where such rivers belong to the standard inventory of descriptions of the Other World.

Dietrich, 'Die deutsche Wasserhölle' (*ZfdA* 9) 1853.

Slíðrugtanni (ON, 'the one with the dangerously sharp tusks'). One of the names of the boar → Gullinborsti, only mentioned in Snorri (*Gylfaginning* 48 and *Skáldskaparmál* 7). As Snorri only invented the name Gullinborsti as a result of an older kenning, it seems possible that the name Slíðrugtanni is of a similar origin.

Snær (ON, 'snow'). A legendary king in the pre-history of Norway according to Old Icelandic texts (*Hversu Nóregr byggðisk* in the *Flateyjarbók* and *Fundinn Nóregr* at the beginning of the *Orkneyinga saga*). Snær is Frosti's (or Jǫkul's) and Kári's son and as such one of → Fornjótr's descendants, whose genealogy is similar to that of the mythological frost giant families. It appears, therefore, that Snær was originally a frost giant, possibly even a personification of snow.

P. Herrmann, *Die Heldensagen des Saxo Grammaticus*, Leipzig 1922; J. de Vries, *Altgermanische Religionsgeschichte*, Berlin ³1970.

Snakes. Even if we cannot speak of an distinct snake cult, snakes would appear to ve had a not insignificant symbolic value in the religious life of the Germanic peoples, in particular in the Bronze Age (de Vries). Snakes were frequently drawn on rock carvings and cult razor blades, sometimes even as horse-headed snakes which pull the sun.

In one myth Odin turns himself into a snake in order to reach the giantess Gunnlǫð, → Mead of the skalds.

Snakes were presumably a symbol in an early fertility cult and the connexion with the → Midgard serpent and the dragon → Niðhǫggr which gnaws at the roots of the world-ash Yggdrasill could possibly reveal a significance in the cult of the dead.

E. F. Halvorsen, 'Niðhǫggr' (*KLNM* 12) 1967; J. de Vries, *Altgermanische Religionsgeschichte*, Berlin [3]1970.

Snio (Lat.). Legendary king in Saxo (*Gesta Danorum* VIII, 281f.), → Snær.

Snjór → Snær.

Snorra Edda ('Snorri's → *Edda*'). A didactic work about the art of skaldic poetry, written around 1220 by → Snorri Sturluson. The work is divided into three sections: the → *Gylfaginning*, a presentation of pagan mythology; the → *Skáldskaparmál*, a book teaching about → *kenningar*; and the *Háttatal*, a list of 102 stanzas in 100 different forms with metrical commentary. The whole book is introduced by a short prologue. The *Skáldskaparmál* contains comments on mythology, since a knowledge of this was essential for skaldic verse because of the numerous mythological kennings. The *Gylfaginning* presents, however, a systematic presentation of Old Scandinavian mythology and therefore makes the *Snorra Edda* the most important source for Germanic mythology. Nonetheless, Snorri's presentation is not unadulterated, not only because of the possible Christian influences, but also because of Snorri's own creativity in the handling and combination of myths known to him. Snorri's role in writing the *Snorra Edda* has been appraised in different ways in the course of the history of scholarly research; at the beginning of the 19th century Simrock and Grimm considered it to be a pure source of Old Norse religion, and even towards the end of the 19th century Bugge saw no reason to doubt the case. Mogk, on the other hand, saw Snorri in particular as a creative literary artist and as an author of mythical stories which could hardly be used as sources for Old Germanic religion, a view subsequently shared by Baetke.

Dumézil, on the other hand, came to Snorri's rescue and Turville-Petre, de Vries and Holtsmark all show a cautiously positive attitude towards Snorri's mythographical competence. Holtsmark pointed out three levels in Snorri's mythology: the heathen *Weltbild*, the Christian *Weltbild*, and Snorri's combination of them both.

However, Schier has recently remarked yet again that Christian thoughts had already flowed into Snorri's Eddic and skaldic sources. This presents complex problems for criticism of the sources, as not all influences can be traced back to Snorri. Despite many questions, the *Snorra Edda* retains its intrinsic value as a source of Germanic mythology.

Editions: *Edda Snorra Sturlusonar* 1–3, Hafniæ 1848–1887; F. Jónsson, *Snorri Sturluson, Edda*, Copenhagen 1900; F. Jónsson, *Edda Snorra Sturlusonar*, Copenhagen 1931.

Bibliographies: H. Hermansson, *Bibliography of the Eddas*, Ithaca, N.Y. 1920, reprint 1966 (= *Islandica* 13); H. Hermansson, *Bibliography of the Eddas. A Supplement*, Ithaca, N.Y. 1955 (= Islandica 37); G. W. Weber, 'Edda, jüngere' (*Hoops* 5) [2]1985–87.

Lit.: J. Grimm, *Deutsche Mythologie*, Berlin 1835. K. Simrock, *Handbuch der deutschen Mythologie mit Einschluß der nordischen*, Bonn 1853; S. Bugge, *Studier over de nordiske Gude- og Heltesagns Oprindelse*, Christiania 1881–89; A. Heusler, *Die gelehrte Urgeschichte im altnordischen Schrifttum*, Berlin 1908; E. Mogk, *Novellistische Darstellung mythologischer Stoffe Snorris und seiner Schule*,

Helsinki 1923; E. Mogk, *Zur Bewertung der Snorra Edda als religionsgeschichtliche und mythologische Quelle des nordgermanischen Heidentums*, Leipzig 1923; E. Mogk, 'Die Überlieferung von Thors Kampf mit dem Riesen Geirrǫd' (*Festschrift H. Pipping*), Helsingfors 1924; E. Mogk, *Lokis Anteil an Balders Tod*, Helsinki 1925; E. Mogk, *Zur Gigantomachie der Vǫluspá*, Helsinki 1925; R. C. Boer, 'Studien über die Snorra Edda' (*APhSc* 1) 1926; F. v. d. Leyen, *Die Götter der Germanen*, Munich 1938; B. Pering, *Heimdall*, Lund 1941; D. O. Zetterholm, *Studier i en Snorre-Text*, Stockholm/Copenhagen 1949; W. Baetke, *Die Götterlehre der Snorra Edda*, Berlin 1950; S. Beyschlag, 'Die Betörung Gylfis' (*ZfdA* 85) 1954; A. Holtsmark, *Studier i norrøn diktning*, Oslo 1956; A. Holtsmark, 'Den yngre Edda' (*KLNM* 3) 1958; E. O. G. Turville-Petre, *Myth and Religion of the North*, London 1964; A. Holtsmark, *Studier i Snorres mytologi*, Oslo 1964; J. de Vries, *Altgermanische Religionsgeschichte*, Berlin [3]1970; K. Schier, 'Zur Mythologie der Snorra Edda: Einige Quellenprobleme' (*Speculum Norrœnum. Studies G. Turville-Petre*) Odense 1981; G. W. Weber, 'Edda, Jüngere' (*Hoops* 6) [2]1986; M. Clunies Ross, *Skáldskaparmál*, Odense 1987; K. v. See, *Mythos und Theologie im skandinavischen Hochmittelalter*, Heidelberg 1988.

Snorri Sturluson, Icelandic scholar and politician (1179 Hvamm – 1241 Rekjaholt). Snorri belonged to the Sturlung family, the most influential family in Iceland at the beginning of the 13th century. We know a lot about Snorri's life from the *Sturlunga saga* ('the story of the Sturlung family') which was written towards the end of the 13th century. From 1215 to 1219 Snorri was the law speaker, and as such held the highest office in Iceland. Following this period of office he travelled to Norway (c.1220) where he negotiated a peaceful integration of Iceland into the Norwegian kingdom with King Hakon; a plan which made him many enemies in Iceland, and which caused him to fall out of Hakon's favour when the plan came to nothing. Nevertheless, Snorri was called upon to be the law speaker from 1222 to 1231 and in 1237 he undertook a second journey to Norway. His life was brought to a sudden end on the night of September 23, 1241, when he was murdered for political motives by his son-in-law, Gizurr.

It is not as a politician that Snorris is remembered today but on a literary level. He was a prolific writer, and the author of the *Heimskringla* (a history of the Norwegian kings), *Olafs saga*, and possibly also *Egils saga*, but he is best known for his *Edda*, a didactic book for skalds known as the → *Snorra Edda* ('Snorri's *Edda*'). In the parts of this work entitled → *Skáldskaparmál* and *Háttatal*, he gave the rules of skaldic poetry, giving numerous examples. The → *Gylfaginning* offers a scholarly portrayal of Old Norse mythology, which is admittedly heavily influenced by Christian education, but remains nonetheless our most important source for North Germanic mythology.

G. Vigfusson (ed.), *Sturlunga saga*. I–II, Oxford 1878; H. Naumann, *Versuch über Snorri Sturluson*, Bonn 1943; S. Nordal, *Snorri Sturluson*, Reykjavík 1920; Jón Jóhannesson, *Islendinga saga*, Manitoba 1974; S. Hauksdottir, 'Snorri Sturluson og konungsvaldið' (*Mimir* 21) 1974; G. Turville-Petre, *Origins of Icelandic Literature*, Oxford 1975; J. Simon, 'Snorri, His Life and Times' (*Parergon* 15) 1976; M. Ciklamini, *Snorri Sturluson*, Boston 1978.

Snotra (ON, 'the clever one'). A goddess in Snorri (*Gylfaginning* 34) and in the *Þulur*, whose name is not mentioned elsewhere. Snorri calls this Æsir goddess 'clever and well behaved'. Snotra is possibly an invention of Snorri's whom he derived from *snotr* 'clever' and placed next to other insignificant goddesses.

Sœkin (ON, 'the one who pushes forward'). One of the mythical rivers in the river catalogue in *Grímnismál* 27 and in the *Þulur*.

Sǫkkmímir (ON, 'Mímir the deep' or 'the warlike Mímir'). A giant according to *Þulur* and *Ynglingatal* 2. In *Grímnismál* 50 it is clear that he is involved with one of Odin's exploits. It is uncertain if Sǫkkmímir is really identical with → Mímir in this context, but the name is not unsuitable for a being which lives in a spring.

J. Simpson, 'Mímir: Two Myths or One?' (*Saga Book* 16) 1962.

Sǫkkvabekkr (ON, 'sunken bank' or 'treasure bank'). One of the gods' residences, which according to *Grímnismál* 7 belongs to both Odin and the goddess Sága in *Grímnismál* 7. In Snorri (*Gylfaginning* 34) it only belongs to Sága.

Sǫnnungr (ON, 'the true one'?). A name given in the *Þulur* to the god Thor.

Sól (ON, 'sun'). According to Eddic mythology, Sol is one of the Æsir goddesses, but in fact she is only the personification of the sun and only played a role in poetry. Basing his tale on two Eddic stanzas (*Grímnismál* 37 and *Vafþrúðnismál* 23), Snorri relates the following tale in *Gylfaginning* 10: 'A man called Mundifari had two children; they were so fair and pretty that he called his son Moon, and his daughter Sun; he gave her in marriage to a man called Glenr. The gods were angry about this impudence and they took the brother and sister and set them in the sky. They made Sól drive the horses which pulled the chariot of the sun which the gods had created to illuminate the world from a spark which had flown from Muspellsheimr. These horses are called Arvakr and Alsviðr. Under the shoulders of the horses the gods fastened two bellows to cool them and in some sources this is called "Iron cooling". Sól is pursued over the sky by a wolf called Hati, and the moon by a wolf called Skǫll' (*Gylfaginning* 11 following *Grímnismál* 39).

There is much evidence for a devotion to the sun in the Bronze Age (rock carvings; sun chariot of Trundholm), and certainly as a life giving heavenly body, the sun probably always received a certain veneration. It is only evident from the occurrence of the Æsir goddess Sól in Old Norse literature and the goddess Sunna in the Second Merseburg Charm that it was also considered to be a divine person, but both these occurrences are insufficient evidence to assume a sun cult. On the other hand the great age of the concept is evident from the Trundholm chariot, which supports the idea recorded by Snorri and *Grímnismál*, namely that the sun is drawn across the sky by horses. The combination of sun symbols with the ship in cult contexts, which occurs frequently from the Bronze Age to medieval times, seem to go back to a cult of a fertility god (Njǫrðr or Freyr), hardly however to a personified sun.

J. de Vries, *Altgermanische Religionsgeschichte*, Berlin [3]1970; A. Holtsmark, 'Sól' (*KLNM* 16) 1971; R. Simek, 'Skíðblaðnir' (*Northern Studies* 9) 1977.

Sólbjartr (ON, 'sun-bright'). The father of the hero, Svipdagr, according to *Fjǫlsvinnsmál* 47.

Sólblindi (ON, 'the sun-blind one'). Possibly a dwarf in *Fjǫlsvinnsmál* 10. The interpretation that Sólblindi is a dwarf seems to be likely as his three sons are said to have forged the gate (Þrymgjǫll) to Menglǫð's residence. The name fits the dwarfs who are blinded by the sun (or who even turn to stone in sunlight).

Sómr (ON). A giant in the *Þulur*. The name is unclear; perhaps it is cognate to *sómi* 'honour', less likely to *sómr* 'bow'.

F. Jónsson, 'Þulur' (*APhSc* 9) 1934.

Són (ON). According to Snorri, Són is one of the vessels in which the dwarfs Fjalarr and Galarr collect the blood of the giant Kvasir (*Skáldskaparmál* 1); in this version of the myth of → mead of the skalds they use the vessels Són and Boðn, as well as the cauldron Óðrœrir. However, it is most likely that Són was originally the cauldron in which the Æsir and the Vanir mixed their spittle at the conclusion of peace following the Vanir wars. It was from this spittle that Kvasir was then created. The etymology of the name, probably cognate to OHG *suona, sôna* 'reconciliation, atonement', supports this theory.

Sonargǫltr (ON, 'sacrificial boar'). A boar in Old Scandinavian cult. *Helgakviða Hjǫrvarðssonar* 4 Pr and *Hervarar saga* 10 record that on Yule evening hands were laid on the back of this boar whilst an oath (*heitstrenging*) was sworn and Sonargǫltr was then sacrificed in a *sonarblót* ('Sonar-sacrifice') to assure a good harvest. In the *Ynglinga saga* 18 the *sonarblót* is held as an oracle (*til frétts*).

Whereas earlier Sonargǫltr used to be interpreted as meaning 'atonement boar, atonement sacrifice', Sievers' suggestion that Sonargǫltr actually means nothing more than 'herd boar, leading boar' has been generally accepted. The *sonarblót*, the sacrifice of the boar, was originally unquestionably a sacrifice to the fertility god Freyr, whose attribute was a boar → Gullinborsti.

E. Sievers, 'Sonargǫltr' (*PBB* 16) 1892; A. Holtsmark, 'Sonargǫltr' (*KLNM* 16) 1971.

Soul. There is no direct reference to the concept of a soul separate from the body in our sources for Germanic religion. Nevertheless, it is apparent from various religious ideas that at least the North Germanic peoples seem to have had a concept closely related to a belief in the soul. In this belief only living people had a soul and the belief in a soul played no role in → death and life after death (→ *draugr*). The concept of a shadow soul which separates itself from the body after death (a belief held by the Ancient Greeks) is unknown in Germanic beliefs.

The concept of a soul, detachable (or perhaps even totally separate) from the body, is most clearly seen in the northern belief in → *fylgjur*. These occur in the shape of animals or in the shape of the person to whom this 'soul' (*fylgja*) belongs, and they are very closely connected with his fate, becoming visible at critical points in his life (at least according to saga literature). However, the existence of the *fylgja* also ends with the death of the person. The *hamingjur* appear to have been soul-like beings related in some way to *fylgjur*. It is extremely questionable whether we can draw upon the shape-changing into animal shapes in the sagas as evidence for a belief in a soul, and it is an over-interpretation of the sources to call the custom of passing on the name to a grandchild, evident in medieval Scandinavia, a re-birth.

H. Falk, '"Sjelen" i Hedentroen' (MoM) 1926; E. Mandl, *Über den Seelen- und Jenseitsglauben der alten Skandinavier*, Diss. Wien 1927; G. Neckel, *Walhall*, Dortmund 1931; H.-J. Klare, 'Die Toten in der altnordischen Literatur' (*APhSc* 8) 1933/34; H. R. Ellis, *The Road to Hel*, Cambridge 1943; Å. V. Ström, H. Biezais, *Germanische und baltische Religion*, Stuttgart 1975; D. Strömbäck, 'The concept of Soul in Nordic Tradition' (*Arv* 31) 1975.

Sources of Germanic mythology. The earliest sources for the religion of early northern Europe are found on Bronze Age → rock carvings which undoubtedly reveal religious features. However, it is questionable if we can call the people who left these traces of their cult (or rather, cults) Germanic without any limitation. The reason for this is that over the period of at least two millenium during which the rock carvings were made essential changes also took place in the religion, and so it is impossible to draw final conclusions about any particular stage. Archaeological finds also give us a great deal of information about religious concepts: of foremost importance here are the burial finds which indicate the religious attitude of the people involved with regard to → burial traditions and thus to their concepts of a life after death. In addition to this there are also votive gifts which were left, usually in a deliberately broken state, to honour a particular god. In third place with regard to archaeological sources come the finds made in various places of → cult objects which do not only give information about the cult by their function and decoration, but also, more rarely, even about the gods who were worshipped there. – A further non-literary source is the evidence offered by → place-names, insofar as they contain theophorous elements or else references to former cult places. – The oldest written sources are the names of the gods written on ancient votive stones (→ matrons) and information from classical authors. → Tacitus' *Germania* (written c.98 A.D.), Caesar's *De bello Gallico* (c.50 B.C.) and *De bello Gothico* by Procopius (died c.558) are of particular interest, but in addition to these there are further references to Germanic religion in Ammianus Marcellinus, Vellejus Paterculus, Strabo, Sueton, Plutarch and many more. Furthermore, there are numerous references concerning the religion of the Germanic peoples in the writings of the European clerics from late classical times until the High Middle Ages: especially, Paulus Orosius' *Historia* (after 410), Jordanes' work *De origine actibusque Getarum* (551), Gregory of Tour's *Historia Francorum* (591), Venerable Bede's *Historia ecclesiastica gentis Anglorum* (731), Paul the Deacon's *Historia Langobardorum* (after 787), Alcuin's works (died in 804) and the *Res gestae Saxonicae* written by Widukind of Corvey (c.967). In addition to these there are various legends of the saints and other information concerning the missionaries to the Germanic peoples, such as Willibald, Columban, Bonifatius and Ansgar. Two of the most important works are those by Adam of Bremen in his *Gesta Hammaburgensis Ecclesiae Pontificum* (c.1072) and also the extremely important work compiled by the Dane → Saxo Grammaticus at the beginning of the 13th century, *Gesta Danorum*. The oldest written documents in a Germanic language are the → runic inscriptions dating from the heathen period in the 2nd century. The majority of these are concerned more with → magic than religion but nevertheless they hand down to us valuable information, in particular formulae of blessing and protection. Also extant are → spells handed down to us from southern Germanic regions.

Although we have sources, however sparse, for most areas settled by Germanic peoples, the richest sources we have dealing with religion and mythology are those concerning the North Germanic peoples and are found in Medieval Icelandic literature. Indeed, the most unique sources for Germanic religion are the → mythological lays of the *Edda*. Skaldic poetry, which partly reaches back to heathen times, as well as the systematic presentation of Germanic mythology given in the → *Snorra Edda*, must be viewed with discretion and even then it will not always lead to the oldest layers of Germanic religion. Even though the Icelandic → sagas contain frequent references to the heathen religion of their forefathers, the relatively late composition dates (13th and 14th centuries) and the predominantly literary character of these works make them hardly usable as reliable sources as we must constantly reckon here with the dominating influence of Medieval scholarship and thus with scholarly reconstructions and anachronisms.

C. Clemen, *Fontes Historiae Religionis Germanicae*, Berlin 1928; W. Capelle, *Das alte Germanien*, Jenor 1929; F. R. Schröder, *Quellenbuch zur germanischen Religionsgeschichte*, Berlin, Leipzig 1933; O. Almgren, *Nordische Felszeichnungen als religiöse Urkunden*, Frankfurt 1934; S. Gutenbrunner, *Die germanischen Götternamen der antiken Inschriften*, Halle 1936; W. Baetke, *Die Religion der*

Sources

Germanen in Quellenzeugnissen, Frankfurt [2]1938; A. Holtsmark, 'Mytologi' (*KLNM* 12) 1967; R. L. M. Derolez, *Götter und Mythen der Germanen*, Wiesbaden 1974.

spádísir (ON, 'sibill goddesses') are told of in the late Old Norse literature partly as (valkyrie-like) women who appear to heroes in dreams and tell them about their future destiny (e.g. *Asmundar saga kappabana* 8), and who, somewhat like a kind of norn, are able to determine the fate of a person already at his birth (cf. *Vǫlsunga saga* 9). *Spádísir* should not be confused with the word *spákona* 'seeress'. The concepts of the *spádísir* and other such beings have little to do with Germanic mythology and are at best part of medieval Icelandic folk-belief where they originate from unclear memories of norns, *dísir* ('lesser goddesses') and valkyries.

spákóna (ON, 'seeress') → Seeresses.

spámaðr (ON, 'seer, sorcerer') → Seeresses, → Magic.

Spells (ON, *galdar*). Spells are used in → magic to set into motion the magical powers which the person in question wants to bring into his service through the power of the rhymed word. A great number of Germanic spells have been handed down to us. However most of them only come from the Christian Middle Ages and consequently heathen gods are mentioned only extremely rarely. It may seem somewhat surprising that something as inherently heathen as magical spells should continue to be used in Christian times, but the recommended invocation of Christ in the Lord's Prayer after the conclusion of the actual spell made it acceptable for Christians and it could even be retained in monastical writings. In fact most of the spells extant today come down to us in such manuscripts.

Most of the spells we know are for healing and blessing. The → Second Merseburg Charm is one such healing spell which is of particular interest because of the naming of the gods Wodan, Baldr, Frija, Volla, Sintgunt and Phol. The → First Merseburg Charm was supposed to bring about freedom from imprisonment.

In Old Norse there is a poetic metre especially for spells (ON *galdar*) namely the *galdralag*. However, there are no real spells to be found in ON literature, only the announcements of them (*Hávamál*, *Grógaldr*), and in the *Eireks saga rauða* 4 the procedure for the singing of a magical spell is described in some detail (→ *varðlokkur*, → Þorbjǫrg lítilvǫlva). This is admittedly not necessarily historical.

Spells were not always spoken or sung. Wooden staves with spells carved into them were also used in magic, whereby the earliest → runes had a magical character, and magical effect could be achieved not only by well-formulated spells but also by individual magical conceptual runes.

A. F. Hälsig, *Der Zauberspruch*, Leipzig 1910; F. Genzmer, 'Germanische Zaubersprüche' (*GRM* 32) 1950; L. Forster, 'Zum 2. Merseburger Zauberspruch' (*Archiv* 192) 1956; G. Eis, *Altdeutsche Zaubersprüche*, Berlin 1964; O. Bø, 'Trollformlar' (*KLNM* 18) 1974; K. A. Wipf, 'Die Zaubersprüche im Althochdeutschen' (*Numen* 22) 1975.

Sprettingr (ON, 'the jumping up one' or 'the starting out one'). A giant in the *Þulur*.

Springs, cult of. The worship of springs, which manifests itself in the laying down of → votive offerings in or near springs, is well documented archaeologically speaking for the Bronze and Iron Ages, and a veneration of the waters is mentioned also by early Medieval authors (Gregory of Tours, *Historia Francorum* II, 10, Procopius, *Bell.*

Goth. II, 25). Church books of repentence and Christian laws forbade the worship of springs just as they did the worship of trees and groves.

In mythology, the springs reflected the significance of the mythical springs to which → Urd's well, → Mímir's well count as well as the spring called → Hvergelmir, in which the primeval mythical rivers (→ Élivágar) have their source.

The worship of springs is not only documented for Germanic peoples, but also for other Indo-Germanic peoples, especially for the Celts. The origin of the cult of springs is undoubtedly connected with the belief in the sanctity of → water.

stallahringr (ON, 'altar ring') → Temple ring.

stalli or stallr (ON, 'cultic construction, altar') → altar.

Starkaðr (1) (ON). A giant who is named in a fragmentary stanza by the Icelander Verliði Sumarliðason (10th century). The stanza suggests that Starkaðr was one of the many other giants and giantesses who were supposedly killed by Thor. It is uncertain whether he might be identical with the known saga hero Starkaðr (2).

Starkaðr (2) (ON). An Odinic hero of Germanic heroic poetry. His life is dominated by predestinies which the gods have given him: Odin gives him the span of three lives, victory in battles, the gift of poetry and other things; Thor, on the other hand, gives him three nefarious deeds, frequent injury, and a bad memory (*Gautreks saga* 7). Particularly in the case of Starkaðr the ambivalence of the dedication to Odin shows that this dedication not only makes the hero victorious but also ensnares him more and more in his own fate.

Starkaðr also plays a decisive role in Odin's sacrifice in which his friend and king → Víkarr is killed.

O. Höfler, *Germanisches Sakralkönigtum*, Tübingen 1952.

State. If state is defined as an independent community, organized by a government with its own territory, then it is only possible to talk of the formation of states in Germanic Europe in the Iron Age. Before this time the larger forms of community were the family and age groups.

Certain constructions dating from the Neolithic and Bronze Age point to some kind of organized sizeable community and this has resulted in attempts to date the formation of states to these times. Examples are the monumental passage graves and stone settings of West European Megalithic culture, which were undoubtedly the result of a centralized cult community. However, we know too little about ruling conditions and the independence of these community forms.

In the 1st century A.D. Tacitus tells of the state (*civitas*) among the Germanic peoples (*Germania* 10, 13) and mentions state offices: kings and army leaders (*Germania* 7). From Scandinavian sources we know of two Germanic forms of state, the state of kings and the Thing-state (or free state). The repeatedly discussed question about whether the origins of the formation of the state lie in sacral or secular areas, whether there was a 'sanctity of the state' among Germanic peoples, is closely connected with the question of → sacred kingship and → sanctity of the Thing. The existence of a sacred kingship among the Germanic peoples is virtually certain today, and even the sanctity of the Thing may hardly be seriously doubted and the question about the sanctity of the state for the Germanic people must also be affirmed.

W. Schulz, *Staat und Gesellschaft in germanischer Vorzeit*, Leipzig 1926; J. de Vries, *Die geistige Welt der Germanen*, Tübingen [3]1964; Å. V. Biezais, *Germanische und baltische Religion*, Stuttgart 1975; O. Höfler, 'Staatsheiligkeit und Staatsvergottung' (*Festschrift* A. *Erler*) Aalen 1976.

Stave churches. Norwegian medieval wooden churches. It is thought by some that they were modelled on Germanic → temples.

Stígandi (ON, 'the climber'). A giant in the *Þulur*, referring no doubt to the giants as mountain dwellers.

Stórverkr (ON, 'the one who does great deeds'). Stórverkr is the name (or a synonym) for a giant in the *Þulur*. Folklore associated the giants with great building feats because of their strength. The same is true in tales such as the → giant master builder.

Strǫnd (ON, 'beach'). One of the (mythical?) rivers in the river catalogue of *Grímnismál* 28 and in the *Þulur*.

Stúmi (ON, 'stumbler'?). A giant in the *Þulur*.

Suðri (ON, from *suðr* 'south'). A dwarf in *Vǫluspá* 11. According to *Gylfaginning* 7 he supports the vault of heaven created from Ymir's skull. → Vestri.

Suebae. Epithet of → matrons on three votive inscriptions. Two of them come from Cologne, Germany, and the third from Deutz can be dated to the year 223 A.D. The name means 'the Suebian matrons' and the votive stones were probably dedicated by members of this particular tribe.

S. Gutenbrunner, *Die germanischen Götternamen*, Halle 1936; H. Reichert, *Lexikon der altgermanischen Namen*, Vienna 1987–90.

Sulevia. Name of a goddess. Sulevia should be understood as a goddess in her own right, at least according to an inscription from Trier (CIL XIII 3664) (*D[e]ae Sulev[ae]*). In numerous other inscriptions the → Suleviae are a group of goddesses and matrons.

Suleviae. Name of → matrons or goddesses. Nearly 40 inscriptions on Roman votive stones are dedicatd to the *Sulevis*. The inscriptions are found spread over the greater part of the Roman Empire in Europe, and are particularly numerous in Rome (here with the addition of *matribus*) and on the Lower Rhine. These inscriptions give more information than other matron inscriptions and allow conclusions to be drawn about the function of the goddesses. The additions *meae*, *suae*, *domesticae suae* and other such formulae show quite clearly that the Suleviae were deities of the private sphere and as such can be compared with the Roman *genii* and the Christian idea of guardian angels (Gutenbrunner). The meaning of the name Suleviae has not been fully explained, but it can most likely be interpreted in a similar way to the goddess Sulis (recorded in Bath, England) as 'goddesses of the warm springs', or perhaps even 'sun goddesses'. It has not even been possible up to now to make a clear-cut assignment to the Celtic or Germanic religion. Some of the inscriptions have been dated and nearly all of these fall into the time period between 130–160 A.D., and only one inscription from Xanten can be placed before 89 A.D. Therefore, the Suleviae fall into the earliest period of the cult of matrons.

S. Gutenbrunner, *Die germanischen Götternamen*, Halle 1936; E. A. Philippson, 'Der germanische Mütter- und Matronenkult am Niederrhein' (*GR* 19) 1944; H. Reichert, *Lexikon der altgermanischen Namen*, Vienna 1987–90.

Sumarr (ON, 'summer'). The personification of summer in *Vafþrúðnismál* 27 (and in Snorri who used this stanza). His father is Svásuðr. In heathen mythology there was no personified summer, and as such Sumar is a late literary construction, perhaps adopted from older riddle poetry.

Sun → Sól.

Sunna. A goddess who is only mentioned in the → Second Merseburg Charm, and should probably only be understood as a literary personification of 'sun', since there is no other evidence for the worship of a personified sun among Germanic peoples. Even the ON goddess → Sól is only very rarely mentioned in the sources.

H. Gering, 'Der zweite Merseburger Spruch' (*ZfdPh* 26) 1894; S. Gutenbrunner, 'Ritennamen – Kultnamen – Mythennamen' (*Namenforschung. Festschrift A. Bach*) Heidelberg 1965.

Sunucsal (or Sunuxsal). Name of a goddess mentioned in ten inscriptions from the Lower Rhine, of which one can be dated to 239 A.D. Sunucsal is probably the goddess belonging to the tribe of the Sunuci whom Tacitus referred to as being Germanic.

S. Gutenbrunner, *Die germanischen Götternamen*, Halle 1936; J. de Vries, *Altgermanische Religionsgeschichte*, Berlin [3]1970; H. Reichert, *Lexikon der altgermanischen Namen*, Vienna 1987–90.

Surtalogi (ON, 'Surtr's fire', actually; 'Surti's fire'). The fire with which the giant → Surtr will set the world on fire and thus destroy it, according to *Vafþrúðnismál* 50, 51 and also Snorri (*Gylfaginning* 16, 52).

Surti (ON). A sub-form of → Surtr which presupposes the term *Surta logi* (*Vafþrúðnismál* 50, 51). Neckel rejected the existence of such an additional form, however, and considered the form *Surta logi* merely to be a peculiarity of the *Codex Regius*.

G. Neckel, 'Zu den Eddaliedern' (*ANF* 43) 1927.

Surtr (ON, 'the black one'). The fire giant of Nordic mythology. The concept of Surtr is undoubtedly old, as it is already referred to by the 10th-century skalds (Eyvindr, Hallfreðr) as well as in the *Edda* (*Vǫluspá* 47, 52, 53; *Vafþrúðnismál* 18, 50, 51; *Fáfnismál* 14). It is also referred to in the name of the volcanic caves Surtshellir in western Iceland which was already recorded as such in the *Landnámabók*. In the Eddic lays Surtr is especially the enemy of the gods at Ragnarǫk, and he and Freyr, who has to fight without his sword, kill each other. The fact that Surtr lives in the south (*Vǫluspá* 52), although the giants usually live in the east, surely has to do with his association with fire and heat. The world conflagration which destroys everything at Ragnarǫk is called *surta(r)logi* 'Surt's fire' (*Vafþrúðnismál* 50, 51). Snorri links Surtr with the sons of Muspell, or even with → Muspell himself whose guardian he is and 'who has a flaming sword; at the end he will come and wage war and will conquer all the gods and will destroy the whole world by fire' (*Gylfaginning* 4); 'Surtr rides in the vanguard and before him and behind him there will be burning fire; his sword is splendid and shines brighter than the sun.' (*Gylfaginning* 50). In Iceland Surtr was obviously thought of as being a mighty giant who ruled the powers of (volcanic) fire of the Underworld. The concept of Surtr as the enemy of the gods probably did not, however, originate in Iceland. Surtr lives on as a fire-giant in the minds of modern Icelanders even today as can be seen by the name given to the volcanic island, Surtsey ('Surtr's island'), which suddenly appeared as an addition to the Westmannaeyjar as recently as 1963, although the name surely is partially a result of the impressive Surtshellir already mentioned.

B. S. Phillpotts, 'Surt' (*ANF* 21) 1905; G. Neckel, 'Zu den Eddaliedern' (*ANF* 43) 1927; J. de Vries, *Altgermanische Religionsgeschichte*, Berlin ³1970; A. Holtsmark, 'Surtr' (*KLNM* 17) 1972; S. Nordal, *Vǫluspá*, Darmstadt 1980.

R: Snorri's interpretation of Surtr as Muspell's guard is adopted by J. C. Dollmann's painting *The Giant with the Flaming Sword*.

Suttungr (ON). Name of the giant who owned the → mead of the skalds before Odin stole it for the gods and mankind. Snorri tells in *Skáldskaparmál* 1 that the giant Suttungr had forced the dwarfs Galarr and Fjalarr to give him the mead as compensation for the killing of his father Gillingr. Then he reports how Odin moves into action, first bringing about the deaths of the giant Baugi's nine mowers and then by working for the unsuspecting Baugi, Suttungr's brother, under the pseudonym of Bǫlverkr. At the end of the summer, after Baugi has been unable to persuade Suttungr to give Odin a sip of the mead of the skalds as reward for his work, Baugi, using his drill Rati, drills a hole through the mountain. Then Odin in the shape of a snake is able to creep into Suttungr's domicile Hnitbjǫrg and sleep with Suttungr's daughter Gunnlǫð for three nights, after which she allows him three sips of the mead of the skalds. He empties the three vessels Boðn, Són and Óðrœrir and then, changing into the shape of an eagle, he flies back to Asgard, pursued in vain by Suttungr, also in the shape of an eagle.

Snorri's account of Suttungr apparently rests only on the embellishment of several youngish kennings. Suttungr is a giant in *Skírnismál* 34 and *Alvíssmál* 34 (also in the *Þulur*), but only *Hávamál* 104–110 connects Suttungr with the tale of the skaldic mead. Snorri gives another kenning using the name *Suttunga mjǫð* for the mead of the skalds, but this expression and its context are otherwise not documented. This information in skaldic poetry corresponds to Suttungr's position in Snorri's tale which is somewhat colourless and without any real function. Indeed, Snorri's account does not go further than what is related in *Hávamál*: Gunnlǫð lives in Suttungr's hall, and Odin steals the mead from her. It seems almost certain that the idea of Suttungr pursuing Odin in the shape of an eagle is taken from the myth of → Þjazi.

The name Suttungr perhaps comes from *suþþungr* 'heavy with drink', though possibly related to Norwegian *sutta* 'to move quickly' (but unlikely because of the pursuit of Odin). Because there is no clear etymological interpretation of the name, it is extremely uncertain if Suttungr indeed played a role in the myth of the theft of the mead of the skalds, or if Snorri was the first to link the giant with this deed.

A. Holtsmark, 'Suttungr' (*KLNM* 17) 1972; R. Doht, *Der Rauschtrank im germanischen Mythos*, Vienna 1974.

Svaði (ON, 'careless fellow'). A giant (?) in the various versions of the mythologising Norwegian pre-history, where he is called the father of the giantess Hadda and of Hrolfr. Hadda marries Norr and Hrolfr Gói, both of whom are Thor's children belonging to the family of the legendary ancestor Fornjótr.

Svaðilfari (ON, 'the one making an unlucky journey'). The name of the stallion which according to Eddic mythology (*Hyndluljóð* 40) begat Odin's eight-legged horse Sleipnir by a mare who was actually Loki in the shape of a horse. Snorri integrated this myth into the story of the building of Asgard which is a mythological variant of the tale of the → giant master builder.

R: D. Hardy, *Loki and Svadifari* (drawing, c.1900).

Sváfnir (1) (ON, 'the one who puts to sleep = death?'). A name for Odin in *Grímnismál* 54, the *Þulur* and the skaldic poem *Hrafnsmál*, written by Þorbjǫrn hornklofi (c.900).

H. Falk, *Odensheite*, Kristiania 1924.

Sváfnir (2) (ON). One of the snakes which live under the roots of the World-tree, Yggdrasill (*Grímnismál* 34). According to Snorri (*Gylfaginning* 15), these snakes live in the spring there called Hvergelmir.

Svafrþorinn (ON). The father of Menglǫð in *Fjǫlsvinnsmál* 8. As Menglǫð is usually identified as Freyja, it could be that Svafrþorinn is a name for her father Njǫrðr. However, the name is not totally clear: *þorinn* means 'brave', but *svafr* 'gossip' or else a connexion with *sofa* 'sleep' hardly make sense. A more daring, but more meaningful assumption would be that the poet of *Fjǫlsvinnsmál* took the Svefnþorn ('sleeping thorn'), which occurs as a fairy-tale motif in the *fornaldarsǫgur*, together with the motif of the wall of fire (*Fjǫlsvinnsmál* 31) from the legend of Brynhild (which can be found in the Eddic lay *Sigdrífumál*, in Snorri and in the *Vǫlsunga saga*), and at the same time personified the sleeping thorn in this context.

Svára (ON, 'the heavy one'). A giantess in a stanza by the skald Gunnlaugr ormstungu (*Sigtryggsdrápa* 3).

Svárangr (ON, 'the clumsy one'). A giant in the *Þulur* and *Hárbarðsljóð* 29 where Thor tells about a battle with Svárangr's sons. 'Svárangr's sons' is probably quite a general kenning for giants, however, and need not necessarily indicate a lost myth.

Svartálfaheimr (ON, 'world of the black-elves'). The name Snorri (*Gylfaginning* 33, *Skáldskaparmál* 37) gives to the underground home of the dwarfs which suggests that for Snorri black elves and dwarfs were identical. → Elves.

Svartálfar (ON, 'black elves'). A category of → elves which can be traced to the name Svartálfaheim 'world of the black elves' found in Snorri (*Gylfaginning* 33; *Skáldskaparmál* 37). As Snorri calls Svartálfaheim the home of the dwarfs in both cases, it may be assumed that he thought of dwarfs and Svartálfar as being identical. The indistinct transitions between both categories of mythical beings would also speak in favour of this identification.

Svarthǫfði (ON, 'blackhead'). A giant in → *Vǫluspá in skamma* (*Hyndluljóð* 33) who is called the mythical ancestor of all *seiðberandar* ('sorcerers').

Svartr (ON, 'the black one'). A giant in the *Þulur*. Many of the giants' names suggest their dark, hairy, ugly appearance.

Svásuðr (ON, 'the lovable one'). The father of summer in *Vafþrúðnismál* 27 and in Snorri (*Gylfaginning* 18, *Skáldskaparmál* 28). Snorri adds: 'Svásuðr has such a happy life that everything which is pleasant (*svásligt*) is called after him.' However, even in *Vafþrúðnismál*, from which Snorri acquired his information, Svásuðr is a poetic creation, governed by the rules of alliteration.

Sváva (ON, probably from *svæfa* 'to put to sleep', thus perhaps 'the one who puts people to sleep, the killing one'?). A name for a → valkyrie which is only recorded in heroic poetry (*Helgakviða Hjǫrvarðssonar*).

Svebdeg → Svipdagr (1).

Sveið (ON, 'vibration'?, 'noise'?). A valkyrie in the *Þulur*.

Sveipinfalda (ON, 'the one hidden by a hood'). A giantess in the *Þulur*.

Svíagríss (ON, 'Sweden-piglet'). A ring. According to Snorri (*Skáldskaparmál* 41) it was owned by King Aðil of Sweden and was an heirloom of the Yngling kings.

The name, which was unlikely to have been invented by Snorri, suggests that the ring probably bore a small figure of a pig on it (as did Swedish decorative helmets); as Freyr's → boar was sacred and the Yngling kings are said to be descended from Yngvi-Freyr, it would not be surprising if this treasure was a kind of regal insignia of the Ynglings. With regard to the sacral function of rings among the Germanic people see → temple ring, and → Draupnir.

Svibdavus. A hero in Saxo's *Gesta Danorum* (VI, 186), → Svipdagr (2).

Sviðrir (ON). A name for Odin in *Grímnismál* 50 and in the *Þulur*. Although both *Grímnismál* and Snorri (*Gylfaginning* 2 and 19) include the name independently in both cases it would appear that Sviðrir, Sviðurr and the manuscript variant Sviðuðr are only forms of the same name for Odin. Snorri traces the name Svíþjóð 'Sweden' back to Sviðurr, a name for Odin (*Skáldskaparmál* 63), but it is extremely questionable if these names do indeed belong together. The derivation from *sviða* 'spear', which would mean that Sviðrir meant 'spear-god', is possible; other interpretations (as 'swinger' or 'protector') are no more convincing.

H. Falk, *Odensheite*, Kristiania 1924; J. de Vries, *Altgermanische Religionsgeschichte*, Berlin [3]1970.

Sviðuðr (ON). Listed in the *Þulur* as a name for Odin. It is a variant of Sviðurr and → Sviðrir.

Sviðurr (ON). A name for Odin in *Grímnismál* 50 and in Snorri, which is probably related to → Sviðrir.

Svipall (ON, 'changeable'). A name for Odin (*Grímnismál* 47, *Þulur*). It quite obviously refers to Odin's frequently changing names and disguises which both Saxo (*Gesta Danorum* VIII, 263) and Snorri (*Ynglinga saga* 6) expressly mention.

H. Falk, *Odensheite*, Kristiania 1924.

Svipdagerus. A Norwegian king in Saxo's *Gesta Danorum* (I, 18), → Svipdagr 1.

Svipdagr (1) (ON). This is the name of the hero of the young Eddic lay → *Svipdagsmál*. Although the lay appears to have been composed only in the late 13th century and is the youngest of the Eddic lays, it is possible that a figure belonging to heathen mythology could indeed be hidden behind this hero.

The name Svipdagr means approximately 'the suddenly dawning day'. Snorri names him as being one of Odin's descendants (*Edda*, Prologue 4) and comments that he is really called Svebdeg. A Swǣfdæg can also be found in the mythical genealogies of Anglian royal houses as the descendants of Woden. Höfler showed that Swǣfdæg was a 'Dagr of the Suebi', a god Dagr specific to a particular people who was still worshipped by the Angles (who were part of the North Suebi) after their emigration. Thus, Svipdagr should probably be understood as being a mythical ancestor of the Suebi who was possibly a god of fertility (Höfler, Schröder). In the *Svipdagsmál* he is the son of Sólbjartr ('the sun-light': a god of the skies?) and of Gróa (from *gróa* 'grow'; a goddess of growth?). The interpretation of the *Svipdagsmál* as a myth which shows Svipdagr, the son of the gods wooing → Menglǫð (= Freyja?) agrees with the interpretation given above. As with the *Skírnismál*, which served the poet of the *Svipdagsmál* as a model, the younger *Svipdagsmál* might also be ultimately based on a cult myth according to this interpretation. In his *Gesta Danorum* (I, 18), Saxo mentions a Norwegian king Svipdagerus, who is even associated with a certain Groa whose husband he kills in this version.

O. Höfler, 'Das Opfer im Semnonenhain' (*Edda, Skalden, Saga. Festschrift F. Genzmer*) Heidelberg 1952; A. M. Sturtevant, 'The Old Norse Proper Name Svipdagr' (*SS* 30) 1958; F. R. Schröder, 'Svipdagsmál' (*GRM* 47) 1966; J. de Vries, *Altgermanische Religionsgeschichte*, Berlin ^{3}1970.

Svipdagr (2), or to be more exact: Svipdagr blindi (ON, 'blind Svipdag'). A pseudonym for Odin in the *Ynglinga saga* (34ff.) which is related to Svipall, another name for Odin. He is found as a hero both in Saxo (*Gesta Danorum* VI, 186 as Svibdavus) and in *Hrólfs saga kraka* which tells that Svipdagr loses an eye. Höfler sees the direct opposition to Svipdagr (1) in this dark and blind Svipdagr and interprets both as aspects of the same godly figure, a polarity not unknown with vegetation gods.

H. Falk, *Odensheite*, Kristiania 1924; O. Höfler, 'Das Opfer im Semnonenhain' (*Edda, Skalden, Saga. Festschrift F. Genzmer*) Heidelberg 1952; P. Fisher, H. E. Davidson, *Saxo Grammaticus: The History of the Danes*, Cambridge 1980.

Svipdagsmál (ON, 'the lay of Svipdag'). This title is a creation of S. Bugge's who used it in 1860 to designate two very young Eddic lays which obviously belong together, namely *Grógaldr* and *Fjǫlsvinnsmál*. They are both only found in extremely late manuscripts (from the 17th century), although the lays themselves appear to originate from the latest phase of the scholarly Icelandic Renaissance period, i.e. the end of the 13th century. Svipdagr is the hero of both lays; in the 16 stanzas which make up the → *Grógaldr* ('spell of Gróa') he awakens his dead mother and asks her for magical spells with which he might be able to succeed in his quest for Menglǫð's hand in marriage. His mother tells him of nine magical spells for all occasions, but the spell formulae themselves are unfortunately not given in the lay.

The 50 stanzas of → *Fjǫlsvinnsmál* relate how Svipdagr comes to the mountain where Menglǫð lives, and to her home surrounded by a wall of flames. At this point Svipdagr calls himself Vindkaldr, and the giant guard Fjǫlsviðr ('know-all') asks him many questions. The knowledge revealed in this lay at first concerns Menglǫð's followers and home and then continues on mythological topics. Finally, Fjǫlsviðr declares that Menglǫð can belong to no other man but Svipdagr, whereupon Svipdagr makes his true identity known and he and Menglǫð greet each other with mutual declarations of love.

Bugge and Grundtvig used the late Medieval Danish and Swedish ballads of *Ungen Svejdal* ('Yound Svejdal') in order to demonstrate the connexion between *Grógaldr* and *Fjǫlsvinnsmál* and it is clear from this that originally it was a stepmother fairy-tale. The fairy-tale elements and the resemblance of heroic poetry should not lead us away from the fact that the *Svipdagsmál* is a product of the High Middle Ages, in which didactic poetry (following the model of *Grímnismál* and *Vafþrúðnismál*) with fairy-tale motifs (Sleeping Beauty motif; stepmother motif) was reworked to create an Eddic lay. Beneath the fairy-tale-like adventures, however, there are the remains of a mythical tale of wooing (as in the *Skírnismál*). The name of the hero → Svipdagr also points the way to older mythological concepts. Consequently, *Svipdagsmál* should be seen as the mythical wooing of a god (Svip-)Dagr for Menglǫð (= Freyja?) (Schröder), although possibly features of an initiation rite are also retained in the tale (Motz).

S. Bugge, *Forbindelsen mellem Grógaldr og Fjǫlsvinnsmál*, Christiania 1860; T. Rupp, 'Fiölsvinnsmâl' (*Germania* 10) 1865; H. Falk, 'Om Svipdagsmál' (*ANF* 9) 1893; F. R. Schröder, 'Svipdagsmál' (*GRM* 47) 1966; H. Beck, 'Svipdagsmál' (*KLL* 6) 1971; A. Holtsmark, 'Svipdagsmál' (*KLNM* 17) 1972; L. Motz, 'The King and the Goddess' (*ANF* 90) 1975; E. O. Sveinsson, 'Svipdag's Long Journey' (*Hereditas. Essays S. O'Duilearga*) Dublin 1975; A. Kragerud, 'De mytologiske spørsmål i Fåvnesmål' (*ANF* 96) 1981.

Svipul (ON, 'changeable'; also a seldomly used synonym for 'battle' in the *Þulur*). A → valkyrie in → *Darraðarljóð* and once in the *Þulur*. The name presumably refers to the changeable nature of fate, whose directors the valkyries are represented as being, especially in the *Darraðarljóð*.

Svíurr, also Sviárr, Síarr (ON, 'the vanishing one'). A dwarf in *Vǫluspá*.

Svívǫr (ON). One of the giantesses of whom the skald Þórbjǫrn dísarskáld tells that she was killed by Thor, but of whom we otherwise know nothing. The name could mean 'shame-mouth' (from *vǫrr* 'lip'), but the names ending in *-vǫr* (Fjǫlvǫr, Leirvǫr, Sívǫr) could also point to the goddess (of marriage?) Vǫr, whereby Svívǫr would be a kenning-like construction and thus would mean 'shame-goddess' = giantess. Considering the other Old Norse names for giantesses, the first possibility is admittedly far more likely.

Svǫl (1) or Svalin (ON, 'the cool one'). The shield which is situated in front of the sun, and without which the whole world would burn up (*Grímnismál* 38).

Svǫl (2) (ON, 'the cool one'). A river in the catalogue of mythical rivers in *Grímnismál* 27. In Snorri it is one of the Élivágar which flow from the spring called Hvergelmir (*Gylfaginning* 3 and 40).

Svǫlnir (ON). A name for Odin, recorded several times in skaldic poetry. There would appear to be a close connexion with the mythical sun-shield Svǫl so that Falk interprets it as 'shield-bearer', which is however not totally satisfactory.

H. Falk, *Odensheite*, Kristiania 1924.

Svǫsuðr or Svasuðr (ON, 'the delightful one'?). A giant who is called the father of Sumar (the personification of summer) in *Vafþrúðnismál* 27.

Svǣfdæg (Anglo-Saxon). Woden's descendant in the mythical genealogy of the Anglo-Saxon kings, → Svipdagr (1).

Sylgr (ON, 'devourer'). One of the mythical rivers in the catalogue of rivers in *Grímnismál* 28. In Snorri (*Gylfaginning* 3) Sylgr is one of the Élivágar rivers which flow from the spring called Hvergelmir.

Syn (ON, 'refusal, denial'). A goddess in Snorri (*Gylfaginning* 34) and in the *Þulur*, who, according to Snorri, is the guardian of the gates. Syn appears no more closely defined as a mythological figure in skaldic poetry in kennings for 'woman'. Thus, Syn ranks among the female protective goddesses who are given names here in the late heathen period, but who were cumulatively known as → *dísir* and correspond to the ancient Germanic → *matronae*.

Sýr (ON, 'sow'). A name for the goddess Freyja, to be found in the writings of Hallfreðr the skald, and then later in Snorri (*Gylfaginning* 34) as well as in the *Þulur*. The pig was obviously closely connected with the Vanir in cult and sacrificial practices, in particular with the brother and sister Freyr and Freyja, as Freyr's attribute, the boar → Gullinborsti, indicates.

Tacitus, Cornelius. Born c. A.D. 55, died after A.D. 117, this Roman historian is an important informant concerning the religion of the heathen Germanic peoples in his works *Historiae Annales* and *De origine et situ Germanorum*. Tacitus used older sources for his *Germania* (written c. A.D. 90), which, apart from Caesar, included in particular a work by Pliny about the Germanic wars (written around the middle of the first century). As a result of this source, his information seems to reproduce the religion of Continental Germanic peoples shortly after the birth of Christ relatively faithfully, and it is on the whole fairly untouched by external influences. As one would expect from other historical writings of the period, Tacitus does not give a systematic presentation but rather gives individual comments about the religion of the Germanic peoples. Tacitus' tendency elsewhere to depict the Germanic peoples as a model of the 'noble barbarian', thus giving an example to the (in his opinion) increasingly uncivilized Romans, does not appear to have played a particularly significant role in his presentation of Germanic religion.

The most important comments concerning the religion of the Germanic peoples in Tacitus' *Germania* include the description of the cult in the grove of the Semnones (ch. 39), the cult of Nerthus (ch. 40) and the myth of the descendence of the Germanic peoples who can be traced back to Tuisto and Mannus (ch. 2). Some information which Tacitus gives about legal practices among the Germanic tribes (e.g. sinking of criminals into heath bogs) has been confirmed through archaeology.

K. Müllenhoff, *Die Germania des Tacitus*, Berlin ²1920; E. Norden, *Die germanische Urgeschichte in Tacitus' Germania*, Leipzig, Berlin ³1923; R. Much, *Die Germania des Tacitus*, Heidelberg ³1967; R. Syme, *Tacitus*, Oxford 1958; H. Jankuhn, *Archäologische Bermerkungen zur Glaubwürdigkeit des Tacitus in der Germania*, Göttingen 1966; J. de Vries, *Altgermanische Religionsgeschichte*, Berlin ³1970; N. Wagner, 'Zwei Triaden in Tacitus' "Germania" ' (ZfdA 108) 1979; K. v. See, 'Der Germane als Barbar' (*Jahrbuch für Internationale Germanistik* 13) 1981.

Tamfana. A Germanic goddess. Tacitus records (*Annales* I, 51) that during a campaign in the area of the Marsae, who had settled between the upper Lippe and the Ruhr, the Roman troops led by Germanicus in the year A.D. 4 destroyed the shrine (*templum*) of a certain Tamfana while the Germanic tribe was in the process of celebrating a festival there. According to the details given by Tacitus, the only possible dates for this enterprise were September 28th or October 27th which makes it an autumn festival. As we have evidence for an autumnal sacrifice held for the *dísir* in Scandinavia (*dísablót*), the cult of Tamfana should perhaps be considered to be within the framework of the West Germanic cult of matrons, which in the first centuries A.D. played a great role and had certain similarities with the Scandinavian worship of the *dísir*.

J. Wormstall, *Der Tempel der Tamfana*, Münster 1906; H. Krahe, 'Tamfana' (*PBB* 58) 1934; M. Schönfeld, *Wörterbuch der altgermanischen Personen- und Völkernamen*, Heidelberg [2]1965; R. Much, *Die Germania des Tacitus*, Heidelberg [3]1967; J. de Vries, *Altgermanische Religionsgeschichte*, Berlin [3]1970.

R: Tanfara is a Germanic goddess in Klopstock's ode *Wingolf* (1747).

Tanngnidr (ON, 'teeth-grinder'). A valkyrie in the *Þulur*.

Tanngnjóstr (ON, 'teeth grinder'). One of → Thor's goats according to Snorri (*Gylfaginning* 20) and the *Þulur*; the descriptive name was probably invented by Snorri.

Tanngrísnir (ON, 'teeth barer, snarler'). One of → Thor's goats according to Snorri (*Gylfaginning* 20) and the *Þulur*. The name is young and was probably invented by Snorri.

Temples. There are no Germanic temples left standing, and even archaeological investigations cannot confirm the existence of temples. In addition to this the sparse literary references to heathen temples are all extremely late and hardly reliable, and even the research of place-names has not brought conclusive evidence about possible temples. Even so, speculation concerning the form, kind and distribution of Germanic temples has continued uninterrupted since the 16th century.

As the Germanic words for temple prove, the meaning 'temple' is on the whole merely secondary, and originally it designated probably only a → 'sacred grove, holy place'. Anglo-Saxon *ealh*, *alh*, Gothic *alhs*, as well as Anglo-Saxon *bearo*, OHG *baro*, Anglo-Saxon *heargh*, and Old Norse *hǫrgr* were glossed as 'temple' and at the same time as 'holy place, sacred grove'. Whatever the case, there were sacred woods long before there were temples and altars.

Literary tradition concerning Germanic temples begins in the first century A.D. with Tacitus' writings. He writes that the Germanic tribes did not have any temples but had rather put up idols in sacred groves (*Germania* 9). Elsewhere he mentions a temple (*templum*) in the cult of Nerthus (*Germania* 40) and of → Tamfana (*Annales* I, 51). Around the year A.D. 730 the English historian Bede repeatedly refers to pre-Christian temples (*Historia ecclesiastica* I, 30; II, 15; III, 30). It is doubtful whether he really knew any Germanic temples or whether he merely allowed himself to transfer his own classical knowledge of Roman heathendom onto Germanic circumstances. The Eddic lays refer to the → *hǫrgr* three times. It is possible that this is an indication of a wooden construction which could be interpreted as a kind of protective roof. The descriptions of Icelandic temples (*hof*) in the sagas around the middle of the 13th century (*Eyrbyggja saga* 4, *Kjalnesinga saga* 2) correspond more or less to the appearance of larger Icelandic farmhouses. Archaeological investigations around 1900 at Hofstaðir, which have unearthed a ressemblence of the building there to the *hof* of the sagas (Ohlmarks, de Vries) are of little significance as *hof* obviously only received its meaning of 'temple' in the literature of the High Middle Ages in Iceland, i.e. in the post-heathen era. The Christian skald Sigvatr Þórðarson (c.1020) mentions a *hof* in Sweden at which an → *álfablót* was held. However, this might simply refer to a farm called Hof. The ON word *hof* is most likely the name for a large farmhouse at which cult festivals for a large number of people could be held (O. Olsen). The great number of place-names based on *hof* in Scandinavia, which would be surprisingly high for proper temple buildings, thus refers rather to farms which combined their secular function with a sacred one. This interpretation is also justifiable in the cases of both the *hofs* called Hofstaðir (in Mývatnsveit and in Þorskafjọrður) in Iceland whose religious significance is obvious from striking sacrificial pits near to the entrances.

The only remotely contemporary description of a Germanic temple is given by the ecclesiastical historian, Adam of Bremen, using eye-witness accounts (*Gesta Hammaburgensis Ecclesiae Pontificum* IV, 26 and Scholion 138f.): 'This people has a very famous temple in Uppsala, which does not lie very far from Sigtuna. In this temple, which is made totally out of gold, the people worship the statues of three gods. Thor, as the mightiest of them, has his seat in the middle of the room and the places to the left and right of him are taken by Wodan and Fricco.' Scholion 139: 'The temple is encircled by a golden chain which hangs down from the gable of the house and shines from afar to the people arriving, for the shrine which lies in the valley is surrounded all the way round by mountains, like an amphitheatre.'

Archaeological investigations in 1926 discovered post holes underneath the church at Gamla Uppsala in the penultimate layer which could possibly be connected up to make concentric rectangles. As a result of this discovery there have been a variety of widely differing attempts at reconstruction, most of which have been influenced by the form of Norwegian stave churches, even though a connexion with temples cannot be proven.

The stave churches present one of the most pressing arguments for the assumption of complex Viking Age temple buildings, as the building style and structure of the stave churches had already been brought to a standard of perfection which can only be explained by referring back to a long tradition native to Norway. As there are no foreign models which could have been followed, predecessors of the stave churches must be sought in secular and sacral buildings in heathen Norway. However, more detailed explanation from archaeological research has not as yet been forthcoming.

To sum up the question regarding the existence of Germanic temples, it can only be said that presumably there were sacral buildings which were originally simply roofed versions of the *hǫrgr*, whilst a purely sacral function for the buildings known as *hof* cannot be proven. These were presumably farms at which sacrificial ceremonies were held.

F. Jónsson, 'Hǫrgr' (*Festschrift K. Weinhold*), Straßburg 1896; A. Thümmel, 'Der germanische Tempel' (*PBB* 35) 1909; B. S. Phillpotts, 'Temple-administration and chieftainship in pre-christian Norway and Icland' (*Saga-Book* 8) 1913/14; S. Lindqvist, 'Hednatamplet i Uppsala' (*Fornvännen*) 1923; Å. Ohlmarks, 'Isländska hov och gudahus' (*Bidrag til Nordiska Filologi, till. E. Olson*) Lund 1936; W. Gehl, 'Das Problem des germanischen Tempels' (*ZfdA* 78) 1941; T. Palm, 'Uppsalalunden och Uppsalatemplet' (*Vetenskaps-societeten i Lunds Arbok*) 1941; K. Eldjárn, P. Hovda, K. Hald, O. Bø, H. Stahl, 'Hov og horg' (*KLNM* 7) 1962; H. Jankuhn, *Archäologische Bemerkungen zur Glaubwürdigkeit des Tacitus in der Germania*, Göttingen 1966; O. Olsen, *Hørg, Hov og Kirke*, Copenhagen 1966; O. Olsen, 'Vorchristliche Heiligtümer' (H. Jankuhn, *Vorgeschichtliche Heiligtümer*) Göttingen 1970; J. de Vries, *Altgermanische Religionsgeschichte*, Berlin [3]1970; L. Markey, 'Germanic Terms for Temple and Cult' (*Studies for Einar Haugen*) The Hague 1972.

R: (art) The artistic depiction of Germanic temples is partly dependent on research

regarding the great temple in Uppsala. The Swedish historian Olaus Magnus drew the temple in Uppsala in 1554 as an impressive church-like stone building and was followed in this by the historians Erik Dahlberg and Olof Verelius at the beginning of the 17th century. From 1679 onwards Olof Rudbeck's theory that the temples were a kind of Romanic square church was particularly influential. This idea only lost its validity towards the end of the 19th century. T. Brunn's stage design for *Heiligtum der Göttin Hertha* (Shrine of the goddess Hertha) in 1785 shows a strange mixture of dolmens and Greek temples. J. Flintoe's drawing *Thors Heiligtum* (Thor's shrine) in 1818 reminds the observer of a Gothic cathedral. On the other hand, A. Malmström's book illustrations to the edition of I. Tegner's *Frithjofs saga* in 1888, which also shows Baldr's shrine, try to achieve a little more historical accuracy.
(literature) I. Tegner's *Frithjofs saga* refers in detail to a temple to the god Baldr which also occurs in the ON original, *Friðþjófs saga frœkna*.

Temple ring. The Icelandic *Landnámabók* (H 268) and a number of Icelandic sagas (*Eyrbyggja saga* 4, *Droplaugarsonar saga* 6, *Kjalnesinga saga* 2, *Víga-Glúms saga* 25, *Þorsteins þáttr uxafóts*, *Þórðar saga hreðu* 94), which are interdependent to a great extent, mention the existence of a temple ring or else an altar ring which was supposed to lie on the altars of the temple as an oath ring (→ ring oath) and at sacrifices would be sprinkled with the blood of the victim by the priests.

In the above named texts the temple ring is already a literary motif and the lengthy accounts of its use in some of the sagas mainly come from the imagination of the authors.

However, oath rings do not only appear in unreliable sources, but also in the Eddic lays (*Atlakviða* 30; *Hávamál* 110). The *Anglo-Saxon Chronicle* records an oath of peace between the Angles and the Danes sworn on a ring in the year 876.

In addition to the literary accounts of the cultic significance of the ring for the heathen Germanic peoples, there are, apart from the mythical necklace, → Brísingamen and the necklace by which King → Agni was hanged, other important rings; examples are a golden ring laid down on the heath at Jelling as a sign of the legal security during the → Peace of Fróði, as well as the ring Svíagríss which belonged to the Swedish Yngling kings.

Pictorial Scandinavian depictions from the migration era, such as bracteates and pictorial stones, show the ring in a function of legitimizing the sacred right of the king to power. The ring appears to be the mythical counterpart of Odin's ring → Draupnir.

As the Icelandic sagas describe the temple ring mostly as a small ring of around 50 gm in weight, hardly larger than a present day signet-ring, and as such hardly a particularly imposing object, Magoun compared the oath ring/temple ring in the *Eyrbyggja saga* (weight around 550 gm and therefore probably an arm ring) with the slightly heavier Gothic rune ring found at Pietrossa (before A.D. 380). The latter was undoubtedly a sacral object as the inscription 'inheritance of the Goths. I am holy' proves. A letter from Bishop Ambrosianus of Milan in 381 confirms that such arm rings were worn by heathen Gothic priests – and to the horror of the bishops, also by Arian-Christian priests.

Although the close parallels seen in the description of the temple ring in the *Eyrbyggja saga* and the ring from Pietrossa are probably only accidental, nonetheless the religious significance of the ring for the Germanic peoples, and probably also its importance as a ring of oath, can hardly be disputed. The presentation of the role of the ring in the cult, as seen in the Icelandic sagas, is, however, certainly too greatly influenced by Christian concepts and ceremonies to be valuable as source material.

F. P. Magoun, 'On the Old-Germanic Altar- or Oathring (Stallahringr)' (*APhSc* 20) 1947/49; J. de Vries, *Altgermanische Religionsgeschichte*, Berlin [3]1970; A. Kabell, 'Baugi und der Ringeid' (*ANF* 90) 1975; A. Ebenbauer, 'Fróði und sein Friede' (*Festgabe f. O. Höfler*) Vienna 1976.

Teniavehae. Matron name found only once in an inscription on a Roman votive stone from Blankenstein near Aachen, Germany (CIL XIII, 8847). The interpretation is uncertain although Gutenbrunner supposes a derivation from a place-name.

S. Gutenbrunner, *Die germanischen Götternamen*, Halle 1936.

(**Teut**). A god invented by poets in the 18th century who was 'derived' from the name of the ancestral father Tuisto in Tacitus and the tribal name of the Teutons, whilst in the Middle Ages the name only refers to a giant (Chronicles of Colmar, 13th century).

R: Teut often serves as a symbol for German Nationalism in German literature, especially in the 19th century: cf. L. A. Hoffmann's poem *Beschluss*, where he talks of his 'audience of Teut's family' (1778). A rare example of a comedy on the subject is R. Hamerling's two part drama *Teut*. Teut was also the name of two periodicals of nationalist societies (both Nuremberg, 1859 and 1860).

Textumeihae. Matron name on three votive stones from the Lower Rhine. The name either means 'the gods of the southern people' (cf. Gothic *taihswa*; Old Irish *dess* 'right, south': Gutenbrunner) or 'the bringer of joy' (Birkhan).

S. Gutenbrunner, *Die germanischen Götternamen*, Halle 1936; G. Alföldy, 'Epigraphisches aus dem Rheinland III' (*Epigraphische Studien* 5) 1968; H. Birkhan, *Germanen und Kelten*, Vienna 1970; H. Reichert, *Lexikon der altgermanischen Namen*, Vienna 1987–90.

Þekkr (1) (ON, 'the well-liked one'). A name for Odin in the *Grímnismál* 46 and the *Þulur*. 'He was so handsome and noble to look at that everyone was glad if he sat together with his friends. But with his army he appeared terrible to his enemies', according to Snorri in the *Ynglinga saga* 6.

H. Falk, *Odensheite*, Kristiania 1924.

Þekkr (2) (ON). A dwarf in the *Vǫluspá* 12 and in the *Þulur*.

Thing (ON *Þing*, OE *ðing*, Old Franconian, Old Saxon *thing*, OHG *ding*, Langobardian *thinx*). The legislative and executive assembly of free men in Germanic antiquity. In the free state of Iceland the *Allthing* (as opposed to the regional Thing of each individual quarter) was the latter day successor of the Germanic Thing and was a proper legislative and jurisdictional parliament between the 10th and 14th centuries. It was admittedly controlled by the more powerful families so that the formally parliamentarian Iceland was in fact an oligarchy.

The origins of the Germanic Thing lie far back in history: the sacral association of this institution ('sanctity of the Thing') is recorded as early as the Roman Iron Age from the inscription to → Mars Thingsus on a votive stone in North England dating from the 2nd century. Mars Thingsus can only be the ancient Germanic god of the skies *Tīwaz (→ Týr/Ziu). At the end of the first century Tacitus records that the Germanic Thing was opened by the priest's command for silence (*Germania* 11) and he mentions the fact that admission to the Thing was only open to members of the cult community (*Germania* 6).

The expression *at helga þing* ('to sanctify the Thing') repeatedly occurs in the medieval Icelandic law book *Grágás*. The cult function of the location of the Thing, of the peace of the Thing and the invulnerability of the Thing can similarly only be imperfectly explained by attempts at explaining the significance of the Thing from a profane view-point. In the early Middle Ages in Sweden the Thing even had the right to institute the king and if necessary to depose him. The institution of → sacred kingship does not contradict the Thing kingdom, as the Germanic sacred kingship was not principally separated from the people, but rather the king was considered to be *primus inter pares* of the whole people whose representation was the equally sacral Thing.

O. Höfler, 'Der Sakralcharakter des germanischen Königtums' (*Sacral Kingship*) Leiden 1959; K. v. See, *Altnordische Rechtswörter*, Tübingen 1964; K. v. See, *Kontinuitätstheorie und Sakraltheorie*, Frankfurt 1972; O. Höfler, ' "Sakraltheorie" und "Profantheorie" in der Altertumskunde' (*Festschrift S. Gutenbrunner*) Heidelberg 1972; O. Höfler, 'Staatsheiligkeit und Staatsvergottung' (*Festschrift A. Erler*) Aalen 1976; O. Höfler, 'Mars Thingsus' (*Handwörterbuch zur deutschen Rechtsgeschichte* 3) 1979.

Thingsus → Mars Thingsus.

Þistilbarði (ON, 'Thistle-beard'). A giant in the *Þulur*.

Þjálfi (ON Þjálfi or Þjalfi). The servant of the god Thor. He is mentioned in the earliest source, Eilífr Guðrúnarson's *Þórsdrápa* in the 10th century, as a battle companion of Thor's, which also mentions Þjálfi's sister Rǫskva, and then also in *Harbarðsljóð* 39. These references do not suggest that Þjálfi is Thor's servant; in fact, he could just as well be another god in these sources.

Snorri tells repeatedly and in detail of Þjálfi and records also in his version of the myth of → Thor's he-goats how Thor came to acquire Þjálfi and Rǫskva: as Þjálfi was to blame for the laming of one of Thor's goats, Þjálfi's father (→ Egill?) gives him both his children as retribution (*Gylfaginning* 43 and 44). Þjálfi is also present as Thor's companion on his journeys as well as in battle in the story of Thor's journey to → Utgarðaloki where he has to race against Hugi ('thought') and naturally enough loses (*Gylfaginning* 45/46), and also in the myth of Thor's fight with the giant → Hrungnir, when Thor kills the clay giant Mǫkkurkálfi. Only in *Skáldskaparmál* 4, where Thor is called 'Þjálfi's lord' and in the already mentioned tale of Thor's goats is Þjálfi expressly called Thor's servant, which is not necessarily an old concept. The only thing that is clear is Þjálfi's connexion with Thor.

The etymology of the name Þjálfi has not been satisfactorily solved as yet, despite numerous attempts at interpretation. Even the explanation that it derives from *þewa-alfaR 'serving elf' is not altogether satisfactory in that there is nothing to point to the fact that Þjálfi was an elf; however, this quibble is probably immaterial as the name also appears as a personal name in over a dozen Swedish runic inscriptions, and therefore Þjálfi probably was predominantly used as such.

A. Olrik, 'Tordenguden og hans dreng' (*Danske Studier*) 1905; A. M. Sturtevant, 'Etymological Comments' (*PMLA* 67) 1952; J. de Vries, *Altgermanische Religionsgeschichte*, Berlin ^{3}1970; J. de Vries, *Altnordisches etymologisches Wörterbuch*, Leiden ^{2}1977.

R: Klopstock, *Braga* and *Die Kunst Tialfs* (odes, 1771).

Þjazi (ON Þjazi; etymology uncertain). A giant who plays an important role in one of the myths about Loki. The tale is told in *Haustlǫng*, composed by the scald Þjóðólfr ór Hvíni in the 9th century, and is re-told in detail by Snorri (*Skáldskaparmál* 1), for whom other sources were probably still accessible in addition to *Haustlǫng*. – The Æsir Odin, Loki and Hǫnir are on a journey; when they try to roast an ox, Þjazi prevents this in the guise of an eagle. When he has finally forced them to give him a share, he takes so much of the meat that Loki wants to kill him with a staff. However, this miraculously sticks to the eagle and he drags Loki after him over sticks and stones until Loki cries for mercy. Þjazi demands that he gets him Idun's rejuvenating apples. With Loki's help, Þjazi is able to steal → Idun along with all her apples, and the Æsir begin to age without them. Loki is forced to bring Idun back again and with the help of Freyja's falcon cloak he carries Idun, who has been turned into a nut (only in Snorri's version) away, pursued by Þjazi in the shape of an eagle, whom the Æsir bring down by fire and then kill inside the gates of Asgard.

Skaði, Þjazi's daughter, gets ready to take revenge for her father, but the Æsir offer her, as compensation, the choice of one of the Æsir for a husband, but without being able to see more of him than his feet. She chooses the most beautiful feet, expecting that it will be Baldr, but they belong to Njǫrðr. Her second condition is that the Æsir should make her laugh, a matter which she considers to be impossible. Loki, however, ties the ends of a piece of rope around the beard of a goat and around his own testicles. The pulling to and fro and the pitiful screams of both of them make even Skaði laugh. Finally, as additional compensation, Odin throws Þjazi's eyes into the heavens and lets them become stars there. – This mythical tale is composed from the abduction of the goddess Idun and → Skaði's courtship, but nonetheless both of these myths quite certainly belong to old layers of Germanic mythology, and Þjazi's role must have been fixed as early as the 9th century more or less in the form we have today. This is evident from kennings and references in the writings of the older skalds (apart from Þjóðólfr also Kormákr Ǫgmundarson in the *Sigurðardrápa*) and in the Eddic lays (*Lokasenna* 50, *Hyndluljóð* 30, *Grottasǫngr* 9). We hear more about Þjazi, namely that his home is called Þrymrheimr (*Grímnismál* 11) and that he was killed by Thor (*Harbarðsljóð* 19); here Þjazi is also called → 'Allvaldis's son'. – The myth of Þjazi is not without its contradictions in the form extant today: from the trio of gods in *Skáldskaparmál* 1 only → Loki, who is the actual hero of the tale, really has a mythical function. The kennings for Loki used in the *Haustlǫng* (Odin's, Thor's Hǫnir's friend) do not at all fit the role that he usually plays. Thor maintains that he killed Þjazi (*Harbarðsljóð* 19), and in other places Loki boasts about this deed (*Lokasenna* 50). At one time it is said that Odin threw Þjazi's eyes into the sky, at another that they were thrown by Thor. These inconsistencies need not necessarily prove that there were once several myths about Þjazi (de Vries) as the embedded fairy-tale elements are prone to variation in tradition, but they could possibly point to an originally more positive role for Loki in Germanic mythology.

E. Hellquist, 'Ett par mytologiska bidrag 1. Om jättenamnet Þjaze' (*ANF* 21) 1905; E. Mogk, 'Þjazi' (*Hoops* 4) 1918–19; H. Gering, *Kommentar I*, Halle 1927; J. de Vries, *The Problem of Loki*, Helsinki 1933; A. Holtsmark, 'Myten om Idun og Tjatse i Tjodolvs Haustlǫng' (*ANF* 64) 1949; J. de Vries, *Altgermanische Religionsgeschichte*, Berlin ^{3}1970; J. de Vries, *Altnordisches etymologisches Wörterbuch*, Leiden ^{2}1977.

R: Þjazi is usually depicted in the shape of an eagle: D. Hardy, *Loki and Thiassi* (painting, c.1909); C. Hansen, *Iduns Rückkehr nach Valhalla*, and C. Hammer's woodcut after Hansen's painting (1862); C. G. Qvarnström, *Iduna som bortrövas av jätten Tjasse i örnhamn* (statue, 1856).

Þjóðnuma (ON Þjóðnuma 'the man-eating'). One of the (mythical?) rivers in the catalogue of rivers in the *Þulur*.

Þjóðólfr ór Hvíni (ON Þjóðólfr). A Norwegian skald from the 9th century, whose poems *Ynglingatal* and → *Haustlǫng* are still extant, apart from several individual stanzas. The *Ynglingatal* is recorded in Snorri's *Heimskringla* and deals in 38 stanzas with the ancestors of the Norwegian king Rǫgnvald back to mythical times; if one is to believe Snorri's evidence, the poem was composed around 870. The *Haustlǫng* is a shield poem which sings the praise of the mythical scenes depicted on a shield, and as such belongs to one of the oldest literary sources of Nordic mythology we have.

J. de Vries, *Altnordische Literaturgeschichte*, Berlin [2]1964–67; L. M. Hollander, *The Skalds*, Ann Arbor 1968.

Þjóðrœrir (ON Þjóðrœrir). A dwarf well versed in magical matters in *Hávamál* 160. The name could mean either 'the bellowing one' (from *rjósa* 'to sound') or 'the one who moves the people' (from Þjóðhrœrir), if one should not read Þjóðreyrir 'the famous one in the burial mound', as Gould does. None of these interpretations seem particularly convincing for a dwarf's name.

K. Müllenhoff, 'Die alte Dichtung von den Nibelungen' (*ZfdA* 23) 1879; N. C. Gould, 'Dwarf-Names in Old Icelandic' (*PMLA* 44) 1929; J. de Vries, *Altnordisches etymologisches Wörterbuch*, Leiden [2]1977.

Þjóðvarta (ON Þjóðvarta or Þjóðvara). One of → Menglǫð's maidens in *Fjǫlsvinnsmál* 38; the meaning of the name is uncertain.

Þjódvitnir (ON, 'people's wolf'). A name for the Fenris wolf in *Grímnismál* 21.

Þjórr (ON, 'bull'). A dwarf in *Vǫluspá* 12.

Þǫgn (ON, 'silence'). The name of a valkyrie in the *Þulur*.

Þǫkk (ON, 'gratitude, joy'). A giantess (only *Gylfaginning* 48), who according to Snorri is Loki in disguise. Þǫkk is the only living being in the world who does not weep for → Baldr after his death, thereby preventing him from being able to return from the underworld; perhaps the name that Snorri gives her is connected with this, as Þǫkk is the only one who does not mourn.

Þǫll (ON). One of the (mythical?) rivers in *Gylfaginning* 27 and in the *Þulur*. The etymology of the river name has not yet been satisfactorily explained.

Thor (ON Þórr, in southern areas → Donar). The Germanic god of thunder, the strongest of the Æsir and the giant-killer among them.

1. Thor as seen in literary sources.

(a) Thor is called Odin's son throughout Old Norse literature (*Skáldskaparmál* 4; *Þrymskviða* 21 and 32, *Hymiskviða* 2 and 35; frequently in skaldic poetry) and as such he is also the brother of the god Baldr (Þjóðólfr, *Haustlǫng* 16). In *Skáldskaparmál*, Snorri talks about Thor's other relatives: he is the son of the giantess → Jǫrð ('earth', according to *Lokasenna* 58 and *Þrymskviða* 1), who is also known as Hlóðyn or Fjǫrgyn (*Vǫluspá* 56). The idea that Thor is the son of the earth-goddess, the personification of the earth, surely derives from an ancient tradition. Thor's children are all personifications of his strength: his sons are → Moði ('angry') and → Magni ('strong') (*Hymiskviða* 34, *Harbarðsljóð* 53) and his daughter is → Þrúðr ('powerful'). His wife is the goddess → Sif, and he is said to be the stepfather of the god Ullr. All this information given by Snorri is also backed up by skaldic kennings. Snorri alone, however, calls him Vingnir and also Hlóra's foster son, but this might be a pure invention of Snorri's, resulting from the names for Thor, Vingþórr and Hlórriði.

Thor's companion on his journeys to the land of the giants is usually Loki, although in *Hymiskviða* it is Týr. His servants are the peasant children → Þjálfi and Rǫskva who have to serve him as a punishment for having injured one of his goats (*Gylfaginning* 43; *Hymiskviða* 38).

(b) Thor lives in Þrúðheimr or Þrúðvangr (*Grímnismál* 4; *Gylfaginning* 20, *Skáldskaparmál* 17); both of these names point to Thor's strength; his hall there is called Bilskírnir (*Grímnismál* 24; *Gylfaginning* 20, *Skáldskaparmál* 4). He owns a chariot drawn by two he-goats, Tanngrísnir and Tanngnjóstr (*Hymiskviða*; *Gylfaginning* 43), so that he is called the 'lord of the goats' (*hafra dróttin*: *Hymiskviða* 20 and 31) as well as the 'chariot god' (*reiðar Týr*: *Skáldskaparmál* 1). He owns a strength-giving belt and an iron gauntlet and in addition to these the giantess, Gríðr, gives him a staff, Gríðarvǫlr; all these are attributes with which folk-belief in Thor's strength was magically embellished.

Thor's most characteristic attribute, however, is his hammer, → Mjǫllnir, which on the one hand is a fearful weapon in combat with the giants, and on the other hand, in the last few decades of the heathen era, became a symbol for the Germanic-heathen religion and was used as a pagan symbol, much as the newly converted Christians wore the cross. Archaeological evidence supporting this supposition are the stone moulds which allowed either a Thor's hammer or a cross to be made side by side in the same mould.

Thor was imagined as being big in stature, strong, with a red beard and a fierce look (*Thrymskviða*) and as a man with a voracious appetite for both food and drink. Although he is said to be both strong and to have a fiery nature, as the names of his sons suggest, he is also depicted as being gullible to the point of simple-mindedness.

(c) Thor is the defender of gods and men alike against the forces threatening → Utgarð, especially against the giants and the Midgard serpent. In this role he is the hero of a number of adventures, which are related by Snorri in a series of short mythological tales in the *Snorra Edda* and in the younger Eddic lays; the great age of some of these tales can be seen from their being mentioned by the skalds in the 9th and 10th centuries.

The hammer → Mjǫllnir plays a significant role in most of Thor's battles. The mere threat of its use brings the drunken giant → Hrungnir, who has broken into Valhall, to his senses, and when the two of them do finally fight each other in single combat, Thor hurls Mjǫllnir which is so powerful that even the projectile, a large whetstone, which the giant flings at him, shatters on impact in mid-air. Whether, mythologically speaking, it is a matter here of a battle of the elements, between the god of thunder and the mountain giant, or a mythicized version of the battle of the old and the new cultures, between the new metal weapons and the weapons of the Stone Age, is uncertain. Nonetheless, whatever the origin is, this myth in particular shows the importance of projectiles at a very early stage of the culture and as such it must be very old.

In the myth of → Thor's journey to Geirrǫðargarð Thor has to meet the challenge of the giant, Geirrǫðr, without his hammer, but is given the staff Gríðarvǫlr by the giantess Gríðr, and with this he is able to wade through the river Vimur and then later he uses it as a prop to hold up the roof at Geirrǫðr's, thus breaking the backs of the giantess daughters, Gjálp and Greip, who are lifting up his chair against the ceiling in the hope of crushing him to death. In the battle against the giant himself, he uses a glowing piece of iron, which Geirrǫðr has thrown at him, as a replacement for Mjǫllnir, hurling it with such force that it goes straight through an iron pillar, the giant and the house wall as well. These mythical adventure stories were obviously extremely popular as they are frequently retold: in the 10th century in Eilífr's *Þórsdrápa* and later in Snorri, and a reference is even made to them in Saxo's *Gesta Danorum*.

A tale, also dealing with the loss of Mjǫllnir but in a completely different way, is to be found as a delightful medieval comic tale in → *Þrymskviða* in which the giant Þrymr has stolen the hammer, Mjǫllnir, and only agrees to give it back in exchange for the goddess Freyja; as the gods are not prepared to do this, Thor, on Heimdall's advice, disguises himself as the bride, and, accompanied by Loki disguised as his serving girl, sets out for Þrymr. Only after the wedding feast, when the giant brings out the hammer as a bridal gift, does Thor end his disguise and kill Þrymr along with all his family. This tale is recorded neither by the skalds nor by Snorri, and as such it appears to be a purely literary product of the 12th or 13th century.

Just as in *Þrymskviða*, in the myth of Thor's journey to Utgarðaloki, Thor is at first the butt of ridicule before being proved to be the sovereign god at the end of the tale. In this fairy-tale-like story Thor is defeated in every way by his opponent Utgarðaloki (also called → Skrýmir), a circumstance which later turns out to have been the result of magical trickery. This mythical story, which is a combination of different elements, is extremely difficult to date as, although there are parallels outside Germanic areas, the skalds and the Eddic lays do not mention it, which suggests that its origin is somewhat late.

The myth of → Thor and the Midgard serpent and his confrontation with the giant Hymir, as told both in → *Hymiskviða* and also in Snorri, lies much further back in the heathen past. Even the oldest skalds (Bragi, Eystein Valdason, Ulfr Uggason) deal in detail with the myth, and pictorial representations on memorial stones date it back to the 8th century. In the version we have today, this myth is a combination of one of Thor's characteristic fights with giants (with Hymir) and Thor's fishing, where Thor baits the Midgard serpent with the head of an ox, but Hymir, who is scared to death, cuts the fishing line at the last moment before Thor can kill it, thus letting the serpent escape.

Apart from the giants, the → Midgard serpent is Thor's greatest enemy, not only in the myth of the catch of fish. Thor has to struggle with the serpent in one of the confrontations with → Skrýmir, and at Ragnarǫk he will meet it again in battle; then, however, he will succeed in killing it, although he will only be able to take nine steps before fatally succumbing to the serpent's poisonous vapours (*Vǫluspá* 56, *Gylfaginning* 50).

The numerous myths about Thor's giant-killing feats have the effect that he appears as a giant-killer even in places where he perhaps originally did not have this role, such as the killing of Þjazi and that of the → giant master builder who built Asgard. Skaldic stanzas by Þorbjǫrn dísarskáld and Vetrliði Sumarliðarson (from the 10th century) give a whole list of giants and giantesses who have allegedly been killed by Thor.

(d) Although in fact Odin is usually considered to be the supreme god of the Germanic Pantheon, the gods can nonetheless be seen to be dependent on Thor in many myths in which they rely on him for their own protection. This discrepancy is probably the result of a differing position in the cult (see below). Whilst Odin's function as ruler was increasingly superseded by his role as the god of poetry, of magic and runic knowledge and, in addition to that, was limited to a cult of the ruling class (including the skalds and rune-masters who themselves identified with it), Thor's function of strength, which was the reason for the farmer-warriors to honour him as a god of war, shifted more and more towards the function of fertility; one reason for this is because Thor extended his divine role from being the god of thunder to include everything to do with the weather, as Adam of Bremen (IV, 26) commented upon: 'Thor is in charge of the air and directs the thunder and lightning, wind and rain in it.' This extension of Thor's role in this way meant that his function was not only that of a war-god, but also tended towards that of a fertility god (see below). Another major factor in this shift of Thor's responsibilities was the social position of the followers of Thor as farmer-warriors.

The gods call upon Thor time and again whenever danger threatens them, whether the danger takes the form of the giants, Þjazi or Hrungnir, or even silencing Loki (*Lokasenna*) when necessary. In all these cases, it is said that Thor was 'on a journey to the east to fight the giants', but as soon as the gods need his aid, he is there at once, ready, willing and successful.

Loki is Thor's most frequent companion on his journeys, a fact which is unquestionably the consequence of the still extant sources, as the contrast between the strong, honest and yet simple-minded Thor and the crafty and sly Loki, easily lead to the comic situations characteristic of the majority of mythological stories about Thor; in *Þrymskviða*, for example, Thor is made to look ridiculous beside Loki, whilst in *Lokasenna* Thor alone is able to silence Loki.

Only sparse comments are to be found about Thor's wife, Sif, in literary sources and nothing at all is known about her relationship to Thor; it is a matter, too, of pure speculation as to whether Sif can be given a role in Thor's tendency to shift his role towards the third (fertility) function, as the etymology of her name is by no means clear. It is, however, likely that a wife was found for Thor early on because of his important role in the cult as a whole, and as such her name may really only mean 'the wife' (that is, Thor's) and she had no other function.

Apart from in the social standing of his worshippers, Thor's antagonism towards Odin is found nowhere so pronounced as in the → *Hárbarðsljóð*, an Eddic lay composed towards the end of the heathen era. The poet supports Odin, who, disguised here as the ferryman Hárbarðr, refuses to ferry him home after a battle against the giants. Odin mocks the weary and bedraggled Thor and the poet gives his opinion quite clearly: 'The lords, who have fallen in battle, belong to Odin, whereas the thralls are Thor's.' As a result of this comment, older scholarship in particular greatly emphasized the contrast between Odin and Thor: Odin was the god of the nobility, and Thor the god of the farmer-warriors, and as such Thor was subordinate to Odin. His position as Odin's son could also be interpreted as clarifying this still further. Although the two gods are indisputably very different, the similarities between them should not be overlooked: both are said to be the forefathers of royal families, and just as Odin shows his wisdom in *Vafþrúðnismál*, so Thor shows his in *Alvíssmál*. Odin may be the god of runes, but, according to the inscriptions themselves, Thor is called upon to consecrate them (→ *wigiþonar*); Odin makes stars from Þjazi's eyes whereas Thor makes a star from Aurvandill's toe. Both have connexions with warfare: Odin through magic, Thor because of his strength. Indeed, it is in the function of strength, as war-gods, that they have most in common; whereas Odin is firmly established in the function of ruler, Thor's position shifts more towards the third (fertility) function, and Thor to a certain extent at least is indeed the god of the peoples' and farmers' army, whereas Odin's domain is that of the bands of warriors and Vikings, bound by oath to Odin.

2. Evidence of faith and cult.

(a) In late heathen skaldic poetry at the end of the 10th century there are more and more poems which are directed entirely at Thor or else are dedicated to him. The more extensive of these are Eilífr Goðrúnarson's → *Þórsdrápa* (1) and Eysteinn Valdason's → *Þórsdrápa* (2). Shorter poems to Thor were written by Thorbjǫrn dísarskáld and Vetrliði Sumarliðarson, and a fragment of a stanza by Bragi is still extant from the 9th century. This evidence of heathen religious poetry appears alongside purely descriptive mythological poems such as *Húsdrápa* and *Haustlǫng*.

In both the *Landnámabók* and also in the sagas there are numerous references which point to a belief in the god Thor among Icelandic settlers. Although the evidence of these late sources should not be overestimated in detail, the mere amount of extant material points to the great importance of Thor in Icelandic folk-belief during the 9th and 10th centuries. Of about 4,000 people mentioned in the *Landnámabók*, about a quarter have a name which is based in some way on Thor. As family tradition in name-giving frequently plays a major role here, this points to a massive cult of Thor in their original homeland, Norway; personal names deriving from other gods' names (Freyr-, Ing-) are in contrast relatively seldom. The Icelandic settlers entrusted themselves to Thor's protection when it was a case of finding where to build their new farm. They brought highseat pillars with them from their homeland (→ *ǫndvegissúlur*), in which either a picture of Thor had been carved (*Landnámabók* H 73 = S 85) or which were marked as being devoted to Thor by the → *reginnaglar* which had been hit into them (perhaps a reference to Hrungnir's whetstone in Thor's head: *Eyrbyggja saga*). These pillars were then thrown into the sea off the coast of Iceland, and wherever they drifted to land, the settlers built their farms. Thor was most likely also called upon to direct their landfall in the first place (*Eyrbyggja saga*).

According to the sagas (*Eyrbyggja saga*, *Kjalnesinga saga*), there were temples in Iceland as well as in Norway where a statue of Thor was worshipped. One such example is said to have been in Mærin in Trondheim (*Oláfs saga Tryggvasonar*) where it was destroyed by Olaf with an axe; a hollow statue of Thor in Guðbrandsdal was destroyed by St Olaf (*Oláfs saga hins helga*). However, as place-names deriving from Þórshof ('Thor's temple') are totally absent in these areas, these reports must be met with some scepticism. Adam of Bremen mentions the existence of statues of Thor in temples in Sweden (one of which was destroyed around the year 1030 by the English missionary Wilfried: II, 62; another one was the great temple in Uppsala: IV, 26).

Thor's picture was apparently also to be found carved onto the stem of earl Eirek's ship (*Oláfs saga hins helga*) and even onto chairs (*Fóstbrœðra saga*). The cultic use of a small statuette of Thor is very likely, although admittedly only mentioned once (*Hallfreðar saga*), but finds of similar figures of Freyr and perhaps also of Thor substantiate this assumption. Although it is clear from substantial archaeological evidence that the wearing of small metal Thor's hammers (→ Mjǫllnir) as amulet-necklaces was very widespread, this seems to have been more a reaction in the late heathen era to the symbol of the Christian crucifix than based on an ancient tradition.

Sacrifices to Thor are also recorded in medieval literature. Dudo of St Quentin in the 11th century reports a human sacrifice to Thur of the Normans, but his chronicle is extremely unreliable. The *Landnámabók* reports human sacrifice in Iceland, at which the backs of those sacrificed were said to be broken on a Thor's stone (H 73); but it also mentions vows for less harmful sacrifices, probably votive offerings, made by a certain Kollr, who called for Thor's protection during a storm off Iceland (*Landnámabók*: H 15). The memory of a sacrifice to Thor seems to be contained in the tale of Thor's goats, and this would seem to be more ancient than the gory examples mentioned above and written about by Christian authors: when Thor was staying with a farmer, he had both his goats slaughtered and then cooked; afterwards everyone ate, throwing the bones onto the goatskins. Next morning Thor blessed the goatskins with his hammer and the goats sprang to life again. This short tale could be based on a sacrifice of goats to Thor, which is more likely than the rather more fantastic reports of human sacrifice in Iceland.

(b) The widespread devotion to Thor is, however, not only evident from literary sources. Three Danish (Glavendrup, Virring, Sœnder-Kirkeby) and a Swedish (Velanda Skattegården) rune-stone from the 10th century carry the formula 'May Thor bless these runes' after the actual inscription; three Danish (Læborg, Spentrup, Gårdstanga 3) and three Swedish (Stenkvista Kirka, Åby, Bjärby) stones have an engraved Thor's hammer itself instead of this formula. The → Nordendorf fibula from the first half of the 7th century has *wigiþonar* on it, as well as names of other gods. It would be wrong, however, to try to construct from all of this a role for Thor as a consecratory god. Towards the end of the heathen era a devotion to Thor with the formal characteristics of a cult sprang up in many parts of South Scandinavia and the Continent; although it was surely a reaction to the rising popularity of Christianity among the Germanic people, the new upsurgence of a cult based on Thor was an attempt to combat the rapid advance of totally new beliefs (which would neccessarily bring new culture in their wake). The dedication formulas and the hammer symbols on grave stones are as much a pagan reaction to encroaching Christianity as the hammer amulets have been seen to be. It is possible that Thor became the symbolic figure for this heathen renewal movement, in particular because of the hammer symbol.

(c) The flood of personal names deriving from a Thor root may have similar reasons, although it would be wrong to interpret from this that the people with such names living in Christian times were associated in any way with a continuing tendency towards heathen beliefs, as far-reaching family traditions surely play a significant role here. The increasing popularity of Thor in Viking times is also evident from the upsurge of Thor names at this time, whereas previously (before the Viking Era) there were no Thor names to be found in rune inscriptions.

(d) The numerous place names based on Thor also point to the extensive cult of Thor, but caution is necessary here as many place names which link Thor with some general geographical element could possibly simply be based on a personal name based on Thor. Indeed, a certain degree of scepticism is needed with most of the Scandinavian and English place-names based on Thor. The names of places of real cultic significance can only be presumed where the second element of the name points quite obviously to a cultic place, such as *-vé*, *-hof*, *-lundr*. Names based on *-lundr* 'grove' are especially frequent in Denmark and Thorshof in South Norway.

It is less certain whether Thorsåker in Sweden can be considered a cultic place, and a similar problem arises in England with regard to names based on Thunor, whereas those based on Thunores hlæw correspond exactly to Thorslundr, and even in Ireland Coill Tomair is recorded with the same meaning from the year 1000 A.D. Alongside these, the English name Thurstable 'Thor's pillar' suggests devotion to Thor. In Germany the place-name material is sparse, although there are a number of places called Donnersberg which would seem to derive their names from Thor/Donar.

(e) The name of the day Thursday, a translation of Latin *dies Jovi*, is one of the oldest references to the veneration of Thor. This translation is in keeping with the *interpretatio germanica*, which identified Jupiter as Thor; Thursday retained a certain sanctity in German folk-belief up to the 17th century and was a popular day for weddings.

(f) The Bronze Age Scandinavian rock carvings enable us to trace a definite cult of Thor back even further into the past. On the rock carvings at Stora Hoglem and Hvitlycke next to a picture of a copulating couple there is a larger phallic figure carrying a hammer or an axe. This scene has been interpreted as marriage vows (here of a → *hierós gámos*?) supervised by Thor whose hammer was understood as a fertility symbol right into the Middle Ages. Thus, the role of the god of the heavens in a fertility function is documented in the Germanic past. References to a bridal consecration of marriage by Thor have to be seen in the light of the symbolism of his hammer.

3. Function and Position.

The name Thor, ON Þórr, Þunarr, West Germanic Þonar, OHG Donar, AS Þunor, from Germanic *þunraR, originally meaning not 'thunderer' but 'thunder', marks him out as the god of thunder. His hammer, which he hurls as lightning and thunder, is surely originally linked with this role, although Thor principally represents the second Dumézilian theory (function of strength). The shift to the third function is ancient as the hammer as a fertility-giving symbol can be traced back to the Bronze Age. Therefore Thor is not only god of thunder and lightning, but also of wind and rain.

Exactly what Thor's position was in the Germanic world of the gods can be seen from the *interpretatio germanica* whereby Thor is identified as Jupiter. This is clear from Anglo-Saxon glosses and in the translation of the Roman week-day names.

Functionally speaking, Thor is related to the mythical Herakles/Hercules of the ancient world, and Tacitus mentions a → Hercules among the main Germanic gods; Hercules and Thor have, indeed, so much in common (weapon, function as giant-killer and defender of the gods) that it is rather surprising that Thor was identified as Jupiter in the *interpretatio germanica* of the week-day names.

Thor corresponds to the warrior and thunder god Taranis in Celtic mythology whose variant name Tanarus agrees etymologically with Donar; the form Taranis, however, is supported by Celtic *taran* 'thunder' so that a parallel development of thunder gods is conceivable.

The Indian god of war and weather, Indra, is also functionally related to Thor; Indra is the representative of the second function in Indian mythology. Like Thor, he is a son of the gods, the son of the primeval ancestors; like Thor who fights against the Midgard serpent, Indra must combat the snake demon Vrta. Thor's hammer corresponds to Indra's *vajra* (club) and both weapons were made by a godly smith, Sindri and Tvastr in the Norse and Indian myths respectively. Thor and Indra are both great eaters and drinkers, both are chariot gods, both undertake extensive journeys to fight against demons. Despite many differences Thor and Indra can be seen to have so many similarities that a primeval relationship between the two gods ought to be accepted (Dumézil, F. R. Schröder). This would mean that Thor's position can be traced back to the Indo-European era.

F. Jónsson, 'Odin og Tor i Norge og på Island i det 9. og 10. Århundret' (*ANF* 17) 1901; H. Lindroth, 'Om gudanamnet Tor' (*NoB* 4) 1916; R. Jente, *Die mythologischen Ausdrücke im altenglischen Wortschatz*, Heidelberg 1921; F. R. Schröder, 'Thor im Vimurfluß' (*PBB* 51) 1927; E. A. Philippson, *Germanisches Heidentum bei den Angelsachsen*, Leipzig 1929; H. Ljungberg, *Tor*, Uppsala 1947; E. O. G. Turville-Petre, 'Professor Georges Dumézil' (*Saga-Book* 14) 1953–55; F. R. Schröder, 'Indra, Thor und Herakles' (*ZfdPh* 76) 1957; V. Kiil, 'Fra andvegissula til omnkall' (*Norveg* 7) 1960; J. de Vries, *Altgermanische Religionsgeschichte*, Berlin [3]1979; E. O. G. Turville-

Petre, 'Thurstable' (in: *Nine Norse Studies*) London 1972; Å. V. Ström, H. Biezais, *Germanische und baltische Religion*, Stuttgart 1975; E. Marold, ' "Thor weihe diese Runen" ' (*Frühmittelalterliche Studien* 8) 1975; E. O. G. Turville-Petre, *Myth and Religion of the North*, New York, 1975; E. F. Halvorsen, 'Þórr' (*KLNM* 20) 1976; H. Klingenberg, 'Die Drei-Götter-Fibel' (*ZfdA* 105) 1976; G. Dumézil, *Gods of the Ancient Northmen*, Berkeley 1977.

R: in most cases the artistic interpretation of the figure of Thor follows the description of the god in the Nordic sources: as the strength-exuding god of thunder, mostly in the battle against the giants. Especially in the case of statues there is frequently an influence from classical statues of Hercules. Thor is only to be found as the god of war in Klopstock, Thorild, Pottner. Thor is the representative of the Æsir in a polemic confrontation with the Nordic Renaissance in the Romantic with the Scandinavians Stiernstolpe and Grundtvig.
(literature) F. J. Klopstock, *Wir und Sie* (ode addressed to Thor, 1776); A. Oehlenschläger, *Hammeren hentes; Thors fiskeri; Thor besøger Hymir* (poems in: *Nordens Guder*, 1819); A. Oehlenschläger, *Thors reise til Jotunheim* (epic poem, 1807); W. Hertz, *Thors Trunk; Thor kam als Gast ins Riesenlande* (1859); J. M. Stiernstolpe, *Mythologierne eller Gudatvisten* (satirical poem, 1820); N. F. S. Grundtvig, *Nordens Mythologie eller Sinnbilled-Sprog* (1832); Thor Thorild, *Harmen* (poem); L. Uhland, *Der Mythus von Thor* (1836; this poet's attempt marks the beginning of detailed scholarly research on ON mythology in Germany); W. Schulte v. Brühl, *Der Hammer Thors* (1915); H. F. Blunck, *Herr Dunnar und die Bauern* (in: *Märchen und Sagen*, 1937); O. Erler, *Thors Gast* (play, 1937); H. C. Artmann, *Die Heimholung des Hammers* (1977); in the cartoon series *Der mächtige Thor* Thor plays a sort of mythological superman.
(fine art) J. H. Füssli, *Thor in Hymirs Boot bekämpft die Midgardschlange* (painting, 1780); H. E. Freund, *Thor* (statue, 1821/22); B. E. Fogelberg, *Thor* (marble statue, 1844); M. E. Winge, *Thors Kampf mit den Riesen* (charcoal drawing, 1880); K. Ehrenberg, *Odin, Thor und Magni* (drawing, 1883); E. Doepler, *Thor; Thor und die Midgardschlange; Thor den Hrungnir bekämpfend; Thor bei dem Riesen Þrym als Braut verkleidet; Thor bei Hymir; Thor bei Skrymir; Thor den Fluß Wimur durchwatend* (illustrations in: E. Doepler, W. Ranisch, *Walhall*, 1901); J. C. Dollman, *Thor and the mountain; Sif and Thor* (drawings, 1909); G. Poppe, *Thor* (painting); E. Pottner, *Thors Schatten* (= war; drawing, 1914); H. Natter, *Thor* (marble statue); U. Bremer, illustrations to H. C. Artmanns, *Die Heimholung des Hammers* (1977).
(music) The role of Donner in R. Wagner's opera *Das Rheingold* was written for a baritone voice.
(other) Thor, Icelandic coast patrol ship, built 1951; Thor, Swedish icebreaker, built 1963.

Thor and the Midgard serpent. A well-known Nordic myth about Thor's attempt to go fishing for the Midgard serpent from the giant → Hymir's boat in order to kill it. The most detailed version is to be found in the *Snorra Edda* (*Gylfaginning* 47). Thor leaves Midgard alone and disguised as a young man. He spends the night at Hymir's dwelling and next morning accompanies the giant on his fishing trip, despite the giant's reluctance. He has to find his own bait and so he pulls off the skull of one of Hymir's bulls. Then Thor sits at the back of the boat and rows strongly and further out than the giant wants. He fastens the head of the ox to a sturdy fishing line and the Midgard serpent bites immediately. Thor pulls so hard on the line that his feet break through the planks of the boat and standing on the bottom of the sea he pulls the monster up to the edge of the boat. The mere sight of the serpent fills the giant with terror and just as Thor is pulling out Mjǫllnir in order to kill the serpent, Hymir cuts the line and the monster sinks back into the sea, even though Thor throws the hammer after it, 'and some people say that the hammer cut off its head at waterlevel. I believe that the truth is that the Midgard serpent is still alive and out there in the seas which surround the world'. Thor hits the giant with his fist and sends him flying overboard and then finally wades to land himself.

This myth is to be found in a somewhat more concise version in Hym 18–25, where Thor and Hymir both row back, after Thor's lack of success, with the two whales the giant managed to catch.

The *Hymiskviða*, which is not very much older than the *Snorra Edda*, is not the only other record for Snorri's text of Thor and the Midgard serpent; the skalds from the 9th and 10th centuries also indicate knowledge of the myth (Bragi, *Ragnarsdrápa* 14–20; Eystein Valdason 1–2; Gamli gnævaðarskáld; Ulfr Uggason, *Húsdrápa* 3–6) of which Ulf's version is interesting insofar as that in it Thor kills the monster. Other important evidence for the popularity of the myth are four Viking Age pictorial stones; the story can be recognized most clearly of all in the depiction on the pictorial stone of Altuna, Sweden (c.1050), which shows Thor with Mjǫllnir in one hand, the fishing line with a serpent-like monster on the end in the other, with both his feet pushed through the floor of the boat; on the other hand all of the other pictures show a boat with two (armed) people on board, who are fishing for an object which cannot be identified any closer; the mythological context of the rest of the pictures on this stone puts it beyond doubt that the depiction on the pictorial stone Ardre VIII (8th century, Gotland) is of Thor's fight with the Midgard serpent. Because of the bull's skull used as bait, we can be certain also that the grave stone from Gosforth, England (10th century) is of the same story. In the case of the stone from Hœrdum church in Denmark (8th – 11th century), the myth can only be recognized because of the similarity between it and the depiction on Ardre VIII.

Ulfr Uggason's *Húsdrápa*, composed in 983, points to yet another pictorial representation: he describes some wood-carvings in the hall of Oláfr Pá in Hjarðarholt. At any rate a knowledge of the myth can be assumed for the whole of Viking Age and medieval Scandinavia.

Thor is brought into contact with the Midgard serpent elsewhere in Germanic mythology, although this is more the consequence than the reason for his role in the myth. Snorri tells of how, during Thor's journey to Utgarðaloki, which immediately precedes the myth of the fishing of the Midgard serpent, Thor is unable to lift the Midgard serpent, which because of an optical illusion he thinks is a cat (→ Skrýmir); Snorri sees the fishing trip as a direct act of revenge for this. Even in the final battle of the gods at Ragnarǫk Thor is the opponent of the Midgard serpent which he is able to kill, but he himself is overcome by its poisonous breath and dies (*Vǫluspá* 56; *Gylfaginning* 50).

The struggle of a god with a monster is undoubtedly an ancient mythical motive in the Indo-European peoples (Indra fights against Vrtra, Apollo/Helios against Python), but it is nonetheless arguable whether indeed the myth of Thor and the Midgard serpent is a purely Germanic myth or whether it has been influenced by the Old Testament dragon Leviathan which was baited by using Behemoth, and which has been seen by the Church Fathers as the personification of the devil who was baited by God through Christ and then destroyed. It may even come from Jewish apocryphal literature from the 8th century (which Kabell cannot prove absolutely convincingly). Whatever the genesis of this myth was, there can be no doubt that during the conversion of Scandinavia to Christianity the myth of Thor and the

Midgard serpent and the concept of Christ's victory over the Leviathan influenced each other (Gschwantler). The discovery of the depiction on the grave stone from Gosforth found in a Christian context and also the linguistic equation of the Midgard serpent as the translation for Leviathan in later Icelandic religious translated literature serve as evidence.

O. v. Friesen, 'Tors fiske pa en uppländske runsten' (*Festschrift E. Mogk*) Halle 1924; F. R. Schröder, 'Das Hymirlied' (*ANF* 70) 1955; J. Brœndsted, 'Thors fiskeri' (*Fra Nationalmuseets Arbejdsmark*) 1955; O. Gschwantler, 'Christus, Thor und die Midgardschlange' (*Festschrift O. Höfler* 1) Vienna 1968; J. de Vries, *Altgermanische Religionsgeschichte*, Berlin [3]1970; A. Kabell, 'Der Fischfang Thors' (*ANF* 91) 1976; A. Wolf, 'Sehweisen und Darstellungsfragen in der *Gylfaginning*' (*Skandinavistik* 7) 1977; P. Meulengracht Sørensen, 'Thors's Fishing Expedition' (G. Steinsland: *Words and Onjects; towards a Dialogue between Archaeology and History of Religion*) Oslo 1986.

R: (literature) A. Oehlenschläger, *Thors Fiskeri*; and, *Thor besøger Jetten Hymir* (poems in: *Nordens Guder*, 1819).
(fine art) J. H. Füssli, *Thor in Hymirs Boot bekämpft die Midgardschlange* (painting, 1790); E. Doepler, *Thor bei Hymir* (in: E. Doepler, W. Ranisch, *Walhall*, 1901).

Thor's goats. Tanngrísnir and Tanngnóstr, two goats, draw Thor's chariot according to Snorri (*Gylfaginning* 20). There is a short mythological tale about them inserted into the tale of Thor's journey to → Utgarðaloki (*Gylfaginning* 43) which tells of what happened when Thor and Loki stayed overnight with a farmer's family. 'In the evening Thor took his goats and slaughtered them; then the skin was pulled off them and they were thrown into the cooking cauldron. When they were cooked, Thor and his companions sat down to eat and Thor invited the farmer, his wife and his children to join them; the farmer's son was called → Þjálfi, and his daughter Rǫskva. Thor spread the two goatskins out away from the fire and told the farmer and his family to throw the bones onto them. The farmer's son, Þjálfi, took the thighbone of one of the goats and split it with a knife in order to get at the marrow inside. Thor stayed the night, got up before daybreak, dressed, took Mjǫllnir, lifted it and blessed the goatskins. Thereupon the goats stood up again, but one of them was lame in its back leg. Thor saw this and asked if the farmer or one of his family had played around with the goat's legs: he noticed that the bone was broken.' The farmer is able to calm Thor's anger down somewhat by offering him his children as recompense and these accompany Thor thereafter as his servants.

The story of the lame goat is also mentioned in *Hymiskviða* 37, and here too, two children are offered as recompense; even though the context is somewhat different, both versions seem to be re-tellings of the same well-known myth.

A sacrificial rite which is well documented outside Germanic areas is behind the myth. After the slaughter of the sacrificial animal it is then dedicated to the god and resurrected: in shamanic rites especially the slaughter, skinning and cooking, together with the final resurrection of the animal are well documented as a way of making contact with the gods. In Germanic mythology there is further evidence of the old rite in the boar → Sæhrímnir, who is cooked and eaten daily, only to come to life anew next day (*Gylfaginning* 37).

The meaningful names of the goats are surely a young invention and probably come from Snorri himself as they are nowhere to be found except in *Gylfaginning* 20 and the *Þulur*.

F. R. Schröder, 'Das Hymirlied' (*ANF* 70) 1955; J. de Vries, *Altgermanische Religionsgeschichte*, Berlin [3]1970.

Thor's goats

R: apart from his hammer, Thor's goats are among his attributes and depicted on Romanesque German churches (Sts Peter and Paul in Hirsau; Oberröblichen near Halle, Saale), but even more frequently in modern artists' impressions of Thor, such as M. E. Winge's painting, *Tors strid med jättarna* (1872) or E. Doeplers illustration in E. Doepler, W. Ranisch, *Walhall* (1901).

Thor's Journey to Geirrǫðargarð → Geirrǫðargarð.

Þorbjǫrg lítilvǫlva (ON, 'Þorbjǫrg, the little prophetess'). A prophetess in *Eiríks saga rauða* 4. How she makes predictions about the future at a farm on Greenland is described in some detail: a small dais is set up for the seeress who carries a staff with a stud as a sign of her profession, and the women form a circle around this seat. One of them – a Christian, as is deliberately emphasized – begins to sing a magical song (called Varðlokkur) which according to the seeress will call the spirits to her. After this she predicts the future for everyone present.

Even if it is a matter in this report of a literary embellished tale, nonetheless certain elements of the séance, for example the staff of the seeress and the pedestal carry authentic characteristics of practices in Germanic heathendom. The hint is also interesting that the seeress's nine sisters (who have died in the meantime) were also prophetesses; the ability to see into the future was considered by Icelanders to run in the family, as a passage in *Laxdœla saga* confirms.

Þorbjǫrn dísarskáld ('skald of the dísir'). An Icelandic poet of the later 10th century, of whose work hardly more than one and a half stanzas are preserved; they belong to a poem directed to the god Thor, but the poet's nickname suggests that he also composed some religious poetry dedicated to female goddesses.

Þordis spákona (ON, 'Þordís the soothsayer'). The name of a soothsayer in *Vatnsdœla saga* 44; probably a purely literary figure. The only thing she has in common with the Germanic soothsayers is the staff which is the sign of her profession: this had already become a characteristic attribute for soothsayers in medieval literary convention.

Þorgerðr Hǫlgabrúðr (ON, 'Þorgerðr, Hǫlgi's bride') is a goddess to whom a temple was dedicated in the 10th century in Gudbrandsdal, Norway. She was worshipped here together with the goddess → Irpa.

Old Norse prose texts, as well as *Jómsvíkingadrápa* 32, written by Bishop Bjarni Kolbeinson, who died in 1222, tell of the adoration of this goddess in a richly decorated temple. In the description of the temple in the *Færeyinga saga* (where the temple is described as having glass windows!) only the goddess Thorgerðr Hǫlgabrúðr is mentioned, from whose hands Hakon requests a golden ring as a good omen. In the *Jómsvíkinga saga* the goddess Irpa is mentioned as well as Þorgerðr Hǫlgabrúðr, and the *Njáls saga* adds that Thor was also to be seen in the temple on his chariot (88). While these texts all agree that the temple was situated in Norway, *Harðar saga* 19 places it in Iceland. This saga also agrees with *Njáls saga* in that it mentions the burning of the temple and the pictures of the gods.

Snorri reports (*Skáldskaparmál* 42) that 'the king called Hǫlgi, after whom Hálogaland is called, is the father (!) of Þorgerðr Hǫlgabrúðr. Sacrifices were made to both of them, and the burial mound which was built up over Hǫlgi consisted of alternate layers of sacrifice money of gold and silver and layers of earth and gravel.'

The fact that Snorri names Hǫlgi as Þorgerðr Hǫlgabrúðr's father is surprising as the name Hǫlgi as Þorgerðr Hǫlgabrúðr's husband seems obvious. Some other sources replace the form -brúðr with -troll, whilst instead of Hǫlga- other versions such as Hǫrða-, Hǫrga-, Hǫlda- are to be found. Snorri's link of Þorgerðr Hǫlgabrúðr with Hálogaland concurs with what other sources say. In fact she is probably a local deity from Hálogaland, perhaps even a family goddess connected in some way with the family of Hakon who was ruling over Hálogaland at the time (Storm), since in the extant sources the cult of the goddess is almost always associated with Hakon.

The name Þorgerðr probably comes from the name of the giantess Gerðr. Þorgerðr Hǫlgabrúðr is also described as a troll, i.e. a giantess. Presumably Þorgerðr Hǫlgabrúðr should be considered as one of the fertility deities. Irpa, who is named alongside her, belongs etymologically to *jarpr* 'dark brown'; thus perhaps she is also a chthonic deity (Schröder).

The way in which Þorgerðr Hǫlgabrúðr interferes in the battle in Hjǫrungavágr, where she causes a hailstorm and appears in the clouds firing arrows from her fingertips, reminds us, however, more of the valkyries; her function in the temple on the other hand, where she is not asked for a gift, but rather for a prophecy, is more reminiscent of the role of soothsayers than of goddesses.

All our sources are, however, too fictional and far too interdependent to allow details of the description to tempt us too far in attempts to interpret Þorgerðr Hǫlgabrúðr.

G. Storm, 'Om Thorgerd Hölgebrud' (*ANF* 2) 1885; F. R. Schröder, *Quellenbuch zur germanischen Religionsgeschichte*, Berlin, Leipzig 1933; J. de Vries, *Altgermanische Religionsgeschichte*, Berlin [3]1970; E. F. Halvorsen, 'Þorgerðr Hǫlgabrúðr' (*KLNM* 20) 1976.

Þorinn (ON Þorinn 'the brave one'). A dwarf in *Vǫluspá* 12 and in the *Þulur*.

R: in J. R. R. Tolkien's novel, *The Hobbit* (1937), Thorinn is the eldest of the 13 dwarfs.

Þorri (ON; otherwise the name of the winter month from mid-January to mid-Feburary). A giant in the genealogies of → Fornjótr. According to them, Þorri was the son of King Snær and had three children. His sons were Norr and Gorr, and his daughter was Gói. The introductory chapter to the *Orkneyinga saga* (*Fundinn Nóregr*) records: 'Þorri cared a lot about sacrifices and had one every year at mid-winter, which was called Þorri's sacrifice (*Þorrablót*), and the name of the month comes from this.' The tale obviously serves to explain aetiologically the meaning of the name of the month and the sacrifice. The sacrifice, however, probably took its name from the month and not vice versa so there is no need to assume a vegetation god Þorri, as the name of the month is quite adequately explained by 'frost'.

J. de Vries, *Altgermanische Religionsgeschichte*, Berlin 31970; E. F. Halvorsen, 'Þorri' (*KLNM* 20) 1976.

Þórsdrápa (1) (ON, 'eulogy to Thor'). A poem by the skald Eilífr Goðrúnarson from the end of the 10th century. Only 19 whole and two half stanzas in *dróttkvætt* metre are still extant in the *Snorra Edda*. The lay describes with great artistic skill and numerous complicated kennings Thor's journey to → Geirrǫðargarð which was brought about by Loki, the crossing of the river Vimur, the killing of Geirrǫð's daughters Gjálp and Greip, and finally the fight with the giant Geirrǫðr himself, in which Thor and Geirrǫðr fling a piece of glowing iron at each other until it finally fells Geirrǫðr. Snorri describes this journey in great detail (*Gylfaginning* 18) using the *Þórsdrápa* as a source.

K. Reichardt, 'Die *Þórsdrápa* des Eilífr Goðrúnarson: Textinterpretation' (*PMLA* 63) 1948; V. Kiil, 'Eilífr Goðrúnarsons Þórsdrápa' (*ANF* 71) 1956; H. Lie, 'Þórsdrápa' (*KLNM* 20) 1976; H. Kuhn, *Das Dróttkvætt*, Heidelberg 1983; R. Frank, 'Eilífr Goðrúnarson' (*Dictionary of the Middle Ages* 4) 1984; R. Frank, 'Hand tools and power tools in Eilífr's Þórsdrápa' (*Structure and Meaning in Old Norse Literature*) Odense 1986.

Þórsdrápa (2) (ON). A skaldic poem by the Icelander, Eysteinn, of which only three stanzas still remain which Snorri used as a source in his Edda, thus keeping them for posterity. The fragment of *Þórsdrápa* deals with the central part of the mythological tale of → Thor and the Midgard serpent.

Þráinn (ON, 'the threatening one'). A dwarf in *Vǫluspá* 12.

Þrar (ON, 'the stubborn one'). A dwarf in the *Þulur*.

Þrasarr (ON, 'the furious one'). A name for Odin in the *Þulur*. The mythical names Þrasir, Lífþrasir, MǫgÞrasir, Dolgþrasir are related to it, as are the male personal names ON Þrasi, OHG Thraso. The etymology of his name suggests that → Odin has something to do with (cultic) fury and ecstasy.

H. Falk, *Odensheite*, Kristiania 1924; J. de Vries, *Altgermanische Religionsgeschichte*, Berlin [3]1970.

Þrasir (ON, 'the furious, threatening one'). A dwarf in the *Þulur*.

A. M. Sturtevant, 'Semantic and etymological Notes' (*SS* 20) 1948.

Þriði (ON, 'the third one'). A name for Odin in *Grímnismál* 46. In *Gylfaginning*, Þridi is said to be a god in an otherwise unknown divine triad, together with Hárr and Jafnhárr.

H. Falk, *Odensheite*, Kristiania 1924; J. de Vries, *Altgermanische Religionsgeschichte*, Berlin [3]1970.

Þrígeitir (ON, 'three-Geitir'). A giant in *Þulur*; perhaps merely a strengthening of the giant's name Geitir?

Þrima (ON, 'fight'). The name of a valkyrie in the *Þulur*.

Þrívaldi (ON, 'the three-mighty', 'very mighty'). A giant with whom Thor, according to Snorri (*Skáldskaparmál* 4), had one of his battles. Snorri quotes in this context a fragment of verse written by the skald Vetrliði (end of the 10th century) in which it is said that Thor killed Þrívaldi, but already in the 9th century there is a fragment of another stanza composed by Bragi the skald where Thor obviously is referred to (as a chariot driver) and where Bragi mentions that Thor split open the nine heads of Þrívaldi. In spite of the naming of a many-headed giant in the Eddic lays (with 900 heads: *Hymiskviða* 8; with 6: *Vafþrúðnismál* 33; with 3: *Skírnismál* 31) a nine-headed giant appears nowhere else in ON poetry. Even taking into account that the number nine had a particular significance in Germanic religion, Þrívaldi's name suggests a three-headed giant.

Nevertheless, there are the remains here of yet another adventure of the god Thor, which can be counted in the list of fights with giants (Hrungir, Þrymr, Hymir, Skrýmir, Geirrǫðr), although we no longer have any more details about the contents.

Þróinn (ON). A dwarf in *Vǫluspá* 12 and *Gylfaginning* 13. Etymologically, perhaps like

→ Þrór to *þróast* 'to grow', thus 'the thriving one' or 'the growing one'; possibly, however, as the manuscripts seem to suggest, a variant of → Þráinn.

Þrór (1) (ON). A pseudonym for Odin in *Grímnismál* 49 and a few times in skaldic poetry. The name is cognate to ON *þróast* 'thrive', so that Jónsson supposed that it was originally the name for (the fertility god) Freyr, as Þrór is also a name for a boar (Freyr's attribute). Höfler pointed out that the boar, when connected with Odin, is associated with the battle order called the 'boar snout' (*svinfylking*), and therefore Odin's name Þrór is probably better translated as 'attacker'.

F. Jónsson, 'Gudenavne – dyrenavne' (*ANF* 35) 1919; H. Falk, *Odensheite*, Kristiania 1924; O. Höfler, *Germanisches Sakralkönigtum*, Münster/Köln 1952; J. de Vries, *Altnordisches etymologisches Wörterbuch*, Leiden [2]1977.

Þrór (2) (ON, 'the thriving one'). A dwarf in *Vǫluspá* 12 and in the *Þulur*, where also a boar named Þrór is mentioned.

Þróttr (ON, 'might, power'). A name frequently found for Odin in skaldic poetry which probably refers to Odin's various skills, not least to his magical powers.

H. Falk, *Odensheite*, Kristiania 1924.

Þrúðgelmir (ON, 'the powerfully shouting one'). A giant in *Vafþrúðnismál* 29 who is the six-headed son of → Aurgelmir, a giant who fathers him by pairing his feet together. Aurgelmir is probably identical to the primordial giant Ymir. Þrúðgelmir's son is called Bergelmir and is the ancestor of the frost giants.

Þrúðheimr (ON, 'power-home'). The name given in *Grímnismál* 4 to the residence of the god Thor, in the *Snorra Edda* (*Gylfaginning* 20, *Skáldskaparmál* 17), however, Thor's residence is called Þrúðvangr. In his pseudo-history in the prologue to his *Edda* Snorri tells how Thor conquered a kingdom Thrákíá (Thracia) which 'we call Þrúðheimr'.

Þrúðr (1) (ON, 'power; woman'). One of the 13 → valkyries, who in *Grímnismál* 36 offer beer to the *einherjar*. In Snorri's *Edda* (*Skáldskaparmál* 4), Þrúðr is counted among Thor's daughters, rather surprisingly for a valkyrie; it is therefore uncertain whether she is the same person. Although the name Þrúðr is common as the second part of female personal names (e.g. ON Geirþrúðr, German Gertrud), in medieval times and later MHG *trute*, German *Trud*, *Drud* took on the meaning of witch, sorceress (night-)mare. This development in the meaning of the name has more to do with the name of a valkyrie than with the more neutral meaning of 'woman'. Kluge, nevertheless, separates *Trud* from Þrúðr and puts it to ON *troða*, Gothic *trudan* 'to tread'; according to this interpretation *Trud* would have its origin in nightmares.

J. Grimm, *Deutsche Mythologie*, Berlin [4]1875–78; O. A. Erich, R. Beitl, *Wörterbuch der deutschen Volkskunde*, Stuttgart 1974; F. Kluge, *Etymologisches Wörterbuch*, Berlin, New York [22]1989.

Þrúðr (2) (ON). The name given to Thor's daughter by both Snorri (*Gylfaginning* 4) and the skalds. She is, like Thor's son, Magni, a personification of her father's strength. In Bragi's *Ragnarsdrápa* (1) (9th century) the giant Hrungnir, with whom Thor fights, is called 'Þrúðr's abductor' (*þjófr Þrúðar*). However, we have no other indication of a myth telling about this episode.

Þrúðvangr (ON, 'power-field'). Thor's residence, according to Snorri (*Gylfaginning* 20, *Skáldskaparmál* 17, *Ynglinga saga* 5). However, in *Grímnismál* it is called → Þrúðheimr. In Þrúðvangr Thor's hall Bilskírnir is also to be found. All these names are late mythographical embellishments.

Þrymgjǫll (ON, 'the loud resounding one'). The door to → Menglǫð's hall in *Fjǫlsvinnsmál* 10; it was wrought by three dwarfs, Sólblindi's sons. The name is surely a young formation, but is connected with the river in Hel Gjǫll and the bridge to the Other World, Gjallarbrú, and as such it could be understood as the gate to hell. The description of dogs and the wall of flames which guard Menglǫð's residence fits this as well. More likely, however, is that the poet of *Fjǫlsvinnsmál* consciously tried to invent a name connected with these associations.

Þrymheimr (ON). The home of the giant → Þjazi and his daughter → Skaði (*Grímnismál* 11; *Gylfaginning* 22, *Skáldskaparmál* 1). *Gylfaginning* 22 tells of how Skaði and her husband, the god Njǫrðr, spend nine nights in Þrymheimr in the snow-covered mountains where Skaði goes hunting on skis, and then nine nights in Nóatún where Njǫrðr wants to live near the sea. Þrymheimr means 'noisy home'; manuscripts of the *Snorra Edda* read Þrumheimr and Þruþheimr as well, and in the last case it means 'power house' which would also fit the dwelling of a giant.

Þrymr (ON, 'noise'). A giant after whom the Eddic lay → *Þrymskviða* is named, which tells of the theft of Thor's hammer Mjǫllnir by Þrymr and its recovery by Thor. Þrymr is mentioned nowhere else in Old Norse poetry apart from in this lay, neither by Snorri nor by the skalds, only in the list of giants' names in the *Þulur*. This seems to indicate that Þrymr is unlikely to have had a place in Nordic mythology, but was rather a creation of the young poem *Þrymskviða*. Admittedly the home of a giant (namely Þjazi) is called Þrymheimr but this need have nothing to do with Þrymr as the giants are often considered to be noisy, as can be seen from many giants' names (such as Gillingr, Hrungnir, Skerkir, Herkir, Glaumarr, Aurgelmir etc.).

E. F. Halvorsen, 'Þrymr' (*KLNM* 20) 1976.

Þrymskviða (ON, 'Lay of Þrymr', also called Hamarsheimt 'the bringing home of the hammer'). An Eddic lay in which the story of the theft of the hammer Mjǫllnir by the giant Þrymr and Thor's recovery of it is told.

The lay in the *Codex Regius* described under the name of *Þrymskviða* tells in 32 stanzas how Thor awakens one day and discovers that his hammer is missing. He asks Freyja for her cloak of feathers with which Loki flies to the giants' home and there hears from the giants' ruler → Þrymr that he has taken it and has hidden it eight miles under the earth; he will only return it if he gets Freyja as his wife (11). Loki informs the Æsir of this condition and Freyja refuses indignantly. Heimdall, however, suggests that Thor disguises himself as the bride and after initial hesitation on Thor's part, the plan is put into operation; Thor as the bride and Loki as the handmaid travel to the giant's home (21). At the wedding feast which has been prepared there, the bride eats an ox and eight salmon and drinks three barrels of mead dry which somewhat disconcerts the would-be bridegroom, but Loki pacifies Þrymr by pointing out that the bride has fasted for eight days out of longing for her new husband; when Þrymr catches a glimpse of Thor under the veil, he reels back in horror, but again Loki can calm him with the excuse that the bride has not slept for eight nights. Finally the giant king brings out the hammer and lays it in the lap of the bride, but as soon as Thor has his hammer safely in his hands again, he kills Þrymr and all his family with it (31–32).

The tale of the theft of Mjǫllnir is told nowhere else in the sources, and other motives from the lay, such as the custom of laying a Thor's hammer in the lap of the bride, are not otherwise recorded. Only the blessing of the bridal couple by the goddess Vǫr (here called Vár) would seem to go back to heathen concepts; the reference to Freyja's necklace Brísingamen and the extremely few kennings are only used by the poet to add a more ancient touch.

It is difficult to date exactly when this comic lay was written, but as the subject matter was known neither to Snorri nor to the skalds, a very late composition would appear to be most likely (12th/13th century); another possibility would be that the lay is not Icelandic and was only known there at a very late time (de Vries). The idea of seeing Snorri of all people as the author of *Þrymskviða* (Hallberg), is relatively unlikely by the mere lack of any reference to it in the *Snorra Edda* (Magerøy).

From the late Middle Ages on this lay gained great popularity in Scandinavia and in Iceland there are ballad-like rhyme versions (*rímur*) of it under the name *Þrymlur* as early as the 14th century; folk-song versions of this were written in Norway, Denmark, Sweden and in the Faeroes.

P. Hallberg, 'Om Þrymskviða' (*ANF* 69) 1954; H. Magerøy, 'Þrymskviða' (*Edda* 58) 1958; B. Nerman, 'Två unga eddadikta' (*ANF* 78) 1963; J. de Vries, *Altnordische Literaturgeschichte*, Berlin [2]1967; F. R. Schröder, 'Thors Hammerholung' (*PBB West* 87) 1965; H. R. Ellis Davidson, 'Thor's Hammer' (*Folklore* 76) 1965; H. Beck, '*Thrymskviða*' (*KLL* 6) 1971; H. M. Heinrichs, 'Satirisch-parodistische Züge in der Þrymskviða' (*Festschrift H. Eggers*) Tübingen 1972; G. E. Rieger, 'Þrk. 20 við scolom aca tvau' (*skandinavistik* 5) 1975; A. Jakobsen, 'Þrymskviða som allusjonsdikt' (*Edda* 84) 1984.

R: (literature) N. F. S. Grundtvig, *Þrymskvide* (Gedicht in *Kvædlinger* I, 1808); A. Oehlenschläger, *Hammaren hentes* (Gedicht in: *Nordens Guder*, 1819); H. C. Artmann, *Die Heimholung des Hammers* (Gedicht 1977);
(fine art) E. Doepler d. J., *Thor bei dem Riesen Thrym als Braut verkleidet* (in: E. Doepler, W. Ranisch, *Walhall*, 1901); U. Bremer, Illustrations for Artmann's *Die Heimholung des Hammers* (1977).

Þulinn (ON Þulinn 'the murmurer' or 'the counted up one?'). A dwarf in the *Þulur*.

Þulr (ON *Þulr*, 'poet, see, cult speaker'). The function of the Germanic *þulr* can no longer be determined exactly because of the sparse source material. The identical OE *þyle* is glossed with Latin *orator* and in *Beowulf* it simply means 'poet'.

In skaldic poetry, too (*Íslendinga drápa* 18, Jarl Rǫgnvald 29) *þulr* is a name, in particular for the skalds. *Þulr* is found on the Danish rune stone of Snoldelev from the 9th century where it is used to refer to the function of a certain Gunnwaldr Hróaldsson. This *þulr* was employed *á Salhaugum* (literally c. ' at the mounds of the hall') and this reference to hills suggests an extended cult function of the *þulr*. *Hávamál* 111 speaks of the 'chair of the *þulr* at Urd's well'. The speaker in the *Hávamál* 134 who proclaims sententious advice calls himself the 'old *þulr*', and the giant Vafþruðnir in the Eddic mnemonic poem *Vafþrúðnismál* calls himself by the same name (*Vafþrúðnismál* 9). Odin is called *fimbulþulr* 'mighty *þulr*' in *Hávamál* 80 and 142 which corresponds to his position as god of the poets and of magic.

The *þulr*, whose name is connected to *þylja* 'murmur' and the genre of the → *Þulur*, is the speaker of the *Þulur*, alliterative mnemonic poetry, originally probably of magical-religious content which, by its metre, was designed with the aim of passing on knowledge. *Þulr* could, thus, be seen as the guardian of tradition, especially religious but perhaps also legal tradition, as the speaker of the tradition, as 'cult speaker' (Vogt).

The etymology of *þulr* is not quite clear, but it could belong to Gothic *þulan* 'lift', Hittite *talliia* 'to call upon the gods' (Polomé).

W. H. Vogt, *Stilgeschichte der eddischen Wissensdichtung* 1, Breslau 1927; W. H. Vogt, 'Der frühgermanische Kultredner' (*APhSc* 2) 1927; W. H. Vogt, *Die Þula zwischen Kultrede und eddischer Wissensdichtung*, Göttingen 1942; J. de Vries, *Altgermanische Religionsgeschichte*, Berlin [3]1970; E. Polomé, 'Old Norse Religious Terminology' (*The Nordic Languages and Modern Linguistics* 2) Stockholm 1975; E. F. Halvorsen, 'Þulr' (*KLNM* 20) 1976.

Þulur (ON *þula*, pl. *þulur*). Collections of ON mnemonic verses, lists of synonyms or names which served to pass on knowledge to the following generations orally, using mnemotechnical aids such as alliteration, rhythm and factual associations. Although Eddic lays such as the *Alvíssmál* or the *Rígsþula* are also based on such *Þulur* and in others (*Vǫluspá*, *Grímnismál*) mnemonic verses are similarly worked in, the lists of synonyms and names in the manuscripts of Snorri's *Edda* are understood as *Þulur* in the narrower sense of the word. They originated together with the increasing interest in → skaldic poetry in Iceland at the end of the 12th century and were thought of as an aid for skalds. The *Þulur* include wide areas of poetic vocabulary and give the names of gods, dwarfs, giants, valkyries, sea kings as well as synonyms for man, woman, weapons, battle, sea, ship etc. The *Þulur* derived their onomastic material from older poetry and where this has been lost, the *Þulur* have handed down numerous antiquated or seldomly used words which would otherwise have been irretrievably lost. As the *Þulur* in the more extended sense of the word (that is the lists of names integrated into several of the Eddic lays) convey mythological knowledge, it would seem natural to see the origin of the *Þulur* as part of the cult education of the → *þulr*, the cult speaker.

W. H. Vogt, *Stilgeschichte der eddischen Wissensdichtung* 1, Breslau 1927; W. H. Vogt, *Die Þula zwischen Kultrede und eddischer Wissensdichtung*, Göttingen 1942; J. de Vries, *Altnordische Literaturgeschichte*, Berlin [2]1964–67.

Thunaer. Old Saxon form of the name of the god Thor/Donar. It occurs in a Saxon abjuration oath (baptismal formula) from the 9th century. → Saxon baptismal vow.

Þund (ON, 'the roaring one'?). The river in front of Valhall, according to *Grímnismál* 21.

Þundr (or Þudr? ON). A name given to Odin in the *Grímnismál* (21, 46, 54) and the *Hávamál* 145. The meaning of the name is obscure, but it is probably related to OE *ðunian* 'swell'. 'God of the stormy sea' (Falk) is hardly convincing. Perhaps it simply meant 'the mighty one'?

H. Falk, *Odensheite*, Kristiania 1924; M. Olsen, 'Þundarbenda' (MoM) 1934; J. de Vries, *Altnordisches etymologisches Wörterbuch*, Leiden [2]1977.

Þunor (OE). The OE of the Germanic name for the god of thunder → Thor/Donar. However, the English sources of the 9th and 10th centuries used predominantly the name Þor, Þur, the ON form to refer to the god. This suggests that the native name Thunor had already been forgotten and that as a result of the very early Christianization of England the ON form had to be borrowed. Only place-names give any information about the devotion to the god Thunor on the British Isles. It is interesting to note that in the distribution as an element in pre-Christian place-names the name Thunor is almost exclusively limited to areas settled by Saxons. The place names of Thunderley, Thursley and Thurstable in Essex and Surrey in particular are obvious cult place-names, deriving from *Þunores hlæw* ('Þunor's grove') and from *Þunres stapol* ('Þunor's pillar'). However, many English place-names based on Thunor can be traced to personal names based on Thor.

R. Jente, *Die mythologisches Ausdrücke im altenglischen Wortschatz*, Heidelberg 1921; E. A. Philippson, *Germanisches Heidentum bei den Angelsachsen*, Leipzig 1929; K. Cameron, *English Place-Names*, London 1961; G. Turville-Petre, 'Thurstable' (in: *Nine Norse Studies*) London 1972; G. Turville-Petre, *Myth and Religion of the North*, Westport 1975.

Þurbǫrð (ON, 'the one with the dried out cheeks'). A giant in the *Þulur*.

Þuríðr spákona (ON, 'Þuríðr the seeress'). An Icelandic seeress in the 10th century who is mentioned in the predominantly historical account of the settlement of Iceland, the *Landnámabók* (H 37).

Þuríðr sundafyllir (ON, 'Þuríðr the sound-filler'). A woman listed in the *Landnámabók* as one of the Norwegian settlers of Iceland. Her name means that she filled the fjords with fish by means of magical practices during a famine in Norwegian Halogaland. If this explanation of her nickname is indeed correct then she is one of the numerous women mentioned in Icelandic literature who are well-versed in magic. Admittedly, she is one of the few whose historical existence is recorded with a fair degree of certainty. Þuríðr is a name frequently found in ON literature for seeresses and witches.

þurs (ON, 'giant'). One of the terms for 'giant' in ON literature. In contrast to the predominantly neutral term *jǫtunn*, *þurs* and *troll* are both names for evil-minded giants with demonic characteristics. This distinction does not only stem from Christian tendencies to demonize heathen elements, as it was already used in this way in heathen times. This is borne out since *þurs* is also the name of a rune which (as far as it is used as a symbolic sign) has a damaging property: for example in *Skírnismál* 36 where it is used for *ergi*, *œði* and *óþola* as a threat towards the giant daughter Gerðr, and, here as elsewhere, is obviously associated with ignoble sexual practices. In the concept of *þurs* as being evil giants there are possibly also characteristics of a demon of disease which derives from Medieval Scandinavian folklore in which a *þurs* can particular damage women in body and spirit.

I. Reichborn-Kjennerud, 'Eddatidens medisin' (*ANF* 40) 1924; J. de Vries, *Altgermanische Religionsgeschichte*, Berlin [3]1970.

Thursday. The name of a day of the week which derives from a pagan god's name, just as Friday and Tuesday do. In the *interpretatio germanica* the Roman name *dies Iovi* ('day of Jupiter', which resulted in French *jeudi*) was rendered as 'the day of → Donar/Thor': Gmc **þonares dag*, from which OHG *donarestag* (German *Donnerstag*), OE *þunresdæg* (English Thursday) and ON *þórsdagr* (Danish, Swedish *torsdag*) derive. The identification of the Roman chief god Jupiter as the Germanic god Donar/Thor indicates the status of the Germanic god during the first centuries A.D.

Þviti (ON, 'hitter, batterer'). A stone. The rock on which the Fenris wolf was chained was hit into the ground using Thviti, according to Snorri (*Gylfaginning* 33). The name is clearly one of Snorri's numerous inventions.

Þyn (ON, 'the roaring one'). One of the (mythical?) rivers in the river catalogue of the *Grímnismál* 27, in the *Þulur* and in a stanza in the *Njáls saga*.

Þyrs (OE, 'giant'). One of the terms for giants, corresponding to ON → *þurs* which is possibly retained in English place-names such as Thursford.

E. A. Philippson, *Germanisches Heidentum bei den Angelsachsen*, Leipzig 1929.

Tigvæ or Tigr (ON). A dwarf in the *Þulur*. The meaning is obscure.

Time. Time does not seem to have played a particular role in the ON mythology of the Eddas. Nonetheless, several eras are clearly differentiated: the mythical prehistory of the creation 'when Ymir was alive'; the mythical present which bears aspects of eternity as is stressed by the constant youth of the gods who eat → Idun's apples to achieve their longevity; the Ragnarǫk as the eschatological end of time; and finally the distant time of the new world which will be created after the destruction of this world.

It is partially possible to order the individual myths into the particular parts of the mythical present, but this leads nowhere as such compilations have shown (Ciklamini). On the other hand, the assumption of a new world after the Ragnarǫk speaks against an apocalyptic-linear expectation of the end of time and for an escatological-cyclic concept of time among the Germanic peoples.

M. Ciklamini, 'The Chronological Concept in Norse Mythology' (*Neophilologus* 47) 1963; A. Y. Gurevich, 'Space and Time' (*Medieval Scandinavia* 2) 1969.

Tīw or **Tīg** (Anglo-Saxon). Form of the Germanic god's name → *Tīwaz, ON Týr, found in Anglo-Saxon glosses, who was identified by the Germanic peoples as being identical with the Roman god Mars, as is confirmed by, among other things, the translation of the week-day name *dies Marti* by Anglo-Saxon *tiswesdæg, tīwesdæg* (Tuesday). Place-names based on Tīw have not been recorded with certainty in England.

R. Jente, *Die mythologischen Ausdrücke im altenglischen Wortschatz*, Heidelberg 1921; E. A. Philippson, *Germanisches Heidentum bei den Angelsachsen*, Leipzig 1929; G. Turville-Petre, *Myth and religion of the North*, Westport 1975.

***Tīwaz.** The Germanic god of war, the skies and the Thing (ON → Týr, OHG *Ziu). The Germanic peoples identified him as the Roman god of war Mars. The translation of *dies Martis* by Anglo-Saxon *tīwesdæg*, ON *týsdagr* confirms this, whilst OHG *dingesdag* (→ Tuesday) is probably derived from another form of *Tīwaz found in the name → Mars Thingsus.

Toki (ON, 'fool'?). The name of a dwarf, cf. → Jaki.

Travala(e)ha. A goddess on a recently found fragment of a Roman votive stone from Cologne, Germany. The undoubtedly Germanic name of the goddess is probably connected with the name *þrāwija* on the Swedish rune stone from Kalleby (Tanum, Bohuslän) (*þrāwijan haitanaR was namne*; c. A.D. 400). This name is probably derived from *þrāwijan*, cognate to Proto-Norse *þrāwō* 'long, desire'. The *(Dea) Travala(e)ha* could signify 'the desired goddess'.

B. u. H. Galsterer, *Die römischen Steininschriften aus Köln*, Köln 1975; H. Reichert, *Lexikon der altgermanischen Namen*, Vienna 1987–90.

Trees. The Germanic peoples worshipped → sacred groves and thought of individual trees as sacred. Christian authors of the early Middle Ages repeatedly condemned the worship of trees practised by southern Germanic tribes. A large tree is mentioned in Adam of Bremen's description of the temple at Uppsala (*Gesta ecclesiae Hammaburgensis pontificum* IV, 26), which is green in both winter and summer and nobody knows what kind of tree it is (Scholion 138). This tree was probably seen as the earthly counterpart to the mythological World-ash → Yggdrasill on which Odin hung for nine nights during his self-sacrifice. Trees were generally not worshipped because of their link with a particular god, but rather because of their symbolic characteristic of growth.

T. Palm, *Trädkult*, Lund 1948; J. de Vries, *Altgermanische Religionsgeschichte*, Berlin [3]1970.

trénið (ON, 'wooden derision') → magic.

Troll (ON *troll*, 'fiend, monster, giant'). One of the terms for giants in ON (together with *jǫtunn* and *þurs*). It is a name denoting only hostile giants. In the literature of the High Middle Ages the trolls take on more of the meaning 'fiend' so that they become a being in their own right among the beings of lower mythology to whom certain magical powers were ascribed, especially in the areas of illness and black magic. In late medieval Icelandic legendary fiction and in West Scandinavian folklore even in modern times the trolls play a greater role than the giants. They are described as being bigger than people but extraordinarily ugly. They live in mountain caves and frequently harm people. They are partly identical with the living dead, the → *draugr*.

In Swedish and Danish folklore on the other hand troll is the name used in general to denote all the beings of lower mythology, as well as being the name for a kind of brownie-like being, the *huldrefolk* which often plays a role in changeling tales.

E. Hartmann, *Die Trollvorstellungen*, Stuttgart, Berlin 1936; T. H. Wilbur, 'Troll, an etymological note' (*SS* 30) 1958.

Troy-castles. Low, round rows of stones similar to other ancient labyrinths and formed by loops which lead inwards. They are frequently found in southern Scandinavia, but also occur in other parts of Europe (Russia, Italy and the Greek islands). They are certainly very old and their function is still unknown. They possibly served for cult dance; the representation of the way into the underworld in initiation rites would also be conceivable. The widespread distribution in early Scandinavian, Italian and Cretan cultures suggest that they are part of Indo-European tradition.

E. Krause, *Die Trojaburgen Nordeuropas*, Glogau 1893; W. Hunke, *Die Trojaburgen und ihre Bedeutung*, Diss. Munich 1941; R. Simek, 'Domus Daedali – Vǫlundarhús' (Festskrift H. Bekker-Nielsen) Odense 1993.

Tuesday. Of all → names of the days of the week, Latin *dies Martis* (resulting in French *mardi*) 'day of Mars' has been translated into Germanic languages in the most varied ways. Anglo-Saxons and Scandinavians simply replaced the Roman god Mars with the Germanic god *Tīwaz (OHG Zīu, OE Tīg, Tīw, ON Týr), which resulted in the week-day names OE *Tīwesdæg* (Engl. Tuesday), ON *týsdagr*. In German speaking areas the god *Tīwaz appeared only in Frisian *tīesdi*, OHG *zīostag*, MHG *zīestac*,

Allemanic *zīstac*. In German, however, the variants as in Middle Dutch *dinxendach*, *dingsdag*, German *Dienstag* prevailed, which are probably derived from another name for *Tīwaz, namely **Þingsaz* 'Thing-god' (→ Mars Thingsus), if, indeed, the name does not come from the Thing ('council') in the first place. However, this latter suggestion does not seem very likely because of the significant role played by the names of various gods in the translation of the week-day names. De Vries' theory of *Dienstag* being a subsidiary form for an original *Diestag* is not really convincing. – The southern Bavarian name *Ertag* ('day of Ares') and *Aftermontag*, a non-heathen term used in the area around Augsburg, are two more names for this day in German.

J. de Vries, 'Dinsdag' (*TNTL* 48) 1929; J. de Vries, *Altgermanische Religionsgeschichte*, Berlin [3]1970; F. Kluge, *Etymolgogisches Wörterbuch*, Berlin, New York [22]1989; O. Höfler, 'Mars Thingsus' (*Handwörterbuch zur deutschen Rechtsgeschichte* 18) 1979.

Tuisco → Tuisto.

Tuisto. According to Tacitus (*Germania* 2, 9) this is the mythical ancestor of the Germanic peoples, a god born of Earth whom they celebrate in ancient lays. His son is Mannus whose three sons were in turn the ancestors of the Germanic peoples, the Ingaevones, Herminones and Istaevones. This succession father-son-three sons has parallels in both Germanic and non-Germanic areas (→ Myth of descendency) and can therefore be assumed to be authentic.

Tuisto seems to be related to the proto-giant → Ymir as the earth-born hermaphrodite ancestor of the race of man, and therefore the meaning of the name Tuisto as 'hermaphrodite' is quite likely. The form of the name Tuisco (the actual manuscript reading) can also be traced back etymologically to the same basic meaning.

F. Kluge, 'Tuisco deus et filius Mannus' (*Zeitschrift für deutsche Wortforschung* 2) 1902; E. Adinsky, *Tuisko oder Tuisto?*, Königsberg 1903; R. Much, *Die Germania des Tacitus*, Heidelberg [3]1967.

R: (literature) in his play *Hermann* (1743), J. E. Schlegel imagined a cult of Tuisto complete with wooden statues.

Tummaestiae. A votive stone from Sinzenich (near Euskirchen, Germany; CIL XIII 7902) is dedicated to the *Matronis Tum(m)aesti(i)s*. Gutenbrunner suggested that the name meant 'the helping goddesses of the house, or the building site'.

S. Gutenbrunner, *Die germanischen Götternamen*, Halle 1936; H. Reichert, *Lexikon der altgermanischen Namen*, Vienna 1987–90.

Turstuahenae. Matron name on two votive stones from Derichsweiler (Düren, Germany) from the 2nd or 3rd centuries. The nearest words etymologically are Old Saxon *thurstian* 'to thirst', Gothic *þaurstei* 'thirst' but this hardly seems probable. It is more likely related (with superlative suffix?) to OHG *duris*, *thuris*, ON *þurs* 'giant', thus 'the mightiest', or else, with metathesis, to trust, cf. Old Franconian *antrustio* 'follower' see the matron name → Andrusteihae.

S. Gutenbrunner, 'Zur Matroneninschrift von Derichsweiler' (*Bonner Jahrbücher* 152) 1952; M. Clauss, 'Neue Inschriften im rheinischen Landesmuseum Bonn' (*Epigraphische Studien* 11) 1976; H. Reichert, *Lexikon der altgermanischen Namen*, Vienna 1987–90.

Tveggi (ON, 'the hermaphrodite, the double'). A name for Odin in *Vǫluspá* 23, in the *Þulur* and in Egill's *Sonatorrek* 25. As Odin could hardly be called a hermaphrodite, the name probably refers to his double role as god and man in numerous disguises, perhaps also to the dark and light aspects of his character. Odin has hardly anything in common with the two-faced Roman god Janus.

H. Falk, *Odensheite*, Kristiania 1924.

Tviblindi (ON, 'double-blind'). A name for Odin in the *Þulur* which could refer to the fact that Odin is blind (one-eyed) as well as being able to blind his enemies (cf. *Ynglinga saga* 6; → Herblindi).

H. Falk, *Odensheite*, Kristiania 1924.

Týr (ON). The Old Scandinavian name for the Germanic god of the sky, war and council → *Tīwaz (OHG Ziu), who is the only Germanic god who was already important in Indo-European times: Old Indian Dyaus, Greek Zeus, Latin Jupiter, as well as Old Indian *deva*, Old Irish *día*, Latin *dei*, ON *tívar* (plural to Týr) 'gods' are all closely related etymologically to each other.

Despite his early importance, Týr is relatively unimportant in the ON mythology of the Eddas although he is repeatedly mentioned in the younger Eddic lays (*Lokasenna* 38 and 40, *Hymiskviða* 4 and 33, *Sigrdrífumál* 6), and Snorri names him frequently as one of the more important of the Æsir. However, even he has little more to say about Týr except that he was the god of war and battle (*Gylfaginning* 24, *Skáldskaparmál* 9), that he lost his right arm whilst fettering the wolf → Fenrir and that he will fight against the wolf Garmr (= Fenrir?) at Ragnarǫk (*Gylfaginning* 50). Týr also stands outside the usual bonds of relationship of the Æsir which are normally so carefully given. There is no indication that Týr had a wife (except for an unimportant reference in the *Lokasenna*) and it is even unclear who his father was. *Hymiskviða* calls Týr a son of the giant Hymir (because the gods are descended from the giants?), and Snorri calls him a son of Odin's (because nearly all the gods are sons of the Alfaðir Odin according to Snorri). There is little more to be found than hints of Týr's role as god of war. On the other hand he must have played a more important role at some stage as is clear from the plural of his name *tívar* meaning 'gods', as well as the fact that in skaldic poetry his name could be used as the basic word in kennings for other gods, especially for Odin; this proves that his name originally, but still in Viking times, could simply mean 'god'.

The idea that Týr was one-armed, which is only explained by Snorri in the myth of the fettering of Fenrir, is mentioned both in Norwegian and Icelandic folklore and appears to represent an old feature of the myth. There are several parallels with non-Germanic gods since both the Irish god Nuadu and the Indian god Sūrya are one-armed, with the difference that Týr lost his hand as a pledge. The loss of the hand used for swearing oaths is documented in many cultures as a punishment for perjury, alienating but predominating in the case of a god of justice such as Týr. Dumézil has found a counterpart in a Roman legend in which the hero sacrifices his hand in order to prove his innocence. The myth of Týr shows how a god wants to pay for the security of the cosmic order by telling a necessary lie which results in the loss of his hand (de Vries).

Týr also plays a role in rune-magic; the T-rune bears his name in historical time, ON *týr*, Anglo-Saxon *ti*, Gothic *tyz*. The *Sigrdrífumál* 6 teach that one puts victory runes onto a sword by carving Týr twice, and in Migration Age runic inscriptions (also on bracteates) the T-rune frequently appears as a sign of magical significance.

There are indications of a cult of Týr in particular in certain place-names in Denmark, whereby Tislund (from *lundr* 'grove') occurs even more frequently; the cult place-names are rarer and sparser in Norway (Tysnesø, Tysnes); here the cult appears to have been adopted from Denmark. It is possible, too, that a cult of the god Týr was already waning at the time when the extant theophorous place-names were formed.

O. Bremer, 'Der germanische Himmelsgott' (*IF* 3) 1894; R. Much, 'Der germanische Himmelsgott' (*Festgabe für R. Heinzel* 1) Halle/S 1898; K. Krohn, 'Tyrs hǫgra hand' (*Festskrift F. Feilberg*) Copenhagen 1911; G. Dumézil, *Mitra-Varuna*, Paris 1940; W. Krause, *Ziu* (Nachrichten der gesellschaft der Wissenschaften, Göttingen, Phil.-hist. Kl., N. F. 3/6) 1940; B. Nerman, 'Fimbultýs fornar rúnar' (*ANF* 85), 1970; J. de Vries, *Altgermanische Religionsgeschichte*, Berlin [3]1970; O. Höfler, ' "Sakraltheorie" und "Profantheorie" ' (*Festschrift S. Gutenbrunner*) Heidelberg 1972; G. Turville-Petre, *Myth and Religion of the North*, Westport 1975; A. Holtsmark, 'Týr' (*KLNM* 19) 1975; G. Dumézil, *Gods of the Ancient Northmen*, Berkeley 1977.

R: (fine art) K. Ehrenberg, *Tyr und Heimdal; Widar und Uller* (drawing, 1882); E. Doepler, *Fesselung des Fenriswolfs* (E. Doepler, W. Ranisch, *Walhall*, 1901).
(literature) F. Blunck, in: *Kampf der Gestirne* (novel, 1926), invents a cult of Týr; M. A. Hansen, *Orm og Tyr* (novel, 1952).
(other) Tyr, Norwegian mine-laying vessel, built 1942.

Uðr (1) or Unnr (ON). A name for Odin in *Grímnismál* 46. Uðr is possibly related to *unna*, thus meaning 'the patron', perhaps however to *vinr* 'friend' where the name would refer to the god of the followers.

H. Falk, *Odensheite*, Kristiania 1924; J. de Vries, *Altnordisches etymologisches Wörterbuch*, Leiden [2]1977.

Uðr (2) (ON, 'wave'). One of the nine daughters of the sea-giant → Ægir and his wife Rán (*Skáldskaparmál* 22 and 58; Einarr Skúlason; *Þulur*) who correspond in Old Norse poetry to the waves of the sea.

Udravarinehae or Udrovarinehae. Matron name found on two Roman inscriptions from the Lower Rhine. Gutenbrunner interprets Udravarinehae as 'goddesses of the Otter-defence' which seems most unlikely despite the frequency with which matrons names are derived from river names.

S. Gutenbrunner, *Die germanischen Götternamen*, Halle 1936; H. Reichert, *Lexikon der altgermanischen Namen*, Vienna 1987–90.

Uggerus. An old seer who appears in Saxo (*Gesta Danorum* V, 158) and is probably identical to Odin, since the Latin form Uggerus corresponds to the ON name for Odin → Yggr.

Ulauhinehae. Matron name on a votive stone from Gleich near Füssenich (Kreis Düren, Germany; CIL XIII 9732). The meaning of this name has never been explained satisfactorily. Gutenbrunner assumed a base form **uwa-lauha-* 'owl-grove', but the name is more likely based on Vlauh- (from the Indo-Germanic root **plau-/pleu-* 'flow'), hence 'river goddess'.

S. Gutenbrunner, *Die germanischen Götternamen*, Halle 1936; H. Reichert, *Lexikon der altgermanischen Namen*, Vienna 1987–90.

Ulfheðnar (ON, 'wolf-skins'). These are mentioned in Old Norse literature in connexion with → berserks, and belong like them to the type of warrior in animal guise who had their origin in the cult bands of warriors dedicated to Odin.

The name Ulfheðnar is also reflected in personal names, ON Ulfheðin, Old Franconian Wolfhetan, which originally marked the men thus named as members of bands of warriors in animal-disguise.

G. Müller, 'Zum Namen Wolfhetan' (*Frühmittelalterliche Studien* 1) 1967.

Ulfr Uggason. 10th century Icelandic poet; author of the → Húsdrápa. We only know about his life, our single source being a few short remarks in *Landnámabók* (S 76 = H 64) and *Njáls saga.*

L. M. Hollander, *The Skalds*, Ann Arbor 1968; E. O. G. Turville-Petre, *Scaldic Poetry*, Oxford 1976.

Ulfrún (ON, 'wolf-rune', 'wolf-woman'). One of Heimdall's nine giant mothers, according to *Vǫluspá in skamma* (*Hyndluljóð* 37). Ulfrún is also recorded as an ON female personal name.

A. M. Sturtevant, 'Etymological Comments upon certain Old Norse Proper Names' (*PMLA* 67) 1952; L. Motz, 'Giantesses and their Names' (*FmSt* 15) 1981.

Ullinn. A secondary form of the name for the god → Ullr, which occurs in several Norwegian place-names.

Ullr (ON). A Germanic god who is only mentioned in Scandinavian sources. Snorri says that Ullr is Sif's son and Thor's step-son (*Gylfaginning* 30, *Skáldskaparmál* 4 and 14). All his other information comes from kennings (*Gylfaginning* 30, *Skáldskaparmál* 14): Ullr is a good archer and an accomplished skater and skier; he is handsome and of warlike appearance and it is useful to invoke his aid in duels.

According to *Grímnismál* 5, Ullr's home is Ýdalir, and in the *Atlakviða* 30 an oath is sworn on Ullr's ring. Ullr is often named in skaldic poetry, mostly in kennings for 'warrior', and → Ullr's ship is repeatedly referred to.

In Saxo Grammaticus (*Gesta Danorum* III, 81) Ollerus (= Ullr) can travel over the sea on a bone, an ability which Saxo attributes to sorcery, but is more likely to be parallel to Snorri's comments that Ullr is a good skater and the god of skis. According to Saxo, this same Ollerus took on the regency over the Æsir during Odin's exile. Whereas the literary sources are extremely sparse in their information about Ullr, the numerous place-names based on the god's name, in particular in Sweden (apart from in Scania) and in East Norway, point to an especial devotion to the god in these parts. As a result of Saxo's indications of a cult of Ullr in Sweden, there have been attempts to assume that it stood in conflict with the predominating Odin's cult. It is interesting to note that there was a fairly frequent association of place-names based on Ullr with those of another god, i.e. Freyr in Norway and Njǫrðr in Sweden (in Denmark there no place-names based on Ullr). Care must be taken when drawing conclusions from the abundance of place-names, as not all of them based on Ull- are indeed cult place-names (cf. Norwegian Ullerö). Even an association with the place-names on Freyr or Njǫrðr are not sufficient to allow us to count Ullr with any certainty as one of the Vanir and a god of fertility. Ullr should by no means be identified with Freyr (Nielsen).

R. Much, 'Ulls Schiff' (*PBB* 20) 1895; I. Lindquist, 'Eddornas bild av Ull – och guldhornens' (*NoB* 14) 1926; E. Wessén, 'Schwedische Ortsnamen und altnordische Mythologie' (*APhSc* 4) 1929/30; J. de Vires, Studien over Germaansche mythologie VI' (TNTL 53) 1934; S. K. Amtoft, *Nordiske Gudeskikkelser*, Copenhagen 1948; W. Elgqvist, *Ullvi och Ullinshov*, Lund 1955; N. Å. Nielsen, 'Freyr, Ullr, and the Sparlösa Stone' (*Medieval Scandinavia* 2) 1969; J. de Vries, *Altgermanische Religionsgeschichte*, Berlin ^{3}1970; A. Holtsmark, 'Ullr' (KLNM 19) 1975;

N. Å. Nielsen, 'Myten om krigen' (*Nordiska Studier i filologi och lingvistik, Festskrift* G. *Holm*) Lund 1976; B. Falck-Kjällquist, 'Namnet Ullerö' (*NoB* 71) 1983.

Ullr's ship (ON *Ullar skip*, *Ullar kjóll* or *Ullar askr*). A kenning for 'shield' which plays upon the idea that the god Ullr used his shield as a ship (or as a ski?). However, the corresponding myth is no longer extant. Nonetheless, the shield as the ship of a fertility god appears to have been a well-known part of myth, as is shown by a certain Skjǫldr ('shield') mentioned as the husband of Gefjon, as well as → Scyld Scefing who was found drifting in a boat lying on a sheaf.

R. Much, 'Ulls Schiff' (*PBB* 20) 1895; H. Rosenfeld, 'Nordische Schilddichtung' (*ZfdPh* 61) 1936; K. v. See, *Skaldendichtung*, Munich, Zürich 1980.

Undensakre → Odáinsakr.

Underworld → Other World, → Hel.

Uni (ON, 'the satisfied one'?). A dwarf (?) in *Fjǫlsvinnsmál* 34.

Unngerðr (ON, 'wave-Gerðr'). A giantess in the *Þulur*. Gerðr frequently occurs as one of the most well-known giantesses in Nordic mythology. Unngerðr could be formed from the name of Ægir's daughter, Unnr (or Uðr), unless the name is a scribal error for Imgerðr.

L. Motz, 'Giantesses and their Names' (*FmSt* 15) 1981.

Underworld → Other World, → Hel (1).

Uppsala. Uppsala, or, to be more exact, Old Uppsala (Gamla Uppsala), situated somewhat to the north of the modern city, was the Old Swedish royal seat and was not only the secular but also the religious centre of Sweden from the Migration Era at the latest. According to Adam of Bremen, there was a temple in Uppsala (→ Uppsala temple), where great sacrificial festivals took place every nine years (→ Uppsala sacrifice). Even today the three huge Migration Age burial mounds of the kings and a church can be seen on the site of the heathen temple.

Uppsala sacrifice. After his description of the → Uppsala temple, Adam of Bremen (c.1070) gives an account of the sacrifices held there: 'Every nine years all the Swedish tribes celebrate a festival in Uppsala; nobody is dispensed from attending. King and people, the community and the individuals bring their sacrificial offerings to Uppsala, and those – and this is the hardest punishment – who have already converted to Christianity must buy themselves out of these ceremonies. The sacrifice is as follows: nine of every male living being are sacrificed, and it is hoped that their blood will make atonement to the gods. The bodies are hung up in a grove which lies close to the temple. This grove is so holy to the heathens that divinity is attributed to the individual trees because of the death and decay of their sacrificial victims. Dogs and horses hang there next to humans, and one Christian has told me that he has seen 72 cadavers of various kinds hanging there. Apart from this, the songs which are sung at these sacrificial rites are manifold and obscene; therefore, I had better be silent about them.' (*Gesta Hammaburgensis Ecclesiae Pontificum* IV, 27). Scholion 141: 'Feasting and sacrifices such as these are celebrated for nine days long. Every day they sacrifice a human and one of every other kind of animal so that in nine days 72 living beings have been sacrificed. This sacrifice takes place roughly at the equinox in Spring.'

Bishop Thietmar of Merseburg gives a much shorter account of a very similar sacrifice in Danish → Lejre at the beginning of the 11th century. – Like Adam, he also mentions pictures of Thor, Odin and Freyr in the previous description of the temple, and therefore the question has repeatedly been asked which of the three gods the sacrifice was for. The human sacrifice and also the form of sacrifice would speak in favour of a sacrifice to Odin: the hanging and the mythical number nine are known from Odin's sacrifice. Snorri mentions (*Ynglinga saga* 8) that the Scandinavian Spring sacrifice was held *tils sigrs* (for victory). On the other hand Snorri repeatedly links the temple and sacrifice in Uppsala with Freyr (*Ynglinga saga* 6, 10). As Uppsala was the cult centre of the Swedish kings, who were descended from Yngvi-Freyr, a link between the sacrifice and Freyr is likely. In addition, it appears that the Uppsala sacrifice was a fertility sacrifice (cf. *Ynglinga saga* 15), a factor which the obscene songs mentioned by Adam and the date in Spring would indicate. In this case it must be a sacrifice to Freyr.

However, as the Swedish rune stones prove, Thor played a role in the Swedish cult of the Viking Age, and so sacrifices to him cannot be excluded either. Thus it is probably best not to attempt to assume that the sacrifice was made to one particular god. If Adam is correct in the names of the three gods which he cites – and there is no reason to assume otherwise – then the Uppsala sacrifice should be seen as being a sacrifice to all three gods.

→ Sacrifice, → Uppsala temple.

Uppsala temple. The temple at Uppsala, which played a significant role in heathen times as the seat of the Swedish kings and an important cult centre, was described c.1070 by Adam of Bremen who based his record on eye-witness accounts made at a time when Sweden was not yet fully Christianized (*Gesta Hammaburgensis Ecclesiae Pontificum* IV, 26 and Scholion 139): 'This people owns a very famous temple at Uppsala, not far from Sigtuna. In this temple, which is made exclusively of gold, the people worship the statues of three gods. Thor, the mightiest of them, has his seat in the middle of the room, and the places to the left and right of him are taken by Wodan and Fricco.' Scholion 139: 'The temple is encompassed by a golden chain which hangs down from the gable of the building and shines towards the people approaching, for the shrine, which lies in the valley, is surrounded by mountains like a theatre.'

Admittedly, Adam's sources for this information are of extremely varying reliability, but the existence of a temple at Uppsala is undisputed. The details have often been questioned as some influences from descriptions of the Temple of Solomon in the Old Testament have been assumed, but the chain mentioned has counterparts in European churches of the 8th and 9th centuries, even if the idea that it was made of gold is an exaggeration.

Archaeological investigations beneath the church at Gamla Uppsala carried out by Lindqvist in 1926 have revealed a row of post holes which possibly belonged to a heathen temple. Numerous attempts at reconstruction based on Lindqvist's hypothetic ordering of the holes probably overestimated the size of the Uppsala temple. These holes were arranged in two concentric rectangles and were modelled on early forms of Nordic stave churches. More recent investigations based on Medieval documents only indicate that the 11th century temple described by Adam was located adjoining the choir of today's church whilst the post holes found by Lindquist possibly went back to an older, burnt down temple (Norberg).

S. Lindqvist, 'Hednatemplet i Uppsala' (*Fornvännen*) 1923; S. Lindqvist, 'Gamla Uppsala kyrka' (*Fornvännen*) 1951; H. Widéen, 'Till diskussionen om Uppsalas hednatempel' (*Fornvännen*) 1951; T. Palm, 'Uppsalalunden och Uppsalatemplet' (*Vetenskapssocieteten i Lunds Årsbok*) 1941; O. Olsen, *Hǫrg, Hov og Kirke*, Copenhagen 1966; R. Norberg, 'Uppsala tempel' (*KLNM* 19) 1975.

R: → temple.

Urðar brunnr (ON, 'Urd's well' or 'well of fate', cognate to ON *urðr* 'fate'). One of the springs under the roots of the World-ash → Yggdrasill, according to Snorri (*Gylfaginning* 14, 15). It is near to this spring that the gods hold their council and also where the hall is situated in which live the three norns, Urd, Verdandi and Skuld, who determine men's fates. 'And it is told that the norns, who live at Urd's well, take water from the spring every day and also mud which is around the spring, and they spray it over the ash so that its branches neither dry out nor rot'. We do not learn much more from other sources (*Vǫluspá* 19, *Hávamál* 111 and two skalds) except that Urd's well lies under Yggdrasill, and the skalds (Kormákr: *Sigurðardrápa* 4 from the 10th century, Eilífr Goðrúnarson from the 10th/11th centuries) only mention the name of the well. Eilífr even mentions it in a highly Christian-influenced context, when he describes Christ as sitting 'in the south at Urd's well'. Snorri alone writes in more detail about Urd's well, telling of two birds who feed there. He calls them the ancestors of all swans, indicating the sanctity of these birds.

The afore mentioned association of Urd's well with the south and with Rome, found in Eilífr's stanza, has caused a lot of problems for scholarly research and has led to *Urðar brunnr* even being identified as the river Jordan (Bugge). Ohrt's quite convincing suggestion is that the phonetic and typological similarity between the holy spring in the north and the holy 'Jurdan' could have played a role for the strange occurrence in Eilífr, even if there is no causative connexion.

Urd's well is nowhere mentioned explicitly as a 'well of fate'. The only justification of such a supposition is that the norns live there and that the name of the norn, Urd, may be derived from *Urðar brunnr*. Adam von Bremen's reference to a spring at the holy tree in Uppsala, which would correspond to the Urd's well beneath Yggdrasill, points to a spring into which sacrifical victims were thrown. → Water.

S. Bugge, *Studien*, Munich 1889; F. Ohrt, 'Sunnr at Urðarbrunni' (*APhSc* 12) 1937/38 (mit älterer Literatur); G. W. Weber, *Wyrd*, Bad Homburg 1969.

Urðr (1) (ON, 'fate'). A → norn (*Vǫluspá* 19, 20, *Hávamál* 111, *Grógaldr* 7). She is associated in virtually all the sources with the concept of the *Urðar brunnr*. In Snorri (*Gylfaginning* 14 following *Vǫluspá* 20), Urðr is one of the three norns who live at *Urðar brunnr* (→ 'Urd's well') and who determine the fates of men. The author of *Vǫluspá*, and possibly also Snorri, probably interpreted Urðr, Verdandi and Skuld as past, present and future (Urðr from the plural *urðum* 'became'), but were equally aware of the relationship to the concept of *urðr* 'fate'. De Vries' suggestion that Urðr (as the personification of fate) had already earlier become a norn, is not totally convincing despite evidence from the end of the 10th century in Kormákr's *Sigurðardrápa* 4, because Urðr cannot be found at all in the *Codex Regius* of the *Edda*. Also, it is possible to read Kormák's line not as *komsk Urðr ór brunni* ('Urðr came out of the spring') but as *komsk Uðr at brunni* (Uðr = Odin came to the spring'), whereby the passage loses every connexion with the norns. But even if one does take the first, more generally accepted, interpretation, Urðr is in spite of everything most likely a derivation from *Urðar brunnr*, which as 'well of fate' would be older than the name Urðr. ON *urðr* 'fate' in turn corresponds to the frequently used OE → *wyrd*, which was considered by past scholars to be the central concept of a Germanic belief in fate.

L. Mittner, *Wurd*, Bern 1955; G. W. Weber, *Wyrd*, Bad Homburg 1969.

Urðr (2) (ON 'fate') → Wyrd.

Urd's well → Urðar brunnr.

Uri (ON, 'the smith'). A dwarf in the *Fjǫlsvinnsmál* 34.

Utgarðr (ON, 'the outer world', 'area outside'). According to Nordic cosmology, Utgarðr is the area outside the part of the world inhabited by gods and men (Asgard and Midgard respectively) and is the dwelling place of demons and giants. Originally it was thought to surround the whole world, but in the mythological stories of the Middle Ages Utgarð tended to be located in the east of Midgard. In later Medieval times, as a result of increasing awareness and geographical knowledge acquired on journeys, the home of dangerous creatures such as giants and monsters was pushed increasingly further northwards until some fairy-tale sagas of the 14th and 15th centuries even locate their giants and trolls in the polar sea. – In Snorri's tale of Thor and → Utgarðaloki, Utgarðr has a limited importance and is merely the castle of the giant Utgarðaloki where Thor undertook several tests in which he was defeated.

J. de Vries, *Altgermanische Religionsgeschichte*, Berlin ³1970; A. Holtsmark, 'Utgarðr' (*KLNM* 19) 1975.

Utgarðaloki (ON). A giant who is (according to Snorri) also called → Skrýmir. Snorri reports a journey of Thor's to Utgarðaloki where Thor and his companions, Loki and Þjálfi, match themselves against the giant in competitions which are finally all revealed to have been pure illusions. There are parallels in Thor's journey to Utgarðaloki and his journey to the giant → Geirrǫðr, such as Loki's company and the competition, and also in Saxo (*Gesta Danorum* VIII, 286f. and 292f.) the visit of the hero Thorkillus to Geruthus (= Geirrǫðr) is not dissimilar to his visit in *Uthgarthi locus* (probably identical with Utgarðaloki), so that Thor's opponents Utgarðaloki and Geirrǫðr probably originally had the same model which in time underwent a slightly different epic re-working.

The name Utgarðaloki ('Loki of Utgarðr, of the Other World') is clearly young, since it presupposes the demonization of Loki; thus it seems that the myth was probably not originally linked to the name Utgarðaloki. In the Eddic lays the story is referred to twice, once in *Lokasenna* 60–62, where the giant is called Skrýmir, the other time in *Hárbarðsljóð* 26, where he is called Fjallar.

In spite of the change in the giant's name, the myth itself appears to be ancient – even if the original myth itself is hidden in Snorri's version by fairy-tale elements. Not only the giant Svyatogor in Russian folk-tales but also the figures of a Ossetic legend show extensive parallels with the Nordic Utgarðaloki/Skrýmir, for example the sleep in the glove or the giant's bag and the tests of strength.

Concerning the literary handling of the myth of Thor's journey to Utgarðaloki, see → Skrýmir.

G. Dumézil, 'Légendes sur les Nartes' (*Revue del'histoire des religions* 125) 1943; N. K. Chadwick,

'The Russia Giant Svyatogor and the Norse Utgarðaloki' (*Folklore* 75) 1964; J. de Vries, *Altgermanische Religionsgeschichte*, Berlin ³1970.

útiseta (ON, 'sitting outside'). A form of magical practice mentioned in the ON sources which was used in black magic (*Gulathingslǫg* 32) as well as in the magic of prophecy, of which the latter does not necessarily correspond to pagan customs (→ Seeress). The nightly *útiseta* served the purpose of coming into contact with the dead in their own area (i.e. outside human habitation). → Black magic.

Vacallinehae. Matron name. The *Matronae Vacallinehae* are among the best documented matron names, and are possibly even the most frequent names found. Over 130 inscriptions from the 2nd and 3rd centuries A.D. which were certainly dedicated to the Vacallinehae come from the temple area at Pesch (Kreis Aachen; more exactly Bad Münstereifel-Nöthen, Kreis Euskirchen, Germany) and its immediate surroundings. In addition to these 10 inscriptions are dedicated to the Vocallinehae (and similar), and a further 150 fragments of inscriptions appear to come from votive inscriptions to these matrons. At Pesch a cult centre with temple buildings dedicated to these matrons has been discovered. It is not certain whether the name of the Vacallinehae is purely Germanic, as the first word element could be Celtic. The cult of the *Matronae Vacallinehae* was carried out, according to the information given in the inscriptions, by a mixed Germanic-Celtic population. The name Vacallinehae is most likely derived from a place-name *Vacall-, perhaps from Wachendorf (near Antweiler) on the stream Wachenbach (earlier Wachlenbach) or else from the river name Waal, Gallic Vacalus, Germanic Vahalis. In three cases the Vacallinehae bear the additional name → Leudinae which could mean the inhabitants of a place *Leudium.

S. Gutenbrunner, *Die germanischen Götternamen*, Halle 1936; E. A. Philippson, 'Der germanische Mütter- und Matronekult am Niederrhein' (*GR* 19) 1944; G. Alföldy, 'Epigraphisches aus dem Rheinland III' (*Epigraphische Studien* 5) 1968; M. Clauss, 'Neue Inschriften im Rheinischen Landesmuseum Bonn' (*Epigraphische Studien* 11) 1976; H. Reichert, *Lexikon der altgermanischen Namen*, Vienna 1987–90.

Vaðgelmir (ON, 'ford screamer'). A river which punishes liars (only *Reginsmál* 4). The concept of a river in the underworld as a place of punishment certainly derives from Medieval Christian visionary literature. The rivers of the Underworld Slíðr and Geirvimull in late Nordic mythography also come from the same Christian source.

Vættir → Landvættir.

vafrlogi → Wall of flames.

Vafþrúðnir (ON Vafþrúðnir, 'the mightily entangling one'). A wise giant who, in the Eddic lay → *Vafþrúðnismál*, is challenged to a battle of wits by Odin and loses. Apart from this lay, Vafþrúðnir occurs only in the *Þulur* and in Snorri (*Gylfaginning* 4) where he quotes the Eddic lay. The giant Vafþrúðnir is a purely literary creation in order to present Odin with a sparring partner. Further proof that giants in Germanic heathendom could be considered wise – in contrast to medieval and later poetry where they are usually shown to be rather stupid – is the giantess Hyndla (*Hyndluljóð*) and also Mímir.

Vafþrúðnismál (ON *Vafþrúðnismál* 'the lay of Vafþrúðnir'). An Eddic lay from the area of mythological didactic poetry, to which also *Alvíssmál* and *Grímnismál* belong.

The lay comprises 55 stanzas in the *ljóðaháttr* metre and is stringently organized. Apart from stanza 5 the whole lay is in the form of a dialogue, a form otherwise characteristic of didactic poetry. The first five stanzas form a short introduction: Odin asks his wife Frigg for advice as he wants to visit the wise giant Vafþrúðnir. Frigg warns him that Vafþrúðnir is stronger than other giants, but nonetheless Odin sets out and is received at the giant's, where he uses a pseudonym for himself, Gangráðr. Stanzas 7–19 are devoted to Vafþrúðnir's questioning of Odin, in which the giant asks him who moves day and night, what the border river between the giants and gods is called, where Surtr will fight with the gods (at Ragnarǫk). Odin answers all these questions, and in the remaining stanzas he questions the giant about the origin of the sky and the earth, sun and moon, day and night, the giants, Njǫrðr, the *einherjar*, and the world and the gods after Ragnarǫk; Odin's last question is: what did Odin whisper into his son's (Baldr) ear before he was put onto the funeral pyre? The giant is unable to answer this and has to concede victory to Odin in this battle of wits.

The knowledge given in *Vafþrúðnismál* is exclusively mythological information, and Snorri utilized the lay to the full for the mythography in his *Edda*. The composition date of the lay has been assumed to be the beginning of the 10th century, as only then could such well-founded mythological knowledge be expected (de Vries), but this assumption is undoubtedly wrong. The interest in heathen mythology was peaking shortly before the end of the 10th century when heathendom was being seriously threatened by Christianity, and then again in the Icelandic Renaissance in the 12th and 13th centuries. Whereas the style of the lay points rather towards the end of the 10th century, its dialogue form, which was probably adopted from medieval scholarly literature, means that a composition date as late as the 13th century is not impossible.

ED: G. Neckel, H. Kuhn, *Edda*, Heidelberg [5]1983.

J. de Vries, *Altnordische Literaturgeschichte*, Berlin [2]1967;P. H. Salus, 'More "Eastern Echoes" in the Eddas?' (*MLN* 79) 1964; A. Holtsmark, 'Den uløselige gåten' (MoM) 1964; H. Beck, 'Vafþrúðnismál' (*KLL* 7) 1972; E. Salberger, 'Heill þú farir!' (*Scripta Islandica* 25) 1974; A. Holtsmark, 'Vafþrúðnismál' (*KLNM* 19) 1975.

Váfuðr (ON, 'wind'). A name for Odin in *Grímnismál* 54 which probably refers to Odin's self-sacrifice when he hung 'on a wind-swept gallows for nine long nights', and not to Odin as a 'god of the wind'.

H. Falk, *Odensheite*, Kristiania 1924.

Vagdavercustis (also Vagevercustis, Vagdaevercustis; lagdaarcustus?). A Germanic goddess whose name is preserved on seven votive stones dedicated to her. The geographic dispersion of the locations of the finds is great: five inscriptions come from the Lower Rhine, one from Plumtonwall on Hadrian's wall in North England, and one from Hungary. Two of the stones could be dated to the first half of the 3rd century. Although the meaning of the name is by no means clear, the elements of the name allow an interpretation of her as a goddess of war (Vagdavercustis = 'warlike virtue'?).

R. Much, 'Vagdavercustis' (*ZfdA* 55) 1917; S. Gutenbrunner, *Die germanischen Götternamen*, Halle 1936; J. de Vries, *Altgermanische Religionsgeschichte*, Berlin [3]1970; H. Reichert, *Lexikon der altgermanischen Namen*, Vienna 1987–90.

Vagnhǫfði (ON, 'whale-head'?). A giant in the *Þulur*. He is not recorded anywhere else in Old Norse literature but does occur in Saxo in a Latinized form Vagnophtus. In

Saxo's tale of Haddingus, the giants Vagnophtus and Haphlius (Hafli) are the Swedish tutors of Gram's sons Guthorm and Hadding (*Gesta Danorum* I, 19). Subsequently, Saxo tells of the giantess Harthgrepa (= Harðgreip) who is Vagnophtus' daughter. In his description of her, Saxo unites the Nordic folklore belief of the High Middle Ages and the concept of the giant in Germanic mythology in one picture, more than he does with Vagnhǫfði and Hafli.

Vagnophtus (Latin). A giant in Saxo, identical with → Vagnhǫfði.

Valaskjálf (ON). One of the homes of the gods covered in silver, and described in *Grímnismál* 6 as being extremely ancient. In contrast to the other homes of the gods listed, it is not allotted to any particular god, and only Snorri (*Gylfaginning* 16) mentions that Valaskjálf belongs to Odin. The name Valaskjálf has not been explained completely, but it is probable that it is a mythological place associated with Odin's son Vali. Valaskjálf can be found in a Norwegian place-name, today Valaskioll. As there was possibly a place-name *Viðarsskjálf (today Viskiǫl), it is possible that Odin and his sons Vali and Víðarr were brought in direct connexion with place-names based on *-skjálf* – cf. Odin's throne → Hlíðskjálf. The possibility that it is a cult place-name should not be ignored.

E. O. G. Turville-Petre, *Myth and Religion of the North*, Westport 1975; J. de Vries, *Altnordisches etymologisches Wörterbuch*, Leiden [2]1977.

Valfǫðr (ON, 'father of the slain'). A name for Odin (*Vǫluspá* 1, 27, *Grímnismál* 48 and in the *Þulur*), which refers to the concept that those slain in battle are welcomed by Odin in Valhall, as Snorri (*Gylfaginning* 19) explains: 'He [Odin] is also called Valfǫðr, since everyone who falls in battle [*falla i val*], are his adopted sons; he assigns them places in Valhall and Vingólf and they are then called *einherjar*.' The names for Odin based on *-fǫðr* (Valfǫðr, Herfǫðr) are probably older and more likely to be heathen than those based on *-faðir* (Sigfaðir, Alfaðir). The German word *Walvater* is a modern translation of Valfǫðr, which first appeared in K. Simrock's *Handbuch der deutschen Mythologie* (1853), and it is from here that R. Wagner adopted it for use in his 'Walküre'.

H. Kuhn, *Das nordgermanische Heidentum* (ZfdA 79) 1942; F. Kluge, *Etymologisches Wörterbuch der deutschen Sprache*, Berlin, New York [22]1989.

Valgautr (ON, 'Gautr of the fallen ones'). A name for Odin in a stanza by the skald Refr. It is an extension of Odin's name, Gautr.

Valglaumnir or Valglaumr (ON, 'the noisy one in front of Valhalla'). According to *Grímnismál* 21, it is perhaps the name of the river flowing past the front of Valhall, which is otherwise known as Thund.

Valgrind (ON, 'fence of the fallen ones'). The name of 'an old gate', according to *Grímnismál* 22; probably just as with Nágrind or → Helgrind, the fence around → Hel is meant by Valgrind, but hardly the gate to Valhall.

Valhall or Valhalla (ON Vallhǫll, 'hall of the slain') is the name of Odin's home in Asgard where he gathers the warriors slain in battle around him.

The most detailed description of Valhall is in the list of godly residences in *Grímnismál* (8–10, 18–26) and subsequently in Snorri (*Gylfaginning* 37–40). Valhall is situated in the part of → Asgard called Glaðsheimr; the hall is thatched with spears and shields and armour lies on the benches. The valkyries lead the slain heroes (the → *einherjar*) to this hall, to Odin, and they serve them with meat from the boar Sæhrímnir (which the cook Audhrímnir prepares in the cauldron Eldhrímnir). Everyone has enough to eat from the boar, which renews itself constantly. The *einherjar* drink mead with this meal which flows from the udders of the goat, Heiðrun. The goat stands on the roof of Valhall and, like the stag Eikthymir, grazes on the foliage of the tree Læraðr (= Yggdrasill). Odin, however, only drinks wine, and he feeds the wolves Geri and Freki with his own food. One gate to Valhall is called Valgrind (perhaps the one through which the slain warriors enter) and a wolf lies in front of it and an eagle soars above. The *einherjar* fight the whole day with each other, but in the evening they are all alive again and sit around together, drinking (*Vafþrúðnismál* 41). This seems to give an impression of how Viking Age warriors imagined paradise. At Ragnarǫk, however, the *einherjar* will march out – 800 through each of the 540 gates of Valhall – and will fight on the side of the gods against Fenrir and the powers of the Underworld.

The poetic image of the warriors' paradise given in *Grímnismál* derives, although not in all details, without a doubt from folk-belief, but nonetheless several elements can be found already in 9th and 10th century skaldic poetry: in Þórbjǫrn Hornklofi's *Hrafnsmál* (the shield-covered hall), in Eyvind's *Hákonarmál* and in the *Eiríksmál*.

M. Olsen's provocative theory that the constantly fighting warriors and the 540 gates to Valhall were a recalling of the experiences gathered by a Scandinavian traveller to the Colosseum with its constant combats of gladiators in Rome, aroused much attention. Even if this recall was not the basis for the actual Nordic myth of Valhall, it is nonetheless a possible source of the later poetic treatment of the material. The number of 800 times 540 = 432,000 *einherjar* mentioned in the *Grímnismál* can possibly be traced back to Hellenic influence, and is not a number of any particular symbolic significance. It is also by no means certain if the number is at all correct and if the *Grímnismál* did not use the Germanic value of hundred (= 120).

The ON Valhǫll (German *Walhalla* first used by H. Schütze in 1750) derives from *valr* 'those slain on the battlefield' and *hǫll* 'hall' and was understood, at least in the late heathen period, as 'hall of the slain'; however, some mountains in South Sweden which in folk-belief are thought to be the place where the dead live, as mountains of the dead, are also called Valhall. Perhaps the belief in Valhall also comes from the concept of life after death within barrows and mountains (→ Burial mound), as described in the sagas of the 13th century, where the dead are seen by the living to be celebrating with their ancestors in mountains (*Gisla saga* 11, *Eyrbyggja saga* 11, *Njáls saga* 14). In this case it would be possible that ON Valhǫll does not derive from *hǫll* 'hall' but from *hallr* 'rock'.

The origin of the concept is by no means older than the name: in the beginning there was the battlefield strewn with corpses, from which the demons of death (valkyries) led the fallen heroes to a god of the dead; the description of this place, whether as a place in a mountain, or else a heavenly drinking hall, only came secondarily.

A. Schullerus, 'Zur Kritik des altnordischen Valhollglaubens' (*PBB* 12) 1887; G. Neckel, *Walhall*, Dortmund 1931; E. Mogk, 'Walhall' (J. Hoops, *Reallexikon der germanischen Altertumskunde* 4) 1918/19; M. Olsen, 'Vallhall med de mange dörer' (*APhSc* 6) 1931/32; O. Höfler, *Kultische Geheimbünde der Germanen*, Frankfurt 1934; E. O. G. Turville-Petre, *Myth and Religion of the North*, Westport 1975; E. Marold, 'Das Walhallbild in den Eiríksmál und den Hakonarmál' (*Medieval Scandinavia* 5) 1972; E. F. Halvorsen, 'Valhall' (*KLNM* 19) 1975.

R: in modern times Valhall has assumed the meaning of a gathering of chosen dead people or else a hall of honour for these; this is also the idea behind the Walhalla built by L. v. Klenze (1830–47) near Regensburg (Germany) for Ludwig I of Bavaria, which contains the portraits of great Germans, and also behind the museum of the same name containing the figure-heads of ships wrecked on the island of Tresco in the Scillies (SW of England). This meaning also occurs in literature, namely in H. Rebenstock's poem *Walhalla der Menschheit* (1847) and in K. v. Gerstenber's comedy *Walhalla der Heiligen* (1873), as well as in H. v. Fallersleben's political poem: *Walhalla, Walhalla, was soll denn das sein* (1842).
On the other hand K. Ehrenberg's charcoal drawing *Gastmahl in Walhalla (mit einziehenden Einheriern* (1880) and even R. Wagner's concept of Valhalla in his opera *Der Ring des Nibelungen* are based on Nordic mythology. Valhall as a symbol for Germanic heathendom can be found in the magazine *Walhalla* (Munich 1905–13) and, on a less serious note, in the Danish comic series *Valhalla* (since the seventies).

Valhǫll (ON) → Valhall.

Vali (1) (ON) Baldr's avenger in the mythology of the *Edda*. He is called → Bous in Saxo. According to both traditions Rindr/Rinda is the mother of the avenger (*Baldrs draumar* 11) who Odin was only able to conquer by magic and deception. Vali is otherwise only named as Baldr's avenger in *Hyndluljóð* 29 and this is the only deed which we know about. If Baldr's avenger, as mentioned in *Vǫluspá* 32f., is also Vali, then he performed this act of revenge when he was only one day old. There is no mention of this in Saxo's version, although he does comment that Bous was interested in the art of war from an early age; according to Saxo, Bous is killed as soon as he has taken revenge on Hötherus (→ Hǫðr). However, *Vafþrúðnismál* 51 names Vali as the god of the younger generation who will live on after the Ragnarǫk. The god, Ali, mentioned by Snorri (a son of Loki's) appears to be derived from Vali through a misunderstanding.

Etymologically speaking, the name Vali has not been fully explained, and the interpretation from *Wanilo 'the little Vanir' is supported by nothing factual, but even Nordenstreng's interpretation as 'the arguing one' (from **waihalaR*) cannot be positively claimed. The god's name Vali is presumably to be found in the Norwegian place name Valaskioll (from *Valaskíalf), a name which is given in *Grímnismál* 6 as one of the homes of the gods; as with Viskjøl (from *Víðarsskjálf) it could be a cult place-name for one of Odin's sons, but the evidence of this information should not be given too much weight.

R. Nordenstren, 'Guden Váli' (*Festskrift H. Pipping*) Helsingfors 1924; J. de Vries, *Altgermanische Religionsgeschichte*, Berlin ^{3}1970; A. Holtsmark, 'Vali' (*KLNM* 19) 1975.

Vali (2) (ON). Loki's son in *Lokasenna* 65 Pr, *Gylfaginning* 49, and also *Vǫluspá* 34. The etymology of the name is obscure, as it is with Odin's similarly named son (→ Vali 1). We know nothing more about Vali than his name.

Váli (3). A dwarf in *Vǫluspá* 13 according to some of the manuscripts (instead of Náli).

Valkjósandi (ON, 'the one who chooses the fallen ones'). A young poetic name for

Odin used by the skald Kormákr which refers to Odin's bringing home to Valhall the heroes slain in battle.

valkyries. Originally probably demons of the dead to whom the warriors slain on the battle field belonged. The name valkyries (ON pl. *valkyrjar*) derives from ON *valr* 'the corpses lying on the battlefield' and *kjósa* 'to choose', thus 'those who choose the slain' (cf. also OE cognate *wælcyrge*, although the surviving OE texts show little understanding of the Norse concept, but rather identify them with furies or witches). There was a shift in the interpretation of the valkyries when the concept of Valhall changed from a battlefield to a warriors' paradise. The original concept was superseded by the shield girls – Irish female warriors who lived on like the → *einherjar* in Valhall. They were closely associated with Odin, just as they surely were earlier in their role as demons of death. Now their function is interfering in battle, and thus determining the fate of the combatants, as supernatural female warriors (*Darraðarljóð*) who fulfil Odin's wishes and lead the heroes slain in battle to Odin. Hence they are called *Oðins meyar* 'Odin's girls' and *óskmeyjar* 'wish-girls', 'girls who fulfil Odin's wishes'. As a result of this shift in the concept, they became a popular element in heroic poetry where they lost to a great extent their demonic characteristics and became more human, and therefore capable of falling in love with mortals, as in the case of the valkyrie Sigrdrífa in the *Sigrdrífumál*. The number of valkyries is given as either 9 (*Helgakviða Hjǫrvarðssonar*) or 12 (*Darraðarljóð*), but it seems to have been limitless. In *Grímnismál* 36 the names of 13 valkyries who serve the *einherjar* in Valhalla with beer listed are: Hrist, Mist, Skeggjǫld, Skǫgull, Hildr, Þrúðr, Hlǫkk, Herfjǫtur, Gǫll, Geirǫlul (or: Geirrǫmul, Geirahǫd), Randgríðr, Radgríðr and Reginleifr. In addition *Darraðarljóð* gives the names Hjǫrthrimul, Sanngríðr, Svipull, Guðr and Gǫndull; the *Þulur* add Herja, Geiravǫr, Skuld, Geirrǫndul, Randgnid, Geirskǫgull, Hrund, Geirdriful, Tanngniðr, Sveid, Þǫgn, Hjalmþrimull, Þrima and Skalmǫld. Other valkyries are only encountered in heroic poetry: Sigrun, Kara (*Helgakviða Hundingsbana* II), Svafa (*Helgakviða Hjǫrvarðssonar*) and Brynhildr (*Grípsspá*). Hardly one of these mostly expressive names, of which the majority point to the warlike function, seems to be particularly old, and they mostly come from poetic creativity rather than from real folk-belief.

E. Mogk, 'Walküren' (J. Hoops, *Reallexikon der germanischen Altertumskunde* 4) 1918/19; A. H. Krappe, 'The Valkyries' (*MLR* 21) 1926; H. R. Ellis, *The Road to Hel*, Cambridge 1943; F. Ström, *Diser, nornor, valkyrjor*, Stockholm 1954; J. de Vries, *Altgermanische Religionsgeschichte*, Berlin [3]1970; A. Holtsmark, 'Valkyrje' (*KLNM* 19) 1975; G. Müller, 'Zur Heilkraft der Walküre' (*FmSt* 19) 1976; L. Motz, 'Sister in the Cave' (*ANF* 95) 1980; M. I. Steblin-Kamenskij, 'Valkyries and Heroes' (*ANF* 97) 1982.

R: (literature) H. Heine, *Die Walküren* (poem in *Romanzero*, 1847); H. v. Linge, *Die Walküren* (poem, 1864); K. Boye, *Sköldmön* (poem in *Gömda Land*, 1924).
(fine art) J. G. Sandberg, *Die Walküren* (sketch, 1818); M. Echter, *Reitende Walküre* (fresco in Munich palace, 1865/66, now destroyed); P. N. Arbo, *Valkyrien*, and *Valkyriens død*, (paintings, 1860); A. Welti, *Walkürenritt* (etching, 1871); T. Pixis, *Walkürenritt* (woodcut, 1871); A. v. Heyde, *Walkürenritt* (1873) reproducing the etching *Walkürenritt* by A. Becker (1872); K. Ehrenberg, *Die Walkyren* (charcoal drawing, 1880), and *Walkyren wählen und wecken die gefallenen Helden (Einherier), um sie vom Schlachtfeld nach Walhall zu geleiten* (painting, 1882), and *Walkyrenschlacht* (oilpainting, 1884); A. Welti, *Walkürenritt*, (oilpainting, 1888; etching, 1890); H. Günther, *Walküre* (statue); H. Hendrich, *Walkürenritt* (oilpainting); F. Leeke, *Walkürenritt* (painting); K. Dielitz, *Einherier* (painting, c.1900); J. C. Dollman, *The*

Ride of the Valkyries (painting, c.1900); S. Sinding, *Valkyrie* (statue, 1910), and the *Walhalla-freeze* in the Ny Carlsberg Glyptotek (1886/7); A. Kolb, *Walkyrien* (print, 1915); E. Hansen, *Valkyrier* (drawing, 1925).
(music) R. Wagner's opera *Die Walküre* takes its material in a modified form from the *Vǫlsunga saga* where the concept has already been worked into Germanic heroic legend and has little to do with ancient mythological concepts.

Vallabnaehiae (also Valabneiae). Matron name in two inscriptions on Roman votive stones in Cologne, Germany, which, as with the matron name Vallamaeneihiae, are probably not Germanic, but rather belong to the Celtic personal name, Valamni.

S. Gutenbrunner, *Die germanischen Götternamen*, Halle 1936; H. Reichert, *Lexikon der altgermanischen Namen*, Vienna 1987–90.

Vallamaeneihiae. Matron name in an inscription from Cologne, Germany (CIL XIII 8228); → Vallabnaehiae.

Valþǫgn (ON, 'receiver of the slain'?). A valkyrie in a stanza by the Norwegian skald Guttormr Sindri from the middle of the 10th century.

Valþǫgnir (ON, 'receiver of the slain'). A name given to Odin by Víga-Glúmr; cf. the names for Odin Valkjósandi and the valkyrie-name Valþǫgn.

Valtýr (ON, 'god of the slain'). A name for Odin in Eyvindr Finnsson's *Háleygjatal* 15 (end of the 10th century) which refers to Odin's function as the god of war who takes those slain in battle to himself. Apart from Valtýr the plural of the word, *valtívar*, is found as a kenning for 'gods' (*Vǫluspá* 62, *Hymiskviða* 1); → Sigtýr.

H. de Boor, 'Die religiöse Sprache der Vǫluspá' (*Deutsche Islandforschung* 1) Breslau 1930.

Ván, also Vón (ON, 'hope'?). One of the (mythological?) rivers in the catalogue of rivers given in the *Grímnismál* 28. Since 'hope' does not fit particularly well to one of these dangerous rivers, Sturtevant suggested that a euphemism for 'danger' was seen in it, but this is hardly more convincing. In Snorri's description of the fettering of the Fenris wolf (*Gylfaginning* 33) Ván is the name of the river which is formed from the spittle flowing out of the open jaws of the wolf.

A. M. Sturtevant, 'Etymological Comments upon Certain Old Norse Proper Names' (*PMLA* 67) 1952.

Vanadís (ON, 'Vanir-dís'). This name for the goddess Freyja is only found in Snorri (*Gylfaginning* 34) and is merely a kenning for the goddess who is one of the Vanir ('Vanir-woman'), although a connexion with the → *dísir* is possible.

R: I. Kurz, *Vanadis* (novel, 1931).

Vanaheimr (ON, 'residence of the Vanir'). The name Snorri gives to the fictitious home of the Vanir (*Gylfaginning* 32) where Njǫrðr is supposed to have grown up. Snorri unquestionably invented the name as a counterpart to Asgard.

Vánargandr (ON, 'the monster of the river Ván'). The name Snorri gives to the Fenris wolf, probably because he says in *Gylfaginning* 33 that the river Ván (or Vón) springs from the foam flowing from the mouth of the chained Fenris wolf. It is by no means certain that Vánargandr in the kenning 'father of Vánargandr' = 'Loki', only recorded in Snorri, really means the Fenris wolf, or whether the Midgard serpent might be intended.

J. de Vries, *The Problem of Loki*, Helsinki 1933.

***Vandill** (1) (ON, 'god of the Vandals'?). Possibly a god's name, formed from an interpretation of the legendary place-name Vandilsvé ('shrine of the Vandill': *Helgakviða Hundingsbana* II 35). R. Much combined Vandilsvé with the sacred grove of the Naharvali mentioned by Tacitus in *Germania* 43 and assumed the existence of a Vandal god *Vandill from this, whose name was also present in the mythical name Aurvandill. As brilliant as this theory may be, it can hardly be proved by the source material available at the present time.

R. Much, 'Wandalische Götter' (*Mitteilungen der schlesischen Gesellschaft für Volkskunde* 27) 1926; R. Much, *Die Germania des Tacitus*, Heidelberg ^{3}1967.

Vandill (2) (ON). A giant in the *Þulur*.

Vandilsvé (ON, 'shrine of Vandill') → *Vandill (1).

Vaningi (ON, 'member, relative of the Vanir'). A name for Freyr used in *Skírnismál* 37 as he is the typical representative of the divine family of the Vanir. In the *Þulur* Vaningi is a term meaning 'boar', but as the boar → Gullinborsti is a typical attribute of Freyr's, this name could be an indirect one for the god himself.

Vanir (ON). The second Germanic family of gods, the most important being the Æsir.

Although primarily all Germanic gods are called Æsir, a group of them, Njǫrðr, Freyr and Freyja, belong to another family, the Vanir, which did not always live in peace with the Æsir. Snorri tells of the → Vanir wars at the end of which both families of gods made peace and exchanged hostages.

The Vanir are in particular fertility gods who were called upon for good harvests, sun, rain and good winds especially by the agrarian population, and for favourable weather conditions by the seafarers and fishermen. The Vanir practised a form of magic deemed to be ignoble by the Æsir who became acquainted with it through Freyja. In addition to this, according to Snorri in *Ynglinga saga* 4, incest between brothers and sisters was allowed by the Vanir, again in contrast to the Æsir, a circumstance which could indicate matriarchal conditions among the original followers of a Vanir cult. The differences between devotion to the Vanir and to the Æsir are derived from different social levels: the Vanir are the gods of the farming population, and the Æsir those of the warlike lords and their followers.

Devotion to the Vanir can be traced far back: the god Nerthus, etymologically identical to Njǫrðr, was mentioned as early as Tacitus, and the fertility gods who appear on Bronze Age rock carvings should certainly be seen as representing Vanir. It is interesting to note, too, that in Scandinavia there are far more place-names based on the names of the Vanir gods than of all other gods added together (with the exception of Ullr).

Apart from Njǫrðr and his two children Freyr and Freyja, the god Ing, who later in Scandinavia became one with the god Freyr, should be added to the list of the Vanir. The idea that Fróði (= Freyr) was once worshipped as a god in his own right is, however, doubtful. The belief that the god Ullr was also one of the Vanir can hardly be proven.

The etymology of the name, despite numerous attempts at explanation, has still not been convincingly interpreted.

W. Schulz, 'Archäologisches zur Wodan- und Wanenverehrung' (*Wiener Prähistorische Zeitschrift* 19) 1932; J. de Vries, *Altgermanische Religionsgeschichte*, Berlin [3]1970; A. Holtsmark, 'Vanir' (*KLNM* 19) 1975; G. Dumézil, *Gods of the Ancient Northmen*, Berkeley 1977.

R: A. Oehlenschläger, *Om vanerne* (poem in *Nordens Guder*, 1819).

Vanir wars. The name given to the battle between the two families of gods, the Æsir and the Vanir, which only Snorri and a few not especially clear stanzas in the *Vǫluspá* relate. Snorri gives two short accounts of the Vanir wars (*Ynglinga saga* 4, *Gylfaginning* 22), and an extremely short one is found in *Skáldskaparmál* 1:

'It began with the gods making war on the people who were called the Vanir. But they agreed on having a peace meeting and decided upon peace in such a way that both groups should go to a vessel and spit into it. When the gods went away again, they took this sign of atonement and did not want to forget about it and instead created out of it a man who was called → Kvasir.'

The other, more detailed version is in *Ynglinga saga* 4: 'Odin took his army to war against the Vanir, but they noticed it early and defended their land so that neither of them could conquer the other. Each one laid waste the other's land and did a lot of damage. When they were both tired of this, they agreed to have a peace meeting and made their peace and exchanged hostages. The Vanir took their most distinguished men, Njǫrðr the Rich and his son Freyr, but the Æsir took a man called Hœnir and they called him an ideal chieftain. He was a big and handsome man. They sent → Mímir with him, a very wise man, but the Vanir gave the cleverest of their group and he was called Kvasir.'

Apart from this Snorri mentions (*Gylfaginning* 22) the way that Njǫrðr and Hœnir were made hostage thus indirectly refering to the Vanir wars.

Although the stanzas 21–26 of *Vǫluspá* also supposedly depict the Vanir wars and Snorri knew these stanzas, nonetheless the contents of both of Snorri's versions deviate tremendously from the *Vǫluspá*. In *Vǫluspá* there is no mention of the taking of hostages, and the cause of the Vanir wars is the Vanir seeress, Gullveig, a person not mentioned in Snorri's versions.

In older scholarship the myth of the Vanir wars was mostly seen as a reflection of a historical war which took place in the 2nd millenium B.C. At that time the established South Scandinavian-West European megalithic culture was overrun by the north-westward advancing battle-axe culture, whence came the mixture of the (non-Indo-European? matriarchal?) champions of the megalithic culture (= Vanir) with the Indo-Germanic battle-axe people (= string ceramics culture = Æsir). These historical processes would have stayed in memory in the form of the myth of the Vanir and the pact of peace between the Æsir and the Vanir (Eckhardt).

In opposition to this theory, Dumézil pointed out the related myths and legends among other Indo-Germanic peoples (the Romans, Indians) and interpreted the Vanir wars as a result of this as the social conflict within a society in which the hierarchical followers of the kings (= Æsir?) and the farming population (for whom the vegetation cult and magic were of significance) stood against each other. Only through the pact of peace between these social classes – which in the myth of the Vanir wars indeed did take on a central position – was the ordered social and religious structure of the Indo-Germanic society created (Dumézil, de Vries).

K. A. Eckhardt, *Der Wanenkrieg*, Bonn 1940; G. Dumézil, *Tarpeia*, Paris 1947; J. de Vries, *Altgermanische Religionsgeschichte*, Berlin [3]1970; N. Å. Nielsen, 'Mythen om krigen og fredsslutningen mellem aserne og vanerne' (*Nordiska Studier i filologi och lingvistik. Festschrift G. Holm*) Lund 1976; C. Dumézil, *Gods of the Ancient Northmen*, Berkeley 1977.

Vapthiae. Name of Germanic matrons found on an inscription on a Roman votive stone from the Lower Rhine (after 150 A.D.); as the inscription has been lost, the evidence is not verifiable.

S. Gutenbrunner, *Die germanischen Götternamen*, Halle 1936; H. Reichert, *Lexikon der altgermanischen Namen*, Vienna 1987–90.

Vár (also Vór, ON, 'beloved'). A goddess in Old Norse mythology. Snorri (*Gylfaginning* 34) relates that she was responsible for contracts between men and women. In this Snorri was led astray by the word *várar* ('contracts') into making an etymological interpretation. The meaning 'beloved' is highly probable for Vár (cf. *Svǫlnis Var* 'Odin's beloved'= 'earth' in Eyvindr). Even Snorri's explanation still suggests this. In *Þrymskviða* 30 it is Vár who dedicates marriage. Thus Vár is a goddess of marriage and of love.

J. de Vries, *Altgermanische Religionsgeschichte*, Berlin [3]1970; A. Holtsmark, 'Vár' (*KLNM* 19) 1975.

Varðlokkur or Varðlokur (ON, 'temptor of the soul'). The name of a magical song (*galdr*) which was sung at prophetic sessions by Scandinavian seeresses, and in this shamanistic practice probably had a function of calling up the spirits from whom the seeresses received their knowledge.

The name Varðlokkur is given in *Þorfinns saga Karlsefnis* and it is not certain whether the expression was commonly known. In the *Landnámabók* such a song is called a *seiðlæti* 'magic tune'.

M. Olsen, 'Varðlokkur' (MoM) 1916.

Varðrun (ON, 'guard-rune'?). A giantess in Arnorr Þórðarson's *Haraldsdrápa* 13 and in the *Þulur*.

Vargr (ON). A term meaning both 'wolf' as well as 'outlaw', 'peaceless criminal'. Like a wolf he had to live in the woods outside human society and like a wolf was considered to be dangerous for man and could be killed by anyone.

C. v. Unruh, 'Wargus' (*Zeitschrift der Savigny-Stiftung für Rechtsgeschichte* 74) 1957.

Várkaldr (ON, 'Spring-cold'). The name given in *Fjǫlsvinnsmál* 6 to the father of Svipdagr who calls himself Vindkaldr here. Várkaldr and the name of his father, Fjǫlkaldr, are only poetic embellishments and are the creation of the poet.

Varr (ON, 'the careful one'). A dwarf in the *Þulur*.

Vartari (ON, 'belt, strap'). The name Snorri gives (*Skáldskaparmál* 33) to the thread with which Loki's mouth is sewn up in → Loki's punishment. In the *Þulur*, however, Vartari is a name for 'fish' and Snorri used the name as an embellishment of his tale, but whether he had a source or not, we have no means of knowing.

Vataranehae. Matron name. There are three inscriptions from Embeken near Düren, Germany, dedicated to the *Matronis Vataranehabus* (CIL XIII 7903–05). It is probably another form of the name → Veteranehae, as the evidence for this name comes from the same location.

S. Gutenbrunner, *Die germanischen Götternamen*, Halle 1936; H. Reichert, *Lexikon der altgermanischen Namen*, Vienna 1987–90.

vatni ausa (ON, 'to sprinkle with water', or *ausa barn vatni* 'sprinkle a child with water). This Germanic baptism is the supposed Germanic custom of sprinkling the newly born babies with water, a custom which would correspond to Christian baptism, and which was called *ausa vatni* whilst the term used for Christian baptism is always *skíra* ('cleanse; baptise'). According to the sagas, the new baby was picked up by the father, put on his knee and then sprinkled with water whilst being given his name; if another person (uncle, lord) took the father's place, then supposedly a kind of godfather-gift was given (*nafnfesti*). When the sprinkling had been performed, the child had the same rights as after taking his first nourishment: the child could no longer be exposed and had to be avenged if murdered with the full *wergeld*.

This heathen baptism is mentioned over 30 times in ON literature (*Hávamál* 158; *Rígsþula* 7, 21, 31; *Landnámabók* H 314; frequently in Snorri's *Heimskringla*, but also in the sagas of the Icelanders and the *fornaldarsǫgur*). However, none of these sources is dated before the 12th century, and in skaldic poetry the custom is not mentioned at all. The oldest source for heathen baptism is a letter written around 732 by Pope Gregory III to Boniface where he writes about a kind of heathen baptism. It is not clear from this passage whether this means the custom described in the Icelandic sources or not. The Nordic references are not very sound as evidence of a heathen baptism and, as with other 'heathen' rites which have been gleaned from saga literature, the possibility of scholarly borrowing of Christian customs should be considered. The fact that the custom was not borrowed in the last few pre-Christian centuries from Christian baptism, possibly in the cultural contact zone of the British Isles, can be seen from the fact that at this time total immersion was the most common form of Christian baptism whilst the description of the supposed heathen baptism presupposes the transition to the sprinkling of the new-born child.

Two things admittedly speak in favour of the existence of a heathen baptism among the heathen Germanic peoples. On the one hand the legal consequences of baptism were so well established in the 13th century that Maurer considered that baptism must have presupposed at least a similar heathen custom as a legal act. However, the established nature of baptism might be the result of the 200 years that had passed since the Christianization of Iceland. On the other hand a cult ablution after birth is so common among Indo-European peoples that the Germanic tribes would have been rather an exception if they did not have some sort of baptism. These arguments, naturally enough, are by no means sufficient evidence to prove the truth of the heathen baptism for Germanic heathendom.

K. Maurer, 'Über die Wasserweihe des germanischen Heidenthumes' (*Abhandlungen der philol.-histor. Klasse der königl. bayer. Akademie der Wissenschaften* 15/3) 1881; W. Baetke, 'Christliches Lehngut in der Sagareligion' (*Berichte über die Verhandlungen der sächsischen Akademie der Wissenschaften* 98/6) 1952; R. Simek, *Die Wasserweihe bei den heidnischen Germanen*, Vienna 1979.

Vatviae. Matron name. Twelve inscriptions have been found to date recording the name Vatviae. Three of the inscriptions come from Rödingen (Kreis Jülich) and five from Morken-Harff (Kreis Bergheim, Germany). Half of the inscriptions give the dative *Vatviabus*, and the others *Vatvims*, which confirms the Germanic character of the name. The most frequent interpretation relates the Vatviae etymologically to a

Germanic word base meaning 'water', but the exact application of this is disputed. More original, but not more likely, is the connexion of the Vatviae with Latin *vates* 'seer'.

S. Gutenbrunner, *Die germanischen Götternamen*, Halle 1936; E. A. Philippson, 'Neues über den Mütter- und Matronenkult am Niederrhein' (*MLN* 65) 1950; J. de Vries, *Altgermanische Religionsgeschichte*, Berlin ³1970; H. Birkhan, *Germanen und Kelten*, Vienna 1970; H. Reichert, *Lexikon der altgermanischen Namen*, Vienna 1987–90.

Vé (ON, 'shrine'), Germanic god, → Víli.

vé (ON, 'shrine'). The term derives from Germanic **wīha* and designates heathen shrines and sacred places in the widest sense of the word. Even the homes of the gods in mythological poetry of the *Edda* (*Vafþrúðnismál* 51) are called *vé*, and the word occurs repeatedly in skaldic poetry. The place of the → Thing was also considered as a *vé*; this is born out by the expression *vébǫnd* ('bands which form the boundaries of the shrine'), which is the name used in legal texts (*Frostaþingslǫg* I) for the fencing around the court at the Thing.

Place-names reveal the wide distribution of shrines with the name *vé* in Scandinavia: in Sweden there are more than 80 place-names based on *-vé*, 18 of them formed with the name of the god Ullr, 16 with Skaði, 8 with Freyr, but only 4 with Odin and 2 with Thor. In addition to this there are a large number of place-names based on *-vé* which use geographical elements (e.g. Visby). In Denmark, on the other hand, all 5 place-names based on *-vé* are combined with Odin (e.g. Odense). Most of the few Norwegian places called Ve are not compound, and in Iceland there are none whatsoever.

In the scholarship of the 1940s and '50s attempts were made to identify *vé* as a specific kind of shrine which would have been characterised by a long extended V-shaped marking (e.g. a stone setting). Such constructions have been supposedly discovered (by Dyggve, Ljunggren) in Jelling (Jutland), Tibirke (Zealand) and Tingsted (Falster). In the meantime scholars have stopped limiting the term *vé* in such a way to an actual form of Old Germanic shrines because the term *vé* in literary sources appears to have had a much more extensive meaning.

M. Olsen, *Ættegård og Helligdom*, Oslo 1926; E. Wessén, 'Schwedische Ortsnamen und altnordische Mythologie' (*APhSc* 4) 1929/30; W. Baetke, *Das Heilige im Germanischen*, Tübingen 1942; E. Dyggve, 'Eine Gruppe südskandinavischer Heiligtümer' (*Festschrift W. Baetke*) Weimar 1966; J. de Vries, *Altgermanische Religionsgeschichte*, Berlin ³1970; O. Olsen, 'Vorchristliche Heiligtümer' (H. Jankuhn, *Vorgeschichtliche Heiligtümer*) Göttingen 1970; O. Olsen, 'The "sanctuary" in Jelling' (*Mediaeval Scandinavia* 7) 1974; O. Olsen, H. Ståhl, 'Vi' (*KLNM* 19) 1975.

Vecha → Rindr.

Vegdeg (ON). One of Odin's sons. Only Snorri mentions him in the prologue to his *Edda*.

Vegdrasill (ON, 'way-horse' or 'famous horse'?). A dwarf in the *Fjǫlsvinnsmál* 34.

C. N. Gould, 'Dwarf-Names in Old Icelandic' (*PMLA* 44) 1929; L. Motz, 'New Thoughts on Dwarf-Names' (*Frühmittelalterliche Studien* 7) 1973.

Vegetation cult → Fertility cult.

Veggr (ON, 'wedge'). A dwarf in the *Vǫluspá* 12 according to the version given in the *Hauksbók*; in other manuscripts he is called → Veigr.

Vegsvinn (ON, 'the traveller'?). One of the (mythical?) rivers in the catalogue of rivers in *Grímnismál* 28 and in the *Þulur*.

Vegtamr (ON, 'the one used to journeys'). A pseudonym which Odin assumes on his journey to Hel to the dead seeress in → *Baldrs draumar*. Like others of Odin's names (Gangráðr and Gestr), Vegtamr shows Odin as the wandering god who turns up on people frequently unexpectedly and under various names and in various disguises.

H. Falk, *Odensheite*, Kristiania 1924; J. de Vries, *Altgermanische Religionsgeschichte*, Berlin [3]1970.

Vegtamskviða → *Baldrs draumar*.

Veigr, also Veggr or Vigr (ON). A dwarf in *Vǫluspá* 12. His name is related either to *veig* 'drink', hence 'the mead-possessing dwarf' or 'the one gifted with the powers of the healing potion'. Gutenbrunner does not see a name in Veigr but rather only an attribute to the dwarf name Gandálfr, related to OHG *weigar* 'defiant'. Since an ON **veigr* is otherwise not recorded and all manuscripts obviously understand Veigr as being a name, this theory seems to be most unlikely.

S. Gutenbrunner, 'Eddastudien 1' (ANF 70) 1955; J. de Vries, *Altnordisches etymologisches Wörterbuch*, Leiden [2]1977.

Veleda. A Germanic seeress from the tribe of the Bructeri who (according to Tacitus) was worshipped almost like a god by her own people in the first century A.D., and who also attracted a certain amount of fame among the Romans. Veleda played a vital political role in the Batavi war: in 69 A.D. the Germanic Batavi living on the Lower Rhine under Julius Civilis rose against the Roman occupation at a time when the majority of the Roman army on the Rhine had been withdrawn to Italy as a result of political confusion back home. Civilis sent the captured legion commander of the fallen Castra Vetera as a gift to Veleda, of whom Tacitus reports at this time (*Historiae* IV, 61): 'She was a maiden from the tribe of the Brukteri who possessed extensive powers, according to the old custom of the Germanic peoples to regard many women as seeresses, and in an extended superstition to consider them even to be goddesses. The respect afforded to Veleda increased tremendously at this time as she had prophesied success for the Germanic tribe and the destruction of the legion.' Admittedly, the commander of the legion was murdered on the way to Veleda, but this did not lessen the honour given to Veleda; when the Germanic people on the right bank of the Rhine led by the Tenkteri, threatened the town of Cologne, the citizens of Cologne called upon Civilis and Veleda, who was seen as being decisive, as arbitrators; 'Envoys were sent with various gifts to Civilis and Veleda who organized everything to the satisfaction of the people of Cologne: however, they were not allowed to appear themselves in front of Veleda or to speak with her. It was forbidden to look at her in order to encourage still greater respect. She lived in a high tower and a relative, specially chosen for the purpose, brought questions and answers to her as if a go-between to a deity.' (Tacitus, *Historiae* IV, 65). Soon after this (70 A.D.) in a night-time attack the Germanic people seized the flag ship of the Roman Rhine fleet, a Trireme, and dragged it as a gift for Veleda up as far as the river Lippe. The commander, Petilius Cerialis (who was not taken prisoner as he had spent the night with a Germanic woman on land), knew and appreciated the power of Veleda, since he asked her in secret messages to allow the fate of war to take another direction if he promised a pardon for both Civilis and the Batavi (Tacitus, *Historiae* V, 24); we do not know how Veleda reacted here as Tacitus' account breaks off shortly afterwards. From other sources, however, we know about the fate of Veleda later on because a poem written by Papinius Statius (*Silvae* I, 4, 89) mentions Veleda as being a prisoner in the year 77 A.D. A little later it appears that Veleda was deported to Italy and lived the remainder of her days in a temple in the town of Ardea in Latium (South Italy); a Greek satirical poem on a small fragment of marble from this town is aimed at Veleda and mentions her name with the addition 'the tall, arrogant virgin whom the Rhine water drinkers worship' so that it is probably indeed a matter of the same Germanic seeress who appears to have remained a temple servant for the rest of her life.

Although the name Veleda reminds us phonetically of ON *vǫlva* 'seeress', it should more likely be linked with Celtic *fili(d)* 'poet, scholar'; it is however not very likely that Veleda should be considered as a term for her profession rather than a name.

J. Weisweiler, 'Die Stellung der Frau bei den Kelten und das Problem des "keltischen Mutterrechts"' (Zeitschrift für celtische Philologie 21) 1938–40; M. Guarducci, 'Veleda' (*Rendiconti della Pontificia Accademia Romana di Archaeologia* 21) 1945/46; J. Keil, 'Ein Spottgedicht auf die gefangene Seherin Veleda' (*Anzeiger der österreichischen Akademie der Wissenschaften, Phil.-hist. Klasse* 84/19) 1947; A. Wilhelm, 'Das Gedicht auf Veleda' (*Anzeiger der österreichischen Akademie der Wissenschaften, Phil.-hist. Klasse* 85) 1948; H. Krahe, 'Altgermanische Kleinigkeiten 4. Veleda' (*IF* 66) 1961; C.-J. Guyonvarch, 'Notes d'etymologie et de lexicographie celtiques et gauloises 9' (*Ogam* 13) 1961; W. Meid, 'Der germanische Personenname Veleda' (*IF* 69) 1964; H. Volkmann, *Germanische Seherinnen in römischen Diensten*, Krefeld 1964; R. Much, *Die Germania des Tacitus*, Heidelberg [3]1967; J. de Vries, *Altgermanische Religionsgeschichte*, Berlin [3]1970; H. Birkhan, *Germanen und Kelten*, Vienna 1970.

R: (literature) F. de la Motte-Fouqué, *Welleda und Ganna* (novel, 1818).
(fine art) E. H. Maindron, *Velleda* (marble statue, 1843/4); K. Sigrist, *Veleda, die Prophetin der Brukterer* (drawing).
(music) Sobolewsky, *Velleda* (opera, 1836).

Venus. The Roman goddess of love Venus was identified by the Germanic peoples with the goddess Frîja (ON Frigg), as the translation of the → week-day name *dies Veneris* to 'day of Frîja', → Friday confirms.

Veratýr (ON, 'Týr of mankind'). A name for Odin in *Grímnismál* 3 and the *Þulur*. Like Aldafaðir it refers to Odin's role in creating man (→ Anthropogeny).

Vercana. A goddess on two Roman votive inscriptions, one from Bad Bertrich (CIL XIII 7667), the other from Ernstweiler near Zweibrücken, Germany (CIL XIII 4511). It is disputable whether the name is Celtic or Germanic; in the latter case it could be connected to Germanic **werka* 'work', or else to the name of the b-rune, ON *bjarkan* (then Vercana for *Berkana). As the birch tree played a role in folk medicine, this interpretation would be semantically most appealing.

S. Gutenbrunner, *Die germanischen Götternamen*, Halle 1936; M. Schönfeld, *Wörterbuch der altgermanischen Personen- und Völkernamen*, Heidelberg [2]1965; H. Birkhan, *Germanen und Kelten*, Vienna 1970; H. Reichert, *Lexikon der altgermanischen Namen*, Vienna 1987–90.

Verdandi (ON, 'becoming'). One of the three → norns in Snorri (*Gylfaginning* 14) following *Vǫluspá* 20. It is supposed that Verdandi – certainly a young name – should personify the present, whilst Urd stands for the past and Skuld for the future.

R: this norn is found as Werandi in Klopstock's ode *Skulda* (1766).

Verr (ON, 'man'). One of the synonyms for giants in the *Þulur*.

Vestri (ON, from *vestr* 'west'). A dwarf in *Vǫluspá* 11, who according to *Gylfaginning* 7 supports the sky made from Ymir's skull in the west, helped by the dwarfs Austri, Nordri and Sudri in the other appropriate directions. The idea could just possibly be influenced by Greek concepts since Atlas, too, supports the vault of heaven in the west, but the four dwarfs suggest rather a link with the four angels at the ends of the world in St John's *Revelation* 7, 1. The concept of the dwarfs who carry the sky cannot, however, merely be traced back to Snorri, as a kenning *niðbyrðra Norðra* 'burden of the relations of Norðris' for 'sky' may already be found in the 10th century in Hallfreðr vandræðaskáld's *Olafsdrápa* (26). It is not really particularly surprising that in ON the beams supporting the roof (also the sky of the domestic microcosmos) were called *dvergar* 'dwarfs', but whether there is indeed a connexion here is somewhat questionable. – There is apparently a depiction of dwarfs supporting the sky to be found on a relief from a Viking Age grave in Haysham, England.

S. Gutenbrunner, 'Über die Träger des Himmelsgewölbes im germanischen Mythos' (*ARW* 37) 1941/42; J. de Vries, *Altgermanische Religionsgeschichte*, Berlin [3]1970; L. Motz, 'On Elves and Dwarfs' (*Arv* 29/30) 1973/74.

Vesuniahenae. Matron name which is recorded on five Roman votive inscriptions of which four come from Vettweis (Kreis Düren, Germany). Whether the name of the Vesuniahenae is derived from an earlier form of the place-name Vettweis (older Wisse) appears to be questionable; a Celtic origin is also a possibility.

M. Ihm, 'Der Mütter- und Matronenkultus und seine Denkmäler' (*Bonner Jahrbücher* 83) 1887; S. Gutenbrunner, *Die germanischen Götternamen*, Halle 1936; H. Reichert, *Lexikon der altgermanischen Namen*, Vienna 1987–90.

Veterahenae. Matron name, recorded twice in Embken. Another form of → Veteranehae.

S. Gutenbrunner, *Die germanischen Götternamen*, Halle 1936.

Veteranehae. Matron name. A number of inscriptions on votive stones from Embken and Wollersheim (Kreis Düren, Germany) are dedicated to the *matronibus Veteranehis*. In addition to this there are two monuments with the name variant Veterahenae and three with Vataranehae from the same area, so that a cult centre in Embken may be postulated; four of the inscriptions with the Veteranehae come from donors from the same family. Another newly found inscription, of which only Veter . . . is extant is not found in the same area of the other stones (Rommerskirchen, Kreis Neuß), but it was used as a building stone and could therefore also come from Embken originally. – The link of the name with *veteranus* 'veteran' is unlikely. Gutenbrunner suggested the form Vataranehae was the correct one and related the name etymologically to Germanic **watar-* 'water' as numerous matron names are derived from river names. The great frequency of the form on Veter-, however, makes this interpretation somewhat improbable, and a derivation from the name of a camp Castra Vetera is to be preferred.

S. Gutenbrunner, *Die germanischen Götternamen*, Halle 1936; M. Clauss, 'Neue Inschriften im Rheinischen Landesmuseum Bonn' (*Epigraphische Studien* 11) 1976; H. Reichert, *Lexikon der altgermanischen Namen*, Vienna 1987–90.

Véþormr (ON, 'protector of the shrine'). Possibly a name for the god Thor, considering the other name for the god Thor, Véurr; the context in which the name occurs (Egill, *Arinbjarnarkviða* 19: *vinr Véþorms* 'friend of Véþorm' = Arinbjǫrn) however leaves every possibility open.

J. de Vries, *Altgermanische Religionsgeschichte*, Berlin [3]1970.

Vetr (ON, 'winter'). Vetr (in *Vafþrúðnismál* 27 and then also in Snorri, *Gylfaginning* 18) is a purely literary personification of winter whose father is named here as being Vindsvalr. In actual mythology there is no 'winter' as a mythical person.

Véuðr or Véoðr (ON). A name of the god Thor mentioned in the *Þulur*, which is possibly only a variant of → Véurr.

Véurr (ON, 'guard of the shrine'?). Thor is called Véurr in *Hymiskviða* (11, 17, 21) and in *Vǫluspá* he is called *Midgards Véurr* 'protector of the world'(?). The etymology of the name is controversial, but probably it is derived from a **vé-vǫrr* or **vé-vǫrþr* (to *vé* 'shrine' and *verja* 'protect'). The origin from **wihi-þonraR* 'dedication-Thor' (Krause) can be rejected as the other evidence for Thor as a dedicatory god is extremely questionable.

W. Krause, 'Vingþorr' (*ZfdA* 64) 1927; E. Marold, ' "Thor weihe diese Runen" ' (*FmSt* 8) 1974: J. de Vries, *Altnordisches etymologisches Wörterbuch*, Leiden [2]1977.

Víð or Víl (ON Víð 'the broad one' or Víl 'plight'?). One of the mythical rivers in the catalogue of rivers in *Grímnismál* 28. In Snorri (*Gylfaginning* 3) Víð is one of the Élivágar rivers, which flow from the spring Hvergelmir.

A. M. Sturtevant, 'Etymological Comments Upon Certain Old Norse Proper Names' (*PMLA* 67) 1952.

Víðarr (ON, 'the wide ruling one'?). One of the Æsir who is mainly known as Odin's avenger on the wolf Fenrir at the Ragnarǫk (*Vǫluspá* 55; *Vafþrúðnismál* 53; *Grímnismál* 17). It is only mentioned in the *Þulur* that he is a son of Odin's. In Snorri he is called the son of the giant Gríðr (*Skáldskaparmál* 18). Víðarsland or Viði is named in *Grímnismál* 17 as Víðarr's abode, and Víðarr belongs, along with Vali, Móði and Magni, to the generations of gods who will live in the new world, after the downfall of the gods at Ragnarǫk.

Snorri calles Víðarr the 'silent god'. He has the 'strong shoe'; he is the strongest of the gods after Thor and the gods rely on him in all difficulties (*Gylfaginning* 28). The reference to the shoe alludes to a tale told by Snorri within the framework of the events at Ragnarǫk (*Gylfaginning* 50): 'The wolf devours Odin who is thus killed; but immediately afterwards Víðarr appears and kicks the lower jaw of the wolf with his foot. He wears a shoe on this foot which was made at the beginning of the world; it consists of leather strips which men cut off their shoes at the front or at the heel; therefore everybody who wants to help the Æsir should throw away these strips. – Then Víðarr takes the wolf's upper jaw in one hand and rips his mouth apart whereupon he dies.' A similar fragment of folk-belief is told by Snorri with reference to the ship → Naglfar.

Víðarr is not mentioned in skaldic poetry and there have been tendencies to see him as a purely literary figure of mythological Eddic poetry (*Vǫluspá, Vafþrúðnismál, Grímnismál, Lokasenna*). It is questionable whether the seldomly occurring place-names in Norway, Virsu (from Viðarshof) and Viskjøl (from Víðarsskjálf) can prove that there was a cult dedicated to Víðarr in the later heathen period, but Víðarr is definitely not an ancient deity.

An interpretation of the relief on the stone crosses from Gossforth (North England) and Kirk Andreas (Isle of Man), both from the time around 900, tried to see Víðarr in a picture of a man tearing apart a wolf's mouth. It can, however, be just as easily a picture of Christ, because the Viking Age allowed a fusion of heathen and Christian traditions (→ Thor and the Midgard serpent, → *interpretatio christiana*).

J. de Vries, *Altgermanische Religionsgeschichte*, Berlin [3]1970; A. Holtsmark, 'Víðarr' (*KLNM* 19) 1975.

R: K. Ehrenberg, *Tyr and Heimdall, Widar and Ullr* (drawing, 1882); *Widar: Deutschgläubige Gemeinde* was the name that one of the so-called neo-Germanic belief movements called themselves around 1935.

Víðbláinn (ON, 'the far-blue'). The name given by Snorri (and in the *Þulur*) to the third heaven where according to Snorri the hall Gimlé is situated and where light-elves (= angels?) live (*Gylfaginning* 16). The whole concept is Christian; for information about Snorri's possible source cf. → Andlangr.

Víðblindi (ON, 'the very blind one'?). A giant in skaldic poetry. Snorri explains the kenning 'Víðblindis's boar' = whale, which occurs in a stanza by Hallar-Stein, as follows: whales are called Víðblindi's boar here. He was a giant and went fishing in the sea for whales as others do for fish' (*Skáldskaparmál* 44). This explanation of Snorri's for the kenning is obviously insufficient, but Víðblindi is nowhere else referred to. The only giant in mythological poetry who catches whales is Hymir in the tale of Thor and the Midgard serpent, but he was never called Víðblindi.

Viddi (ON). A giant in a poem by Egill Skalagrímsson and in the *Þulur*. The meaning of the name is uncertain. If it were possible to read Víddi, then 'the wide one = fat one' would be plausible.

Viðfinnr (ON, 'the opposing Finn'?, more likely, 'the finder'). The father of Bil and Hjuki in an aetiological tale told by Snorri (*Gylfaginning* 10) about the picture in the moon. → Máni.

Viðgrípr (ON, 'the far grasping one'). A giant in the *Þulur*.

Viðofnir (ON). A cock in *Fjǫlsvinnsmál* (18, 24, 25) who sits in the branches of the tree Mimameiðr at Menglǫð's home and whose meat is the only thing with which the guard dog can be calmed down. There are several different interpretations for the name Viðofnir; considering *víð-*: *víðopnir* 'the far shouting one' (Jónsson); reading Viðófnir 'the tree glower' (from *váfa* 'flicker': Bergmann) or 'tree kicker' (from *við-þófnir*: Olsen).

F. W. Bergmann, *Vielgewandts Sprüche*, Strassburg 1874; J. de Vries, *Altnordisches etymologisches Wörterbuch*, Leiden [2]1977.

Viðólfr (ON → Vittólfr.

Viðr (ON *viðr* 'tree'). A dwarf in the *Þulur*.

Viðrir (ON, 'weather god'). A name for Odin in *Lokasenna* 26, *Helgakviða Hundingsbana* I 13, as well as several times in skaldic poetry. Snorri also includes the name (*Gylfaginning* 2) and in the *fornaldarsǫgur* Odin often appears repeatedly under this name. Odin is naturally not the actual weather god of Nordic mythology; he influences it, however, by magic (cf. *Reginsmál* 16 Pr).

H. Falk, *Odensheite*, Kristiania 1924.

Viðurr (ON). A name for Odin in *Grímnismál* 49 is recorded in skaldic poetry several times since Bragi in the 9th century, although in Bragi Viðurr may well be a dwarf-name.

The meaning of this name for Odin is somewhat obscure: either 'killer' (from *viða*), or else it is dervived from the name of a people Wederas or Weder-Geatas, whereby Viðurr would be a eponymous ancestor of this Gautland tribe.

H. Falk, *Odensheite*, Kristiania 1924; J. de Vries, *Altnordisches etymologisches Wörterbuch*, Leiden ^{2}1977.

Vigglǫð (ON, 'the one happy in battle'). A giantess in the *Þulur*.

Viggr (ON). A dwarf in *Vǫluspá* 12 (in the majority of manuscripts however → Veigr). Etymologically the connexion to *vigg* 'horse' – thus, 'the one with the staggering gait' – is more likely than a link to Norwegian *vigg* 'part of an axe'.

C. N. Gould, 'Dwarf-Names in Old Icelandic' (*PMLA* 44) 1922; J. de Vries, *Altnordisches etymologisches Wörterbuch*, Leiden ^{2}1977.

Vígríðr (ON, 'place on which battle surges') The name given in *Vafþrúðnismál* 18 to the battlefield on which Surtr (and his Underworld forces) will take their stand for the final battle against the gods at Ragnarǫk.

Vihansa. Name of a Germanic goddess. A centurion from the III. legion dedicates shield and spear to Vihansa in an inscription on a bronze plaque from Tongern in Belgium; the name is therefore connected to Germanic **wīhan* 'to fight' and Vihansa is seen as a goddess of war. On the other hand the derivation from Germanic **wīhan* 'to dedicate' would certainly be possible.

S. Gutenbrunner, *Die germanischen Götternamen*, Halle 1936; J. de Vries, *Altgermanische Religionsgeschichte*, Berlin ^{3}1970; H. Reichert, *Lexikon der altgermanischen Namen* I. Vienna 1987.

Víkarr (in Saxo Wicarus). A legendary Norwegian king who died according to the legend as a sacrifice to Odin which originally was only supposed to have been a mock sacrifice.

The tale of this sacrifice is given both in the Old Norse *Gautreks saga* and the poem recorded in it, *Víkarsbálkr*, as well as in Saxo (*Gesta Danorum* VI, 184).

According to *Gautreks saga*, Víkarr and his blood-brother Starkaðr were on a Viking expedition and were becalmed; as a last chance they drew lots to decide which of them was going to be sacrificed, and the lot fell to Víkarr. The sacrifice was only supposed to be an imitation one and Starkaðr knotted the rope, fastened it to a thin branch and then put it round Víkarr's neck; Starkaðr then struck the king with a reed which he had received from Odin. Suddenly the twig became a thick branch, the gut cord became a strong rope, and the reed a spear, so that Víkarr was both hanged and pierced.

Saxo's version is only slightly different; however, he refutes quite explicitly the tale of the metamorphosis of the gut cord and rationalizes Víkarr's death as resulting from the knot in the noose being too tight. In this version, too, Starkaðr kills Víkarr, with a sword.

The form of this sacrificial death by hanging and being pierced is closely connected with → Odin's self-sacrifice and was already characterized through this as a sacrifice to Odin. Víkarr had already fallen to Odin through a prophesy, and in this sacrifice his fate was simply realized, and the return in death to Odin is verbalized in the *Gautreks saga* as follows: 'Now I give you to Odin'. The name Víkarr even indicates the dedication of Víkarr to a god, as Höfler showed, as Víkarr can be compared to *vé-/vi-* 'holy' and *-kárr* 'hair', which points to the religious meaning of long hair in the dedication to Odin.

P. Herrmann, *Die Heldensagen des Saxo Grammaticus*, Leipzig 1922; O. Höfler, *Germanisches Sakralkönigtum*, Tübingen, Münster, Köln 1952.

Vili (ON, 'will'). Vili and Vé are Odin's brothers. These three gods are the first gods according to Snorri's myth of the creation (*Gylfaginning* 5) and are the sons of the mythical ancestor Borr with the giantess Bestla. In *Ynglinga saga* 3 Vili and Vé are the lords who take over the rule of the Æsir during → Odin's exile, and they share Odin's wife Frigg until Odin returns. *Lokasenna* 26 refers to this, saying that Frigg deceived Odin with Vili and Vé. Odin is called Vili's brother in skaldic poetry, too (Þjóðólfr, *Ynglingatal* 3; Egill, *Sonatorrek* 23).

The triad of Borr and Odin's sons, Vili and Vé corresponds to another divine triad in the → myth of descent (→ Cosmogony, → Anthropogeny) of the Germanic peoples, which Tacitus reports: Mannus, the son of Tuisto, was the father of three brothers, who gave their names to the three Germanic peoples Ingaevones, Istaevones and Hermiones. The alliteration used in Germanic poetry is reflected also in the names of Odin, Vili and Vé; at the time of the composition of this genealogy the alliteration of the initial W in Wodan/Odin was still retained, thus allowing a dating to primitive Germanic times.

F. R. Schröder, 'Germanische Schöpfungsmythen' (*GRM* 19) 1931; J. de Vries, *Altgermanische Religionsgeschichte*, Berlin ³1970; E. F. Halvorsen, 'Vé' (*KLNM* 19) 1975.

Víli (ON). A dwarf in *Vǫluspá* 13; → Fíli, → Heptifíli.

Vilmeiðr (ON, meaning obscure: *meiðr* 'tree, beam', the first part of the word as in Vilhjálmr and so on). According to *Vǫluspá in skamma* (*Hyndluljóð* 33; *Gylfaginning* 4) Vilmeiðr is the mythical ancestor of all sorcerers; whether the name is semantically connected to this, is conceivable, but the question must remain open.

Vimur (ON, 'the bubbling one'? cf. Geirvimul). A mythological river, which is named in skaldic poetry (e.g. Ulfr's *Húsdrápa* 6) and in the *Þulur* and which also occurs in Snorri's tale of Thor's journey to → Geirrǫðargard (*Skáldskaparmál* 18). In this passage Thor has to wade through the torrential river which is swollen even more by the urine from the giant's daughter Gjálp, and Thor is only able to save himself by grasping a branch of an ash. The stanza in Ulfr could perhaps suggest that Vimur was one of the names for the river on the border between men and giants.

Vin (ON). A (mythical?) river in the catalogue of rivers in *Grímnismál* 27; perhaps identical with → Vína.

Vína (ON, the Dwina in Russia). One of the rivers in the mythological catalogue of rivers in *Grímnismál* 28 and in the *Þulur*.

Vindálfr (ON, 'wind-elf' or 'the bent dwarf'). A dwarf in *Vǫluspá* 12 and in the *Þulur*.

Vindkaldr (ON, 'wind-cold'). The name the hero Svipdagr adopts for himself in *Fjǫlsvinnsmál* 6 in his battle of wits with Menglǫð's guard. The names given here for his father and grandfather Várkaldr and Fjǫllkaldr should be considered to be poetic embellishments, just as his own name is.

Vindlér or Vindhlér (ON). A name for the god → Heimdall (*Skáldskaparmál* 8, *Háttatal* 7) which either means 'the one protecting against the wind' (from *hlé* 'lee, protection') or 'wind-sea' (from Hlér = Ægir = sea). The link between the name and the role of the god Heimdall is totally obscure.

Vindljóni (ON). A name for → Vindsvalr, the father of winter in Snorri (*Gylfaginning* 18).

Vindr (ON, 'wind, storm'). A giant in the *Þulur*. In Snorri (*Skáldskaparmál* 26) he is said to be the son of Fornjótr and the brother of Ægir and Eldr. In the other genealogies of Fornjótr this son is, however, called Kari ('wind, squall, gust') so that Vindr as the son of Fornjótr would represent only an invention of Snorri's from a synonym for wind instead of Kari.

Vindsvalr (ON, 'the wind-coolness'). The father of winter in *Vafþrúðnismál* 27 and in Ormr Steinþórsson and also in Snorri (*Gylfaginning* 18, *Skáldskaparmál* 27), but this name is little more than a poetic embellishment of mythology. In the *Þulur*, Vindsvalr is listed as being among the giants. Snorri also adds Vindljóni as the synonymous name for Vindsvalr.

Vingnir (1) (ON). A name for Odin listed in the *Þulur*. The name has not been satisfactorily explained, but 'the weapon-shaking god' would be possible, which would suit Odin as well as Thor. The similarity to the name for Thor, Vingthor, is obvious.

J. de Vries, *Altnordisches etymologisches Wörterbuch*, Leiden [2]1977.

Vingnir (2) (ON). A name for Thor (in the *Þulur*), which means either the same as Vingnir (1) or else is derived from Vingthor.

In the prologue to his *Edda*, Snorri names Vingnir in Thor's genealogy along with many other names for Thor, thus identifying him also with Thor. On the other hand, in *Skáldskaparmál* 4 Snorri names Vingnir as being Thor's foster-father, whereby either a mythological figure whom we otherwise do not know is meant, which is not especially likely, or else Odin → Vingnir (1).

Vingnir (3) (ON). A giant in *Haustlǫng* 19 and in the *Þulur*.

Vingólf (ON, perhaps: 'the friendly house'). The beautiful building in Asgard, according to Snorri (*Gylfaginning* 13), which served the female gods as a temple. On the other hand, he mentions in *Gylfaginning* 19 that the warriors slain in battle and brought home by Odin will not only be housed in Valhall, but also in Vingólf.

Braune thought that the word which was obviously first invented by Snorri should actually be read as Víngólf 'wine house' and is only another name for Valhall; this alteration is not necessary at all as 'hall of friends' or even 'hall of lovers' is sufficient for an interpretation of the place where the warrior paradise of the *einherjar* is.

W. Braune, 'Vingólf' (*PBB* 14) 1889; F. Jónsson, 'Vingólf' (*ANF* 6) 1890; F. Kauffmann, 'Vingólf' (*ZfdA* 36) 1892.

R: F. G. Klopstock wrote an ode *Wingolf* in 1762, whicht was adopted as the name of a German student club in Prague in 1848.

Vingþor (ON, 'battle-Thor'?). A name given to Thor in *Þrymskviða* 1, *Alvíssmál* 6 and in the *Þulur*. The interpretation of the name is disputed; the interpretation of it as 'fetter-Thor, dedication-Thor' (from **ueik-* 'fetter, dedicate': Krause) is linguistically and factually implausible. The most likely explanation is 'battle-Thor' (from *vega* 'fight' cf. Latin *vincere*), whereby Vingthor would be related to the runic → wigithonar.

It is clear from Snorri's naming in the scholarly pre-history in the prologue of his *Edda* of a Ving(e)þórr as being the son of a certain Einriði, the grandson of Lóriði (= Hlóriði) and the father of Vingener (= Vingnir) that Snorri understood Vingthor to be a name for Thor, as this genealogy consists exclusively of names for Thor.

A. Kock, 'Etymologisch-mythologische Untersuchungen' (*IF* 10) 1889; W. Krause, 'Vingþorr' (*ZfdA* 64) 1927; E. Marold, ' "Thor weihe diese Runen" ' (*FmSt* 8) 1974; J. de Vries, *Altnordisches etymologisches Wörterbuch*, Leiden [2]1977.

Víparr (ON). A giant in the *Þulur*. The name most likely means 'the bristly one' (cf. Norwegian *vipa* 'bristle, beard'). Jónsson's interpretation of 'the moving one' is not convincing.

F. Jónsson, 'Þulur' (*APhSc* 9) 1934.

Viradecdis (other forms Viradestis, Viratehtis, Virodact(h)is). Name of a goddess in a Roman votive inscription from Vehten (CIL XIII 8815). Although this inscription and the one with Virodactis are on Germanic ground, the name itself (from Irish *ferdaht* 'masculinity') indicates a Celtic goddess.

S. Gutenbrunner, *Die germanischen Götternamen*, 1936; J. de Vries, *Altgermanische Religionsgeschichte*, Berlin [3]1970; H. Birkhan, *Germanen und Kelten*, Vienna 1970; H. Reichert, *Lexikon der altgermanischen Namen*, Vienna 1987–90.

Viradesthis. Name of a goddess on a Roman votive inscription from Birrens, North England (CIL VII 1073); → Viradecdis.

Viratehtis. Name of a goddess in a Roman votive inscription from Streé-lez-Huy, Belgium: *D(eae) Viratehti Superina Supponis*; → Viradecdis.

H. Reichert, *Lexikon der altgermanischen Namen*, Vienna 1987–90.

Virodact(h)is. Name of a goddess in two Roman votive inscriptions on the Lower Rhine from Mainz (CIL XIII 6761) and from Trebur (CIL XIII 11944); → Viradecdis.

Virvir, also Virfir and Virpir (ON). A dwarf in the *Vǫluspá* 15 and in the *Þulur*. De Vries considers Virvir as a phallic word just like the obscure sea-king's name Virfill. Gould interprets it, however (with a borrowing from Old Frisian) as 'colourer, dyer'.

C. N. Gould, 'Dwarf-Names' (*PMLA* 44) 1929; J. de Vries, *Altnordisches etymologisches Wörterbuch*, Leiden [2]1977.

Visna. A warrior-like queen in Saxo (*Gesta Danorum* VIII, 256f.); → Alvilda.

Vitazgjafi (ON, 'the one certain to give'). A field in Iceland in the *Víga-Glúms saga* (7ff.), 'because it was never infertile'. As there was supposed to have been a temple to Freyr immediately in the vicinity of this, Vitazgjafi has been seen as being a Freysakr, that is a field dedicated to Freyr, as is recorded in place-names in mainland Scandinavia. The field never failed to bear fruit because it was dedicated to the god of fertility. – However, one should not overestimate the source value of anecdotes like this, which were part of the (partly romantic) interest in heathen religion in Iceland during the 13th century.

A. Holtsmark, 'Vitazgjafi' (MoM) 1933; J. de Vries, *Altgermanische Religionsgeschichte*, Berlin [3]1970.

Vitolfus (Med. Latin) → Vittólfr.

Vitr (ON, 'the wise one'). A dwarf in *Vǫluspá* 12 and in the *Þulur*.

Vittólfr (ON). He is, according to *Vǫluspá in skamma* (*Gylfaginning* 4), the ancestor of all seers and prophets. In *Hyndluljóð* 33 he is called Viðólfr ('Wood-Wolf'), but the variant with *vitt* (meaning 'magic') seems more convincing. Saxo (*Gesta Danorum* VII, 219) mentions a certain Vitolfus, who is well versed in the magical arts, and may therefore be identified with Vittólfr.

H. Gering, *Kommentar*, Bd. 1, Halle 1927.

Vlauhinehae. Name of Matrons, → Ulauhinehae.

Vocallinehae. Matron name. Another form of → Vacallinehae, a fact which is confirmed by the seven inscriptions bearing this name which come from the cult area of Pesch, Germany.

S. Gutenbrunner, *Die germanischen Götternamen*, Halle 1936.

Vōden → Woden.

Vǫlsi (ON, 'penis'). A horse penis, the cult worship of which is told of in an episode of the *Oláfs saga hins helga*, the so-called *Vǫlsa þáttr* ('tale of Vǫlsi').

King Olaf (the Saint) hears about some farmers who are still heathen; one of these is a northern Norwegian farmer, his wife, son and daughter. One autumn when the farmer's horse dies, the family eat its meat (as befits good heathen tradition), but the thrall cuts the penis off the horse and wants to throw it away. However, the farmer's wife thinks that whatever is of some use should not wasted and so she wraps it in linen and → leek and other herbs so that it will not rot and so that the penis can continue growing until it can stand alone next to the farmer's wife, who places all her belief in this 'Vǫlsi'. Every evening the Vǫlsi is passed around and everyone says a stanza over it which ends with the refrain: *þiggi Mǫrnir (Maurnir) þetta blœti* ('Accept, Mǫrnir, this sacrifice') until King Olaf descends on the family one day and puts an end to their heathen superstitions.

The various previous interpretations of the *Vǫlsa þáttr* have led to several conclusions which contradict each other.

Ström understood one of the unknowns in the story of Vǫlsi, the name Mǫrnir, as being the plural of Marn, which could be a name for the goddess Skaði in *Haustlǫng* 12; the sacrifice to the Mǫrnir was, according to Ström, directed towards a plurality of fertility goddesses among whom he also counted the *dísir*.

Turville-Petre pointed out that Mǫrnir is also recorded as a sword name, so that Mǫrnir was, like Vǫlsi, nothing more than a phallus; as Freyr was characterized by the phallus as a fertility god, the Vǫlsi-sacrifice would be directed towards Freyr.

In a detailed critical investigation into the sources Düwel considers the tale of Vǫlsi to be unhistorical and the invention of the 13th/14th centuries, the whole tale being created by an author of the High Middle Ages who invented more or less freely the elements considered up to now to have been old, that is the names Vǫlsi and Mǫrnir.

Even if Düwel may not be correct in all his suppositions, careful consideration should be given before reconstructing an ancient Nordic phallic cult from the tale of Vǫlsi.

H. Rosén, 'Phallosguden i Norden' (*Antikvarisk Tidsskrift för Sverige* 20) 1914; F. Ström, *Diser, nornor, valkyrjor*, Stockholm 1954; J. de Vries, *Altgermanische Religionsgeschichte*, Berlin [3]1970; K. Düwel, *Das Opferfest von Lade und die Geschichte vom Völsi*, Göttingen 1971; G. Turville-Petre, *Myth and Religion of the North*, Westport 1975; G. Steinsland, K. Vogt, ' "Aukin ertu Uolse ok vpp vm tekinn". En religionshistorisk analyse av *Vǫlsaþáttr* i *Flateyjarbók*' (*ANF* 96) 1981.

Vǫluspá (ON, 'the prophesy of the seeress'). Without question the most famous of the mythological poems of the Poetic *Edda*. The *Vǫluspá* comprises 66 stanzas (of which 62 are given in the *Codex Regius*, four others in another version in the *Hauksbók*, the second main manuscript) and has the form of a visionary monologue; the first two stanzas as well as stanza 28, and other shorter references in other places, give the vision a frame in which a gigantic seeress gives information to Odin. Nonetheless, the monologue is neither didactic nor really epic, but rather is composed of extremely effective individual images.

The oldest manuscript of the *Vǫluspá*, the *Codex Regius*, dates from the 2nd half of the 13th century, but the lay itself is considerably older. Whether it was written at the beginning of the 10th century (Jónsson) or else in the first half of the 11th century (Heusler), it cannot have been later as a borrowing from the *Vǫluspá* used by Arnórr Járlaskáld around 1065 in his *Þorfinnsdrápa* makes an earlier composition date for the *Vǫluspá* indisputable. Since Nordal's work, the ideas in *Vǫluspá* have been seen to reflect the period of religious change and the expectation of the end of the world shortly before 1000. In his *Edda*, Snorri not only quoted numerous stanzas from *Vǫluspá* and used them extensively as a source for his mythology, but also handed on to us the title of the lay.

The *Vǫluspá* gives an account of the creation of the world from the proto-giant → Ymir, of the pre-history of the gods and men, of giants and dwarfs, and of the first war between the Æsir and the Vanir. Baldr's death then leads on to a description of the powers dangerous both to gods and man, and then comes a broad depiction of the events at the end of the world, → Ragnarǫk (stanzas 43–58). However, the extinguishing of the sun, the fall of the gods and the destructive fire of the world does not mean the end: the last stanzas of the *Vǫluspá* depict the creation of a new, better world in the future.

Vǫluspá is extremely rich not only as a result of its topic, but also because of the concepts contained within it. It soon became clear that the most impressive of all the mythological poems did not reflect exclusively heathen-Germanic mythology (still the opinion of Müllenhoff), but an interpretation which tries to see the lay predominantly as the product of Early Medieval Christian concepts (Meyer) also does the *Vǫluspá* injustice. There have been attempts to see not only Christian, but also Indian-Iranian-Indo-European parallels (Rydberg, Ström) as well as Persian-Manichean parallels in the *Vǫluspá*. – Even though there have been attempts to distinguish clearly between Germanic and Christian traits within the lay (Olrik), this way cannot lead to a final clarification of the sources of the *Vǫluspá*. Nordal has suggested, on the other hand, that the lay, whose poet reworked predominantly native material, should be seen as a unity, even though Christian influences are most likely present. Nonetheless, this still means that neither the wealth of material nor the means of recording it have been clarified. The bringing together of these concepts of varying origin in a lasting form is the work of a single author, even if his work is perhaps not even representative of the late heathen period, but rather reflects his personal confession in artistic form. These limitations should not be forgotten in using the *Vǫluspá* as a source for Germanic mythology. → Cosmogony, → Cosmology, → Baldr, → Ragnarǫk, → Eschatology.

K. Müllenhoff, *Über die Vǫluspá*, Berlin 1883; V. Rydberg, *Undersökningar i Germanisk Mythologi* 1–2, Stockholm 1886–89; E. H. Meyer, *Vǫluspá*, Berlin 1889; R. C. Boer, 'Kritik der Vǫluspá' (*ZfdPh* 36) 1904; F. Jónsson, 'Vǫluspá' (*Skírnir* 81) 1907; R. Meissner, 'Zum Wortschatz der Vǫluspá' (*ZfdPh* 43) 1911; E. Brate, 'Vǫluspá' (*ANF* 30) 1914; A. Olrik, *Ragnarǫk*, Berlin 1922; A. Heusler, *Die altgermanische Dichtung*, Berlin 1923; R. Reitzenstein, 'Weltuntergangsvorstellungen' (*Kyrkohist. Årsskrift*) 1924; E. Mogk, *Zur Gigantomachie der Vǫluspá*, Helsinki 1925; H. de Boor, 'Die religiöse Sprache der Vǫluspá und verwandter Denkmäler' (*Dt. Islandforschung* 1) Breslau 1930; F. R. Schröder, 'Germanische Schöpfungsmythen' (*GRM* 19) 1931; J. de Vries, 'Die Vǫluspá' (*GRM* 24) 1936; S. Gutenbrunner, 'Über Vortragsregeln für die Vǫluspá' (*ZfdPh* 77) 1958; F. T. Wood, 'The Transmission of the Vǫluspá' (*GR* 34) 1959; Olafur M. Olafsson, 'Vǫluspá Konungsbókar' (*Landsbókasafn Islands. Arbók* 22) 1965; H. A. Grahn, 'Vǫluspá, Versuch einer Deutung' (*Wirkendes Wort* 17) 1967; Å. V. Ström, 'Indogermanisches in der Vǫluspá' (*Numen* 14) 1967; H. Dölvers, 'Text, Gliederung und Deutung der Vǫluspá' (*ZfdA* 98) 1969; W. Butt, 'Zur Herkunft der Vǫluspá' (*PBB* 91) 1969; M. Lundgren, 'Vǫluspá' (*KLL* 7) 1972; H. Klingenberg, *Edda – Sammlung und Dichtung*, Basel 1974; H. Magerøy, 'Vǫluspá' (*KLNM* 20) 1976; S. Nordal, 'The Author of Vǫluspá' (*Saga-Book* 20) 1978–79; P. Schach, 'Some Thoughts on Vǫluspá' (*Edda. A Collection of Essays*) Winnipeg 1983; R. Boyer, 'On the Composition of Vǫluspá' (*Edda. A Collection of Essays*) Winnipeg 1983.

R: A. Oehlenschläger, *Volas Spaadom* (poem in *Nordens Guder*, 1819); H. W. v. Gerstenberg, *Gedicht eines Skalden, 5. Gesang* (1766); in P. F. Suhm's story *De tre Venner* (1775) fishermen sing (!) the *Vǫluspá* during their work.

Vǫluspá in skamma (ON, 'the short *Vǫluspá*', 'the short prophesy of the seeress'). An imitation of the → *Vǫluspá* which is embedded as stanza 29–44 in the → *Hyndluljóð*. Snorri proves that the *Vǫluspá in skamma* existed as a poem in its own right, separate from the *Hyndluljóð*, since he cites it in *Gylfaginning* 4 under its own title. The *Hyndluljóð* dates from the 13th century, but the *Vǫluspá in skamma* is not much older and probably dates from the 12th century. Despite word-for-word borrowings from the *Vǫluspá* it remains artistically speaking far behind its original; it hardly even brings a cosmological course of events, but rather gives predominantly lists of relationships between the gods and the giants. Apart from Loki, Heimdall is dealt with in particular detail (35–39), but Ragnarǫk is only briefly referred to, although the lay gives the impression that it is planned eschatologically. – The way of presentation presupposes already a reflection on a systematic mythography and should therefore be dated as coming from a time of awakening scholarly interest in heathen mythology in the 12th/13th centuries. Apart from the genealogy of giants (32), the lay produces few puzzles but rather only confirms mythological facts which we know from other Eddic sources; on the other hand, the fact should be taken into account that *Vǫluspá in skamma* itself uses material from these same sources and can therefore be considered at best as secondary and not as a parallel source to other Eddic lays for mythology.

→ *Hyndluljóð*.

Vǫlva (ON, 'prophetess, seeress', actually 'wand-bearer'). The ON term for a seeress. In the *Edda*, particularly in the *Vǫluspá* and *Baldrs draumar*, Vǫlva has a significant role as a seeress, and in the sagas a Vǫlva frequently appears as a woman with magical powers and is hence the typical representative of Germanic heathendom in Medieval Scandinavian literature which shows slight characteristics of a Christian demonization of seeresses. → Seeresses.

E. F. Halvorsen, 'Vǫlva' (*KLNM* 20) 1976.

Vǫnd (ON, 'the difficult one'). One of the (mythical?) rivers in the catalogue of rivers in *Grímnismál* 28 and in the *Þulur*.

Vǫr (ON, 'the careful one'?). A goddess, according to Snorri (*Gylfaginning* 34), 'who is so wise and careful that she never misses anything'. Vǫr occurs only twice otherwise in kennings for 'woman' and it is not certain whether she really was a goddess and if Snorri's etymological explanation (from *vǫrr* 'careful') is correct.

Vǫr → Var.

Vǫrnir (ON, 'the careful one'?). The name of a giant who only occurs in the *Þulur*. Phonetically speaking Vǫrnir corresponds to the name of the Indian god Varuna but a direct link is extremely unlikely. On the other hand Vǫrnir could be an eponymous hero of the tribe of the Varni (in Jordanes), if indeed he is not a 'fallen' god.

F. R. Schröder, 'Der Riese Vörnir' (*PBB* West 84) 1962.

Volla (probably instead of Folla). A goddess in the → Second Merseburg Charm. She is not mentioned elsewhere in this form, but is probably identical with the Scandinavian goddess → Fulla. Presumably, Volla and the god Phol, named in the same charm, are a South Germanic counterpart to the Scandinavian divine pair Freyr and Freyja.

H. Gering, 'Der zweite Merseburger Spruch' (*ZfdPh* 26) 1894; E. Brate, 'Andra Merseburg-besvärjelsen' (*ANF* 35) 1919; F. Genzmer, 'Die Götter' (*ANF* 63) 1948; J. de Vries, *Altgermanische Religionsgeschichte*, Berlin 31970.

Vón → Ván.

Votive gifts. Gifts dedicated to a deity which could be intended as petitions as well as offerings of gratitude. For the Germanic peoples the custom of laying down votive gifts in springs or on moors is archaeologically well-documented from the late Bronze Age onwards. Leaving gifts at such inaccessible places served the purpose that the gifts should be solely reserved for the gods; this could be achieved by deliberately making the gifts unusable or breaking them before laying them down, so that nobody else could make use of them; another typical kind of votive gift which has survived far into the Christian period and even to the present day, is the reproduction of objects in miniature form so that the content of the petition or the gratitude could be given actual expression.

The 100 or so golden miniature ships from a moor near Nors in Jutland, which are all decorated with sun symbols and were sunk into the moor in an earthern pot around 200–400 A.D. and which unquestionably are linked with the desire for safe seafaring, are an example of this latter kind of votive gifts. The sun-chariot of Trundholm was a purely cult object from the beginning, which was finally destroyed and buried. The most frequent votive gifts, however, are women's jewelry and other objects of the particularly female sphere which were probably dedicated to female deities. The Germanic votive altars to the → matrons which were dedicated on

Germanic soil after Roman tradition in the first century A.D. should be considered as votive stones set up in order to ameliorate the domestic life of the period.

Votive inscriptions. Such inscriptions have survived from Germanic antiquity on the Roman altars in Rhineland. In these inscriptions Germanic gods and → matrons were called upon for help. The form and the origin of these votive inscriptions is Roman; the petitioners themselves, however, and the deities to whom they appealed were Germanic.

De Vries, Jan (1890–1964). A scholar who spent a life time occupied with Old Norse language, literature and Germanic mythology. Apart from many individual articles, his most important work on mythology is his *Altgermanische Religionsgeschichte* ('History of Old Germanic Religion') (1935–37; 2nd edn 1956–57, reprinted 1970) which is the most extensive and best modern complete representation of Germanic religion. De Vries attempted in this work not only to present the religion of the Germanic peoples from the beginnings to the Middle Ages, encompassing all known sources, but he also considered critically the whole of scholarship up to his time and tried to bring about a synthesis of the various theories. This work is still viewed as the standard work on Germanic mythology and it has not been outdated by more recent works (Ström, Turville-Petre).

***Vrindr** → Rindr.

Waberlohe (German). Richard Wagner's version of ON *vafrlogi* → Wall of flames.

wælcyrge (Anglo-Saxon) → valkyries.

Wagner, Richard (1813–1883), German composer who brought Germanic mythology an unexpected popularity through his opera *Der Ring des Nibelungen*. Wagner's enthusiasm for Germanic mythology and his original reproduction of mythological material has led, however, to numerous wrong concepts about Germanic mythology which are still popular today.

Wagner's use of alliteration which corresponded completely to the level of knowledge in his time and still has its effect when sung today, is alienating when spoken, but in particular the enthusiastic reception and integration of Wagnerian art by the Nazi regime have led to an ideological rejection of Germanic mythology which has only been overcome in recent years.

Wagner's preoccupation with Germanic gods and heroic poetry goes back to the 1840s and by 1843 he knew J. Grimm's *Deutsche Mythologie* (1st edition 1835). In 1848 he composed the essay *Wibelungen (World history from Legend)* in which he made connexions between current politics and the legend of the Nibelungs; in the same year he began work for the first time on *Siegfried's death*. In 1850 the draft of the drama *Wieland der Schmied* after K. Simrock's version of the *Vilkina saga* came into being. After 1851 F. H. v. d. Hagen's translation of the *Vǫlsungs saga* (in *Nordische Heldenromane*, Breslau 1814–28) became the source for Wagner's preoccupation with the Nibelung material. Wagner learnt Old Norse and also used the original of the *Edda* and the *Vǫlsunga saga* during his work on the *Ring*. By 1851 the complete text to *Der junge Siegfried* (later *Siegfried*) was finished, and by 1852 the composition of the text to the whole *Ring* was completed, the text of which Wagner published privately in 1853. Between the years 1853 and 1874 the music to the *Ring* was composed, which in the final version consists of the Prelude *Das Rheingold* and the three operas *Die Walküre*, *Siegfried* and *Götterdämmerung* ('Twilight of the Gods').

Wagner reworked most areas of the heroic and mythological poetry known to him according to his ideas about the Nibelung material with artistic licence. It is Wagner who gives Wotan a vital role in the Siegfried story which makes change the entire basic structure; the death of Signy and Odin's role are Wagner's most important inventions with regard to the material, but more frequent are the deviations in the finished product: Wagner's coarse picture of the valkyries, the introduction of the giants, the merging of Loki with the fire-giant Logi (a confusion which can probably be excused from the level of scholarship at his time), to mention only a few which directly affect the mythology. But it is the success of Wagner's poetic reworking, together with his impressive musical interpretation of the material, which has led to an expansion of Germanic mythological and heroic legend surpassing all other modern actualizations of figures of Germanic mythology.

W. Golther, *Die sagengeschichtlichen Grundlagen der Ringdichtung*, Charlottenburg 1902; R. Wagner, *Mein Leben*, hg. v. M. Gregor-Dellin, Munich 1976; D. Ingenschay-Goch, *Richard Wagners neu erfundener Mythos*, Bonn 1982; M. Gregor-Dellin, M. v. Soden, *Richard Wagner*, Düsseldorf 1983.

Wall of flames (ON *vafrlogi*). A wall of flames can surround the place where a virgin lives and which must be broken through by the hero so that he can reach her. In the *Edda* the wall of flames is mentioned expressly in *Fjǫlsvinnsmál* 31f. and *Sigrdrífumál* 1 Pr, also in *Skírnismál* 17f. Skírnir has to cross through fire to get to Gerðr. However, the wall of flames is not an element of old Germanic mythology.

The ON word *vafrlogi* occurs in Old English as *wæfrelieg* and is (according to Sahlgren) borrowed from there. The concept of the wall of flames, however, probably originates from scholarly Medieval literature where an impenetrable wall of flames surrounding paradise is frequently mentioned, as at the beginning of the 7th century in the work of Isidor of Sevilla (*Etymologiae*: PL 82, 492). As Isidor's work was one of the most popular reference works in the Middle Ages, it is not unlikely that the idea was adopted from him directly.

J. Sahlgren, 'Sagan om Frö och Gärd' (*NoB* 16) 1928.

R: A. v. Heyden, *Siegfried in der Waberlohe* (painting, 1888); R. Wagner, *Die Walküre* (opera, 1866).

(**Waltraute**). One of the valkyries (mezzo-soprano) in R. Wagner's opera *Die Walküre*. The name is a free invention of Wagner's.

Waluburg. A Germanic seeress whose name has been found inscribed in Greek on an ostracon (inscribed potsherd) from the second century A.D. on the Egyptian island of Elephantine. The name, the occupation and the origin of the seeress are given: *Waluburg. Se[m]noni Sibylla* ('Waluburg, sibyl from the tribe of the Semnoni') is found in the penultimate line of a list of Roman and Graeco-Egyptian soldiers, which was possibly a pay-roll. Senoni is certainly a misspelling of Semnoni, and so the sibyl came from the Germanic tribe of the Semnoni and not from the Celtic Senones, because her name is quite clearly Germanic, even if *-burg* is otherwise not recorded in personal names before the 7th century. *Walu-* probably derives from Germanic ***walus** 'stave, wand', thus the wand, the symbol of a seeress (as with the other sibyl from the same tribe, Ganna). Waluburg has nothing whatsoever to do with the German name Walpurga (from Wald-burga).

How the Germanic seeress came to be in Egypt, where she was obviously in service to the Romans, is an open question. If she did not go there as a slave, then perhaps she was in some form of service to a Roman officer, which would explain her lowly rank on the salary list, but possibly she was deported by the Romans, like her seeress-colleague → Veleda, which is not unlikely considering the significant political influence the seeress had upon the Germanic peoples.

E. Schröder, 'Walburg, die Sibylle' (*ARW* 19) 1916–19; K. Helm, 'Waluburg, die Wahrsagerin' (*PBB* 43) 1918; L. Franz, 'Seherinnen-Schicksale' (*Anzeiger der österreichischen Akademie der Wissenschaften, Phil.-hist. Kl.* 87) 1950.

Walvater → Valfǫðr.

Wanderer. Odin/Wotan/Woden often appears as a wanderer, in particular in the *fornaldarsǫgur*, in order to influence a combat or else to make prophesies. In this role, with cloak, floppy hat, and wanderer's staff he is also found in modern literature and art, for example in R. Wagner's opera *Siegfried*, or as Gandalf in Tolkien's *The Lord of the Ring.*

Water. The belief in the sanctity of life-giving water is common to all Indo-Germanic peoples. Sacrifices and the laying down of votive gifts near to holy springs are documented from the earliest times, and in Eddic mythology springs such as → Urðar brunnr and → Mímir's well are seats of wisdom. Water, drawn at particular times under certain conditions, was regarded as having healing qualities (cf. OHG *heilwac*). On the other hand it is not certain whether the Germanic peoples really did know a form of sprinkling of water (→ *vatni ausa*) on the newly born.

Week-day names. The names of pagan Germanic gods are to be found in three German and English week-day names, Thursday, Friday and perhaps also Tuesday.

The seven day week did not only find its entrance to the Occidental world through the expansion of Christianity, but had already been adopted from the Orient during the Roman Empire. When the Germanic peoples came into closer contact with the Roman Empire from the last pre-Christian century onwards, they partly adopted the Roman designations for the days of the week, translating them into Germanic. This process of adoption was completed at the latest in the 4th century A.D.

In the *interpretatio germanica* the Roman god Mars was equated with the Germanic god *Tīwaz (→ Ziu, Týr), so that it seems possible that Tuesday (German *Dienstag*) emerged from the Roman *dies Martii* (French *mardi* comes from this) OHG *zî(o)stag*, OE *tiwesdæg*, and possibly German *Dienstag*. *Dies Iovi* ('Day of Jupiter' resulting in French *jeudi*) became the day of Donar/Thor: OHG *donarestag*, German *Donnerstag*, OE *thunresdæg*, Thursday, and Friday comes from the name of the goddess Frîja/Frigg, which shows a correspondance between the Germanic goddess and the Latin goddess Venus in the translation of the *dies Veneris* (French *vendredi*). The Latin *Dies Mercurii* (French *mecredi*) was translated by Germanic **Wodanesdag*, and finds its correspondance in OHG *wōdnesdæg*, Wednesday, Middle Low German *wōdensdach* (Dutch *Woensdag*), ON *Óðinsdagr* (Danish *Onsdag*). Although this term was still apparent in OHG, it was later ousted and replaced by the translation of the Church Latin *media hebdomas* 'middle of the week' (German *Mittwoch*).

F. Kluge, 'Die deutschen Namen der Wochentage' (*Wissenschaftliche Beihefte zur Zeitschrift des allgemeinen deutschen Sprachvereins* 8) 1885; H. Eggers, *Deutsche Sprachgeschichte* 1., Reinbek 1963; J. de Vries, *Altgermanische Religionsgeschichte*, Berlin 31970; R. L. M. Derolez, *Götter und Mythen der Germanen*, Wiesbaden 1974.

Weird's well → Urðar brunnr.

(**Wellgunde**). One of the Rhine-daughters in Richard Wagner's operas *Das Rheingold* and *Die Götterdämmerung*. The name was invented by Wagner himself.

Werwolves also werewolves ('man-wolves'). The term used for people who have changed into wolves. The belief in such metamorphosis into animal shape was common in the whole of Europe, indeed the oldest references to it may be found in Herodot and Pliny (*lykánthrópos*). In Germanic regions the belief in werwolves is recorded documentarily in Burchard of Worms (c.1000 A.D.). In medieval Scandinavia the wearing of a wolfskin is assumed to be the means to enable the shape-change (*Vǫlsunga saga* 5 and 8) and Snorri's mention of Odin's warriors who became 'wild like wolves or bears' is also probably connected with this. In Old Norse literature such → berserks clothed in wolfskins are called Ulfheðnar. The Swedish scholar and archbishop Olaus Magnus in 1555 writes in great detail about these shape-changes into wolves. Höfler has linked these shape-changes which took place within the ecstatic states peculiar to the cult of Odin, to the belief in the → Wild Hunt. The belief in werwolves may be traced back partly to shape-change cults, but also to lycanthropy, a mental illness in which there is an identification of the patient, in a schizophrenic condition, with a wolf. Both these explanations are probably the basis for the concept of werwolves.

J. Grimm, *Deutsche Mythologie*, Berlin [4]1875–78; L. Weiser-Aal, 'Zur Geschichte der altgermanischen Todesstrafe und Friedlosigkeit' (*ARW* 30) 1933; O. Höfler, *Kultische Geheimbünde der Germanen*, Frankfurt 1934; J. de Vries, *Altgermanische Religionsgeschichte*, Berlin [3]1970; O. A. Erich, R. Beitl, *Wörterbuch der deutschen Volkskunde*, Stuttgart [3]1974.

R: (literature) W. Hertz, *Der Werwolf* (in *Sagen*, 1862); C. Morgenstern, *Der Werwolf* (poem in *Galgenlieder*, 1905); H. Löns, *Der Werwolf* (novel, 1910); A. Sandemose, *Varulven* (novel, 1958).
(fine art) J. C. Dollman, *The Were-Wolves* (painting, c.1900).

Wicarus → Víkarr.

Wigiþonar (runic wigiþonar). The name of a god on the → Nordendorf fibula which bears the names of other gods Logaþore and Wodan as well. Wigiþonar is obviously identical with the god Donar/Thor, and only the origin of the first element of the word is debatable. On the one hand there is the opinion that it is a question of one name, contrary to the idea that it is a dedication formula ('Thor, dedicate!'); on the other hand the name-element *Wigi-* is interpreted partly as 'dedication-' (cognate to **wīgian* 'to dedicate'), partly as 'battle-' (from OHG *wīgan* 'to fight'), so that the latter attempt at a solution is linguistically speaking the most convincing; the name 'battle-Thor', with its corresponding Thor's name in Old Norse, Vingþórr, would thus be handed down in the rune name Wigiþonar.

W. Krause, 'Vingþorr' (*ZfdA* 64) 1972; W. Steinhauser, 'Die Wodansweihe von Nordendorf bei Augsburg (Runenspange A)' (*ZfdA* 97) 1968; E. Marold, ' "Thor weihe diese Runen" ' (*FmSt* 8) 1975; H. Klingenberg, 'Die Drei-Götter-Fibel von Nordendorf' (*ZfdA* 105) 1976.

Wild Hunt (MHG. *Wuotanes her*, Swed. *Odens jakt*, Norw. *Oskoreidi*, *jolareidi*, German *Wildes Heer*, *Wilde Jagd*). The term used for the concept common to the entire Germanic regions to denote the ghostly riders who ride through the storms at the head of a ghostly army during the Twelve Nights of Yuletide.

Older scholarship considered the legends of the Wild Hunt to be a fusion of two concepts: on the one hand the fear of the community of the dead – of links with the living which were stronger at midwinter than usual. On the other hand there was fear of the howling gales during winter nights; in particular this natural-mythological view has continued right up to the recent past. However plausible this suggestion might be at first sight, such a simplified explanation cannot justify the widespread common traits in the description of the Wild Hunt throughout the whole of Europe.

Höfler was the first scholar (following up work done by Weiser and Meuli) to prove with great probability that the legends of the Wild Hunt are 'in an exceptional majority reflections of ancient cults of secret societies' (Höfler 1934). Supporters of these cults who stood in connexion with Odin/Wodan who is clearly evident in the sources as the leader of the Wild Hunt in all the folk-tales were warrior bands. A significant factor in the activity of these warrior bands was the cult ecstasy with which Odin was still directly associated in the 11th century (Adam of Bremen, IV, 26: *Wodan, id est furor*: 'Wodan, that is to say fury'). The nightly cult activity of the Wild Hunt was interpreted very early, even by outsiders, to be an army of the dead (thus, also in Tacitus, → Harii). In a Munich exorcism from the 14th century the hanged and those broken on the wheel were called *Wûtanes her und alle sine man*. Dogs and horses were among the most frequent companions of the Wild Hunt as they were death-demonic animals. The cult-ecstastic connexion with the dead as a special form of the veneration of the dead is also the basis for processions of the Wild Hunt, with Odin as the god of the dead and ecstasy.

L. Weiser, *Altgermanische Jünglingsweihen und Männerbünde*, Baden 1927; K. Meuli, 'Bettelumzüge im Totenkultus, Opferritual und Volksbrauch' (*Schweizerisches Archiv für Volkskunde* 28) 1928; O. Höfler, *Kultische Geheimbünde der Germanen*, Frankfurt 1934; O. Huth, 'Der Durchzug des Wilden Heeres' (*ARW* 32) 1935; O. Höfler, 'Der germanische Totenkult und die Sagen vom Wilden Heer' (*Oberdeutsche Zeitschrift für Volkskunde* 10) 1936; J. de Vries, *Altgermanische Religionsgeschichte*, Berlin [3]1970; O. Höfler, *Verwandlungskulte, Volkssagen und Mythen*, Vienna 1974; O. A. Erich, R. Beitl, *Wörterbuch der deutschen Volkskunde*, Stuttgart [3]1974.

Wind. According to Nordic mythology, the wind is produced by the beating of the wings of a gigantic eagle, called → Hræsvelgr (according to Snorri) who lives in the north at the end of the world.

In *Gylfaginning* 22 Snorri mentions → Njǫrðr, whom he thinks of as the god of seafarers, being the god of the wind and the weather; however, because both Njǫrðr and also his son Freyr are called upon in their role as fertility gods for good weather, Snorri's comment must surely be extended also to Freyr, who was seen to be a god of shipping just as much as Njǫrðr was.

When Adam of Bremen calls Thor the god of the wind and rain (*Gesta Hammaburgensi Ecclesiae Pontificum* IV, 26), he probably means a generalization of his role as god of thunder and storms, and it should not be forgotten that Thor increased in significance during the last years of heathendom as the god of the farming community.

Wodan (Old Franconian). One of the West Germanic forms of the name for the god, worshipped in Scandinavia under the name of Odin, who was called Woden by the Saxons and Anglo-Saxons and Wotan/Godan by the Langobards. Documentary evidence for belief in a Wodan is far fewer in the south than in Scandinavia, but are nonetheless well documented. Wodan appears in the divine triad on the → Nordendorf fibula, and also in the → Second Merseburg Charm where he heals a horse. According to all records available Wodan corresponded to the Roman god → Mercury, even if the translation of the Roman weekday name *dies Mercurii* by *Wodanesdag* (OHG *Woutenestac*) has not been retained in German. Wodan is mentioned by Tacitus under the name of Mercury as the chief god of the Germanic peoples in the first century. Tacitus comments on the fact that human sacrifices are offered to him (*Germania* 9).

Woden (OE). The Anglo-Saxon form of the name for the god who is worshipped as → Odin in Scandinavia and as → Wodan by the Franconians. The records of a cult of Woden among the Anglo-Saxons are admittedly sparse as a result of the early Christianization of Great Britain in the 6th and 7th centuries, but are more frequent on the Continent.

Woden appears as the healing magician in the Old English *Nine Herb Blessing*, and a dozen place-names speak in favour of a cult of Woden's in England (Wodnes beorh, Wenslow, Wedynsfeld, Wodnesfeld, as well as Wansdyke, the name for the late Roman wall of defence). It is questionable whether Odin's other name Grímr is retained in names such as Grim's ditch and Grim's dyke. The retention of the → weekday name *Wodnesdæȝ* (English Wednesday) speaks in favour of the importance of Woden in England, whereas in German it was replaced by the ecclesiastically more acceptable version Mittwoch (from Church Latin *media hebdomas*). The descent of the Anglo-Saxon royal houses from Woden (→ Myth of descendency) was widespread, as reported by the Venerable Bede with regard to Hengist and Horsa (*Historia ecclesiastica* I, 15). Later the Anglo-Saxon Chronicle repeats the descent of Angle, West Saxon and Kent royal houses as coming from Woden.

E. Hackenberg, *Die Stammtafeln der angelsächsischen Königreiche*, Berlin 1918; E. A. Philippson, *Germanisches Heidentum bei den Angelsachsen*, Leipzig 1929; J. S. Ryan, 'Othin in England' (*Folklore* 74) 1963; A. L. Meaney, 'Woden in England' (*Folklore* 77) 1966; E. O. G. Turville-Petre, *Myth and Religion of the North*, Westport 1975.

(**Woglinde**). One of the Rhine-daughters in Richard Wagner's operas *Das Rheingold* and *Die Götterdämmerung*. The name was invented by Wagner.

World-view → Cosmology.

World-fire → Surtarlogi, → Ragnarǫk.

World-pillar → Irminsûl.

World, End of the → Ragnarǫk, → Eschatology.

Wuotes Her, *Wuotanes Her* (MHG.) → Wild Hunt.

Wurd → Urd, → Wyrd.

Wyrd (OE, 'fate'; OHG *wurt*, ON *urðr*). This was understood by past scholars as the central concept in Germanic ideas about fate. In contrast to this Weber has been able to show that the expression *wyrd* (which glosses Latin *fortuna*) is unlikely to hand down heathen-Germanic thought, but rather a Medieval view of the world based on late Classical-Christian beliefs and therefore ought not to be brought into dispute as evidence for a belief in fatalism among Germanic peoples.

B. Timmer, 'Wyrd in Anglo-Saxon Prose and Poetry' (*Neophilologus* 26) 1941; L. Mittner, *Wurd*, Bern 1955; G. W. Weber, *Wyrd*, Bad Homburg 1969.

Walkürenlied → *Darraðarljóð*.

Ýdalir (ON, 'yew-valley'). The domicile of Ullr, according to *Grímnismál* 5. This connexion of the god with the yew-tree, of whose wood bows were made (cf. ON *ýbogi* 'yew bow'), has led to Ullr being seen as a bow-god.

M. Olsen, 'Yddal' (MoM) 1931.

Yggdrasill (ON, 'Odin's horse'). The name of the world-tree of Eddic mythology. According to *Vǫluspá* 19, 47, *Grímnismál* 35, 44, Yggdrasill is an ash tree. Its roots reach out on three sides over the whole world. Men live under one, the giants under another and Hel under the third (*Grímnismál* 31). The squirrel → Ratatoskr runs up and down the trunk, an eagle sits in the branches and the dragon Níðhǫggr and numerous snakes (Góinn, Móinn, Grafvitnir, Grábakr, Grafvǫlluðr, Ofnir, Svafnir) gnaw at its roots. Four stags graze in the branches of the ash tree – Dáinn, Dvalinn, Duneyrr and Duraþrór (*Grímnismál* 32–35). Yggdrasill is an evergreen and beneath it, according to *Vǫluspá* 19, lies Urd's well. According to Snorri, there are three springs there, namely → Urd's well, → Mímir's well and → Hvergelmir. The gods meet and hold council beneath Yggdrasill before the Ragnarǫk (*Grímnismál* 29, 30) and the world-tree quivers as a sign of the coming of the end of the world (*Vǫluspá* 47). Snorri adds further details to the picture of Yggdrasill which only receives the properties of a world-tree in his version (*Gylfaginning* 14): 'This ash-tree is the biggest and best of all trees. Its branches reach out over the whole world and up into the sky above; three of the tree's roots hold it upright and reach far out, one to the Æsir, the other to the frost-giants where previously Ginnungagap was, and the third stands over Niflheim, and beneath this root Hvergelmir is found, but → Níðhǫggr gnaws at the root from beneath. Mímir's well, which hides all wisdom and understanding, lies under the root which goes towards the frost-giants; the owner of the spring is called → Mímir; he is full of wisdom as he drinks water from the spring using the horn Gjallarhorn. [. . .] The third root of the tree reaches up to the sky and under this root lies the very holy spring, which is known as Urd's well; it is there that the gods have their tribunal.' – Yggdrasill is also called Læraðr (*Grímnismál* 25, 26) and Mímameiðr (*Fjǫlsvinnsmál* 20).

Opinions about the meaning of the name Yggdrasill differ widely, especially on the question whether Yggdrasill can be understood as the name of a tree alone, or else whether only the full term *askr Yggdrasil* means the tree. Yggdrasill means 'Ygg's horse', i.e. 'Odin's horse' (→ Yggr); according to that, *askr Yggdrasils* would be the world-tree on which the horse of the highest god is bound. The more generally held opinion, however, is that Yggdrasill alone in the meaning 'Odin's horse' means 'tree'. This could therefore be called Odin's 'horse' because the gallows can be understood as the horse of the hanged; the tree would, according to this, be Odin's gallows on which he hung during his self-sacrifice (→ Odin's self-sacrifice, *Hávamál*). In both cases, however, the fact that Yggdrasill stands for an expected *Yggsdrasill, is taken for granted. Another possible interpretation would be to relate Yggdrasill to the base word *yggr* 'terror' instead of to the name for Odin Yggr, thus Yggdrasill could be interpreted as the 'tree of terror, gallows' (Detter). A completely different way of explaining Yggdrasill has been suggested by Schröder who thinks of Yggdrasill as 'yew-pillar' (*yggia* from **igwja*) 'yew-tree', *drasill* from **dher-* 'support').

The mythical world-tree Yggdrasill corresponds in earthly regions to the mighty evergreen tree near the temple in → Uppsala of which Adam of Bremen tells (*Gesta*

Hammaburgensis Ecclesiae Pontificum, IV, Scholion 138) that nobody knows its kind; the same is said of Mímameiðr in *Fjǫlsvinnsmál* 19, 20. Just as this tree is the image of Yggdrasill at a main shrine on earth, so too did farmsteads have their own protective trees. The manifold symbols which fall together in Yggdrasill as the world-tree, world-axis, support of the skies, Odin's tree of sacrifice have led to attempts being made to show that this myth has Christian characteristics (cf. the legend of the Rood); it is more likely, however, that Indo-European concepts, if not indeed archetypal concepts, have mingled together in the concept of the world-tree in Yggdrasill. – Although the *Vǫluspá* and the *Grímnismál* speak of Yggdrasill expressly as an ash tree, the pointless discussion about which type of tree the world-tree is has never died. From Läffler to de Vries it has been assumed that it was a yew tree (*taxus baccata*), on the one hand because of the expression *barr* (*Fjǫlsvinnsmál* 20) whereby a conifer must be meant, on the other hand because Tacitus mentions that the Celts worshipped such a tree. In spite of this, there is naturally no reason to 'refute' the concepts given in the *Edda* with regard to which type of tree Yggdrasill is, even if something different might be correct for the holy tree in Uppsala.

E. Magússon, *Odins Horse Yggdrasill*, London 1895; F. Detter, 'Review of E. Magnússon' (*ANF* 13) 1897; E. Magnússon, 'Yggdrasill' (*ANF* 13) 1897; F. Detter, 'Erwiderung' (*ANF* 13) 1897; L. F. Läffler, 'Det evigt grönskande trädet' (*Festskrift Feilberg*) Copenhagen 1911; A. Olrik, 'Yggdrasill' (*DS*) 1917; U. Holmberg, *Der Baum des Lebens*, Helsinki 1922; R. Nordenstreng, 'Namnet Yggdrasill' (*Festschrift A. Kock*) Lund 1929; O. Höfler, *Kultische Geheimbünde der Germanen*, Frankfurt 1934; F. R. Schröder, *Ingunar-Freyr*, Tübingen 1941; A. M. Sturtevant, 'Etymological Comments Upon Certain Old Norse Proper Names' (*PMLA* 67) 1952; S. Einarson, ' "Askr Yggdrasils", "Gullnar töflar" ' (*Festschrift Schlauch*) Warschau 1966; J. de Vries, *Altgermanische Religionsgeschichte*, Berlin [3]1970; E. F. Halvorsen, 'Yggdrasill' (*KLNM* 20) 1976; G. Steinsland, 'Treet i Vǫluspá' (*ANF* 94) 1979.

R: illustrations of Yggdrasill are already found in the Middle Ages: the reliefs on the interior wall of the Medieval stave church at Sogne in Norway are usually interpreted as being Yggdrasill with the stags and Níðhǫggr, and a rich illustration with Yggdrasill can be found in the Old Icelandic manuscript AM 738, 4to, from 1680. Modern versions can be found in the painting, *Die Nornen* by K. Ehrenberg (1888); in the fresco Yggdrasil by Axel Revold (1933) in the auditorium of the University Library in Oslo; in the wood relief *Hjortene beiter i løvet på Yggdrasil asken* by D. Werenskiold (1938) in Oslo town hall; the bronze relief doors of the historical museum in Stockholm, executed by B. Marklund (c.1950).
(literature) V. Rydberg, *Vårdträdet* (poem); J. Linke, *Yggdrasill* (poem).

Yggiungr (ON). In *Vǫluspá* 28 Odin is called *Yggiungr asa* 'God from the house of Yggr; → Yggr is, however, Odin himself.

Yggr (ON, 'the terrible'). A name for Odin in *Hávamál* 3, *Grímnismál* 53 and 54, *Vafþrúðnismál* 5, *Hymiskviða* 2, *Fáfnismál* 43 and frequently in skaldic poetry, where he is mentioned by Bragi already in the 9th century.

The ancient and widespread name for Odin has led to several derivations. Among them is Yggdrasill (actually, 'Ygg's horse', which probably does not mean Sleipnir, but rather the tree on which Odin hung in his self-sacrifice, thus the world-tree) and Yggjungr (*Vǫluspá* 28), which could actually mean somebody from Odin's family but stands here for Odin himself. In Saxo (*Gesta Danorum* V, 158) Yggr appears in the form of Uggerus, where an ancient seer, who can influence the outcome of battle, is called this; this is undoubtedly Odin in one of his numerous roles.

H. Falk, *Odensheite*, Christiania 1924; → Sleipnir.

Ylgr (ON, 'she-wolf'). One of the mythical rivers in the catalogue of rivers in *Grímnismál* 28; in Snorri (*Gylfaginning* 3) Ylgr is one of the → Élivágar rivers which originate from the spring Hvergelmir.

Ymir (ON). Proto-giant of the Nordic myth of creation. The Poetic *Edda* names Ymir repeatedly (*Vǫluspá* 3, *Vafþrúðnismál* 21 and 28, *Grímnismál* 40, *Hyndluljóð* 33) and kennings in the skaldic poetry of Arnórr Jarlaskáld (Ymir's skull = sky) and Ormr Barreyjarskáld (Ymir's blood = sea) from the 11th and 10th centuries respectively give evidence of the expansion of the myth of Ymir. Snorri gives a detailed account in *Gylfaginning* 4–7: Ymir originated in → Ginnungagap from the melting ice drops of the rivers → Élivágar and grew to gigantic proportions, fed by the proto-cow → Auðumla. Ymir is the progenitor of all the giants – the frost-giants (Hrimþursar), as Snorri calls them here. The birth of his descendants occurs by autogamy: when Ymir was asleep (Snorri writes), he sweated and beneath his left armpit a man and a woman grew, and one of his legs begat a son with the other leg. The giants descend from these children of Ymir's. After the birth of the first gods Odin, Vili and Vé, Ymir is killed by the same and all the giants drown in his blood, except for Bergelmir (and his wife?) who escapes on a *lúðr* in the flood (*Gylfaginning* 6; the meaning of *lúðr* is unclear in this connexion: perhaps it refers to a raft). Burr's sons Odin, Vili and Vé then brought Ymir into the middle of Ginnungagap and began to create the world out of his body; his blood became the sea and all the waters, his flesh the earth, his bones the mountains, his teeth and splinters of bone the rocks, his skull the sky; *Grímnismál* 40 and 41 tell in addition that from his hair the trees came, from his brain the clouds and from his brows → Midgard was created. – In *Vǫluspá* 9 Ymir is no doubt meant with the giants' names Bláinn and Brimir, and if this is so, then Ymir is also the ancestor of the dwarfs. Snorri had also understood the name Aurgelmir in the *Vafþrúðnismál* as being a name for Ymir. On the other hand the *Vafþrúðnismál* 29 and 33 tell a different tale to Snorri's: in this one Aurgelmir and not Ymir is the hermaphrodite ancestor of the giants and his son is called Þruðgelmir and his grandson Bergelmir. The *lúðr* on which Bergelmir was laid is mentioned here (*Vafþrúðnismál* 35), but there is no mention of a flood. De Vries has tried to interpret the flood as a Christian addition made by Snorri and *lúðr* as the cradle, namely of the whole giant family; however according to *Vafþrúðnismál* it is not Bergelmir but Aurgelmir who is the ancestor of the giants. Obviously, the mixing of the concepts of two different giants occured before the composition of *Vafþrúðnismál*, and is not merely Snorri's fault; the doubling of the offspring which was certainly not original speaks in favour of this. In Snorri the come from Ymir and in the *Vafþrúðnismál* from Aurgelmir: on the one hand the brother and sister who come from the armpit of the giant, and on the other hand the six-headed son produced by the legs of the proto-giant. Which descendents should be deemed to have come from which giant must remain an open question, but Snorri certainly equated Ymir with Aurgelmir with good reason, and his sources would seem to have been no richer in this particular case than ours. – Not only the myth recorded by Snorri but also the etymology reveal Ymir as a hermaphrodite being because the name is etymologically related to Sanskrit Yama, Avedic Yima (likewise mythical ancestors), Lat. *geminus*, Middle Irish *gemuin* 'twin' from the Indo-Germanic root **iemo-* 'twin, hermaphrodite'. Also → Tuisto who Tacitus names as being the ancestor of the Germanic tribes Ingvaeones, Hermiones and Istvaeones is revealed to be a hermaphrodite being according to the etymology, so that here too common concepts within Germanic cosmogeny may be assumed. – There might possibly be a cult myth present in the myth of the creation of the world from Ymir's body in which the dismembering of the sacrificial victim represented the creation of the world from the dismembered proto-giant.

F. R. Schröder, 'Germanische Schöpfungsmythen' (*GRM* 19) 1931; F. Börtzler, 'Ymir' (*ARW* 33) 1936; J. de Vries, *Altgermanische Religionsgeschichte*, Berlin 31970; Å. V. Ström, *Germanische Religion*, Stuttgart 1975; E. F. Halvorsen, 'Ymir' (*KLNM* 20) 1976.

R: N. A. Abilgaard, *Ymer dier Koen Ødhumble* (painting).

Ynglinga saga ('Saga about the → Ynglings'). The first part of the *Heimskrinlga* by → Snorri Sturluson, dealing with the part-mythical prehistory of Scandinavia and Sweden. Snorri's main source for it was the → *Ynglingatal*.

Ynglingatal ('Poem about the → Ynglings'). A remarkable poem by the skald Þjóðólfr ór Hvíni from the 9th century. The poem deals in 38 stanzas with the mythical origins and early history of the Yngling dynasty up to the 9th century and dwells in some detail on the deaths of the early kings of Sweden, thereby allowing some insight into the religious role of Scandinavian kingship.

Ynglings (ON Ynglingar). The Swedish royal dynasty of the early Middle Ages from which the first Norwegian king, Harald Fairhair (died c.933) and afterwards the Norwegian royal dynasty of the Ynglings are descended until as far down as the 14th century.

The beginning of the genealogy of the Swedish Ynglings is interesting for mythological purposes; the names of these kings are retained in the poem *Ynglingatal* written by the skald Þjóðólfr ór Hvíni in the 9th century, and from there they are adopted into Old Norse prose texts, into Snorri's *Ynglingasaga* and Ari's *Islendingabók*, as well as the Latin *Historia Norvegiae*. According to *Ynglingatal* the first king is Fjǫlnir, but the prose texts name three gods' names before this; in Ari and in the *Historia* these are Yngvi, Njǫrðr and Freyr, in Snorri Odin, Njǫrðr and Yngvi-Freyr. Angvi-Freyr (also in the form Ingunar-Freyr) was considered to be the ancestor of the Ynglings by both Ari and Snorri. We are not acquainted with their sources for this derivation, since it is by no means certain whether any opening stanzas of *Ynglingatal* are missing. The frequent reference to Yngvi as the ancestor of the Ynglings in heathen skaldic poetry and in Tacitus' report (*Germania* 2) speaks in favour of the fact that Ari and Snorri were not the first to associate the ancestor Yngvi with the Ynglings (as Baetke assumed in 1964). Tacitus tells at the end of the first century that the Germanic tribe of the Ingaevones are descended according to old traditions from a son of Mannus who gave them the name (→ Myth of descendency). The assumption of an ancestor called *Inguaz or *Inguan as the godly ancestor of the Nordic Germanic group strengthens Snorri's information about the sacred descendency of the Ynglings.

A. Heusler, *Die gelehrte Urgeschichte*, Berlin 1908; A. Noreen, 'Yngve, Inge, Inglinge m.m.' (*NoB* 8) 1920; K. A. Eckhardt, *Ingwi und die Ingweonen*, Weimar 1939; H. Schück, 'Ingunar-Freyr' (*Fornwännen* 35) 1940; F. R. Schröder, *Ingunar-Freyr*, Tübingen 1941; O. Höfler, 'Der Sakralcharakter des germanischen Königtums' (*Vorträge und Forschungen herausgegeben vom Institut für geschichtliche Landesforschung des Bodenseegebiets in Konstanz* 3) 1956; W. Baetke, *Yngvi und die Ynglinge*, Leipzig 1964.

Yngvi (1). An additional name for the god → Freyr who is therefore also known as → Yngvi-Freyr, and from whom, according to Snorri (*Ynglinga saga* 10f.) the Swedish royal dynasty of the → Ynglings took its name. Snorri also tells that the Ynglings bore the name Yngvi or Ynguni as an honorary name (*Ynglinga saga* 16); this comment will have to be restricted to the reigning king at any one time since not all of the living Ynglings bore this honorary name at the same time.

The meaning of the name Yngvi is largely unexplained, and there is not even agreement on its meaning as the additional name of the Ynglings: the most illuminating idea is to see the respective king as the representative of the divine ancestor Yngvi-Freyr, but there is nothing against the meaning being 'the Ing-supporter' or else 'the Ingaevone'. → Yngvi-Freyr.

Yngvi (2), also Ingi (ON). A dwarf in *Vǫluspá* 16. The meaning is as uncertain as in the case of Yngvi (1).

Yngvi-Freyr. The name which Snorri gives to the god Freyr (*Ynglinga saga* 11); this name has developed from Freyr's other name → Yngvi which was also held by the Swedish Yngling-kings as a result of this.

The original meaning of Yngvi is quite uncertain; it is only certain that there is a connexion with the god's name Ing (from *Ingwaz), the mythical ancestor of the Germanic tribe of Ingaevones (in Tacitus, *Germania* 2). The Gothic name of the yew-rune, *enguz*, also points to the great age of the god Ing.

Yngvi could as a result be a derivation from *Ingwaz and be interpreted as 'the Ingaevone', and Yngvi-Freyr from *Ingwia-fraujaz 'lord of the Ingaevones' whereby a great age for the construction Yngvi-Freyr must also be assumed.

A. Heusler, *Die gelehrte Urgeschichte*, Berlin 1908; A. Noreen, 'Yngve, Inge, Inglinge m.m.' (*NoB* 8) 1920; K. A. Eckhardt, *Ingwi und die Ingweonen*, Weimar 1939; H. Schück, 'Ingunar-Freyr' (*Fornvännen* 35) 1940; F. R. Schröder, *Ingunar-Freyr*, Tübingen 1941; A. H. Krappe, 'Yngvi-Freyr and Aengus mac Oc' (SS 18) 1942/43; W. Krause, *Ing*, Göttingen 1944; W. Baetke, *Yngvi und die Ynglinger*, Leipzig 1964.

Yule (ON *jól*). The pagan-Germanic festival of sacrifice at mid-winter which is still the Scandinavian name for Christmas.

The temporal coincidence with the mid-winter festival is rather problematic as the older Germanic evidence, the names of the month in Gothic *fruma jiuleis* (4th century) and Anglo-Saxon *giuli* (8th century, from the Venerable Bede), refer to December or else December and January, whilst the etymologically likewise related Old Norse name of the month *ýlir* (recorded only once in the 13th century) covers the time between the 14th of November and the 13th of December, and thus offers no point of reference for the sacrificial feast. Admittedly, the identification with the mid-winter time of sacrifice is the most likely.

The pre-Christian Yule-feast also had a pronounced religious character. According to the *Gulathingslǫg* 7 it was celebrated *til árs oc til friðar* (roughly: 'for a fertile and peaceful season'), and was a fertility sacrifice. It was not so much the Vanir gods who were venerated through this sacrifice but rather Odin, who bore the name Jólnir, and was associated with Yule, an association to which undoubtedly the concept of the → Wild Hunt contributed. It is uncertain whether the Germanic Yule feast still had a function in the cult of the dead and in the veneration of the ancestors, a function which the mid-winter sacrifice certainly had for the West European Stone and Bronze Ages.

The Christian Icelandic sources of the High Middle Ages describe the heathen Yule in the light of the Christmas celebrations which their authors knew. Especially in the sagas, Yule-tide stands out as a time for the special activity of → *draugar*. On the one hand surely the literary reworking of un- (or else pre-)Christian patterns of behaviour is responsible for this, but on the other hand also the concept of the Wild Hunt as retained in folklore. The fact that 'Yule drinking' was synonymous for celebrating the festival shows the form of the feast as a drinking feast in historical time, but could in fact point back to an older drink-sacrifice. In Snorri's writings, heathen Yule is understood throughout as a mid-winter sacrifice, which he presents as a communal feast. Otherwise, the Old Norse sources do not generally show Yule to be a community or family feast.

The sparsity of literary sources for the pagan feast of Yule stands in contrast to the richness of Scandinavian (and partly Anglo-Saxon) Yule-tide customs (Yule-block, Yule-goat, Yule-boar, Yule-log, Yule-singing and others) which indicate the significance of the feast in pre-Christian times.

The etymology of the name of the Yule feast (ON *jól*, Anglo-Saxon *geohol*, *gehol*) and the winter month (Anglo-Saxon *giuli*, *geóla*, Gothic *fruma jiuleis*, ON *ýlir*) has not been explained completely, but a derivation from 'magic', 'feast of entreaty' or similar ideas would be conceivable (Meringer).

G. Bilfinger, *Das germanische Julfest*, Stuttgart 1901; R. Meringer, 'Der Name des Julfests' (*Wörter und Sachen* 5) 1913; M. P. Nilsson, 'Studien zur Vorgeschichte des Weihnachtsfestes' (*ARW* 19) 1916–19; H. Celander, *Förkristen Jul*, Stockholm 1955; M. P. Nilsson, 'At Which Time of the Year was the Pre-Christian Yule Celebrated?' (*Arv* 14) 1958; A. Björnsson, 'Hjátrú á jólum' (*Skírnir* 135) 1961; L. Weiser-Aall, 'Jul' (*KLNM* 8) 1963.

***Ziu.** The OHG form of the name belonging to the Germanic god → *Tīwaz, ON → Týr; the OHG translation of the Roman week-day name *dies Marti* ('day of Mars') was *Ziostag* (Alemannic *Ziestag*) and thus confirms that the identification of the Roman god of war Mars with the Germanic god *Tīwaz was also prevalent on the Continent, as well as among Scandinavians and Anglo-Saxons. The god Ziu is otherwise not expressly mentioned in OHG texts, although one gloss to the so-called Wessobrunn prayer names the Alemanni *Cyowari* (probably: 'worshippers of Cyo') and their capital Ciesburc, and this Cyo was probably Ziu.

In West Germanic areas there was obviously another form of the god's name apart from *Tīwaz which is recorded in Mars Thingsus and is derived from the German week-day name *Dienstag* (from the older form *dingesdach*).

W. Krause, 'Ziu' (*Nachrichten der Gesellschaft der Wissenschaften Göttingen, Phil.-hist. Klasse*, N. F. 3/6) 1940; H. Rosenfeld, 'Alemannischer Ziu-Kult' (*Archiv für Kulturgeschichte* 37) 1955; O. Höfler, ' "Sakraltheorie" und "Profantheorie" ' (*Festschrift S. Gutenbrunner*) Heidelberg 1972.

BIBLIOGRAPHY

Aakjær, Svend, 'Danske stednavne fra hedenold' (*Dansk udsyn*) 1927, 123–125.
Aakjær, Svend, Hilla, 'Hleiðra og Skialf' (*Studier tilegnede Verner Dahlerup paa femoghalvfjerdsdagen*) Aarhus 1934, 52–62.
Aakjær, Svend, 'Hoveri, Hovgaard og Hov' (*Danske folkemål* 3) 1929, 25–34.
Aakjær, Svend, 'Odins Vi i Salling' (*Skivebogen*) 1943, 33–42.
Abrahamson, David, 'Solkult i nordisk bebyggelse' (*Ymer* 44) 1924, 239–259.
Achterberg, Herbert, *Interpretatio Christiana*, Leipzig 1930 (= Form und Geist. 19).
Aðalsteinsson, Jón Hnefill, *Kristnitakan á Íslandi*, Reykjavík 1971.
Aðalsteinsson, Jón Hnefill, *Under the Cloak: The Acceptance of Christianity with Particular Reference to the Religious Attitudes Prevailing at the Time*. Stockholm 1978 (= Studia Ethnologica Upsaliensia. 4).
Adinsky, E., *Tuisko oder Tuisto?* Königsberg 1903.
Agrell, Sigurd, 'Der Ursprung der Runenschrift und die Magie' (*ANF* 43) 1927, 97–109.
Agrell, Sigurd, *Zur Frage nach dem Ursprung der Runennamen*. Lund 1928 (= Skrifter udgivna av vetenskaps-societeten i Lund. 10).
Alföldy, Géza, 'Epigraphisches aus dem Rheinland III. Die Inschriften aus dem Tempelbezirk bei Pesch (Kr. Schleiden)' (*Epigraphische Studien* 5) 1968, 33–89.
Alföldy, Géza: *Die Personennamen der römischen Provinz Dalmatia*, Heidelberg 1969 (= Beiträge zur Namenforschung, N. F. Beiheft 4).
Allén, Sture, ' "Baldrs draumar" 14 och Guðrúnarkviða II, 9-två samhöriga eddaställen' (*ANF* 76) 1961, 74–95.
Allen, W. E. D., 'The Poet and the Spae-Wife' (*Saga-Book* 15) 1957–61, 149–258.
Almgren, Bertil, 'Hällristningar och bronsålderdräkt' (*Tor* 6) 1960, 19–50.
Almgren, Oskar, *Nordische Felszeichnungen als religiöse Urkunden*, Frankfurt/M. 1934.
Almgren, Oskar, 'Det runristade guldhornets datering' (*NoB* 2) 1914, 217–225.
Almgren, Oscar, 'Symboliska miniatyryxor från den yngre järnåldern' (*Fornvännen* 4) 1909, 39–42.
Almgren, Oskar, 'Tanums härads fasta fornlämnigar fran bronsaldern. 1. Hällristningar' (*Bidrag till kännedom om Göteborgs och Bohusläns Fornminnen och Historie* 8) 1906–13, 473–575.
Almgren, Oskar, 'Vikingatidens grafskick i verkligheten och i den fornordiska litteraturen' (*Nordiska Studier till. A. Noreen*) Upsala 1904, 309–346.
Amira, Karl von, 'Die germanischen Todesstrafen' (*Abh. d. bayer. Ak. d. Wiss., Phil.-hist. Kl.* 31/3) 1922, 1–415.
Amtoft, S. K., *Nordiske Gudeskikkelser i bebyggelseshistorisk Belysning*, Copenhagen 1948.
Amtoft, S. K., 'Stednavne som bebyggelses-og religionshistorisk Kildestof. En kritisk-historisk Oversigt' (*Aarbøger for nordisk Oldkyndighed og Historie*) 1941, 177–312.
Andersen, Harry, 'Smaa kritiske Strejftog' (*ANF* 52) 1936, 66–75.
Andersen, Harry, 'Viborg' (*Sprog og kultur* 4) 1935, 97–99.
Andersen, Lise Præstgaard, *Skjoldmøer: En kvindemyte*, Copenhagen 1982.
Anderson, Philip N., 'Form and Content in Lokasenna: a Re-evaluation' (*Edda* 81) 1981, 215–225.
Anderson, William, 'Das altnordische Paradies' (*Mannus* 24) 1931, 19–32.
Andersson, Thorsten, 'Eigennamen als erstes Glied nordischer Ortsnamen' (*Namn och bygd* 67) 1979, 123–146.
Anholm, M, 'Den bundene jætte i Kavkasus' (*DS* 1) 1904, 141–151.
Arren, J., 'Om Ragnarok' (*Dania* 10) 1903, 112–125.
Arrhenius, Birgit, 'Det flammande smycket' (*Fornvännen* 57) 1962, 79–101.

Arrhenius, Birgit, 'Snorris Asa-Etymologie und das Gräberfeld von Altuppsala' (*Tradition als historische Kraft. [Festschrift] K. Hauck*) Berlin, New York 1982, 65–77.
Arrhenius, Birgit, 'Zum symbolischen Sinn des Almadin im früheren Mittelalter' (*FmSt* 3) (1969), 47–59.
Auld, Richard, L., 'The Psychological and Mythic Unity of the God "Oðinn" ' (*Numen* 23) 1976, 145–160.
Bachlechner, Joseph, 'Eine Göttin Zisa' (*ZfdA* 8) 1851, 587–588.
Bachlechner, Joseph, 'Vuldor-Ullr' (*ZfdA* 8) 1851, 201–208.
Bächtoldi-Stäubli, Hanns (Hg.), *Handwörterbuch des deutschen Aberglaubens*, 10 vols, Berlin 1972–1942, reprint Munich 1987.
Baesecke, Georg, 'Muspilli II' (*ZfdA* 82) 1948/50, 199–239.
Baetke, Walter, *Art und Glaube der Germanen*, Hamburg [3]1938.
Baetke, Walter, *Arteigene germanische Religion und Chrstentum*. Berlin and Leipzig, [2]1936.
Baetke, Walter, *Die Aufnahme des Christentums durch die Germanen*, reprint Darmstadt 1959.
Baetke, Walter, 'Der Begriff der "Unheiligkeit" im altnordischen Recht' (*PBB* 66) 1942, 1–54.
Baetke, Walter, *Christentum und Germanische Religion*, Berlin 1934.
Baetke, Walter, *Christliches Lehngut in der Sagareligion*, Berlin 1952 (= Berichte über die Verhandlungen der sächsischen Akademie der Wissenschaften Leipzig, 98/6).
Baetke, Walter, 'Germanischer Schicksalsglaube' (*Neue Jahrbücher für Wissenschaft und Jugendbildung* 10), 226–236.
Baetke, Walter, *Die Götterlehre der Snorra-Edda*, Berlin 1950 (= Berichte über die Verhandlungen der sächsischen Akademie der Wissenschaften Leipzig, 97/3).
Baetke, Walter, 'guð in den altnordischen Eidesformeln' (*PBB* 70) 1948, 351–371.
Baetke, Walter, *Das Heilige im Germanischen*, Tübingen 1942.
Baetke, Walter, *Kleine Schriften*, Weimar 1973.
Baetke, Walter, *Die Religion der Germanen in Quellenzeugnissen*, Frankfurt/M. [2]1938.
Baetke, Walter, *Vom Geist und Erbe Thues*, Göttingen 1944.
Baetke, Walter, *Yngvi und die Ynglinger*, Berlin 1964 (= Sitzungsberichte der sächsischen Akademie der Wissenschaften Leipzig, 109/3).
Baetke, Walter, 'Zur Religion der Skalden' (*Atti dell' VIII congresso internazionale di storia delle religione*) Firenze 1956, 361–364.
Bang, A. C., *Völuspaa og de Sibyllinske Orakler*, Oslo 1879.
Bauchhenss, Gerhard, *Jupitergigantensäulen*, Köln 1976 (= Kleine Schriften zur Kenntnis der römischen Besetzungsgeschichte Südwestdeutschlands, 14).
Bauschatz, Paul C., 'The Germanic Ritual Feast' (*The Nordic Languages and Modern Linguistics*) Stockholm 1978, 289–294.
Beck, Heinrich, *Das Ebersignum im Germanischen*, Berlin 1965 (= Quellen und Forschungen zur Sprach- und Kulturgeschichte der germanischen Völker, N.F. 16).
Beck, Heinrich, 'Eddische Dichtung' (J. Hoops, *Reallexikon der germanischen Altertumskunde*, hg. v. H. Beck 6) [2]1986, 413–426.
Beck, Heinrich, 'Germanische Menschenopfer in der literarischen Überlieferung' (H. *Jahnkuhn*, *Vorgeschichtliche Heiligtümer und Opferplätze in Mittel- und Nordeuropa*) Göttingen 1970, 240–258.
Beck, Heinrich, 'Grottasǫngr' (*KLL* 3) Munich 1967, 1213–1215.
Beck, Heinrich, 'Hávamál' (*KLL* 3) Munich 1967, 1514–1516.
Beck, Heinrich, 'Reginsmál' (*KLL* 6) Munich 1971, 75–77.
Beck, Heinrich, 'Svipdagsmál' (*KLL* 6) Munich 1971, 2232–2233.
Beck, Heinrich, 'Thrymskviða' (*KLL* 6) Munich 1971, 2646–2647.
Beck, Inge, *Studien zur Erscheinungsform des heidnischen Opfers nach altnordischen Quellen*, Munich 1967.
Behm-Blancke, Günter, 'Germanische Mooropferplätze in Thüringen' (*Ausgrabungen und Funde* 2) 1957, 129–135.

Behm-Blancke, Günter, 'Ein westgermanisches Moor- und Seeheiligtum in Nordwestthüringen' (*Ausgrabungen und Funde* 3) 1958, 264–166.
Behm-Blancke, Günter, 'Das germanische Tierknochenopfer und sein Ursprung' (*Ausgrabungen und Funde* 10) 1965, 233–239.
Behn, Friedrich, *Die Bronzezeit in Nordeuropa*, Stuttgart etc. 1967.
Behn, Friedrich, 'Die nordischen Felsbilder' (*ARW* 34) 1937, 1–13.
Berendson, Walter A., 'Zauberunterweisung in der Edda' (*ANF* 50) 1934, 250–259.
Bergeron, Tor, Magnus Fries, Carl-Axel Moberg, Folke Ström, 'Fimbulvinter' (*Fornvännen* 51) 1956, 1–18.
Bertholet, Alfred, *Wörterbuch der Religionen*, Stuttgart [3]1976 (= Kröners Taschenausgabe 125).
Betz, Werner, 'Die altgermanische Religion' (*Deutsche Philologie im Aufriß* 3) Berlin [2]1962, 1547–1648.
Betz, Werner, 'Die Laima und der zweite Merseburger Zauberspruch' (*Latomus* 45) 1960, 45–50.
Betz, Werner, 'Sose gelimida sin' (*Rheinische Vierteljahresblätter* 21) 1956, 11–13.
Betz, Werner, 'Vom "Götterwort" zum "Massentraumbild". Zur Wortgeschichte von "Mythos" ' (*Mythos und Mythologie in der Literatur des 19. Jahrhunderts*) Frankfurt 1979, 11–24.
Beyschlag, Siegfried, 'Die Betörung Gylfis' (*ZfdA* 85) 1954, 163–181.
Bibire, Paul, 'Freyr and Gerðr: The story and its Myths' (*Sagnaskemmtun. Studies H. Pálsson*) Vienna 1986, 19–40.
Bibliographie zur archäologischen Germanenforschung. Deutschsprachige Literatur 1941–1955. Berlin 1966.
Bickel, Ernst, 'Die Glaubwürdigkeit des Tacitus und seine Nachrichten über den Nerthuskult und den Germanennamen' (*Bonner Jahrbücher* 139) 1934, 1–20.
Biezais, Haralds, 'Die vermeintlichen germanischen Zwillingsgötter' (*Temenos* 5) 1969, 22–36.
Bilfinger, G., *Untersuchungen über die Zeitrechnung der alten Germanen II*. Das germanische Julfest. Programm, Stuttgart 1901.
Bing, Just, 'Germanische Religion der älteren Bronzezeit' (*Mannus* 6) 1914, 149–180.
Bing, Just, 'Die Götter der südskandinavischen Felszeichnungen' (*Mannus* 14) 1922, 259–274.
Bing, Just, 'Der Götterwagen' (*Mannus* 6) 1914, 261–282.
Bing, Just, 'Götterzeichen' (*Mannus* 7) 1915, 263–280.
Bing, Just, 'Das Kivikdenkmal' (*Mannus* 7) 1915, 61–77.
Bing, Just, 'Ull, en mytologisk undersøkelse' (MoM) 1916, 107–124.
Birkeli, Emil, *Fedrekult i Norge*, Oslo 1939.
Birkeli, Emil, *Huskult og hinsidighetstro*, Oslo 1941.
Birkhan, Helmut, 'Gapt und Gaut' (*ZfdA* 94) 1965, 1–17.
Birkhan, Helmut, *Germanen und Kelten bis zum Ausgang der Römerzeit*, Vienna 1970.
Björkman, Erik, 'Skialf och Skilfing' (*NoB* 7) 1919, 163–181.
Björnsson, A., 'Hjátrú á jólum' (*Skírnir* 135) 1961, 110–128.
Blaney, H., *The Berserkr: His Origin and Development in Old Norse Literature*, Diss. Univ. of Colorado 1972.
Blind, Karl, 'The Meaning of "Edda" ' (*Academy* 48) 1895, 547.
Blum, Ida, *Die Schutzgeister in der altnordischen Literatur*, Diss. Straßburg, Zabern 1912.
Bø, Olav, 'Hammarseng' (*KLNM* 6) Malmö 1961, 81.
Bø, Olav, 'Torshamrar' (*KLNM* 18) Malmö 1974, 502–503.
Bø, Olav, 'Trollformlar' (*KLNM* 18) Malmö 1974, 674–678.
Bø, Olav, 'Vær og vind' (*KLNM* 20) Malmö 1976, 332–334.
Boer, R. C., 'Gylfes mellemværende med Aserne' (*Festskrift H. Pipping*) Helsingfors 1924, 17–24.
Boer, R. C., 'Kritik der Vǫluspá' (*ZfdPh* 36) 1904, 289–370.

Boer, R. C., 'Studien über die Snorra-Edda' (*APhSc* 1) 1926/27, 54–150.
Börtzler, Friedrich, 'Ymir. Ein Beitrag zu den eddischen Weltschöpfungsvorstellungen' (*ARW* 33) 1936, 230–245.
Bolle, Kees W., 'In Defense of Euhemeros' (*Myth and Law among the Indo-Europeans*) London 1970, 19–38.
Bondevik, Kjell, 'Truer og førestellingar i stadnamn' (*Norske stedsnavn/stadnamn*) Oslo 1975, 132–144.
de Boor, Helmuth, 'Die religiöse Sprache der Vǫluspá und verwandter Denkmäler' (*Deutsche Islandforschung* 1) Breslau 1930, 68–142.
de Boor, Helmuth, 'Der Zwerg in Skandinavien' (*Festschrift E. Mogk*) Halle/S. 1924, 536–557.
Bork, Ferdinand, 'Germanische Götterdreiheiten' (*Mannus* 15) 1923, 1–19.
Bornhausen, Karl, 'Die nordische Religionsvorstellung vom Sonnengott und ihr Gestaltwandel' (*ARW* 33) 1936, 15–20.
Boudriot, Wilhelm, *Die altgermanische Religion in der amtlichen kirchlichen Literatur des Abendlandes vom 5. bis 11. Jahrhundert*, Bonn 1928 (= Untersuchungen zur allgemeinen Religionsgeschichte. 2).
Boyer, Regis, 'On the Composition of Vǫlospá' (*Edda. A Collection*) Winnipeg 1983, 117–133.
Boyer, Regis, 'Paganism and literature: the so-called "Pagan survivals" in the samtiðarsǫgur' (*Gripla* 1) 1975, 135–167.
Branston, Brian, *Gods of the North*, London, New York 1955.
Branston, Brian, *The lost Gods of England*, London 1957.
Brate, Erik, 'Andra Merseburg-besvärjelsen' (*ANF* 35) 1919, 287–296.
Brate, Erik, 'Disen' (*Zeitschrift für deutsche Wortforschung* 13) 1912, 143–152.
Brate, Erik, *Nyare forskning i nordisk mytologi*, Stockholm 1907.
Brate, Erik, 'Voluspa' (*ANF* 30) 1914, 43–60.
Brate, Erik, 'Wrindawi' (*ANF* 29) 1913, 109–119.
Braune, Walter, 'Irmindeot und Irmingot' (*PBB* 21) 1896, 1–7.
Braune, Walter, 'Muspilli' (*PBB* 40) 1915, 425–445.
Braune, Walter, 'Vingolf' (*PBB* 14) 1889, 369–376.
Breiteig, Byrge, 'Snorre Sturlason og Æsene' (*ANF* 79) 1964, 117–153.
Bremer, Otto, 'Der Germanische Himmelsgott' (*IF* 3) 1894, 301–302.
Briem, Olafur, 'Fenrisúlfr' (*KLNM* 4) Malmö 1959, 220–221.
Briem, Olafur, *Heiðina siður á Íslandi*, Reykjavík 1945.
Briem, Olafur, *Vanir og Æsir*, Reykjavík 1963 (= Studia Islandica, 21).
Brím, Eggert Ó., 'Bemærkniger angående en del vers i "Noregs konungasǫgur I" ' (*ANF* 11) 1895, 1–32.
Brix, H., 'Noter til Hávamál' (*Edda* 58) 1958, 100–105.
Brøndsted, Johannes, *Nordische Vorzeit 1–3*, Neumünster 1960–1963.
Brøndsted, Johannes, 'Thors Fiskeri' (*Fra Nationalmuseets Arbejdsmark*) 1955, 93–104.
Brunner, Heinrich, 'Der Todtentheil in germanischen Rechten' (*Zeitschrift der Savigny-Stiftung für Rechtsgeschichte, Germ. Abt.* 19) 1898, 107–139.
Buchholz, Peter, 'Im Himmel wie auf Erden. Gedanken zu Heiligtum und Kultprovinz in der frühgeschichtlichen Religion Skandinaviens' (*Acta Germanica* 7) 1972, 1–17.
Buchholz, Peter, 'Perspectives for historical research in Germanic religion' (*History of Religions* 8) 1968, 111–138.
Buchholz, Peter, 'The religious geography of pagan Scandinavia. A new research project' (*Medieval Scandinavia* 5) 1972, 89–91.
Buchholz, Peter, *Schamanistische Züge in der altisländischen Überlieferung*, Münster 1968.
Bugge, Sophus, 'Altnordische Namen' (*Zeitschrift für vergleichende Sprachforschung* 3) 1854, 26–34.
Bugge, Sophus, *Fricco, Frigg und Priapos*, Christiania 1904.
Bugge, Sophus, 'Germanische Etymologien' (*PBB* 21) 1896, 421–428.

Bugge, Sophus, 'Der Gott Bragi in den norrönen Gedichten' (*PBB* 13) 1888, 187–201.
Bugge, Sophus, 'Iduns Æbler' (*ANF* 5) (1889), 1–45.
Bugge, Sophus, 'Rigsþula' (*ANF* 1) 1883, 305–313.
Bugge, Sophus, *Studien über die Entstehung der nordischen Götter- und Heldensagen*, Munich 1889.
Bugge, Sophus, *Studier over de nordiske Gude-og Heltesagns Oprindelse*, Christiania 1881–1889.
Buschan, Georg, *Altgermanische Überlieferung in Kult und Brauchtum der Deutschen*, Munich 1936.
Butt, Wolfgang, 'Zur Herkunft der Vǫluspá' (*PBB West* 91) 1969, 82–103.
Butt, Wolfgang, *'Sterben' und 'Töten' in der Sprache der altnordischen Dichter*, Diss. Kiel 1967.
Byvanck, A. W., 'De inscriptionibus traiectensibus nuper repertis' (*Mnemosyne* N. S. 60) 1933, 193–198.
Cameron, Kenneth, *English Place-Names*, London 1961.
Cassidy, Vincent H. de P., 'The Location of Ginnunga-gap' (*Scandinavian Studies. Essays H. G. Leach*) Seattle 1965, 27–38.
Celander, Hilding, *Förkristen jul enligt norröna källor, Stockholm*, Gothenburg 1955.
Celander, Hilding, 'Loke-Problemet' (*DS*) 1914, 65–93.
Celander, Hilding, 'Lokes mytiska ursprung' (*SSUF*) 1906–09, 18–140.
Celander, Hilding, *Nordisk Jul*, Stockholm 1928.
Celander, Hilding, 'Oskoreien och besläktade forestellningar i äldre och nyare nordisk tradition' (*Saga och Sed*) 1943, 71–175.
Chadwick, Henry Munro, *The cult of Othin*, London 1899.
Chadwick, Nora K., 'The Russian giant Svyatogor and the Norse Utgartha-Loki' (*Folklore* 75) 1964, 243–259.
Chambers, Raymond Wilson, *Beowulf. An introduction to the study of the poem with a discussion of the stories of Offa and Finn*, Cambridge [3]1959.
Chaney, William Albert, *The cult of kingship in Anglo-Saxon England*, Manchester 1970.
Chantepie de la Saussaye, Pierre Daniel, *Lehrbuch der Religionsgeschichte* 1–2, Tübingen [4]1925.
Chantepie de la Saussaye, Pierre Daniel, *The religion of the Teutons*, Boston, London 1902.
Christiansen, H., 'En untolketsstrofe av Grógaldr' (*Norsk Tidsskrift for Sprogvitenskap* 17) 1954, 425–427.
Christiansen, H., 'Eyluðr' (*Norsk Tidsskrift for Sprogvitenskap* 19) 1960, 383–392.
Christiansen, Inger, 'Rimtusser' (*KLNM* 14) Malmö 1969, 319.
Christiansen, Inger, 'Vetter' (*KLNM* 19) Malmö 1975, 678–679.
Christiansen, Reidar Thoralf, *The dead and the living*, Oslo 1946 (= Studia Norvegica, 2).
Christiansen, Reidar Thoralf, *Die finnischen und nordischen Varianten des zweiten Merseburger Spruches*, Helsinki 1914 (= FFC, 18).
Christiansen, Reidar Thoralf, 'Til de norske sjøvetters historie' (*MoM*) 1935, 1–25.
Ciklamini, Marlene, 'The chronological conception in Norse mythology' (*Neophilologus* 47) 1963, 138–151.
Ciklamini, Marlene, 'Óðinn and the giants' (*Neophilologus* 46) 1962, 145–157.
Clauss, Manfrd, 'Neue Inschriften im Rheinischen Landesmusuem Bonn' (*Epigraphische Studien* 11) 1976, 1–40.
Clemen, Carl, *Altgermanische Religionsgeschichte*, Bonn 1934.
Clemen, Carl, 'Die Bedeutung anderer Religionen für die altnordische Religionsgeschichte' (*ARW* 34) 1937, 13–18.
Clemen, Carl, *Der Einfluß des Christentums auf andere Religionen*, Leipzig 1933.
Clemen, Carl, *Fontes historiæ religionis Germanicæ*, Berlin 1928.
Clemen, Carl, 'Mithrasmysterien und germanische Religion' (*ARW* 34) 1937, 217–226.
Clemen, Carl, 'Südöstliche Einflüsse auf die nordische Religion?' (*ZfdPh* 55) 1930, 148–160.

Clemen, Carl, *Urgeschichtliche Religion* 1–2, Bonn 1932–1933.
Closs, Alois, *Heidentum der Altgermanen* (Kirche in der Zeitenwende) Salzburg [3]1939.
Closs, Alois, 'Die Heiligkeit des Herrschers' (*Anthropos* 56) 1961, 469–480.
Closs, Alois, 'Irdisches Wiedererstehen im Glauben der alten Nordeuropäer' (*Kairos* 7) 1965, 216–234.
Closs, Alois, 'Loki und die germanische Frömmigkeit' (*Kairos* 2) 1960, 89–100.
Closs, Alois, 'Neue Problemstellungen in der germanischen Religionsgeschichte' (*Anthropos* 29) 1934, 477–496.
Closs, Alois, 'Die Religion der Germanen in ethnologischer Sicht' (*Christus und die Religionen der Erde*) Freiburg [2]1961, 2, 267–366.
Closs, Alois, 'Die Religion des Semnonenstammes' (W. Koppers, *Die Indogermanen- und die Germanenfrage*) Salzburg, Leipzig, 1936, 549–674.
Closs, Alois, 'Das Versenkungsopfer' (*Kultur und Sprache* 9) 1952, 66–107.
Clover, Carol J., 'Hárbarðsljóð as generic farce' (*SS* 51) 1979, 124–145.
Clunies-Ross, Margaret, 'An Interpretation of the Myth of Þórr's Encounter with Geirrøðr and his daughters' (*Speculum norrœnum. Studies G. Turville-Petre*) Odense 1981, 370–391.
Clunies-Ross, Margaret, 'The myth of Gefjon and Gylfi and its function in *Snorra Edda* and *Heimskringla*' (*ANF* 93) 1978, 149–165.
Clunies-Ross, Margaret, *Skáldskaparmál. Snorri Sturluson's ars poetica and the medieval theories of language*. Odense 1987 (= The Viking Collection, 4).
Clunies-Ross, Margaret, 'Snorri Sturluson's use of the Norse origin-legend of the sons of Fornjótr in his Edda' (*ANF* 98) 1983, 47–66.
Coles, J. M., A. F. Harding, *The Bronze Age in Europe*, London 1979.
Collinder, Björn, 'Till frågan om de äldsta Eddakvädenas ålder' (*ANF* 80) 1965, 61–63.
Collitz, Hermann, 'Wodan, Hermes und Pushan' (*Festskrift H. Pipping*) Helsingfors 1924, 574–587.
Cordes, August, 'Lassen sich "urgermanische Menschenopfer" mit Tacitus beweisen?' (*Heimat* 67) 1960, 88–89.
Cornelius, Friedrich, *Indogermanische Religionsgeschichte*, Munich 1942.
Cour, Vilhelm la, 'Heimdalls navne' (*DS*) 1923, 61–68.
Cramer-Peeters, Elisabeth, 'Frija – Isis – Nehalennia' (*Amsterdamer Beiträge zur älteren Germanistik* 3) 1972, 15–24.
Cramer-Peeters, Elisabeth, 'Zur Deutung des Namens der Göttin Nehalennia' (*Amsterdamer Beiträge zur älteren Germanistik* 3) 1972, 1–14.
Davidson, Hilda R. Ellis, *The Battle God of the Vikings*, York 1972 (= University of York Medieaval Monograph Series, 1).
Davidson, Hilda R. Ellis, *Gods and Myths of Northern Europe*, London 1964.
Davidson, Hilda R. Ellis, 'Hostile Magic in the Icelandic Sagas' (*The Witch Figure. Studies K. M. Briggs*) London, Boston 1973, 20–41.
Davidson, Hilda R. Ellis, *Pagan Scandinavia*, London 1967 (= Ancient Peoples and Places, 58).
Davidson, Hilda R. Ellis, 'Progress on the Northern Front' (*Religion* 4) 1974, 151–155.
Davidson, Hilda R. Ellis, *The road to Hel. A study of the conception of the dead in Old Norse literature*, Cambridge 1943, reprint New York 1968.
Davidson, Hilda R. Ellis, *Scandinavian Mythology*, London 1969.
Davidson, Hilda R. Ellis, 'Thor's Hammer' (*Folklore* 76) 1965, 1–15.
Davidson, Hilda R. Ellis, David Fisher, *Saxo Grammaticus: The History of the Danes*, 1–2, Cambridge 1979–1980.
Davidson, Thomas, 'The needfire ritual' (*Antiquity* 29) 1955, 132–136.
Derolez, R. L. M., *Götter und Mythen der Germanen*, Wiesbaden 1974.
Detter, Ferdinand, 'Der Baldrmythus' (*PBB* 19) 1894, 495–516.
Detter, Ferdinand, 'Erwiderung' (*ANF* 13) 1897, 207–208.

Detter, Ferdinand, 'Review of E. Magnússon, *Odin's horse Yggdrasil*. London 1895' (*ANF* 13) 1897, 99–100.
Detter, Ferdinand, 'Review of E. H. Meyer, *Die eddische Kosmogonie*. Freiburg 1891' (*ANF* 8) 1892, 304–306.
Detter, Ferdinand, 'Der Mythus von Hölgi, Þórgerðr und Irpa' (*ZfdA* 32) 1888, 394–402.
Detter, Ferdinand, 'Zur Ragnarsdrápa' (*ANF* 13) 1897, 363–369.
Detter, Ferdinand, 'Zur Ynglinga saga' (*PBB* 18) 1894, 72–105.
Detter, Ferdinand, Richard Heinzel, 'Hœnir und der Vanenkrieg' (*PBB* 18) 1894, 542–560.
Dick, Ernst S., *Ae. dryht und seine Sippe*, Münster 1965 (= Neue Beiträge zur englischen Philologie, 3).
Dieck, Alfred, *Die europäischen Moorleichenfunde (Hominidenmoorfunde)* 1, Neumünster 1965 (= Göttinger Schriften zur Vor- und Frühgeschichte, 15).
Dietrich, [Franz], 'Die deutsche Wasserhölle' (*ZfdA* 9) 1853, 175–186.
Dillmann, François-Xavier, 'Georges Dumézil et la religion Germanique-l'interprétation du dieu Odhinn' (*Jean-Claude Riviere, Georges Dumézil à la découverte des Indo-Européens*) Paris 1979, 157–186.
Dillmann, François-Xavier, 'Le maître-des-runes: essai de détermination socioanthropologique: quelques réflexions méthodologiques' (*Michigan Germanic Studies* 7) 1981, 27–37.
Dinzelbacher, Peter, *Die Jenseitsbrücke im Mittelalter*, Diss. Vienna 1973.
Döbler, Hannsferdinand, *Die Germanen*, Munich 1975.
Döhring, A., 'Kastors und Balders Tod' (*ARW* 5) 1902, 38–63, 97–104.
Dölvers, Horst, Text, 'Gliederung und Deutung der Vǫluspá' (*ZfdA* 98) 1969, 241–264.
Dörries, Hermann, *Germanische Religion und Sachsenbekehrung*, Göttingen 1934.
Doht, Renate, *Der Rauschtrank im germanischen Mythos*, Vienna 1974 (= Wiener Arbeiten zur germanischen Altertumskunde und Philologie, 3).
Domaszewski, A. von, 'Die Juppitersäule in Mainz' (*ARW* 9) 1906, 303–311.
Domaszewski, A. von, 'Die Religion des römischen Heeres' (*Westdeutsche Zeitschrift* 14) 1895, 1–124.
Drescher Hans, Karl Hauck, 'Götterthrone des heidnischen Nordens' (*FmSt* 16) 1982, 237–301.
Drexel, Friedrich, 'Die Gottheiten der Equites Singulares und die Juppitersäulen' (*Germania* 8) 1924, 49–60.
Drobin, Ulf, 'Myth and epical motifs in the Loki-research' (*Temenos* 3) 1968, 19–39.
Dronke, Ursula, 'Art and tradition in Skírnismál' (*English and Mediaeval Studies pres. to J. R. R. Tolkien*) Oxford 1962, 250–268.
Dronke, Ursula, 'Reginsmál v. 8' (*MoM*) 1960, 97–98.
Dronke, Ursula, 'Vǫluspá and satiric tradition' (*Annali* 21) 1979, 57–86.
Düwel, Klaus, 'Buchstabenmagie und Alphabetzauber. Zu den Inschriften der Goldbrakteaten und ihrer Funktion als Amulette' (*FmSt* 22) 1988, 70–110.
Düwel, Klaus, 'Germanische Opfer und Opferriten im Spiegel altgermanischer Kultworte' (H. Jahnkuhn, *Vorgeschichtliche Heiligtümer und Opferplätze in Mittel- und Nordeuropa*) Göttingen 1970, 219–239.
Düwel, Klaus, *Das Opferfest von Lade. Quellenkritische Untersuchungen zur germanischen Religionsgeschichte*, Wien 1985 (= Wiener Arbeiten zur germanischen Altertumskunde und Philologie, 27).
Düwel, Klaus, *Das Opferfest von Lade und die Geschichte vom Völsi*, Göttingen 1971.
Düwel, Klaus, 'Runen und interpretatio christiana. Zur religionsgeschichtlichen Stellung der Bügelfibel von Nordendorf I' (*Tradition als historische Kraft. [Festschrift] K. Hauck*) Berlin, New York 1982, 78–99.
Düwel, Klaus, 'Zu den Umschreibungen für "Gott" in der altnordischen Dichtung' (*Die vielen Namen Gottes. Festschrift G. H. Mohr*) Stuttgart 1974, 65–77.

Dumézil, Georges, 'Balderiana minora' (*Indo-Iranica. Mélanges prés. a G. Morgenstierne*) Wiesbaden 1964, 67–72.
Dumézil, Georges, 'Deux petits dieux scandinaves: Byggvir et Beyla' (*La nouvelle Clio* 3) 1952, 1–31.
Dumézil, Georges, 'Le dieu scandinave Víðarr' (*Revue de l'histoire des religions* 168) 1965, 1–13.
Dumézil, Georges, *Du mythe au roman*, Paris 1970.
Dumézil, Georges, *From myth to fiction*. The saga of Hadingus, Chicago, London 1973.
Dumézil, Georges, *Gods of the Ancient Northmen*, Berkeley 1977.
Dumézil, Georges, 'Hotherus et Balderus' (*PBB West* 83) 1961–62, 259–270.
Dumézil, Georges, *L'ideologie tripartie des Indo-Européens*, Bruxelles 1968 (= Latomus. 31).
Dumézil, Georges, 'Légendes sur les Nartes' (*Revue de l'histoire des religions* 125) 1943, 97–128.
Dumézil, Georges, *Loki*, Paris 1948.
Dumézil, Georges, *Loki*, Darmstadt 1959.
Dumézil, Georges, 'Njǫrðr, Nerthus et le folklore scandinave de génies de la mer' (*Revue de l'histoire des religions* 147) 1961, 210–226.
Dumézil, Georges, *De nordiska gudarna*, Stockholm ²1966.
Dumézil, Georges, 'Notes sur le bestiaire cosmique d'Edda et du Rg Veda' (*Mélanges de linguistique et de philologie. F. Mossé in memoriam*) Paris 1959, 104–112.
Dumézil, Georges, 'Remarques comparatives sur le dieu scandinave Heimdallr' (*Etudes Celtiques* 8) 1959, 268–283.
Dumézil, Georges, 'La Rígsþula et la structure sociale indo-européenne' (*Revue de l'histoire des religions* 154) 1958, 1–9.
Dumézil, Georges, *Tarpeia*, Paris 1947.
Dyggve, Einar, *Three Old Danish sanctuaries of the Jelling type*, Lund 1961.
Ebenbauer, Alfred, 'Bifröst' (J. Hoops, *Reallexikon der germanischen Altertumskunde*, hg. v. H. Beck 2) ²Berlin, New York 1982, 1–3.
Ebenbauer, Alfred, 'Blutaar' (J. Hoops, *Reallexikon der germanischen Altertumskunde*, hg. v. H. Beck 3) ²Berlin, New York 1978, 80–81.
Ebenbauer, Alfred, 'Fróði und sein Friede' (*Festgabe für O. Höfler*) Vienna 1976, 128–181.
Ebenbauer, Alfred, 'Ursprungsglaube, Herrschergott und Menschenopfer: Beobachtungen zum Semnonenkult (Germania c. 39)' (*Antiquitates Indogermanicae. Gedenkschrift für H. Güntert*) Innsbruck 1974, 233–249 (= Innsbrucker Beiträge zur Sprachwissenschaft. 12).
Eckhardt, Karl August, *Ingwi und die Ingweonen in der Überlieferung des Nordens*, Weimar 1939.
Eckhardt, Karl August, *Irdische Unsterblichkeit*, Weimar 1937.
Eckhardt, Karl August, *Der Wanenkrieg*, Bonn 1940.
Edzardi, A., 'Fensalir und Vegtamskviða 12,5ff.' (*Germania* 27) 1882, 330–338.
Edzardi, A., 'Über die Heimat der Eddalieder' (*PBB* 8) 1882, 349–370.
Edzardi, A., 'Zur Lokasenna' (*Germania* 23) 1878, 418–421.
Einarsson, Stefán, ' "Askr Yggdrasils", "Gullnar tǫflur" (Vǫluspá)' (*Festschrift M. Schlauch*) Warschau 1966, 111–115.
Einarsson, Stefán, 'Some Parallels in Norse and Indian Mythology' (*Scandinavian Studies. Essays H. G. Leach*) Seattle 1965, 21–26.
Eis, Gerhard, *Altdeutsche Zaubersprüche*, Berlin 1964.
Eis, Gerhard, 'Eine neue Deutung des ersten Merseburger Zauberspruchs' (*Forschungen und Fortschritte* 32) 1958, 27–29.
Eitrem, S., 'Lina laukar' (*Festskrift till. A. Kjær*) Christiania 1924, 85–94.
Ejder, Bertil, 'Eddadikten Vafþrúðnismál' (*Vetenskaps-Societeten i Lunds Årsbok*) 1960, 5–20.
Ejder, Bertil, 'Eine Vǫluspá-Stelle' (*Die Sprache* 22) 1976, 49–52.

Ejerfeldt, Lennart, 'Germanische Religion' (*Handbuch der Religionsgeschichte*) Göttingen 1971, 1, 277–342.
Eldjárn, Kristján, 'The Bronze Image from Eyrarland' (*Speculum Norrœnum. Studies* G. *Turville-Petre*) Odense 1981, 73–84.
Eldjárn, Kristján, *Kuml og Haugfé*, Reykjavík 1956.
Eldjárn, Kristján, Per Hovda, Kristian Hald, Olav Bø, Harry Ståhl, 'Hov og Horg' (*KLNM* 7) Malmö 1962, 8–15.
Elgqvist, Eric, 'Guden Höner' (*ANF* 72) 1957, 155–172.
Elgqvist, Eric, *Studier rörande njordkultens spridning bland de nordiska folken*, Lund 1955.
Elgqvist, Eric, *Ullvi och Ullinshov*, Lund 1955.
Ellekilde, Hans, 'Om Sighvat skjalds Alfeblotsstrofer og Alfhildsagnet i Hervararsaga' (*APhSc* 8) 1933, 182–192.
Elliot, Ralph, W. V., 'Runes, yews and magic' (*Speculum* 32) 1957, 250–261.
Ellis, Hilda Roderick → Davidson, H. R. Ellis.
Elmevik, Lennart, 'fsv. *lytir (*Lytir). Ett etymologiskt och religionshistoriskt bidrag' (*NoB* 54) 1966, 47–61.
Elmevik, Lennart, 'Glömskans häger. Till tolkningen av en Hávamál-strof' (*Scripta Islandica* 19) 1968, 39–45.
Elstad, Kåre, 'Om tremenn og solulvar i Edda. To små merknader om poesi og mytologi' (*ANF* 102) 1987, 13–17.
Emsheimr, Ernst, 'Horn' (*KLNM* 6) Malmö 1961, 672–673.
Erben, Johannes, 'Der Schluß des zweiten Merseburger Zauberspruchs' (*Festschrift W. Baetke*) Weimar 1966, 118–121.
Erich, Oswald A., Richard Beitl, *Wörterbuch der deutschen Volkskunde*, Stuttgart [3]1974 (= Kröners Taschenausgabe. 127).
Espeland, Anton, 'Njarðarlaug – Onarheim – Tingstad' (MoM) 1919, 62–65.
Esterle, Gert, *Die Boviden in der Germania*, Vienna 1974 (= Wiener Arbeiten zur germanischen Altertumskunde und Philologie, 2).
Ettlinger, Ellen, 'The mythological relief of the Oseberg wagon found in southern Norway' (*Folklore* 87) 1976, 81–88.
Ettmüller, Ludwig, 'Beiträge zur Kritik der Eddalieder' (*Germania* 14) 1869, 305–323.
Evans, David A. H., 'King Agni: myth, history or legend?' (*Speculum norrœnum. Studies* G. *Turville-Petre*) Odense 1981, 89–105.
Fabing, H. D., 'On going berserk: a neurochemical inquiry' (*Scientific Monthly* 83) 1956, 232–237.
Falck-Kjällquist, Birgit, 'Namnet Ullerö' (*NoB* 71) 1983, 152–156.
Falk, Hjalmar, 'Begravelseterminologien i den oldnorsk-islandske litteratur' (*Festskrift til* A. *Torp*) Kristiania 1913, 1–18.
Falk, Hjalmar, 'Mytologiens gudesønner' (*Festskrift til.* A. *Kjær*) Christiania 1924, 1–8.
Falk, Hjalmar, 'De nordiska hovedguders utviklingshistorie' (*ANF* 43) 1927, 34–44.
Falk, Hjalmar, *Odensheite*, Kristiania 1924.
Falk, Hjalmar, 'Om Svipdagsmál' (*ANF* 9) 1893, 311–362, (10) 1894, 26–82.
Falk, Hjalmar, ' "Sjelen" i Hedentroen' (*MoM*) 1926, 169–174.
Falk, Hjalmar, 'Martianus Capella og den nordiske mythologi' (*ANOH*) 1891, 266–300.
Moltke Moe, 'Middelalderens Visionsdigtning' (*Festskrift til* H. F. *Feilberg*) Copenhagen 1911, 421–448.
Farwerck, F. E., 'Het Wilde Heir' (*Nehalennia* 2) 1957, 120–132.
Faulkes, Anthony, 'Descent from the gods' (*Medieval Scandinavia* 11) 1978–79, 92–125.
Faulkes, Anthony, 'Edda' (*Gripla* 2) Reykjavík 1977 (= Rit 16), 32–39.
Feilberg, Henning Frederik, *Jul*, Copenhagen 1904.
Feilberg, Henning Frederik, 'Der Kobold in nordischer Überlieferung' (*Zeitschrift für Volkskunde* 8) 1898, 1–20, 130–146, 264–277.
Feist, Siegfried, 'Runen und Zauberwesen im germanischen Altertum' (*ANF* 35) 1919, 243–287.

Feist, Siegfried, 'Zur Deutung der deutschen Runenspangen' (*ZfdPh* 47) 1918, 1–10.
Fischer, Rudolf W., 'Gullveigs Wandlung' (*Antaios* 4) 1963, 581–596.
Fischer, Rudolf W., 'Vinculo ligatus. Zur Akzessionsvorschrift des Kultes im Semnonenhain' (*Antaios* 5) 1963, 285–300.
Fleck, Jere, 'Drei Vorschläge zu Baldrs draumar' (*ANF* 84) 1969, 19–37.
Fleck, Jere, 'The "knowledge-criterion" in the Grimnismál: the case against "shamanism"' (*ANF* 86) 1971, 49–65.
Fleck, Jere, 'Konr – Óttar – Geirroðr: a knowledge criterion for succession to the germanic sacred kingship' (*SS* 42) 1970, 39–49.
Fleck, Jere, 'Óðinn's self-sacrifice – a new interpretation' (*SS* 43) 1971, 119–142, 385–413.
Foote, Peter, *Aurvandilstá. Norse Studies*, Odense 1984.
Forster, Leonard, 'Zum 2. Merseburger Zauberspruch' (*Archiv* 192) 1956, 155–159.
Franz, Bernhard, *Der Wanenkrieg und seine historische Grundlage*, Diss. Vienna 1921.
Franz, Leonhard, 'Seherinnen-Schicksale' (*Anzeiger der österreichischen Akademie der Wissenschaften* 87) 1950, 276–278.
Franz, Leonhard, 'Zur altnordischen Religionsgeschichte' (*Mannus* 19) 1927, 135–148.
Franzén, Gösta, 'Aspen i hultet. Till tolkningen av en strof i Hamðismál' (*ANF* 78) 1963, 134–139.
Frazer, James George, *The golden bough. A study in magic and religion*, 1–7, London [3]1911–1935.
Friedrichs, Gustav, *Grundlage, Entstehung und genaue Einzeldeutung der bekanntesten germanischen Märchen, Mythen und Sagen*, Leipzig 1909.
Friesen, Otto von, 'Har det nordiska kungadömet sakralt ursprung?' (*Saga och Sed*) 1932, 15–34.
Friesen, Otto von, 'Tors fiske på en uppländsk runsten' (*Festschrift* E. *Mogk*) Halle/S. 1924, 474–483.
Fromm, Hans, 'Lemminkäinen und Baldr' (*Märchen, Mythos, Dichtung. Festschrift F. v. d. Leyen*) Munich 1963, 287–302.
Fuglesang, Signe Horn, 'Viking and medieval amulets in Scandinavia' (*Fornvännen* 84) 1989, 15–25.
Gade, Kari Ellen, 'Skjalf' (*ANF* 100) 1985, 59–71.
Galsterer, Brigitte, Hartmut Galsterer, 'Neue Inschriften aus Köln – Funde der Jahre 1974–1979' (*Epigraphische Studien* 12) 1981, 225–264.
Galsterer, Brigitte, Hartmut Galsterer, *Die römischen Steininschriften aus Köln*, Wiss. Katalog RGZM, Köln 1975.
Gaster, M., 'Naglfar' (*Germania* 26) 1881, 204–207.
Gehl, Walther, *Der germanische Schicksalsglaube*, Berlin 1939.
Gehl, Walther, 'Das Problem des germanischen Tempels' (*ZfdA* 78) 1941, 37–49.
Gehrts, Heino, 'Die Gullveig-Mythe der Vǫluspá' (*ZfdPh* 88) 1969, 321–378.
Gelling, Peter, Hilda Ellis Davidson, *The chariot of the sun and other rites and symbols of the northern bronze age*, London 1969.
Genzmer, Felix, 'Die Gefjonstrophe' (*PBB* 51) 1932, 414–436.
Genzmer, Felix, 'Germanische Zaubersprüche' (*GRM* 32) 1950, 21–35.
Genzmer, Felix, 'Die Götter des Zweiten Merseburger Zauberspruchs' (*ANF* 63) 1948, 55–72.
Genzmer, Felix, 'Das Walkürenlied' (*ANF* 71) 1956, 168–171.
Gering, Hugo, 'Ottar heimski' (*ANF* 36) 1920, 326–331.
Gering, Hugo, *Über Weissagung und Zauber im nordischen Altertum*, Kiel 1902.
Gering, Hugo, 'Der zweite Merseburger Spruch' (*ZfdPh* 26) 1894, 145–149.
Gering, Hugo, B. Sijmons, *Kommentar zu den Liedern der Edda*, Halle/S. 1927.
Gimmler, Heinrich, 'Rígsþula' (*KLL* 6) Munich 1971, 284–286.
Gimmler, Heinrich, 'Skírnismál' (*KLL* 6) Munich 1971, 1517–1519.
Gjessing, Guttorm, 'Hesten i førhistorisk kunst og kultus' (*Viking*) 1943, 5–143.

Glob, Vilhelm Peter, *Danske Oldtidsminder*, Copenhagen [2]1967.
Glob, Vilhelm Peter, 'Kultbåde fra Danmarks bronzealder' (*Kuml*) 1961, 8–18.
Glob, Vilhelm Peter, *Mosefolket*, Copenhagen 1965.
Glob, Vilhelm Peter, *The Mound People*, London 1974.
Glob, Vilhelm Peter, *Vorzeitdenkmäler Dänemarks*, Neumünster 1967.
Golther, Wolfgang, *Handbuch der germanischen Mythologie*, Leipzig 1895.
Gould, Chester Nathan, 'Dwarf-Names: A study in Old Icelandic religion' (*PMLA* 44) 1929, 939–967.
Gould, Chester Nathan, 'Which are the norns who take children from mothers?' (*MLN* 42) 1942, 218–221.
Graf, Heinz-Joachim, *Orientalische Berichte des Mittelalters über die Germanen. Eine Quellensammlung*, Krefeld 1971.
Grahn, Heinz A., 'Vǫluspá. Versuch einer Deutung' (*Wirkendes Wort* 17) 1967, 289–301.
Gras, Elizabeth Johanna, *De Noords Loki-mythen in hun onderling verband*, Haarlem 1931.
Gras, Elizabeth Johanna, 'Mistiltein' (*Neophilologus* 17) 1932, 293–298.
Grieg, Sigurd, 'Amuletter og gudebilder' (*Viking* 18) 1954, 157–209.
Grienberger, Theodor von, 'Dea Garmangabis' (*ZfdA* 38) 1894, 189–198.
Grienberger, Theodor von, 'Germanische Götternamen auf rheinischen Inschriften' (*ZfdA* 35) 1891, 388–401 (36) 1892, 308–316.
Grienberger, Theodor von, 'Die Merseburger Zaubersprüche' (*ZfdPh* 27) 1895, 433–462.
Grienberger, Theodor von, 'Muspell' (*IF* 16) 1904, 40–63.
Grienberger, Theodor von, 'Niederrheinische Matronen. Die Beinamen nach dem Typus -ehae und -henae' (*Eranos Vindobonensis*) 1893, 253–268.
Grienberger, Theodor von, *Über germanische Götternamen auf Inschriften des Niederrheins mit besonderer Berücksichtigung der Matronensteine*, Diss. Vienna 1890.
Grienberger, Theodor von, 'Zwischenvokalisches h in germanischen und keltischen Namen der Römerzeit' (*PBB* 19) 1894, 527–536.
Grimm, Jakob, *Deutsche Mythologie*, Berlin [4]1875–78, reprint Frankfurt 1981.
Grönbech, Vilhelm, 'Die Germanen' (P. D. Chantepie de la Saussaye, *Lehrbuch der Religionsgeschichte* 2) Tübingen [4]1925, 540–600.
Grönbech, Vilhelm, *Kultur und Religion der Germanen*, 1–2, Darmstadt [5]1954.
Grönbech, Vilhelm, *Nordiske myter og sagn*, Copenhagen [4]1973.
Grönbech, Vilhelm, *Vor Folkeaet i Oldtiden*, Copenhagen 1909–12.
Gröndal, Benedikt Sveinbjarnarson, *Clavis poetica antiquae linquae Septemtrionalis*, Hafniæ 1864.
Gschwantler, Otto, 'Asen' (*Lexikon des Mittelalters* 1) Munich, Zurich 1980, 1104–1106.
Gschwantler, Otto, 'Christus, Thor und die Midgardschlange' (*Festschrift für Otto Höfler* 1) Vienna 1968, 145–168.
Gschwantler, Otto, 'Edda' (*Lexikon des Mittelalters* 3) Munich 1986, 1555–1558.
Gschwantler, Otto, 'Die Überwindung des Fenriswolfs und ihr christliches Gegenstück bei Frau Ava' (*Proceedings of the VIIth International Saga Conference*) Spoleto 1990, 1–26.
Guarducci, Margherita, 'Veleda' (*Rendiconti della Pontifica Academia Romana di Archaeologia* 21) 1945/46, 163–176.
Gubernatis, Angelo de, *Die Tiere in der indogermanischen Mythologie*, Leipzig 1874.
Güntert, Hermann, *Altgermanischer Glaube nach Wesen und Grundlage*, Heidelberg 1937.
Güntert, Hermann, *Über altisländische Berserkergeschichten*, Heidelberg 1912.
Güntert, Hermann, *Von der Sprache der Götter und Geister*, Halle/S. 1921.
Gurevich, Aron Ya, 'Edda and Law. Commentary upon Hyndloliόð' (*ANF* 88) 1973, 72–84.
Gurevich, Aron Ya, 'Space and time in the *Weltmodell* of the Old Scandinavian peoples' (*Mediaeval Scandinavia* 2) 1969, 42–53.
Gustafson, Gabriel, *Gotlands Bildsteine* 1–2, Stockholm 1941–1942.

Gutenbrunner, Siegfried, 'Altnordische Spruchdichtung in den Reginsmál' (*ZfdA* 74) 1937, 135–139.
Gutenbrunner, Siegfried, 'Balders Wiederkehr. Südostgermanisches in der Völuspa?' (*GRM* 37) 1956, 62–72.
Gutenbrunner, Siegfried, 'Der Büchertitel Edda' (*PBB* 66) 1942, 276–277.
Gutenbrunner, Siegfried, 'Eddastudien I. Über die Zwerge in der Völuspa Str. 9–13' (*ANF* 70) 1955, 61–75.
Gutenbrunner, Siegfried, 'Eddica' (*ZfdA* 77) 1040, 17–25.
Gutenbrunner, Siegfried, 'Fanesii und Fenrir' (*ZfdA* 77) 1940, 25–26.
Gutenbrunner, Siegfried, *Germanische Frühzeit in den berichten der Antike*, Halle/S. 1939.
Gutenbrunner, Siegfried, *Die germanischen Götternamen der antiken Inschriften*, Halle/S. 1936.
Gutenbrunner, Siegfried, 'Die Harier im Markomannenkrieg' (*ZfdA* 77) 1940, 27–28.
Gutenbrunner, Siegfried, 'Der Kult des Weltherrschers bei den Semnonen und ein altnorwegischer Rechtsbrauch' (*APhSc* 14) 1939/40, 102–108.
Gutenbrunner, Siegfried, 'Ostern' (*Festschrift W. Baetke*) Weimar 1966, 122–129.
Gutenbrunner, Siegfried, 'Ritennamen – Kultnamen – Mythennamen' (*Namenforschung. Festschrift A. Bach*) Heidelberg 1965, 17–31.
Gutenbrunner, Siegfried, 'Über die Redewendung "láttu grǫn sía þá" ' (*ZfdA* 72) 1935, 175–176.
Gutenbrunner, Siegfried, 'Über die Träger des Himmelsgewölbes im germanischen Mythos' (*ARW* 37) 1941/42, 270–272.
Gutenbrunner, Siegfried, 'Über Vortragsregeln für die Vǫluspá' (*ZfdPh* 77) 1958, 1–25.
Gutenbrunner, Siegfried, 'Über zwei germanische Heiligtümer bei Plinius und bei Ptolemaios' (*ZfdA* 83) 1951/52, 157–162.
Gutenbrunner, Siegfried, 'Versteckte Eddagedichte' (*Edda, Skalden, Saga. Festschrift f. F. Genzmer*) Heidelberg 1952, 72–86.
Gutenbrunner, Siegfried, 'Zur Matroneninschrift von Derichsweiler' (*Bonner Jahrbücher* 152) 1952, 162–164.
Gutenbrunner, Siegfried, 'Der zweite Mersebuger Spruch im Lichte nordischer Überlieferung' (*ZfdA* 80) 1944, 1–5.
Gutenbrunner, Siegfried, Heinz Klingenberg, 'Runenschrift. Die älteste Buchstabenschrift der Germanen' (*Studium generale* 20) 1967, 432–448.
Guyonvarch, Christian-J., 'Notes d'etymologie et de lexicographie celtiques et gauloises 9' (*Ogam* 13) 1961, 321–330.
Gysseling, Maurits, 'Nordostgallische Götternamen' (Rolf Bergmann et al., *Althochdeutsch* 2) Heidelberg 1987, 1296–1304.
Haas, Hans, *Bilderatlas zur Religionsgeschichte*, Leipzig, Erlangen 1924.
Hachmann, Rolf, *Die Goten und Skandinavien*, Berlin 1970.
Hachmann, Rolf, Georg Kossack, Hans Kuhn, *Völker zwischen Germanen und Kelten*, Neumünster 1962.
Hackenberg, Erna, *Die Stammtafeln der angelsächsischen Königreiche*, Diss. Berlin 1918.
Haegstad, Marius, 'Um navnet Oskoreidi' (MoM) 1912, 80–85.
Hälsig, Arthur Friedrich, *Der Zauberspruch bei den Germanen bis um die Mitte des XVI. Jahrhunderts*, Diss. Leipzig 1910.
Hagen, S. N., 'Om navnet Fenrisulfr' (MoM) 1910, 57–59.
Hagen, S. N., 'On the origin of the name Kvasir' (*ANF* 28) 1912, 127–139.
Hagman, N., 'Kring nagra motiv i Hávamál' (*ANF* 72) 1957, 13–24.
Hald, Kr., 'The cult of Odin in Danish place-names' (*Early English and Norse Studies, pres. to H. Smith*) London 1963, 99–109.
Hale, Christopher S., 'The river names in Grimnismal 27–29' (*Edda. A Collection*) Winnipeg 1983, 165–186.
Hallberg, Peter, 'Om Þrymskviða' (*ANF* 69) 1954, 51–77.

Hallberg, Peter, 'Världsträdet och Världsbranden. Ett Motiv i Vǫluspá' (*ANF* 67) 1952, 145–155.
Halvorsen, Eyvind Fjeld, 'Aegir' (*KLNM* 20) Malmö 1976, 470–471.
Halvorsen, Eyvind Fjeld, 'Åsgard' (*KLNM* 20) Malmö 1976, 457–458.
Halvorsen, Eyvind Fjeld, 'Dverger' (*KLNM* 3) Malmö 1958, 376–378.
Halvorsen, Eyvind Fjeld, 'Élivágar' (*KLNM* 3) Malmö 1958, 597–598.
Halvorsen, Eyvind Fjeld, 'Freyja' (*KLNM* 4) Malmö 1959, 617–618.
Halvorsen, Eyvind Fjeld, 'Freyr' (*KLNM* 4) Malmö 1959, 618–620.
Halvorsen, Eyvind Fjeld, 'Frigg' (*KLNM* 4) Malmö 1959, 631–632.
Halvorsen, Eyvind Fjeld, 'Hel' (*KLNM* 6) Malmö 1961, 304–305.
Halvorsen, Eyvind Fjeld, 'Iðunn' (*KLNM* 7) Malmö 1962, 330–331.
Halvorsen, Eyvind Fjeld, 'Lóðurr' (*KLNM* 10) Malmö 1965, 668–669.
Halvorsen, Eyvind Fjeld, 'Miðgarðr' (*KLNM* 11) Malmö 1966, 610.
Halvorsen, Eyvind Fjeld, 'Mímir' (*KLNM* 11) Malmö 1966, 629–630.
Halvorsen, Eyvind Fjeld, 'Muspell' (*KLNM* 12) Malmö 1967, 32–33.
Halvorsen, Eyvind Fjeld, 'Naglfar' (*KLNM* 12) Malmö 1967, 202–203.
Halvorsen, Eyvind Fjeld, 'Niðhǫggr' (*KLNM* 12) Malmö 1967, 303–304.
Halvorsen, Eyvind Fjeld, 'Njǫrðr' (*KLNM* 12) Malmö 1967, 322–324.
Halvorsen, Eyvind Fjeld, 'Norner' (*KLNM* 12) Malmö 1967, 347–348.
Halvorsen, Eyvind Fjeld, 'Óðinn' (*KLNM* 12) Malmö 1967, 503–509.
Halvorsen, Eyvind Fjeld, 'Ódr' (*KLNM* 12) Malmö 1967, 514.
Halvorsen, Eyvind Fjeld, 'Þorgerðr Hǫlgabruðr' (*KLNM* 20) Malmö 1976, 382–384.
Halvorsen, Eyvind Fjeld, 'Þórr' (*KLNM* 20) Malmö 1976, 391–395.
Halvorsen, Eyvind Fjeld, 'Þorri' (*KLNM* 20) Malmö 1976, 395–397.
Halvorsen, Eyvind Fjeld, 'Þrymr' (*KLNM* 20) Malmö 1976, 402.
Halvorsen, Eyvind Fjeld, 'Þulr' (*KLNM* 20) Malmö 1976, 402–403.
Halvorsen, Eyvind Fjeld, 'Valhall' (*KLNM* 19) Malmö 1975, 364–465.
Halvorsen, Eyvind Fjeld, 'Vé' (*KLNM* 19) Malmö 1975, 591–593.
Halvorsen, Eyvind Fjeld, 'Vǫlva' (*KLNM* 20) Malmö 1976, 355–358.
Halvorsen, Eyvind Fjeld, 'Yggdrasill' (*KLNM* 20) Malmö 1976, 357–359.
Halvorsen, Eyvind Fjeld, 'Ymir' (*KLNM* 20) Malmö 1976, 359–360.
Hamel, A. G. van, 'The conception of fate in early Teutonic and Celtic religion' (*Saga-Book* 11) 1928–36, 202–214.
Hamel, A. G. van, 'The game of the gods' (*ANF* 50) 1934, 218–242.
Hamel, A. G. van, 'Gambanteinn' (*Neophilologus* 17) 1932, 136–143, 234–239.
Hamel, A. G. van, 'Gods, skalds and magic' (*Saga-Book* 11) 1928–36, 129–152.
Hamel, A. G. van, 'The mastering of the mead' (*Studia Germanica till. E. A. Kock*) Lund 1934, 76–85.
Hamel, A. G. van, 'Óðinn hanging on the tree' (*APhSc* 7) 1932–33, 260–288.
Hamel, A. G. van, 'The prose-frame of "Lokasenna" ' (*Neophilologus* 14) 1929, 204–214.
Hamel, A. G. van, 'Vǫluspá 27–29' (*ANF* 41) 1925, 293–305.
Hammarstedt, N. E., 'Olsmessa och Torsblo' (*Fataburen*) 1915, 32–40, 89–91.
Harder, Hermann, *Die Religion der Germanen*, Leipzig ^{2}1941.
Harris, Joseph, 'Cursing with the thistle' (*Neuphilologische Mitteilungen* 76) 1975, 26–33.
Harris, Joseph, 'The masterbuilder tale in Snorri's Edda and two sagas' (*ANF* 91) 1976, 66–101.
Hartmann, Elisabeth, 'Der Ahnenberg. Eine altnordische Jenseitsvorstellung' (*ARW* 34) 1937, 201–217.
Hartmann, Elisabeth, *Die Trollvorstellungen in den Sagen und Märchen der skandinavischen Völker*, Stuttgart, Berlin 1936.
Hartner, Willy, *Die Goldhörner von Gallehus*, Wiesbaden 1969.
Hauck, Karl, 'Bildforschung als historische Sachforschung' (*Geschichtsschreibung und geistiges Leben im Mittelalter', Festschrift f. H. Löwe*) Köln, Vienna 1978, 27–70.
Hauck, Karl, 'Die bildliche Wiedergabe von Götter- und Heldenwaffen im Norden seit

der Völkerwanderungszeit. Zur Ikonologie der Goldbrakteaten XVIII' (*Wörter und Sachen im Lichte der Bezeichnungsforschung*) Berlin, New York 1981, 168–269.
Hauck, Karl, 'Dioskuren, 4–6: Die Bildzeugnisse des Nordens' (J. Hoops, *Reallexikon der germanischen Altertumskunde*, hg. v. H. Beck, vol. 5) ²Berlin, New York 1981, 168–269.
Hauck, Karl, 'Dioskuren in Bildzeugnissen des Nordens vom 5. bis. 7. Jahrhundert. Zur Ikonologie der Goldbrakteaten XXVIII' (*Jahrbuch des Römisch-germanischen Zentralmuseums* 32) 1983, 435–464.
Hauck, Karl, 'Ein neues Drei-Götter-Amulett von der Insel Fünen. Zur Ikonologie der Goldbrakteaten V' (*Geschichte in der Gesellschaft. Festschrift für K. Bosl*) Stuttgart 1974, 93–153.
Hauck, Karl, 'Gemeinschaftsstiftende Kulte der Seegermanen. Zur Ikonologie der Goldbrakteaten XIX' (*FmSt* 14) 1980, 463–617.
Hauck, Karl, 'Germanische Bilddenkmäler des frühen Mittelalters' (*DVjS* 31) 1957, 349–379.
Hauck, Karl, 'Die geschichtliche Bedeutung der germanischen Auffassung von Königtum und Adel' (*Rapports du XIe Congrès International des Sciences Historiques*) Stockholm 1960, 96–120.
Hauck, Karl, *Goldbrakteaten aus Sievern*, Munich 1970.
Hauck, Karl, 'Gott als Arzt. Zur Ikonologie der Goldbrakteaten XVI' (*Text und Bild*) Wiesbaden 1980, 19–62.
Hauck, Karl, 'Herrschaftszeichen eines wodanistischen Königtums' (*Jahrbuch für fränkische Landesforschung* 14) 1954, 9–65.
Hauck, Karl, 'Kontext-Ikonographie' (*Verbum et Signum* 2) Munich 1975, 25–69.
Hauck, Karl, 'Lebensnormen und Kultmythen in germanischen Stammes- und Herrschergenealogien' (*Saeculum* 6) 1955, 186–223.
Hauck, Karl, 'Politische und asketische Aspekte der Christianisierung' (*Dauer und Wandel der Geschichte. Festgabe für K. v. Raumer*) Münster 1965, 45–61.
Hauck, Karl, 'Text und Bild in einer oralen Kultur' (Zur Ikonologie der Goldbrakteaten XXV) (*FmSt* 17) 1983, 510–599.
Hauck, Karl, 'Völkerwanderungszeitliche Bilddarstellungen des zweiten Merseburger Spruchs als Zugang zu Heiligtum und Opfer' (H. Jankuhn, *Vorgeschichtliche Heiligtümer und Opferplätze*) Göttingen 1970, 297–319.
Hauck, Karl, 'Völkerwanderungszeitliche Bildzeugnisse eines Allgotts des Nordens und ihre älteren mediterranen Analogien' (*Zur Ikonologie der Goldbrakteaten XVII*), *Pietas. Festschrift für B. König*) Münster 1980, 566–583.
Hauck, Karl, 'Zur Ikonologie der Goldbrakteaten I. Neue Windgott-Amulette' (*Festschrift für H. Heimpel*) Göttingen 1972, 627–660.
Hauck, Karl, 'Zur Ikonologie der Goldbrakteaten IV. Metamorphosen Odins nach dem Wissen von Snorri und von Amulettmeistern der Völkerwanderungszeit' (*Festschrift für S. Gutenbrunner*) Heidelberg 1972, 47–70.
Hauck, Karl, 'Zur Ikonologie der Goldbrakteaten VIII. Ikonographie des Opfers' (*Festschrift für O. Höfler*) Vienna, Stuttgart 1976, 269–296.
Hauck, Karl, 'Zur Ikonologie der Goldbrakteaten X: Formen der Aneignung spätantiker ikonographischer Konventionen im paganen Norden' (*Settimane di studio del centro italiano di studi sull'alto medioevo XXIII*) Spoleto 1976, 81–121.
Hauck, Karl, 'Zur Ikonologie der Goldbrakteaten XII. Die Ikonographie der C-Brakteaten' (*Archäologisches Korrespondenzblatt* 6) 1976, 235–242.
Hauck, Karl, 'Zur Ikonologie der Goldbrakteaten XIII: Schlüsselstücke zur Entzifferung der D-Brakteaten' (*Studien zur Sachsenforschung. [Festschrift] A. Genrich*) Hildesheim 1977, 161–196.
Hauck, Karl, 'Zur Ikonologie der Goldbrakteaten XIV: Die Spannung zwischen Zauber- und Erfahrungsmedizin, erhellt an Rezepten aus zwei Jahrtausenden' (*FmSt* 11) 1977, 414–510.
Hauck, Karl, 'Zur Ikonologie der Goldbrakteaten XV: Die Arztfunktion des seegermani-

schen Götterkönigs, erhellt mit der Rolle der Vögel auf den goldenen Amulettbildern' (*Festschrift für H. Beumann*) Sigmaringen 1977, 98–116.

Haugen, Einar, 'The Edda as ritual: Odin and his masks' (*Edda. A Collection of Essays*) Winnipeg 1983, 3–24.

Hauksdóttir, Sólveig, 'Snorri Sturluson og konungsvaldið' (*Mímir* 21) 1974, 5–11.

Heinemann, Frederik, J., 'Ealuscerwen-Meoduscerwen, the cup of death, and Baldrs draumar' (*Studia Neophilologica* 55) 1983, 3–10.

Heinrichs, Heinrich Matthias, 'Satirisch-parodistische Züge in der Þrymskviða' (*Festschrift für H. Eggers*) Tübingen 1972 (= *PBB* 94, Sonderheft) 501–510.

Heinzel, Richard, 'Über die ostgotische Heldensage' (*Sitzungsberichte der kaiserlichen Akademie der Wissenschaften in Wien* 119) 1889, 1–98.

Heizmann, Wilhelm, *Laukr ("Lauch") in der altnordischen Literatur, Mythologie und Heilkunde*, Diss. Munich 1981.

Heizmann, Wilhelm, 'Bildformel und Formelwort. Zu den laukaR-Inschriften auf Goldbrakteaten der Völkerwanderungszeit' (*Runor och runinskrifter*) Stockholm 1985, 145–153 (= Kungliga Vitterhets Historie och Antikvitets Akademien, Konferenser, 15).

Helgadóttir, Guðrún P., 'Laukagarðr' (*Speculum Norrœnum. Studies G. Turville-Petre*) Odense 1981, 171–184.

Hellmuth, Leopold, *Die germanische Blutsbrüderschaft*, Vienna 1975 (= Wiener Arbeiten zur germanischen Altertumskunde und Philologie, 7).

Hellquist, Elof, 'Ett par mytologiska bidrag' (*ANF* 21) 1905, 132–140.

Hellquist, Elof, 'Om Fornjótr' (*ANF* 19) 134–140.

Hellquist, Elof, 'Om naturmytiska element i Hymiskviða' (*ANF* 18) 1902, 353–368.

Helm, Karl, *Altgermanische Religionsgeschichte*, 1–2/2, Heidelberg 1913–1953.

Helm, Karl, 'Balder in Deutschland?' (*PBB* 67) 1944, 216–222.

Helm, Karl, 'Die Entwicklung der germanischen Religion; ihr Nachleben in und neben dem Christentum' (H. Nollau, *Germanische Wiedererstehung*) Heidelberg 1926, 292–422.

Helm, Karl, 'Erfundene Götter?' (*Studien zur deutschen Literatur des Mittelalters*, F. Panzer dargebracht) Heidelberg 1950, 1–11.

Helm, Karl, 'Die germanische Weltschöpfungssage und die Alvísmál' (*PBB* 32) 1907, 99–112.

Helm, Karl, 'Hluðana' (*PBB* 37) 1912, 337–338.

Helm, Karl, 'Isis Sueborum?' (*PBB* 43) 1918, 527–533.

Helm, Karl, 'Mythologie auf alten und neuen Wegen' (*PBB* West 77) 1955, 333–365.

Helm, Karl, 'Religionsgeschichte und Volkskunde' (*Zum Verständnis des religiösen Phänomens. Festschrift für R. Otto*) Berlin 1940, 1–9.

Helm, Karl, 'Waluburg, die Wahrsagerin' (*PBB* 43) 1918, 337–341.

Helm, Karl, 'Weltwerden und Weltvergehen in altgermanischer Sage, Dichtung und Religion' (*Hessische Blätter für Volkskunde* 38) 1940, 1–35.

Helm, Karl, *Wodan. Ausbreitung und Wanderung seines Kultes*, Gießen 1946.

Helten, W. van, 'Über Marti Thincso, Alaesiagis Bede et Fimmilene (?), Tuihanti (langob.) thingx (got.) þeihs und mnl. dinxen-, dijssendach etc. (mnd.) dingsedagh' (*PBB* 27) 1902, 137–153.

Hempel, Heinrich, 'Hellenistisch-orientalisches Lehngut in der germanischen Religion' (*GRM* 16) 1928, 185–202.

Hempel, Heinrich, 'Matronenkult und germanischer Mütterglaube' (*GRM* 27) 1939, 245–270.

Henning, R., 'Die Alaisiagen' (*ZfdA* 42) 1898, 193–195.

Herrmann, Ferdinand, 'Das Tier als Schöpfer. Ein Beitrag zu vergleichenden Mythologie' (*Studium generale* 20) 1967, 129–138.

Herrmann, Paul, *Das altgermanische Priesterwesen geschildert*, Jena 1929.

Herrmann, Paul, *Deutsche Mythologie in gemeinverständlicher Darstellung*, Leipzig ²1906.

Herrmann, Paul, *Die Heldensagen des Saxo Grammaticus*, Leipzig 1922 (= P. Herrmann, Dänische Geschichte des Saxco Grammaticus, 2).
Herrmann, Paul, *Nordische Mythologie in gemeinverständlicher Darstellung*, Leipzig 1903.
Hertlein, Friedrich, *Die Juppitergigantensäulen*, Stuttgart 1910.
Hertlein, Friedrich, 'Juppitersäulen' (J. Hoops, *Reallexikon der germanischen Altertumskunde* 2) Straßburg 1914–15, 619–621.
Hettema, F. Buitenrust, 'Fosete, Fosite Foste' (*TNTL* 12) 1893, 281–288.
Hettner, Felix, 'Juppitersäulen' (*Westdeutsche Zeitschrift* 4) 1885, 365–388.
Heusler, Andreas, 'Die Geschichte vom Völsi' (*Zeitschrift für Volkskunde* 13) 1903, 25–39.
Heusler, Andreas, *Die gelehrte Urgeschichte im altisländischen Schrifttum*, Berlin 1908.
Heusler, Andreas, 'Heimat und Alter der eddischen Gedichte' (*Archiv* 116) 1906, 249–281.
Heusler, Andreas, 'Sprichwörter in den eddischen Sittengedichten' (*Zeitschrift für Volkskunde* 25) 1915, 108–115 (26) 1916, 42–57.
Hirschfeld, Max, *Untersuchungen zur Lokasenna*, Berlin 1889 (= Acta Germanica, 1).
Höckert, Robert, *Vǫluspá och Vanakulten*, 1–2, Stockholm 1926–1930.
Höfler, Otto, 'Abstammungstraditionen' (J. Hoops, *Reallexikon der germanischen Altertumskunde*, hg. v. H. Beck, vol. 1) 2Berlin, New York 1973, 18–22.
Höfler, Otto, 'Antwort' (*Oberdeutsche Zeitschrift für Volkskunde* 11) 1973, 97–102.
Höfler, Otto, 'Balders Bestattung und die nordischen Felszeichnungen' (*Anzeiger der phil.-hist. Klasse der österr. Akademie der Wissenschaften* 88) 1951, 343–372.
Höfler, Otto, 'Berserker' (J. Hoops, *Reallexikon der germanischen Altertumskunde*, hg. v. H. Beck, Vol. 1) 2Berlin, New York 1973, 298–304.
Höfler, Otto, 'Brakteaten als Geschichtsquelle' (*ZfdA* 101) 1972, 161–186.
Höfler, Otto, 'Das germanische Kontinuitätsproblem' (*Historische Zeitschrift* 157) 1938, 1–26.
Höfler, Otto, *Germanisches Sakralkönigtum 1: Der Runenstein von Rök und die germanische Individualweihe*, Tübingen, Münster/Köln 1952.
Höfler, Otto, 'Götterkomik. Zur Selbstrelativierung des Mythos' (*ZfdA* 100) 1971, 371–389.
Höfler, Otto, 'Herkunft und Ausbreitung der Runen' (*Die Sprache* 17) 1971, 134–156.
Höfler, Otto, *Kultische Geheimbünde der Germanen*, Frankfurt/M. 1934.
Höfler, Otto, 'Mars Thingsus' (*Handwörterbuch der deutschen Rechtsgeschichte* 3) Berlin 1979, 344–348.
Höfler, Otto, 'Die nordischen Kultortsnamen' (*Disputationes ad montium vocabula* 1) Vienna 1969, 191–199.
Höfler, Otto, 'Das Opfer im Semnonenhain und die Edda' (*Edda, Skalden, Saga. Festschrift für F. Genzmer*) Heidelberg 1952, 1–67.
Höfler, Otto, 'Der Sakralcharakter des germanischen Königtums' (*Vorträge und Forschungen, hg. v. Institut für geschichtliche Landesforschung des Bodenseegebiets in Konstanz* 3) Lindau, Konstanz 1956, 75–104.
Höfler, Otto, ' "Sakraltheorie" und "Profantheorie" in der Altertumskunde' (*Festschrift für S. Gutenbrunner*) Heidelberg 1972, 71–116.
Höfler, Otto, 'Staatsheiligkeit und Staatsvergottung' (*Rechtsgeschichte als Kulturgeschichte. Festschrift für A. Erler*) Aalen 1976, 109–133.
Höfler, Otto, 'Der germanische Totenkult und die Sagen vom Wilden Heer' (*Oberdeutsche Zeitschrift für Volkskunde* 10) 1976, 33–49.
Höfler, Otto, 'Über germanische Verwandlungskulte' (*ZfdA* 73) 1936, 109–115.
Höfler, Otto, *Verwandlungskulte, Volkssagen und Mythen*, Vienna 1973.
Höfler, Otto, 'Zur Bestimmung mythischer Elemente in der geschichtlichen Überlieferung' (*Beiträge zur deutschen und nordischen Geschichte. Festschrift für O. Scheel*) Schleswig 1952, 9–27.
Höfler, Otto, 'Zwei Grundkräfte im Wodankult' (*Antiquitates Indogermanicae. Gedenkschrift für H. Güntert*) Innsbruck 1974, 133–144.

Høeg, Ove Arbo, 'Mistiltein' (*KLNM* 11) Malmö 1966, 651–653.
Højrup, Ole, 'Mjød-gudernes drik' (*Fra Nationalmuseets Arbejdsmark*) 1957, 53–62.
Hoffmann, Erich, *Die heiligen Könige bei den Angelsachsen und den germanischen Völkern*, Neumünster 1975.
Hoffory, Julius, 'Der germanische Himmelsgott' (*Nachrichten von der königl. Gesellschaft der Wissenschaften zu Göttingen*) 1888, 426–443.
Hollander, Lee M., 'The Old Norse god Óðr' (*JEGPH* 49) 1950, 304–308.
Hollander, Lee M., 'Recent works and views on the poetic Edda' (*SS* 35) 1963, 101–109.
Holmberg, Uno, *Der Baum des Lebens*, Helsinki 1922.
Holmqvist, Wilhelm, 'The dancing gods' (*Acta Archaeologica* 31) 1960, 101–127.
Holthausen, Ferdinand, 'Requalivahanus' (*PBB* 16) 1892, 342–345.
Holtsmark, Anne, 'Bil og Hjuke' (*MoM*) 1945, 139–154.
Holtsmark, Anne, 'Eddadiktning' (*KLNM* 3) Malmö 1958, 480–488.
Holtsmark, Anne, 'Gevjons plog' (*MoM*) 1944, 169–179.
Holtsmark, Anne, 'Grotta sǫngr' (*KLNM* 5) Malmö 1960, 482–483.
Holtsmark, Anne, 'Haustlǫng' (*KLNM* 6) Malmö 1961, 254–255.
Holtsmark, Anne, 'Iðavǫllr' (*Festschrift K. Reichardt*) Bern, Munich 1969, 98–102.
Holtsmark, Anne, 'Lokasenna' (*KLNM* 10) Malmö 1965, 678–680.
Holtsmark, Anne, 'Loki' (*MoM*) 1962, 81–89.
Holtsmark, Anne, 'Måne' (*KLNM* 12) Malmö 1967, 140–143.
Holtsmark, Anne, 'Myten om Idun og Tjatse i Tjodolvs Haustlǫng' (*ANF* 64) 1949, 1–73.
Holtsmark, Anne, 'Mytiske dikt' (*KLNM* 12) Malmö 1976, 105–106.
Holtsmark, Anne, 'Mytologi' (*KLNM* 12) Malmö 1967, 107–110.
Holtsmark, Anne, *Norrøn mytologi*, Oslo 1970.
Holtsmark, Anne, 'Ragnarǫk' (*KLNM* 13) Malmö 1968, 649–652.
Holtsmark, Anne, 'Rán' (*KLNM* 13) Malmö 1968, 654–655.
Holtsmark, Anne, 'Ratatoskr' (*KLNM* 13) Malmö 1968, 677.
Holtsmark, Anne, 'Reginnaglar' (*KLNM* 13) Malmö 1968, 712–713.
Holtsmark, Anne, 'Rígsþula' (*KLNM* 14) Malmö 1969, 234–236.
Holtsmark, Anne, 'Rindr' (*KLNM* 14) Malmö 1969, 326–327.
Holtsmark, Anne, 'Rǫkstólar' (*KLNM* 14) Malmö 1969, 624.
Holtsmark, Anne, 'Sæhrimnir' (*KLNM* 17) Malmö 1972, 685.
Holtsmark, Anne, 'Sága' (*KLNM* 14) Malmö 1969, 650–651.
Holtsmark, Anne, 'Skaði' (*KLNM* 15) Malmö 1970, 381–382.
Holtsmark, Anne, 'Skíðblaðnir' (*KLNM* 15) Malmö 1970, 494.
Holtsmark, Anne, 'Skírnismál (*KLNM* 15) Malmö 1970, 570–572.
Holtsmark, Anne, 'Sleipnir' (*KLNM* 16) Malmö 1971, 200–201.
Holtsmark, Anne, 'Sol' (*KLNM* 16) Malmö 1971, 401–402.
Holtsmark, Anne, 'Sonargǫltr' (*KLNM* 16) Malmö 1971, 433.
Holtsmark, Anne, *Studier i norrøn diktning*, Oslo 1956.
Holtsmark, Anne, *Studier i Snorres mytologi*, Oslo 1964.
Holtsmark, Anne, 'Surtr' (*KLNM* 17) Malmö 1972, 440–442.
Holtsmark, Anne, 'Suttungr' (*KLNM* 17) Malmö 1972, 445–446.
Holtsmark, Anne, 'Svipdagsmál' (*KLNM* 17) Malmö 1972, 585–587.
Holtsmark, Anne, 'Til Hávamál str. 52' (*MoM*) 1959, 1.
Holtsmark, Anne, 'To Eddasteder' (*Arv* 13) 1957, 21–30.
Holtsmark, Anne, 'Týr' (*KLNM* 19) Malmö 1975, 122–123.
Holtsmark, Anne, 'Ullr' (*KLNM* 19) Malmö 1975, 280–281.
Holtsmark, Anne, 'Den uløselige gåten' (*MoM*) 1964, 101–104.
Holtsmark, Anne, 'Útgarðr' (*KLNM* 19) Malmö 1975, 379–380.
Holtsmark, Anne, 'Vafþrúðnismál' (*KLNM* 19) Malmö 1975, 422–423.
Holtsmark, Anne, 'Váli' (*KLNM* 19) Malmö 1975, 465–466.
Holtsmark, Anne, 'Valkyrje' (*KLNM* 19) Malmö 1975, 468–469.

Holtsmark, Anne, 'Vanir' (*KLNM* 19) Malmö 1975, 493–494.
Holtsmark, Anne, 'Vár' (*KLNM* 19) Malmö 1975, 529–530.
Holtsmark, Anne, ' "Vefr Darraðar" ' (*MoM*) 1939, 74–96.
Holtsmark, Anne, 'Víðarr' (*KLNM* 19) Malmö 1975, 690–691.
Holtsmark, Anne, 'Vitazgjafi' (MoM) 1933, 111–133.
Holtsmark, Anne, 'Den yngre Edda' (*KLNM* 3) Malmö 1958, 475–480.
Hommel, Hildebrecht, 'Die Hauptgottheiten der Germanen bei Tacitus' (*ARW* 37) 1941/42, 144–173.
Hondius-Crone, Ada, *The temple of Nehalennia at Domburg*, Amsterdam 1955.
Horn, Heinz-Günter, 'Eine Weihung für Hercules Magusanus aus Bonn' (*Bonner Jahrbücher* 170) 1970, 233–251.
Huitman, Johannes A., 'Odin auf dem Holzweg, oder die Irrfahrt eines altgermanischen Zauberspruchs' (*Altgermanische Beiträge, J. v. Dam zum 80. Geburtstag*) Amsterdam 1977, 1–9.
Hunke, Waltraud, 'Odins Geburt' (*Edda, Skalden, Saga. Festschrift F. Genzmer*) Heidelberg 1952, 68–71.
Hunke, Waltraud, *Die Trojaburgen und ihre Bedeutung*, Diss. Kiel o.J.
Huth, Ott, 'Der Durchzug des Wilden Heeres' (*ARW* 32) 1935, 193–210.
Huth, Ott, 'Der Feuerkult der Germanen' (*ARW* 36) 1939, 108–133.
Huth, Ott, Vesta. *Untersuchungen zum indogermanischen Feuerkult*, Leipzig, Berlin 1943 (= Beihefte zum *ARW*. 2).
Hvidtfeldt, Arild, 'Mistilteinn og Balders Død' (*Arbøger f. nord. Oldkyndighed og Historie*) 1941, 169–175.
Hyenstrand, Åke, 'Gravformer och symboltecken under yngre bronsålder' (*Fornvännen* 63) 1968, 185–189.
Ihm, Max, 'Der Mütter- und Matronenkultus und seine Denkmäler' (*Bonner Jahrbücher* 83) 1887, 1–200.
Die Iupitersäulen in den germanischen Provinzen. Gerhard Bauchhenss, 'Die Iupitergigantensäulen in der römischen Provinz Germania superior'. Peter Noelke, 'Die Iupitersäulen und -pfeiler in der römischen Provinz Germania inferior', Köln, Bonn 1981 (= Beihefte der Bonner Jahrbücher. 41).
Jaekel, Hugo, 'Die Alaisiagen Bede und Fimmilene' (*ZfdPh* 22) 1890, 257–277.
Jaekel, Hugo, 'Ertha Hludana' (*ZfdPh* 23) 1891, 129–145.
Jaekel, Hugo, 'Die Hauptgötter der Istvaeen' (*ZfdPh* 24) 1892, 289–311.
Jakobsen, Alfred, 'Strofe 33 i Grímnismál' (ANF 80) 1965, 87–94
Jakobsen, Alfred, 'Til strofe 2^{5-6} i Vǫluspá' (MoM) 1963, 79–93.
Jankuhn, Herbert, *Archäologische Bemerkungen zu Tier- und Menschenopfern bei den Germanen in der Römischen Kaiserzeit*, Göttingen 1967.
Jankuhn, Herbert, *Archäologische Bemerkungen zur Glaubwürdigkeit des Tacitus in der Germania*, Göttingen 1966.
Jankuhn, Herbert (Hg.), *Vorgeschichtliche Heiligtümer und Opferplätze in Mittel- und Nordeuropa*, Göttingen 1970.
Jankuhn, Herbert, Hans Kuhn, 'Altar' (J. Hoops, *Reallexikon der germanischen Altertumskunde*, hg. v. H. Beck 1) Berlin, New York ^{2}1973, 200–202.
Jankuhn, Herbert, Heinrich Beck, 'Axtkult' (J. Hoops, *Reallexikon der germanischen Altertumskunde*, hg. v. H. Beck 1) Berlin, New York ^{2}1973, 562–568.
Jarausch, Konrad, 'Der Zauber in den Isländersagas' (*Zeitschrift für Volkskunde* 39) 1930, 237–268.
Jensen, Knud B., 'Til Gefjon-spørgsmaalet' (*DS*) 1919, 92–94.
Jente, Richard, *Die mythologischen Ausdrücke im altenglischen Wortschatz*, Heidelberg 1921 (= Anglistische Forschungen. 56).
Jóhannesson, Jón, *Íslendinga saga. A History of the Old Icelandic Commonwealth*, [Winnipeg] 1974.
Johansson, K. F., 'German. Alcis (germ. Dioskurer)' (*ANF* 35) 1919, 1–22.

Jones, Gwyn, *A History of the Vikings*, Oxford 1973.
Jónsson, Finnur, 'Brage skjald' (*APhSc* 5) 1930–31, 237–286.
Jónsson, Finnur, 'Gudenavne – dyrenavne' (*ANF* 35) 1919, 309–314.
Jónsson, Finnur, 'Hǫrgr' (*Festschrift K. Weinhold*) Straßburg 1896, 13–20.
Jónsson, Finnur, 'Mytiske forestillinger i de ældste skjaldekvad' (*ANF* 9) 1893, 1–22.
Jónsson, Finnur, 'Odin og Tor i Norge og på Island i det 9. og 10. århundret' (*ANF* 17) 1901, 219–247.
Jónsson, Finnur, 'Rígsþula' (*ANF* 33) 1917, 157–171.
Jónsson, Finnur, 'Þulur. Søkonge-og Jættenavneremserne' (*APhSc* 9) 1934, 289–308.
Jónsson, Finnur, 'Um galdra, seið, seiðmenn og vǫlur' (*Þrjár ritgǫrðir til einkaðar Páli Melsteð*) Copenhagen 1892, 5–28.
Jónsson, Finnur, 'Vingolf' (*ANF* 5) 1890, 280–284.
Jónsson, Finnur, 'Vǫluspá' (*Skírnir* 81) 1907, 326–341.
Jung, Erich, *Germanische Götter und Helden in christlicher Zeit*, Munich, Berlin [2]1939.
Jungner, Hugo, *Gudinnan Frigg och Als Härad*, Uppsala 1922.
Jungner, Hugo, 'Om Friggproblemet' (*NoB* 12) 1924, 1–36.
Kaalund, Kristian, *Bidrag til en historisk-topografisk beskrivelse af Island*, 1, Kjøbenhavn 1877.
Kabell, Aage, *Balder und die Mistel*, Helsinki 1965 (= FFC. 196).
Kabell, Aage, 'Baugi und der Ringeid' (*ANF* 90) 1975, 30–40.
Kabell, Aage, 'Der Fischfang Þórs' (*ANF* 91) 1976, 112–129.
Kabell, Aage, 'Harja' (*ZfdA* 102) 1973, 1–15.
Kabell, Aage, 'Nordendorf A.' (*PBB* West 92) 1970, 1–16.
Kahle, Bernhard, 'Der Ragnarökmythus' (*ARW* 8) 1905, 431–455 (9) 1906, 61–72.
Kahle, Bernhard, 'Zum Nerthuskult' (*ARW* 14) 1911, 310–313.
Karsten, T. E., 'Tīwaz' (*NoB* 2) 1914, 195–204.
Kaspers, Wilhelm, 'Germanische Götternamen' (*ZfdA* 83) 1951/52, 79–91.
Kauffmann, Friedrich, 'Altgermanische Religion' (*ARW* 8) 1905, 114–128 (11) 1908, 105–126 (20) 1920, 205–229 (27) 1929, 334–345 (31) 1934, 124–136.
Kauffmann, Friedrich, *Balder: Mythus und Sage nach ihren dichterischen und religiösen Elementen untersucht*, Straßburg 1902.
Kauffmann, Friedrich, *Deutsche Mythologie*, Stuttgart [2]1893.
Kauffmann, Friedrich, 'Der Matronenkultus in Germanien' (*Zeitschrift des Vereins für Volkskunde* 2) 1892, 24–46.
Kauffmann, Friedrich, 'Mercurius Cimbrianus' (*ZfdPh* 38) 1906, 289–297.
Kauffmann, Friedrich, 'Mythologische Zeugnisse aus römischen Inschriften.'
'I. Hercules Magusanus' (*PBB* 15) 1891, 553–562.
'II. Mars Thingsus et deae Alaisiagae' (*PBB* 16) 1892, 200–210.
'III. Dea Nehalennia' (*PBB* 16) 1892, 210–234.
'IV. Dea Hludana' (*PBB* 18) 1894, 134–157.
'V. Deus Requalivahanus' (*PBB* 18) 1894, 157–194.
'VI. Dea Garmangabis' (PBB 20) 1895, 195–207.
Kauffmann, Friedrich, 'Oðinn am Galgen' (*PBB* 15) 1891, 195–207.
Kauffmann, Friedrich, 'Über den Schicksalsglauben der Germanen' (*ZfdPh* 50) 1926, 361–408.
Kauffmann, Friedrich, 'Vingolf' (*ZfdA* 36) 1892, 32–41.
Kauffmann, Friedrich, 'Der zweite Merseburger Zauberspruch' (*PBB* 15) 1891, 207–210.
Keil, Joseph, 'Ein Spottgedicht auf die gefangene Seherin Veleda' (*Anzeiger der österreichischen Akademie der Wissenschaften* 84) 1947, 185.
Kiessling, Edith, *Zauberei in der germanischen Volksrechten*, Jena 1914.
Kiil, Vilhelm, 'Eilífr Goðrúnarson's Þórsdrápa' (*ANF* 71) 1956, 89–167.
Kiil, Vilhelm, 'Fra andvegissula til omnkall. Grunndrag i Torskulten' (*Norveg* 7) 1960, 183–246.
Kiil, Vilhelm, 'Gevjonmyten og Ragnarsdråpa' (*MoM*) 1965, 63–70.

Kiil, Vilhelm, 'Hliðskjálf og seiðhjallr' (*ANF* 75) 1960, 84–112.
Kiil, Vilhelm, 'The Norse prophetess and the ritually induced prostitution' (*Norveg* 9) 1962, 159–174.
Kiil, Vilhelm, 'Tjodolvs Haustlǫng' (*ANF* 74) 1959, 1–104.
Kirchner, Horst, 'Eine steinzeitliche "Nerthus"-Darstellung. Zur Innenverzierung der Steinkammer von Züschen' (*Studien aus Alteuropa. K. Tackelberg gewidmet.* Teil 1.) Köln, Graz 1964, 82–92.
Klare, Hans-Joachim, 'Die Toten in der altnordischen Literatur' (*APhSc* 8) 1933/34, 1–56.
Klein, Ernst, 'Der Ritus des Tötens bei den nordischen Völkern' (*ARW* 28) 1930, 166–182.
Klingenberg, Heinz, 'Alvíssmál. Das Lied vom überweisen Zwerg' (GRM N.F. 17) 1967, 113–142.
Klingenberg, Heinz, 'Die Drei-Götter-Fibel von Nordendorf bei Augsburg' (*ZfdA* 105) 1976, 167–188.
Klingenberg, Heinz, *Edda – Sammlung und Dichtung*, Basel, Stuttgart 1974.
Klingenberg, Heinz, 'Gylfaginning. Tres vidit unum adoravit' (*Germanic dialects*) Amsterdam, Philadelphia 1986, 627–693.
Klingenberg, Heinz, 'Hávamál' (*Festschrift für S. Gutenbrunner*) Heidelberg 1972, 117–144.
Klingenberg, Heinz, *Runenschrift – Schriftdenken – Runeninschriften*, Heidelberg 1973.
Klingenberg, Heinz, 'Types of Eddic mythological poetry' (*Edda. A Collection of Essays*) Winnipeg 1983, 134–164.
Klose, Olaf, *Handbuch der historischen Stätten. Dänemark*, Stuttgart 1982 (= KTA. 327).
Kluge, Friedrich, 'Die deutschen Namen der Wochentage' (*Wissenschaftliche Beihefte zur Zeitschrift des allgemeinen deutschen Sprachvereins.* 8) 1895, 89–98.
Kluge, Friedrich, *Etymologisches Wörterbuch der deutschen Sprache*, Berlin, New York [22]1989.
Kluge, Friedrich, 'Tuisco deus et filius Mannus' (*Zeitschrift für deutsche Wortforschung* 2) 1902, 43–45.
Knudsen, Regnar, 'Vi og Vis i Stednavne' (*Studier til. V. Dahlerup*) Aarhus, Copenhagen 1934, 196–204.
Kock, Axel, 'Besvärjelseformler i forndanska runinskrifter' (*ANF* 38) 1922, 1–21.
Kock, Axel, 'Etymologisch-mythologische Untersuchungen' (*IF* 10) 1899, 90–111.
Kock, Axel, 'Die Göttin Nerthus und der Gott Njǫrðr' (*ZfdPh* 28) 1896, 289–294.
Kock, Axel, 'Ordforskning i den äldre Eddan' (*ANF* 27) 1911, 107–140.
Kock, Axel, 'Studier i de nordiska språkens historia' (*ANF* 14) 1898, 213–270.
Köbler, Gerhard, 'Ewart. Ein Beitrag zur Lehre vom altgermanischen Priesteramt' (*Zeitschrift der Savigny Stiftung für Rechtsgeschichte* 89, Kanonist. Abteilung) 1972, 306–319.
Kögel, Rudolf, 'Idis und die Walküre' (*PBB* 16) 1892, 502–509.
Kölbing, Eugen, 'Zur Œgisdrekka' (*Germania* 21) 1876, 27–28.
Koepp, Friedrich, *Germania Romana IV. Die Weihedenkmäler*, Bamberg [2]1928.
Kohl, R., 'Die Augsburger Cisa – eine germanische Göttin?' (*ARW* 33) 1936, 21–40.
Koht, Halvdan, 'Var "finnane" alltid finnar?' (MoM) 1923, 161–175.
Kolbe, Hans-Georg, 'Neue Inschriften aus Bonn' (*Bonner Jahrbücher* 161) 1961, 85–107.
Kolbe, Hans-Georg, 'Die neuen Matroneninschriften von Morken Harff' (*Bonner Jahrbücher* 160) 50–124.
Konow, Sten, 'Njord und Kali' (*Festschrift till. A. Kjær*) Oslo 1924, 53–60.
Koppers, Wilhelm, 'Pferdeopfer und Pferdekult der Indogermanen' (*Wiener Beiträge zur Kulturgeschichte und Linguistik* 4), 279–412.
Kragerud, Alv, 'De mytologiske spørsmþl i Fåvnesmål' (*ANF* 96) 1981, 9–48.
Krahe, Hans, 'Altgermanische Kleinigkeiten. 4. Veleda.' (*IF* 66) 1961, 39–43.
Krahe, Hans, 'Tamfana' (*PBB* 58) 1934, 282–287.

Krahe, Hans, 'Zu einigen Namen westgermanischer Göttinnen' (*Beiträge zur Namenforschung* 13) 1962, 268–276.
Kralik, Dietrich von, 'Niblung, Schilbung und Balmung' (*Wiener Prähistorische Zeitschrift* 19) 1932, 324–348.
Krappe, Alexander Haggerty, 'Alces' (*PBB* 57) 1933, 226–230.
Krappe, Alexander Haggerty, 'Anses' (*PBB* 56) 1932, 1–10.
Krappe, Alexander Haggerty, 'Die Blendwerke der Æsir' (*ZfdPh* 62) 1937, 113–124.
Krappe, Alexander Haggerty, 'Les dieux jumaux dans la religion germanique' (*APhSc* 6) 1931, 136–145.
Krappe, Alexander Haggerty, 'Odin entre les feux (Grímnismál)' (*APhSc* 8) 1933–34, 136–145.
Krappe, Alexander Haggerty, 'The Valkyries' (MLR 21) 1926, 55–73.
Krappe, Alexander Haggerty, 'Yngvi-Freyr and Aengus mac Oc' (*SS* 18) 1942–43, 174–178.
Krause, Ernst, *Die Trojaburgen Nordeuropas*, Glogau 1893.
Krause, Wolfgang, *Beiträge zur Runenforschung*, Halle/S. 1932.
Krause, Wolfgang, 'Gullveig und Pandora' (*Skandinavistik* 5) 1975, 1–6.
Krause, Wolfgang, *Ing*, Göttingen 1944 (= Nachrichten der Gesellschaft der Wissenschaften zu Göttingen, Phil.-hist. Kl. N. F. 3 M).
Krause, Wolfgang, *Die Kenning als typische Stilfigur der germanischen und keltischen Dichtersprache*, Halle/S. 1930.
Krause, Wolfgang, *Die Runeninschriften im älteren Futhark*, Göttingen 1966.
Krause, Wolfgang, 'Vingþorr' (*ZfdA* 64) 1927, 269–276.
Krause, Wolfgang, *Was man in Runen ritzte*, Halle/S. ^{2}1943.
Krause, Wolfgang, 'Ziu' (*Nachrichten der Gesellschaft der Wissenschaften zu Göttingen*, Phil.-hist. Kl. N. F. 3/6) 1940, 155–172.
Kreutzer, Gerd, 'Berserker' (*Lexikon des Mittelalters* 1) Munich 1980, 2019–2020.
Kristensen, Marius, 'Skjaldenes Mytologi' (*APhSc* 5) 1930–31, 67–92.
Kroes, H. W. J., 'Die Balderüberlieferungen und der zweite Merseburger Zauberspruch' (*Neophilologus* 35) 1951, 201–213.
Kroes, H. W. J., 'Muspilli' (*GRM* 38) 1957, 393–394.
Kroesen, Riti, 'One Hadingus – two Haddingjar' (*SS* 59) 1987, 404–435.
Krogmann, Willy, 'Die Edda' (*ANF* 52) 1936, 243–249.
Krogmann, Willy, 'Eine neue Vermutung über as. mûdspelli' (*Niederdeutsches Jahrbuch* 84) 1961, 43–54.
Krogmann, Willy, *Die heilige Insel. Ein Beitrag zur altfriesischen Religionsgeschichte*, Assen 1942.
Krogmann, Willy, 'Hœnir' (*APhSc* 6) 1932, 311–327.
Krogmann, Willy, 'Loki' (*APhSc* 12) 1937–38, 59–70.
Krogmann, Willy, 'Mudspelli' (*WuS* 14) 1932, 68–85.
Krogmann, Willy, *Mudspelli auf Island. Eine religionsgeschichtliche Untersuchung*, Wismar 1933.
Krogmann, Willy, 'Muspilli und Muspellsheim' (*Zeitschrift für Religions-und Geistesgeschichte* 5) 1953, 97–118.
Krogmann, Willy, 'Neorxna wang und Iða vǫllr' (*Archiv* 191) 1954–55, 30–43.
Krohn, Kaarle, 'Das schiff Naglfar' (*Finnisch-ugrische Forschungen* 11) 1911, 154–155.
Krohn, Kaarle, *Skandinavisk Mytologi*, Helsingfors 1922.
Krohn, Kaarle, 'Tyrs hǫgr hand, Freys svärd' (*Festskrift til H. F. Feilberg*) Copenhagen 1911, 541–547.
Krohn, Kaarle, 'Zum schiffe Naglfar' (*Finnisch-ugrische Forschungen* 11) 1911, 317–320.
Krüger, Emil, 'Die gallischen und die germanischen Dioskuren' (*Trierer Zeitschrift* 15) 1940, 8–27 und (16/17) 1941–42, 1–66.
Krüger, Emil, 'Das Tierfries-Beschlagstück aus dem Moorfund von Thorsberg' (*Prähistorische Zeitschrift* 34/35, Teil 2) 1949–50, 112–124.

Kuhn, Adalbert, *Die Herabkunft des Feuers und des Göttertranks*, Gütersloh ²1886.
Kuhn, Adalbert, 'Zur Mythologie' (*ZfdA* 6) 1848, 117–134.
Kuhn, Hans, 'Alben' (J. Hoops, *Reallexikon der germanischen Altertumskunde*, hg. v. H. Beck 1) Berlin, New York ²1973, 130–132.
Kuhn, Hans, 'Asen' (J. Hoops, *Reallexikon der germanischen Altertumskunde*, hg. v. H. Beck 1) Berlin, New York ²1973, 457–458.
Kuhn, Hans, 'Es gibt kein balder "Herr" ' (*Erbe der Vergangenheit. Festschrift für K. Helm*) Tübingen 1951, 37–45.
Kuhn, Hans, 'Das Fortleben des germanischen Heidentums nach der Christianisierung' (*Settimane di Studio del centro Italiano di Studi sull'Alto Medioevo* 14) Spoleto 1967, 743–757.
Kuhn, Hans, 'Gaut' (*Festschrift für J. Trier*) Meisenheim 1954, 417–433.
Kuhn, Hans, 'Germanisches Sakralkönigtum?' (H. Kuhn, *Kleine Schriften* 4) Berlin, New York 1978, 242–247.
Kuhn, Hans, 'Kämpen und Berserker' (*FmSt* 2) 1968, 218–227.
Kuhn, Hans, 'Die negation des verbs in der altnordischen dichtung' (*PBB* 60) 1936, 431–444.
Kuhn, Hans, 'Das nordgermanische Heidentum in den ersten christlichen Jahrhunderten' (*ZfdA* 79) 1942, 133–166.
Kuhn, Hans, 'Die Religion der nordischen Völker in der Wikingerzeit' (*Settimane di Studio del centro Italiano di Studi sull'Alto Medioevo* 16) Spoleto 1969, 117–129, 161–163.
Kuhn, Hans, 'Rund um die Vǫluspá' (*Medievalia litteraria. Festschrift für H. de Boor*) Munich 1971, 1–14.
Kummer, Bernhard, *Midgards Untergang. Germanischer Kult und Glaube in den letzten heidnischen Jahrhunderten*, Zeven ²1972.
Kummer, Bernhard, 'Sverre und Magnus' (*Atti dell'VIII congresso internazionale di storia della religioni*) Firenze 1956, 368–371.
Kunze, Richard, *Die Germanen in der antiken Literatur*, Leipzig 1906–07.
Kvillerud, Reinert, 'Några anmärkningar till Þrymskviða' (*ANF* 80) 1956, 64–86.
Läffler, L. Fr., 'Det evigt grönskade trädet vid Uppsala hednatämpel' (*Festskrift til H. F. Feilberg*) Copenhagen 1911, 617–696.
DeLaet, Sigfrid J., 'Nehalennia, déesse germanique ou celtique?' (*Helinium* 11) 1971, 154–162.
La Farge, Beatrice, *"Leben" und "Seele" in den altgermanischen Sprachen*, Heidelberg 1991.
Lang, Andrew, 'Mythology and fairy tales' (*Fortnightly Review* N. S. 13) 1873, 618–631.
Lange, Johan, 'Løg-LaukaR. Studier over en ordgruppe i nordiske sprog' (*Sprog og Kultur* 23) 1963, 1–27.
Lecouteux, Claude, 'Zwerge und Verwandte' (*Euphorion* 75) 1981, 366–378.
Lee, Alvin A., 'Heorot and the "Guest-Hall" of Eden' (*Mediaeval Scandinavia* 2) 1969, 78–91.
Lehmann, K., 'Die Rígsþula' (*Festschrift für J. v. Amsberg*) Rostock 1904, 1–34.
Lehmann, Winfried P., '*Lín* and *laukr* in the Edda' (GR 30) 1955, 163–171.
Leitzmann, Albert, 'Ags. neorxnawong' (PBB 32) 1907, 60–66.
Leitzmann, Albert, 'Saxonica I. Das Taufgelöbnis und der Indiculus Superstitionum' (*PBB* 25) 1900, 567–591.
Leo, Heinrich, *Über Odins Verehrung in Deutschland*, Erlangen 1822.
Leyen, Friedrich v. d., 'Alte Zaubersprüche und Segen in der Münchener Staatsbibliothek' (*Bayerisches Jahrbuch für Volkskunde*) 1958, 103–104.
Leyen, Friedrich v. d., 'Die Entwicklung der Göttersagen in der Edda' (GRM 1) 1909, 284–291.
Leyen, Friedrich v. d., 'Der gefesselte Unhold. Eine mythologische Studie' (*Untersuchungen und Quellen zur germanischen und romanischen Philologie*, J. v. Kelle dargebracht. Teil 1) Prag 1908, 7–35.

Leyen, Friedrich v. d., 'Die germanische Runenreihe und ihre Namen' (*Zeitschrift für Volkskunde* 40) 1930, 170–182.
Leyen, Friedrich v. d., *Die Götter der Germanen*, Munich 1938.
Leyen, Friedrich v. d., 'Die Götter der Germanen' (*GR* 30) 1955, 5–13.
Leyen, Friedrich v. d., 'Mythus und Märchen' (*DVjS* 33) 1959, 343–360.
Leyen, Friedrich v. d., 'Utgardaloke in Irland' (*PBB* 33) 1908, 382–391.
Leyen, Friedrich v. d., 'Zur größeren Nordendorfer Spange' (*PBB* West 80) 1958, 208–213.
Libermann, Anatoly, 'Germanic *sendan* "to make a sacrifice" ' (*JEGPh* 77) 1978, 473–488.
Lid, Nils, 'Altnorw. Þorri' (*Norsk Tidsskrift for Sprogvidenskap* 7) 1934, 163–169.
Lid, Nils, 'Berserkr' (*KLNM* 1) Malmö 1956, 501–502.
Lid, Nils, 'Díar' (*KLNM* 3) Malmö 1958, 63–64.
Lid, Nils, 'Drikkeoffer' (*KLNM* 3) Malmö 1958, 322–323.
Lid, Nils, 'Scandinavian heathen cult-places' (*Folk-Liv* 21/22) 1957–58, 79–84.
Lid, Nils, 'Til varulvens historia' (*Saga och Sed*) 1937, 3–25.
Lidén, Evald, 'Om nagra ortnamn' (*ANF* 23) 1907, 259–269.
Lie, Hallvard, 'Naglfar og Naglfari' (MoM) 1954, 152–161.
Lie, Hallvard, 'Ragnarsdrápa' (*KLNM* 13) Malmö 1968, 647–649.
Lie, Hallvard, 'Þórsdrápa' (*KLNM* 20) Malmö 1976, 397–400.
Liestøl, Knut, 'Jøtarne og Joli' (*Festskrift til* H. F. *Feilberg*) Copenhagen 1911, 192–205.
Lincoln, Bruce, 'On the imagery of paradise' (*IF* 85) 1980, 151–164.
Lindow, John, 'Adressing Thor' (*SS* 60) 1988, 119–136.
Lindow, John, 'Mythology and Mythography' (*Old Norse-Icelandic Literature: A Critical Guide*) Ithaca, London 1985, 21–67 (= Islandica 45)
Lindow, John, *Scandinavian Mythology*, New York, London 1988.
Lindquist, Ivar, 'Eddornas bild av Ull – och guldhornens' (*NoB* 14) 1926, 82–103.
Lindquist, Ivar, *Die Urgestalt der Hávamál*, Lund 1956.
Lindquist, Sune, 'Gamla Uppsala kyrka' (*Fornvännen*) 1951, 219–250.
Lindquist, Sune, *Gotlands Bildsteine* 1, Stockholm 1941.
Lindquist, Sune, 'Hednatemplet i Uppsala' (*Fornvännen*) 1923, 85–118.
Lindquist, Sune, 'Snorres Uppgifter um hednatidens gravskick och gravar' (*Fornvännen* 15) 1920, 56–105.
Lindquist, Sune, 'Ynglingatidens gravskick' (*Fornvännen* 16) 1921, 83–194.
Lindroth, Hjalmar, 'Boðn, Són och Óðrœrir' (MoM) 1915, 174–177.
Lindroth, Hjalmar, 'En nordisk gudagestalt i ny belysning genom ortnamn' (*Antikvarisk tidsskrift for Sverige* 20) 1915, 1–76.
Lindroth, Hjalmar, 'Om gudanamnet Tor' (*NoB* 4) 1916, 161–169.
Lindroth, Hjalmar, 'Yggdrasils "Barr" och eviga grönska' (*ANF* 30) 1914, 218–226.
Littleton, C. Scott, 'The "kingship in heaven" theme' (*Myth and Law among the Indo-Europeans*) Berkely 1970, 83–121.
Littleton, C. Scott, *The new comparative mythology. An anthropological assessment of the theories of Georges Dumézil*, Berkely ^{2}1973.
Ljungberg, Helge, 'Das sakrale Königtum im Norden während der Missionszeit im 10. und 11. Jahrhundert' (*Atti dell'VIII congresso internazionale di storia della religioni*) Firenze 1956, 364–366.
Ljungberg, Helge, Tor. *Undersökningar i indoeuropeisk och nordisk religionshistoria*, Uppsala, Leipzig 1947.
Ljunggren, Karl Gustav, 'Eine Gruppe südskandinavischer Altertümer in philologischer Beleuchtung' (*Festschrift W. Baetke*) Weimar 1966, 261–270.
Ljunggren, Karl Gustav, 'Anteckningar till Skírnismál och Rígsþula' (*ANF* 53) 1937, 190–232.
Lönnroth, Lars, 'Dómaldi's death and the myth of sacral kingship' (*Structure and Meaning in Old Norse Literature*) Odense 1986, 73–93.

Lönnroth, Lars, 'Iǫrð fannz æva né upphiminn: A Formula Analysis' (*Speculum Norrœnum. Studies G. Turville-Petre*) Odense 1981, 310–327.
Lönnroth, Lars, 'Skírnismál och den fornisländska äktenskapsnormen' (*Opuscula Septentrionalia. Festskrift til O. Widding*) Copenhagen 1977, 154–178.
Loewenthal, John, 'Alcis' (*PBB* 51) 1927, 287–289.
Loewenthal, John, 'Altnord. Loki' (*IF* 39) 1921, 113–114.
Loewenthal, John, 'Cultgeschichtliche Fragen' (*PBB* 49) 1925, 63–88.
Loewenthal, John, 'Drei Götternamen. Yngvi, Phol, Loki' (*ANF* 31) 1915, 153–154.
Loewenthal, John, 'Fricco' (*PBB* 50) 1927, 287–296.
Loewenthal, John, 'Germanische Cultaltertümer' (*PBB* 47) 1922, 261–289.
Loewenthal, John, 'Religionswissenschaftliche Parerga' (*PBB* 45) 1921, 239–265.
Loewenthal, John, 'Wirtschaftsgeschichtliche Parerga' (*WuS* 9) 1926, 173–191.
Loewenthal, John, 'Zur germanischen Wortkunde' (*ANF* 32, 33, 35) 1916, 1917, 1919, 270–301, 97–131, 229–242.
Lorenz, Gottfried, *Snorri Sturluson, Gylfaginning. Texte, Übersetzung, Kommentar*. Darmstadt 1984 (= Texte zur Forschung, 48).
Losch, Friedrich, 'Mythologische Studien im Gebiet des Baldermythus' (*ARW* 3) 1900, 358–374.
Lütjens, August, *Der Zwerg in der deutschen Heldendichtung*, Breslau 1911 (= Germanistische Abhandlungen, 38).
Lukman, Niels, 'Gefion' (*KLNM* 5) Malmö 1960, 228–229.
Lund, Allan A., *Moselig*, Copenhagen 1976.
Lundgren, Michael, 'Vǫlospá' (*KLL* 7) Munich 1972, 764–766.
McCreesh, Bernardine, 'How pagan are the Icelandic family sagas?' (*JEGPh* 79) 1980, 58–66.
Mackensen, Lutz, 'Baumseele' (*Zeitschrift für Deutschkunde*) 1924, 1–21.
Magerøy, Hallvard, 'Þrymskviða' (*Edda* 58) 1958, 256–270.
Magerøy, Hallvard, 'Vǫluspá' (*KLNM* 20) Malmö 1976, 352–355
Magnusen, Finn, *Priscae veterum borealium mythologiae lexicon*, Havniae 1828.
Magnússon, Eiríkr, 'The derivation of "Edda" ' (*Academy* 49) 1896, No. 1235, 15–16.
Magnússon, Eiríkr, 'Edda' (*Academy* 48) 1895, No. 1230, 464–465.
Magnússon, Eiríkr, *Odin's Horse Yggdrasil*, London 1895.
Magnússon, Eiríkr, 'Yggdrasil' (*ANF* 13) 1897, 205.
Magoun, Francis Peabody, 'On some survivals of pagan belief in Anglo-Saxon' (*Harvard Theological Review* 40) 1947, 33–46.
Magoun, Francis Peabody, 'On the Old-Germanic altar- or oath-ring (*stallahringr*)' (*APhSc* 20) 1947–49, 277–293.
Mahr, Alexander, *Wodan auf südgermanischem Gebiet*, Diss. Vienna 1921.
Mahr, Alexander, 'Wodan in der deutschen Volksüberlieferung' (*Mitteilungen der anthropologischen Gesellschaft in Wien* 58) 1928, 143–167.
Mandl, Emilie, *Ueber den Seelen- und Jenseitsglauben der alten Skandinavier*, Diss. Vienna 1927.
Mannhardt, Wilhelm, *Germanische Mythen*, Berlin 1858.
Mannhardt, Wilhelm, *Die Götter der deutschen und nordischen Völker*, Berlin 1860.
Mannhardt, Wilhelm, *Die Korndämonen*, Berlin 1868.
Mannhardt, Wilhelm, *Wald- und Feldkulte*, 1–2, Berlin [2]1904.
Markey, Thomas L., 'Germanic *þ/laiþ- and funerary ritual' (*FmSt* 8) 1974, 179–194.
Markey, Thomas L., 'Germanic terms for temple and cult' (*Studies for E. Haugen*) The Hague, Paris 1972, 365–378.
Markey, Thomas L., 'Nordic Níðvísur: An Instance of Ritual Inversion?' (*Medieval Scandinavia* 5) 1972, 7–18.
Marold, Edith, *Kenningkunst*, Berlin, New York 1983.
Marold, Edith, *Der Schmied im germanischen Altertum*, Diss. Vienna 1967.
Marold, Edith, ' "Thor weihe diese Runen" ' (*FmSt* 8) 1975, 195–222.

Marold, Edith, 'Das Walhallabild in den Eiríksmál und den Hákonarmál' (*Medieval Scandinavia* 5) 1972, 19–33.
Marstrander, Carl J. S., 'Isis chez les Germains du Nord' (*Norsk tidsskrift for sprogvidenskap* 3) 1929, 236–238.
Marstrander, Carl J. S., 'De nordiska runeinnskrifter i eldre Alfabet' (*Viking* 16) 1953, 1–277.
Marstrander, Carl J. S., 'Tor i Irland' (MoM) 1915, 80–89.
Marstrander, Sverre, *Østfolds jordbruksristninger*: Skjeberg. 1–2, Oslo 1963.
Martin, John Stanley, 'Ár vas alda: Ancient Scandinavian Creation Myths Reconsidered' (*Speculum Norroenum. Studies* G. *Turville-Petre*) Odense 1981, 357–369.
Martin, John Stanley, 'Baldr's death and The Golden Bough' (*Iceland and the Mediaeval World*. Studies I. Maxwell) Melbourne 1974, 26–32.
Martin, John Stanley, 'The development of the figure of Baldr in Old Norse mythology' (*Australasian Universities Language and Literature Association*. Proceedings and Papers 14) 1972, 248–249.
Martin, John Stanley, *Ragnarök*, Assen 1972.
Martin, John Stanley, 'Some comments on the perception of heathen religious customs in the sagas' (*Parergon* 6) 1973, 45–50.
Maurer, Conrad, *Die Bekehrung des norwegischen Stammes zum Christenthume*, 1–2, Munich 1855–56.
Maurer, Conrad, 'Über die Wasserweihe des germanischen Heidenthumes' (*Abhandlungen der phil.-hist. KLasse der königl. bayer. Akademie der Wissenschaften* 15/3) 173–253.
Maurer, Conrad, 'Zur Urgeschichte der Godenwürde' (*ZfdPh* 4) 1873, 125–130.
Meaney, A. L., 'Woden in England: A reconsideration of the evidence' (*Folklore* 77) 1966, 105–115.
Meid, Wilhelm, 'Der germanische Personenname Veleda' (*IF* 69) 1964, 256–258.
Meissner, Rudolf, 'Ganga til fréttar' (*Zeitschrift für Volkskunde* 27) 1917, 1–13 und 97–105.
Meissner, Rudolf, *Die Kenningar der Skalden*, Bonn, Leipzig 1921.
Meissner, Rudolf, 'Rígr' (*PBB* 57) 1933, 109–130.
Meissner, Rudolf, 'Die Sprache der Götter, Riesen und Zwerge in den "Alvíssmál" ' (*ZfdA* 61) 1924, 128–140.
Menzel, Wolfgang, *Odin*, Stuttgart 1855.
Meringer, Rudolf, 'Indogermanische Pfahlgötzen (Alche, Dioskuren, Asen)' (*WuS* 9) 1926, 107–123.
Meringer, Rudolf, 'Der Name des Julfests' (*WuS* 5) 1913, 184–194.
Meringer, Rudolf, 'Wörter und Sachen III. Der verehrte Pflock' (*IF* 18) 1905–06, 277–282.
Meringer, Rudolf, 'Wörter und Sachen V. Die Pflock- und Säulenverehrung bei den Indogermanen' (*IF* 21) 1907, 296–306.
Merkel, R. F., 'Anfänge der Erforschung der germanischen Religion' (*ARW* 34) 1937, 18–41.
Meulengracht Sørensen, Preben, 'Thors's Fishing Expedition' (G. Steinsland: *Words and Objects; towards a Dialogue between Archaeology and History of Religion*) Oslo 1986, 257–278.
Meuli, Karl, 'Bettelumzüge im Totenkultus, Opferritual und Volksbrauch' (*Schweizerisches Archiv für Volkskunde* 28) 1928, 1–38.
Meyer, Elard Hugo, *Die Eddische Kosmogonie*, Freiburg 1891.
Meyer, Elard Hugo, *Germanische Mythologie*, Berlin 1891.
Meyer, Elard Hugo, 'Hercules Saxanus' (*PBB* 18) 1894, 106–133.
Meyer, Elard Hugo, *Völuspá. Eine Untersuchung*, Berlin 1889.
Meyer, Richard Moses, *Altgermanische Religionsgeschichte*, Leipzig 1910.
Meyer, Richard Moses, 'Beiträge zur altgermanischen Mythologie' (*ANF* 23) 1907, 245–255.
Meyer, Richard Moses, 'Ikonische Mythen' (*ZfdPh* 38) 1906, 166–177.

Meyer, Richard Moses, 'Mythologische Fragen' (*ARW* 9) 1906, 417–428, 10 (1907) 88–103.
Meyer, Richard Moses, 'Schwurgötter' (*ARW* 15) 1912, 435–450.
Meyer, Richard Moses, 'Snorri als Mythograph' (*ANF* 28) 1912, 109–121.
Meyer, Richard Moses, 'Der Urriese' (*ZfdA* 41) 1897, 180–187.
Meyer, Richard Moses, 'Ymi und die Weltschöpfung' (*ZfdA* 37) 1893, 1–8.
Mikkola, J. J., 'Zur Vanenmythe' (*Festskrift till. H. Pipping*) Helsingfors 1924, 376–378.
Mitchell, Stephen A., 'Fǫr Scírnis as mythological model: frið at kaupa' (*ANF* 98) 1983, 108–122.
Mitchell, Stephen A., 'The Whetstone as Symbol of Authority in Old English and Old Norse' (*SS* 57) 1985, 1–31.
Moberg, Lennart, 'The languages of *Alvíssmál*' (*Saga-Book* 18) 1973, 299–323.
Mogk, Eugen, 'Das angebliche Sifbild im Tempel zu Guðbrandsdalir' (*PBB* 14) 1889, 90–93.
Mogk, Eugen, 'Bragi' (*PBB* 14) 1889, 81–90.
Mogk, Eugen, 'Bragi als Gott und Dichter' (*PBB* 12) 1887, 383–392.
Mogk, Eugen, *Germanische Religionsgeschichte und Mythologie*, Leipzig [3]1927.
Mogk, Eugen, 'Ginnungagap' (*PBB* 8) 1882, 153–160.
Mogk, Eugen, *Lokis Anteil an Balders Tod*, Helsinki 1925 (= FFC. 57).
Mogk, Eugen, *Die Menschenopfer bei den Germanen*, Leipzig 1909.
Mogk, Eugen, 'Ein Nachwort zu den Menschenopfern bei den Germanen' (*ARW* 15) 1912, 422–434.
Mogk, Eugen, 'Nordgermanische Götterverehrung nach den Kultquellen' (*Germanica. [Festschrift] E. Sievers*) Halle/S. 1925, 258–272.
Mogk, Eugen, *Novellistische Darstellung mythologischer Stoffe Snorris und seiner Schule*, Helsinki 1923 (= FFC. 51).
Mogk, Eugen, 'Die Überlieferung von Thors Kampf mit dem Riesen Geirrǫd' (*Festschrift till. H. Pipping*) Helsingfors 1924, 379–388.
Mogk, Eugen, 'Untersuchungen über die Gylfaginning' (*PBB* 6) 1879, 477–537 (7) 1880, 203–334.
Mogk, Eugen, 'Veleda' (Hoops, *Reallexikon der germanischen Altertumskunde* 4) Straßburg 1918–19, 389.
Mogk, Eugen, *Zur Bewertung der Snorra Edda als religionsgeschichtliche und mythologische Quelle des nordgermanischen Heidentums*, Leipzig 1923.
Mogk, Eugen, *Zur Gigantomachie der Vǫluspa*, Helsinki 1925 (= FFC. 58).
Mohr, Wolfgang, 'Mephistopheles und Loki' (*DVjS* 18) 1940, 173–200.
Mohr, Wolfgang, Walter Haug, *Zweimal "Muspilli"*, Tübingen 1977.
Moltke, Erik, 'The origins of the runes' (*Michigan Germanic Studies* 7) 1981, 3–7.
Mosher, Arthur D., 'The story of Baldr's death: the inadequacy of myth in the light of Christian faith' (*SS* 55) 1983, 305–315.
Motz, Lotte, 'The Conquest of Death: the Myth of Baldr and its Middle Eastern Counterparts' (*Collegium Medievale* 4) 1991, 99–116.
Motz, Lotte, 'The Families of Giants' (*ANF* 102) 1987, 216–236.
Motz, Lotte, 'Gerðr' (*MoM*) 1981, 121–136.
Motz, Lotte, 'Giantesses and their names' (*FmSt* 15) 1981, 495–511.
Motz, Lotte, 'Giants in Folklore and Mythology: A New Approach' (*Folklore* 93) 1982, 70–84.
Motz, Lotte, 'Gods and Demons of the Wilderness. A Study in Norse Tradition' (*ANF* 99) 1984, 175–187.
Motz, Lotte, 'The king and the goddess, An interpretation of Svipdagsmál' (*ANF* 90) 1975, 133–150.
Motz, Lotte, 'New thoughts on dwarf-names in Old Icelandic' (*FmSt* 7) 1973, 100–115.
Motz, Lotte, 'On elves and dwarfs' (*Arv* 29/30) 1973–74, 93–127.

Motz, Lotte, 'Sister in the cave: the stature and the function of the female figures of the Eddas' (*ANF* 95) 1980, 168–182.

Motz, Lotte, 'Snorri's Story of the Cheated Mason and its Folklore Parallels' (MoM 1977) 115–122.

Motz, Lotte, 'The Winter Goddesses: Percht, Holda, and Related Figures' (*Folklore* 95) 1984, 151–166.

Much, Rudolf, 'Aurvandils tá' (*Festschrift H. Seger*) Breslau 1934, 387–388 (= Altschlesien. 5).

Much, Rudolf, 'Balder' (*ZfdA* 61) 1924, 93–124.

Much, Rudolf, 'Baudihillia und Friagabis' (*Festschrift M. H. Jellinek*), Vienna, Leipzig 1928, 75–85.

Much, Rudolf, 'Dea Harimella' (*ZfdA* 36) 1892, 44–47.

Much, Rudolf, 'Eddica' (*ZfdA* 37) 1893, 417–419.

Much, Rudolf, 'Die Eruler' (*Deutsch-Nordische Zeitschrift*. Festnummer) 1929, 43–57.

Much, Rudolf, *Die Germania des Tacitus*, Heidelberg [3]1967.

Much, Rudolf, 'Germanische Dative aus der Römerzeit' (*ZfdA* 31) 1887, 354–358.

Much, Rudolf, 'Der germanische Himmelsgott' (*Festgabe für R. Heinzel* 1) Halle/S. 1898, 189–278.

Much, Rudolf, 'Harimalla – Harimella' (*ZfdA* 63) 1926, 19–22.

Much, Rudolf, 'Heruler' (Hoops, *Reallexikon der germanischen Altertumskunde* 2) Straßburg 1915, 517–519.

Much, Rudolf, 'Mercurius Hanno' (*ZfdA* 35) 1891, 207–208.

Much, Rudolf, 'Der Namensatz der Germania' (*Anzeiger der österreichischen Akademie der Wissenschaft* 27) 1928, 275–297.

Much, Rudolf, 'Nehalennia' (*ZfdA* 35) 1891, 324–327.

Much, Rudolf, 'Der nordische Widdergott' (*Deutsche Islandforschung 1930*) 1, Breslau 1930, 63–67.

Much, Rudolf, 'Requalivahanus' (*ZfdA* 35) 1891, 374–376.

Much, Rudolf, 'Der Sagenstoff der Grimnismal' (*ZfdA* 46) 1902, 309–329.

Much, Rudolf, 'Ulls Schiff' (*PBB* 20) 1895, 35.

Much, Rudolf, 'Undensakre – Untersberg' (*ZfdA* 47) 1904, 67–72.

Much, Rudolf, 'Unfachlas' (*ZfdA* 35) 1891, 204–376.

Much, Rudolf, 'Vagdavercustis' (*ZfdA* 55) 1917, 284–296.

Much, Rudolf, 'Wandalische Götter' (*Mitteilungen der schlesischen Gesellschaft für Volkskunde* 27) 1926, 20–41.

Much, Rudolf, 'Zauberzeichen auf germanischen Eisenwaffen' (*Wiener Prähistorische Zeitschrift* 7/8) 1920–21, 78–81.

Much, Rudolf, 'Zur Rígsþula' (*Prager deutsche Studien* 8) 1908, 225–239.

Müllenhoff, Karl, 'Die alte Dichtung von den Nibelungen' (*ZfdA* 23) 1879, 113–173.

Müllenhoff, Karl, *Deutsche Altertumskunde* 1–5, Berlin 1870–1908.

Müllenhoff, Karl, 'Frija und der Halsbandmythos' (*ZfdA* 30) 1886, 217–260.

Müllenhoff, Karl, 'Irmin und seine Brüder' (*ZfdA* 23) 1879, 1–22.

Müllenhoff, Karl, 'Sceáf und seine Nachkommen' (*ZfdA* 7) 1849, 410–419.

Müllenhoff, Karl, 'Tanfana' (*ZfdA* 23) 1879, 23–25.

Müllenhoff, Karl, *Über die Vǫluspá*, Berlin 1883.

Müllenhoff, Karl, 'Um Ragnaröckr' (*ZfdA* 16) 1873, 146–148.

Müller, Max, *Essays 1–4*, Leipzig 1869–1876.

Müller, Gunther, 'Altnordisch Vífill – ein Weihename' (*Festschrift für O. Höfler* 2) Vienna 1968, 363–371.

Müller, Gunther, 'Zum Namen Wolfhetan und seinen Verwandten' (*FmSt* 1) 1967, 200–212.

Müller, Gunther, 'Zur Heilkraft der Walküre' (FmSt 10) 1976, 350–361.

Müller, Sophus, *Nordische Altertumskunde*, 1–2, Straßburg 1897–98.

Müller, Werner, *Die Jupitergigantensäulen und ihre Verwandten*, Meisenheim 1975 (= Beiträge zur klassischen Philologie, 66).
Müller, Wilhelm, 'Gefjon' (*ZfdA* 1) 1841, 95–96.
Müller-Wille, Michael, 'Bestattung im Boot' (*Offa* 25/26) 1970, 7–203.
Müller-Wille, Michael, 'Boat-graves in Northern Europe' (*The International Journal of Nautical Archaeology and Underwater Exploration*) 1974, 187–204.
Munch, P. A., *Norrøne gude- og heltesagn*, Oslo 1967.
Mundal, Else, *Fylgjemotiva i norrøn litteratur*, Oslo 1974.
Murray, Margaret A., 'The divine king in England' (*Atti dell'VIII congresso internazionale di storia della religioni*) Firenze 1956, 378–380.
Naert, Pierre, 'Grímnismál 33' (*ANF* 81) 1966, 117–119.
Naumann, Hans, *Germanischer Schicksalsglaube*, Jena 1934.
Naumann, Hans, 'Die Götter Germaniens' (*DVjS* 8) 1930, 13–32.
Naumann, Hans, 'Neue Beiträge zum altgermanischen Dioskurenglauben' (*Bonner Jahrbücher* 150) 1950, 91–101.
Naumann, Hans, *Versuch über Snorri Sturluson*, Bonn 1943.
Naumann, Hans-Peter, 'Viktor Rydbergs "Undersökningar i germansk Mythologi" ' (*Studien zur dänischen und schwedischen Literatur des 19. Jahrhunderts*) Basel, Stuttgart 1976, 185–205 (= Beiträge zur Nordischen Philologie, 4).
Nebel, Gerhard, *Die Not der Götter. Welt und Mythos der Germanen*, Hamburg 1957.
Neckel, Gustav, 'Aisl. Edda "Urgroßmutter" ' (*ZfdA* 49) 1908, 314–320.
Neckel, Gustav, *Die altgermanische Religion*, Berlin 1932.
Neckel, Gustav, 'Die Götter auf dem goldenen Horn' (*ZfdA* 58) 1921, 225–233.
Neckel, Gustav, 'Irmin' (*Festschrift T. Siebs*) Breslau 1933, 1–9 (= Germanistische Abhandlungen, 67).
Neckel, Gustav, *Die Überlieferungen vom Gotte Balder*, Dortmund 1920.
Neckel, Gustav, *Walhall*, Dortmund 1931.
Negelein, Julius von, *Germanische Mythologie*, Leipzig ^{3}1919.
Nerman, Birger, 'De äldsta Eddadikterna' (*ANF* 86) 1971, 19–37.
Nerman, Birger, 'Baldersagans äldsta form' (Edda 3) 1915, 1–10.
Nerman, Birger, 'Fimbultýs fornar rúnar' (*ANF* 85) 1970, 206–207.
Nerman, Birger, 'Det heliga tretalet och Vǫluspá' (*ANF* 74) 1959, 264–267.
Nerman, Birger, 'Rígsþula 16:8 *dvergar á ǫxlom*, arkeologiskt belyst' (*ANF* 69) 1954, 210–213.
Nerman, Birger, 'Rígsþulas ålder' (*ANF* 84) 1969, 15–18.
Nerman, Birger, 'Två unga eddadikter. Arkeologisk belysning av Þrymskviða och Atlamál' (*ANF* 78) 1963, 126–133.
Nerman, Birger, 'Vǫluspá 61:3 gullnar tǫflor' (*ANF* 78) 1963, 122–125.
Nesheim, Asbjörn, 'Omkring harpen i Volospå' (*By og Bygd* 29) 1967, 1–10.
Neumann, Eduard, *Das Schicksal in der Edda 1*, Gießen 1955 (= Beiträge zur deutschen Philologie, 7).
Neumann, Eduard, Helmut Voigt, 'Germanische Mythologie' (*Wörterbuch der Mythologie* 2) Stuttgart 1963, 21–98.
Neumann, G., 'Germani cisrhenani – die Aussage der Namen' (*Germanenprobleme in heutiger Sicht*) Berlin, New York 1986, 105–129 (= Ergänzungsbände zu J. Hoops, *Reallexikon der germanischen Altertumskunde*, hg. v. H. Beck. 1).
Niedner, Felix, 'Baldrs Tod' (*ZfdA* 41) 1897. 305–334.
Niedner, Felix, 'Bemerkungen zu den Eddaliedern 3. Lokasenna' (*ZfdA* 36) 1892, 286–290.
Niedner, Felix, 'Die Dioskuren im Beowulf' (*ZfdA* 42) 1898, 229–258.
Niedner, Felix, 'Eddische Fragen' (*ZfdA* 41) 1897, 33–64.
Niedner, Felix, 'Der Mythus des zweiten Merseburger Zauberspruchs' (*ZfdA* 43) 1899, 101–112.
Niedner, Felix, 'Ragnarǫk in der Vǫluspá' (*ZfdA* 49) 1908, 239–298.

Niedner, Felix, 'Skírnis Fǫr' (*ZfdA* 30) 1886, 132–150.
Nielsen, Niels Åge, 'Freyr, Ullr, and the Sparlösa Stone' (*Medieval Scandinavia* 2) 1969, 102–128.
Nielsen, Niels Åge, 'Myten om krigen og fredsslutningen mellem aserne og vanerne' (*Nordiska Studier i filologi og lingvistik. Festskrift* G. *Holm*) Lund 1976, 310–315.
Nilsson, Martin P., 'At which time of the year was the pre-Christian Yule celebrated?' (*Arv* 14) 1958, 109–114.
Nilsson, Martin P., 'Studien zur Vorgeschichte des Weihnachtsfestes' (*ARW* 19) 1916–19, 50–150.
Nilsson, Martin P., 'Zur Deutung der Juppitergigantensäulen' (*ARW* 23) 1925, 175–184.
Ninck, Martin, *Die Bedeutung des Wassers im Kult und Leben der Alten*, Leipzig 1921 (Philologus. Suppl. 14. H. 2).
Ninck, Martin, *Wodan und der germanische Schicksalsglaube*, Jena 1935.
Nissen, Carl, 'Der "Norden" auf dem Theater' (*Märchen, Mythos, Dichtung. Festschrift f. F. v. d. Leyen*) Munich 1963, 423–446.
Nollau, Hermann (Hg.), *Germanische Wiedererstehung*, Heidelberg 1926.
Norberg, Rune, 'Uppsala tempel' (*KLNM* 19) Malmö 1975, 334–336.
Nordal, Sigurður, 'The Author of Vǫluspá' (*Saga-Book* 20) 1978–79, 114–130.
Nordal, Sigurður, 'Billings mær' (*Bidrag till nordisk filologi till. E. Olson*) Lund 1936.
Nordal, Sigurður, 'Three Essays on Vǫluspá' (*Saga-Book* 18) 1971, 79–135.
Nordal, Sigurður, *Vǫluspá*, Darmstadt 1980 (= Texte zur Forschung, 33).
Norden, Eduard, *Die germanische Urgeschichte in Tacitus Germania*, Leipzig, Berlin [3]1923.
Nordenstreng, Rolf, 'Guden Vali' (*Festskrift till. H. Pipping*) Helsingfors 1924, 392–394.
Nordenstreng, Rolf, 'Namnet Yggdrasill' (*Festskrift till. A. Kock*) Lund 1929, 194–199.
Nordland, Odd, 'Offer' (*KLNM* 12) Malmö 1967, 514–524.
Nordland, Odd, 'Stalli' (*KLNM* 17) 1972, 38–41.
Noreen, Adolf, 'Mytiska beståndsdelar i Ynglingatal' (*Uppsalastudier til. S. Bugge*) Uppsala 1892, 194–225.
Noreen, Adolf, 'Urkon Audhumla och några hennes språkliga släktningar' (*NoB* 6) 1918, 169–172.
Noreen, Adolf, 'Yngve, Inge, Inglinge m.m.' (*NoB* 8) 1920, 1–8.
Noreen, Evald, 'Ett hedniskt kultcentrum i värmland' (*NoB* 8) 1920, 17–31.
Noreen, Evald, 'Ordet bärsärk' (*ANF* 58) 1932, 242–254.
Northcott, Kenneth, 'An interpretation of the second Merseburg Charm' (*MLR* 54) 1959, 45–50.
Nutt, Alfred, 'The fairy mythology of English literature: its origin and nature' (*Folk-Lore* 8) 1897, 29–53.
Nylén, Erik, *Bildstenar*, Visby 1978.
Ohlmarks, Åke, 'Arktischer Schamanismus und altnordischer seiðr' (*ARW* 36) 1939, 171–180.
Ohlmarks, Åke, *Gravskeppet*, Stockholm 1946.
Ohlmarks, Åke, *Gudatro i nordisk forntid*, Stockholm 1970.
Ohlmarks, Åke, *Heimdalls Horn und Odins Auge*, Lund 1937.
Ohlmarks, Åke, 'Isländska hov och gudahus' (*Bidrag till Nordisk Filologi*, till. E. Olsen) Lund 1936, 339–355.
Ohlmarks, Åke, 'Totenerweckungen in Eddaliedern' (*ANF* 52) 1936, 264–297.
Ohrt, Ferdinand, 'Eddica og magica' (*APhSc* 52) 1934–35, 161–176.
Ohrt, Ferdinand, 'Gondols ondu' (*APhSc* 10) 1935, 199–207.
Ohrt, Ferdinand, 'Hammerens lyde – Jærnets last' (*Festskrift til F. Jónsson*) Copenhagen 1928, 294–298.
Ohrt, Ferdinand, 'Odin paa træet' (*APhSc* 4) 1930, 273–286.
Ohrt, Ferdinand, 'Sunnr at Urðarbrunni' (*APhSc* 12) 1937–38, 91–101.
Ólafsson, Ólafur M., 'Vǫluspá Konungsbókar' (*Landsbókasafn Íslands*. Arbók 22) 1965, 86–124.

Olrik, Axel, 'En Oldtidshelligdom' (*DS*) 1911, 1–14.
Olrik, Axel, 'Gefion' (*DS*) 1910, 1–31.
Olrik, Axel, 'Irminsul og gudestøtter' (*MoM*) 1–10.
Olrik, Axel, 'Loke i nyere folkeoverlevering' (*DS*) 1908, 193–207, 1909, 69–84.
Olrik, Axel, 'Myterne om Loke' (*Festskrift til H.F. Feilberg*) Copenhagen 1911, 548–593.
Olrik, Axel, *Nordisches Geistesleben*, Heidelberg 1908.
Olrik, Axel, 'Odins Ridt' (*DS*) 1925, 1–18.
Olrik, Axel, *Ragnarǫk*, Berlin 1923.
Olrik, Axel, 'The sign of the dead' (*Finnisch-ugrische Forschungen*) 1912, 40–44.
Olrik, Axel, 'Skjaldenmjøden' (*Edda* 24) 1926, 236–241.
Olrik, Axel, 'Tordenguden og hans dreng' (*DS*) 1905, 129–146.
Olrik, Axel, 'Yggdrasill' (*DS*) 1917, 49–62.
Olrik, Axel, Hans Ellekilde, *Nordens Gudeverden*, 2 vols, Copenhagen 1926–1951.
Olrik, Jörgen, Axel Olrik, 'Asgård' (*DS*) 1914, 1–8.
Olsen, Björn M., 'Um nokkra staði i Svipdagsmálum' (*ANF* 33) 1917, 1–21.
Olsen, Emil, 'Neue Beiträge zur altnordischen Religionsgeschichte' (*ARW* 31) 1934, 213–271.
Olsen, Magnus, *Aettegård og Helligdom*, Kristiania 1926.
Olsen, Magnus, *Farms and Fanes of ancient Norway*, Oslo 1928.
Olsen, Magnus, 'Fra Eddaforskningen. "Grímnismál" og den höiere tekstkritik' (*ANF* 49) 1933, 263–278.
Olsen, Magnus, 'Fra gammelnorsk mythe og kultus' (*MoM* 1) 1909, 17–36.
Olsen, Magnus, *Det gamle norske Ønavn Njarðarlög*, Christiania 1905 (= Skrifter utg. av det Norske vidensk. Ak. i Christiania, Hist.-Filos. Kl. 1905.5.)
Olsen, Magnus, *Hærnavi. En gammel svensk og norsk gudine*, Christiania 1908 (= Forhandl. utg. a. d. Norske vidensk. Selsk. i Christiania. 1908.6.)
Olsen, Magnus, *Hedenske Kultminder i norske stedsnavne* 1, Kristiania 1915 (= Skrifter utg. av det Norske vidensk. Selsk. i Kristiania, Hist.-Filos. Kl. 1914.4.)
Olsen, Magnus, 'Hjadningekampen og Hallfreds Arvedrapa over Olav Tryggvason' (*Heidersskrift til* M. *Hægstad*) Oslo 1925, 23–33.
Olsen, Magnus, 'Möjebrostenen' (*ANF* 33) 1917, 276–283.
Olsen, Magnus, *Norges innskrifter med de yngre runer*, Oslo 1941.
Olsen, Magnus, 'Om Balder-digtning og Balder-kultus' (*ANF* 40) 1924, 148–175.
Olsen, Magnus, 'Le prêtre-magicien et le dieu-magicien dans la Norvége ancienne' (Revue de l'histoire des religiones 111) 1935, 177–221, and (112) 1935, 5–49.
Olsen, Magnus, *Stedsnavne og Gudeminner i Land*, Oslo 1929 (= Skrifter utg. av Norske vidensk. Ak. i Oslo, Hist.-Filos. Kl. 1929.3.)
Olsen, Magnus, 'þundarbenda' (*MoM*) 1934, 92–97.
Olsen, Magnus, 'Valhall med de mange dører' (*APhSc* 6) 1931–32, 151–170.
Olsen, Magnus, 'Varðlokur' (*MoM*) 1916, 1–21.
Olsen, Magnus, 'Yddal (Ydlar) i Strandvik' (*MoM*) 1931, 131–133.
Olsen, Olaf, *Høg, Hov og Kirke*, Copenhagen 1966
Olsen, Olaf, 'The "sanctuary" in Jelling' (*Mediaeval Scandinavia* 7) 1974, 226–234.
Olsen, Olaf, 'Vorchristliche Heiligtümer in Nordeuropa' (H. Jankuhn, *Vorgeschichtliche Heiligtümer und Opferplätze in Mittel- und Nordeuropa*) Göttingen 1970, 259–278.
Olsen, Olaf, Harry Ståhl, 'Vi' (*KLNM* 19) Malmö 1975, 684–689.
Orluf, F., 'Gefionmythen hos Brage den Gamle' (*DS*) 1923, 22–30.
Palm, Thede, 'Der Kult der Naharvalen' (*ARW* 36) 1939, 398–405.
Palm, Thede, *Trädkult. Studier i germansk religionshistoria*, Lund 1948.
Palm, Thede, 'Uppsalalunden och Uppsalatemplet' (*Vetenskaps-societeten i Lunds Årsbok*) 1941, 79–109.
Palmér, Johan, 'Baldersbrå' (*ANF* 34) 1918, 138–147.
Pálsson, Hermann, 'Áss hin almáttki' (*Skírnir* 130) 1956, 187–192.
Panzer, Friedrich, *Hilde-Gudrun*, Halle a.S. 1901.

Pappenheim, Max, 'Zum ganga undir jarðarmen' (*ZfdPh* 24) 1892, 157–161.
Pering, Birger, *Heimdall*, Lund 1941.
Persson, Axel W., 'Åkerbruksriter och hällristningar' (*Fornvännen* 25) 1930, 1–24.
Peters, R.A., 'OE. Aelf, -Aelf, Aelfen, -Aelfen' (*Philological Quarterly* 42) 1963, 250–257.
Peuckert, Will Erich, 'Germanische Eschatologien' (*ARW* 32) 1935, 1–37.
Pfannenschmid, Heino, *Das Weihwasser im heidnischen und christlichen Cultus*, Hannover 1869.
Pfister, Friedrich, 'Die Religion und der Glaube der germanischen Völker und ihrer religiösen Führer' (*ARW* 33) 1936, 1–14.
Philippson, Ernst Alfred, 'Die agrarische Religion der Germanen nach den Ergebnissen der der Nordischen Ortsnamenforschung' (*PMLA* 51) 1936, 313–327.
Philippson, Ernst Alfred, *Die Genealogie der Götter in germanischer Religion, Mythologie und Theologie*, Urbana, Ill. 1953.
Philippson, Ernst Alfred, 'Der germanische Mütter- und Matronenkult am Niederrhein' (*GR* 19) 1944, 81–142.
Philippson, Ernst Alfred, *Germanisches Heidentum bei den Angelsachsen*, Leipzig 1929.
Philippson, Ernst Alfred, 'Neuere Forschung auf dem Gebiet der germanischen Mythologie' (*GR* 11) 1935, 4–19.
Philippson, Ernst Alfred, 'Neues über den Mütter- und Matronenkult am Nierrhein' (*MLN* 65) 1950, 462–465.
Philippson, Ernst Alfred, 'Phänomenologie, vergleichende Mythologie und germanische Religionsgeschichte' (*PMLA* 77) 1962, 187–193.
Philippson, Ernst Alfred, 'Phol, Pholesleah und Poling' (*Archiv* 150) 1926, 228–231.
Philippson, Ernst Alfred, 'Die Volkskunde als Hilfswissenschaft der germanischen Religionsgeschichte' (*GR* 13) 1938, 237–251.
Phillpotts, Berta S., *The Elder Edda and Ancient Scandinavien Drama*, Cambridge 1920.
Phillpotts, Berta S., 'Surt' (*ANF* 21) 1905, 14–30.
Phillpotts, Berta S., 'Temple-administration and chieftainship in pre-christian Norway and Iceland' (*Saga-Book* 8) 1913–14, 264–284.
Picard, Eve, *Germanisches Sakralkönigtum?*, Heidelberg 1991.
Piepers, Wilhelm, 'Neue Matronensteine aus Morken-Harff, Ldkr. Bergheim (Erft)' (*Germania* 37) 1959, 298.
Piggot, Stuart, *Ancient Europe from the beginnings of agriculture to Classical Antiquity*, Edinburgh 1965.
Pipping, Rolf, *Odin i Galgen*, Helsingfors 1928 (= Studier i nordisk Filologi. 18.2.)
Pipping, Rolf, 'Om Gullveig-stroferna i Vǫluspá' (*Festskrift til F. Jónsson*) Copenhagen 1928, 225–228.
Pittioni, Richard, *Urzeit von etwa 80000 bis 15 v. Ch. Geb.*, Vienna 1980 (= Geschichte Österreichs 1).
Polomé, Edgar, 'Á propos de la déesse Nerthus' (*Latomus* 13) 1954, 167–200.
Polomé, Edgar, 'L'étymologie du terme germanique *ansuz "dieu souverain" ' (*Études Germaniques* 8) 1953, 36–44.
Polomé, Edgar, 'The Indo-European component in Germanic Religion' (*Myth and Law among the Indo-Europeans*) London 1970, 55–82.
Polomé, Edgar, 'Notes sur le vocabulaire religieux du germanique I. Runique alu' (*Nouvelle Clio* 6) 1954, 40–55.
Polomé, Edgar, 'Old Norse Religious Terminology in Indo-European Perspective' (*The Nordic Languages and Modern Linguistics* 2) Stockholm 1975, 654–665.
Polomé, Edgar, 'Quelques notes á propos de l'énigmatique dieu scandinave Loðurr' (*Revue Belge de Phil.* 33) 1955, 493–494.
Polomé, Edgar, 'Some aspects of the cult of the mother goddess in Western Europe' (*Vistas and Vectors. Festschrift H. Rehder*) Austin 1980, 493–494.
Polomé, Edgar, 'Some Comments on Vǫluspá, Stanzas 17–18' (*Old Norse Literature and Mythology*) Austin 1969, 265–290.

Porter, Mary Gray, *A Dictionary of the Personal Names in the Eddic Poems (Elder Edda and Eddica minora)*, Diss. Chapel Hill 1960.
Prosdocimi, Aldo Luigi, Piergiuseppe Scardigli, 'Negau' (*Italia linguistica nuova et antica 1, Miscellanea in onore di O. Parlangi*) Galantina 1976, 178–229.
Puhvel, Martin, 'The Deicidal Otherworld Weapon in Celtic and Germanic Mythic Tradition' (*Folklore* 83) 1972, 210–219.
Ralph, Bo, 'The Composition of the Grímnismál' (*ANF* 87) 1972, 97–118.
Ranke, Kurt, 'Ahnenglaube und Ahnenkult' (J. Hoops, *Reallexikon der germanischen Altertumskunde* 1) Straßburg 1911–13, 112–114.
Redlich, Clara, 'Zur Trinkhornsitte der Germanen der älteren Kaiserzeit' (*Prähistorische Zeitschrift* 52) 1977, 61–120.
Reichardt, Konstantin, ' "Hymiskviða". Interpretation, Wortschatz, Alter' (*PBB* 57) 1937, 130–156.
Reichardt, Konstantin, 'Odin am Galgen' (*Festschrift H. F. Weigand*) New Haven 1957, 15–28.
Reichardt, Konstantin, 'Die Thórsdrápa des Eilífr Guðrunarson: Textinterpretation' (*PMLA* 63) 1948, 329–391.
Reichborn-Kjennerud, I., 'Eddatidens medisin' (*ANF* 40) 1924, 104–148.
Reichborn-Kjennerud, I., 'Den gamle dvergetro' (*Festschrift E. A. Kock*) Lund 1934, 278–288.
Reichborn-Kjennerud, I., 'Mimameiðs aldin' (*Studier i Nordisk Filologi* 17) 1926, Heft 2, 1–3.
Reichborn-Kjennerud, I., 'Den norske Dvergetradition' (*Norsk Folkekultur* 20) 1934, 85–141.
Reichborn-Kjennerud, I., *Vår gamle Trolldomsmedisin*, Oslo 1927–1940 (= Skrifter utg. av. Norske videnskaps Ak. i Oslo, Hist.-Filos. Kl. 1927.6, 1933.2, 1940.1).
Reichert, Hermann, *Lexikon der altgermanischen Namen*, Vienna 1987–90 (= Thesaurus Palaeogermanicus. 1, 1–2).
Reichert, Hermann, 'Zum Sigrdrífa-Brünhild-Problem' (*Antiquitates Indogermanicae. Gedenkschrift f. H. Güntert*) Innsbruck 1974, 251–265.
Reinbold, Ernst Th., *Die Nacht im Mythos, Kultus, Volksglauben und in der transpersonalen Erfahrung*, Köln 1970.
Reitzenstein, Richard, 'Die nordischen, persischen und christlichen Vorstellungen zum Weltuntergang' (*Vorträge der Bibliothek Marburg* 26) 1923–34, 149–169.
Reitzenstein, Richard, 'Weltuntergangsvorstellungen' (*Kyrkohistorisk Årsskrift* 24) 1924, 129–212.
Renauld-Krantz, P., 'Odin' (*Les Vikings et leur civilisation*) Paris 1976, 191–208.
Renauld-Krantz, P., *Structures de la mythologie nordique*, Paris 1972.
Reuschel, Helga, *Untersuchungen über Stoff und Stil der Fornaldarsaga*, Bühl 1933.
Rieger, Gerd Enno, 'Þrk. 20 *við scolom aca tvau*' (*skandinavistik* 5) 1975, 7–10.
Rieger, Max, 'Über den altnordischen Fylgjenglauben' (*ZfdA* 42) 1898, 277–290.
Riese, Alexander, 'Zur Geschichte des Götterkults im rheinischen Germanien' (*Westdeutsche Zeitung* 17) 1898, 1–40.
Riviere, Jean Claude, *Georges Dumézil à la découverte des Indo-Européens*, Paris 1979.
Rooth, Anna Birgitta, 'Loke' (*KLNM* 10) Malmö 1965, 680–684.
Rooth, Anna Birgitta, *Loki in Skandinavian Mythology*, Lund 1961.
Rosén, Helge, 'Freykult och djurkult' (*Fornvännen* 8) 1913, 213–244.
Rosén, Helge, *Om dödsrike och dödsbruk i fornnordisk religion*, Lund 1918.
Rosén, Helge, 'Phallosguden i Norden' (*Antikvarisk Tidsskrift för Sverige* 20/2) 1920, 1–24.
Rosenberg, G., 'Et Gudebillede fra Broncealderen' (*DS*) 1929, 1–9.
Rosenfeld, Hellmut, 'Alemannischer Ziu-Kult und SS. Ulrich- und Afra-Verehrung in Augsburg' (*Archiv für Kulturgeschichte* 37) 1955, 306–355.
Rosenfeld, Hellmut, 'Die germanischen Runen im kleinen Schulerloch und auf der Nordendorfer Bügelfibel A.' (*ZfdA* 113) 1984, 159–173.

Rosenfeld, Hellmut, 'Germanischer Zwillingsgottkult und indogermanischer Himmelsgottglaube' (*Märchen. Festschrift f. F. v. d. Leyen*) Munich 1963, 269–286.
Rosenfeld, Hellmut, 'Name und Kult der Istvionen (Istwäonen), zugleich Beitrag zu Wodankult und Germanenfrage' (*ZfdA* 90) 1960–61, 161–181.
Rosenfeld, Hellmut, 'Nordische Schilddichtung und mittelalterliche Wappendichtung' (*ZfdPh* 61) 1936, 232–269.
Rosenfeld, Hellmut, 'Die vandalischen Alkes "Elchreiter", der ostgermanische Hirschkult und die Dioskuren' (*GRM* 28) 1940, 245–258.
Ross, Margaret Clunies, 'The myth of Gefjon and Gylfi and its function in Snorra Edda and Heimskringla' (*ANF* 93) 1978, 149–165.
Rostvik, Allen, *Har och Harg*, Uppsala 1967.
Rudolph, O. E., *Die Göttergestalt der Frigg in ihrem historischen Entwicklungsgang*, Leipzig 1875.
Rückert, Hans, *Die Christianisierung der Germanen*, Tübingen 1932.
Rupp, Theophil, 'Fiölsvinnsmâl' (*Germania* 10) 1965, 433–446.
Ryan, J. S., 'Germanic Mythologie Applied – The Extension of the Literary Folk Memory' (*Folklore* 77) 1966, 45–59.
Ryan, J. S., 'Othin in England. Evidence from the Poetry for a Cult of Woden in Anglo-Saxon England' (*Folklore* 74) 1963, 460–480.
Rydberg, Viktor, *Undersökningar i Germanisk Mythologie*, 2 vols, Stockholm 1886–1889.
Sahlgren, Jöran, 'Lunden Barre i Skírnismál' (*NoB* 50) 1962, 193–203 and 233.
Sahlgren, Jöran, 'Sagan om Frö och Gärd' (*NoB* 16) 1928, 1–19.
Sahlgren, Jöran, 'Skírnismál' (J. Sahlgren, *Eddica et Scaldica* 2) Lund 1928, 209–243.
Salberger, Evert, 'Ett stafrimsproblem i Vafþrúðnismál 34' (MoM) 1955, 113–120.
Salberger, Evert, 'Heill Þú farir! Ett textproblem i Vafþrúðnismál 4' (*Scripta Islandica* 25) 1974, 23–30.
Salberger, Evert, 'Rístu nú, Skírnir! Ett textställe i Skírnismál 1' (*ANF* 72) 1957, 173–192.
Salus, Peter H., 'More "Eastern Echoes" in the Edda? An Addendum' (*MLN* 79) 1964, 426–428.
Salus, Peter H., Paul B. Taylor, 'Eikinskjaldi, Fjalarr, and Eggþér. Notes on Dwarves and Giants in the Vǫluspá' (*Neophilologus* 53) 1969, 76–81.
Sandklef, Albert, 'De Germanska Dödsstraffen, Tacitus och Mossliken' (*Fornvännen* 39) 1944, 27–44.
Sarrazin, G., 'Der Balder-Kultus in Lethra' (*Anglia* 19) 1897, 392–397.
Sarrazin. G., 'Die Hirsch-Halle' (*Anglia* 19) 1897, 368–392.
Sauvé, James L., 'The Divine Victim: Aspects of Human Sacrifice in Viking Scandinavia and Vedic India' (*Myth and Law among the Indo-Europeans*) London 1970, 173–191.
Schade, Oskar, 'Über Jünglingsweihen' (*Weimararisches Jahrbuch* 4/2) 1857, 241–416.
Schahl, A., 'Freyr-Fro-Phôl' (*ARW* 35) 1938, 174–178.
Scheltema, F. Adam von, 'Um eine deutsche Runeninschrift' (*Mannus* 24) 1932, 211–215.
Scher, S. P., 'Rígsþula as poetry' (*MLN* 78) 1963, 397–407.
Scherer, Wilhelm, 'Mars Thingsus' (*Sitzungsber. d. kl. preuß. Ak. d. Wiss. zu Berlin* 1) 1884, 571–582.
Schier, Kurt, 'Alvísmál' (*KLL* 1) Munich 1967, 506–507.
Schier, Kurt, 'Balder' (J. Hoops, *Reallexikon der germanischen Altertumskunde*, hg. v. H. Beck 2) Berlin, New York [2]1976, 2–7.
Schier, Kurt, Balder, Loki, *Heimdall. Untersuchungen zur germanischen Religion. Teil 1: Balder und die sterbenden Gottheiten des Orients*, Habil. Munich 1969.
Schier, Kurt, 'Balder-Lieder' (*KLL* 1) Munich 1967, 1278–1279.
Schier, Kurt, 'Baldrs draumar' (*KLL* 1) Munich 1967, 1282–1283.
Schier, Kurt, 'Edda' (*KLL* 2) Munich 1967, 1814–1828.

Schier, Kurt, 'Edda, Ältere' (J. Hoops, *Reallexikon der germanischen Altertumskunde*, hg. v. H. Beck 6) ²1986, 355–394.
Schier, Kurt, 'Die Erdschöpfung aus dem Urmeer und die Kosmogonie der Vǫluspá' (*Märchen. Festschrift f. F. v. d. Leyen*) Munich 1963, 303–334.
Schier, Kurt, 'Freys und Fróðis Bestattungen' (*Festschrift f. O. Höfler* 2) Vienna 1968, 389–409.
Schier, Kurt, 'Die Literaturen des Nordens' (*Neues Handbuch der Literaturwissenschaft* 7) Wiesbaden 1981, 535–574.
Schier, Kurt, 'Zur Mythologie der Snorra Edda: Einige Quellenprobleme' (*Speculum Norroenum. Studies* G. *Turville-Petre*) Odense 1981, 405–420.
Schirokauer, Arno, 'Der 2. Merseburger Zauberspruch' (A. *Schirokauer, Germanistische Studien*) Hamburg 1957, 169–197.
Schjødt, Peter, 'Om Loke endnu engang' (*ANF* 96) 1981, 49–86.
Schlerath, B., 'Zu den Merseburger Zaubersprüchen' (*Zweite Fachtagung für indogerm. und allgem. Sprachwissenschaft*) Innsbruck 1962, 139–143.
Schlund, Erhard, *Neugermanisches Heidentum im heutigen Deutschland*, Munich ²1924, reprint 1977.
Schmidt, Kurt Dietrich, *Die Bekehrung der Germanen zum Christentum*, vol. 1, Göttingen 1939.
Schneider, Hermann, 'Beiträge zur Geschichte der nordischen Götterdichtung' (*PBB* 69) 1947, 301–350.
Schneider, Hermann, 'Die Geschichte vom Riesen Hrungnir' (*Edda. Skalden. Saga, Festschrift für F. Genzmer*) Heidelberg 1952, 200–210.
Schneider, Hermann, *Die Götter der Germanen*, Tübingen 1938.
Schneider, Hermann, 'Muspilli' (H. Schneider, *Kl. Schriften*) Berlin 1962, 165–194.
Schneider, Hermann, 'Der Mythus von Thor' (*Archiv* 143) 1922, 165–176, and (144) 1922, 1–30.
Schneider, Hermann, 'Über die ältesten Götterlieder der Nordgermanen' (*PBB* 67) 1947, 301–350.
Schneider, Karl, 'Runische Inschriftzeugnisse zum Stieropfer-Kult der Angelsachsen' (*Festschrift f. E. Mertner*) Munich 1969, 9–54.
Schnippel, E., 'Der Grottasong und die Handmühle' (*ZfdA* 61) 1924, 41–48.
Schönfeld, Markus, *Wörterbuch der altgermanischen Personen- und Völkernamen*, Heidelberg ²1965.
Schomerus, Rudolf, *Die Religion der Nordgermanen im Spiegel christlicher Darstellung*, Diss. Göttingen 1936.
Schoning, O., *Dødsriger i nordisk hedentro*, Copenhagen 1903.
Schopper, Karl, *Die Irminsul. Forschungen über ihren Standort*, Paderborn 1947.
Schreiner, K., *Die Sage von Hengest und Horsa*, Berlin 1921.
Schreuer, Hans, 'Altgermanisches Sakralrecht 1' (*Zeitschrift der Savignystiftung für Rechtsgeschichte*, German. Adt. 34) 1913, 313–404.
Schreuer, Hans, 'Das Recht der Toten' (*Zeitschrift für vergleichende Rechtswissenschaft* 33) 1916, 333–423, und (34) 1917, 1–208.
Schröder, Edward, 'Balder in Deutschland' (*NoB* 10) 1922, 13–19.
Schröder, Edward, 'Dea Harimella' (*ZfdA* 61) 1924, 59–60.
Schröder, Edward, 'Irminsûl' (*ZfdA* 72) 1935, 292.
Schröder, Edward, 'Walburg und Sibylle' (*ARW* 19) 1916–19, 196–200.
Schröder, Franz Rolf, *Altgermanische Kulturprobleme*, Berlin, Leipzig 1929.
Schröder, Franz Rolf, 'Ase und Gott' (*PBB* 51) 1927, 29–30.
Schröder, Franz Rolf, 'Balder und der zweite Merseburger Spruch' (*GRM* 34) 1953, 161–183.
Schröder, Franz Rolf, 'Balder-Probleme' (*PBB* West 84) 1962, 319–357.
Schröder, Franz Rolf, 'Die eddischen "Balders Träume" ' (*GRM* N. F. 14) 1964, 329–337.
Schröder, Franz Rolf, 'Erce und Fjǫrgyn' (*Festschrift f. K. Helm*) Tübingen 1951, 15–36.

Schröder, Franz Rolf, *Die Germanen*, Tübingen 1929.
Schröder, Franz Rolf, *Germanentum und Hellenismus*, Heidelberg 1924.
Schröder, Franz Rolf, 'Germanische Schöpfungsmythen' (*GRM* 19) 1931, 1–26 und 81–99.
Schröder, Franz Rolf, 'Germanische Urmythen' (*ARW* 35) 1939, 201–236.
Schröder, Franz Rolf, 'Die Göttin des Urmeeres und ihr männlicher Partner' (*PBB* West 82) 1960, 221–264.
Schröder, Franz Rolf, 'Grimnismál' (*PBB* West 80) 1958, 341–378.
Schröder, Franz Rolf, 'Heimdall' (*PBB* West 89) 1967, 1–41.
Schröder, Franz Rolf, 'Helgi und Heimdall?' (*GRM* N. F. 19) 1969, 454–456.
Schröder, Franz Rolf, 'Hœnir' (*PBB* 43) 1918, 219–252.
Schröder, Franz Rolf, 'Das Hymirlied. Zur Frage verblaßter Mythen in den Götterliedern der Edda' (*ANF* 70) 1955, 1–40.
Schröder, Franz Rolf, 'Indra, Thor und Herakles' (*ZfdPh* 76) 1957, 1–41.
Schröder, Franz Rolf, 'Ingunar-Freyr', Tübingen 1941.
Schröder, Franz Rolf, 'Mythos und Heldensage' (*Zur Germanisch-deutschen Heldensage*) Bad Homburg 1961, 285–315 (= Wege der Forschung, 14.)
Schröder, Franz Rolf, 'Neuere Forschungen zur germanischen Altertumskunde und Religionsgeschichte' (*GRM* 17) 1929, 177–192, und 241–255, und 401–420.
Schröder, Franz Rolf, 'Njǫrds nackte Füße' (*PBB* 51) 1927, 31–32.
Schröder, Franz Rolf, 'Odins Verbannung' (GRM N. F. 17) 1967, 1–12.
Schröder, Franz Rolf, *Quellenbuch zur germanischen Religionsgeschichte*, Berlin, Leipzig 1933.
Schröder, Franz Rolf, 'Der Riese Vǫrnir' (*PBB* West 84) 1962, 1–4.
Schröder, Franz Rolf, *Skadi und die Götter Skandinaviens*, Tübingen 1941.
Schröder, Franz Rolf, 'Svipdagsmál' (GRM N. F. 16) 1966, 132–119.
Schröder, Franz Rolf, 'Das Symposion der Lokasenna' (*ANF* 67) 1972, 1–29.
Schröder, Franz Rolf, 'Thor im Vimurfluß' (*PBB* 51) 1927, 33–34.
Schröder, Franz Rolf, 'Thor und der Wetzstein' (*PBB* West 87) 1965, 3–42.
Schröder, Franz Rolf, 'Thors Hammerholung' (*PBB* West 87) 1965, 3–42.
Schröder, Franz Rolf, 'Ursprung und Ende der germanischen Heldendichtung' (GRM 27) 1939, 325–367.
Schroeder, Leopold von, *Arische Religion*, 2 vols, Leipzig 1914–16.
Schück, Henrik, 'Ingunar-Freyr' (*Fornvännen* 35) 1940, 289–296.
Schück, Henrik, 'Odin, Vili och Vé' (*Fornvännen* 36) 1941, 22–29.
Schütte, Gudmund, 'The Cult of Nerthus' (*Saga-Book* 8) 1913–14, 29–43.
Schütte, Gudmund, 'Dänisches Heidentum', Heidelberg 1923.
Schütte, Gudmund, 'Eponyme Götter und Heroen' (*ZfdA* 69) 1932, 129–136.
Schütte, Gudmund, *Gotthiod, Die Welt der Germanen*, Jena 1939.
Schütte, Gudmund, *Gotthiod und Utgard. Altgermanische Sagengeographie in neuer Auffassung*, 2 vols, Copenhagen, Jena 1935–1936.
Schütte, Gudmund, 'Die Schöpfungssage in Deutschland und im Norden' (*IF* 17) 1905, 444–457.
Schullerus, A., 'Zur Kritik des altnordischen Valhollglaubens' (*PBB* 12) 1887, 221–282.
Schultz, Bruno, *Beiträge zu den Jenseitsvorstellungen der Germanen*, Diss. Vienna 1924.
Schultz, Wolfgang, 'Die Felsritzung von Hvitlycke und das Edda-Lied von Thrym' (*Mannus* 21) 1929, 52–71.
Schultz, Wolfgang, 'Grundsätzliches über Religion und Mythos der Arier' (*Mannus* 16) 1924, 193–225.
Schultz, Wolfgang, 'Thors Bergung' (*Mannus* 6, Erg.-Heft. Festgabe G. Kossina) Leipzig 1928, 316–323.
Schultz, Wolfgang, 'Zeitrechnung und Weltordnung bei den Germanen' (*Mannus* 16) 1924, 119–126.

Schulz, Walter, 'Archäologisches zur Wodan- und Wanenverehrung' (*Wiener Prähistorische Zeitschrift* 19) 1932, 160–172.
Schulz, Walter, *Staat und Gesellschaft in germanischer Vorzeit*, Leipzig 1926.
Schulz-Halle, Walther, *Kartographische Darstellungen zur altgermanischen Religionsgeschichte*, Halle/S. 1926.
Schulze, W., 'Alaferhviae' (*ZfdA* 54) 1913, 172–174.
Schwab, Ute, 'The Inscription of the Nordendorf Brooch I: A Double Reading Line III?' (*Michigan Germanic Studies* 7) 1981, 38–49.
Schwartz, Wilhelm, *Der heutige Volksglaube und das alte Heidentum*, Berlin 1849.
Schwartz, Wilhelm, *Der Ursprung der Mythologie dargelegt an griechischer und deutscher Sage*, Berlin 1860.
Schwarz, Ernst, 'Die Herkunft der Juthungen' (*Jahrbuch für fränk. Landesforschung* 14) 1954, 1–8.
Schwarz, Werner, 'Germanische "Dioskuren"?' (*Bonner Jahrbücher* 167) 1967, 1–10.
Schwietering, J., 'Wodans Speer' (*ZfdA* 60) 1923, 290–292.
Scovazzi, Marco, 'Nerthus e la völva' (*Einarsbók. Afmæliskveðja E. Ól. Sveinssson*) Reykjavík 1970, 309–323.
See, Klaus von, 'Das Alter der RígsÞula' (*APhSc* 24) 1957, 1–12.
See, Klaus von, *Altnordische Rechtswörter*, Tübingen 1964 (= Hermea. N. F. 16.)
See, Klaus von, 'Berserker' (*Zeitschrift f. deutsche Wortforschung* N. F. 2) 1961, 129–135.
See, Klaus von, *Deutsche Germanen-Ideologie. Vom Humanismus bis zur Gegenwart*, Frankfurt/M 1970.
See, Klaus von, 'Disticha Catonis und Hávamál' (*PBB* West 94) 1972, 1–18.
See, Klaus von, 'Review of: E. Hoffmann, "Die heiligen Könige" ' (*Skandinavistik* 8) 1978, 72–75.
See, Klaus von, 'Der Germane als Barbar' (*Jahrbuch für internationale Germanistik* 13) 1981, 42–72.
See, Klaus von, *Die Gestalt der Hávamál*, Frankfurt/M. 1972.
See, Klaus von, 'Götter und Mythen der Germanen' (*AfdA* 79) 1968, 1–5.
See, Klaus von, 'Common sense and Hávamál' (*Skandinavistik* 17) 1987, 135–147.
See, Klaus von, *Kontinuitätstheorie und Sakraltheorie in der Germanenforschung*, Frankfurt/M. 1972.
See, Klaus von, *Mythos und Theologie im skandinavischen Hochmittelalter*, Heidelberg 1988.
See, Klaus von, 'Probleme der altnordischen Spruchdichtung' (*ZfdA* 104) 1975, 91–118.
See, Klaus von, 'Rígsþula Str. 47 und 48' (*PBB* West 82) 1960, 318–320.
See, Klaus von, 'Sonatorrek und Hávamál' (*ZfdA* 99) 1970, 26–33.
See, Klaus von, 'Das Walkürenlied' (*PBB* West 81) 1959, 1–15.
Seggewiss, Hermann-Josef, *Goði und hǫfðingi. Die literarische Darstellung und Funktion von Gode und Häuptling in den Isländersagas*, Frankfurt, Bern, Las Vegas 1978.
Siebourg, Max, 'Der Matronenkult beim Bonner Münster' (*Bonner Jahrbücher* 138) 1933, 103–123.
Siebourg, Max, 'Matronen-Terrakotta aus Bonn' (*Bonner Jahrbücher* 105) 1900, 78–102.
Siebourg, Max, 'Zum Matronenkultus' (*Westdeutsche Zeitschrift* 7) 1888, 99–116.
Siebs, Theodor, 'Beiträge zur deutschen Mythologie' (*ZfdPH* 24) 1892, 145–157 and 433–461.
Siebs, Theodor, 'Der Gott Fos(e)te und sein Land' (*PBB* 35) 1909, 535–553.
Siebs, Theodor, 'Neues zur germanischen Mythologie' (*Mitteilungen der schlesischen Gesellsch. f. Volkskunde* 25) 1924, 1–17.
Sieg, G., 'Zu den Merseburger Zaubersprüchen' (*PBB* Ost 82) 1960, 364–370.
Sievers, Eduard, 'Grammatische Miscellen' (*PBB* 18) 1894, 582–584.
Sievers, Eduard, 'Sonargǫltr' (*PBB* 16) 1892, 540–544.
Sievers, Eduard, 'Zur Lokasenna' (*PBB* 18) 1894, 208.
Simek, Rudolf, *Altnordische Kosmographie. Studien und Quellen zu Weltbild und Weltbe-*

schreibung in Norwegen und Island vom 12. bis zum 14. Jahrhundert, Berlin, New York 1990 (= Ergänzungsbände zum Reallexikon der Germanischen Altertumskunde, 4).
Simek, Rudolf, *Die Schiffsnamen, Schiffsbezeichnungen und Schiffskenningar im Altnordischen*, Vienna 1982 (= Wiener Arbeiten zur germanistischen Altertumskunde und Philologie, 14).
Simek, Rudolf, 'skíðblaðnir. Some Ideas on Ritual Connections between Sun and Ship' (*Northern Studies* 9) 1977, 31–39.
Simek, Rudolf, *Die Wasserweihe der heidnischen Germanen*, Thesis, Vienna 1979.
Simon, John, 'Snorri Sturluson: His Life and Times' (*Parergon* 15) 1976, 3–15.
Simpson, Jacqueline, 'Mímir, Two Myths or One?' (*Saga-Book* 16) 1962, 41–53.
Simpson, Jacqueline, 'Otherworld adventures in an Icelandic Saga' (*Folklore* 77) 1966, 1–20.
Simpson, Jacqueline, 'Some Scandinavian Sacrifices' (*Folklore* 78) 1967, 190–202.
Simrock, Karl, *Handbuch der deutschen Mythologie*, Bonn [3]1869.
Singer, Samuel, 'Die Religion der Germanen' (*Schweizerisches Archiv für Volkskunde* 43) 1946, 327–342.
Slawik, Alexander, 'Kultische Geheimbünde der Japaner und Germanen' (*Wiener Beiträge zur Kulturgeschichte und Linguistik* 4) 1926, 675–763.
Sluyter, P. C. M., *Ijslands Volksgeloof*, Haarlem 1936.
Söderberg, Barbro, 'Lokasenna – egenheter och ålder' (*ANF* 102) 1987, 18–99.
Solheim, Svale, 'Landvætte' (*KLNM* 10) Malmö 1965, 300–302.
Sommerfelt, Alf, 'Har syden og vesten vært uten betydning for nordisk hedenskap?' (*MoM*) 1962, 90–96.
Spamer, A., 'P(h)ol ende Uodan. Zum zweiten Merseburger Spruch' (*Deutsches Jahrbuch für Volkskunde* 3) 1957, 347–365.
Sperber, Hans, 'Embla' (*PBB* 34) 1910, 219–222.
Sperber, Hans, 'Der Name Loki und die Wortfamilie von germ. *lukan' (*Saga och Sed*) 1962, 48–63.
Sperber, Hans, 'Två mytologiska namn: "Hǫrn och Mǫrn" ' (*Svio-Estonica* 14) 1958, 231–237.
Ståhl, Harry, 'Vi' (*KLNM* 19) Malmö 1975, 685–689.
Steblin-Kamenskij, M. I., 'Myte og medvit' (*Syn og segn* 84) 1978, 468–481.
Steblin-Kamenskij, M. I., *Myth. The Icelandic Sagas and Eddas*, Ann Arbor 1982.
Steblin-Kamenskij, M. I., 'On the Etymology of the Word Skáld' (*Afmælisrit Jóns Helgasonar*) Reykjavík 1969, 421–430.
Steblin-Kamenskij, M. I., 'Valkyries and Heroes' (*ANF* 97) 1982, 81–93.
Steenstrup, Johannes C. H. R., 'Nogle Undersøgelser om Guders Navne i de nordiske Stedsnavne' (*Historisk Tidskrift* 6. R. 6) 1895, 353–388.
Steffensen, J., 'Lækningagyðjan Eir' (*Skírnir* 134) 1960, 34–46.
Steinhauser, Walter, 'Kultische Stammesnamen in Ostgermanien' (*Die Sprache* 2) 1950, 1–22.
Steinhauser, Walter, 'Die Wodansweihe von Nordendorf bei Augsburg (Runenspange A)' (*ZfdA* 97) 1968, 1–29.
Steinsland, Gro, 'Antropogonimyten i Vǫluspá' (*ANF* 98) 1983, 80–107.
Steinsland, Gro, *Det hellig bryllup og norrøn kongeideologi*, Oslo 1991.
Steinsland, Gro, 'Giants as Recipients of Cult in the Viking Age?' (G. Steinsland, *Words and Objects; towards a Dialogue between Archaeology and History of Religion*) Oslo 1986, 212–222.
Steinsland, Gro, 'Treet i Vǫluspá' (*ANF* 94) 1979, 120–150.
Steinsland, Gro, Kari Vogt, ' "Aukin ertu Uolse ok vpp vm tekinn". En religionshistorisk analyse av *Vǫlsaþáttr* i *Flateyjarbók*' (*ANF* 96) 1981, 87–106.
Steller, Walter, 'Phol ende Wodan' (*Zeitschrift für Volkskunde* 40) 1930, 61–71.
Stjerna, Knut, 'Mossfynden och Valhallstron' (*Från Filologiska Föreningen i Lund. Språkliga uppsater till. A. Kock*) 1906, 137–161.

Stjernfelt, Frederik, *Baldr og verdensdramaet*, Copenhagen 1990.
Stjernquist, Berta, 'Germanische Quellenopfer' (H. Jankuhn, *Vorgeschichtliche Heiligtümer und Opferplätze in Mittel- und Nordeuropa*) Göttingen 1970, 78–99.
Stjernquist, Berta, 'New light and Spring-Cults in Scandinavian Prehistory' (*Archeology* 17) 1964, 180–184.
Stokes, Whitley, 'A few Parallels between the Old-Norse and the Irish Literatures and Traditions' (*ANF* 2) 1885, 339–341.
Storm, Gustav, 'Ginnungagap i Mythologien og i Geografien' (*ANF* 6) 1890, 340–350.
Storm, Gustav, 'Om Thorgerd Hölgebrud' (*ANF* 2) 1885, 124–135.
Straubergs, Karlis, 'Zur Jenseitstopographie' (*Arv* 13) 1957, 56–110.
Ström, Åke V., 'Änkebegravning' (*KLNM* 20) Malmö 1976, 544–546.
Ström, Åke V., 'Die Hauptriten des wikingerzeitlichen nordischen Opfers' (*Festschrift W. Baetke*) Weimar 1966, 330–342.
Ström, Åke V., 'Das indogermanische Erbe in den Urzeit- und Endzeitschilderungen des Eddaliedes Vǫluspá' (*10. Kongreß für Religionsgeschichte*) Marburg 1961, 83–84.
Ström, Åke V., 'Indogermanisches in der Vǫluspá' (*Numen* 14) 1967, 167–208.
Ström, Åke V., 'The King-God and his Connection with Sacrifice in Old Norse Religion' (*Sacral Kingship*) Leiden 1959, 702–715.
Ström, Åke V., 'Scandinavian Belief in Fate' (*Fatalistic Beliefs*) Stockholm 1967, 63–88.
Ström, Åke V., Haralds Biezais, *Germanische und baltische Religion*, Stuttgart 1975 (= Die Religionen der Menschheit, 19).
Ström, Folke, 'År och fred' (*KLNM* 20) Malmö 1976, 450–452.
Ström, Folke, 'Bog Corpses and *Germania*, Ch. 12' (G. Steinsland, *Words and Objects; towards a Dialogue between Archaeology and History of Religion*) Oslo 1986, 223–239.
Ström, Folke, 'Diser' (*KLNM* 3) 1958, 101–103.
Ström, Folke, *Diser, nornor, valkyrjor. Fruktbarhetskult och sakralt kungadöme i Norden*, Stockholm 1954.
Ström, Folke, 'Döden och de döda' (*KLNM* 3) Malmö 1958, 432–438.
Ström, Folke, *Den döendes makt och Odin i trädet*, Göteborg 1947.
Ström, Folke, 'Einherjar' (*KLNM* 3) Malmö 1958, 532–533.
Ström, Folke, 'Fylgja' (*KLNM* 5) Malmö 1960, 38–39.
Ström, Folke, 'Gudarnas vrede' (*Saga och Sed*) 1952, 5–40.
Ström, Folke, 'Guden Hœnir och odensvalen' (*Arv* 12) 1956, 41–68.
Ström, Folke, 'Hieros gamos – motivet i Hallfreðr Óttarsons Hákonardrápa och den nordnorska jarlavärdigheten' (*ANF* 98) 1983, 67–79.
Ström, Folke, 'Hœnir' (*KLNM* 7) Malmö 1962, 301–302.
Ström, Folke, 'Kung Domalde i Svitjod och "kungalyckan" ' (*Saga och Sed*) 1967, 52–66.
Ström, Folke, *Loki. Ein mythologisches Problem*, Göteborg 1956.
Ström, Folke, 'Nid och ergi' (*Saga och Sed*) 1972, 27–47.
Ström, Folke, *Nordisk hedendom*, Göteborg ^{2}1967.
Ström, Folke, *On the sacral Origin of the Germanic Death Penalties*, Stockholm 1942.
Ström, Folke, 'Poetry as an instrument of Propaganda. Jarl Hakon and his poets' (*Speculum Norrœnum. Studies G. Turville-Petre*) Odense 1981, 440–458.
Ström, Folke, 'Straff. Sakrala element i straff' (*KLNM* 17) Malmö 1972, 275–280.
Ström, Folke, 'Tro och blot' (*Arv* 7) 1951, 23–38.
Strömbäck, Dag, 'The Concept of Soul in Nordic Traditon' (*Arv* 31) 1975, 5–22.
Strömbäck, Dag, *The Conversion of Iceland*, London 1975.
Strömbäck, Dag, 'Hade de germanska dödsstraffen sakralt ursprung?' (*Saga och Sed*) 1942, 51–69.
Strömbäck, Dag, 'Lytir – en fornsvensk gud?' (*Festskrift til F. Jónsson*) Copenhagen 1928, 283–293.
Strömbäck, Dag, 'Philologisch-kritische Methode und altnordische Religionsgeschichte' (*APhSc* 12) 1937–38, 1–24.

Strömbäck, Dag, 'Resan til den andra världen kring medeltidsvisionerna och Draumkvædet' (*Saga och Sed*) 1976, 15–29.
Strömbäck, Dag, 'Sejd' (*KLNM* 15) Malmö 1970, 76–79.
Strömbäck, Dag, *Sejd. Textstudier i nordisk religionshistoria*, Stockholm, Copenhagen, Lund 1935.
Strömberg, Märta, 'Kultische Steinsetzungen in Schonen' (*Meddelanden från Lunds Universitets Historiska Museum*) 1962–63, 148–185.
Stübe, R., 'Kvasir und der magische Gebrauch des Speichels' (*Festschrift E. Mogk*) Halle/S. 1924, 500–509.
Stumpfl, Robert, *Kultspiele der Germanen als Ursprung des mittelalterlichen Dramas*, Berlin 1936.
Sturtevant, Albert Morey, 'Comments on Mythical Name-Giving in Old Norse' (*GR* 29) 1954, 68–71.
Sturtevant, Albert Morey, 'Etymological Comments on Certain Words and Names in the Elder Edda' (*PMLA* 66) 1951, 278–291.
Sturtevant, Albert Morey, 'Etymological Comments Upon Certain Old Norse Proper Names in the Eddas' (*PMLA* 67) 1952, 1145–1162.
Sturtevant, Albert Morey, 'The Old Norse Proper Name Svipdagr' (*SS* 30) 1958, 30–34.
Sturtevant, Albert Morey, 'Regarding the Name Ása-þórr' (*SS* 25) 1953, 15–16.
Sturtevant, Albert Morey, 'Regarding the Old Norse Name Gefjon' (*SS* 24) 1952, 166–167.
Sturtevant, Albert Morey, 'Semantic and Etymological Notes on Old Norse Poetic Words' (*SS* 20) 1948, 129–142.
Sturtevant, Albert Morey, 'A Study of the Old-Norse Word Regin' (*JEGPh* 15) 1916, 251–266.
Sturtevant, Albert Morey, 'Three Old Norse Words: Gamban, Ratatǫskr, and Gymir' (*SS* 28) 1956, 109–114.
Sveinsson, Einar Ólafur, 'Celtic Elements in Icelandic Tradition' (*Béaloideas* 15) 1959, 3–24.
Sveinsson, Einar Ólafur, *Íslenzkar Bókmenntir í Fornǫld*, Reykjavík 1962.
Sveinsson, Einar Ólafur, 'Svipdags Long Journey. Some Observations on Grógaldr and Fjǫlsvinnsmál' (*Hereditas*. Studies S. O'Duilearga) Dublin 1975, 298–319.
Svennung, Josef, 'Jordanes' beskrivning av ön Scandia' (*Fornvännen* 59) 1964, 1–23.
Svennung, Josef, 'Jordanes Scandia-Kapitel' (*Fornvännen* 60) 1965, 1–41.
Sverdrup, G., *Rauschtrank und Labetrank in Glaube und Kultus*, Oslo 1940.
Sverdrup, Jakob, 'Bemerkungen zum Hildebrandslied' (*Festschrift E. Mogk*) Halle/S. 1924, 99–118.
Sydow, C.W. von, 'Jättarna i mytologi och folktro' (*Folkminnen och Folktankar* 6) 1919, 52–96.
Sydow, C.W. von, 'Jättens Hymers bägare' (*DS*) 1915, 113–150.
Sydow, C.W. von, 'Scyld Scéfing' (*NoB* 12) 1924, 90–91.
Sydow, C.W. von, 'Tors färd till Utgård' (*DS*) 1910, 65–105 and 145–182.
Syme, Ronald, *Tacitus*, 2 vols, Oxford 1958.
Tally, Joyce Ann, *The Dragon's Progress: The significance of the dragon in "Beowulf", the "Volsunga saga", "Das Nibelungenlied", and "Der Ring des Nibelungen"*, Diss. Denver 1983.
Tapp, Henry L., 'Hinn almáttki áss – Thor or Odin?' (*JEGPh* 55) 1956, 85–99.
Taylor, Paul B., 'The Rythm of Vǫluspá' (*Neophilologus* 55) 1971, 45–57.
Taylor, Paul B., 'Searoniðas: Old Norse Magic and Old English Verse' (*Studies in Philology* 80) 1983, 109–125.
Þórðarson, Matthías, 'Álvissmál' (*Árbók hins Islenzka Fornleifafjelags*) 1924, 61–78.
Þórðarson, Matthías, 'Um dauða Skalla-Gríms og hversu hann var heygður' (*Festskrift til F. Jónsson*) Copenhagen 1928, 95–112.
Thrane, T., T. Capelle, H. Jankuhn, W. Krause, K. Ranke, 'Amulett' (J. Hoops, *Reallexi-*

kon der germanischen Altertumskunde, hg. v. H. Beck 1) [2]Berlin, New York 1973, 268–274.
Thümmel, Albert, 'Der germanische Tempel' (*PBB* 35) 1909, 1–23.
Thun, Nils, 'The Malignant Elves. Notes on Anglo-Saxon Magic and Germanic Myth' (*Studia Neophilologica* 41) 1969, 378–396.
Timmer, B. J., 'Wyrd in Anglo-Saxon Prose and Poetry' (*Neophilologus* 26) 1941, 24–33 and 213–228.
Toldberg, Helge, 'Dvaergekongen Laurin' (*KLNM* 3) Malmö 1958, 378–380.
Tovar, Antonio, 'Germanische Wortbildungen in römischen Inschriften am Rhein' (*Scritti in onore di Giuliano Bonfante* 2) Brescia 1976, 1079–1106.
Traetteberg, Hallvard, 'Åks. Sakralt, ikon. og herald.' (*KLNM* 20) Malmö 1976, 667–674.
Trathnigg, Gilbert, 'Glaube und Kult der Semmonen' (*ARW* 34) 1937, 226–249.
Trier, Jost, 'Irminsul' (*Westfälische Forschungen* 4) 1941, 99–133.
Turville-Petre, E. O. Gabriel, 'A Note on the Landdísir' (*Early English and Norse Studies, Pres. to H. Smith*) London 1963, 196–201.
Turville-Petre, E. O. Gabriel, 'The Cult of Freyr in the Evening of Paganism' (*Proceedings of Leeds Philos. and Literary Society* 3) 1935, 317–333.
Turville-Petre, E. O. Gabriel, 'Fertility of Beast and Soil in Old Norse Literature' (*Old Norse Literature and Mythology*) Austin 1969, 244–264.
Turville-Petre, E. O. Gabriel, *Myth and Religion of the North*, London 1964, Reprint Westport 1975.
Turville-Petre, E. O. Gabriel, 'Professor Georges Dumézil' (*Saga-Book* 14) 1953–55, 131–134.
Turville-Petre, E. O. Gabriel, 'Thurstable' (G. Turville-Petre, *Nine Norse Studies*) London 1972, 20–29.
Tveitane, Mattias, 'Omkring det mytologiske navnet Aegir m. "vannmannen" ' (*APhSc* 31) 1976, 81–95.
Uecker, Heiko, *Die altwestnordischen Bestattungssitten in der literarischen Überlieferung*, Diss. Munich 1966.
Uecker, Heiko, 'Darraðarljóð' (J. Hoops, *Reallexikon der germanischen Altertumskunde*, hg. v. H. Beck, 5) Berlin, New York [2]1983, 254–256.
Uhland, Ludwig, *Uhlands Schriften zur Geschichte der Dichtung und Sage*, vol. 6, Stuttgart 1868.
Ulvestad, Bjarne, 'How old are the Mythological Eddic Poems?' (*SS* 26) 1954, 49–69.
Unruh, Christoph v., Wargus, 'Friedlosigkeit und magisch-kultische Vorstellungen bei den Germanen' (*Zeitschrift der Savignystiftung für Rechtsgeschichte* 74, German. Abt.) 1957, 1–40.
Unwerth, Wolf von, 'Fjolnir' (*ANF* 33) 1917, 320–335.
Unwerth, Wolf von, 'Óðinn und Rota' (*PBB* 39) 1914, 213–223.
Unwerth, Wolf von, *Über Totenkult und Ódinnverehrung bei Nordgermanen und Lappen*, Breslau 1911.
Unwerth, Wolf von, 'Zur Deutung der längeren Nordendorfer Runenschrift' (*Zeitschrift für Volkskunde* 26) 1916, 81–85.
Vesper, Ekkehard, 'Das Menschenbild der älteren Hávamál' (*PBB* Ost 79) 1957, 13–21.
Vetter, Ferdinand, 'Zum Muspilli' (*Germania* 16) 1891, 121–155.
Visted, K., 'Frodes Fred – Julefred' (*Norsk Folkekultur* 8) 1922, 1–10.
Vogt, Walter Heinrich, 'Bragis Schild. Maler und Skalde' (*APhSc* 5) 1930, 1–28.
Vogt, Walter Heinrich, 'Thors Fischzug, Eine Betrachtung über ein Bild auf Bragis Schild' (*Studier till A. Kock*) Lund 1929, 200–216.
Vogt, Walter Heinrich, 'Fluch, Eid, Götter – altnordisches Recht' (*Zeitschrift der Savigny-Stiftung für Rechtsgeschichte* 57, German. Abt.) 1937, 1–57.
Vogt, Walter Heinrich, 'Der frühgermanische Kultredner' (*APhSc* 2) 1927, 250–263.
Vogt, Walter Heinrich, 'Hroptr Rǫgna' (*ZfdA* 62) 1925, 41–48.

Vogt, Walter Heinrich, *Stilgeschichte der eddischen Wissensdichtung*, vol.1, Der Kultredner (þulr), Breslau 1927.
Vogt, Walter Heinrich, *Die þula zwischen Kultrede und eddischer Wissensdichtung*, Göttingen 1942.
Vogt, Walter Heinrich, 'Zum Problem der Merseburger Zaubersprüche' (*ZfdA* 65) 1928, 97–130.
Volkmann, Hans, *Germanische Seherinnen in römischen Diensten*, Krefeld 1964 (= Kölner Universitätsreden. 32.)
Vollgraff, C.W., 'Romeinsche Inscripties uit Utrecht' (*Verslagen en Mededelingen der Akademie van Wetenschapen te Amsterdam*, Afd. Letterk. 70 B 5) 1930, 127–148.
Volz, R., 'Balder' (*Lexikon der Mittelalters* 1) Munich, Zurich 1980, 1362–64.
Vordemfelde, Hans, *Die germanische Religion in den deutschen Volksrechten*. 1. Der religiöse Glaube, Giessen 1923.
Vries, Jan de, *Altgermanische Religionsgeschichte*, 2 vols, Berlin [3]1970.
Vries, Jan de, *Altnordische Literaturgeschichte*, Berlin [2]1964–67.
Vries, Jan de, *Altnordisches etymologisches Wörterbuch*, Leiden [2]1977.
Vries, Jan de, 'Der altnordische Rasengang' (*APhSc* 3) 1928–29, 106–135.
Vries, Jan de, 'Die Bedeutung der Volkskunde für mythologische und religionsgeschichtliche Untersuchungen' (*GRM* 20) 1932, 27–39.
Vries, Jan de, 'Celtic and Germanic Religion' (*Saga-Book* 16) 1963–64, 109–123.
Vries, Jan de, *Contributions to the study of Othin especially in his relation to agricultural practises in modern popular lore*, Helsingfors 1931 (= FFC. 94.)
Vries, Jan de, 'Dinsdag' (*TNTL* 48) 1929, 145–184.
Vries, Jan de, *Forschungsgeschichte der Mythologie*, Freiburg, Munich 1961.
Vries, Jan de, *Die geistige Welt der Germanen*, Tübingen [3]1964.
Vries, Jan de, 'Ginnungagap' (*AphSc* 5) 1930–31, 41–66)
Vries, Jan de, 'Heimdallr, dieu énigmatique' (*Études Germanique* 10) 1955, 257–268.
Vries, Jan de, 'Der heutige Stand der germanischen Religionsforschung' (*GRM* 33) 1951–52, 1–11.
Vries, Jan de, 'Kenningen und Christentum' (*ZfdA* 87) 1956–57, 125–131.
Vries, Jan de, 'Das Königtum bei den Germanen' (*Saeculum* 7) 1956, 289–309.
Vries, Jan de, 'Loki . . . und kein Ende' (*Festschrift F.R. Schröder*) Heidelberg 1959, 1–10.
Vries, Jan de, 'Der Mythos von Balders Tod' (*ANF* 70) 1955, 41–60.
Vries, Jan de, 'Odin am Baume' (*Studia Germanica*, till. E.A. Kock) Lund 1934, 392–395.
Vries, Jan de, 'Om Eddaens Visdomsdigtning' (*ANF* 50) 1934, 1–59.
Vries, Jan de, 'Over de dateering der þrymskviða' (*TNTL* 47) 1928, 251–322.
Vries, Jan de, *The Problem of Loki*, Helsingfors 1933 (= FFC. 110.)
Vries, Jan de, *De Skaldenkenningen met mytologischen Inhoud*, Haarlem 1934.
Vries, Jan de, 'Studien over Germaansche mythologie.'
'I. Fjǫrgyn en Fjǫrgynn' (*TNTL* 50) 1931, 1–25.
'II. De nederrijnsche Matronenvereering' (*TNTL* 50) 1930, 85–125.
'III. Franeker en Vroonloo' (*TNTL* 51) 1932, 97–121.
'IV. De goden der West-Germanen' (*TNTL* 51) 1932, 277–304.
'V. De Wodanvereering bij West- en Noord-Germanen' (*TNTL* 52) 1933, 165–216.
'VI. Over enkele godennamen' (*TNTL* 53) 1934, 192–210.
'VII. De skaldenkenningen met de namen der godinnen Freyja en Frigg' (*TNTL* 53) 1934, 210–217.
'VIII. Ward en Werf' (*TNTL* 53) 1934, 257–269.
'IX. De Oudnoorsche god Heimdallr' (*TNTL* 54) 1935, 53–76.
'X. Bilrǫst en Gjallarbru' (*TNTL* 54) 1935, 77–81.
Vries, Jan de, 'Sur certain glissements fonctionnels de divinités dans la religion germanique' (*Hommages à Georges Dumézil*) Brüssel 1960, 83–95.
Vries, Jan de, 'Über das Verhältnis von Óðr und Óðinn' (*ZfdPh* 73) 1954, 337–353.
Vries, Jan de, 'Über Sigvats Álfablót-Strophen' (*APhSc* 7) 1932, 169–180.

Vries, Jan de, 'La valeur religieuse du mot germanique irmin' (*Cahiers du Sud* 36) 1952, 18–27.
Vries, Jan de, 'Die Vǫluspá' (*GRM* 24) 1936, 1–14.
Vries, Jan de, 'Vǫluspá Str. 21 und 22' (*ANF* 77) 1962, 12–47.
Vries, Jan de, *Die Welt der Germanen*, Leipzig [1934].
Vries, Jan de, 'Wodan und die Wilde Jagd' (*Die Nachbarn*. Jahrbuch für vergleichende Volkskunde 3) 1962, 31–59.
Vries, Jan de, 'Das Wort goðmálugr in der Hymiskviða' (*GRM* 35) 1954, 336–337.
Wagner, Norbert, 'Dioskuren, Jungmannschaften und Doppelkönigtum' (*ZfdPh* 79) 1960, 1–12 and 225–247.
Wagner, Norbert, '(Hercules) Magusanus' (*Bonner Jahrbücher* 177) 1977, 417–422.
Wagner, Norbert, 'Zu zwei Triaden in Tacitus' "Germania" ', *ZfdA* 108 (1979), 209–218.
Wagner, Norbert, 'Zum Mars der Goten. Eine religions- und sozialgeschichtliche Marginalie' (*Volkskultur und Geschichte. Festgabe f. J. Dünninger*) Berlin 1970, 557–561.
Wagner, Norbert, 'Zur Neunzahl von Lejre und Uppsala' (*ZfdA* 109) 1980, 202–208.
Wais, Kurt, 'Ullikummi, Hrungnir, Armilius und Verwandte' (*Edda, Skalden, Saga. Festschrift F. Genzmer*) Heidelberg 1952, 211–261.
Walter, Ernst, 'Quellenkritisches und Wortgeschichtliches zum Opferfest von Hlaðir in Snorris Heimskringla (Hák. góð. c. 17)' (*Festschrift W. Baetke*) Weimar 1966, 359–367.
Ward, Donald J., 'An Indo-European mythological theme in Germanic tradition' (*Indo-European and the Indo-Europeans*) Philadelphia 1970, 405–420.
Ward, Donald J., 'The Divine Twins: An Indo-European Myth in Germanic Tradition' (*Folklore Studies* 19) 1968, 8–29.
Ward, Donald J., 'The separate functions of the Indo-European divine twins' (*Myth and Law among the Indo-Europeans*) Berkeley 1970, 193–202.
Ward, Donald J., 'The threefold death: An Indo-European trifunctional sacrifice?' (*Myth and Law among the Indo-Europeans*) Berkeley 1970, 123–142.
Warde Fowler, W., 'The Oak and the Thundergod' (*ARW* 16) 1913, 317–320.
Warnatsch, Otto, 'Phol und der 2. Merseburger Zauberspruch' (*ZfdPh* 64) 1939, 148–155.
Watkins, Calvert, 'Language of gods and language of men' (*Myth and Law among the Indo-Europeans*) Berkeley 1970, 1–17.
Weber, Gerd Wolfgang, 'Edda, Jüngere' (J. Hoops, *Reallexikon der germanischen Altertumskunde*, hg. v. H. Beck 6) ²1986, 394–412.
Weber, Gerd Wolfgang, 'Grímnismál' (*KLL* 3) Munich 1967, 1171–1172.
Weber, Gerd Wolfgang, 'Harbardsljóð' (*KLL* 3) Munich 1967, 1470–1471.
Weber, Gerd Wolfgang, 'Háttatal' (*KLL* 3) 1967, 1498–1499.
Weber, Gerd Wolfgang, 'Hymiskviða' (*KLL* 3) 1967, 2291–2293.
Weber, Gerd Wolfgang, 'Die Literatur des Nordens' (*Neues Handbuch der Literaturwissenschaft* 8) Wiesbaden 1978, 487–518.
Weber, Gerd Wolfgang, 'Lokasenna' (*KLL* 4) Munich 1968, 1592–1593.
Weber, Gerd Wolfgang, 'Odins Wagen' (FmSt 7) 1973, 88–89.
Weber, Gerd Wolfgang, 'Das Odinsbild des Altunasteins' (*PBB* West 94) 1972, 323–334.
Weber, Gerd Wolfgang, 'Siðaskipti. Das religionsgeschichtliche Modell Snorri Sturlusons in Edda und Heimskringla' (*Sagnaskemmtun. Studies Hermann Pálsson*) Vienna 1986, 309–329.
Weber, Gerd Wolfgang, "*Wyrd*". *Studien zum Schicksalsbegriff der altenglischen und altnordischen Literatur*, Bad Homburg 1969.
Weinhold, Karl, 'Die Riesen des germanischen Mythus' (*Sitzungsber. d. kl. preuß. Ak. d . Wiss. zu Berlin* 26) 1858, 225–306.
Weinhold, Karl, 'Die Sagen von Loki' (*ZfdA* 7) 1849, 1–94.
Weinhold, Karl, 'Tius Things' (*ZfdPh* 21) 1889, 1–16.
Weinhold, Karl, 'Über den Mythus vom Wanenkrieg' (*Sitzungsber. d . kl. preuß. Ak. d. Wiss. zu Berlin*) 1890, 611–625.
Weiser-Aall, Lily, *Altgermanische Jünglingsweihen und Männerbünde*, Bühl 1927.

Weiser-Aall, Lily, 'Jul' (*KLNM* 8) Malmö 1963, 6–14.
Weiser-Aall, Lily, 'Zur Geschichte der altgermanischen Todesstrafe und Friedlosigkeit' (*ARW* 30) 1933, 209–227.
Weisweiler, Josef, 'Seele und See. Ein etymologischer Versuch' (*IF* 57) 1940, 25–55.
Weisweiler, Josef, 'Die Stellung der Frau bei den Kelten und das Problem des "keltischen Mutterrechts" ' (*ZfceltPh* 21) 1938–40, 205–279.
Weninger, Ludwig, 'Feralis exercitus' (*ARW* 9) 1906, 201–247, and (10) 1907, 229–256.
Werner, Joachim, 'Herkuleskeule und Donar-Amulett' (*Jahrbuch des römisch-germanischen Zentralmuseums Mainz* 11) 1964, 176–197.
Wesche, Heinrich, *Der althochdeutsche Wortschatz im Gebiet des Zaubers und der Weissagung*, Halle/S. 1940.
Wesche, Heinrich, 'Beiträge zu einer Geschichte des deutschen Heidentums' (*PBB* 61) 1937, 1–116.
Wessén, Elias, 'Athuganir á stíl Hávamála' (*Andvari* N.F. 5) 1965, 193–209.
Wessén, Elias, 'Gestumblinde' (*Festskrift till. H. Pipping*) Helsigfors 1924, 537–548.
Wessén, Elias, *Havamal. Några stilfrågor*, Stockholm 1959.
Wessén, Elias, 'Ordspråk och lärodikt. Några stilformer i Hávamál' (*Septentrionalia et Orientalia. Studia B. Kalgren ded.*) Stockholm 1959, 455–473.
Wessén, Elias, 'Schwedische Ortsnamen und altnordische Mythologie' (*APhSc* 4) 1929–30, 97–115.
Westergaard, Kai-Erik, 'Die vergessenen Göttinnen der Fruchtbarkeit' (*Frauen und Frauenbilder dokumentiert durch 2000 Jahre*) Oslo 1983, 203–226.
Widéen, Harald, 'Till diskussionen om Uppsala hednatempel' (*Fornvännen*) 1951, 127–131.
Wieden, Helge bei der, 'Bragi' (*ZfdPh* 80) 1961, 83–86.
Wieden, Helge bei der, 'Zum religionsgeschichtlichen Ort der Lokasenna' (*ZfdPh* 83) 1964, 266–275.
Wiens, Gerhard Lebrecht, *Die frühchristlichen Gottesbezeichnungen im Germanisch-Althochdeutschen*, Diss. Berlin 1935.
Wilbur, Terence H., 'The Interpretation of Vǫluspá 22,4: Vitti Hon Ganda' (SS 31) 1959, 129–136.
Wilbur, Terence H., 'Troll, an etymological note' (*SS* 30) 1958, 137–139.
Wild, Friedrich, *Odin und Euhemeros*, Vienna 1941.
Wilhelm, Adolf, 'Das Gedicht auf Veleda' (*Anz. d. öst. Ak. d. Wiss.* 85) 1948, 151.
Wilken, E., 'Der Fenriswolf' (*ZfdPh* 28) 1896, 165–198 and 297–348.
Wipf, K. A., 'Die Zauberspüche im Altnordischen' (*Numen* 22) 1975, 42–69.
Wirth, W., *Der Schicksalsglaube in den Isländersagas*, Stuttgart 1940.
Wislicenus, Hugo, *Loki und seine Stellung in der germanischen Mythologie*, Zurich 1867.
Wissowa, Georg, 'Interpretatio Romana. Götter im Barbarenlande' (*ARW* 19) 1918–19, 1–49.
Wolf, Alois, 'Sehweisen und Darstellungsfragen in der Gylfaginning. Thors Fischfang' (*Skandinavistik* 7) 1977, 1–27.
Wolf-Rootkay, W. H., 'Balder and the Mistletoe. A Note' (*SS* 39) 1967, 340–344.
Wolff, Ludwig, 'Die Merseburger Zaubersprüche' (*Festschrift für F. Maurer*) Stuttgart 1963, 305–319.
Wood, F. T., 'The age of the Vǫluspá' (GR 36) 1961, 94–107.
Wood, F. T., 'The transmission of the Vǫluspá' (GR 34) 1959, 247–261.
Wormstall, Joseph, *Der Tempel der Tanfana. Ein altgermanisches Heiligtum in neuer Beleuchtung*, Münster 1906.
Wrede, Ferdinand, 'Zu den Merseburger Zaubersprüchen' (F. Wrede, *Kleine Schriften*) Marburg 1963, 364–369.
Wrenn, C. L., 'Some earliest Anglo-Saxon cult symbols' (*Franciplegus. [Festschrift] F. P. Magoun*) New York 1965, 40–55.
Wrigth, T., *Anglo-Saxon and Old English vocabularies* 1–2, London ^{2}1884.

Wyss, Ulrich, 'Zur Interpretation der Ynglingasage' (*Philologische Untersuchungen gewidmet E. Stutz*) Wien 1984, 469–486 (= Philologica Germanica, 7).
Young, J. I., 'Does Rígsþula betray Irish influence?' (*ANF* 49) 1933, 97–107.
Zacher, K., 'Loki und Typhon' (*ZfdPh* 30) 1898, 289–301.
Zangemeister, Karl, 'Römische Inschriften' (*Bonner Jahrbücher* 81) 1886, 78–86.
Zangemeister, Karl, 'Zur germanischen Mythologie' (*Neue Heidelberger Jahrbücher* 5) 1895, 46–60.
Zetterholm, D. O., *Studier i en Snorre-Text*, Stockholm, Copenhagen 1949.
Zimmer, H., 'Parjanya, Fiǫrgyn, Vâta, Wôdan. Ein Beitrag zur vergleichenden Mythologie' (*ZfdA* 19) 1976, 164–180.

www.ingramcontent.com/pod-product-compliance
Ingram Content Group UK Ltd.
Pitfield, Milton Keynes, MK11 3LW, UK
UKHW020755060125
453221UK00002B/3

9 780859 915137